ECONOMIC TORTS AND ECONOMIC WRONGS

This book explores contemporary issues in respect of causes of action which operate to protect a plaintiff's economic interests.

It examines the question from across the spectrum of private law. Focusing mainly on common law principles, it looks in particular at the treatment of such causes of action in the United Kingdom, Australia, Canada and Singapore as well as other common law jurisdictions. Addressing both theoretical and doctrinal issues, this important book will appeal to both private law scholars and practitioners.

Volume 39 in the series Hart Studies in Private Law

Economic Torts and Economic Wrongs

Edited by
John Eldridge
Michael Douglas
and
Claudia Carr

•HART•
OXFORD • LONDON • NEW YORK • NEW DELHI • SYDNEY

HART PUBLISHING
Bloomsbury Publishing Plc
Kemp House, Chawley Park, Cumnor Hill, Oxford, OX2 9PH, UK
1385 Broadway, New York, NY 10018, USA
29 Earlsfort Terrace, Dublin 2, Ireland

First published in Great Britain 2021

A catalogue record for this book is available from the British Library.

Library of Congress Cataloging-in-Publication data

Names: Eldridge, John (Law teacher), editor. | Douglas, Michael C., editor. | Carr, Claudia (Lawyer), editor.

Title: Economic torts and economic wrongs / edited by John Eldridge, Michael Douglas and Claudia Carr.

Description: Oxford ; New York : Hart, 2021. | Series: Hart studies in private law ; volume 39 | Includes bibliographical references and index.

Identifiers: LCCN 2021032680 (print) | LCCN 2021032681 (ebook) | ISBN 9781509934751 (hardback) | ISBN 9781509954506 (paperback) | ISBN 9781509934775 (pdf) | ISBN 9781509934768 (Epub)

Subjects: LCSH: Torts—Economic aspects—English-speaking countries.

Classification: LCC K923 . E36 2021 (print) | LCC K923 (ebook) | DDC 346.03—dc23

LC record available at https://lccn.loc.gov/2021032680

LC ebook record available at https://lccn.loc.gov/2021032681

ISBN: HB: 978-1-50993-475-1
ePDF: 978-1-50993-477-5
ePub: 978-1-50993-476-8

Typeset by Compuscript Ltd, Shannon

FOREWORD

THE HON. SIR ANTHONY MASON AC KBE GBM QC*

The chapters in this book seek to bring clarity to the development of the law relating to economic torts and economic wrongs. In the introduction to the book reference is made to Lord Hoffmann's hope that

> "cases on the economic torts will become rare curiosity of little practical consequence".

The authors of the introduction maintain, however, that, despite a reduction in the scope of the economic torts, they continue to play a vital role. They will continue to do so until legislative action is taken to mandate a different course. And, even if such action is contemplated, the chapters in this book will contribute to an understanding of the law which needs to be replaced and why it should be replaced.

The contributors to the book have endeavoured to explore the unresolved uncertainties surrounding economic torts and economic wrongs with a view to clarifying and assisting the development of the law as it applies to the various issues. In this endeavour they have been very largely successful.

As you would expect in matters where economic torts and wrongs are involved, at times the issues are economic policy issues. Recognition of this aspect of the discussion is no doubt one of the reasons why Lord Hoffmann favoured a legislative approach. But the economic issues are broad and can be handled by people who are not economic experts. The same point cannot be made confidently with issues that arise as a matter of competition policy when specific understanding of the particular issues at stake may prove to be invaluable.

It remains for me to mention some specific chapters in the book. First, I refer to Chapter 10 by the Hon. Geoffrey Nettle AC QC and Daniel Farinha on "Misfeasance by Directors". It contains an illuminating account of the history of this form of liability and possible future developments.

Then there is Chapter 13 by Elise Bant and Jeannie Marie Paterson on "Developing a Rational Law of Misleading Conduct". This Chapter is part of an ongoing project and summarises the effect of the work done to date. The authors discuss the confusing legislation on the topic – "an Increasingly Convoluted and

* The Hon Sir Anthony Mason AC KBE GBM QC is a former Chief Justice of the High Court of Australia and a former Non-Permanent Judge of the Hong Kong Court of Final Appeal.

Conflicting Landscape" – and make the point that the combination of statute and general law has become "almost unmanageably complex".

Chapter 5 by Dr Katy Barnett on "Inducing Breach of Contract" describes the history of the tort, its modern operation in Australia and the United Kingdom, identifying uncertainties in the scope of the tort. The Chapter then considers how these uncertainties might be resolved, with particular regard to the need to protect performance interests.

Chapter 7 by Paula Giliker on "Economic Wrongs and Private Nuisance" deals, among other things, with the tensions and inconsistencies in this area of the law, particularly private nuisance. The Chapter points to the Civil law on this subject and its tendency to seek general principles of tort law to overcome these inconsistencies.

Chapter 11 by Simone Degeling deals with Fiduciaries, Equitable Compensation and Lost Commercial Opportunity and reconciles the need for financial loss. The Chapter seeks to resolve what is an apparent inconsistency between offering compensation for lost commercial opportunity and insistence on the need for financial loss.

I mention these chapters because they offer a taste of what this book is about. It will be of interest and of value to practitioners, academics and students.

Anthony Mason

ACKNOWLEDGEMENTS

We have incurred many debts in the course of editing this collection of essays. Sydney Law School, UWA Law School and Curtin Law School have each generously placed their resources at our disposal. We are particularly grateful for the support of Sydney Law School's Ross Parsons Centre of Commercial, Corporate and Taxation Law, which provided funds to support the editing of the manuscript.

Books such as these owe their success to the industry and scholarship of their contributors. It has been our privilege to work with an exceptional group of authors in the course of compiling this collection. We hope the finished volume is a fitting showcase of their labours.

We are grateful to William Gummow, James Goudkamp and Barbara McDonald, each of whom provided invaluable advice at various stages of the book's development. Thanks must also go to the exceptional staff at Hart Publishing, and to Brendan Hord for his skilful editing work. Finally, the editors are greatly indebted to the Honourable Sir Anthony Mason AC KBE HonFAIB DistFRSN QC, who generously agreed to author the foreword to this collection.

The publication of this book was beset by a number of unforeseen delays. The bulk of the chapters were settled in early 2020, and they accordingly state the law as at that date.

John Eldridge
Michael Douglas
Claudia Carr
July 2021

TABLE OF CONTENTS

NOTES ON CONTRIBUTORS

Elise Bant is Professor of Private Law and Commercial Regulation at the University of Western Australia and Professorial Fellow at the University of Melbourne.

Katy Barnett is Professor of Law at the University of Melbourne.

Samuel Beswick is an Assistant Professor at the Peter A Allard School of Law, University of British Columbia.

Anna Bunn is a Senior Lecturer in Law at Curtin University.

Claudia Carr is an Associate at Clifford Chance.

Simone Degeling is Professor of Law at the University of New South Wales.

Michael Douglas is a Senior Lecturer in Law at the University of Western Australia.

John Eldridge is a Barrister at Serle Court, London.

Daniel Farinha is a Reader at Eleven Wentworth, Sydney.

Paula Giliker is Professor of Comparative Law at the University of Bristol.

Bobby Lindsay is a Lecturer in Law at the University of Glasgow.

Shae McCrystal is Professor of Labour Law at the University of Sydney.

Geoffrey Nettle is a former Justice of the High Court of Australia.

Jeannie Marie Paterson is Professor of Law at the University of Melbourne.

Andrew Stewart is the John Bray Professor of Law at the University of Adelaide.

Zhong Xing Tan is an Assistant Professor of Law at the National University of Singapore.

Hilary Young is Professor in Law at the University of New Brunswick.

1

Introduction

JOHN ELDRIDGE, MICHAEL DOUGLAS AND CLAUDIA CARR

The expression 'economic torts' is commonly understood to denote a bundle of related but distinct causes of action. As Lord Sumption and Lord Lloyd-Jones explained in *JSC BTA Bank v Khrapunov*:

> Conspiracy is one of a group of torts which tend to be loosely lumped together as 'economic torts', the others being intimidation, procuring a breach of contract and unlawful interference with economic and other interests (sometimes called the 'intentional harm' tort).[1]

To this list may be added, at the very least, deceit and malicious falsehood.[2] Each of these torts protect economic interests: things for which 'a finite sum of money can provide recompense'.[3] In particular, they protect economic interests in circumstances where there has been no physical damage to a plaintiff's person or property.

Just as private nuisance regulated land use prior to the emergence of the modern regulatory state,[4] the economic torts instanced above were once the principal means by which commercial competition and industrial action were subject to legal control.[5] In charting the modern history of the economic torts,[6] it is conventional to begin with the landmark decision of *Lumley v Gye*.[7] That case established that the knowing and direct inducement of a breach of contract is an actionable wrong. For a considerable time thereafter, the decision remained an aberration,[8]

[1] *Khrapunov* [2018] UKSC 19; [2018] 2 WLR 1125, 1132 [6].

[2] H Carty, *An Analysis of the Economic Torts*, 2nd edn (Oxford University Press, 2010) 1.

[3] P Cane, *Tort Law and Economic Interests*, 2nd edn (Clarendon Press, 1996) 5.

[4] See JPS McLaren, 'Nuisance Law and the Industrial Revolution – Some Lessons from Social History' (1983) 3(2) *Oxford Journal of Legal Studies* 155.

[5] H Carty, 'The Modern Functions of the Economic Torts: Reviewing the English, Canadian, Australian, and New Zealand Positions' [2015] *Cambridge Law Journal* 261, 265–68.

[6] What follows draws heavily upon the pellucid account of the modern history of the economic torts given in L Hoffmann, 'The Rise and Fall of the Economic Torts' in S Degeling, J Edelman and J Goudkamp (eds), *Torts in Commercial Law* (Thomson Reuters, 2011). For a discussion of Lord Hoffmann's contribution to the development of the economic torts, see R Bagshaw, 'Lord Hoffmann and the Economic Torts' in PS Davies and J Pila (eds), *The Jurisprudence of Lord Hoffmann* (Hart Publishing, 2015).

[7] *Lumley v Gye* (1853) 2 El & Bl 216; (1853) 118 ER 749 (QB).

[8] Hoffmann (n 6) 108.

neither approved nor disapproved in subsequent decisions that considered it.[9] It was not until three decades later, in *Bowen v Hall*,[10] that the decision was approved by the Court of Appeal.

In 1889, in *Mogul Steamship v McGregor, Gow and Co*[11] ('*Mogul Steamship*'), the Court of Appeal considered a case in which the plaintiff was put out of business by the joint actions of his competitors. The defendants were held not to be liable on the basis that:

> No man, whether trader or not, can … justify damaging another in his commercial business by fraud or misrepresentation. Intimidation, obstruction and molestation are forbidden; so is the intentional procurement of violation of individual rights, contractual or other, assuming always that there is no just cause for it … [but] the defendants have been guilty of none of these acts. They have done nothing more against the plaintiffs than pursue to the bitter end a war of competition wages in the interests of their own trade.[12]

The decision of the Court of Appeal was upheld by the House of Lords.[13] While liability was not made out, the passage above nonetheless suggests the recognition of a tort of conspiracy. The case established the proposition that it is not tortious for a group of traders to join forces in order to advance their own interests, though doing so may injure the business of rival traders, so long as no unlawful means are employed in doing so.

Less than a decade later, the tort recognised in *Lumley v Gye* was considered at length by the House of Lords. In *Allen v Flood*,[14] a union official was held not liable for the making of a threat that, unless the plaintiff employees were dismissed, certain other employees would be called upon to strike. The House of Lords held that, in circumstances where the plaintiffs were able to be lawfully dismissed upon short notice, the threat made by the defendant did not procure an act which amounted to a breach of contract. Significantly, it was noted that the fact that a defendant acts maliciously does not render an act tortious where it would otherwise not be.[15]

At the beginning of the nineteenth century, this sphere of the law continued to offer little in the way of certainty or coherence. In 1901, the House of Lords held in *Quinn v Leathem*[16] that a conspiracy aimed at harming the plaintiff in his or her trade or business was actionable as a tort if it involved malice. The defendants in that case were union members who had a dispute with the plaintiff, their employer,

[9] See, eg, *Cattle v Stockton Water Works Co* [1875] LR 10 QB 453 (DC); *Couper & Sons v Macfarlane* [1879] SLR 16 379.

[10] *Bowen v Hall* (1881) LR 6 QBD 333 (CA), 342.

[11] *Mogul Steamship v McGregor, Gow and Co* (1889) LR 23 QBD 598.

[12] *Ibid* 614.

[13] *Mogul Steamship v McGregor, Gow and Co* [1892] AC 25.

[14] *Allen v Flood* [1898] AC 1 (HL).

[15] See also *Stevenson v Newnham* (1853) 13 CB 297; *Bradford v Pickles* [1895] AC 597 (CA); *Haron bin Mundir v Singapore Amateur Athletic Association* [1992] 1 SLR 18, 31–32.

[16] *Quinn v Leathem* [1901] AC 495.

over his employment of non-union members. The plaintiff refused to discharge the non-union employees and the defendants retaliated by forcing the plaintiff's main customer to cease to deal with the plaintiff by threatening that they would otherwise call on the customer's employees to strike. The House of Lords found that, as the defendants acted out of spite and malice, rather than the protection of their own interests, they were liable for conspiracy, even though no unlawful means had been used. This was an evident departure from the rule in *Allen v Flood* that the presence of malice alone could not render an act tortious. Indeed, more than 60 years after the decision in *Quinn v Leathem*, Lord Devlin said that he was not sure that it could be said with certainty what was actually decided by that case.[17]

Five years after the decision in *Quinn v Leathem*, Australia saw a similar case in which the High Court heavily qualified the rule in *Allen v Flood*. The Court held that any interference with the rights of another, including the right to trade and seek employment, which occasions damage to him or her is actionable unless the interference is authorised, justified or excused by law.[18] However, it was said that interference which results from the exercise of free competition, such as the acts in *Mogul Steamship* and *Allen v Flood*, are not actionable.[19] Interference that is not authorised or expressly forbidden by law is justified and excused unless the plaintiff can show that the interference was deliberate and the defendant intended to cause harm.[20] The High Court said that it considered each of these principles to be consistent with earlier English authorities, including *Allen v Flood*. Subsequent Australian decisions, however, followed English principles more closely,[21] leaving the status of the economic torts open and with as little certainty as in England.

As is no doubt plain, the development of the principles discussed above was driven in large measure by the rise of the trade union movement in the nineteenth century.[22] Over a series of cases involving actions founded upon the torts of conspiracy and inducing breach of contract, employers sought to combat unions' actions in court.[23] The frequency with which the torts of conspiracy and inducing breach were relied upon in the context of industrial action eventually resulted in the enactment of the *Trade Disputes Act 1906* (UK) ('*Trade Disputes Act*').

The *Trade Disputes Act* was an attempt on the part of the legislature to render the economic torts toothless in the industrial sphere.[24] Although, in the words of Lord Hoffmann, the Government 'did not quite foresee the ingenuity of future lawyers in finding even more obscure economic torts which were not covered

[17] *Rookes v Barnard* [1964] AC 1129, 1216.

[18] *Brisbane Shipwrights Provident Union v Heggie* (1906) 3 CLR 686, 697–98.

[19] *Ibid* 698.

[20] *Ibid* 699.

[21] See, eg, *McKernan v Fraser* (1931) 46 CLR 343, 380–81; *James v Commonwealth* (1939) 62 CLR 339, 362–66.

[22] Hoffmann (n 6) 108.

[23] In addition to the cases discussed above, see: *Temperton v Russel* [1893] 1 QB 715 (CA); *South Wales Miners Federation v Glamorgan Coal Co Ltd* [1905] AC 239 (HL); *Taff Vale Railway Co v Amalgamated Society of Railway Servants* [1901] AC 426 (HL).

[24] Hoffmann (n 6) 110.

by the Act',[25] the role of the economic torts was nonetheless circumscribed for some time after the Act's entry into force. In addition to the *Trade Disputes Act*, the courts narrowed the economic torts' scope of potential application by introducing new requirements as to the defendant's state of mind.[26] In *Crofter Hand Woven Harris Tweed Co Ltd v Veitch*,[27] the House of Lords determined that a finding of bad motive conspiracy required that the defendant have an intention to injure without any desire to advance his or her own interests. This requirement was, as Lord Hoffmann has observed, 'virtually impossible to satisfy'.[28] In *Lumley v Gye* the Court noted that the inducement of the breach of contract was malicious on the basis that Mr Gye was aware of Miss Wagner's contract and intended to cause the breach that eventuated. As a result, findings of inducing breach were limited to circumstances where the defendant intended to cause such breach – a subjective inquiry which limited the subsequent application of *Lumley v Gye*.[29] Lord Hoffmann has suggested that the confines within which judges interpreted *Lumley v Gye* represented a 'determination to keep its application within very narrow limits'.[30]

It was not until the 1960s that the economic torts experienced a revival in order to combat the perceived 'excessive use' of trade union power.[31] That decade and the two that followed saw a gradual expansion in the tort of inducing breach of contract. In *Torquay Hotel Co Ltd v Cousins*,[32] liability was imposed on a trade union official who called for industrial action to disrupt the supply of oil to the business of the plaintiff. The Court of Appeal held that a tort was made out where 'a third person prevents or hinders one party from performing his contract, even though it not be a breach'.[33] Winn LJ said in obiter:

> Where a contract between two persons exists which gives one of them an optional extension of time or an optional mode for his performance, or part of it, but, from the normal course of dealing between them, the other person does not anticipate such postponement, or has come to expect a particular mode of performance, a procuring of the exercise of such an option should, in principle, be held actionable …[34]

Thus, not only did the tort offer protection from interference with contractual relations, it seemed that it might also grow to protect *expectancies* under contracts.[35]

[25] *Ibid* 111.
[26] *Ibid.*
[27] *Crofter Hand Woven Harris Tweed Co Ltd v Veitch* [1942] AC 435 (HL).
[28] Hoffmann (n 6) 111.
[29] See, eg, *British Industrial Plastics Ltd v Ferguson* [1940] 1 All ER 479 (HL) ('*Ferguson*'); Hoffmann (n 6) 111.
[30] Hoffmann (n 6) 111.
[31] *Ibid* 112.
[32] *Torquay Hotel Co Ltd v Cousins* [1969] 2 Ch 106 (CA).
[33] *Ibid* 138.
[34] *Ibid* 147.
[35] This suggestion has not been picked up. See *Woolley v Dunford* (1972) 3 SASR 243, 299; *J T Stratford & Son Ltd v Lindley* [1965] AC 269 (HL) 339; *Bowles & Son v Lindley* [1965] I Ll R 207, 213; *Torquay Hotel* (n 32)141.

Further, it was said that it was not necessary for the defendant to have had precise knowledge of the relevant contract; it was enough that he had been aware of the contract's existence and acted with a reckless disregard for, or turned a blind eye to, the consequences of his actions with respect to interference with that contract. These principles were subsequently affirmed in *Merkur Island Shipping Corp v Laughton*.[36]

Building on those principles, in *Dimbleby & Sons Ltd v NUJ*,[37] the plaintiff was granted an injunction to prevent interference with commercial contracts to which he was a party. Had the injunction not been granted, the interference with the contracts would have had the effect of making it more difficult or expensive for the contracts to be carried out. In *Emerald Construction Co Ltd v Lowthian*, Lord Denning MR suggested another expansion, whereby a defendant would be liable in tort if a contract were lawfully terminated by the conduct of a defendant who intended or was reckless as to breach.[38]

In 1964 in *Rookes v Barnard (No 1)*[39] ('*Rookes v Barnard*'), precedents concerning 'the use of violence to frighten away a competitor's customers or suppliers were generalised into the tort of intimidation'.[40] That decision brought greater clarity to the decisions in *Quinn v Leathem* and *Crofter*. The formulation of the tort – whereby threats of unlawful action against a third party are used to damage the target – was relied on in the context of threatened strikes in breach of no-strike agreements. The Court made it clear that if a defendant intentionally injures a plaintiff in his trade or business, the defendant will be liable in tort if the means used to afflict such injury were unlawful, in that they involved an act or threatened act not permitted by civil or criminal law. *Rookes v Barnard* also clarified that a threatened breach of contract is adequate to satisfy the unlawful means requirement and that malice is only required to be shown if purely lawful means were used.

Rookes v Barnard was not an uncontroversial decision.[41] The tort had already been accepted,[42] but *Rookes v Barnard* recognised that if the defendant threatened an illegal act against a third party who then caused the defendant loss, the tort of intimidation was committed and that a threat of breach of contract was sufficient as an 'illegal act' for the purpose of such tort. Unlike the torts of inducing breach of contract and conspiracy, the tort of intimidation was not covered by the *Trade Disputes Act*, and so could still be readily wielded in court against the

[36] *Merkur Island Shipping Corp v Laughton* [1983] 2 AC 570 (HL).
[37] *Dimbleby & Sons Ltd v NUJ* [1983] 1 WLR 427 (HL).
[38] *Emerald Construction Co Ltd v Lowthian* [1966] 1 WLR 691 (CA) 701.
[39] *Rookes v Barnard* (HL) (n 17).
[40] Hoffmann (n 6) 112.
[41] See, eg, JD Heydon, 'The Future of the Economic Torts' (1975) 12 *University of Western Australia Law Review* 1, 5.
[42] *J T Stratford & Son* (n 35); *Torquay Hotel* (n 32); *Pete's Towing Services Ltd v NIUW* [1970] NZLR 32; *Sid Ross Agency Pty Ltd v Actors and Announcers Equity Association of Australia* (1970) 90 WN (Pt 1) NSW 743, [1971] NSWR 760, 768; *Morgan v Fry* [1968] 2 QB 710 (CA).

trade unions.[43] In the 1970s, the Labour Government passed legislation extending the scope of the *Trade Disputes Act* to curtail the use of the new economic torts.[44]

The legislative framework based on the *Trades Disputes Act* was replaced by Margaret Thatcher's government in the early 1980s and has not been substantially altered since.[45] The current legislative scheme is somewhat peculiar, as explained by Lord Hoffmann:

> [The legislation] starts from accepting that, as a result of the development of the economic torts, virtually all forms of industrial action are unlawful at common law. It then re-enacts the 1906 Act and the legislation of the 1970s, which makes virtually all forms of industrial action lawful. But then it carves out some important exceptions in which strike action will not be protected from the common law, notably, strikes without a previous secret ballot of the members and secondary action against customers or suppliers ... The result ... is that in the area of industrial relations, there is no longer any interest in the common law economic torts. It is simply assumed that unprotected industrial action is unlawful. Parliament has taken over the role of delimiting what industrial action should be lawful or unlawful, without regard to contractual relationships.[46]

By the 1980s, the economic torts were distinct enough that they could be seen to fall into three categories of tortious liability.[47] The first comprises cases in which the tort involves direct interference with the pre-existing legal rights of the plaintiff. This category includes the tort of inducing breach of contract, along with lesser-known torts such as inducing the breach of a statutory or fiduciary duty owed to the plaintiff. The second category, derived from *Rookes v Banard*, comprises cases in which the defendant intentionally interferes with the plaintiff's trade, business or livelihood using unlawful means. Third, there stands apart the tort of lawful means conspiracy – distinct in that tortious liability can be found even if no unlawful means were used and no interference with a pre-existing legal right has taken place. Instead, the tort is based on the concept of 'unjustified combination leading to economic pressure or harm, so that, in effect, malice was required'.[48]

The decision in *OBG Ltd v Allan*[49] stands out as a landmark in the modern history of the economic torts.[50] The majority decision reflects a continued determination on the part of the judiciary to 'confine the economic torts as narrowly as possible, on the grounds that they have little rational basis in social or economic policy and that such matters are best left to the legislature'.[51]

[43] Hoffmann (n 6) 112.

[44] *Trade Union and Labour Relations Act 1974* (UK); *Trade Union and Labour Relations (Amendment) Act 1976* (UK); Hoffmann (n 6) 112.

[45] Originating with the *Employment Act 1980* (UK). The current provisions are consolidated in the *Trade Union and Labour Relations (Consolidation) Act 1992* (UK).

[46] Hoffmann (n 6) 112–13.

[47] S Deakin and J Randall, 'Rethinking the Economic Torts' (2009) 72(4) *MLR* 519, 519.

[48] *Ibid* 523.

[49] *OBG Ltd v Allan* [2007] UKHL 21, [2008] AC 1 (HL).

[50] J O'Sullivan, 'Intentional Economic Torts in the House of Lords' [2007] *CLJ* 503, 503.

[51] Hoffmann (n 6) 113.

Indeed, Lord Hoffmann has, extracurially, expressed hope that 'cases on the economic torts will become rare curiosities, of little practical consequence'.[52]

A different view, however, is that despite the reduction in scope of the economic torts, they continue to play a vital role.[53] While it may be true that the role of the economic torts in the industrial sphere is today much attenuated, and while their role in regulating commercial competition may have been largely overtaken by the emergence of modern competition law, it would nonetheless be quite wrong to relegate the economic torts to the dustbin of history. Indeed, this volume proceeds on the footing that an examination of the economic torts remains a worthwhile undertaking today. It seeks to examine a number of important questions in respect of this body of doctrine. Importantly, it also seeks to shed light on the place of the economic torts in the broader scheme of the law of obligations. It thus grapples with questions in respect of other doctrines and rules which operate to protect economic interests. In addition to showing that 'the economic torts' is a wider and more diverse legal category than has heretofore been acknowledged, it situates the economic torts alongside other bodies of doctrine which share similar rational underpinnings. It is hoped that by doing so, new light may be thrown on old problems, and scholarly interest in the economic torts will be stimulated anew.

[52] *Ibid* 116.
[53] Deakin and Randall (n 47) 524.

2

The 'Property' Paradigm in Torts Protecting Contractual Interests

ZHONG XING TAN*

I. Introduction

It is often suggested that there is something proprietary in the nature of the contractual obligation. The idea is of considerable vintage. Peter Benson, one of the most well-known figures in the 'property' or 'transfer' theory of contract camp,[1] argues as follows:

> At the moment of agreement and in accordance with its terms, what one party transfers to the other is the exclusive authority to exercise control over the thing promised (whether the thing is an external object or a service) … This exclusive authority to exercise control over a thing *is* ownership … The right acquired at contract formation is a right of ownership and therefore includes all the incidents of ownership: the right to possess, use, and alienate.[2]

In this chapter I aim to reconsider the property paradigm of contract through a particular angle: the economic tort of inducing breach of contract, its close cousin the unlawful means tort, and the tort of conversion. The centripetal force for the modern restatement of these torts has been the much-dissected House of Lords decision in *OBG v Allan*,[3] which provided the platform for the authoritative clarification of the ingredients of these torts.

* I am grateful to Hans Tjio and Andrew Simester for the chance to discuss some of the ideas in this chapter. The usual caveats apply.

[1] See P Benson, 'Contract as Transfer of Ownership' (2007) 48 *William and Mary Law Review* 1673; A Gold, 'A Property Theory of Contract' (2009) 103 *Northwestern University Law Review* 1; SA Smith, *Contract Theory* (Oxford University Press, 2004); H Dedek, 'A Particle of Freedom: Natural Law Thought and the Kantian Theory of Transfer by Contract' (2012) 25 *Canadian Journal of Law and Jurisprudence* 313; S Serafin, 'Transfer by Contract in Kant, Hegel and Comparative Law' (2018) 31 *Canadian Journal of Law and Jurisprudence* 151.

[2] Benson (n 1) 1725–26.

[3] *OBG v Allan* [2007] UKHL 21, [2008] 1 AC 1.

For inducing breach of contract, the 'standard case' of inducement or procurement is direct persuasion, coupled with subjective knowledge of an existing contract (including a conscious decision not to inquire but drawing the line at objective recklessness) and intention to procure the breach as a means to an end or an end in itself (not requiring malice but drawing the line at knowledge of foreseeable but incidental consequences).[4]

As to unlawful means (previously often conflated with the tort of inducing breach of contract),[5] this may cover situations where the claimant's interests falling short of a contractual right are interfered with, but requiring that the defendant intended to cause the claimant loss as an intended end or means of achieving that end (malice again not being necessary but likewise drawing the line at foresight of probable harm), and moreover that the defendant used unlawful means in doing so, defined as acts unlawful against a third party which interfered with the freedom of the third party to deal with the claimant.[6]

In comparing and contrasting the two, the former is said to be a tort of accessorial liability, dependent upon primary wrongdoing by the contract-breaker, unlike the latter which creates primary liability sparked by the distinctive element of utilising unlawful means.[7]

Conversion, on the other hand, requires a claimant with a superior possessory right in an asset, a deprivation by the defendant of the claimant's full benefit of that right, and an assumption by the defendant of the possessory rights rightfully belonging to the claimant.[8] In *OBG* a divergence of views was seen between the dissenters, Lord Nicholls and Baroness Hale, who were in favour of extending liability for conversion to intangible contractual rights (in circumstances where invalidly appointed administrative receivers had innocently taken control of the claimant's business, terminated contracts and settled claims), and the bare majority of Lord Hoffmann, Lord Walker and Lord Brown, who deemed it too radical to extend strict liability in conversion beyond chattels to choses in action.[9]

If there is something in the nature of 'property' in the contractual obligation, how exactly do we conceive of 'property', and to what extent does a property paradigm motivate the shape of these torts? I will first consider how commentators have used 'property' reasoning in explaining or justifying the torts under consideration, before pointing out where such ideas are ambiguous, misleading or incomplete. While recognising that 'property' serves (at best) as an amplifier for the notion of protected interests, I argue for a shift from a more monistic property

[4] *Ibid* [8], [39]–[44], [172]–[173], [191]–[192], [264], [302]–[303], [319].

[5] See H Carty, 'The Economic Torts in the 21st Century' (2008) 124 *LQR* 641; H Carty, *An Analysis of the Economic Torts*, 2nd edn (Oxford, Oxford University Press, 2010) Ch 3.

[6] *OBG* (n 3) [8], [45]–[64], [270], [302], [320]; Carty (n 5) 78–101.

[7] *OBG* (n 3) [8].

[8] See the concise restatement in S Green and J Randall, *The Tort of Conversion* (Oxford, Hart Publishing, 2009) 75–78.

[9] *OBG* (n 3) [95]–[100], [105]–[106], [271], [319]–[322], [330]; S Douglas, 'The Scope of Conversion: Property and Contract' (2011) 74 *MLR* 329.

paradigm to a pluralistic one where claimant-sided, defendant-sided and wider societal considerations come into play shaping the precise scope of *in rem* liability in a given doctrine.

II. The Property Paradigm

A. Inducing Breach of Contract

A property, or at least quasi-proprietary, rationale is often mooted for the tort of inducing breach of contract, though commentators differ on the manner and extent to which they draw the relevant link with 'property'. We often find passing comments made by judges and commentators to this effect. In *OBG*, Lord Hoffmann observed that the tort:

> [T]reats contractual rights as a species of property which deserve special protection, not only by giving a right of action against the party who breaks his contract but by imposing secondary liability on a person who procures him to do so. In this respect it is quite distinct from the unlawful means principle, which is concerned only with intention and wrongfulness and is indifferent as to the nature of the interest which is damaged.[10]

Extra-judicially, Lord Hoffmann has explained the genesis of the proprietary notion with reference to the historical context in which *Lumley v Gye*[11] (the famous case of an opera singer induced by the defendant to break her contract with the plaintiff) was decided:

> The judges in *Lumley v Gye* must have thought that poaching someone who was contracted to provide her services to a rival was crossing a bright line … It was probably important to the judges that Miss Wagner was an artist of European reputation … Her services were unique … *Lumley v Gye* made the judges think of how they would have felt if someone poached their butler or cook. And so they reached back into the mediaeval law of master and servant, when menial servants and wives were a species of property and an action lay *per quod servitium amisit*, or for loss of consortium, and they applied this to the contract with Miss Wagner.[12]

The property analogy is also invoked at times by various common law courts sharing the heritage of *Lumley*. Chesney, writing in 1999, comments that 'the notion is generations old, and judges reaffirm it regularly',[13] citing for instance *R & W Hat Shop, Inc v Sculley*[14] where the Court commented that the 'contract relation gave to each a property right in the contracts, and any intentional interference

[10] *OBG* (n 3) [32].

[11] *Lumley v Gye* (1853) 2 E & B 216, (1853) 118 ER 749.

[12] L Hoffmann, 'The Rise and Fall of the Economic Torts' in J Edelman, J Goudkamp and S Degeling (eds), *Torts in Commercial Law* (Sydney, Thomson Reuters, 2011) 107.

[13] F Chesney, 'Tortious Interference with Contract Versus "Efficient" Breach: Theory and Empirical Evidence' (1999) 28 *Journal of Legal Studies* 131, 141.

[14] *R & W Hat Shop Inc v Sculley*, 118 A. 55 (Conn. 1922) 58.

with the rights of either by a third party was an interference with his rights of property'.[15] The High Court of Australia in the 2004 decision of *Zhu v Treasurer (NSW)*[16] cited with approval Kitto J's 'quasi-proprietary' analysis of contractual rights in *Attorney-General (NSW) v Perpetual Trustee Co Ltd*,[17] and while it noted that Kitto J's argument had an 'element of circuity' in explaining the proprietary characteristic by reference to its *in rem* reach,[18] it endorsed the property analogy, commenting that the arguments before it 'did not suggest that Kitto J's reasoning does not represent the law in Australia'.[19]

In fleshing out the property notion, one of the most well-known argumentative strategies is Epstein's analogy of the *Lumley* tort as an illustration of the problem of ostensible ownership.[20] As Epstein notes, such problems 'arise where a party, when placed in possession of property he does not own, acts as its owner in dealing with a third party who typically has no notice of the separation of ownership from possession'.[21] As between the owner and the third party, 'people can control misconduct at lower cost as owner than they can as potential purchaser', such as an owner who is able to exercise care and take precaution in selecting a bailee, in contrast to a prospective purchaser who might bear higher costs of verification given the ability of the ostensible owner to conceal defects in his title.[22] As such, the balance of considerations favours a good faith purchaser without notice, and the fault factor is accommodated not through a more costly and litigation-intensifying standard of negligence or comparative fault, but via a default strict liability rule coupled with a defence based on notice.[23] The pièce de résistance of Epstein's analysis is to fit the *Lumley* tort within this frame, suggesting that 'inducement of breach of contract is used to fill the gaps in the law of trespass and conversion' where the problems of ostensible ownership routinely arise, such as in sale of goods scenarios.[24] The property we are concerned with is not a tangible good but the intangible promise (such as one to confer an exclusive service) interfered with by the third party, and the notice element in ostensible ownership is correlated with the *mens rea* in the *Lumley* doctrine – the purchaser of labour with notice 'is no better than … the bad faith purchaser of negotiable instruments, goods, or land', as his 'willingness to proceed with a transaction where there is knowledge that it entails a breach is itself a form of malice, as it indicates a self-interested willingness to defy the basic system of rights created by the legal system'.[25]

[15] *Ibid* 58.
[16] *Zhu v Treasurer (NSW)* [2004] HCA 56, (2004) 218 CLR 530.
[17] *Attorney-General (NSW) v Perpetual Trustee Co Ltd* (1952) 85 CLR 237 (HCA).
[18] *Zhu* (n 16) [126].
[19] *Ibid* [135].
[20] RA Epstein, 'Inducement of Breach of Contract as a Problem of Ostensible Ownership' (1987) 16 *Journal of Legal Studies* 1.
[21] *Ibid* 2.
[22] *Ibid* 13–14.
[23] *Ibid* 15–16.
[24] *Ibid* 19–20.
[25] *Ibid* 25.

Neyers, following Benson, attempts to refract the *Lumley* tort through a different 'proprietary' lens.[26] The aspect of property latched upon is the notion of assignability, which no doubt applies to contractual rights as valuable commercial assets. The basis of such a transfer is typically consent, but it is said that a third party defendant can similarly view the contractual right as a proprietary object susceptible to appropriation (in this case, involuntarily from the standpoint of the claimant).[27] It follows that 'it is the intention to appropriate which creates the protected interest (the quasi-property) and the actual appropriation which constitutes the violation of that right'.[28] In other words, the extension from the *in personam* contractual relationship to *in rem* protection accorded to the claimant against the third party is explicable by reference to the latter's 'free choice to interfere with the contract – without this intention to appropriate there could be no liability'.[29]

Other commentators draw different parallels between *Lumley* liability and conceptions of property. For instance, Bagshaw borrows arguments from the canon of property theory to indicate possible justifications for engrafting *in rem* protection onto the contractual obligation.[30] These include, first, a freedom-enhancing aspect – the stability of contracts, like the stability of ownership, allows persons to increase their options and resources without fear that these might be compromised by external interference; second, a wealth-maximisation justification – like the institution of private property, which creates social wealth, contractual rights are items of commercial value and intangible stores of corporate and individual wealth which warrant legal protection to enhance their security; and third, a desert/incentivisation argument – just as private property is sometimes grounded in Lockean terms on labour[31] and for the economist as a tool to align incentive structures,[32] protecting contract rights from third party interference is said to be appropriate especially in situations where parties have invested effort and resources in contractual relations, both on a backward-looking reward basis as well as a forward-looking reason to encourage productive endeavours.[33]

While Bagshaw's normative justifications for contract as property look somewhat externalist with their consequentialist flavour, Lee offers a different, powerfully-reasoned internalist rationale focussing on rights.[34] Building on Simester and Chan's account of the *Lumley* tort as safeguarding the promisee's right

[26] JW Neyers, 'The Economic Torts as Corrective Justice' (2009) 17 *Torts Law Journal* 162 (discussing P Benson, 'The Basis for Excluding Liability for Economic Loss in Tort Law' in DG Owen (ed), *Philosophical Foundations of Tort Law* (Oxford, Clarendon, 1993)).

[27] *Ibid* 175.

[28] *Ibid.*

[29] *Ibid* 176.

[30] R Bagshaw, 'Inducing Breach of Contract' in J Horder (ed), *Oxford Essays in Jurisprudence*, 4th series (Oxford, Oxford University Press, 2000).

[31] J Locke, *Second Treatise of Government* (New York, Hafner, first published 1689, 1947).

[32] H Demsetz, 'Toward a Theory of Property Rights' (1967) 57 *American Economic Review* 347.

[33] Bagshaw (n 30) 133–37.

[34] PW Lee, 'Inducing Breach of Contract, Conversion and Contract as Property' (2009) 29 *OJLS* 511.

to pre-emptive status in the promisor's reasoning,[35] and adopting Gray's capacious definition of property as a 'power-relation constituted by the state's endorsement of private claims to regulate the access of strangers to the benefits of particular resources',[36] she argues that the property analogy directs 'the court's attention to the nature and degree of control which a claimant seeks to assert over a particular interest or resource, as well as the practical, legal and moral justifications for the same',[37] hence concluding that the promise is property-like to the extent that the promisee is able to restrict or exclude access to the peremptory status of the promise as against third parties.[38]

B. Unlawful Means Tort

In comparison with the *Lumley* tort, property arguments for the unlawful means tort are far less visible within the literature for a glaring reason: the tort does not require a breach of contract, and hence covers 'expectancies' falling short of contract. Hence, Epstein argues that '[i]t is only where the promisor is in breach that the promisee can be said to have lost a property right',[39] and Neyers comments that 'a valid contract is necessary to ground the [*Lumley*] tort since without a valid contract there is no right to performance'.[40] Nonetheless, the possibility of a property analogy is not completely absent, especially if one adopts normative property rationales (such as Bagshaw's consequentialist justifications) for the protection of expectancies falling short of rights created by contract, perhaps where there is substantial investment by parties made prior to contracting, or in more relational scenarios where the contractual relations may not be formalised but embedded within existing longer-term dealings with shared expectations of continued cooperation and commitment.[41]

The most sustained attempt at a property analogy which would apply to the expectancies covered by the unlawful means tort is Fine's strategy of setting out a series of stages where property rights come into being with increasing *in rem* effect, and for this purpose drawing an intriguing parallel between textbook property law cases concerning the pursuit of wild animals and the case law on the acquisition of various types of contractual interests.[42] In Fine's analysis, the first stage is where pursuit has not commenced, and hence a claimant can claim no interest

[35] AP Simester and W Chan, 'Inducing Breach of Contract: One Tort of Two?' (2004) 63 *CLJ* 132.
[36] K Gray, 'Property in Thin Air' (1991) 50 *CLJ* 252, 294.
[37] Lee (n 34) 519.
[38] *Ibid* 524.
[39] Epstein (n 20) 24.
[40] Neyers (n 26) 175.
[41] LR BeVier, 'Reconsidering Inducement' (1990) 76 *Virginia Law Review* 877, 908. See also WJ Woodward Jr, 'Contractarians, Community, and the Tort of Interference with Contract' (1996) 80 *Minnesota Law Review* 1103.
[42] BL Fine, 'An Analysis of the Formation of Property Rights Underlying Tortious Interference with Contracts and Other Economic Relations' (1983) 50 *University of Chicago Law Review* 1116.

'even for the most direct and malign interference' such as the slaying of a wild fox out of spite before the claimant's eyes.[43] When a pursuer begins the pursuit of a wild animal, liability is founded on the defendant's notice of the pursuit plus the absence of any privilege which would otherwise attach in the case where the defendant is also a genuine pursuer.[44] The contractual parallel is where a defendant had 'notice of the expectancy' and a lack of 'genuine commercial interest in the object of the expectancy', the latter element negating the right to pursue which 'would otherwise stand on equal footing with the rights of the party interfered with'.[45] Hence a defendant who jeers a claimant-performer off the stage, causing the claimant's at-will contract to be terminated and consequent harm to his employment prospects, can be found liable under this analysis from 'knowledge plus lack of commercial interest in the expectancy',[46] even though the claimant has no contractual rights to speak of. Once a pursuer obtains some definite degree of physical control over an animal, paralleling the entry into an executory contract, the pursuer or promisee acquires 'an exclusive right to pursue, depriving other pursuers of the privilege of pursuit or commercial interest',[47] even though 'property' in the actual performance is only fully obtained in an executed contract.[48] For our purposes, Fine's analysis suggests that certain types of expectancies falling short of contract warrant property-like protection, which justify the imposition of liability under the unlawful means tort. One thinks of *Tarleton v M'Gawley*,[49] where it could be said that the claimant-shipowner had a property-like interest in the custom of African natives for which it had travelled to pursue, which was interfered with by the defendant's unlawful act of firing guns at the natives, though this interest fell short of a concluded contract.

In conceptualising a property-like foundation for the interests and expectancies covered by the unlawful means tort, we might also have reference to Lord Hoffmann's formulation in *OBG* of the requirement that the unlawful means in question must affect the third party's freedom to deal with the claimant,[50] a significant component of the unlawful means doctrine which was recently re-affirmed by the English Court of Appeal in *Secretary of State for Health v Servier Laboratories Ltd*.[51] In *OBG*, Lord Hoffmann illustrated the operation of this requirement with *RCA Corp v Pollard*,[52] where it was said that the defendant-bootlegger had not interfered with the liberty of Elvis Presley's estate to perform their exclusive recording contract

[43] Adapting for illustration the facts of *Pierson v Post* 3, Cai R 175 (NY Sup Ct, 1805).
[44] Fine (n 42) 1136, discussing *Keeble v Hickeringill* (1707) 3 Salk 9, (1707) 91 Eng Rep 659.
[45] Fine (n 42) 1136.
[46] *Ibid* 1140, citing *Gregory v Duke of Brunswick* (1843) 6 Man & G 205, 953, (1843) 134 Eng Rep 866, 1178.
[47] Fine (n 42) 1144.
[48] *Ibid* 1136.
[49] *Tarleton v M'Gawley* [1793] Peake 270, (1793) 170 Eng Rep 153.
[50] *OBG* (n 3) [51].
[51] *Secretary of State for Health v Servier Laboratories Ltd* [2019] EWCA Civ 1160.
[52] *RCA Corp v Pollard* [1983] Ch 135 (Ch).

with the claimant, merely reducing the latter's profits;[53] as well as *Isaac Oren v Red Box Toy Factory*,[54] where the defendant's sales of articles alleged to have infringed a design right had not interfered with the relations between the owner of the right and the claimant (an exclusive licensee), merely affecting the commercial success of the licensing agreement.[55] Another fairly straightforward illustration is that of Lord Walker's pizza delivery business which obtains more business to the detriment of its rivals by jumping red lights – unlawful means which do not interfere with any third parties' liberty to deal with a competitor potentially suing under this tort.[56] Abstracting away from the case law, the importance of the 'interference with liberty to deal' requirement is that it evinces a taking of a fairly concretised privilege to trade that the claimant has with a commercial partner. This privilege could be said to be quasi-proprietary in a certain sense, in so far as we might see the claimant as exclusively entitled to a certain type of expectancy that the defendant should not interfere with.

C. Conversion

While conversion clearly protects proprietary interests, the question is whether and how far the subject matter of conversion extends from tangible chattels to intangible choses in action. One way around this, as Lee argues, is to identify the gist of conversion as protecting property in the sense of 'control of access to a valued resource'.[57] Possession is relevant only in so far as 'physical control of tangible property was the best proxy of ownership or exclusive control', but 'the precise manifestation of control must surely be context-dependent' and hence there is 'no reason for insisting on physical control when the relevant resource does not exist in physical form'.[58] Accordingly, in a case like *OBG*, the claimant had the 'sole and exclusive right to determine the conduct and discharge of its contracts', which could constitute convertible property.[59] This progressive view finds its echo in the judgment of Lord Nicholls in *OBG*, where he observed that the law already provides remedies where the contractual obligation is embodied or recorded in documentary form, and that:

> The reality is that English law does sometimes provide a remedy for the misappropriation, or conversion, of intangible rights. To that extent the tort of conversion has already jumped the gap between tangibles and intangibles … Rationally the dividing line cannot be the existence or not of a piece of paper.[60]

[53] *OBG* (n 3) [52].
[54] *Isaac Oren v Red Box Toy Factory* [1999] FSR 785.
[55] *OBG* (n 3) [54].
[56] *Ibid* [266].
[57] Lee (n 34) 529.
[58] *Ibid.*
[59] *Ibid* 530.
[60] *OBG* (n 3) [228], [230].

For Green and Randall, who support the extension of liability to intangible contractual rights, the claimant must nonetheless exhibit not only the cognitive indicia of possession – his active intention to control and exclude others from an excludable and exhaustible asset, coupled with passive awareness of the asset's existence and form – but also the manual indicia of possession whether direct (physical contact) or indirect (controlling access).[61] These, however, are not obstacles to contractual debts being the subject of conversion, even those not manifested in any physical form. A debt is said to be an excludable asset, access being limited to the creditor; as well as an exhaustible one, as with *OBG* where the receivers' unauthorised dealings with the claimants' contractual claims deprived them substantially of the value of their corporate assets.[62] As such, it is said that there are 'no convincing reasons, either conceptual or of policy, for excluding many forms of intangible personal property from the ambit of the legal protection afforded to tangible property'[63] under the tort of conversion.

III. Problems with the Property Paradigm

The property paradigm is by no means universally endorsed. At times it has been scathingly dismissed, perhaps without sufficient attention to the depth of sophistication presented by its proponents. Palmer comments that '[i]nstinctively, certainly nonchalantly, common-law judges made recourse to property conceptions, and gave us another instance of Milsom's dictum that "The life of the common law has been the unceasing abuse of its elementary ideas".'[64] In this section I will raise a number of concerns regarding the above-mentioned property arguments.

A. Fit with Doctrinal Data

Some versions of the property analogy incorrectly characterise the *mens rea* required for the *Lumley* tort. For instance, Fine points out that under Epstein's theory of strict liability for the *Lumley* tort, 'the tortfeasor's mental state forms no part of the prima facie case; mental states are relevant only in overcoming a defendant's otherwise affirmative defense'.[65] Recall also Epstein's explicit likening of the *Lumley* tort to conversion, the only difference being that *Lumley* is not confined to sale of goods scenarios but extends to the provision of services and other types of contractual arrangements.[66] This is a deliberate conflation of the elements of the

[61] Green and Randall (n 8) 110.
[62] *Ibid* 134–37.
[63] *Ibid* 139.
[64] VL Palmer, 'A Comparative Study (From a Common Law Perspective) of the French Action for Wrongful Interference With Contract' (1992) 40 *American Journal of Comparative Law* 297, 332.
[65] Fine (n 42) 1123.
[66] Epstein (n 20) 19.

torts inducing breach of contract and conversion, by forcing *Lumley* into the latter's mould despite obvious and well-established differences: in particular that conversion is 'in essence a strict liability tort', the notion of 'intentionality' in conversion being used only in the sense of a 'deliberate or non-accidental conduct' in interfering with possession,[67] while the *Lumley* tort requires subjective appreciation of the contract and intention to procure breach as an end or means to an end.

For Bagshaw, a dilute form of 'intention' in the form of 'a sufficient degree of knowledge of the likelihood that conduct may bring about a breach of contract, and a choice to persist with that conduct despite the knowledge', is the appropriate mental element, as 'a narrow mental element might be thought to offer insufficient protection to an interest in some ways akin to a property interest'.[68] As Carty points out, Bagshaw's dilute conception may suggest that inevitable consequences are sufficient for liability, which is out of tune with *OBG*'s philosophy.[69] Without a firm grip on intention to procure breach as an end or means to an end, we risk opening the door to *Millar v Bassey*[70]-type situations where the defendant-singer's breach of a recording contract inevitably and foreseeably, but not intentionally, led to the recording company's further breach of a downstream contract for technical services for the aborted recording; a decision which Lord Hoffmann commented was wrongly decided by a majority of the Court of Appeal in loosening the *mens rea* of the *Lumley* tort towards a negligence standard.[71]

B. Analytical Extensions

In some cases, a working definition of property is offered and extensions are made from the existence of one or a number of analytical features, to others. For instance, Neyers and Benson appear to reason from transferability or assignability to associated *in rem* protection under the *Lumley* tort.[72] Baroness Hale appears to adopt a similar strategy in arguing for intangible contract rights to be protected through conversion, observing that the

> essential feature of property is that it has an existence independent of a particular person: it can be bought or sold, given and received, bequeathed and inherited, pledged or seized to secure debts, acquired (in the olden days) by a husband on marrying its owner.[73]

No doubt property is at times usefully depicted as a bundle of rights, comprising for instance Honoré's incidents as ownership: 'the right to possess, the right to

[67] Green and Randall (n 8) 165–66.
[68] Bagshaw (n 30) 142–43.
[69] Carty (n 5) 58.
[70] *Millar v Bassey* [1994] EMLR 44 (CA).
[71] *OBG* (n 3) [43].
[72] Neyers (n 26).
[73] *OBG* (n 3) [309].

use, the right to manage, the right to income of the thing, the right to capital, the right to security, the rights or incidents of transmissibility and absence of term' and so on.[74] However, the existence of one or more incidents (say, transmissibility) does not per se lead to the conclusion that a certain level of *in rem* protection is warranted. More generally, we might say that each aspect of property needs to be able to stand on its own justification. For instance, taking the features of property identified by Worthington[75] as relevant to commercial lawyers – excludability, assignability, protection via property rules, carrying entitlements to proceeds, imposing obligations running with the asset, and attracting insolvency protection – we might say that the policy considerations underlying each proprietary characteristic are different. As Worthington notes, 'public policy determines whether a particular bundle of rights is assignable', be they body parts, rights to litigate, and so on.[76] These are different from the considerations taken into account when deciding whether the proprietary remedies of specific performance or disgorgement should be awarded.[77] The question of the scope of *in rem* protection for the contractual obligation must accordingly be answered independently via normative argument, as opposed to reasoning from one proprietary feature to another.

C. Identification of 'Property' and the Subject Matter of the Torts

One major issue in the literature analogising contract to property relates to the malleability of the latter concept. As Wexler observes, '[i]t is not useful to say that one cannot take another's property when the real issue is what rights, if any, the other person "owns" in the property in question'.[78] What precisely has been taken by the defendant in inducing a breach of the claimant's contract or in converting the claimant's contractual rights? For Bagshaw the 'things' in question are the promisor's willingness and existing capacity to perform under the *Lumley* tort.[79] Yet as Simester and Chan explain:

> The metaphor is overtly proprietary: we might say that, by preventing performance, D 'misappropriates' [the promisor's] capacity to perform. But even if we grant such a metaphor, the misappropriation is from [the promisor]. It is not obvious why it is a

[74] AM Honoré, 'Ownership' in AG Guest (ed), *Oxford Essays in Jurisprudence* (Oxford, Oxford University Press, 1961) 107, 113.

[75] S Worthington, 'The Disappearing Divide Between Property and Obligation: The Impact of Aligning Legal Analysis and Commercial Expectation' (2007) 42 *Texas International Law Journal* 917.

[76] *Ibid* 928.

[77] See further G Virgo and S Worthington, *Commercial Remedies: Resolving Controversies* (Cambridge, Cambridge University Press, 2017) chs 5 and 13.

[78] GD Wexler, 'Intentional Interference with Contract: Market Efficiency and Individual Liberty Considerations' (1994) 27 *Connecticut Law Review* 279, 305.

[79] Bagshaw (n 30) 137.

> taking from P … Indeed, at the time the bargain is made, [the promisor] may have *no* existing capacity to perform … Thus what seems to matter is not [the promisor's] existing capacity but her *future* capacity to perform … If P has any right of this sort, it can only be an action-right: a right that strangers not act to prevent [the promisor] from performing. To conceive of the tort as protecting an interest in [the promisor's] existing capacity to perform generates an unstable analysis.[80]

If the focal point of 'property' is not the promisor's capacity to perform, then it has to be something else that the claimant-promisee is able to 'own'. As noted above, one strategy as adopted by Lee is to argue that the relevant property is found in the promisee's exclusive right to the peremptory status of the promisor's promise. Another way of putting the point is that the 'thing' that is taken does not exist in the factual realm of capacity to perform but in the normative landscape of the promisor's will. Similarly, but in Kantian terms:

> By contract I acquire something external. But what is it that I acquire? Since it is only the causality of another's choice with respect to a performance he has promised me, what I acquire directly by a contract is not an external thing but rather his deed, by which that thing is brought under my control so that I make it mine.[81]

The trouble with this promissory/will-based depiction of property is that contract law does not invariably seek to protect the will per se; rather, its concern appears to be with the *legitimate interests* underpinning the contractual obligation.[82] For instance, it is often said that a restraint of trade covenant is enforceable only where there is a legitimate interest which the covenant is intended to protect[83] (sometimes called a legitimate proprietary interest).[84] As Smith notes, the 'classic examples of *legitimate interests* – trade secrets, customer connections, goodwill – are all properly described as investments necessary for the positive endeavour (the job, developing a business)'[85] and hence protected. In the UK Supreme Court decision on the combined cases of *Cavendish Square Holding BV v Talal El Makdessi* and *ParkingEye Limited v Beavis*,[86] it was noted that 'the minimum condition for an order of specific performance is that the innocent party should have a *legitimate interest* extending beyond pecuniary compensation for the breach', the paradigm case being the purchase of unique parcels of land or chattels such as ships.[87] Likewise, in discussing the limits on affirmation following repudiatory breach in

[80] Simester and Chan (n 35) 148–49.
[81] I Kant, *The Metaphysics of Morals*, 2nd edn (translated by MJ Gregor) (Cambridge, Cambridge University Press, 1996) 53.
[82] See S Rowan, 'The "Legitimate Interest in Performance" in the Law of Penalties' (2019) 78 *CLJ* 148.
[83] See *Tilman v Egon Zehnder Ltd* [2019] UKSC 32, [24]: 'The law came to recognise that the employer or purchaser of a business had legitimate interests which might justify his placing limited restrictions on his employee or vendor'.
[84] See *Countrywide Assured Financial Services Ltd v Deanne Smart* [2004] EWHC 1214 (Ch) and the Singapore Court of Appeal in *Mano Vikrant Singh v Cargill TSF Asia Pte Ltd* [2012] 1 SLR 311.
[85] SA Smith, 'Reconstructing Restraint of Trade' (1995) 13 *OJLS* 565, 576 (emphasis added).
[86] *Cavendish Square Holding BV v Talal El Makdessi* [2015] UKSC 67, [2016] AC 1172.
[87] *Ibid* [30] (emphasis added).

the leading decision of *White and Carter (Councils) Ltd v McGregor*,[88] Lord Reid famously observed that:

> it may well be that, if it can be shown that a person has no *legitimate interest*, financial or otherwise, in performing the contract, rather than claiming damages, he ought not to be allowed to saddle the other party with an additional burden with no benefit to himself.[89]

The focus of contract doctrine on legitimate interests often appears to be a significant qualification to property in the will-based obligation.

Another problem with the will/obligation conception of property is seen in the conversion cases. No doubt the 'thing' in question which is convertible can conceivably be thought of as a promisee's exclusive entitlement to conduct or discharge his contracts, or his dominion over obligations owed to him (as in *OBG*), but as Simon Douglas has pointed out in a careful analysis, where a promisor owes the claimant a sum of money, the fact that the defendant has persuaded the promisor to pay him that sum instead (for example by purporting to be the claimant's receiver) does not discharge the promisor's obligation – the defendant has not successfully converted or deprived the claimant of his intangible rights and powers, which remain in place vis-à-vis the promisor.[90]

Rather, the claimant is negatively affected because the promisor may not be in a position (in terms of willingness or ability) to pay out that sum again to the claimant as a result of the defendant's conduct; hence the defendant has potentially deprived the claimant of 'something' which could be characterised as the 'financial value of the right'[91] or perhaps the 'right to a certain likelihood of the promisor fulfilling his obligations', for instance a right to be paid $1,000 in circumstances where the promisor is of a particular financial standing, with a certain quantity of resources, under a given set of economic conditions, all things being equal.

But it is difficult to think of claimants having such rights, and to think of them in proprietary terms as having *in rem* reach, since these would contravene the policy rationale undergirding well-established prohibitions on recovery for pure economic loss, given that the 'holder of a contractual right bears the risk that the contract will not turn out to be as profitable as expected', and that 'third parties come under no duty towards the holders of contractual rights to refrain from doing acts which deprive those contractual rights of their value'.[92] As such, when it comes to intangible contractual rights, it is difficult to identify any 'thing' that constitutes the subject-matter of proprietary protection for the conversion doctrine to operate upon.

[88] *White and Carter (Councils) Ltd v McGregor* [1962] AC 413 (HL).
[89] *Ibid* 431 (emphasis added).
[90] Douglas (n 9) 338–40.
[91] *Ibid* 342.
[92] *Ibid* 346, discussing the representative cases such as *The Aliakmon* [1986] AC 785 (HL).

D. Normative Justifications for *in rem* Reach

If we could grant a working definition of property in contract, such as on a will-based foundation of a claim-right to performance coupled with the power to waive or enforce the obligation viewed as an excludable resource or asset, it is still not abundantly clear how the conclusion to *in rem* protection is derived. To be clear, I am not denying the *in rem* scope of the torts protecting contractual interests, nor arguing that they are ultimately unjustifiable – what I am concerned with is getting to such an *in rem* conclusion by working through a monistic 'property' frame.

For instance, proprietary will-based reasoning in the 'transfer' theory tradition only gets one to promissory remedies such as specific performance or expectation damages *inter partes*, but not beyond that to *in rem* protection. Recall Benson's transfer account where the 'agreement transfers rightful control over a thing (object or service) from one party (alienation) to the other (appropriation), and, by stipulating performance, it determines the time and manner of the promisee's physically taking it (use)'.[93] As Benson emphasises:

> [I]n the case of contract, the right and the object are completely specified by the terms of the parties' agreement, and this analysis holds only as between the parties in accordance with those terms. The right is a non-proprietary [ie non *in rem*] right of ownership that is *wholly transactional as between the parties alone*.[94]

For avoidance of doubt, Benson uses the terms 'property' and 'ownership' in a stipulative fashion where the latter is a general conception consisting of any right to exclusive possession, use or alienation as against another or others. Within the notion of ownership of things, property involves *in rem* ownership rights, while contract involves *in personam* ownership rights.[95] The whole point of Benson's property analogy is to answer the Fuller and Perdue challenge[96] of being able to identify a protected interest to which a contractual claimant is entitled prior to breach, as opposed to mere psychological expectancies of performance.[97] To the extent that a Benson-like account is persuasive, it accordingly demonstrates that contract creates a new baseline of entitlement given the promisee's acquisition of exclusive authority to exercise control, thus justifying the principle in *Robinson v Harman*[98] that the aim of damages for breach of contract is to put the claimant into as good a position as if the contract had been performed. But this rationale does not go further in prescribing the existence or extent of protection as against *non-parties* to the contract.

[93] Benson (n 1) 1725.
[94] *Ibid* 1723.
[95] *Ibid* 1719.
[96] LL Fuller and WR Perdue Jr, 'The Reliance Interest in Contract Damages' (1936) 46 *Yale Law Journal* 52.
[97] *Ibid* 57–58.
[98] *Robinson v Harman* (1848) 1 Exch 850, 855, (1848) 154 ER 363, 365.

Moreover, as Dobbs has argued (and in contrast to the analogy drawn by Bagshaw), the normative consequentialist justifications for contract as property are less compelling compared to other forms of intangible property, such as intellectual property, for in such cases:

> [The claimant] has not merely entered an agreement, but has designed a product, invented a novel machine or process, or written a book. He has created values which may properly be reserved to him … If, then, we ask why it is that contracts should be treated as property, we can find little justification in the other cases where property … is recognized. When property is created by individuals … protection usually is given as a reward and encouragement for creation, or because (in the case of trademarks) the public will be misled if property is not recognized. Even in these cases, property is given for limited periods of time and is defeasible automatically or upon the happening of certain contingencies.[99]

Dobbs is perhaps overreaching in making his point – setting up a straw man comparison between the investment that goes into contracts and that which goes into intellectual property. As BeVier has argued, in some cases the *Lumley* tort might be seen as responsive to under-compensatory contract remedies, in settings involving contract-specific investment such as 'returns-to-information' cases (say, a contract to purchase controlling shares of a company) and 'relational contract' scenarios (joint ventures, franchises, distributorships, and so on) where the relevant performance obligations are difficult to specify and costly to monitor, such that expectation damages will be highly uncertain.[100]

But Dobbs' cautionary note is well-taken. One cannot simply trot out the 'property' label to equate the labour involved in entering a contract with the labour involved in creating a patentable invention. The former may not always involve substantial investment or productive endeavour. This would apply to executory contracts, and *a fortiori* to expectancies, since the latter would involve dealings that have yet to reach the stage of contract formation. Moreover, as Varadarajan has argued,[101] it is not clear that the answer to deficient *in personam* remedies is to create new *in rem* liability, as opposed to rectifying under-compensatory remedies. For example, it is said that an 'expansion of the specific-performance remedy in contract law would likely lead to a corresponding narrowing in the application of the tort remedy',[102] as it 'seems redundant to protect the promise with a property rule in tort when one is already available in contract'.[103] Again, my point is not simply that *in rem* liability under the *Lumley* or unlawful means tort is unjustified, but rather that 'property' analogies are ultimately limited in explaining the shape of these torts.

[99] D Dobbs, 'Tortious Interference with Contractual Relationships' (1980) 34 *Arkansas Law Review* 335, 353, 355.
[100] BeVier (n 41) 899–911.
[101] D Varadarajan, 'Tortious Interference and the Law of Contract: *The Case for Specific Performance* Revisited' (2001) 111 *Yale Law Journal* 735.
[102] *Ibid* 760.
[103] *Ibid* 753.

E. Expressive Considerations in Using the 'Property' Label

More broadly, one might entertain doubts as to the appropriateness of 'contract as property' that stem from expressive considerations, *viz*, the political or moral 'statement' that is conveyed via the label.[104] As Simester and Chan argue:

> Crudely put, people are not objects. When it comes to other persons' attitudes, emotions, intentions, and the like, ownership analogies are entirely misplaced; indeed, they are inconsistent with the principles of individual autonomy that are cornerstones of any liberal society.[105]

In a nutshell, the fear is that 'property' reasoning encourages commodification – the reduction of persons as subjects to objects.[106] There is perhaps a lingering hint of this, say in the *Lumley* tort, recalling its origins. As Kitto J commented in *Attorney-General (NSW)*,[107] the quasi-proprietary idea of contract 'originally was a corollary of the ancient conception of the relationship of master and servant', and that while the ancient conception no longer held sway, 'the notion of a right in the master, as a species of property, that others shall not, by their wrongful acts, deprive him of the benefit of the relation between himself and his servant has not been abandoned'.[108] In this sense the *Lumley* tort is inextricably linked with Blackstonian notions of a 'sole and despotic dominion' over persons, suggesting a questionable view of contract's moral underpinnings even in an era where we have transitioned from status to contract. If so, 'property' cannot provide an appropriate normative justification for interpreting the *Lumley* jurisprudence – rather it provides an *immoral* justification for the existence of the doctrine.

While there is truth in the commodification critique, it should not be pushed too far. Following Radin's leading critique, we might say that while commodification as a general theme is a concern in coarsening the moral landscape by tainting non-monetisable components of social and personal life, more pressing concerns are in play where commodification is associated with distributive injustice, such as where those who lack a baseline of resources necessary for flourishing are more likely to commodify themselves (their bodies, organs, offspring, and so on) for financial gain.[109] This concern may be present in certain kinds of *Lumley* scenarios where there exists a gross disparity of bargaining power as between promisor (eg an employee) and promisee (eg an employer), such that we find it particularly

[104] See C Sunstein, 'On the Expressive Function of Law' (1996) 144 *University of Pennsylvania Law Review* 2021.

[105] Simester and Chan (n 35) 149.

[106] MJ Radin, *Contested Commodities* (Cambridge, Harvard University Press, 1996).

[107] *Attorney-General (NSW)* (n 17).

[108] *Ibid* 295.

[109] M Radin and M Sunder, 'The Subject and Object of Commodification' in MM Ertman and JC Williams (eds), *Rethinking Commodification* (New York, New York University Press, 2005) 10–13.

repugnant to think of such relations as 'proprietary', but it is far from a universal concern in all cases of inducing breach of contract. For instance, in Howarth's survey of the case law in 2005, he noted that the *Lumley* doctrine features in a range of cases, including strikes, poaching of employees, restrictive covenants concerning land, confidentiality or other restraints on competition, complaints about policy changes made by regulators affecting contractual dealings, intra-corporate disputes and so on.[110] A good number of these scenarios do not necessarily concern promisors who are coerced into contractual dealings, but rather operate on a fairly even commercial playing field. Accordingly, it may be going a little too far to accuse the 'property' idea of complicity with contractual injustice perpetuated through commodification, though it certainly gives off an 'illiberal' flavour in suggesting that persons are reducible to objects or means.

F. 'Property' Simply an Amplifier for 'Interests'?

In the final analysis, we might say that the 'property' label is not entirely meaningless, though it is in many respects incomplete or misleading. Those like Epstein who impose a fairly robust and structured notion of property (such as ostensible ownership) onto contract end up distorting doctrine. On the other hand, other commentators are more circumspect and adopt a 'broad and fluid conception of property',[111] such as Lee, who explains that property 'denot[es] a sphere of individual liberty within which a legal person's access to resources is protected against the claims of the state and of other citizens' and that '[w]hen a property analogy is invoked, it is an attempt to adjust the boundaries of this sphere'.[112]

This observation is unimpeachable, though the challenge then is to identify whether the 'property' label itself is doing any work in rationalising the scope of *in rem* protection for any given asset (in our case, the contractual obligation), or whether it simply functions as a placeholder for other sources of normative justification. Carty makes the same point in her observation that 'the focus of commentators on "property" or "quasi-property" really reflects a moral justification for the tort',[113] such as an overall consequentialist calculus that leans in favour of the security and stability of the contractual relations.

In my view, the 'property' label might best be understood as an amplifier for a protected interest that the claimant is said to have in the contract or expectancy (as the case might be), an interest which is one facet of a more capacious overall

[110] D Howarth, 'Against *Lumley v Gye*' (2005) 68 *MLR* 195, 196–97.
[111] Lee (n 34) 519.
[112] *Ibid* 518–19.
[113] Carty (n 5) 59.

inquiry into the justification for a particular scope of *in rem* protection under the relevant tortious doctrine. As Carpenter explains:

> We are not so much concerned in determining whether this is or is not a property right, as we are concerned with the question how far or against what invasions the interest is and should be protected.[114]

Deakin and Randall similarly observe that there is a 'hierarchy of interests … implicit in the current structure of the economic torts: contractual interests are entitled to a higher level of protection than general economic interests'.[115] Ultimately it is the nature and quality of the interest in the contract or the expectancy that appears to matter; our use of the property label is simply shorthand for an intuition that the interest in question should be placed at the higher end of the protective spectrum.

IV. Towards a Pluralistic Conception

A. Forms of Pluralism

If the property idea is found wanting in some respects, what might be a preferable schema for understanding the normative grounding for torts protecting contractual interests? A complete answer is clearly beyond the scope of this chapter, but it is possible to sketch the structure of an alternative pluralistic paradigm that brings more directly and thoroughly to the fore the considerations that shape these torts.

The particular version of pluralism that I believe best accounts for the comparative shape of the torts protecting contractual interests is what Porat and Posner have termed 'normative aggregation',[116] where we find courts aggregating different considerations in amplifying a case for liability. Porat and Posner's examples from American contract doctrine include the normative aggregation of various minor breaches to reach a finding of substantial or material breach entitling termination, or the aggregation of multiple (but taken singly, insufficient) factors of lack of education and failure to read to collectively reach the threshold for unconscionability.[117] In the case of torts protecting contractual interests, some aggregation of normative paradigms is arguably at play. Morality and wrongdoing are reflected in the relevant *mens rea*, the collective concern with the need to adhere to the 'rules of the game' in an otherwise free market economy is reflected in the 'unlawful means' requirement; and substantive values balancing is reflected

[114] CE Carpenter, 'Interference with Contract Relations' (1928) 41 *Harvard Law Review* 728, 733.
[115] S Deakin and J Randall, 'Rethinking the Economic Torts' (2009) 72 *MLR* 519, 535.
[116] A Porat and EA Posner, 'Aggregation and Law' (2012) 122 *Yale Law Journal* 2.
[117] Ibid 29–33.

explicitly or implicitly where courts take into account 'justification' for infringing upon protected interests. These sources of justification are aggregated in different ways as I will outline in brief below.

B. *Mens Rea* and the 'Morality' Paradigm

One counterpoint to the 'property' lens, which focusses on the importance of a claimant's protected interest, is the role and relevance of the defendant's wrongdoing. As Lionel Smith explains:

> It is wrong to get in the way of the performance of other people's obligations. Every system goes that far; they only differ on how generously to protect those who are owed obligations against interference by third parties.[118]

The instinctive rebuttal to this is to cite *Allen v Flood*[119] and the common law's longstanding aversion to dealing with motive and mental states in finding tort liability. The difficulty is equated with 'peer[ing] inside people's souls',[120] or drawing distinctions which are too subtle and slippery, which might 'allow a wider scope for prejudice'.[121]

However, to recognise *mens rea* (intention, foresight, notice and so forth) as a relevant factor is not to argue that liability should turn purely on a mental state, or that the philosophy underlying *Allen* should be completely repudiated. Rather, given that *mens rea* in various forms already forms part of the torts in question, the aim is to explain how it operates alongside other considerations.

For instance, we might note that the level of *mens rea* gets amplified as we move from conversion (with strict liability) to the *Lumley* tort (requiring knowledge of the contract and intention to procure breach) and unlawful means doctrine (requiring intentional harm). As we have noted, *OBG* has clarified that conversion is not available for intangible contractual obligations, but only for documents embodying or recording such debts or obligations. For instance, a negotiable instrument physically embodies a payment obligation in an excludable and exhaustible manner, such that the transfer of the chattel necessitates the transfer of the payment obligation; hence 'the possibility of resorting to the law of conversion when the instrument is taken from its owner unlawfully'.[122] Locating the obligation in a 'thing' is critical for strict liability: a thing is necessary to mediate between owners and non-owners, as non-owners faced with a thing can be taken

[118] L Smith, 'Philosophical Foundations of Proprietary Remedies' in R Chambers, C Mitchell and J Penner (eds), *Philosophical Foundations of the Law of Unjust Enrichment* (Oxford, Oxford University Press, 2009) 292.
[119] *Allen v Flood* [1898] AC 1 (HL).
[120] N McBride and R Bagshaw, *Tort Law*, 6th edn (Pearson, Harlow, 2018) 629.
[121] JD Heydon, *Economic Torts*, 2nd edn (London, Sweet & Maxwell, 1978) 131.
[122] A Barak, 'The Nature of the Negotiable Instrument' (1983) *Israel Law Review* 49, 65.

to know that they should 'keep off' or refrain from interfering with it[123] (subject of course to notice-based defences where owners have not signalled their proprietary interests in an immediately verifiable manner through possession, labelling, registration and so on).[124]

In contrast, when we turn to the intentional economic torts covering intangible obligations not locatable in any 'thing', the property notion recedes as a ground for liability in favour of a more intense focus on *mens rea* and wronging. For unlawful means, the tort protecting the least choate interest of 'expectancies', the *mens rea* is arguably the most demanding: it requires an intention to harm as a desired end or means to an end. As Lord Nicholls explained, a 'high degree of blameworthiness is called for, because intention serves as the factor which justifies imposing liability on the defendant for loss caused by a wrong otherwise not actionable by the claimant against the defendant'.[125] A similar notion was referred to by Sales and Stilitz in emphasising 'the central idea that it is the intention of D to harm P which bridges the remoteness of his unlawful actions from P … and the remoteness of P's loss from D's unlawful actions'.[126]

The *Lumley* tort similarly operates on an 'intentional' basis, but with a number of critical differences. The protected interest here is more crystallised, a contractual right having been acquired. The defendant must intend to procure the breach, and must have knowledge of the contract – it is said that 'without knowledge there can be no intention'.[127] Note, however, that intention to *harm* is not required under *Lumley*, simply to cause a breach which may in fact result in benefit rather than loss to the claimant (as in the well-known cases of *South Wales Miners' Federation v Glamorgan Coal Co Ltd*[128] where a miners' union's strike would have benefitted the miners as well as their employers through higher coal prices). In that sense the intent required for *Lumley* liability is less demanding than that under the unlawful means tort, given that a firmer contractual interest is in play.

Moreover, the *mens rea* of *Lumley* is slightly more dilute given that courts post-*OBG* have understood both 'knowledge' and 'intent' in a slightly more flexible fashion. As to knowledge, recall that Lord Hoffmann required subjective actual knowledge (that one is procuring a breach) rather than constructive or objective knowledge,[129] subject to the important proviso for '*subjective* reckless indifference'[130] or Nelsonian knowledge in the form of consciously deciding

[123] See discussion in KM Wyman, 'The New Essentialism in Property' (2017) 9 *Journal of Legal Analysis* 183, 194–95.

[124] As in Epstein's discussion of the ostensible ownership cases: 'The principle has had even greater application in another commercial context; the maker of a negotiable instrument who has been deceived by his drawee cannot recover from a third party, the so-called holder in due course, who has acquired the instrument for value': Epstein (n 20) 9. See also the equivalent concept in English law under s 29 of the *Bills of Exchange Act 1882* (UK).

[125] *OBG* (n 3) [166].

[126] P Sales and D Stilitz, 'Intentional infliction of harm by unlawful means' (1999) 115 *LQR* 411, 413.

[127] Carty (n 5) 38.

[128] *South Wales Miners' Federation v Glamorgan Coal Co Ltd* [1905] AC 239 (HL).

[129] *OBG* (n 3) [39]–[41], discussing *British Industrial Plastics Ltd v Ferguson* [1940] 1 All ER 479 (HL).

[130] Carty (n 5) 40.

not to inquire[131] or deliberately turning a blind eye.[132] In *Wolff v Trinity Logistics USA Inc*,[133] a recent decision of the English Court of Appeal, the defendant-director was found liable for procuring a breach of an agency agreement providing that the claimant-freight forwarder's agents were not to release goods until the proper shipping documents were presented; the defendant was said to be 'at the very least, recklessly indifferent' to whether the agents were acting in breach of contract, which sufficed to affix him with knowledge.[134]

Moreover, noting that the requisite intention can be a means to an ultimate end or an end in itself (as is the case with unlawful means), it is more likely than not that the former scenario applies in most 'inducing' cases (*viz*, Gye procures Wagner's breach *in order* to get her to sing for him). For instance, in the recent decision of *Lifestyle Equities CV v Sportsdirect.com Retail Ltd*,[135] where the defendant was liable for procuring a breach of terms in a licence agreement restricting the manner of sale of the claimant's goods, the Court held that 'the breach of the Agreement was not an end in itself' but a 'means to an end' for the defendant to achieve its corporate restructuring plans. Intention is thus stretched to cover situations where, say, singing for Gye is 'simply the other side of the same coin' as breaking an exclusive engagement with Lumley.[136] In my view the best way to understand how knowledge of the inevitable breaking of an engagement is elevated to intentionally procuring breach (considering the ultimate intention to get Wagner to sing) is to appreciate that means and ends are united through choice:

> To choose … is essentially to adopt a plan or proposal which one has put to oneself in one's practical reasoning and deliberation … Whatever, then, is included within one's chosen plan or proposal, whether as it ends or as a means to that end, is *intended* …[137]

The *mens rea* of the *Lumley* tort is thus stretched, no doubt more demanding than strict liability in conversion, but perhaps more dilute compared with the unlawful means tort, taking into account the rights which they protect.

C. Unlawful Means and the 'Rules of the Game' Paradigm

Where the protected interest concerned is not that of a contractual right, all things being equal, the case for *in rem* protection is rather less strong. Intention alone may be insufficient to demarcate the boundaries of a harm to an expectancy; hence the need to supplement or aggregate this with another factor: unlawful

[131] *OBG* (n 3) [41].
[132] *Emerald Construction v Lothian* [1966] 1 WLR 691 (CA) 700–701.
[133] *Wolff v Trinity Logistics USA Inc* [2018] EWCA Civ 2765, [2019] 1 WLR 3997.
[134] *Ibid* [47]–[51].
[135] *Lifestyle Equities CV v Sportsdirect.com Retail Ltd* [2018] EWHC 728 (Ch).
[136] *OBG* (n 3) [134], [167].
[137] J Finnis, 'Acts and Intentions' in J Finnis (ed), *Intentions and Identity: Collected Essays Volume II* (Oxford, Oxford University Press, 2013) 176.

means. As explained by the Supreme Court of Canada in *Bram Enterprises Ltd v A.I. Enterprises Ltd*,[138] citing Kain and Alexander,[139] one explanation of the tort is that it catches intentional conduct 'that is a flagrant abuse of the competitive process',[140] amounting in effect to 'cheating or upsetting the fundamental rules of market competition'.[141] Under this explanation:

> While no person has a common law right to trade per se, a person does have a general freedom to participate in the … market and a legitimate expectation that the *basic rules of the game* will be respected. To the extent that the defendant intentionally inflicts economic loss on the plaintiff through *unlawful means which are clearly off-side those basic rules*, the defendant gains an illegitimate advantage and causes the plaintiff to suffer a disadvantage.[142]

In short, when we are concerned with inchoate economic interests such as expectancies, *in rem* protection is given only where there is a high degree of moral blameworthiness *and* conduct infringing those interests which crosses the boundaries of acceptable behaviour as demarcated by the positive law. Outside of these circumstances one is free to pursue, appropriate, or cause harm to a rival or other person's economic interests. This is, of course, what Lord Nicholls meant in *OBG* when he opined that 'by this tort the law seeks to curb clearly excessive conduct' by unacceptable means, defined in this context as all unlawful means.[143] Likewise, as Davies and Sales explain, unlawfulness 'supplies a ready-made and reasonably accessible criterion, understandable to ordinary people, to demarcate the boundary of acceptable behaviour'.[144]

Of course, an important sub-issue is the scope of unlawful means. I do not intend to resolve this issue comprehensively, but a few remarks may be apposite to place the debate within the context of the 'normative aggregation' framework I have suggested. The breadth of the concept extends anywhere from civil wrongs such as torts and breaches of contract, to equitable wrongs, beyond civil liability to criminal and other statutory violations, and potentially further beyond to acts that persons are not at liberty to commit, even if they may not otherwise amount to a private wrong or public violation, such as an act of a public authority which is beyond its power and invalid (eg for procedural fairness reasons) or agreements considered void under restrictive trade practices regulations.[145] At the former end of the spectrum stands Lord Hoffmann's formulation in *OBG*, confining unlawful

[138] *Bram Enterprises Ltd v A.I. Enterprises Ltd* 2014 SCC 12, [2014] 1 SCR 177.

[139] B Kain and A Alexander, 'The "Unlawful Means" Element of the Economic Torts: Does a Coherent Approach Lie Beyond Reach?' in TL Archibald and RS Echlin (eds), *Annual Review of Litigation, 2010* (Toronto, Thomson Carswell, 2010).

[140] *Bram* (n 138) [39].

[141] *Ibid* [40].

[142] *Ibid* [41] (emphasis added). Note that the Supreme Court of Canada ultimately adopted a narrower formulation in line with Lord Hoffmann's test of unlawful means: *ibid* [43], [76].

[143] *OBG* (n 3) [153].

[144] PS Davies and P Sales, 'Intentional Harm, Accessories and Conspiracies' (2018) 134 *LQR* 69, 76–77.

[145] Carty (n 5) 84–95.

means to civil wrongs actionable by a third party (which hinder the third party's liberty to deal with the claimant), subject to the qualification that a non-actionable civil wrong can amount to unlawful means if the only reason for its non-actionability is that the third party has suffered no loss himself.[146] At the opposing end is Lord Nicholls' more capacious formulation of 'all acts which a person is not permitted to do', covering 'common law torts, statutory torts, crimes, breaches of contract, breaches of trust and equitable obligations, breaches of confidence, and so on',[147] supported in part by the observation that in 'seeking to distinguish between acceptable and unacceptable conduct it would be passing strange that a breach of contract should be proscribed but not a crime'.[148]

The preference for Lord Hoffmann's formulation – confining it to civil wrongs actionable by a third party – is not without strong support, for self-evident reasons. It has been described as founded upon a more circumspect 'liability stretching rationale' which sees the tort as extending civil liability without creating new actionable wrongs, closing a perceived gap where the defendant's wrongful acts against a third party immediate victim are intentionally directed at the injured plaintiff.[149] As Carty notes, 'Lord Hoffmann's policy is the one that would lead to greater certainty and ensure that the inner logic of other areas of tort law would not be "casually cast to one side"'.[150] The Supreme Court of Canada in *Bram* likewise describes it as a 'clear "control mechanism" on liability … consistent with tort's law reticence to intrude too far into the realm of competitive economic activity'.[151]

From a justificatory point of view, this restriction is pragmatic rather than principled: Lord Nicholls explained that it 'represents a radical departure from the purpose for which this tort has been developed' and would bring about 'an unjustified and unfortunate curtailment of [its] scope'.[152] The major misgiving with the more expansive principled approach is the alleged 'tortification' of criminal conduct,[153] in other words, the oddness 'about using laws designed for wholly different purposes to provide some of the ingredients for the unlawful means tort governing liability between claimant and defendant'.[154] But as Davies and Sales point out, the 'tortification' concern applies equally to civil wrongs, since it is clear enough that tort or contract liability exists for the most part to 'defin[e] the proper relationship between *those* parties', and not for the purposes of creating fresh third party liability.[155]

In my view, the only coherent reason for distinguishing between civil and non-civil wrongs is that the distinction serves as a *proxy* for where a claimant is

[146] *OBG* (n 3) [45]–[50].
[147] *Ibid* [150].
[148] *Ibid* [152].
[149] *Bram* (n 138) [43]; *OBG* (n 3) [154].
[150] Carty (n 5) 179.
[151] *Bram* (n 138) [44].
[152] *OBG* (n 3) [155].
[153] *Ibid* [150].
[154] Davies and Sales (n 144) 72.
[155] *Ibid*.

likely to have a *protected interest* (sometimes coated in 'proprietary' language) and hence the relevant standing in private law to make a claim. Recall Lord Nicholls' red light-jumping courier service:[156] a rival's unlawful means claim is clearly doubtful here since it requires an extended chain of reasoning to determine how a criminal or regulatory breach has any impact on a protected interest. Civil wrongs against intermediaries dealing with claimants are more likely correlated with infringements on protected interests, as where a rival attacks a claimant through wronging the latter's suppliers or customers, hence Weir's oft-quoted observation: 'to ruin a person financially the action you must take must be indirect, through another person, the source of his earnings or profits'.[157]

However, the civil/non-civil distinction is at best an incomplete marker for when protected interests are implicated. Lord Nicholls was grasping at this point where he suggested that the 'couriers' criminal conduct is not an offence committed against the rival company in any realistic sense of that expression'.[158] On the other hand, there is no doubt that some criminal wrongs can be offences committed *against* the claimant such that a protected interest is intentionally infringed – the obvious example being *Total Network SL v Revenue & Customs Commissioners*[159] where the House of Lords allowed the Revenue's claim in unlawful means conspiracy for lost VAT against the defendant conspirator who had participated in carousel fraud, the recognised unlawful means being broadened to include criminal wrongs; here, the common law crime of cheating the Revenue. The Revenue's protected interests were clearly implicated. As Lord Hope put it, the 'means used by the conspirators were directed at the claimants themselves'.[160] Likewise, for Lord Walker, 'criminal conduct (at common law or by statute) can constitute unlawful means, provided that it is indeed the means (what Lord Nicholls … called "instrumentality") of intentionally inflicting harm'.[161] Lord Mance similarly emphasised that 'the offence exists in its very nature to protect the revenue; where its commission is necessarily, directly and intentionally targeted at and injurious to the revenue'.[162]

Of course, the House of Lord in *Total* did not overrule but rather confined Lord Hoffmann's narrow formulation as limited to three-party situations policed by the unlawful means tort, unlike two-party unlawful means conspiracy,[163] on the basis that Lord Hoffmann had caveated that two-party intimidation cases raise different issues,[164] an observation which applied likewise to two-party (ie direct and non-intermediary-based) unlawful means conspiracy.[165] Nonetheless, it is

[156] *OBG* (n 3) [160].
[157] T Weir, *A Casebook on Tort*, 10th edn (London, Sweet & Maxwell, 2004) 572.
[158] *OBG* (n 3) [159].
[159] *Total Network SL v Revenue & Customs Commissioners* [2008] 2 WLR 711 (HL).
[160] *Ibid* [43].
[161] *Ibid* [95].
[162] *Ibid* [120].
[163] *Ibid* [99]–[100].
[164] *OBG* (n 3) [61].
[165] Carty (n 5) 662.

quite possible that *Total*'s expanded understanding of unlawful means (including non-civil wrongs as long as these intentionally, clearly and directly implicate a distinctively identified protected interest of the claimant), might influence the trajectory of the unlawful means tort as well, for as Carty observes:

> [O]nce the courts become used to dealing with the economic tort of conspiracy in a very different setting to trade conflict, claimants will demand a wider function be ascribed to the unlawful means tort … It may well be, therefore, that the revitalisation process that started with the conspiracy tort will insinuate itself into the application of the unlawful means tort.[166]

Accordingly, if we keep the big picture in view – that the additional normative trigger for liability for interference with expectancies is 'off-side' conduct – we see that it is unnecessary to narrow the aperture to allow only certain types of unlawful conduct to the exclusion of others.

D. Justification and the 'Values Balancing' Paradigm

As Carpenter observed many decades ago in relation to contractual interests:

> Whether a privilege of invasion exists depends upon whether it is of greater moment to society to protect the defendant in the invading activities than it is to protect and guard the plaintiff's interest from such invasions. An evaluation and balancing of the social import of the conflicting interests of the respective parties and of the social interests per se are involved.[167]

The scope of *in rem* protection for a contractual right or interest invariably involves a careful calibration of competing considerations, though it is not always abundantly clear how the balancing exercise features in tort doctrine. Broadly speaking, scope for weighing trade-offs appears more explicitly in the 'justification' defence for *Lumley* liability. At the other end of the scale, the conversion doctrine (dealing with chattels, including contractual rights embodied in documents) tolerates no such defence – given the tangible nature of the interests the doctrine protects, these cannot be easily overridden. This explains our intuitive discomfort with the notion of 'efficient theft' or 'efficient conversion'[168] – the idea that some broader social utility calculus can justify private takings of our physical assets. The position for the unlawful means tort remains unclear, given that the issue of justification was not explicitly considered in *OBG*.[169] On one hand, once the defendant's conduct has been tainted by unlawfulness, it might be said that 'there can be no justification for a civil wrong'.[170] On the other hand, it might be too quick to jump to this

[166] H Carty, 'The Modern Functions of the Economic Torts' (2015) 74 *CLJ* 261, 281.
[167] Carpenter (n 114) 745.
[168] D Friedmann, 'The Efficient Breach Fallacy' (1989) 18 *Journal of Legal Studies* 1, 4.
[169] See B Ong, 'Two Tripartite Economic Torts' [2008] *Journal of Business Law* 723, 744–45.
[170] *Shearson Lehman Hutton Inc v Maclaine Watson & Co* [1989] 2 Lloyd's Rep 570 (QB) 633.

conclusion – a more dilute conception of unlawful means catching a wider range of conduct naturally increases 'the pressure to recognize conflict[ing] public policy as justification'.[171] I share the view of Deakin and Randall who argue that a blanket ban on justification where unlawful means is used 'is an unsatisfactorily rigid position', and that a 'more flexible approach would be to allow the courts to weigh the nature of the illegality involved against the strength of the potential justifying factor'.[172] In this regard, I would venture that a rough parallel might be drawn with the current operation of the illegality doctrine, where the nature and gravity of illegal conduct is but one factor in the calculus, given that we are to weigh with a sense of proportionality the underlying purpose of the prohibition which has been transgressed, as other relevant public policies which may be rendered ineffective or less effective in denying a claim[173] (here, denying the justification defence).

To the extent that balancing is available, its operation as part of a workable model of normative aggregation requires some clarification. Balancing often invites standard rule of law concerns, especially when it is said that 'what constitutes justification is incapable of exact definition',[174] and that a whole litany of incommensurable factors appears relevant to the exercise, including: the nature of the contract broken, the position of the parties, the grounds for breach, the means employed, the relation of the person procuring breach to the contract-breaker, and the object of the person procuring breach.[175] In reality, the balancing exercise proceeds in the manner familiar to the common law – through the evolution of conventional categories and case law that is illustrative of accepted types of justification within these categories, from which analogies are drawn. For instance, in *Royal Bank of Scotland v McCarthy*,[176] a retiring solicitor claimed that the bank had induced the solicitor's firm to act in breach of a retirement deed. Under the deed the firm had agreed to repay the solicitor's loan (which had financed his capital contribution to the firm) to the bank. The Court concluded that the bank's act of requiring the firm not to make repayments of capital of any retiring member without its consent was not intended to procure a breach of the retirement deed, and even if so, it was justified in doing so as a secured lender that possessed a right against the firm, superior to the solicitor's right, applying the well-known principle in *Edwin Hill & Partners v First National Finance Corp*,[177] that allowed inducers a justification defence in taking reasonable steps to protect equal or superior pre-existing rights even where they know that this will cause a breach of the claimant's contract.

[171] J Fleming, *The Law of Torts*, 9th edn (Sydney, LBC Information Services, 1998) 771.
[172] Deakin and Randall (n 115) 551.
[173] *Patel v Mirza* [2016] UKSC 42, [2016] 3 WLR 399 [101].
[174] WE Peel and J Goudkamp (eds), *Winfield and Jolowicz on Tort*, 19th edn (London, Sweet & Maxwell, 2014) [19-016].
[175] *Glamorgan Coal Co Ltd v South Wales Miners' Federation* [1903] 2 KB 545 (KB) 574–575.
[176] *Royal Bank of Scotland v McCarthy* [2015] EWHC 3626 (QB).
[177] *Edwin Hill & Partners v First National Finance Corp* [1989] 1 WLR 225 (CA).

While there may be some divergence in the ways courts and commentators approach the categorisation exercise, there is considerable overlap and stability over time. Carpenter, writing in 1928, identifies as justificatory defences the privilege to protect a contract or property right, the privilege to protect life, reputation and health, to give disinterested advice, to discipline, appeal to authorities for redress, or act in performance of a duty, a privilege not to deal, and the privilege of competition.[178] Heydon, writing in 1978, points to the justification defence of protecting existing contracts, property rights, and financial interests, the privilege of acting under statutory authority, of institutional authorities to protect their charges or carry out duties, to protect the public interest, to give bona fide professional advice to withdraw from a contract, and a number of miscellaneous cases.[179] Carty, writing in the last decade post-*OBG*, discusses similar case law and groups these under the headings of 'private right as justification', 'private interest as justification' and 'public interest as justification'.[180]

The identification of categories in the balancing exercise does not mean that the law is in any way ossified. For instance, as Carty notes, no case has applied the 'public morality' defence since *Brimelow v Casson*,[181] a case where a defendant-association was recognised to be justified in procuring theatre proprietors to break their contracts with the claimant to compel the latter to pay a living wage to their chorus girls. This might be in recognition of the fact that a loose 'public morality' defence smacks of moral vigilantism and judicial paternalism out of place in a society founded on liberal values. In other scenarios, progress in balancing competing considerations is made through statutory intervention, the obvious example being the contest between labour and capital, and the concomitant use of economic torts to curtail strikes or threats of strikes. As Lord Hoffmann notes, unlike *Lumley* where poaching was intuitively unjustified, in

> the trade union cases … the question seemed to be whether it was justified to use strike action … as a form of pressure to get an employer, supplier or customer to do something he did not want to do … the question of justification became far more important than whether or not there had been a breach of contract.[182]

The balance in cases of macro-political significance is best clarified by the legislature, as the position is currently in the UK under section 219 of the *Trade Union and Labour Relations (Consolidation) Act 1992* (UK), which provides statutory immunity for acts done in contemplation or furtherance of a trade dispute,[183] and re-directs litigation toward more manageable sub-issues: for instance whether

[178] Carpenter (n 114) 745–62.
[179] Heydon (n 121) 38–47.
[180] Carty (n 5) 65–70.
[181] *Brimelow v Casson* [1924] 1 Ch 302 (Ch).
[182] L Hoffmann (n 12) 109–10.
[183] The tortured legislative history is beyond the scope of this chapter, see further Peel and Goudkamp (n 174) [19-055]–[19-058]; B Simpson, 'Economic Tort Liability in Labour Disputes: The Potential Impact of the House of Lords' Decision in *OBG Ltd v Allan*' (2007) 36 *Industrial Law Journal 468*.

there exists a relevant 'trade dispute'[184] and whether acts taken were 'in furtherance of' such disputes.[185]

V. Conclusion

If, as Proudhon infamously said, property is theft, it is because the concept robs us of clarity of vision. We have seen that a comprehensive accounting of various torts protecting contractual interests cannot be conducted through the narrow lens of 'contract as property'. Property is a protean and slippery term, one that cannot per se explain the *in rem* reach of these torts. It is at best an amplifier for designating a protected interest. By suggesting an alternative pluralistic justificatory framework, I do not mean to argue that the best approach is necessarily a realist one of immediate resort to the unconstrained fount of 'policy' to decide each individual case. Rather, as an interpretive exercise, the established doctrinal requirements and distinctions across these torts are ultimately explicable through the full range of claimant-sided, defendant-sided, and wider societal considerations canvassed in this chapter.

[184] *Trade Union and Labour Relations (Consolidation) Act 1992* (UK) s 244.

[185] See *Express Newspapers Ltd v McShane* [1980] AC 672 (HL); *Duport Steel Ltd v Sirs* [1980] 1 WLR 142 (HL).

3

Defamation as an Economic Tort

MICHAEL DOUGLAS

I. Introduction

Can defamation be characterised as an economic tort? That question is the focus of this chapter. The answer turns on what we mean by 'economic torts', which is the subject of section II below. It also turns on what we mean by 'defamation'. The modern tort is constituted by publication of defamatory matter of and concerning the plaintiff to a person other than the plaintiff.[1] The chapter argues the modern tort of defamation may be characterised as an economic tort. Indeed, legislative action to deny relief in defamation in the absence of 'serious harm' favours the characterisation that the modern tort is an economic tort. The chapter's focus is common law legal systems, with primary emphasis on Australian law.

The chapter is structured as follows. After briefly considering the criteria which determine the identity of the economic torts in section II, section III focuses on the identity of the interest protected by defamation: reputation. It considers that a proprietary conception of reputation has merit and suggests that this supports defamation's characterisation as an economic tort. Section IV examines how defamation law vindicates plaintiffs' economic interests. Section V argues that the legislative introduction of a threshold of serious harm bolsters the claim that defamation is an economic tort. Section VI concludes by explaining why this characterisation matters.

II. What Criteria Determine the Identity of the Economic Torts?

A. Conventional Views

What makes a tort an economic tort?[2] Beever describes the 'conventional view' of the economic torts as follows: they 'regulate economic activity, specifically to

[1] See generally A Mullis and R Parkes (eds), *Gatley on Libel and Slander*, 12th edn (London, Sweet & Maxwell, 2013) Ch 1.

[2] This question is examined in further detail in this collection's first chapter.

prevent or deter destructive forms of competition'.[3] He cites Carty, who frames the economic torts as a common law mechanism to attack excessive competition.[4] In a similar vein, Deakin and Randall argue that the fundamental rationale of the economic torts 'is to maintain the integrity of the competitive process'.[5] Defamation would not naturally be understood as a tort directed to anti-competitive conduct, and so it is not usually considered in analyses of economic torts. Carty, for example, does not include a chapter on defamation in her monograph. Lords Sumption and Lloyd-Jones identify slander of title as an economic tort in *JSC BTA Bank v Khrapunov*,[6] although that tort is better characterised in terms of malicious falsehood.[7] Even if the economic torts are a common law response to unfair competition,[8] in many cases, defamation will fit that mould, but only contingently so. The same can be said for the other economic torts. The archetypal 'competition' economic torts, like so-called interference with contractual relations, are often not litigated by direct competitors.[9] More broadly, they are often deployed where actors within an economy wrong one another.

A related view of the economic torts is that they protect pure economic interests.[10] That is how Dyson Heydon introduced the subject in his short monograph.[11] Weir took the same approach.[12] In *Khrapunov*, Lords Sumption and Lloyd-Jones explained that the economic torts 'are a major exception to the general rule that there is no duty in tort to avoid causing pure economic loss unless it is parasitic upon some injury to person or property'.[13] From this perspective, defamation might be characterised as an economic tort. Defamation, however, may be actionable even in the absence of provable pecuniary loss. Nonetheless, it is argued below that even where special damages are not available, actionable defamation may be coherently understood in terms of economic loss. That argument is strengthened by the introduction of statutory requirements that defamation cause serious harm, which is the subject of section V.

[3] A Beever, *A Theory of Tort Liability* (Oxford, Hart Publishing, 2016) 103.

[4] H Carty, *An Analysis of the Economic Torts*, 2nd edn (Oxford, Oxford University Press, 2010) 2.

[5] S Deakin and J Randall, 'Rethinking the Economic Torts' (2009) 72 *MLR* 519, 520.

[6] *JSC BTA Bank v Khrapunov* [2018] UKSC 19, [2018] 2 WLR 1125 [6] ('*Khrapunov*').

[7] *Palmer Bruyn & Parker Pty Ltd v Parsons* [2001] HCA 69, (2001) 208 CLR 388. For a discussion of malicious falsehood, see chapter 8 of this volume.

[8] See WL Morrison, 'Unfair Competition at Common Law' (1951) 2 *University of Western Australia Law Review* 34.

[9] See, eg, the old cases involving unionism: *Allen v Flood* [1898] AC 1. A contemporary example: action between small business owners and a developer: *Ooranya Pty Ltd v ISPT Pty Ltd* [2018] WASC 256.

[10] K Barker, P Cane, M Lunney and F Trindade, *The Law of Torts in Australia*, 5th edn (Melbourne, Oxford University Press, 2012) 228.

[11] D Heydon, *Economic Torts*, 2nd edn (London, Sweet & Maxwell, 1978) 1–10.

[12] T Weir, *Economic Torts* (Oxford, Oxford University Press, 1997) 1–2.

[13] *Khrapunov* (n 6) [6].

B. Other Criteria

What other definitional criteria can be identified in respect of the economic torts? Intention appears essential to some of them, like tortious conspiracy and inducement of breach of contract.[14] Yet negligent misstatement should probably be characterised as an economic tort: it is a prime exception to the exclusionary rule with respect to recoverability of pure economic loss in tort. Negligent misstatement does not involve an intention to injure. Intention is not essential to the tort of defamation,[15] and so the tort should not be excluded from 'economic torts' on the basis of that criterion. Defamation may be anomalous among torts for imposing strict liability,[16] but the same has been said about torts involving malice.[17]

For Beever, the key to understanding the economic torts is control and coercion: '[t]he wrongdoing with which they are concerned is coercion of the plaintiff by the defendant through another: indirect control'.[18] If that model is accepted, then defamation may fit within its scope: damaging a plaintiff's reputation might be characterised as an imposition on their freedom,[19] achieved through 'another', being the person or persons to whom the matter is published. Rolph considers that reputation, the interest protected by defamation, is inherently relational: it 'inheres in and is mediated by the mechanisms which connect the plaintiff and others'.[20]

Some of the economic torts, like conversion or inducement of breach of contract, could be justified on the basis of interference with rights which are proprietary in character.[21] If one accepts the property paradigm of those economic torts, then defamation could be grouped with them. Reputation, the interest underlying defamation, may be proprietary in character. That controversial view is explored in section III. If this grouping is recategorised in terms of interference with pre-existing rights (proprietary or otherwise),[22] then defamation would still fit within the category.

[14] See D Stilitz and P Sales, 'Intentional Infliction of Harm by Unlawful Means' (1999) 115 *LQR* 441, 435. Intention is framed as key to the economic torts in RP Balkin and JLR Davis, *Law of Torts* (Sydney, Butterworths, 1991) 625.

[15] *Cassidy v Daily Mirror* [1929] 2 KB 331 (CA) 354 (Lord Mansfield).

[16] Australian Law Reform Commission, *Serious Invasions of Privacy in the Digital Era* (Report 123, 2014) [7.76].

[17] J Murphy, 'Malice as an Ingredient of Tort Liability' (2019) 78(2) *CLJ* 355, 356.

[18] Beever (n 3) 124.

[19] '[J]uries should be free to award damages for injuries to reputation is one of the safeguards of liberty': *Sim v Stretch* [1936] 2 All ER 1237 (HL) 1242 (Lord Atkin).

[20] D Rolph, *Reputation, Celebrity, and Defamation Law* (Hampshire, Ashgate, 2008) 37, considering RC Post, 'The Social Foundations of Defamation Law; Reputation and the Constitution' (1986) 74 *California Law Review* 691.

[21] *OBG Ltd v Allan* [2007] UKHL 21, [2008] 1 AC 1 [32]; P Benson, 'The Basis for Excluding Liability for Economic Loss in Tort Law' in DG Owen (ed), *Philosophical Foundations of Tort Law* (Oxford, Clarendon, 1993); JW Neyers, 'The Economic Torts as Corrective Justice' (2009) 17 *Torts Law Journal* 162. Such ideas are explored further in chapter 2 of this volume.

[22] Deakin and Randall (n 5) 522.

Heydon conceived of the economic torts in three categories: those concerned with the causing of loss by means intrinsically lawful; those concerned with the causing of loss by unlawful means; and actionable representations.[23] His latter category includes injurious falsehood and passing off. If defamation were to be categorised among economic torts, it would fit within that category: defamation turns on publication of false[24] information which affects 'the economic decisions of consumers'.[25] There is a place for defamation among the economic torts. But is it necessary to find a place at all?

C. There is No Unity

In *Torts and Rights*, Stevens argued that the economic torts 'have no inherent unity'.[26] Courts have favoured that view.[27] Murphy argues 'that we must regard as ungrounded the whiggish claim that tort law is in the process of becoming steadily more coherent'.[28] Among other things, all-embracing theories often give insufficient regard to the primacy of statutes.[29] That argument has been well put by Justice Leeming recently in relation to negligence.[30] With respect to defamation, the role of statutes is significant. Theories of economic torts which appeal to coherence are difficult to maintain;[31] if maintainable at all, defamation would not neatly sit within such a theory.

Perhaps the best theory of the economic torts is one that acknowledges or even embraces disunity.[32] Beever floated (but did not necessarily support)[33] the view that it may be wrong to look for a general theory of the economic torts: '[i]nstead, clarity should be sought through the attempt to understand each tort individually'.[34] Defamation may be anomalous within the economic torts, yet all of the economic torts – or perhaps even all torts – are anomalous from one perspective or another. Defamation should be understood individually, but there are nonetheless

[23] Heydon (n 11) chs 2, 3 and 4.

[24] Although falsity is not an element of the cause of action, the strength of truth or justification defences, and the requirement of serious harm, render it essentially required.

[25] Heydon (n 11) 81.

[26] R Stevens, *Torts and Rights* (Oxford, Oxford University Press, 2007) 297.

[27] See *OBG* (n 21) [32]. *Hardie Finance Corporation Pty Ltd v Ahern [No 3]* [2013] WASC 403 [676] (Pritchard J); *Donaldson v Natural Springs Australia Ltd* [2015] FCA 498 [213] (Beach J).

[28] J Murphy, 'Contemporary Tort Theory and Tort Law's Evolution' (2019) 32 *Canadian Journal of Law & Jurisprudence* 413, 415.

[29] *Ibid* 414, citing A Burrows, 'The Relationship Between Common Law and Statute in the Law of Obligations' (2012) 128 *LQR* 232, 234.

[30] See M Leeming, *The Statutory Foundations of Negligence* (Alexandria, Federation Press, 2019) 1–4.

[31] Perhaps the difficulty is why they are 'radically under-theorised': JW Neyers, 'Rights-Based Justification for the Tort of Unlawful Interference with Economic Relations' (2008) 28 *Legal Studies* 215, 233.

[32] See generally, in relation to contract law, P Saprai, *Contract Law Without Foundations: Towards a Republican Theory of Contract Law* (Oxford, Oxford University Press, 2019).

[33] See Murphy (n 28) 413.

[34] Beever (n 3) 107.

benefits to also understanding it as an economic tort. These benefits are explored in section VI.

There are two factors that are shared by the economic torts, including defamation. First, they are torts.[35] Second, in contradistinction to the traditional concern of tort law – tangible physical injury to persons, land or goods – economic torts are primarily concerned with pecuniary damage, not consequential upon tangible damage.[36] The character of the damage caused by economic torts has its counterpart in the interest protected by economic torts: they each protect intangible economic interests. In the following section, it is argued that the interest protected by defamation has an economic character.

III. The Interest Protected by Defamation

Each of the economic torts is concerned with interference with an interest which the law protects. For other economic torts, the interests are usually trade, business or employment.[37] For defamation, the protected interest is reputation.[38]

A. The Character of Reputation

'Reputation' is a multi-faceted concept at the heart of defamation law[39] that is hard to pin down. Its meaning is entwined with that of the word 'defamation' and the adjectival 'defamatory', yet there is no entirely satisfactory conception of 'defamatory', either.[40] The legal tests for what is defamatory[41] could indicate that a reputation is what 'right-thinking members of society generally' think of a person;[42] or what ordinary, reasonable people think of a person;[43] or it could be

[35] Even this is contentious, which is one of the reasons why this book considers 'economic wrongs' in addition to economic torts. Stevens writes, '"Unlawful means conspiracy" has been misclassified alongside other so-called "economic torts". Recovery is not limited to economic losses. And it is not a tort': Stevens (n 26) 297.

[36] Heydon (n 11) 1. However, arguably, damages for psychiatric injury may be available for some economic torts, like conspiracy: *McKellar v Container Terminal Management Services Ltd* [1999] FCA 1101, (1999) 165 ALR 409 [142] (Weinberg J), citing *Huntley v Thornton* [1957] 1 WLR 321 (ChD) 350 (Harman J) and NJ Mullany and PR Handford, *Tort Liability for Psychiatric Damage* (Pyrmont, Lawbook Co, 1993) 46–47.

[37] Deakin and Randall (n 5) 533.

[38] *Radio 2UE Sydney Pty Ltd v Chesterton* [2009] HCA 16, (2009) 238 CLR 460 [32] (French CJ, Gummow, Kiefel and Bell JJ).

[39] E Barendt, 'What is the Point of Libel Law' (1999) 52 *Current Legal Problems* 110, 112.

[40] *Sim v Stretch* (n 19) 1240 (Lord Atkin) (HL); *Berkhoff v Burchill* [1996] 4 All ER 1008 (CA) 1111; L McNamara, *Reputation and Defamation* (Oxford, Oxford University Press, 2007) 1.

[41] See generally D Rolph, *Defamation Law* (Pyrmont, Lawbook Co, 2016) 110–14 [6.220]–[6.270].

[42] *Sim v Stretch* (n 19) 1240.

[43] *Radio 2UE* (n 38) [5]–[6] (French CJ, Gummow, Kiefel and Bell JJ).

various other things, which somehow relate to perceptions of a person within a community.[44]

The different facets of 'reputation' were explored by Post. According to McNamara, Post's account of reputation is 'without question the benchmark in contemporary comment and critique'.[45] In 'The Social Foundations of Defamation: Reputation and the Constitution', Post posited 'three distinct conceptions of reputation that the common law of defamation has at various times in its history attempted to protect: reputation as property, reputation as honor [*sic*], and as dignity'.[46] Cases have disclosed other conceptions of reputation, yet these three, he argued, have had the most significant impact on the development of the common law doctrine. Each conception has strengths and weaknesses. The property dimension is most relevant to the present thesis; the other two are explored here first.

Reputation as honour explains the historical development of defamation law from the common law of libel and slander.[47] The contemporary tort's protection of reputation is the product of the statutory abolition of the distinction between libel and slander, premised by the orthodoxy[48] that slander and libel were two closely-aligned torts.[49] Recently, in *Lachaux v Independent Press Ltd*,[50] Lord Sumption considered the historical differences between libel and slander with respect to the significance of damage.[51] Libel has always been actionable per se. He explained that '[t]he gist of the tort is injury to the claimant's reputation and the associated injury to his or her feelings'. Certain categories of slander were also actionable per se: '(i) words imputing criminal offences, (ii) words imputing certain contagious or infectious diseases, and (iii) words tending to injure a person in his or her office, calling, trade or profession'.[52] Other forms of slander arose as a species of action on the case, requiring proof of special damage. In those cases, the gist of the tort was proof of pecuniary loss.[53] The honour rationale of modern defamation makes most sense where defamation is actionable per se; arguably until recently, that was all cases of defamation.[54] Post justifies the honour rationale with reference to a 'deference society'. In contrast to a 'market society', a deference society is concerned with more than protection of merely individual interests, but of

[44] McNamara (n 40) 35–36; FG Bailey, *Gifts and Poison: The Politics of Reputation* (Oxford, Basil Blackwell, 1971) 4; *Radio 2UE* (n 38) [38] (French CJ, Gummow, Kiefel and Bell JJ).

[45] McNamara (n 40) 37, fn 5.

[46] Post (n 20) 693.

[47] See D Rolph, 'The Sources of Defamation Law' in JT Gleeson, JA Watson and E Peden (eds), *The Historical Foundations of Australian Law: Volume II* (Sydney, Federation Press, 2013) 106.

[48] JM Kaye, 'Libel and Slander: Two Torts or One?' (1975) 40 *LQR* 524, 524.

[49] WS Holdsworth, 'Defamation in the Sixteenth and Seventeenth Centuries' (1924) 40 *LQR* 397.

[50] *Lachaux v Independent Press Ltd* [2019] UKSC 27, [2019] 3 WLR 18 [4]–[6].

[51] On the history before that distinction emerged, see Holdsworth (n 49) 978–79.

[52] *Lachaux* (n 50) [4].

[53] *Ibid* [5], citing *Ratcliffe v Evans* [1892] 2 QB 524, 532 (Bowen LJ).

[54] Applying the proposition that damage is presumed for defamatory matter. In some jurisdictions, that proposition is no longer tenable. See TDC Bennett, 'Why So Serious? Lachaux and the Threshold of 'Serious Harm' in Section 1 Defamation Act 2013' (2018) 10 *Journal of Media Law* 1. See further section V below.

public interests.[55] He appeals to defamation law's historical protection of social status and certain social roles.[56] Yet modern defamation focuses on the generic standard of the ordinary, reasonable person – an everyman concept that deliberately eliminates social stratification.[57] The rationale of defamation as honour is less compelling than it once was. The honour rationale explains why some publications are defamatory, and why some plaintiffs sue,[58] but so does a rationale of reputation in terms of economic interests.

Reputation's dignity rationale aligns with a conception of 'personality rights'[59] as human rights.[60] Article 17 of the *International Covenant on Civil and Political Rights*, an instrument which is prefaced with an appeal to dignity, protects reputation as a human right.[61] Further, there is support for the dignity view in case law – for example, in *Reynolds v Times Newspapers Ltd*, it was said that '[r]eputation is an integral and important part of the dignity of the individual'.[62] In that case it was also recognised that human rights law should play an important part in the development of the common law.[63] Outside of Europe, human rights have had an impact on development of defamation law in common law systems.[64] For example, the emergence of *Lange* qualified privilege came with the emergence of the implied freedom of political communication in the Australian *Constitution*;[65] an appeal to rights also underpinned the emergence of the *Durie v Gardiner* 'responsible communication' public interest defence in New Zealand.[66] Dignity explains why reputation may be a 'right', but so might a proprietary or economic conception. Natural rights theories underpinning dignity-based recognition of legal rights[67] are an awkward fit in a rational secular society.[68] If one ignores the religious stilts on which natural rights rest, that a person *should* have dignity does not mean that they naturally *do* have dignity.[69] An economic rationale is less vulnerable to a charge of circularity. Moreover, it has greater explanatory power with respect to defamation in a common law system like Australia's, which still lacks a developed

[55] Post (n 20) 702.

[56] See also McNamara (n 40) 54–; 61–79.

[57] See *Trkulja v Google LLC* [2018] HCA 25, (2018) 263 CLR 149 [31] (Kiefel CJ, Keane, Nettle, Bell and Gordon JJ).

[58] It may help understand how 'defamation is actually practiced': Post (n 20) 707.

[59] See R Pound, 'Interests of Personality' (1915) 28(4) *Harvard Law Review* 343, 349.

[60] See Rolph (n 20) 31 ff.

[61] See also *Terry v Persons Unknown* [2010] EWHC 119 (QB), [2010] EMLR 16 [96].

[62] *Reynolds v Times Newspapers Ltd* [2001] 2 AC 127 (HL) 201 (Lord Nicholls). See also *Jameel v Wall Street Journal Europe Sprl* [2006] UKHL 44, [2007] 1 AC 359 [91] (Lord Hoffmann).

[63] *Reynolds* (n 62) 223 (Lord Cooke).

[64] *cf* P Giliker, 'The Influence of EU and European Human Rights Law on English Private Law' (2015) 64(2) *ICLQ* 237.

[65] *Lange v Australian Broadcasting Corporation* [1997] HCA 25, (1997) 189 CLR 520. See also D Ibbetson, *A Historical Introduction to the Law of Obligations* (Oxford, Oxford University Press, 1999).

[66] *Durie v Gardiner* [2018] NZCA 278, [2018] 3 NZLR 131 [53].

[67] As explored in Pound (n 59).

[68] See consideration of 'natural' rights of a father in *Secretary, Department of Health and Community Services v JMB and SMB (Marion's Case)* [1992] HCA 15, (1992) 175 CLR 218.

[69] Wartime shows that there is nothing dignified about survival in the state of nature.

rights-based jurisprudence at the federal level.[70] In common law systems lacking entrenched human rights, the other personality right of significance – the right to privacy – is often seen through a proprietary lens.[71]

'Reputation as property' is Post's primary conception of reputation. This view is that 'reputation can be understood as a form of intangible property akin to goodwill'.[72] The proprietary conception of reputation has support in (older) case law.[73] It may be justified on Lockean terms[74] in that a reputation is earned through effort.[75] Even if Locke's theory is dismissed as well-argued colonialism,[76] reputation as property still has merit. If damage to reputation means damage to property, then defences to defamation show that certain property damage is justified (in the same way that a builder would not ordinarily be sued for demolishing a decrepit building), and remedies for defamation explain why reputational damage is ascribed a monetary value. For the modern tort, unless the property (reputation) is actually damaged, then no remedy is justified.[77]

Post argues that reputation as property is 'deeply inconsistent' with common law principles that a communication must be defamatory before being actionable, and that harm to reputation is presumed from defamatory publication.[78] Modern defamation now requires the plaintiff to show serious harm[79] – it no longer matters that the property rationale is contrary to historical principle. Other authorities which criticise reputation as property might be distinguished on that basis.[80]

Rolph offers other critiques of reputation as property. First, reputation is inalienable, and alienability is a key characteristic of property rights.[81] Accepting that reputation is inalienable, that critique may be challenged on the basis that alienability is not a necessary criterion of property, even if it is a common criterion. In *Milirrpum v Nabalco*, Blackburn J held that 'property, in its many forms, *generally* implies the right to use or enjoy, the rights to exclude others, and the right to alienate' (emphasis added).[82] He continued: 'I do not say that these rights must co-exist before there can be a proprietary interest, or deny that each of them may

[70] Rolph (n 20) 33.

[71] See *Prince Albert v Strange* [1849] EWHC Ch J20, 41 ER 1171; *Australian Broadcasting Corporation v Lenah Game Meats Pty Ltd* [2001] HCA 63, (2001) 208 CLR 199.

[72] Post (n 20) 693.

[73] Eg *M'Pherson v Daniels* (1829) 10 B & C 263, (1829) 109 ER 448, 453; *Dixon v Holden* (1869) 7 LR Eq 488, 492.

[74] See J Locke, *Two Treatises of Government* (Cambridge, Cambridge University Press, 2003 edn).

[75] T Starkie, *A Treatise on the Law of Slander, Libel, Scandalum Magnatum and False Rumours* (New York, George Lamson, 1826) xx, quoted in Post (n 20) 694.

[76] See generally B Arneil, *John Locke and America: The Defence of English Colonialism* (Oxford, Oxford University Press, 1996).

[77] See section V below.

[78] Post (n 20) 697.

[79] See section V below.

[80] Eg, *Uren v John Fairfax & Sons Ltd* [1966] HCA 40, (1966) 117 CLR 118, 150 (Windeyer J).

[81] Rolph (n 20) 21.

[82] *Milirrpum v Nabalco Pty Ltd* (1971) 17 FLR 141 (NTSC) 272.

be subject to qualifications'.[83] Alienability is better conceived of as a usual consequence, rather than a necessary component, of property.[84] It can be questioned, however, whether reputation is necessarily inalienable. Corporate persons regularly alienate reputations, through sale of intangible assets – namely, trademarks – and through other mergers and acquisitions. The reputation interest protected by defamation is not just that of human persons.[85]

Second, Rolph argues that '[t]he value of reputation is not determined in an open marketplace … it exists solely in the verdicts of juries and, more recently, judges'.[86] That critique may be countered on the following bases. Non-reputational property is not always valued in an open market.[87] Financial analysts use models to value property not for sale,[88] and even things that money cannot buy.[89] There are numerous examples of where a natural person's reputation is ascribed a market value: the sale of autographs; sale of one's skin to market goods with tattoos,[90] or the less extreme version: celebrity endorsements. Arguably, the modern concept of an Instagram 'influencer' cannot exist unless reputation has a market value. Moreover, accountants often value goodwill when reporting; in fact, in Australia, there are mandatory rules for how goodwill is to be accounted.[91] Judges do ascribe reputation monetary value when assessing remedies, but they are not the only persons who value reputation in this way.

The preceding paragraphs defend Post's conception of reputation as property while assuming that property is an economic interest. That assumption requires a brief defence. The subject of economic interests in torts was thoroughly explored by Cane, who defined them as 'an interest for the invasion of which a finite sum of money can provide complete recompense – *restitutio in integrum* in the fullest sense'.[92] He argued that economic interests are capable of objective valuation. He focused on economic interests, rather than economic losses because focusing on the former may allow us 'to identify relevant differences between cases involving economic loss and be able to explain why such loss is recoverable in some cases but not in others'.[93] In characterising property and 'quasi-property' interests as economic interests, he observed, '[w]e do not normally think of reputation

[83] *Ibid.*

[84] *Commissioner of Stamp Duties (NSW) v Yeend* [1929] HCA 39, (1929) 43 CLR 235, 245.

[85] See further section III.C. below.

[86] Rolph (n 20) 21–22.

[87] See P Cane, *Tort Law and Economic Interests*, 2nd ed (Oxford, Clarendon Press, 1996) 8.

[88] Fundamental analysis often focuses on intrinsic aspects of a business: Troy Segal, 'Fundamental Analysis' (*Investopedia*, 16 March 2020), available at www.investopedia.com/terms/f/fundamentalanalysis.asp.

[89] As explored in M Sandel, *What Money Cannot Buy* (New York, Farrar, Straus and Giroux, 2012).

[90] *Ibid*, 163–84.

[91] Australian Accounting Standard, *Accounting for Goodwill* (AAS 18, June 1996), available at www.aasb.gov.au/admin/file/content102/c3/AAS18_6-96.pdf.

[92] Cane (n 87) 5.

[93] *Ibid* 7.

as property. But the way it is protected by the tort of defamation is, in some respects, analogous to the way property rights are protected'.[94] He considered goodwill to mean 'business reputation', and also characterised it as an economic interest.[95]

Various other sources support the view that reputation as property is an economic interest. Rolph described Post's 'reputation as property' as 'an economic construct'.[96] The use of the term 'credit' as a synonym for 'good character' – once recognised by Weber – indicates the closeness of the relationship between reputation and the economy.[97] For some, however, the argument that reputation is a proprietary and economic interest will remain unconvincing; authorities on 'business' reputations may suggest that courts do not see reputation in terms of economic interests.

B. 'Commercial' Reputation

In *Berkhoff v Burchill* it was said that reputation 'is to be interpreted in a broad sense as comprehending all aspects of a person's standing in the community'.[98] A person's standing within the economy comes within that broad sense. Standing within an economy might be described as a 'commercial reputation', even if the person does not identify as a businessperson.

In the leading Australian case on point, *Radio 2UE Sydney Pty Ltd v Chesterton*, the High Court considered 'whether the general test for defamation has application to imputations concerning a person's business or professional reputation, or whether it is limited to those concerning the character or conduct of that person'.[99] The Court cited the principles in *Berkhoff* in saying:

> The concept of 'reputation' in the law of defamation comprehends all aspects of a person's standing in the community. It has been observed that phrases such as 'business reputation' or 'reputation for honesty' may sometimes obscure this fact. In principle therefore the general test for defamation should apply to an imputation concerning any aspect of a person's reputation. A conclusion as to whether injury to reputation has occurred is the answer to the question posed by the general test, whether it be stated as whether a person's standing in the community, or the estimation in which people hold that person, has been lowered or simply whether the imputation is likely to cause people to think the less of a plaintiff. An imputation which defames a person in their professional or business reputation does not have a different effect. It will cause people

[94] *Ibid* 101.
[95] *Ibid* 78.
[96] Rolph (n 20) 13.
[97] M Weber, 'The Protestant Sects and the Spirit of Capitalism' in M Weber, *Essays in Sociology* (edited by HH Gerth and C Mills) (New York, Oxford University Press, 1958) 302, 308, cited in Post (n 20) 695.
[98] *Berkhoff v Burchill* [1997] EMLR 139 (CA) 151 (Neill LJ), cited *Radio 2UE* (n 38) [36] (French CJ, Gummow, Kiefel and Bell JJ).
[99] *Radio 2UE* (n 38) [8] (French CJ, Gummow, Kiefel and Bell JJ).

> to think the less of that person in that aspect of their reputation. For any imputation to be actionable, whether it reflects upon a person's character or their business or professional reputation, the test must be satisfied.[100]

The Court continued: '[t]he distinction sought to be drawn between the standards which might apply to imputations concerning a person's business or professional reputation and those as to their character may be more theoretical than real'.[101] The plaintiff journalist had pleaded that the matter conveyed that he was not to be taken seriously as a journalist.[102] The Court confirmed that the imputation concerning his professional reputation was to be assessed against the standards of the community generally, not within the standards of the media industry or journalists.[103] Recent authority on the ordinary, reasonable person has reaffirmed that approach.[104]

Rather than presenting a barrier to recognition of defamation as an economic tort, this line of authority supports that recognition. Accepting that a 'commercial reputation' is an economic interest, *Radio 2UE* confirms that, whenever a pleaded imputation alleges damage to a person's reputation, it must include damage to their standing within the economy – whatever that standing may be. Every defamation case will have some economic aspect, but those cases brought by professionals and persons who rely on their reputation to gain work – actors,[105] lawyers,[106] politicians[107] and so on – will certainly have an economic quality. These sorts of individuals tend to be those with the means to see defamation litigation through to judgment. Even where the pleaded imputations do not explicitly concern the plaintiff's profession or trade, the interest which would underpin any monetary remedy is still economic in character. That argument is elaborated upon further in section IV.

C. Whose Reputation? Standing to Sue

Where non-natural persons sue in defamation, they do so to vindicate purely economic interests.[108] At common law, a corporation has standing to sue in defamation to vindicate its reputation, as opposed to the reputation of natural persons associated with the corporation. This is an application of the basic proposition

[100] *Ibid* (citations omitted).
[101] *Ibid* [45] (French CJ, Gummow, Kiefel and Bell JJ).
[102] *Ibid* [14] (French CJ, Gummow, Kiefel and Bell JJ).
[103] See also Rolph (n 41) 116 [6.280].
[104] *Trkulja* (n 57) [31] (Kiefel CJ, Keane, Nettle, Bell and Gordon JJ).
[105] Eg, *Bauer Media Pty Ltd v Wilson (No 2)* [2018] VSCA 154, (2018) 56 VR 674.
[106] Eg, *Rayney v State of Western Australia (No 9)* [2017] WASC 367.
[107] Eg, *Hanson-Young v Leyonhjelm (No 4)* [2019] FCA 1981.
[108] Apply *South Hetton Coal Co Ltd v North-Eastern News Ltd* [1894] 1 QB 133 (CA) 138 (Lord Esher MR); *Lewis v Daily Telegraph Ltd* [1964] AC 234 (HL) 262 (Lord Reid).

that a corporation has a separate legal identity from that of its members.[109] Corporations can sue in respect of defamatory matters which have a tendency to damage the corporation 'by way of its business'.[110] That remains the case in England and Wales following the introduction of the *Defamation Act 2013* (UK), subject to the corporate limb of the serious harm threshold in section 1(2), considered below.[111]

In Australia, the standing of corporate persons to sue in defamation was abrogated by the Uniform Defamation Acts.[112] In this respect, Australia is at odds with other common law countries.[113] The Acts establish the general proposition that corporations cannot sue in defamation, although certain 'excluded corporations', including not-for-profits and certain small companies, may still sue. Proposed amendments to the Uniform Defamation Acts would alter the scope of the class of 'excluded corporations' while retaining the general exclusion of standing to sue for corporations. It is also proposed that Australian jurisdictions adopt the UK's approach to 'serious harm' for (non-excluded) corporations contained in the *Defamation Act 2013* (UK) section 1, discussed below.[114]

In those jurisdictions in which corporate-plaintiff defamation is more commonplace, corporate claims regulate excessive competitive conduct, consistent with conventional functionalist views of the economic torts. In an economic analysis of a decade of corporate-claimant defamation decisions, Acheson observed: 'Corporate defendants tended to be either competitors of the claimant or, less often, media companies; human defendants were more varied, although a substantial number were employees or ex-employees either of the claimant or of a corporate defendant'.[115]

While defamation actions brought by corporations are easily characterised as economic torts, arguably, the general exclusion of corporate standing in Australia pushes natural-person defamation into a different function. Remedial principles, however, suggest otherwise.

[109] *South Hetton Coal*, *ibid*. See generally M Collins, *Collins on Defamation* (Oxford, Oxford University Press, 2015) [2.10] fn 21.

[110] *Derbyshire CC v Times Newspapers Ltd* [1993] AC 534 (HL) 547 (Lord Keith).

[111] See P Coe, 'The Value of Corporate Reputation and the Defamation Act 2013 a Brave New World or Road to Ruin' [2015] 4 *Journal of Business Law* 313.

[112] *Defamation Act 2005* (NSW, Qld, Tas, Vic, WA) s 9(1); *Civil Law (Wrongs) Act 2002* (ACT) s 121(1); *Defamation Act 2006* (NT) s 8(1).

[113] See, eg, *Defamation Act 1992* (NZ) s 6; see further NSW Department of Justice, *Council of Attorneys-General Review of Model Defamation Provisions* (Discussion Paper, February 2019) 43, 13 [2.6], available at www.justice.nsw.gov.au/justicepolicy/Documents/review-model-defamation-provisions/Final-CAG-Defamation-Discussion-Paper-Feb-2019.pdf.

[114] See Defamation Working Party, *Background Paper – Model Defamation Amendment Provisions (Consultation Draft)* (December 2019) 30, 9–10, available at www.justice.nsw.gov.au/justicepolicy/Documents/review-model-defamation-provisions/defamation-final-background-paper.pdf.

[115] DJ Acheson, 'Empirical Insights into Corporate Defamation: An Analysis of Cases Decided 2004–2013' (2016) 8 *Journal of Media Law* 32, 40.

IV. How the Underlying Interest is Protected by Defamation Law: Remedies

The preceding section argued that defamation protects an economic interest. Here, it is argued that principles concerning remedies support that characterisation. Furthermore, it is argued that 'reputation as an economic interest' may explain how some remedial principles operate.

It is worth pausing to consider how the economic interest (reputation) is affected by defamation. Cane posited five ways in which a person's economic interests may be interfered with: '(1) deprivation; (2) appropriation; (3) exploitation or use; (4) interference with use, enjoyment or exercise; (5) damage or destruction'.[116] Defamation interferes with reputational interests, it is submitted, in the fourth and fifth sense. A person suffering reputational damage (the fifth sense) is no longer able to enjoy the fruits of having a 'good name' (or at least, a better name then they would have post-defamation) (the fourth sense). The primary function of monetary remedies is to compensate for damage to and loss of enjoyment of reputation.

An award of damages is the primary remedy for defamation, as for other torts. But as Collins observes, for defamation, an award of damages 'is a blunt instrument'; plaintiffs would prefer to prevent the defamation altogether,[117] or a quick correction.[118] An injunction could prevent defamation continuing, however, the primacy of freedom of expression in common law systems means that injunctions are less likely to be awarded for defamation than they are for other causes of action.[119] Where they are awarded, they may be rationalised through the 'economic lens' as either a *quia timet* injunction to prevent threatened invasion of economic rights,[120] or as an injunction to restrain continuing invasion of quasi-proprietary rights.[121]

Different kinds of damages are awarded for defamation. The orthodox view is that 'general damages' are awarded for non-economic loss,[122] while 'special damages' are awarded for economic loss. Each species of damages is compensatory. Aggravated damages – also compensatory in purpose – are awarded where the defendant's conduct has aggravated the defendant's harm. The prospect of

[116] Cane (n 87) 12.

[117] Collins (n 109) [1.19].

[118] *Wagner v Nine Network Australia* [2019] QSC 284 [1].

[119] *Bonnard v Perryman* [1891] 2 Ch 269 (CA); *Australian Broadcasting Corporation v O'Neill* [2006] HCA 46, (2006) 227 CLR 57.

[120] As each view of the matter is a separate tort: *Dow Jones & Co Inc v Gutnick* [2002] HCA 56, (2002) 210 CLR 575. With respect to *quia timet* injunctions, see generally ICF Spry, *The Principles of Equitable Remedies*, 9th edn (Pyrmont, Lawbook Co, 2014) 390–95.

[121] Taking the property analogy to another level, one may draw a parallel between an injunction to restrain continuing defamation and one to restrain continuing private nuisance; see J Murphy, *The Law of Nuisance* (Oxford, Oxford University Press, 2010) [6.06]–[6.07].

[122] See, eg, Rolph (n 41) [15.40].

exemplary damages for defamation has been abolished in Australia,[123] and so exemplary damages are excluded from the following discussion.

It is not argued here that general damages should be abolished, or that the general/special/aggravated distinctions are meaningless. Rather, it is argued that the substance of monetary compensation awarded for defamation not by way of special damages awards is awarded to compensate for economic loss.

A. General Damages Compensate for Pure Economic Loss

The identity of 'general damages' turns on the context in which the term is used.[124] In the context of torts more broadly, general damages are said to be, by their very nature, 'incapable of calculation'.[125] General damages are compensatory, but are referable to losses more difficult to quantify, like pain and suffering. In the context of defamation, general damages are also compensatory,[126] and are 'at large' in the sense that their quantum was historically left to the jury.[127] They are said to serve three overlapping purposes: 'consolation for the personal distress and hurt caused to the appellant by the publication, reparation for the harm done to the appellant's personal and (if relevant) business reputation and vindication of the appellant's reputation'.[128]

At first, these objects may be thought to be inconsistent with defamation's characterisation as an economic tort. Reparation is easiest to reconcile; general damages compensate, and so 'make good what was done wrongfully'.[129] Vindication is trickier. Young explains that the vindicatory purpose of defamation damages means that 'defamation law seeks to vindicate reputation in the sense of reversing the effects of infringement'.[130] A general damages award achieves that object by proving to the public that the defendant's charge was baseless.[131] Vindicatory damages thus function analogously to a declaration. In the United Kingdom, 'vindicatory damages' have been rejected for other torts.[132] At the time of writing,

[123] See, eg, *Defamation Act 2005* (WA) s 37.

[124] See H Luntz, *Assessment of Damages for Personal Injury and* Death, 4th edn (Chatswood, LexisNexis Butterworths, 2002) 64 [1.6.1]; J Edelman (ed), *McGregor on Damages*, 20th edn (London, Sweet & Maxwell, 2018) [3-001].

[125] *Paff v Speed* [1961] HCA 14, (1961) 105 CLR 549, 558–59 (Fullagar J).

[126] *Bauer Media* (n 105) [246] (Tate, Beach and Ashley JJA).

[127] *Uren* (n 80) 151 (Windeyer J).

[128] *Carson v John Fairfax & Sons Ltd* [1933] HCA 31, (1993) 178 CLR 44, 60 (Mason CJ, Deane, Dawson and Gaudron JJ).

[129] See definition of 'reparation' in T Mann (ed), *Australian Law Dictionary*, 3rd edn (South Melbourne, Oxford University Press, 2017) 765–66.

[130] H Young, 'Adding Insult to Injury in Assessing Damages for Corporate Defamation' (2013) 21 *Tort Law Review* 127, 130.

[131] *Broome v Cassell & Co* [1972] AC 1027 (HL) 1071 (Lord Hailsham).

[132] *R (Lumba) v Secretary of State for the Home Department* [2011] UKSC 12, [2012] 1 AC 245.

the High Court of Australia has yet to deliver judgment on a case that will consider this issue.[133] Whatever the outcome, if it is accepted that a purpose of general damages in defamation is vindication, then that purpose is still of an economic character. As a symbol that the plaintiff has been wronged, general damages can restore a lost reputation, or unsour a newly acquired bad reputation. Even in their vindicatory guise, general damages compensate for damage to an economic interest.

The purpose of consolation for hurt and distress does not sit well with an economic characterisation. To that extent, the thesis of this chapter is limited. Mere hurt feelings are not enough to found a cause of action in defamation, and certainly will not be enough to apply a serious harm threshold.[134] Further research should be dedicated to the question of whether damages should ever be available for hurt feelings caused by defamation. As a matter of policy, it is absurd, for example, that a former Treasurer of Australia was awarded compensation for a newspaper hurting his feelings.[135] The prospect of 'feelings damages' increasing a plaintiff's payout could increase the prevalence of the sort of backyard defamation disputes which legislatures are working to discourage.[136] Lady Hale recently observed that 'some heads of damages which would readily fall within that [compensatory] principle are nevertheless irrecoverable because to allow this would be contrary to legal or public policy'. Defamation damages for hurt feelings ought to be contrary to the policy of the law.[137] Defamation law should not remedy hurt feelings more generously than other torts remedy broken bones.[138]

But for the 'consolation' purpose, orthodox principles of general damages for defamation support the proposition that the cause of action protects an economic interest. More precisely, general damages compensate for the effect of the defamation on the plaintiff's reputational interest. Recently, in *Whittington Hospital NHS Trust (Appellant) v XX*, Lady Hale (with whom Lord Kerr and Wilson agreed) began her reasons by describing the compensatory principle as follows:

> The object of damages in tort is to put the claimant, as far as possible, back in the position in which she would have been had the tort not been committed. Money has to compensate, as far as it can, for those injuries that cannot be cured.[139]

In defamation, general damages compensate 'as far as they can' for reputational damage that is difficult to measure. Merely because such damage is difficult to quantify does not mean that it is impossible to quantify, or that it is not economic damage. As section III argued, analysts could attribute an economic value to

[133] *Lewis v The Australian Capital Territory* (Case C14/2019), on appeal from [2019] ACTCA 16.
[134] *Lachaux* (n 50) [5]. See Rolph (n 41) 314 [15.70].
[135] *Hockey v Fairfax Media Publications Pty Ltd* [2015] FCA 652, (2015) 237 FCR 33.
[136] See Defamation Working Party, *Background Paper* (n 114) 25.
[137] *Whittington Hospital NHS Trust (Appellant) v XX* [2020] UKSC 14, [2020] 2 WLR 972 [42].
[138] See *Groom v Crocker* [1939] 1 KB 194 (CA) 231.
[139] *Whittington* (n 137) [1].

reputation if they want to, and indeed, in some cases, the market *does* attribute reputation an economic value.[140]

One further argument supports the claim made here. Recall that, subject to some statutory carve outs, corporations have standing to sue in defamation. Previously, before amendments relating to serious harm, how could a corporation recover in the absence of provable economic loss? A claim premised on changes in market capitalisation would be very difficult to maintain, for too many factors would impact the stock.[141] Corporations could nevertheless receive general damages for defamation, consistent with (most of) the principles discussed.[142] Those damages would compensate for pure economic loss.

B. Special Damages Compensate for Pure Economic Loss

Special damages in defamation compensate for 'special damage' in the sense of measurable economic loss, to be pleaded and proved.[143] In Australia, the distinction between general and special damages is not expressly contemplated by the Uniform Defamation Acts.[144] Rather, the Act refers to 'damages for non-economic loss' and imposes a cap on the amount recoverable in the absence of aggravation.[145] The cap does not apply to special damages.[146]

Economic loss recoverable as 'special damage' includes lost income or loss of earnings,[147] and potentially even loss of opportunity.[148] Confusingly, that kind of damage might also factor into an assessment of general damages. As Tudgendhat J held in *Cambridge v Makin*, 'Where a libel is likely to cause significant loss of earnings, that can be taken into account of special damages'.[149] What, then, is the basis of the distinction between general and special damages? According to Jolowicz, in one sense, the term 'general damage' denotes that incurred through a cause of action that is actionable *per se*, whereas 'special damage' indicates damage incurred through a cause of action where damage is the gist of the action.[150] This substantive distinction spawns a rule of pleading: special damage must be pleaded and proved for it is a necessary condition of the plaintiff's success. As defamation now requires a plaintiff to show serious harm, it may be that the general–special distinction falls away; all that remains is pure economic loss.

[140] *cf Rogers v Nationwide News Pty Ltd* [2003] HCA 52, (2003) 216 CLR 327 [67] (Hayne J).
[141] See *Collins Stewart Ltd v Financial Times Ltd* [2004] EWHC 2337 (QBD).
[142] Corporations lack emotions and would not be awarded consolation damages.
[143] *Lachaux* (n 50) [5].
[144] *Bauer Media* (n 105) [156] (Tate, Beach and Ashley JJA).
[145] See, eg, *Defamation Act 2005* (NSW) s 35.
[146] See *Bauer Media* (n 105).
[147] Eg, *Rayney* (n 106) [922].
[148] *Wilson v Bauer Media Pty Ltd* [2017] VSC 521.
[149] *Cambridge v Makin* [2011] EWHC 12 (QB) [229].
[150] JA Jolowicz, 'The Changing Use of "Special Damage" and its Effect on the Law' [1960] *CLJ* 214, 214–15.

C. Aggravated Damages Compensate for Pure Economic Loss

Aggravated damages are compensatory and ought to be assessed together with general damages.[151] They are awarded where the defendant engages in 'aggravating conduct' – for example, by repeating allegations they should rationally know to be false.[152] Like general damages, aggravated damages serve more than one purpose. Applegarth J held in *Wagner v Nine Network Australia*: '[w]hile aggravated compensatory damages are awarded for conduct which increases hurt to feelings, they are not so limited. Conduct may have the effect of increasing the injury to the plaintiff's reputation as well'.[153] The remarks above in relation to 'feelings damages' apply equally here. If the law were changed so that aggravated damages were no longer used to console, it should not have a significant impact on defamation practice – except in so far as it would lead to a reduced need for evidence in chief from distressed plaintiffs. Aggravated damages will still be awarded in significant quantities to compensate for the increased reputational damage caused by defendants' aggravating conduct.

D. Conclusion as to Damages for Defamation

All defamation damages, apart from what this chapter terms 'feelings damages', compensate for economic loss. That view runs contrary to authority on the relationship between defamation and other torts, like injurious falsehood.[154] In *Radio 2UE*, the majority explained that the remedy for injury to a business or professional reputation 'must be distinguished from that for malicious statements which result in damage not to the reputation but to the business or goods of a person'.[155] With respect, this is an outdated distinction without a meaningful difference. A GP who receives poor reviews of her services is seen by consumers as a *bad doctor*; a lecturer who receives poor student evaluations is seen as a *bad lecturer*; a sole-trader barista with one star on Google Reviews is a *bad barista*; a bank that charges fees for no service is a *bad bank*. Taking 'reputation' to capture *all aspects* of a person's standing in the community,[156] imputations about goods and services provided by a particular individual reflect on that individual's reputation within the economy. As the distinction between work and homelife is more blurred than ever, the distinction between our 'personal' reputations, and our reputations as actors within the economy, has blurred with it.

[151] *Bauer Media* (n 50) [225] (Tate, Beach and Ashley JJA).
[152] See, eg, *Wilson* (n 148) [90].
[153] *Wagner* (n 118) [190] (citations omitted).
[154] Eg, *Palmer Bruyn* (n 7) [116] (Kirby J).
[155] *Radio 2UE* (n 38) [118] (French CJ, Gummow, Kiefel and Bell JJ).
[156] *Berkhoff* (n 98) 151 (Neill LJ), cited in *Radio 2UE* (n 38) [36] (French CJ, Gummow, Kiefel and Bell JJ).

The distinction which cases draw between the purposes of damages for defamation and damages for injurious falsehood hold up an edifice of coherence between these economic torts which is not principled or necessary. Torts are messy; economic torts are messier; but defamation is messiest of all.

V. The Serious Harm Threshold

Post considered that 'defamation law presupposes an image of how people are tied together, or should be tied together, in a social setting. As this image varies, so will the nature of the reputation that the law of defamation seeks to protect'.[157] In recent years, changes in technology and society have changed how we are tied together. Uptake in social media has seen an explosion in digital defamation.[158] The introduction of the serious harm threshold is how the legislature has intervened to recalibrate the reputation that defamation law will protect. It magnifies defamation's character as an economic tort.

The serious harm threshold is contained in section 1 of the *Defamation Act 2013* (UK):

> (1) A statement is not defamatory unless its publication has caused or is likely to cause serious harm to the reputation of the claimant.
> (2) For the purposes of this section, harm to the reputation of a body that trades for profit is not 'serious harm' unless it has caused or is likely to cause the body serious financial loss.

This provision has inspired a proposed equivalent in Australia's Uniform Defamation Acts.[159] If the serious harm threshold does the work it is intended to do, the future of defamation litigation in Australia will involve more high-profile and large-quantum matters and fewer 'backyard' defamation disputes.[160]

As publication of defamatory matter is the essence of the cause of action, the statutory limitation of 'what is defamatory' imposes a new element for the claimant/plaintiff to plead and prove. Whereas defamation was once actionable *per se*, now, a plaintiff must show that the publication 'has caused or is likely to cause serious harm'. That was the effect of Lord Sumption's judgment in *Lachaux*: the legislature has altered the common law, so that some publications which would have

[157] Post (n 20) 693.
[158] See, eg, J Gibson, 'Identifying Defamation Law Reform Issues: A "Snapshot" View of Defamation Judgment Data' (2019) 23 *Media & Arts Law Review* 4.
[159] Section 7A; see Draft Provisions (12 November 2019), available at www.justice.nsw.gov.au/justicepolicy/Documents/review-model-defamation-provisions/consultation-draft-of-mdaps.pdf. Arguably, the statutory language is unnecessary, for 'serious harm' is already part of the common law; that argument is explored elsewhere; see K Gould, 'Locating a "Threshold of Seriousness" in the Australian Tests of Defamation' (2017) 39 *Sydney Law Review* 333; D Rolph, 'Triviality, Proportionality and the Minimum Threshold of Seriousness in Defamation Law' (2019) 23 *Media & Arts Law Review* 280.
[160] Eg, *Armstrong v McIntosh [No 4]* [2020] WASC 31.

been defamatory under the previous law would no longer be defamatory.[161] His Lordship explained:

> The common law rule was that damage to reputation was presumed, not proved, and that the presumption was irrebuttable. If the common law rule survives, then there is no scope for evidence of the actual impact of the publication. That is the main reason why in my opinion it cannot survive.[162]

It is no longer assumed that (otherwise) defamatory matter causes damage. The need to show evidence or actual impact, or likely impact, will mean that fewer defamation cases succeed. Those that do succeed will involve serious reputational damage which is more amenable to an economic characterisation: 'serious' harm will likely entail economic harm. The modern practice of defamation law shows that Windeyer J's claim that 'money and reputation are not commensurables'[163] must no longer hold true.

VI. Why it Matters

Defamation is an economic tort. So what? There are two reasons why characterisation as an economic tort matters.

First, defamation should no longer be seen as an unusual outlier among torts. If anything, within the family of torts, negligence is more of an outlier than defamation.[164] As leading defamation law scholar David Rolph has explained, defamation is a tort like any other.[165] To this I would add: defamation is an economic tort like any other economic tort. Recognising the parallels between the interest protected by defamation and that protected by other economic torts could motivate useful cross-pollination of legal principle, particularly with respect to remedies, but also in other areas – for example, with respect to participatory liability of publishers.[166]

Second, the economic rationale of reputation explains why some plaintiffs sue: to recover compensation for damaged assets. It also explains why some individuals defame. In their economic analysis of torts, Landes and Posner appealed to Coase to explain why, for some, it would be economically rational to engage in certain tortious conduct.[167] In certain cases, paying for damage caused by one's

[161] See *Lachaux* (n 50) [17].
[162] *Lachaux* (n 50) [20].
[163] *Uren* (n 80) 150 (Windeyer J).
[164] See J Edelman, 'Fundamental errors in *Donoghue v Stevenson*' (2014) 29 *Australian Bar Review* 160.
[165] D Rolph, 'Keynote Address' (Media Law & IP Conference, Melbourne Law School, Melbourne, 5 December 2019).
[166] *cf* the controversy surrounding *Voller v Nationwide News Pty Ltd* [2019] NSWSC 766 and *Fairfax Media Publications v Voller* [2020] NSWCA 102.
[167] WM Landes and RA Posner, *The Economic Structure of Tort Law* (Cambridge, Harvard University Press, 1987) 31–38.

tortious conduct may be justified as it would maximise the tortfeasor's wellbeing. With respect to defamation, the position of mass media defendants comes to mind. For investigative reporters, newspaper, gossip magazine publishers,[168] and even internet intermediaries,[169] liability in defamation may be a justifiable cost of doing business. Landes and Posner reasoned that 'a simple rule of strict liability is optimal when the optimal solution is for the injurer to take measures to avoid damage and for the victim to do nothing'.[170] There is little a would-be defamed person can do to protect their reputation while maintaining a life in a community, and so the economic rationale justifies imposition of strict liability in defamation. When we view defamation as an economic tort, we see it in terms of its function to guard against excessive competition. That policy rationale is notably absent from defamation law reform submissions dominated by defendants – as the New South Wales Law Reform Commission once opined, 'prospective defamers are better organized and more articulate than prospective plaintiffs'.[171] The economic rationale better informs the policy debate on how defamation law should balance freedom of speech with protection of reputation.

The thesis of this chapter is against the grain of countless dicta. It is not suggested that they were wrong. They should, however, be re-examined. Post's proprietary (economic) conception of reputation is more compelling than it once was. With the cause of action requiring serious harm, reputation as an economic interest is emerging as the primary interest which the tort protects. Damages for defamation primarily compensate for pure economic loss. When the next book on economic torts is written, it too should include a chapter on defamation.

[168] See *Bauer Media* (n 105).
[169] See *Google Inc v Duffy* [2017] SASCFC, (2017) 129 SASR 304.
[170] Landes and Posner (n 167) 38.
[171] New South Wales Law Reform Commission, *Defamation* (Report No 11, 1971) [12].

4

Regulating Labour Relations in the Twenty-First Century: What Role for the Economic Torts?

ANDREW STEWART AND SHAE McCRYSTAL*

This chapter examines the ways in which civil liability may be imposed for the intentional infliction of economic loss on an employer, under what are often called the 'economic torts'. Given constraints on length, we concentrate on the position in Australia, and to a lesser extent the United Kingdom (UK), while occasionally noting developments or literature from other common law systems. We have also set to one side the particular issues raised by the picketing of worksites and other premises, given that these tend to involve not just a mixture of civil and criminal issues, but liability in torts such as trespass or nuisance.[1]

Depending on how they are analysed and categorised – a matter to which we return in section II – the torts with which we are concerned for this purpose potentially cover up to four types of deliberate conduct: interference with the performance of contractual or other pre-existing obligations; a conspiracy of two or more persons to cause loss; the threat of wrongful conduct to secure a desired objective; and the infliction of economic loss through wrongful means.[2] The first of those wrongs in particular can be used to impose liability on third parties that procure or facilitate various forms of individual wrongdoing by employees. For example, a firm (or the individuals behind it) may be sued for inducing a competitor's employee to disclose trade secrets or to divert customers or business

* We are grateful to Kate McFarlane for her invaluable research assistance in preparing this chapter.

[1] See A Stewart et al, *Creighton & Stewart's Labour Law*, 6th edn (Annandale, Federation Press, 2016) [26.42]–[26.43], [26.88].

[2] For broader treatments of the economic torts, which also include passing off and injurious falsehood, see MA Jones (ed), *Clerk and Lindsell on Torts*, 22nd edn (London, Sweet & Maxwell, 2018) Ch 24; S Deakin, 'Economic Relations' in C Sappideen and P Vines (eds), *Fleming's The Law of Torts*, 10th edn (Rozelle, Lawbook Co, 2011); H Carty, *An Analysis of the Economic Torts*, 2nd edn (Oxford, Oxford University Press, 2010).

opportunities, in breach of their duties of confidentiality and/or fidelity.[3] The conceptual basis for such liability, and whether it can properly be regarded as 'accessorial' in nature, are considered elsewhere in this collection.[4] Our focus, however, is on a different and more contentious use for the economic torts – or the 'industrial torts' as they are sometimes termed in this connection. This is their deployment to suppress *collective* action by groups of workers and trade unions, or (less commonly in practice) to seek pecuniary relief for loss caused by such action.

I. The Development of Economic Tort Liability for Industrial Action

In the context of commercial disputes, the imposition of liability for the intentional infliction of economic loss raises difficult issues of policy, as Lords Sumption and Lloyd-Jones (with the agreement of Lords Mance, Hodge and Briggs) recently noted in *JSC BTA Bank v Khrapunov*:

> [T]he economic torts are a major exception to the general rule that there is no duty in tort to avoid causing a purely economic loss unless it is parasitic upon some injury to person or property. The reason for the general rule is that, contract apart, common law duties to avoid causing pure economic loss tend to cut across the ordinary incidents of competitive business, one of which is that one man's [sic] gain may be another man's loss. The successful pursuit of commercial self-interest necessarily entails the risk of damaging the commercial interests of others. Identifying the point at which it transgresses legitimate bounds is therefore a task of exceptional delicacy. The elements of the four established economic torts are carefully defined so as to avoid trespassing on legitimate business activities or imposing any wider liability than can be justified in principle.[5]

That task might be thought even more challenging when the common law is used to prevent workers from seeking to exercise what at an international level, as we explain in section V, is regarded as a right to strike or to take other forms of industrial action that involve the withdrawal of labour. If workers cannot do this, then their capacity to engage in collective bargaining over wages, working conditions or other issues is necessarily stultified. They are left to the mercies of whatever individual bargaining power they can muster – which for most, is not much. Yet the courts have often shown far less interest in protecting the legitimacy of the

[3] See, eg, *Goodchild Fuel Distributors Pty Ltd v Holman* (1992) 59 SASR 454 (SASC); *Wilson HTM Investment Group Ltd v Pagliaro* (2012) 226 IR 75 (NSWSC).

[4] See also S Deakin and J Randall, 'Rethinking the Economic Torts' (2009) 72 *MLR* 519, 542–44; J Dietrich and P Ridge, *Accessories in Private Law* (Cambridge, Cambridge University Press, 2015) Ch 6.

[5] *JSC BTA Bank v Khrapunov* [2018] UKSC 19, [2018] 2 WLR 1125 [6] ('*Khrapunov*').

pursuit of self-interest by workers and their representatives, compared to commercial competitors. This was especially apparent during two critical phases in the development of the economic torts in the UK.

The first occurred at the turn of the nineteenth and twentieth centuries, in a key trilogy of cases. In *Mogul Steamship Co v McGregor, Gow & Co*[6] the House of Lords absolved a cartel of shipowners from liability for acting in combination to deny a rival firm access to a market that it wished to monopolise. A mere desire to inflict economic loss on a competitor, no matter how calculated (or indeed effective), should not of itself be regarded as tortious. The subsequent decision in *Allen v Flood*[7] seemed to take a similar view in relation to industrial action. An official who threatened that his members would (lawfully) withdraw their labour unless an employer dismissed members of a rival union was found not to be liable for interfering with their employment.[8] It was stressed that action that was otherwise lawful could not be rendered unlawful merely because of a 'malicious' intent to cause harm to the target of the action. Lord Shand observed that competition in labour was 'in all essentials analogous to competition in trade', so that the approach taken in *Mogul* must necessarily apply.[9]

Yet just a couple of years later the House reached a very different conclusion in *Quinn v Leathem*.[10] In order to induce the plaintiff, a butcher, to employ only union labour, the defendant union officials threatened industrial action to persuade his main customer to cease dealing with him. Even if the defendants' conduct may not have been actionable if undertaken separately, the fact that they had acted in combination (unlike the single official in *Allen*) was enough to render them liable for what was characterised as malicious behaviour. The contrast with *Mogul* was stark. Where the blacklist in that case was considered a 'legitimate business device', in *Quinn* it was an 'object of coercion'.[11]

By this stage it had also been established that the tort of inducing breach of contract, famously recognised in *Lumley v Gye*[12] in a dispute concerning an opera singer's services, would be committed when persuading workers to strike or impose work bans in breach of their employment contracts.[13] In *South Wales Miners' Federation v Glamorgan Coal Co Ltd*[14] the House of Lords confirmed this. The fact

[6] *Mogul Steamship Co v McGregor, Gow & Co* [1892] AC 25 (HL).

[7] *Allen v Flood* [1898] AC 1 (HL).

[8] Importantly, no breach of contract was involved here, either on the part of the employer (who gave notice in dismissing the plaintiffs), or in relation to the threatened industrial action (the workers concerned were engaged on short-term contracts and thus were simply proposing not to enter into further engagements).

[9] *Allen* (n 7) 164.

[10] *Quinn v Leathem* [1901] AC 495 (HL).

[11] P Elias and K Ewing, 'Economic Torts and Labour Law: Old Principles and New Liabilities' (1982) 41 *CLJ* 321, 324.

[12] *Lumley v Gye* (1853) 2 El & Bl 216, 118 ER 749.

[13] See, eg, *Bowen v Hall* (1881) 6 QBD 333 (CA); *Temperton v Russell* [1893] 1 QB 715 (CA).

[14] *South Wales Miners' Federation v Glamorgan Coal Co Ltd* [1905] AC 239 (HL).

that those involved may have been seeking to act out of economic self-interest in improving or defending wages or working conditions, rather than a spiteful desire to cause loss, could not be pleaded as a justification. Coupled with the decision in *Taff Vale Railway Co v Amalgamated Society of Railway Servants*,[15] that a registered trade union could be held liable for the tortious acts of its members and officials, employers now had all the legal means they could wish to suppress the exercise of collective power by their own workers, or by those who served their customers or suppliers.

These developments were all the more notable when set against the background of the reforms introduced by the *Conspiracy and Protection of Property Act 1875* (UK). Besides largely repealing the 'master and servant' laws, which had criminalised breaches of contract by individual workers, section 3 provided that an agreement or combination by two or more persons to do or procure any act 'in contemplation or furtherance of a trade dispute' should not be indictable as a conspiracy if it would not be punishable as a crime if done by one person.[16] In effect then, as the UK Supreme Court has now recognised, the application of the tort of conspiracy in *Quinn v Leathem* was 'a device for imposing civil liability on the organisers of strikes and other industrial action', now that the criminal law was no longer available.[17] It was a step that revealed 'the conviction of late Victorian judges that large-scale collective action in the political and economic sphere by those outside the traditional governing class was a potential threat to the constitution and the framework of society'.[18]

Eventually, Parliament reacted to the circumvention of the protections created by the 1875 Act. Section 4 of the *Trade Disputes Act 1906* (UK) conferred on trade unions a blanket immunity against any action in tort. Sections 1–3 afforded individuals (including union members and officials) lesser but still significant protection against various forms of civil liability, including in conspiracy, for anything done 'in contemplation or furtherance of a trade dispute' – thus reaffirming the status of what Wedderburn would later describe as the 'golden formula' of British labour law.[19] 'Trade dispute' was broadly defined in section 5 as 'any dispute between employers and workmen [sic], or between workmen and workmen, which is connected with the employment or non-employment, or the terms of the employment, or with the conditions of labour, of any person'.

For the most part, this intervention successfully took industrial disputes outside the jurisdiction of the courts. And for a time, the courts' attitude to

[15] *Taff Vale Railway Co v Amalgamated Society of Railway Servants* [1901] AC 426 (HL).

[16] As to the implementation of the 1875 reforms in what were then the Australian colonies, see EI Sykes, *Strike Law in Australia*, 2nd edn (Sydney, Law Book Co, 1982) 100–103, 111–15, 128–51.

[17] *Khrapunov* (n 5) [7].

[18] *Ibid*, citing *Revenue and Customs Commissioners v Total Network SL* [2008] UKHL 19, [2008] 1 AC 1174 [78].

[19] KW Wedderburn, *The Worker and the Law* (Harmondsworth, Penguin, 1965) 222–23.

industrial action also seemed to soften. In *Crofter Hand Woven Harris Tweed Co v Veitch*,[20] Lord Wright went so far as to accept that:

> In commercial affairs each trader's rights are qualified by the right of others to compete. Where the rights of labour are concerned, the rights of the employer are conditioned by the rights of the men to give or withhold their services. The right of workmen to strike is an essential element in the principle of collective bargaining.

The House of Lords held in this case that workers seeking to embargo goods produced by businesses which were in dispute with their union would not be liable in the tort of what we go on below to describe as the tort of 'simple' conspiracy, since they were acting out of economic self-interest, rather than a desire to injure the targets of their action.[21]

After this rare outbreak of judicial restraint, however, what might be regarded as normal service eventually resumed with the ruling in *Rookes v Barnard*.[22] The case concerned an airline employee who had resigned his union membership and then been dismissed by his employer, under pressure of threatened strike action. In holding the defendant union officials liable for the loss caused to him by what were found to be unlawful threats, the House of Lords not only revived the ancient tort of intimidation, but adopted a narrow construction of the protections conferred by the 1906 Act.

Once again, the immediate effect of the decision was reversed by a statutory amendment.[23] But the ruling inspired a further period of 'judicial innovation' which involved 'the continual "outflanking" of the statutory immunities',[24] both through the expansion of the existing torts and the recognition of new wrongs.[25] The attitude of many judges to the immunities created by the 1906 Act was captured by Lord Diplock's comment that the legislation was 'intrinsically repugnant to anyone who has spent his [sic] life in the practice of the law or the administration of justice'.[26]

This period of creative development was eventually halted and (to some extent) reversed in *OBG Ltd v Allan*,[27] a decision which brought together appeals against rulings in three separate cases, none of them involving industrial action.

[20] *Crofter Hand Woven Harris Tweed Co v Veitch* [1942] AC 435 (HL) 463.

[21] The High Court of Australia had already arrived at that position: see *McKernan v Fraser* (1931) 46 CLR 343 (HCA).

[22] *Rookes v Barnard* [1964] AC 1129 (HL). For commentary, see, eg, KW Wedderburn, 'Intimidation and the Right to Strike' (1964) 27 *MLR* 257; T Weir, 'Chaos or Cosmos? *Rookes, Stratford* and the Economic Torts' [1964] *CLJ* 225.

[23] See *Trade Disputes Act 1965* (UK).

[24] S Deakin and G Morris, *Labour Law*, 6th edn (Oxford, Hart Publishing, 2012) 11.

[25] See, eg, *Torquay Hotel Co Ltd v Cousins* [1969] 2 Ch 106 (CA); *Prudential Assurance Co Ltd v Lorenz* (1971) 11 KIR 78 (Ch); *Meade v Haringey London Borough Council* [1979] 1 WLR 637 (CA); *Associated British Ports v Transport and General Workers Union* [1989] 1 WLR 939 (HL).

[26] *Duport Steels v Sirs* [1980] 1 WLR 142 (HL) 156.

[27] *OBG Ltd v Allan* [2007] UKHL 21, [2008] 1 AC 1.

Some of the main features of the decision are explained in section II below. Writing extrajudicially, Lord Hoffmann would later describe it as reflecting 'a wish to confine the economic torts as narrowly as possible'.[28] He suggested that Parliament had now 'taken over the task of delimiting what industrial action should be lawful or unlawful',[29] and that accordingly the torts had 'run their course'.[30] It is far from clear that this wish has been born out in practice, whether in the UK or in other common law countries.[31] But that the suggestion was even made is quite striking.

It would also appear that the attitude of the UK courts to the interpretation of the statutory immunities has changed. As Elias LJ put it in *National Union of Rail, Maritime and Transport Union v Serco Ltd*:

> The common law's focus on the protection of property and contractual rights is necessarily antithetical to any form of industrial action since the purpose of the action is to interfere with the employer's rights. The statutory immunities are simply the form which the law in this country takes to carve out the ability for unions to take lawful strike action. It is for Parliament to determine how the conflicting interests of employers and unions should be reconciled in the field of industrial relations. But if one starts from the premise that the legislation should be strictly construed against those seeking the benefit of the immunities, the effect is the same as it would be if there were a presumption that Parliament intends that the interests of the employers should hold sway unless the legislation clearly dictates otherwise. I do not think this is now a legitimate approach, if it ever was. In my judgment the legislation should simply be construed in the normal way.[32]

Against that background, this chapter examines the state of the current law on the economic torts as they apply in relation to industrial action, the use of legislation to shield workers or unions from liability, and how commonly the torts are invoked in practice. It then focuses on the role that tort liability for industrial action can or should play in any labour regulation system which, as in Australia, is now primarily based in legislation. Does the goal of 'coherence' between the common law and statute, as recently espoused by some higher courts, demand that either legislatures or the courts themselves modify or mitigate the operation of the economic torts in an industrial context?

[28] Lord Hoffmann, 'The Rise and Fall of the Economic Torts' in S Degeling, J Edelman and J Goudkamp (eds), *Torts in Commercial Law* (Sydney, Thomson Reuters, 2011) 113.

[29] *Ibid* 113.

[30] *Ibid* 114.

[31] H Carty, 'The Modern Functions of the Economic Torts: Reviewing the English, Canadian, Australian, and New Zealand Positions' (2015) 74 *CLJ* 261. For other analysis of *OBG*, see, eg, B Simpson, 'Economic Tort Liability in Labour Disputes: The Potential Impact of the House of Lords' Decision in *OBG Ltd v Allan*' (2007) 36 *Industrial Law Journal* 468; Deakin and Randall (n 4).

[32] *National Union of Rail, Maritime and Transport Union v Serco Ltd* [2011] EWCA Civ 226, [2011] ICR 848 [9]. See also *British Airways v British Airline Pilots' Association* [2019] EWCA Civ 1663 [7].

II. The Current State of the Common Law

As the common law currently stands in the UK and Australia, three points seem to be clear.[33] The first is that it is tortious for a defendant (D) to persuade a person (X) to breach their contract with the plaintiff (P). For this purpose, D must generally know and intend that the relevant contract exists and will be breached as a result of their actions.[34] But it also appears to be sufficient that they are recklessly indifferent to the contract's existence, and they do not in any event need to know the precise term that is breached.[35] Industrial action almost invariably involves a breach of an employee's obligation to work in accordance with their employer's instructions. It follows that any form of 'primary' action, in which labour is withdrawn in pursuit of demands being made upon the relevant workers' own employer, will generally mean that anyone who organises the action will have committed this tort.[36] One exception is where the action consists of a mass resignation,[37] or a refusal to accept further employment.[38] But that drastic step will not usually be an appealing option, except in theory to casual or temporary workers – and they are among the least likely to be organised, or to be able to afford the loss of wages involved.

Second, two distinct forms of conspiracy are actionable in tort. One has traditionally been described as 'simple' conspiracy or 'conspiracy to injure'.[39] It involves two or more persons (DD) acting in combination deliberately to inflict economic loss on the plaintiff (P). The potential breadth of this principle is limited by the need to establish that DD were not acting in furtherance of their legitimate economic interests. It now seems clearly established that the pursuit of union objectives such as improvement of employment conditions and organisational security are legitimate for this purpose,[40] so that industrial action will not normally be unlawful on this ground. But difficulties may still be encountered where the court disapproves of the purposes of the conspirators (for example, if the strike is 'political' in nature), or where the predominant purpose of the conspiracy is considered to be a malicious desire to harm P rather than to promote the interests of the conspirators.[41]

[33] Some of what follows is taken from Stewart et al (n 1) Ch 28.6.

[34] *OBG* (n 27).

[35] *Daebo Shipping Co Ltd v The Ship Go Star* [2012] FCAFC 156, (2012) 207 FCR 220 [88]–[89].

[36] But see *Qantas Airways Ltd v Transport Workers Union* [2011] FCA 470, (2011) 280 ALR 503, in which Qantas failed to establish liability on the part of the defendant unions or their officials for organising stop work meetings held during work time, because it could not show that in requesting workers to attend those meetings, they had intended any workers to breach their contracts of employment.

[37] See, eg, *Ansett Transport Industries (Operations) Pty Ltd v Australian Federation of Air Pilots* (1989) 95 ALR 211 (VSC).

[38] See, eg, *Allen* (n 7).

[39] But see *Khrapunov* (n 5) [8], preferring the term 'lawful means' conspiracy.

[40] *McKernan* (n 21); *Crofter* (n 20).

[41] See, eg, *Huntley v Thornton* [1957] 1 All ER 234 (Ch). As to the problem of mixed motives amongst the conspirators, see *McKernan* (n 21) 399–408.

The other and far more practically relevant form of conspiracy is conspiracy by unlawful means. Liability under this head is established if DD, acting in combination, deliberately inflict loss on P by doing an act which is in itself unlawful or for a purpose which is inherently unlawful. What distinguishes this form of liability from simple conspiracy is that the motives of the conspirators are irrelevant, in the sense that the fact that the conspirators are actuated by the desire to further their own interests will not absolve them from liability if they have in fact utilised unlawful means.[42] But there must still be an intention to harm P. This requirement is not satisfied by conduct that merely has the foreseeable consequence of harming *someone* (who turns out to be P).[43] In Australia at least, the requisite 'unlawful means' for these purposes may be furnished by a breach of statute,[44] conduct which is unlawful as a crime or as a tort,[45] or a breach of contract.[46] Since most industrial action involves a breach of contract on the part of those involved, and/or a breach of the statutory restrictions detailed later in the chapter, it follows that for practical purposes virtually *all* industrial action in Australia constitutes an unlawful means conspiracy, and is actionable as such. By contrast, in the UK, the Supreme Court, while accepting that crimes may be unlawful means for this purpose, has refused to confirm that the same would be true of breaches of civil statutory duties, torts actionable at the suit of third parties, or breaches of contract or of fiduciary duty.[47]

In *Khrapunov*, Lords Sumption and Lloyd-Jones acknowledged that:

> [Conspiracy] is an anomalous tort because it may make actionable acts which would be lawful apart from the element of combination. The ostensible rationale, that acts done in combination are inherently more coercive than those done by a single actor, has not always been found persuasive, least of all when the single actor may be a powerful corporation.[48]

Nonetheless, the tort was considered to have 'an established place in the law of tort'.[49]

[42] *Williams v Hursey* (1959) 103 CLR 30 (HCA); *Coal Miners Industrial Union of WA v True* (1959) 33 ALJR 224 (HCA); *Lonrho Plc v Fayed* [1992] 1 AC 448 (HL).

[43] *Dresna Pty Ltd v Misu Nominees Pty Ltd* [2004] FCAFC 169.

[44] See, eg, *Coal Miners Industrial Union of WA* (n 42); *Ansett* (n 37); *Maritime Union of Australia v Patrick Stevedores No 1 Pty Ltd* (1998) 153 ALR 602, 612–13. It appears that a breach of statute may constitute unlawful means even where the person injured has no right to enforce the provision breached: *Dresna* (n 43).

[45] See, eg, *Williams* (n 42); *Latham v Singleton* [1981] 2 NSWLR 843 (NSWSC).

[46] See, eg, *David Jones Ltd v Federated Storemen and Packers Union* (1985) 14 IR 75; *Maritime Union of Australia* (n 44) 612–13.

[47] *Khrapunov* (n 5) [15]. It was held in this case that a criminal contempt of court, even if punishable in civil proceedings, qualified as unlawful means.

[48] *Ibid* [7]. See also *Lonrho Ltd v Shell Petroleum Ltd* [1982] AC 173 (HL) 188–89.

[49] *Khrapunov* (n 5) [7].

The third relevant tort that is clearly recognised in both Australia and the UK is intimidation.[50] As conventionally understood, this form of liability arises where one party (D), intending to cause loss to the plaintiff (P), threatens a third party (TP) with violence or serious damage to property unless TP does something which is harmful to P ('three party' intimidation). In *Rookes*[51] it was held that a threat to break a contract of employment in the course of an industrial dispute could be equated with a threat of violence or injury to property for these purposes. In *Construction, Forestry, Mining and Energy Union v Boral Resources (Vic) Pty Ltd*,[52] for example, the union defendant threatened construction principals and subcontractors that its members would refuse to work on their building sites (in potential breach of their contracts) unless the principals and subcontractors refrained from using Boral's products on those same sites, with the intention of damaging Boral's business.[53] It is also widely recognised that there is a 'two party' version of the tort, where D threatens P that an unlawful act will be committed unless P does something which is detrimental to P's own interests.[54]

Prior to the House of Lords' decision in *OBG*, the first of the three torts listed above, that of inducing or procuring a breach of contract, had been progressively broadened to cover not just direct but *indirect* forms of interference with a contract, provided they involved some form of independently unlawful act. In such situations, there was no need for the target contract actually to be breached as a result of the interference: it was sufficient that performance may have been hampered in some substantial way.[55] The extension had obvious implications for so-called 'secondary' boycotts, where industrial action at one business is taken or threatened in order to put pressure on another, with whom the 'real' (or underlying) dispute exists. For example, a union (D) might exert pressure on an employer (P) by persuading its members (YY) employed by a third party (TP) who is a supplier or client of P to refuse to deal with goods or services emanating from or destined for P. If YY have breached their contracts of employment or otherwise acted unlawfully, P would have a cause of action against D for indirect interference, whilst TP would have an action against D for direct interference.[56]

[50] In *OBG* (n 27) a majority of the House of Lords took the view that intimidation should be regarded as an example of the tort of causing loss by unlawful means, discussed separately below. But in *Khrapunov* (n5) [6] it was identified as a tort in its own right, which is the more conventional view.

[51] *Rookes* (n 22).

[52] *Construction, Forestry, Mining and Energy Union v Boral Resources (Vic) Pty Ltd* [2014] VSCA 348, (2014) 45 VR 571.

[53] The High Court refused the union leave to appeal against the Victorian Court of Appeal's conclusion that the tort of intimidation is part of Australian law.

[54] *Spira v Commonwealth Bank of Australia* [2003] NSWCA 180, (2003) 57 NSWLR 544, 552. See further John Murphy, 'Understanding Intimidation' (2014) 77 *MLR* 33.

[55] *Torquay Hotel* (n 25); *Merkur Island Shipping Corp v Laughton* [1983] 2 AC 570 (CA).

[56] *Stratford & Son Ltd v Lindley* [1965] AC 269 (HL); *Woolley v Dunford* (1972) 3 SASR 243 (SASC).

In *OBG* the House of Lords insisted on confining the tort of contractual interference to situations in which a breach of contract is directly induced. Indirect interference was rationalised instead as falling within a separate tort of unlawful interference with a trade or business. The elements of this head of liability are simple: the commission of an unlawful act by the defendant (D) with intent to inflict economic loss upon the plaintiff (P).[57] In Australia, however, the High Court has previously declined to determine whether 'a tort of interference with trade or business interests by an unlawful act should be recognised in Australia'.[58] Even since *OBG*, the recognition of that tort has been treated as a matter for the High Court alone to consider.[59] That being the case, it would also seem to follow that, at least for the time being, the indirect version of the tort of contractual interference should still be recognised as part of Australian law.[60]

A further possibility left open in *OBG*[61] was that the tort of inducing breach of contract might merely be one example of an actionable interference with pre-existing rights. There is, for example, some authority to the effect that it is a tort to induce the breach of a common carrier's duty to carry,[62] or of an equitable obligation,[63] or even of a statutory duty.[64] But the suggestion that these may simply be examples of some kind of 'genus' tort of (direct) interference with rights[65] has not to date been taken up.

A final note on the current law concerns the possibility, left open in many of the formative cases on the economic torts, of defendants being able to plead 'just cause' or 'justification' for their actions. With the notable exception of conspiracy

[57] *OBG* (n 27) [47]. As to what may be regarded as 'unlawful means' for the purposes of this head of liability, see Jones (n 2).

[58] *Sanders v Snell* [1998] HCA 64, (1998) 196 CLR 329, 341. In *Northern Territory of Australia v Mengel* [1995] HCA 65, (1995) 185 CLR 307, 343, the High Court had previously distinguished this 'embryonic or emerging tort' from the broader suggestion in *Beaudesert Shire Council v Smith* (1966) 120 CLR 145 (HCA) 156 that damages could be recovered by 'a person who suffers harm or loss as the inevitable consequence of the unlawful intentional and positive acts of another'. That extraordinary proposition was decisively rejected in *Mengel.*

[59] See, eg, *Ballard v Multiplex* [2012] NSWSC 426 [84]–[85]; *Construction, Forestry, Mining and Energy Union* (n 52) [31].

[60] *Donaldson v Natural Springs Australia Ltd* [2015] FCA 498 [209]–[223]; but *cf Rajlaw NSW Pty Ltd v Rajlaw Pty Ltd* [2013] NSWSC 1621 [27]. As to whether Australia *should* adopt the rationalisation proposed in the UK, see J Neyers, 'Causing Loss by Unlawful Means: Should the High Court of Australia follow *OGB Ltd v Allan*?' in Degeling, Edelman and Goudkamp (eds) (n 28).

[61] *OBG* (n 27) [189].

[62] *James v Commonwealth* (1939) 62 CLR 339 (HCA).

[63] *Prudential Assurance* (n 25). But *cf Metall und Rohstoff AG v Donaldson Lufkin & Jenrette Inc* [1990] 1 QB 391 (CA); *Coomera Resort Pty Ltd v Kolback Securities Ltd* [2004] 1 Qd R 1 (QSC).

[64] *Meade v Haringey London Borough Council* [1979] 1 WLR 637 (CA). The duty must, however, be one that would be actionable by the plaintiff: see *Lonrho Plc v Fayed* [1990] 2 QB 479 (CA) 488. For statutory incarnations of this form of liability in the UK, see Deakin and Morris (n 24) 1045; and see, eg, *Ministry of Justice v Prison Officers' Association* [2017] EWHC 699 (QB), [2017] IRLR 621.

[65] *Associated British Ports v Transport and General Workers Union* [1989] 1 WLR 939 (HL) 951–52, 959, 963.

to injure, where (as explained above) the pursuit of legitimate self-interest will prevent liability from arising, the possibility of successfully pleading justification has been more theoretical than real. There have been one or two instances in which defendants threatening or organising industrial action have been able to escape liability for inducing breach of contract. But the facts in these cases have been unusual.[66] Furthermore, the courts have been reluctant to allow the defence where unlawful means are used,[67] which in practice will typically be the case. In *Zhu v Treasurer (NSW)*[68] the High Court of Australia held that a defendant wishing to plead justification must ordinarily establish that they are acting in accordance with a 'superior legal right' to that of the plaintiff, but left open the question of whether this was necessary in an employment context.[69]

III. Statutory Limitations

The practical effect of the principles just described was recognised by Simler LJ (with whom Hamblen and Davis LLJ agreed) in *British Airways v British Airline Pilots' Association*:[70]

> At common law … there is no right to strike and those who take part in strike action will usually be acting in breach of their contract of employment, and unions who authorise or endorse such action will be liable for inducing a breach of contract and potentially other economic torts.

A similar point was made by Kiefel CJ, Keane, Nettle and Edelman JJ in *Esso Australia Pty Ltd v Australian Workers' Union*.[71]

In countries from the common law tradition, therefore, the impact of the economic torts necessitates a legislative response if workers are to have any right to take industrial action.[72] Such a legislative response might take the form of

[66] See, eg, *Brimelow v Casson* [1924] 1 Ch 302 (Ch); *Pete's Towing Services Ltd v Northern Industrial Union of Workers* [1970] NZLR 32 (NZSC).

[67] See, eg, *Brisbane Shipwrights Provident Union v Heggie* (1906) 3 CLR 686 (HCA) 702; *Ansett* (n 37) 254–55; *Building Workers Industrial Union of Australia v Odco Pty Ltd* (1991) 29 FCR 104 (FCA) 140–45; but *cf Latham* (n 45); *Ranger Uranium Mines Pty Ltd v Federated Miscellaneous Workers Union of Australia* (1987) 54 NTR 6 (NTSC). The issue was left open in *Zhu v Treasurer (NSW)* [2004] HCA 56, (2004) 218 CLR 530 [174].

[68] *Zhu, ibid* [138].

[69] See further D Goodwin, 'Justification Defences under the Economic Torts' (2019) 26 *Tort Law Review* 143.

[70] *British Airways* (n 32) [4].

[71] *Esso Australia Pty Ltd v Australian Workers' Union* [2017] HCA 54, (2017) 263 CLR 551 [30].

[72] Note however that the Canadian Charter of Rights and Freedoms, appended to the Constitution of Canada, guarantees freedom of association for all Canadian citizens. This guarantee has been interpreted to extend to the right to strike: see *Saskatchewan Federation of Labour v Saskatchewan* 2015 SCC 4, [2015] 1 SCR 245, which necessarily impacts on the manner in which the law in this area is implemented and gives Canadian citizens an alternative source of the right to strike that cannot be abrogated. See further J Fudge and H Jensen, 'The Right to Strike: The Supreme Court of Canada, the Charter of Rights and Freedoms and the Arc of Workplace Justice' (2016) 27 *King's Law Journal* 89.

codification, which would have the effect of legislating all rights and remedies in respect of lawful and unlawful industrial action, and removing any role for the common law in the resolution of industrial disputes.[73] Alternatively, a role for the common law may be preserved through the use of an *immunity* approach, where the legislature carves out an area in which strike action may be taken lawfully, and industrial actors are provided with immunity from liabilities that would otherwise arise. In that case, unprotected conduct which falls outside the immunity remains subject to the application of the economic torts, including potential injunctive relief and/or damages at final judgment where pursued. A third approach is to impose *procedural* limitations on access to common law actions that must be fulfilled before any action can be commenced.

In Australia, there are rare examples of the use of procedural limitations, but they have not had any significant impact in practice. The most notable example was the former section 166A of the *Industrial Relations Act 1988* (Cth), inserted into the Act in 1993 by the *Industrial Relations Reform Act* (Cth), at the same time as the introduction of the immunity discussed below for protected industrial action. Section 166A restricted the capacity of employers to bring 'an action in tort … in relation to conduct … in contemplation or furtherance of claims that are the subject of an industrial dispute', where the employer had not first attempted to conciliate the dispute and such conciliation had failed to resolve the dispute within 72 hours. However, in practice the clause ultimately had no work to do because it was interpreted to apply only to an action in tort, not to an application for an interlocutory injunction in equity to issue against possible tortious conduct.[74] The section was repealed in 2005 as part of the 'Work Choices' reforms.[75] There have also been examples of this approach at State level, in both New South Wales[76] and South Australia.[77]

[73] See, eg, G Anderson, 'Strikes and the Law: The Problems of Legal Intervention in Labour Disputes' (1988) 13 *New Zealand Journal of International Relations* 21, 21; Elias and Ewing (n 11) 356; K Ewing, J Hendy and C Jones (eds), *A Manifesto for Labour Law: Towards a Comprehensive Revision of Workers' Rights* (Liverpool, Institute of Employment Rights, 2016) 52; S McCrystal, 'The Right to Strike and the "Deadweight" of the Common Law' (2019) 50 *Victoria University of Wellington Law Review* 281, 300–301.

[74] See, eg, *Patrick Stevedores No 1 v Maritime Union of Australia* (1998) 79 IR 268 (VSC).

[75] *Workplace Relations Amendment (Work Choices) Act 2005* (Cth) Sch 1, cl 71.

[76] See *Industrial Relations Act 1996* (NSW) ss 141–142, prohibiting actions in tort, and injunctive relief, while an industrial dispute is the subject of conciliation and arbitration by the New South Wales Industrial Relations Commission.

[77] See *Industrial Conciliation and Arbitration Act 1972* (SA) s 143a. Enacted in 1984, this provided that no action could be brought in tort for an act or omission done in contemplation or furtherance of an industrial dispute, unless and until the underlying dispute was resolved by conciliation or arbitration, or the Industrial Commission was satisfied that all means for doing so had been exhausted: see A Stewart, 'Civil Liability for Industrial Action: Updating the Economic Torts' (1984) 9 *Adelaide Law Review* 358, 380–82. An equivalent provision currently exists in the *Fair Work Act 1994* (SA) s 138, but access to the common law is now conditional on conciliation and arbitration having been exhausted, *and* the South Australian Employment Tribunal being satisfied that the dispute was prolonged by unreasonable conduct by the person to be sued. This provision operates in a manner more in keeping with an immunity approach.

In both the UK and Australia, however, it is the immunity approach that legislatures have generally chosen to adopt. Accordingly, the extent of strike action that is permitted by workers is dependent upon the scope of the immunity provided, and any legislative prerequisites for that immunity.

In the UK, section 219 of the *Trade Union and Labour Relations (Consolidation) Act 1992* (TULCRA) sets out the relevant immunity from the economic torts.[78] The substance of the provision reflects the historical development of the economic torts and the efforts by the UK Parliament to counter those developments in the context of industrial disputes. Subsection (1) provides that:

> An act done by a person in contemplation or furtherance of a trade dispute is not actionable in tort on the ground only:
>
> (a) that it induces another person to break a contract or interferes or induces another person to interfere with its performance, or
>
> (b) that it consists in his [sic] threatening that a contract (whether one to which it is a party or not) will be broken or its performance interfered with, or that he will induce another person to break a contract or interfere with its performance.

Subsection (2) further provides that

> [a]n agreement or combination by two or more persons to do or procure the doing of an act in contemplation of a trade dispute is not actionable in tort if the act is one which if done without any such agreement or combination would not be actionable in tort.

'Trade dispute' is defined in section 244(1) as a 'dispute between workers and their employer', and the dispute must relate wholly or mainly to a matter in connection with that work relationship as specified in the section.[79] The term 'worker' is defined for this purpose to include not just employees in the common law sense, but those engaged under 'any other contract whereby he [sic] undertakes to do or perform personally any work or services for another party to the contract who is not a professional client of his'.[80]

The immunity provision is phrased in such a manner that it targets specific torts pursued in the context of a trade dispute, rather than providing a blanket immunity. Specifically, those torts are the tort of inducing breach of contract, the tort of intimidation (where it is based on a threat to breach a contract), and the conspiracy torts. Deakin and Morris observe that the protection also encompasses interference with a contract of employment in the context of the tort of unlawful interference recognised in *OBG*.[81] But the method of listing the torts 'means that

[78] Note that besides this immunity, qualified protections are also accorded by ss 236–239 to individual employees, including against dismissal for taking part in industrial action.

[79] Section 244(1) goes on to list the specific matters which may properly be the subject of a trade dispute. As to the interpretation of this key provision, see Deakin and Morris (n 24) 1061–69.

[80] TULCRA s 296(1)(b). As to the scope of that extension, see B Jones and J Prassl, 'The Concept of "Employee": The Position in the UK' in B Waas and G Heerma van Voss (eds), *Restatement of Labour Law in Europe – Volume 1: The Concept of Employee* (Portland, Hart Publishing, 2017) 753–54, 768–69.

[81] *OBG* (n 27).

those organising industrial action have always been vulnerable to new nominate torts being created'.[82]

As Bogg observes, however, some British judges at least have acknowledged that the UK Parliament has assumed the role of determining the boundaries of lawful and unlawful industrial action, removing the 'need for expansively developed economic torts' and 'providing judges with new techniques of control through the tools of statutory interpretation'.[83]

The necessity for such interpretation arises from the complex prerequisites which exist in order to obtain the protection of the immunity from tort. A number of these relate to the purpose of the action – it must be in connection with a trade dispute, and cannot be:

- in respect of the union membership of persons employed by an employer (TULCRA s 222);
- the dismissal of a worker in connection with strike action that is not immune (section 223);
- where there has been secondary action involving threats of tortious action against an employer that is not the employer of the employees involved in the trade dispute (section 224); or
- an attempt to induce an employer to enter into a contract in respect of recognition of a trade union for the purposes of negotiating an agreement (section 225).

More significantly, there are also procedural prerequisites for protection, most importantly including the requirements that the action be authorised in a ballot conducted in accordance with the Act (sections 226–234),[84] and that sufficient notice of the action has been given (section 234A). These provisions are notoriously complex,[85] and have been the source of extensive litigation, allowing the British courts to restrict the application of the immunity against the economic torts through strict interpretation.[86]

[82] Deakin and Morris (n 24) 1061.

[83] A Bogg, 'Common Law and Statute in the Law of Employment' (2016) 69 *Current Legal Problems* 67, 93, citing the observations of Lord Hoffmann quoted earlier (nn 28–30).

[84] See further T Novitz, 'UK Regulation of Strike Ballots and Notices – Moving Beyond "Democracy"' (2016) 29 *Australian Journal of Labour Law* 226; M Ford and T Novitz, 'Legislating for Control: The Trade Union Act 2016' (2016) 45 *Industrial Law Journal* 277; R Dukes and N Kountouris, 'Pre-strike Ballots, Picketing and Protest: Banning Industrial Action by the Back Door?' (2016) 45 *Industrial Law Journal* 337.

[85] See Novitz, *ibid.*

[86] See, eg, B Simpson, 'Strike Ballots and the Law: Round Six' (2005) 34 *Industrial Law Journal* 331; B Simpson, 'The Labour Injunction and Industrial Action Ballots' (2013) 42 *Industrial Law Journal* 270; G Gall, 'Injunctions as a Legal Weapon in Collective Industrial Disputes in Britain 2005–2014' (2016) 54 *British Journal of Industrial Relations* 1. For recent cases considering the application of the current immunities and their prerequisites, see, eg, *Argos Ltd v Unite the Union* [2017] EWHC 1959 (QB); *Birmingham City Council v Unite the Union* [2019] EWHC 478 (QB); *British Airways* (n 32).

In Australia, Part 3-3 of the country's main labour statute, the *Fair Work Act 2009* (Cth) (FW Act),[87] provides immunity for 'protected industrial action' undertaken in compliance with certain legislative pre-conditions.[88] As far as tort liability is concerned, the principal immunity is expressed in section 415(1).[89] This provides that:

> No action lies under any law (whether written or unwritten) in force in a State or Territory in relation to any industrial action that is protected industrial action unless the industrial action has involved or is likely to involve:
>
> (a) personal injury; or
> (b) wilful or reckless destruction of, or damage to, property; or
> (c) the unlawful taking, keeping or use of property.[90]

By contrast to its UK equivalent, this provision does not quantify or counter the elements of the economic torts.[91] Instead, the immunity is from any action at all (with limited exceptions), leaving no room for judicial creativity to develop causes of action that work around the protection. But everything still turns on meeting the requirements for protected action. For workers and unions who take unprotected action, it is not just the economic torts that are likely to apply. The FW Act has no general prohibition on the taking of unprotected action.[92] But there is a specific bar on industrial action taken during the unexpired term of an enterprise agreement (section 417), while many forms of unprotected action are likely to breach the prohibitions in sections 343 and 348 on the 'coercion' of employers. The Fair Work Commission (FWC) has a general power under section 418 to order that unprotected industrial action that is threatened, impending, happening or being organised cease or not occur. A breach of such an order is unlawful, and enforceable in the Federal Court (section 421). In addition, there are separate

[87] As to the application of the FW Act, which covers some government agencies and the great majority of non-government employers, see Stewart et al (n 1) Ch 6.

[88] The term 'industrial action' is defined expansively in s 19(1) to include both a strike, and action short of a strike, including work bans, work to rule and go slows: see B Creighton, C Denvir and S McCrystal, 'Defining Industrial Action' (2017) 45 *Federal Law Review* 383.

[89] As in the UK, individual participants are also shielded against retaliatory action by employers, under what are called the 'general protections' in Part 3-1 of the FW Act. Among other things, s 340 prohibits the dismissal of, or other forms of 'adverse action' against, employees who have exercised or threatened to exercise their workplace rights in respect of protected industrial action, or the processes involved in taking such action. As to the efficacy of these protections in practice, given narrow judicial interpretations of key concepts and provisions, see J Riley, 'General Protections: Industrial Activities and Collective Bargaining' in S McCrystal, B Creighton and A Forsyth (eds), *Collective Bargaining under the Fair Work Act* (Annandale, Federation Press, 2018).

[90] Section 415(2) creates a further exception to the immunity, so that actions for defamation may still be brought in relation to anything that occurred in the course of the industrial action.

[91] It should be noted that in Queensland, from 1915–1976, State legislation barred tortious claims in a similar manner to the UK, providing immunity against the torts of conspiracy and inducing breach of contract: see *Trade Union Act 1915* (Qld) s 28; *Industrial Conciliation and Arbitration Act 1961* (Qld) ss 70–72. By contrast, s 237 of the *Industrial Relations Act 2016* (Qld) now provides an immunity for protected industrial action in substantively the same terms as section 415 of the FW Act.

[92] *cf Building and Construction Industry (Improving Productivity) Act 2016* (Cth) s 46, which *does* impose such a prohibition in the building and construction industry.

prohibitions on certain kinds of boycott activity in sections 45D and 45DB of the *Competition and Consumer Act 2010* (Cth).

In common with the UK provisions, the prerequisites to taking protected industrial action under the FW Act are focused on the reasons for the industrial action itself, along with procedural requirements that must be fulfilled.

Protected industrial action may only be organised or taken by a bargaining representative and the employees they represent during negotiations for a single-enterprise agreement. Among other requirements, the industrial action must be in support of claims that the bargaining representative reasonably believes may be included within that enterprise agreement (section 409(1)), and the bargaining representative must have been genuinely trying to reach agreement at the enterprise concerned (section 413(3)).

The procedural requirements that must be fulfilled for industrial action to be protected include that:

- any existing enterprise agreement binding on the workers concerned has passed its nominal expiry date (section 413(6));
- the bargaining representative of the employees must not have contravened any orders of a court or the FWC during bargaining for the agreement (section 413(5));[93]
- the industrial action has been authorised by the relevant employees in a protected industrial action ballot ordered by the FWC (section 409(2); Pt 3-3, Div 8);[94]
- appropriate notice of the proposed industrial action has been given to the employer (sections 413(4), 414); and
- the right to take protected industrial action by any of the bargaining parties involved in the negotiations has not been suspended or terminated by the FWC or the Minister on a range of grounds, which include the extent of any economic damage caused by previous action or threatened by proposed action (sections 413(7), 423–426, 431).

In combination, these provisions operate to confine the scope of the legislative immunity against the economic torts, and the protections provided to employees, to a narrow window of time where parties are bargaining for a new enterprise agreement and there is no unexpired existing agreement. They also substantively confine the claims that can be supported by strike action (to only those claims

[93] In *Esso* (n 71), the High Court interpreted this to mean that any breach during bargaining for a proposed agreement removes the right of that bargaining representative (and therefore the workers they represent) to take protected action for the remainder of that bargaining round, irrespective of whether the breach was inadvertent or mistaken, or if it had been remedied. See further S McCrystal (n 73) 295–97; and see also below, text at nn 133–39.

[94] See B Creighton et al, *Strike Ballots, Democracy, and Law* (Oxford, Oxford University Press, 2020) Ch 4. However, this requirement does not apply if the employees take industrial action in response to a lockout initiated by their employer (s 410).

capable of inclusion within an agreement), and significant procedural obstacles are lined up before any action can claim protected status.[95]

IV. Use of the Economic Torts by Employers

The use of the economic torts by employers to suppress or penalise the taking or organisation of industrial action by their own or other workers has waxed and waned over the years. In the UK, where actions in tort have remained one of (if not *the*) most readily available form of legal redress for unlawful work bans or stoppages, their use has risen and fallen with the scope and effectiveness of the statutory immunities first introduced in 1906. The number of exceptions and qualifications that now apply, and the complexity of the current statutory provisions, mean that there can still be a basis for British employers to go to court in the hope of challenging strikes and other action.[96]

In Australia, by contrast, the statutory conciliation and arbitration systems that operated for much of the twentieth century tended to 'soak up' industrial disputation, at the expense of any common law litigation. Although the relevant statutes or the awards that operated under them typically prohibited industrial action, the law was rarely enforced against unions or their members. Employers were far more likely to look to the industrial tribunals to help broker settlements when work stoppages occurred – as they frequently did, at some of the highest rates in the world.[97] In the early years of the century, following the development of the economic torts in the UK, there were some notable instances of proceedings against trade unions or their officials.[98] But after 1918, what few cases there were tended to be brought not by employers, but by individual workers 'black banned' by what was often their former union.[99]

There was a brief revival in the use of the torts in the early 1970s,[100] followed by a further lull after the introduction in 1977 of section 45D of the *Trade Practices*

[95] The complex interplay of these statutory provisions in narrowing the opportunities for employees and their unions to take protected industrial action is explored in S McCrystal, 'Why is it So Hard to Take Lawful Strike Action in Australia?' (2019) 61 *Journal of Industrial Relations* 129.

[96] For recent examples, and besides those cited earlier, see *Thames Cleaning and Support Services Limited v United Voices of the World* [2016] EWHC 1310 (QB); *Govia Thameslink Railway Limited v The Associated Society of Locomotive Engineers and Firemen* [2016] EWHC 985 (QB); *Ministry of Justice v Prison Officers' Association* [2017] EWHC 699 (QB). As to the prevalence of claims for injunctions, a remedy whose significance is discussed further below, see Gall (n 86).

[97] See B Creighton, 'Enforcement in the Federal Industrial Relations System: An Australian Paradox' (1991) 4 *Australian Journal of Labour Law* 197.

[98] See, eg, *Martell v Victorian Coal Miners Association* (1903) 9 ALR 231 (VSC); *Brisbane Shipwrights Provident Union v Heggie* (1906) 3 CLR 686 (HCA); *Southan v Grounds* (1916) 16 SR (NSW) 274 (NSWSC).

[99] See, eg, *McKernan* (n 21); *Williams* (n 42).

[100] See, eg, *Harry M Miller Attractions Pty Ltd v Actors and Announcers Equity Association of Australia* [1970] 1 NSWR 614 (NSWSC); *Sid Ross Agency Pty Ltd v Actors and Announcers Equity Association of Australia (No 2)* [1971] 1 NSWLR 760 (NSWSC).

Act 1974 (Cth), which in prohibiting secondary boycotts covered much of the same ground as the torts, but which offered a number of procedural advantages as compared with the common law. There was then a further revival in the mid-1980s, in part because of a rise in employer militancy (and antagonism to both unions and industrial arbitration) associated with what at the time was being called the 'New Right'.[101] But the number of cases involved was very small. According to research conducted for the Commonwealth Department of Industrial Relations, over the period 1971–1992, only 54 actions brought by employers against trade unions, or their officials or members, resulted in any kind of court decision.[102]

Since the introduction by the *Industrial Relations Reform Act 1993* (Cth) of the current system of enterprise-based collective bargaining, and its associated concept of protected industrial action, the incidence of industrial action in Australia has declined dramatically. At the same time, when work bans or stoppages do occur, employers are now far more likely to seek some kind of legal redress.[103] But only rarely will they turn today to the common law. Over the period 2000–2019, we could find only 28 examples of court proceedings concerning industrial action that involved a claim in one of the economic torts. And of those, only 10 did not involve some parallel claim under legislation – typically the FW Act, the *Competition and Consumer Act 2010* (Cth) or the *Building and Construction Industry (Improving Productivity) Act 2016* (Cth), or predecessor statutes.[104] This contrasts with the 47 applications made to the FWC seeking orders stopping or preventing industrial action in 2018–2019 alone.[105]

In theory, and subject to the statutory immunities described earlier, the economic torts can be used to seek damages from unions, their officials and indeed workers themselves for any loss caused by industrial action, most obviously in the form of lost business or income. Until fairly recently, the only plaintiffs who pursued claims to the point of obtaining damages awards tended to be blacklisted workers of the type mentioned earlier.[106] Employers have always been less likely to pursue an award of damages for any loss inflicted as a result of unlawful industrial action. Once a dispute has been resolved and employees are back at work, most

[101] See L Bennett, *Making Labour Law in Australia: Industrial Relations, Politics and Law* (Sydney, Law Book Co, 1984) 183–91; B Creighton, 'Trade Unions, the Law and the New Right' in K Coghill (ed), *The New Right's Australian Fantasy* (Fitzroy, McPhee Gribble/Penguin, 1987). One case in particular became something of a *cause celebre* for those on the right, that of *Dollar Sweets Pty Ltd v Federated Confectioners Association of Australia* [1986] VR 383 (VSC). The barrister for the company involved, Peter Costello, would later become Australia's longest-serving Treasurer, in the conservative government of John Howard.

[102] B Creighton, W Ford and R Mitchell, *Labour Law: Text and Materials*, 2nd edn (Sydney, Law Book Co, 1993) 1166–71.

[103] Stewart et al (n 1) [26.10].

[104] For two recent examples of claims brought under the common law, both involving picketing, see *Yakult Australia Pty Ltd v National Union of Workers* [2018] VSC 151; *Laverton Cold Storage Pty Ltd v National Union of Workers* [2018] VSC 503.

[105] FWC, *Access to Justice: Annual Report 2018–19* (Melbourne, FWC, 2019) 79.

[106] See, eg, *McKernan* (n 21); *Williams* (n 42); *Latham* (n 45).

employers reason that it will be counter-productive, even provocative, to pursue litigation.[107] However, government agencies such as the Australian Building and Construction Commission (ABCC), whose statutory mandate includes 'promoting respect for the rule of law' and 'ensuring that building industry participants are accountable for their unlawful conduct',[108] have no such compunction when it comes to seeking pecuniary remedies. In 2018–2019 alone, the ABCC secured over $4.25 million in fines against building unions and their officials and members for breaches of industrial legislation, many of them involving unlawful industrial action.[109] Even the Fair Work Ombudsman, whose main enforcement role is undoubtedly to hold employers to account for underpaying or otherwise exploiting workers, has been willing at times to pursue unions for taking unlawful industrial action in other industries.[110] Interestingly, this seems to have encouraged at least some major employers to seek such remedies themselves.[111]

Nevertheless, the main type of remedy likely to be pursued by employers, as opposed to government regulators, continues to be orders preventing industrial action being commenced or continued. This is apparent from the popularity of the 'stop order' proceeding in the FWC under section 418 of the FW Act. Under the equitable principles that govern the award of injunctive relief, whether under the common law or statute, it is especially easy to secure an interlocutory or interim injunction to restrain the unlawful conduct pending a full trial of the action. All the plaintiff need show is that there is a 'serious question to be tried' as to the plaintiff's entitlement to relief, that the plaintiff is 'likely to suffer injury for which damages will not be an adequate remedy', and that 'the balance of convenience favours the granting of an injunction'.[112] If the employer obtains the relief they seek, that is usually the end of the matter. The defendants must comply with the order, or face the fines, imprisonment and sequestration of assets that may follow from being found to be in contempt of court. The industrial campaign that gave rise to the application for injunctive relief will almost inevitably lose its momentum. It is irrelevant in practical terms that the proposed industrial action might proceed if the plaintiff were subsequently to fail at trial.

In the UK, the courts have recognised the reality that 'an interim injunction usually determines in practical terms whether a strike can go ahead or not'.[113]

[107] For a rare exception, see *Ansett* (n 37); *Ansett Transport Industries (Operations) Pty Ltd v Australian Federation of Air Pilots (No 2)* [1991] 2 VR 636 (VSC). But even here, an award of $6.48 million damages against the Australian Federation of Air Pilots was never enforced.

[108] *Building and Construction Industry (Improving Productivity) Act 2016* (Cth) s 3(2)(b),(d).

[109] ABCC, *Annual Report 2018–19* (Canberra, ABCC, 2019) 28.

[110] See, eg, *Fair Work Ombudsman v Maritime Union of Australia* [2012] FCA 1232. See generally T Hardy, 'The State Strikes Back: Supervision and Sanctioning of Unlawful Industrial Activity by Federal Government Agencies in Australia' in McCrystal, Creighton and Forsyth (eds) (n 89).

[111] See, eg, *Woodside Burrup Pty Ltd v Construction, Forestry, Mining & Energy Union* [2011] FCA 949, (2011) 220 FCR 551; *Transport Workers Union v Qantas Airways Ltd* [2012] FCAFC 10, (2012) 199 FCR 190.

[112] *Australian Broadcasting Corp v O'Neill* [2006] HCA 46, (2006) 227 CLR 57 [19].

[113] *British Airways* (n 32) [9].

That being the case, the usual test for the availability of interlocutory relief is not applied. The court must not grant an injunction unless it has assessed the strength of any defence the union concerned might be able to plead.[114] In Australia, an injunction may certainly be refused if there is a strong case for treating the relevant action as protected.[115] But there is no special rule for industrial action.[116] In practice, it is more common for interlocutory relief to be granted, in those cases where employers do choose to go to court rather than the FWC.[117]

One striking point about the availability of injunctive relief, when sought against individual workers taking or proposing to take industrial action, is that it may be tantamount in practice to an order for specific performance of their employment contracts. It is well recognised that, as a general rule, the courts will not compel employees to perform their contractual obligations.[118] But that does not seem to concern Australian judges when ordering a *group* of employees back to work.[119] Here again we find a contrast with the modern position in the UK. Section 236 of TULCRA provides that employees cannot be compelled by a court 'to do any work or attend any place for the doing of any work' through any order of specific performance of a contract of employment, or any injunction restraining a threatened or actual breach of a contract of employment.

V. The Right to Strike as a Normative Justification for Excluding or Limiting the Economic Torts

The right of workers to take industrial action is one component of the principle of freedom of association. In Australian law, protection of that principle arises both at common law and in statute. However, acting in association, including by an organised withdrawal of labour, is not presently a part of the common law construction of association rights, such as they are.[120] The principle of freedom

[114] *Ibid.*

[115] See, eg, *Alcoa of Australia Ltd v Australian Workers Union* [2010] FCA 278, (2010) 196 IR 103.

[116] *cf Australian Paper Ltd v Communications, Electrical, Electronic, Energy, Information, Postal, Plumbing and Allied Services Union of Australia* (1998) 81 IR 15 (FCA) 24–27, where North J outlined a number of recurring features of industrial disputes which make it appropriate to exercise 'particular caution' in granting interlocutory relief. But see *Transfield Construction Pty Ltd v AMWU* [2002] FCA 1413 [28]–[35]; *Amcor Packaging (Australia) Pty Ltd v AMWU* [2006] FCA 1265, (2006) 157 IR 32 [5]–[10].

[117] See, eg, *Ralan St Leonards Pty Ltd v Construction, Forestry, Mining & Energy Union* [2014] FCA 431; *Yakult* (n 104); *Laverton Cold Storage* (n 104).

[118] *De Francesco v Barnum* (1890) 45 Ch D 430 (Ch) 438; *Tradition Australia Pty Ltd v Gunson* [2006] NSWSC 298, (2006) 152 IR 395 [27]–[30].

[119] See, eg, *Skilled Engineering Ltd v Automotive, Food, Metals, Engineering, Printing and Kindred Industries Union* [2001] FCA 1397, (2001) 108 IR 116.

[120] See Australian Law Reform Commission (ALRC), *Traditional Rights and Freedoms – Encroachments by Commonwealth Laws*, Final Report (ALRC Report 129, 2015) Ch 6.

of association for workers is more obviously protected by the general protections in Part 3-1 of the FW Act. Among other provisions, section 346 prohibits employers from taking adverse action against employees for belonging or proposing to join a trade union, or engaging in various 'industrial activities'. But in respect of the capacity of workers to take collective action, the scope of protection of the principles of freedom of association is delineated by the tightly circumscribed concept of 'protected industrial action' in Part 3-3, as explained earlier.

Australia is bound in international law to protect the right to take industrial action. For one thing, it is a signatory to the International Covenant on Economic Social and Cultural Rights,[121] Article 8(1)(d) of which protects 'the right to strike, provided that it is exercised in conformity with the laws of the particular country'. The substance of this right has not been explored in any general comments by the United Nations (UN) Committee on Economic, Cultural and Social Rights. However, it is generally accepted that the nature and scope of the right is to be identified by reference to the International Labour Organization (ILO) Convention No 87 on Freedom of Association and Protection of the Right to Organise 1948 (ILO Convention 87).[122]

Australia is a Member of the ILO, and has ratified ILO Convention 87. Article 2 of the Convention protects the right of 'workers and employers to establish, and subject only to the rules of the organisation concerned, join organisations of their own choosing'. Article 3 provides that:

> (1) Workers' and employers' organisations shall have the right to draw up their constitutions and rules, to elect their representatives in full freedom, to organise their administration and activities and to formulate their programmes.
> (2) The public authorities shall refrain from any interference which would restrict this right or impede the lawful exercise thereof.

While Articles 2 and 3 do not expressly mention the right to strike, the ILO Committee of Experts on the Application of Conventions and Recommendations (CEACR) has consistently found that the principles extend to protection of the right of workers to strike in the protection of their economic and social interests.[123]

[121] International Covenant on Economic, Social and Cultural Rights (IESCR), opened for signature 16 December 1966, 993 UNTS 3 (entered into force 3 January 1976).

[122] Article 8(3) of the ICESCR provides that 'nothing in this article shall authorise State Parties to [ILO Convention 87] to take legislative measures which would prejudice, or apply the law, in such a manner as would prejudice, the guarantees provided for in that Convention'. See further C Fenwick, 'Minimum Obligations with Respect to Art 8 of the International Covenant on Economic, Social and Cultural Rights' in A Chapman and S Russel (eds), *Core Obligations: Building a Framework for Economic, Social and Cultural Rights* (New York, Intersentia, 2002).

[123] See *Giving Globalisation a Human Face: General Survey on the Fundamental Conventions Concerning Rights at Work in Light of the ILO Declaration on Social Justice for a Fair Globalisation 2008*, International Labour Conference, 101st sess, Report III (Part 1B), UN Doc ILC.101/III/1B (2012) [117]–[122]; a summary of the substance of the right is set out at [123]–[161]. This interpretation

The Governing Body's Committee on Freedom of Association also acknowledges protection of the right to strike as a component of the commitment within the ILO Constitution to promote and respect the principles of freedom of association.[124]

The substance of the right to strike, as protected by ILO Convention 87, has been set out elsewhere.[125] Australia's FW Act has repeatedly been criticised for failing to provide for a right to take industrial action that complies with those principles.[126] For our purposes, the central point is that Australia is committed within international law to respect the right of workers to take strike action and the legislative framework within the FW Act is the mechanism through which this obligation is to be given effect.

As noted above, to give effect to the right to strike, an exclusion or limitation of the operation of the economic torts under the common law is necessary, and this is achieved through the immunity for protected industrial action provided within section 415 of the FW Act. However, section 415 does not operate in isolation – it must be read subject to the provisions that define the scope of protected industrial action. How these provisions are approached by the courts, when called upon to interpret their scope, also defines the scope of the statutory immunity, and by consequence, the extent to which the FW Act gives effect to international principles concerning the right to strike.

The exclusion of the right of employers or others impacted by industrial action to bring an action in tort in respect of the economic harm inflicted by industrial action is a limitation on a common law right that would otherwise exist. As such, interpretation of the FW Act, and the extent to which it abrogates an existing common law right, is subject to the 'principle of legality'.

of ILO Convention 87 has been the subject of sustained criticism by employer groups at the ILO, particularly in conferences in the lead up to the publication of the 2012 General Survey. However, the CEACR strongly affirmed the interpretation of the Convention to protect the right to strike within the Survey. See further C La Hovary, 'Showdown at the ILO? A Historical Perspective on the Employers' Group's Challenge to the Right to Strike' (2013) 42 *Industrial Law Journal* 338; J Bellace, 'The ILO and the Right to Strike' (2014) 153 *International Labour Review* 29; J Bellace, 'ILO Convention No. 87 and the Right to Strike in an Era of Global Trade' (2018) 39 *Comparative Labor Law and Policy Journal* 495.

[124] ILO, *Freedom of Association: Compilation of Decisions of the Committee on Freedom of Association*, 6th edn (Geneva, International Labour Office, 2018) [751]–[757]; a summary of the substance of the right is set out in Chapter 10 of that report.

[125] See S McCrystal, *The Right to Strike in Australia* (Annandale, Federation Press, 2010) Ch 2; T Novitz, *International and European Protection of the Right to Strike* (Oxford, Oxford University Press, 2003) Pt IV; B Gernigon, A Odero and H Guido, *ILO Principles Concerning the Right to Strike* (Geneva, International Labour Office, 2000).

[126] See S McCrystal, 'The Fair Work Act 2009 (Cth) and the Right to Strike' (2009) 23 *Australian Journal of Labour Law* 3; B Creighton, 'International Labour Standards and Collective Bargaining under the *Fair Work Act 2009*' in B Creighton and A Forsyth (eds), *Rediscovering Collective Bargaining: Australia's Fair Work Act in International Perspective* (New York, Routledge, 2012). Submissions by the Australian Institute of Employment Rights, the ACTU and the United Services Union to the ALRC Inquiry into Traditional Rights and Freedoms also made this point, with the ALRC itself noting that some of the provisions of the FW Act including those in respect of strike action 'may offend ILO norms': ALRC (n 120) 182–83.

The principle of legality is a rule of statutory interpretation. It has the effect that 'unless the Parliament makes unmistakeably clear its intention to abrogate or suspend a fundamental freedom, the courts will not construe a statute as having that operation'.[127] This means that when interpreting a statute, the courts will presume that Parliament would not 'depart from the general system of law, without expressing its intention with irresistible clearness'.[128] Because section 415 of the FW Act departs from the general system of law by abrogating or limiting the rights that employers or other third parties might have at common law, the principle suggests that any ambiguity within the legislation should be interpreted in a way which least impacts the general system of law. Such an approach is considered by the courts to 'enhance the Parliamentary process by securing a great measure of attention to the impact of legislative proposals on fundamental rights'.[129] However, the principle also has the tendency to suggest that the common law position is more 'natural' or 'fundamental' than that preferred by Parliament. Meagher has pointed out that the rule 'operates to insulate (and so protect in full) the judicial conception of the common law right',[130] leaving other rights and interests that arise only in statutes, such as the right to strike, not balanced or weighed.[131] Given that the common law has not (or at least not yet) developed any fundamental right to strike, the rights to sue in tort for economic loss caused by industrial action weigh more on the judicial scales in matters of interpretation.

In enacting section 415 of the FW Act, Parliament has expressed itself with 'irresistible clarity'. The expression 'no action lies under any law (whether written or unwritten) in force in a State or Territory' clearly and unambiguously abrogates the general system of law that would otherwise apply where workers and their organisations take protected industrial action. However, where the principle of legality has had a role to play in the interpretation of the FW Acts protected action provisions is in the interpretation of the prerequisites to industrial action – which are many, and not always clearly expressed.

The propensity of the courts to interpret the protected action provisions strictly, to reduce or confine the scope of the statutory immunity, has been

[127] *Re Bolton; Ex parte Bean* (1987) 162 CLR 514 (HCA) 523, cited with approval in *Coco v The Queen* [1994] HCA 15, (1994) 179 CLR 427, 437. The principle is also recognised by the British courts: see, eg, *R v Secretary of State for the Home Department; Ex parte Simms* [1999] UKHL 33, [2000] 2 AC 115, 131.

[128] *Potter v Minahan* (1908) 7 CLR 277 (HCA) 304. As to whether the principle of legality is properly to be understood as reflecting parliamentary intention, see R French, 'The Principle of Legality and Legislative Intention' (2019) 40 *Statute Law Review* 40; *cf* P Sales, 'Legislative Intention, Interpretation, and The Principle of Legality' (2019) 40 *Statute Law Review* 53. For further discussion, see B Lim, 'The Normativity of the Principle of Legality' (2013) 37 *Melbourne University Law Review* 372; ALRC (n 120) 36–38.

[129] *Coco* (n 127) 437.

[130] D Meagher, 'The Common Law Principle of Legality in the Age of Rights' (2011) 35 *Melbourne University Law Review* 449, 463.

[131] *Ibid* 462.

demonstrated elsewhere.[132] The approach was most recently manifested in the High Court decision in *Esso*.[133] The decision illustrates how the judicial scales weigh the role of the economic torts more heavily than the statutorily enacted right to strike. It also contrasts starkly with the approach now taken in the UK.[134]

The case revolved around the interpretation of section 413(5) of the FW Act, which is a prerequisite to protected industrial action and provides that the relevant person 'must not have contravened any orders that apply to them and that relate to …. the agreement or a matter that arose during bargaining for the agreement'. There were two competing interpretations of this provision. First, it could be argued that access to protected industrial action was only restricted while a bargaining representative was in breach of any order made by a court or the FWC, and once the breach was corrected or the order was spent, protected industrial action could resume. This was the preferred interpretation of the Federal Court of Australia at first instance,[135] and on appeal by the Full Federal Court.[136] The competing interpretation would restrict access to protected industrial action for the bargaining representative and the employees that they represented for the remainder of the negotiations for the proposed enterprise agreement – effectively removing the right to strike altogether for the relevant set of negotiations.[137]

In the High Court it was acknowledged that the subsection could reasonably be interpreted either way, and was poorly drafted. The High Court, by majority, interpreted it so as to remove access to protected industrial action for any bargaining representative who had breached an order of a court or the commission during bargaining for the agreement, for the remainder of the negotiations. Chief Justice Kiefel and Justices Keane, Nettle and Edelman justified this choice of interpretation by reference to the immunity in section 415 as a 'privilege', whereby the apparent purpose of section 413(5) was 'to ensure that persons who have shown they cannot be trusted to comply with orders …. are not to be trusted with the immunity afforded in relation to protected industrial action'.[138]

By contrast Gageler J, faced with the same choice, refused to invoke any common law presumptions and construed the provision within the context of

[132] See B Creighton and S McCrystal, '*Esso Australia Pty Ltd v The Australian Workers Union*: Recidivism, Coercion and Protected Industrial Action under the *Fair Work Act 2009* (Cth)' (2017) 39 *Sydney Law Review* 233; McCrystal (n 73).

[133] *Esso* (n 71).

[134] See n 32.

[135] *Esso Australia Pty Ltd v Australian Workers' Union* [2015] FCA 758, (2015) 253 IR 304.

[136] *Esso Australia Pty Ltd v Australian Workers' Union* [2016] FCAFC 72, (2016) 245 FCR 39.

[137] Interestingly, in a subsequent case arising out of this dispute, Gostencnik VP suggested that one remedy open to the employees represented by a union who had breached an order of a court or commission in these circumstances would be to change bargaining representative: *Esso Australia Pty Ltd v Australian Workers Union* [2019] FWC 6143 [214].

[138] *Esso* (n 71) [53].

a regime facilitating collective bargaining supported by access to lawful strike action. On his dissenting view, protected action could resume once the breach of an order of a court or the FWC had been rectified. He noted that the preferred approach of the majority constituted a 'harsh and rigid form of industrial discipline' which would be likely to create 'industrial cripples and outlaws'.[139] Despite the existence of international obligations on Australia to respect the right to strike, the 'immunity' from otherwise applicable common law liability acted in this case as a basis on which the High Court could construe access to strike action as a privilege provided only to the industrially 'worthy'.

VI. Towards 'Coherence' in Liability for Industrial Action

Much has been written in recent years, not least by judges, about the appropriate role for the common law in an era dominated by statutory regulation.[140] The High Court of Australia has accepted, as a matter of principle, that it may be appropriate to take account of statutory provisions in adjusting or developing the common law, at least where there is a 'consistent pattern of legislative policy'.[141] Furthermore, common law principles should not be applied in such a way as to contradict or defeat the purposes of a statutory regime. This approach is evident in cases emphasising the need to take a flexible, policy-oriented approach to the effect of statutory breaches on the enforcement of rights under or connected to a contract.[142] The High Court has, in this context, emphasised the desirability of 'coherence' in the law.[143]

In a recent analysis of the relationship between common law and statute as they affect employment regulation, Alan Bogg draws on Lord Hoffmann's judgment

[139] *Ibid* [103].

[140] See, eg, J Beatson, 'The Role of Statute in the Development of Common Law Doctrine' (2001) 117 *LQR* 247; M Leeming, 'Theories and Principles Underlying the Development of the Common Law – The Statutory Elephant in the Room' (2013) 36 *UNSW Law Journal* 1002; A Mason, 'The Interaction of Statute Law and Common Law' (2016) 90 *Australian Law Journal* 324; M Gordon, 'Analogical Reasoning by Reference to Statute: What is the Judicial Function?' (2019) 42 *UNSW Law Journal* 4.

[141] *Esso Australia Resources Ltd v Commissioner of Taxation* [1999] HCA 67, (1999) 201 CLR 49 [23]–[24].

[142] See, eg, *Gnych v Polish Club Ltd* [2015] HCA 23, (2015) 255 CLR 414; A Stewart, W Swain and K Fairweather, *Contract Law: Principles and Context* (Cambridge, Cambridge University Press, 2019) Ch 21. The UK Supreme Court has also begun to adopt this approach: see *Patel v Mirza* [2016] UKSC 42, [2017] AC 467; A Burrows, 'Illegality after *Patel v Mirza*' (2017) 70 *Current Legal Problems* 55.

[143] *Equuscorp Pty Ltd v Haxton* [2012] HCA 7, (2012) 246 CLR 498 [23]. See E Bant, 'Statute and Common Law: Interaction and Influence in Light of the Principle of Coherence' (2015) 38 *UNSW Law Journal* 367; R Grantham and D Jensen, 'Coherence in the Age of Statutes' (2016) 42 *Monash University Law Review* 360; A Fell, 'The Concept of Coherence in Australian Private Law' (2018) 41 *Melbourne University Law Review* 1160.

in *Johnson v Unisys Ltd*[144] to identify three 'modes of interaction'.[145] The first, exemplified by the much criticised ruling in *Johnson* itself to restrict the right of dismissed workers to pursue common law redress in a manner inconsistent with the statutory regime for unfair dismissal,[146] involves statute being treated as pre-emptive of common law developments. The second would see legislation acting as 'analogical stimulus to common law development', while the third, and perhaps most radical, would treat the common law as 'an independent source of protection for fundamental rights'.[147]

In relation to industrial action, the most obvious (and to us desirable) form of statutory pre-emption of the common law would be the explicit kind associated with a codification of rights and liabilities, of the type suggested at the beginning of section III. The more intriguing question, however, is whether any of the methods discussed by Bogg might be used by the judiciary to redress the long-standing imbalance in the common law's respect for the interests of employers and organised labour.

Bogg's own suggestion was that it might be possible for the common law courts to develop an abstract 'common law right to strike', by reference to both state practice in legislating to protect strike action, and international laws that protect the right to strike. Such an approach might protect workers' rights in this respect in the face of ever tighter controls in the UK on the legislative protection of strike action.[148] His specific proposal was to resuscitate the idea, once floated (somewhat ironically given his other views on trade unions) by Lord Denning,[149] but then swiftly rejected,[150] that a notice of intention to take industrial action might be treated as suspending rather than breaching the employment contracts of the workers concerned. This is a well-accepted feature of many systems of labour regulation around the world,[151] and it might potentially remove the most common foundation for strikes and other work bans being treated as tortious.

However, the doctrinal and practical arguments against the concept of contractual suspension are substantial,[152] and it is hard to imagine it being taken up without specific legislative endorsement. The same would likely apply to any

[144] *Johnson v Unisys Ltd* [2003] 1 AC 518.

[145] Bogg (n 83).

[146] For an Australian perspective on that issue, see Carolyn Sutherland, 'Regulating Dismissals: The Impact of Unfair Dismissal Legislation on the Common Law Contract of Employment' in Chris Arup et al (eds), *Labour Law and Labour Market Regulation* (Annandale, Federation Press, 2006).

[147] Bogg (n 83) 71.

[148] *Ibid* 104–107. The irony of a 'progressive' labour lawyer looking to the common law for protection of the right to strike was not lost on the author, who referred to it (at 113) as a 'rather discomforting position'!

[149] *Morgan v Fry* [1968] 2 QB 710 (CA) 725.

[150] *Simmons v Hoover* [1977] ICR 61 (EAT).

[151] TJM Jacobs, 'The Law of Strikes and Lockouts' in R Blanpain (ed), *Comparative Labour Law and Industrial Relations in Industrialised Market Economies*, 11th edn (Boston, Wolters Kluwer, 2014) [57]–[62].

[152] See Creighton et al (n 102) 1320–25.

attempt to develop the defence of justification, and/or to extend the 'legitimate interests' concept from simple conspiracy to unlawful means conspiracy. It is only a few years since the High Court of Australia declined to imply a term protective of the 'mutual trust and confidence' inherent in employment relationships, despite its widespread acceptance in the UK and other common law countries, because (among other reasons) this would involve 'complex policy considerations' that were more appropriate for the legislature to address.[153]

There are perhaps more realistic possibilities at the procedural level. One option might be to ask the courts to defer to the role of specialist tribunals such as the FWC in dealing with industrial conflict, as was sometimes done in the past. For example, in *Harry M Miller Attractions*,[154] Street J refused an interlocutory injunction to restrain industrial action, on the ground that the relevant dispute was before what was then the Australian Conciliation and Arbitration Commission:

> [I]n the ordinary course of resolving an industrial dispute such as this, the parties should be left to pursue their remedies before the Commission … [I]t is a well-settled approach in this Court that injunctive relief will not ordinarily be granted where it can be seen that there is another tribunal particularly suited to deal with the matter in issue and having the requisite power and authority to resolve the issues between the parties.[155]

It is perhaps harder now to expect the courts to adopt this approach, however, given the abolition of the need to gain a certificate from the tribunal before instituting tort proceedings,[156] and indeed the explicit role given to the courts under the FW Act, including in enforcing stop orders made under section 418.[157] A more likely source of judicial restraint might to be to invite the courts to reverse what is in practice an effective presumption in favour of interlocutory relief and, as their UK equivalents have done, to raise the bar for obtaining orders that have the practical effect of suppressing the effective use of collective action.

At the very least too, Australian judges could choose to set less store by the principle of legality and lean in favour of both a narrower operation for the economic torts and more broadly interpreted statutory immunities, so as to recognise and protect what should be seen as a right to take industrial action.

Of course, the very fact that a legislature has framed immunity provisions that cover some but not all instances of presumptively tortious industrial action

[153] *Commonwealth Bank of Australia v Barker* [2014] HCA 32, (2014) 253 CLR 169 [40]. For discussion of this aspect of the decision, see G Golding, 'The Role of Judges in the Regulation of Australian Employment Contracts' (2016) 32 *International Journal of Comparative Labour Law and Industrial Relations* 69.

[154] *Harry M Miller Attractions* (n 100).

[155] *Ibid* 615. For further examples, see *David Jones* (n 46); *Wodonga Meats Pty Ltd v Australasian Meat Industry Employees Union* (1991) 34 AILR 103 (VSC). But *cf National Workforce Pty Ltd v Australian Manufacturing Workers' Union (No 2)* (1997) 76 IR 200 (VSCA) 213–15, rejecting this approach.

[156] See text at nn 74–75.

[157] See text at n 92.

makes it unlikely that the courts would voluntarily limit common law liability in situations falling outside the immunities. This is especially true where, as in Australia, the immunities are specifically and narrowly framed. But to the extent that the immunities rely for their operation on open-textured rules, conditions or provisos that can be given a broad or narrow scope – such as 'in contemplation or furtherance of', or the need for attempts to 'genuinely try to reach agreement' – there is no reason why courts cannot exercise their discretion to favour rather than hinder any interpretation that would comply with rather than flout Australia's international obligations. The view taken in decisions like *Esso*[158] stands in stark contrast to the far more progressive and nuanced approach now being taken by the UK courts to what is conceded (even if only loosely) to be a right to strike.[159] That approach is very far removed from the judicial attitudes that prevailed when the economic torts were first developed, but it is arguably much more attuned to the idea of a balanced system of labour regulation.

[158] See text at nn 133–39.
[159] See n 32.

5

Inducing Breach of Contract

DR KATY BARNETT*

This chapter situates inducing breach of contract as an accessorial tort flowing from the primary wrong of breach of contract. The first part of this chapter describes the history of the tort. In the second part, the modern operation of the tort of inducing breach of contract in Australia and the United Kingdom is considered, and uncertainty as to its scope is outlined. In the third part of this chapter, a tentative solution to some of the issues with regard to scope and normative bases is proposed, reflecting the fundamental nature of the primary wrong itself and the need to protect the performance interests. In keeping with the rules governing the award of specific relief, the limitation which should apply to this tort is whether the subject matter of the contract is substitutable or not.

I. Introduction

Inducing breach of contract is one of a suite of economic torts prohibiting interference with contractual relations, along with interference with contractual relationships and conspiracy. A distinct thread in the history and development of the tort is the way in which it has often been used by employers to control employees, although its application was broadened out to all contracts by the nineteenth century case of *Lumley v Gye*.[1] This may explain its relative rarity and qualms about its use in a modern context. The compass and normative basis of the tort has always been uncertain, including the limitations applying to its availability. While Heydon's book on the topic briefly outlines the history of the tort, this chapter will

* Professor, Melbourne Law School, University of Melbourne (BA/LLB (Hons), PhD (Melb). I am grateful to TT Arvind for recommending *English Law in the Age of the Black Death 1348–1381* to me, for the support of 'Law Twitter' (especially the various labour lawyers who debated with me) and to Michael Bryan, Elise Bant, Sirko Harder and Adam Kramer for their helpful suggestions on earlier drafts.

[1] *Lumley v Gye* [1853] EWHC QB J73, [1853] 118 ER 749. See D Heydon, *Economic Torts*, 2nd edn (Sweet & Maxwell, 1978) 29.

delve more deeply into the historical background,[2] and to make some tentative suggestions from a contract law perspective as to more principled limitations. This chapter will consider both the law of Australia and the United Kingdom.

I will treat inducing breach of contract as an accessorial tort, in accordance with several recent analyses.[3] However, not all inducements of breach of contract should give rise to accessorial liability. A consideration of the history of the tort shows that it arose in the context of the Black Death, when labour suddenly went from being abundant to scarce. Similarly, when the tort underwent a renaissance in the nineteenth century in *Lumley v Gye*,[4] it was in response to a situation where a service was unique and non-substitutable. It is suggested that the scope and normative bases of the tort are presently unclear and confused, but that greater understanding can be gained by stepping back and looking at the nature of breach of contract and the remedies which flow from breach of contract, and how this flows through into the accessorial tort.

II. History of Inducing Breach of Contract

A. Medieval Beginnings with the Black Death

Historically, inducing breach of contract is related to (but distinct from) the action of *per quod servitium amisit* or 'loss of services,' an action for trespass to a servant in medieval England.[5] *Per quod servitium* has its genesis in the fact that the feudal lord was held to own both the services of his servants and his wife, and was entitled to damages against those who trespassed against them.[6]

Until the mid-fourteenth century, a master had no legal recourse if a servant left his employ and broke his contract to serve. However, the first Black Death

[2] Heydon, *ibid* 28–29.

[3] J Dietrich and P Ridge, *Accessories in Private Law* (Cambridge University Press, 2015) Ch 6; PS Davies, *Accessory Liability* (Hart Publishing, 2015) Ch 6.

[4] *Lumley* (n 1).

[5] GH Jones, '*Per quod servitium amisit*' (1958) 74 *LQR* 39, 39.

[6] Sayre situates the origin of *per quod servitium amisit* even further back, in notions of the right of the Roman *paterfamilias* to bring an *actio iniuriarum* and an *actio indirecta* for injuries committed to his wife, children, members of his household and slaves: see FB Sayre, 'Inducing Breach of Contract' (1923) 36 *Harvard Law Review* 663, 663. Injury to the wife therefore gave rise to damages for 'loss of consortium' on the part of the husband, a right that persisted for husbands. In some Australian jurisdictions the action has been abolished; in others it has been extended to all spouses and domestic partners, and the common law form is only retained in the Northern Territory and Victoria. See discussion in K Barnett and S Harder, *Remedies in Australian Private Law*, 2nd edn (Cambridge University Press, 2018) [7.85]–[7.88]. *Per quod servitium amisit* or 'loss of employee's services' was abolished in England and Wales by the *Administration of Justice Act 1982*, s 2 on the basis that an employer's right to his employee's services is a personal right (not a 'quasi-proprietary' right). However, it still exists in Australian law, as the case of *Barclay v Penberthy* [2012] HCA 40, (2012) 246 CLR 258 demonstrates, although limitations upon recovery exist in some States: see discussion in Barnett and Harder (n 6) [7.81]–[7.84].

pandemic decimated the Britain Isles between 1348 and 1350, during which a third to one half of the population in Britain is estimated to have died.[7] In an effort to stem the effects of this on labour, Edward III and the English Parliament passed the *Ordinance of Labourers* in 1349,[8] followed by the *Statute of Labourers* in 1351.[9] The preamble to the *Statute of Labourers* explicitly linked the enactment to the Black Death, saying,

> [b]ecause a great part of the people and especially of the workmen and servants has now died in that pestilence, some, seeing the straights of the masters and the scarcity of servants, are not willing to serve unless they receive excessive wages, and others, rather than through labour to gain their living, prefer to beg in idleness ....

Both the Statute and the Ordinance attempted to fix wages at pre-plague rates.[10] The Statute made it a crime to break an existing contract of service and allowed a master to force a servant to return to his service. In some ways, the Statute reflects the same policy behind the cases in which courts specifically enforce contracts for sale of goods which would not ordinarily be specifically enforceable because of a particular shortage,[11] but the difference is that the Statute remained in force once the shortage was over and continued to shape the law.

Palmer has posited that the Black Death gave rise to broader social changes which necessitated corresponding legal changes, such that, for example, conditional bonds with punitive terms became a frequent part of the legal landscape to ensure people kept to their promises.[12] He explains:

> Before the Black Death England was relatively overpopulated. Skilled labor was valued, but people incompetent in their occupation could be avoided or replaced. ... With the Black Death there no longer was the market situation that had made a successful society possible without a truly comprehensive state structure providing for labor regulation.[13]

The tort of inducing breach of contract is a further example of this trend, as the courts came to interpret the Statute and Ordinance as giving rise to a civil action where, if a servant had entered into the service of a second master, the second

[7] RC Palmer, *English Law in the Age of the Black Death 1348–1381* (University of North Carolina Press, 1993) 3.

[8] *Ordinance of Labourers* (Fordham University Source Books), available at https://sourcebooks.fordham.edu/seth/ordinance-labourers.asp.

[9] *Statute of Labourers* 23 Edw III (Yale Law School Lillian Goldman Law Library), available at https://avalon.law.yale.edu/medieval/statlab.asp.

[10] The Ordinance and the Statute were unsuccessful at achieving their aims of wage-fixing and are thought to be one of the factors leading to Wat Tyler's (unsuccessful) Peasant's Revolt in 1381.

[11] See, eg, *Curtice Brothers Co v Catts*, 72 NJ Eq 831, 833, 66 A 935, 936 (1907) (tomatoes); *Sky Petroleum Ltd v VIP Petroleum Ltd* [1974] 1 WLR 576 (Ch D) (petroleum); *Howard Perry & Co v British Railways* [1980] 1 WLR 1375 (Ch D) (steel).

[12] Palmer (n 7) Ch 7 (on the law of contract and penal bonds before and after the Black Death).

[13] *Ibid* 140.

master would be liable if he had notice of the first master's retainer.[14] Thus, William de Fincheden was able to say in 1372:

> At common law, before the statute, if a man took my servant out of my service, I should have a write of trespass, where he was in my service bodily: now the statute was made for this mischief, that if he never comes into my service, after he has made covenant to serve me, but he eloignes himself from me, I shall have such writ and suggest that he was retaining in my service and departed, as here is: wherefore it is necessary to traverse the retainer.[15]

The action was not based on the Statute itself, although its existence was inferred as being possible from the presence of the criminal provisions in the Statute. It appears to have been a common law action on the case.[16] The economic impetus was clearly the scarcity of labour: prior to the Black Death, there was no need to prevent labourers from working for other masters, but afterwards, it was not easily possible to get a substitute from elsewhere. In later times the action on the case for inducing breach of contract of a servant was divorced from the Statute altogether.[17]

B. The Revival of the Tort in *Lumley v Gye*

The modern tort of inducing breach of contract was established in the case of *Lumley v Gye*,[18] where Lumley (the manager of Her Majesty's Theatre) sued Gye (the manager of Covent Garden Theatre) for inducing an opera singer, Johanna Wagner (Richard Wagner's adopted niece), to breach her contract to perform for Lumley in order to perform at his venue instead. As Stephen Waddams has discussed, this case arose in the context of a notorious and sustained rivalry between London opera houses, where different houses sought to profit from 'taking' the other house's performer.[19] Ultimately, despite the willingness of a majority of the Court to develop the tort,[20] Lumley was unsuccessful, as Gye was found to have lacked the necessary bad faith.[21]

It is important to note that *Lumley v Gye* was preceded by another case, *Lumley v Wagner*, in which Lumley also sued Wagner for breach of a negative covenant not

[14] Jones (n 5) 40. If the second master was in the same county, he was presumed to have knowledge. Otherwise, the second master had to know or be given notice. See also *Lumley* (n 1) 763–67 (Coleridge J, dissenting) who gives a detailed history of the early cases.

[15] Yearbook Michaelmas 47 E 3 fol 14A pl 15 (1373).

[16] Jones (n 5) 40–44.

[17] *Ibid* 48.

[18] *Lumley* (n 1).

[19] SM Waddams, 'Johanna Wagner and the Rival Opera Houses' (2001) 117 *LQR* 431, 448–49. Lumley had induced the opera singer Jenny Lind to perform at his hall, taking Lind's services from Alfred Bunn of Drury Lane Theatre.

[20] *Lumley* (n 1) (Crompton J, Erle J and Wightman J in the majority, Coleridge J dissenting).

[21] Waddams (n 19) 456–57. Waddams suggests that the Court got the law wrong, as Gye seems to have been reckless or to have turned a blind eye to Lumley's contract.

to perform for another venue, and successfully gained an injunction to restrain her from doing so.[22] In Australia and other common law countries, this case has given rise to a line of cases in which injunctions have been granted for a short time against employees, particularly those who possess unique skills.[23] The uniqueness of the service is linked to inadequacy of damages and lack of substitutability: damages are less likely to be adequate where an equivalent employee cannot be found elsewhere. However, courts are also concerned with regard to ordinary employees not to render them effectively unemployable because an ordinary employee will be restrained from a wide variety of ordinary activities,[24] and the doctrine of restraint of trade may also operate to render restrictive covenants unenforceable.[25] Courts refuse to enforce or limit the operation of severe clauses which operate for a long time or which preclude too broad a range of activities.[26] Similarly, if the court considers that the parties are incapable of cooperating,[27] an injunction may not be granted because the practical effect may be to force the employee to resume employment.

As Waddams has also observed, *Lumley v Wagner* and *Lumley v Gye* should be read as different facets of the same problem, but even at the time, the court did not treat them as such.[28] Consequently, injunctions pursuant to *Lumley v Wagner* are available only in limited circumstances, whereas *Lumley v Gye* opened up the availability of inducing breach of contract to all contracts and (as will be seen below) the defences are traditionally narrow.[29]

The majority in *Lumley v Gye* found that there was no reason to confine any action to contracts for services or manual labourers.[30] Indeed two of the judges seemed to open the action up broadly on the basis that the plaintiff should be entitled to a remedy, using the example of debt and goods. Crompton J said:

> Nor is it an answer, to say that there is a remedy against the contractor, and that the parties relies on the contract; for, besides that reason also applying to the case of master and servant, the action on the contract and the action against the malicious wrong-doer may be for a different matter; and the damages occasioned by such malicious injury might be calculated on a very different principle from the amount of the debt which might be the only sum recoverable on the contract.[31]

[22] *Lumley v Wagner* [1852] EWHC J96, [1852] 42 ER 687.

[23] Barnett and Harder (n 6) [11.41]–[11.44].

[24] *Curro v Beyond Productions Pty Ltd* (1993) 30 NSWLR 337 (NSWCA), 348. *cf Page One Records v Britton* [1968] 1 WLR 157 (Ch D), 166.

[25] Barnett and Harder (n 6) [11.41].

[26] *Ehrman v Bartholomew* [1898] 1 Ch 671 (Ch D); *Heine Bros (Aust) Pty Ltd v Forrest* [1963] VR 383 (VSC); *William Robinson & Co Ltd v Heuer* [1898] 2 Ch 451 (CA); *Whitwood Chemical Company v Hardman* [1891] 2 Ch 416 (CA); *Chapman v Westerby* [1913] WN 277. *cf Rely-A-Bell Burglar and Fire Alarm Company Ltd v Eisler* [1926] 1 Ch 609 (Ch D).

[27] *Page One Records v Britton* (n 24); *Warren v Mendy* [1989] 1 WLR 853 (CA).

[28] Waddams (n 19) 448–49.

[29] An exception to this is *Warren* (n 27), where the inducing of a breach of a contract with a manager was treated similarly to a *Lumley v Wagner*-type case.

[30] *Lumley* (n 1) 753 (Crompton J), 755–56 (Erle J), 758–59 (Wightman J).

[31] *Ibid* 754 (Crompton J).

He uses the example of trading rivals, where one party who goes to a banker and begs the banker not to pay the other trader to whom he owes money, and goes on to say that while he is unprepared to decide the more general principle of whether such an action should be extended to other contracts, 'it would seem unjust, and contrary to the general principles of law, if such wrongdoer were not responsible for the damage caused by his more malicious act', but that in any case, the principle between masters and servants extends to this case.[32]

Erle J's judgment is broader:

> He who maliciously procures a damage to another by violation of a right ought to be made to indemnify; and that, whether he procures an actionable wrong or a breach of contract. He who procures the non-delivery of goods according to contract may inflict an injury, the same as he who procures the abstraction of goods after delivery; and both ought on the same ground to be made responsible. The remedy on the contract may be inadequate, as where the measures of damages is restricted … In such cases, he who procures the damage maliciously might justly be made responsible beyond the liability of the contractor.[33]

Coleridge J dissented on the basis that damages for breach of contract should be confined to the parties to the contract, and any exception on the basis of the relationship between master and servant was highly restricted for good reason.[34]

Lumley v Gye was not followed until years later, in a case where a brickmaker was enticed to work for another company in breach of negative covenant not to work for a competitor.[35] However, after that case, it became notorious as a tort which was used to enforce compulsory labour and to suppress trade unions.[36] It is to this part of the history of inducing breach of contract that we turn next.

C. Use of Inducing Breach of Contract to Combat Trade Unions

At the same time as *Lumley v Gye* was decided, the conduct of trade unions was becoming an issue in the United Kingdom, particularly after the 'Sheffield outrages' of the 1860s culminated in a 1869 report by the Royal Commission on Trade Unions.[37] In the 1890s, the tort of inducing breach of contract became

[32] *Ibid* 755 (Crompton J).
[33] *Ibid* 756 (Erle J).
[34] *Ibid* 760 (Coleridge J).
[35] *Bowen v Hall* (1888) 6 QBD 333 (CA).
[36] W Page Keeton et al, *Prosser & Keeton on Torts*, 5th edn (West Publishing Group, 1984) 978–79.
[37] D Brodie, *A History of British Labour Law 1867–1945* (Hart Publishing, 2003) 1. The 'Sheffield outrages' were a series of murders and explosions committed by militant unionists in Sheffield, who were dissatisfied with the poor working conditions of Sheffield grinders, cutlers and tool makers.

part of the private law armoury used by employers to suppress trade unions,[38] along with the contractual doctrine prohibiting restraint of trade,[39] and the tort of conspiracy.[40] Things came to a head in 1901. First, in *Taff Vale Railway Company v Amalgamated Society of Railway Servants*,[41] the tort of inducing breach of contract was used to hold unions liable for losses which companies suffered due to striking workers.[42] Second, *Quinn v Leathem*[43] expanded the operation of conspiracy, despite the prior case of *Flood v Allen*,[44] which had envisaged a narrow doctrine.[45] All these doctrines were ameliorated by statute in due course in the United Kingdom, although the wide immunity enjoyed by unions from *Lumley v Gye* was wound back in the early 1980s in the United Kingdom during the Thatcher years.[46] In Australia, the common law torts have been adopted wholly, and there is no existing statute conferring general immunity on unions or union officials for industrial action.[47]

[38] *Temperton v Russell* [1893] 1 QB 715 (CA), the third case to follow *Lumley v Gye* after *Bowen v Hall* (n 35), was a union case. See also, eg, *South Wales Miners Federation v Glamorgan Coal Co* [1905] AC 239 (HL); *Smithies v National Association of Operative Plasterers* [1909] 1 KB 310 (HL).

[39] *Hornby v Close* [1867] LR 2 QB 153 (QBD) held that union rulebooks were unenforceable as an invalid restraint of trade. This was later reversed by legislation several years later: *Trade Union Act 1871* (34 & 35 Vict c 31) (UK) (a result of the Royal Commission) and *Trade Union Act 1876* (39 & 40 Vict c 22).

[40] *Mogul Steamship v McGregor* [1892] AC 25 (HL) was a cartel case involving conspiracy, but the Court declined to extend Erle J's dictum in *Lumley v Gye* to trade unions. Lord Bramwell said at 47:

> There is one thing that is to me decisive. I have always said that a combination of workmen, an agreement among them to cease work except for higher wages, and a strike in consequence, was lawful at common law; perhaps not enforceable inter se, but not indictable. The Legislature has now so declared.

However, *Quinn v Leathem* [1901] AC 495 (HL) later extended the doctrine to trade unions. *Rookes v Barnard* [1964] AC 1149 (CA) held that closed shop agreements by unions with employers constituted 'unlawful intimidation'. *Rookes v Barnard* was immediately reversed by legislation: *Trade Disputes Act 1965*.

[41] *Taff Vale Railway Company v Amalgamated Society of Railway Servants* [1901] AC 426 (CA) ('*Taff Vale*').

[42] *Taff Vale* was reversed by legislation: *Trade Disputes Act 1906* (6 Edw 7 c 47).

[43] *Quinn* (n 40).

[44] *Flood v Allen* [1898] AC 1 (HL).

[45] See H Carty, 'The Modern Functions of the Economic Torts: Reviewing the English, Canadian, Australian and New Zealand Positions' (2015) 74(2) *Cambridge Law Journal* 261, 263–67.

[46] D Howarth, 'Against *Lumley v Gye* (2005) 68(2) *MLR* 195, 200, citing *Trade Union and Labour Relations (Consolidation) Act 1992*, ss 219–246.

[47] See M Pittard and R Naughton, *Australian Labour Law: Text, Cases and Commentary*, 5th edn (LexisNexis Butterworths, 2010) [17.23] citing the adoption of the English case law in *Sid Ross Agency Pty Ltd v Actors' and Announcers' Equity Association of Australia* [1970] 2 NSWR 47 (NSWCA); *Woolley v Dunford* (1972) 3 SASR 243 (SASC); *Davies and Davies v Nyland and O'Neil* (1975) 10 SASR 76 (SASC); *Dollar Sweets Pty Ltd v Federated Confectioners' Association of Australia* [1986] VR 383 (VSC); *Ranger Uranium Mines Pty Ltd v Federated Miscellaneous Workers' Union of Australia* (1987) 54 NTR 6 (NTSC); *Building Workers' Industrial Union of Australia v Odco Pty Ltd* (1991) 88 ALR 735 (FCAFC); *Ansett Transport Industries (Operations) Pty Ltd v Australian Federation of Air Pilots* [1991] 1 VR 637 (VSC); *Ansett Transport Industries (Operations) Pty Ltd v Australian Federation of Air Pilots (No 2)* [1991] 2 VR 636 (VSC); *Amcor Packaging (Aust) Pty Ltd v Automotive, Foods, Metals, Engineering, Printing and Kindred Industries Union* [1999] VSC 434; *Email Ltd v Automotive, Foods, Metals, Engineering, Printing and Kindred Industries Union* [2000] FCA 1932.

The tort has generally been used by employers, either to prevent employees from working for a rival employer, or to prevent unions from encouraging members from refusing to work for certain organisations. As Howarth has pointed out, around 40 per cent of the cases in which *Lumley v Gye* have been cited involve strikes, and another 20 per cent involve employment or personal services contracts.[48] This is unsurprising given the origins of the tort. Moreover, as Howarth notes, it is difficult for employers to sue employees if they want to have an ongoing relationship with the employees, but there is less compunction with regard to suing third parties such as unions and union organisers.[49]

D. Other Modern Uses of Inducing Breach of Contract

Inducing breach of contract has also been used in contexts other than industrial disputes, and the more general doctrine of inducement has been argued to extend beyond inducing breaches of contract into inducing breaches of trust[50] and inducing breaches of confidence.[51] The economic torts are essentially about protecting economic relations in one way or other,[52] and many of the cases involving inducing breach of contract are highly relational, involving disputes about long term contractual relationships such as employment, leases and long-term business relationships.[53]

Other cases involving inducing breach of contract include a case of third party travel companies inducing the breach of the terms of sale of tickets to a sporting event;[54] a newspaper inducing parties to breach the terms of a contract not to discuss discreditable conduct on the part of a company executive;[55] a case where third parties induced a boxer to breach a contract to only attend fights promoted by a particular company;[56] another case involving a third party inducing a

[48] Howarth (n 46) 197.

[49] *Ibid* 200.

[50] See, eg, *Australian Super Developments Pty Ltd v Marriner* [2014] VSC 464, upheld in *Marriner v Australian Super Developments Pty Ltd* [2016] VSCA 141. Cases of inducing breach of trust have risen after *Farah Constructions Pty Ltd v Say-Dee Pty Ltd* [2007] HCA 22, (2007) 230 CLR 89, 159, 163 held that the primary wrongdoer/fiduciary must be dishonest and fraudulent before an accessory will be liable for knowing assistance, whereas this is not the case for inducing breach of trust so long as the accessory is dishonest. *cf Royal Brunei Airlines Sdn v Tan* [1995] 2 AC 378 (PC), 385 (Lord Nicholls): what matters for knowing assistance of breach of fiduciary duty is the dishonesty of the assistant, and the honesty of the principal wrongdoer is irrelevant.

[51] H Carty, *An Analysis of the Economic Torts*, 2nd edn (Oxford University Press, 2010) 50–54.

[52] Heydon (n 1) 1.

[53] D Partlett, 'From Victorian Opera to Rock and Rap: Inducement to Breach of Contract in the Music Industry) (1991–92) 66 *Tulane Law Review* 771, 775.

[54] *Hospitality Group Pty Ltd v Australian Rugby Union Ltd* [2001] FCA 1040, (2001) 110 FCR 157.

[55] *ABC v Telegraph Media Group Ltd* [2018] EWCA Civ 2329, [2019] 2 All ER 684.

[56] *Fightvision Pty Ltd v Onisforou* [1999] NSWCA 323, (1999) 47 NSWLR 473. Note the similarity to *Lumley v Gye* and the different outcome.

boxer to breach his contract with his manager;[57] a company inducing a related company to breach a contract with a promoter;[58] a tenants' association urging tenants not to pay rent to landlords;[59] and a trade rival poaching customers by offering unfair incentives.[60]

The substitutability of the service in question is not always considered, nor is the effect on the autonomy of the parties. A rare exception to this is *Warren v Mendy*, a case where the plaintiff entered into a three-year contract to act as a manager for a boxer.[61] The boxer agreed to be managed exclusively by the plaintiff, and not to enter into an agreement with any other manager. After several months, the boxer was unhappy with the plaintiff's services and entered into a contract with the defendant to act as his manager. The plaintiff sought an injunction to restrain the defendant for inducing a breach of the management contract. The Court said that it was not prepared to award an injunction on the basis that it would effectively compel the boxer to continue with the plaintiff as manager, and that the boxer's confidence and trust in the plaintiff was destroyed.[62] In any event, damages were adequate.

III. The Tort of Inducing Breach of Contract in Australia Today

The English case of *Crofter Hand-Woven Harris Tweed v Veitch* outlined the tort as follows:

> [I]f C has an existing contract with A and B and is aware of it, and if B persuades or induces C to break the contract with resulting damage to A, this is generally speaking, a tortious act for which B will be liable to A for the injury he has done him. In some cases, however, B may be able to justify his procuring of the breach of contract ...[63]

Dietrich and Ridge usefully summarise the tort as follows: there is a need for a breach of contract by the principal wrongdoer as a result of inducement or procurement by the defendant. The inducement or procurement must be done with an *intent* to procure breach: in other words, there must be knowledge of the existence of the contract such that the defendant *knows* that the inducement or procurement will lead to a breach. Finally, the conduct must result in damage to the plaintiff.[64]

[57] *Warren* (n 27).
[58] *Zhu v Treasurer of New South Wales* [2004] HCA 56, (2004) CLR 530.
[59] *Camden Nominees v Forcey* [1940] Ch 352 (Ch D).
[60] *Multinail Australia Pty Ltd v Pryda (Aust) Pty Ltd* [2002] QSC 105.
[61] *Warren* (n 27).
[62] *Ibid* 116 (Nourse LJ).
[63] *Crofter Hand-Woven Harris Tweed v Veitch* [1972] AC 435 (HL), 442.
[64] Dietrich and Ridge (n 3) 179. See *Sanders v Snell* [1998] HCA 64, (1998) 196 CLR 329, 339; *Fightvision* (n 56) 509; *Scottish Pacific Business v Benchmark Debtor Finance* [2004] FCA 224, [169]; *OBG v Allen* [2007] UKHL 21, [2008] 1 AC 1, [39]; *Tarabay v Bechara* [2009] NSWSC 617 [164].

The expansion of the tort in *Lumley v Gye* beyond the situation of master and servant[65] seems to mean that the tort of inducing breach of contract applies to all contracts as long as the requisite elements can be made out.[66] There have been suggestions that inducing breach of contract protects the institution of contract because it gives rise to a 'quasi-proprietary interest'.[67] My own suggestion in a later section of this chapter is that this is not the best way to conceive of the reason for liability. In keeping with the rules governing the award of specific relief (and arguably gain-based relief for breach of contract), the limitation which should apply to this tort is whether the subject matter of the contract is substitutable or not. While it is certainly true that the rationale of the tort of inducing breach of contract is to deter the primary wrongdoing, it is suggested that we must take care that deterrence does not operate too widely. By stepping back and looking at the primary wrong, we can see that not all breaches of contract should be deterred, and that there should be room for parties to change their minds on the basis of changes in circumstance.

A. Inducing or Procuring

In order to make out the tort, it seems likely that the defendant must exercise *direct persuasion* for the breaching party to breach the contract,[68] via 'encouragement, threat or persuasion'.[69] It may be by means of payments of money[70] or threats.[71] It is not necessary for the acts to be unlawful,[72] but they must be positive acts, not omissions. The defendant's actions must have a sufficient causal relationship with the eventual breach of contract.[73] It does not matter if the breaching party was inclined to breach in any case; it must simply be 'a factor'.[74]

[65] *Lumley* (n 1).

[66] Carty (n 51) 31; C Sappideen, PM O'Grady and J Riley, *Macken's Law of Employment*, 8th edn (Thomson Reuters, 2009) 580.

[67] *Zhu* (n 58) [121]–[122].

[68] When Heydon wrote his text, he included inducing breach of contract through direct persuasion, direct disablement and indirect disablement: Heydon (n 1) 29. However, although there is no High Court authority on point, this has probably been overruled by *OBG* (n 64) [34]–[38] (Lord Hoffmann), [178] (Lord Nicholls). Certainly in *Jaddcal v Minson (No 3)* [2011] WASC 362 [191]–[195], La Miere J accepted the arguments of Carty (n 51) as compelling, and decided that *OBG* should be followed in Australia. Other commentators have suggested that indirect persuasion is no longer covered in Australia: Dietrich and Ridge (n 3) 183–85; S Deakin, 'Economic Relations' in P Vines and C Sappideen (eds), *Fleming's The Law of Torts*, 10th edn (Lawbook Co, 2011) [30.80]; Sappideen, O'Grady and Riley (n 66) 580–82.

[69] *OBG* (n 64) [36] (Lord Hoffmann).

[70] *Smithies* (n 38) 335.

[71] *Emerald Construction Co Ltd v Lowthian* [1966] 1 WLR 691 (CA).

[72] *Independent Oil Industries Ltd v Shell Co of Australia Ltd* (1937) 37 SR (NSW) 394 (NSWSC), 418–19. See Carty (n 51) 36.

[73] *OBG* (n 64) [36] (Lord Hoffmann).

[74] *Fightvision* (n 56) 534–35 (adopting a 'common sense' view of causation from *March v E & MH Stramare Pty Ltd* [1991] HCA 12, (1991) 171 CLR 506.

B. Knowledge and Intention

As Dietrich and Ridge note,[75] there is controversy over whether the central inquiry is primarily as to the defendant's knowledge,[76] the defendant's intention[77] or whether the inquiry is 'twofold', although of course knowledge and intention are necessarily interlinked. The knowledge or intention must relate to the fact that the breaching party was likely to breach as a result of the inducement or procurement.[78]

There is no need to show that the defendant acted with any 'malice' or ill-will, or even an intention to injure.[79] It simply needs to be shown that the defendant acted with knowledge and intention of procuring a breach of contract.[80] It is necessary for the defendant to have known that a contract exists, and to know of the general terms, however, it is not necessary to know of precise terms or the details of the contract.[81] Recklessness and wilful blindness appears to suffice.[82]

C. Justification

Inducing breach of contract is subject to an ill-defined defence of 'justification', which does not reflect any clear public policy.[83] Deakin describes it in the following terms: 'the defendant's ultimate purpose may … be so meritorious as to require sacrifice of the plaintiff's claim to freedom from inference'.[84] The rather dated example given by Viscount Simon in *Crofter Hand-Woven Harris Tweed* above is a father who justifiably persuades his daughter not to marry a 'scoundrel'.[85] The High Court in *Zhu* said that the defence is very narrow and requires 'either

[75] Dietrich and Ridge (n 3) 186–87.

[76] See, eg, *Short v City Bank of Sydney* [1912] HCA 54, (1912) 15 CLR 148, 160.

[77] See, eg, *Allstate Life Insurance Company v Australia and New Zealand Banking Group Ltd* (1995) 58 FCR 26 (FCA), 43 (Lindgren J, with whom Lockhart and Tamberlin JJ agreed), endorsed in *Fightvision* (n 56) 512.

[78] Dietrich and Ridge (n 3) 187–88.

[79] *Zhu* (n 58) [114]; *cf Lumley* (n 1) 732 (Crompton J), 756 (Erle J), 756 (Wightman J), 759 (Coleridge J): the terms 'malicious' or 'maliciously' are used in all judgments. However, Crompton J specifies that 'maliciously' 'is the same thing' as 'with notice' at 224, 752. See also commentary in Sappideen, O'Grady and Riley (n 66) 582.

[80] *Hill and Partners v First National Finance Corporation Plc* [1989] 1 WLR 225 (CA), 234 (Stuart-Smith LJ); Deakin (n 68) [30.90].

[81] Dietrich and Ridge (n 3) 188–89.

[82] *Ibid* 191–94; Deakin (n 68) [30.90].

[83] As per James Goudkamp's analysis, I assert that it is in fact a defence: see J Goudkamp, *Tort Law Defences* (Hart Publishing, 2013) 149. He notes that the defence is hard to place in a taxonomy because of its lack of definition and it contains both private and public justification elements.

[84] Deakin (n 68) [30.100].

[85] *Crofter Hand-Woven Harris Tweed* (n 63) 442–43. It is worth noting that Lord Wright's analysis of justification in *Crofter* is far more convincing: 476–80. Breach of a promise to marry has been abolished in Australia and the United Kingdom: see *Marriage Act 1961* (Cth), s 111A and *Law Reform (Miscellaneous Provisions) Act 1970*, s 1.

the authority of statute or some other superior right if the interference is to be lawful'.[86] In industrial cases, the defence applies to public policy, social or moral duties, and statutory or contractual privilege.[87] Howarth has suggested that the defence of justification should be broadened to take account of legitimate interests of employees in striking.[88]

As Davies has observed, it is easier to say what will *not* constitute justification than to say what positively will establish justification.[89] A lack of malice is not a defence,[90] nor is the argument that one was protecting one's own interests a defence[91] without more (such as an argument that the conduct was reasonably necessary).[92]

D. Remedies

Typically, the remedy will be an injunction preventing the person from continuing to induce the breach[93] or damages 'at large' reflecting the losses suffered as a result of the breach, which may outstrip the damages flowing from the breach of contract.[94] While damages for distress[95] and exemplary damages for a contumelious disregard of the plaintiff's right may be available,[96] an account of profits is presently unavailable for inducing breach of contract.[97]

[86] *Zhu* (n 58) [159]. *cf* American law on this topic which requires a discretionary balancing of interests: Dietrich and Ridge (n 3) 196. See the extensive discussion of equal or superior right in Davies (n 3) 230–34; PS Davies, 'Defences and Third Parties: Justifying Participation' in A Dyson, J Goudkamp, F Wilmot-Smith (eds), *Defences in Tort* (Hart Publishing, 2015) 107, 113–17.

[87] Sappideen, O'Grady and Riley (n 66) 592–95.

[88] Howarth (n 46) 220. For an extraordinary case where this did in fact occur, see *Brimelow v Casson* [1924] 1 Ch 302 (Ch D), where associations for the protection of actors were entitled to compel the plaintiff to pay his chorus girls decent wages. *Brimelow v Casson* has been received in an inconsistent manner in Australia – frequently rejected but sometimes adopted: Sappideen, O'Grady and Riley (n 66) 592–93.

[89] Davies (n 3) 226; Davies (n 86) 111.

[90] *Smithies* (n 38); *Glamorgan* (n 38) 266 (McCardie J).

[91] *De Jetley Marks v Lord Greenwood* [1936] 1 All ER 863 (KBD), 873 (Porter J).

[92] *Zhu* (n 58) [159].

[93] *Esso Petroleum v Kingswood* [1974] QB 142 (QBD), 156; *Crestford v Tesco Stores* [2005] EWHC 805.

[94] *Ansett v Australian Federation of Air Pilots (No 2)* (n 47).

[95] *Ibid.*

[96] *Ibid.* In order to obtain exemplary damages in Australia, it is necessary to show 'conscious wrongdoing in contumelious disregard of another's rights': *Whitfield v De Lauret & Co Ltd* [1920] HCA 75, (1920) 29 CLR 71, 77 (Knox CJ); *Australian Consolidated Press Ltd v Uren* [1969] 1 AC 590, (1967) 117 CLR 221, 232–34; *XL Petroleum (NSW) Pty Ltd v Caltex Oil (Australia) Pty Ltd* [1985] HCA 12, (1985) 155 CLR 448, 471 (Brennan J); *Gray v Motor Accident Commission* [1998] HCA 70, (1998) 196 CLR 1 [22] (Gleeson CJ, McHugh, Gummow and Hayne JJ). It has been said that in relation to inducing breach of contract that something 'bordering on the malicious' is probably necessary: *Hospitality Group Pty* (n 54).

[97] *Hospitality Group Pty Ltd* (n 54) [162] (Finkelstein and Hill JJ). *cf* [166]–[173] (Emmett J, dissenting).

IV. Stepping Back: The Nature of the Primary Wrong

Inducing breach of contract is treated in this chapter as an accessorial wrong; in other words, there must be a primary wrong of breach of contract for the defendant to have induced, involvement in the wrong by the defendant, and a requisite mental state on the part of the defendant.[98] However, like Dietrich and Ridge, who have also advanced an accessorial view, I accept that there are other claimed normative bases behind the tort, including the promotion of efficiency, the necessity of enforcing bargains and the 'quasi-proprietary' nature of interests under contract. Before I consider the justificatory principles of the tort, it is necessary to outline my understanding of the justificatory principles for the primary wrong. The limitations upon the availability of the tort of inducing breach of contract should be understood in this context.

A. The Justifications for Liability in Contract

The High Court of Australia in *Zhu* has offered the typical justifications for imposing liability in contract within the context of a claim of inducing breach of contract. The Court justifies its approach to inducing breach of contract in the following terms:

> … [S]ubject to the established limits on the grant of specific performance and injunctions, in Australian law each contracting party may be said to have a right to the performance of the contract by the other. It is not true here to say: 'The duty to keep a contract at common law means a prediction that you must may damages if you do not keep it, – and nothing else'.[99]

My own position is that, despite the rhetoric of courts in Australia, England and Wales, there is, in fact, no straightforward 'right to performance of the contract' when the reality of contractual remedies is taken into account. The most a plaintiff can say is that there is a 'right to damages substituting for performance', or in the case of contracts which are specifically performable, there is a 'defeasible right

[98] Dietrich and Ridge (n 3) 3–4. See also *OBG* (n 64). Dietrich and Ridge note that an accessorial rationale has been rejected by some commentators, including R Stevens, *Torts and Rights* (Oxford University Press, 2007) 256–57, 276–77; S Deakin and J Randall, 'Rethinking the Economic Torts' (2009) 72(4) *MLR* 519. Carty and Lee accept an accessorial rationale, but do not think that it adds to the analysis: Carty (n 51) 60–62, 304–307; P-W Lee, 'Inducing Breach of Contract: Conversion and Contract as Property' (2009) 29 *OJLS* 511, 522.

[99] *Zhu* (n 58) [128]. The quotation is from OW Holmes, 'The Path of the Law' (1897) 10 *Harvard Law Review* 457, 462.

to performance'.[100] This is why some earlier writings on the topic call it a 'performance interest',[101] not a 'right to performance'.

In asserting this, I must acknowledge first that the rhetoric of both English and Australian courts suggests otherwise,[102] and second, that other academics argue that there is a right to performance.[103] Most recently, Chen-Wishart has argued that there is a contractual right to performance (and a corresponding duty to perform), but that the remedies do not simply aim to enforce the right to performance because of contract's concern for autonomy. As part of that argument, she has argued that the existence of the tort of inducing breach of contract assumes and illustrates that there is a right to performance.[104] Certainly, if it is accepted that inducing breach of contract applies to *all* contracts (and presently that seems to be the assumption) there is strength to this argument.

The qualification at the beginning of the passage from *Zhu* is instructive and illuminating. While the Court says that there is a right to performance (subject to limitations on the availability of specific relief), in fact, specific performance and injunctions are not the presumptive remedy for breach of contract. The primary remedy for breach of contract is expectation damages, with the aim of placing the plaintiff in the position it would have been in if the contract had been performed.[105] Compensatory damages will be adequate if a substitute performance can be purchased with damages. While the plaintiff has a 'performance interest',[106] the law favours expectation damages because they represent a less intrusive way of vindicating this interest, one which favours the parties' autonomy.[107]

In assessing what a primary wrongdoer's liability for breach of contract will be, it is vital to assess the *substitutability* of the subject matter of the contract.[108]

[100] See K Barnett, 'Review Article: A Critical Consideration of Substitutive Awards in Contract Law' (2018) 81(6) *MLR* 1064, 1071; K Barnett, 'Great Expectations: A Dissection of Expectation Damages in Contract in Australia and England' (2016) 33 *Journal of Contract Law* 1.

[101] D Friedmann, 'The Performance Interest in Contract Damages' (1995) 111 *LQR* 628; B Coote, 'Contract Damages, Ruxley, and the Performance Interest' (1997) 56 *CLJ* 537, 566; see also B Coote, 'The Performance Interest, Panatown, and the Problem of Loss' (2001) 117 *LQR* 81.

[102] Other than *Zhu* itself, see, eg, *Alley v Deschamps* [1806] 33 ER 278 (Ch D), 279 (Lord Erskine); *Coulls v Bagot's Executor and Trustee Co Ltd* (1967) 119 CLR 460 (HCA), 504 (Windeyer J); *Placer Development Ltd v Commonwealth of Australia* (1969) 121 CLR 353 (HCA), 373 (Windeyer J); *Cehave NV v Bremer Handelgesellschaft mbH ('The Hansa Nord')* [1976] QB 44 (CA), 71 (Roskill LJ); *In Re T & N Ltd* [2005] EWHC 2870, [2006] 1 WLR 1728 [26] (David Richards J).

[103] See, eg, R Stevens, 'Damages and the Right to Performance: A Golden Victory or Not?' in J Neyers, R Bronagh and S Pitel (eds), *Exploring Contract Law* (Hart Publishing, 2009) 172; D Winterton, *Money Awards in Contract Law* (Hart Publishing, 2015) 146–48; M Chen-Wishart, 'Specific Performance and Change of Mind' in G Virgo and S Worthington (eds), *Commercial Remedies: Resolving Controversies* (Cambridge University Press, 2017) 98, 100.

[104] Chen-Wishart, *ibid*.

[105] *Robinson v Harman* (1848) 1 Ex 850, 855, [1848] 154 ER 363, 365.

[106] Friedmann (n 101); Coote, 'Contract Damages' (n 101) 566; see also Coote, 'The Performance Interest' (n 101).

[107] Chen-Wishart (n 103).

[108] See K Barnett, *Accounting for Profit for Breach of Contract: Theory and Practice* (Hart Publishing, 2012) Ch 3. Professor Kronman first coined the term 'substitutability' in A Kronman, 'Specific Performance' (1978) 45 *University of Chicago Law Review* 351, 359.

Substitutability looks to what the plaintiff hoped to gain from the contract, and therefore what remedy the defendant must give the plaintiff as a substitute for the performance which was denied as a result of the breach. Thus, sometimes a defendant is 'free' to breach his contract, subject to his obligation to pay damages (as the supporters of 'efficient breach' allege).[109] In addition, there may be situations where we *want* to allow breach, for example, when unforeseen circumstances mean that the defendant breaches to avoid a loss (as opposed to the situation of 'efficient breach' where the defendant breaches to obtain a gain).[110] In this way, contract maximises the autonomy of both plaintiff and defendant.

Certain things follow from this. It is suggested that we only want to make an accessory liable for inducing breach of contract in circumstances where damages would be inadequate to compensate for the primary breach.[111] In fact, if one looks at the cases (even if one includes the cases of inducing breach of confidence and inducing breach of trust) courts primarily seem to apply the doctrine in these circumstances: where there is a unique service involved in the primary contract (as for *Lumley v Wagner* and several of the cases involving promotion of celebrities or sports people), or where the contracted-for right is otherwise difficult to adequately compensate for (as with breach of confidence or breach of trust). Before this proposition is explored, however, it is first necessary to consider the policy justifications for the existence of inducing breach of contract, and particularly the 'quasi-proprietary' justification.

B. The Justifications for Liability for Inducing Breach of Contract

Carty notes that there are two general justifications given for liability for inducing breach of contract: social theory and property theory.[112] Ultimately,

[109] The main advocate of this view (although it is widely followed in the United States) is Richard Posner: R Posner, *Economic Analysis of Law*, 9th edn (Aspen, 2014) §4.10.

[110] D Friedmann, 'Economic Aspects of Damages and Specific Performance Compared' in D Saidov and R Cunnington (eds), *Contract Damages: Domestic and International Perspectives* (Hart Publishing, 2008) 65 introduces the concept of 'tolerated breach'. See also D Campbell, 'The Relational Constitution of Remedy: Co-operation as the Implicit Second Principle of Remedies for Breach of Contract' (2005) 11 *Texas Wesleyan Law Review* 455; D Campbell, 'A Relational Critique of the Third Restatement of Restitution § 39' (2011) 68 *Washington and Lee Law Review* 1063, 1093–1109; D Campbell, 'What Do We Mean by the Non-Use of Contract?' in J Braucher, J Kidwell and WC Whitford (eds), *Revisiting the Contracts Scholarship of Stewart Macaulay: On the Empirical and Lyrical* (Hart Publishing, 2013) 179–18; Chen-Wishart (n 103); and K Barnett, 'Mitigation in Contract Law: Policy and Principle' (2019) 36(1) *Journal of Contract Law* 5.

[111] This is arguably implicit in *Lumley* itself: (n 1) 754, 755 (Crompton J); 756 (Erle J).

An example of this is where the primary wrongdoer can claim a defence or an immunity, but the accessory cannot avail herself of this: Davies (n 86) 108–10.

[112] Carty (n 51) 54–60.

Carty herself rejects both theories, and considers that the tort reflects a notion of joint-tortfeasance.[113]

i. Social Theory

The social theory as to why the tort of inducing breach of contract is useful relates to the importance of contracting as a social institution. In other words, by protecting contracting parties from having bargains undermined by deliberate inducement, the institution of contract is itself protected.[114] Here, as with contract more generally, there is a balance between enforcing bargains and party autonomy. Some have objected to the tort of inducing breach of contract on the basis that it does not respect autonomy,[115] or it reduces competition in a labour law context.[116]

More broadly, law and economists who adhere to 'efficient breach' theory[117] tend to argue that the tort should have a limited operation.[118] The High Court of Australia, on the other hand, has explicitly rejected Holmes' disjunctive theory of contractual remedies in this context,[119] and has also explicitly rejected the notion of 'efficient breach' in another case.[120] I have argued elsewhere that efficient breach theory is based on doubtful doctrinal and theoretical grounds, because it fails to take into account the substitutability of the contractual performance.[121] Partlett's criticisms of the use of 'efficient breach theory' in a highly relational context are apposite.[122] Nonetheless, as will be evident from my description of the performance interest above, I consider that there must be some room for allowing breach of contract, for the reasons of autonomy advanced by Chen-Wishart. Indeed, one can see these concerns played out in *Warren v Mendy*, mentioned above.

[113] *Ibid* 60.

[114] J Danforth, 'Tortious Interference with Contract: A Reassertion of Society's Interest in Commercial Stability and Contractual Integrity' (1981) *81 Columbia Law Review* 1491; AP Simester and W Chan, 'Inducing Breach of Contract: One Tort or Two?' (2004) 62 *CLJ* 132, 144; W Landes and R Posner, The Economic Structure of Intellectual Property Law (Harvard University Press, 2003) 118–19. Landes and Posner were cited approvingly by the High Court of Australia in *Roadshow Films Pty Ltd v iiNet Ltd (No 2)* [2012] HCA 16, (2012) 248 CLR 42 [110] (Gummow and Hayne JJ).

[115] D Dobbs, 'Tortious Interference with Contractual Relationships' (1980) 34 *Arkansas Law Review* 335.

[116] Howarth (n 46) 202.

[117] Posner (n 109) §4.10.

[118] See, eg, H Perlman, 'Interference with Contract and Other Economic Expectancies: A Clash of Tort and Contract Doctrine' (1982) 49 *University of Chicago Law Review* 61; L BeVier, 'Reconsidering Inducement' (1990) 76 *Virginia Law Review* 877; W Landes and R Posner, 'Joint and Multiple Tortfeasors: An Economic Analysis' (1980) 9 *Journal of Legal Studies* 517, 552–55.

[119] *Zhu* (n 58) [128].

[120] *Tabcorp Holdings Ltd v Bowen Investments Pty Ltd* [2009] HCA 8, (2008) 236 CLR 272 [13].

[121] Barnett (n 108) 106–16.

[122] Partlett (n 53) 795–806. On the other hand, David Campbell has argued that even in a relational context, there may be reasons why parties wish to breach their contracts, including the fact that performance may no longer be feasible or profitable, and that allowing such a facility may in fact improve relations between the parties: see Campbell's articles and chapters listed in n 110.

ii. Property Theory

Property theory is reflected in the two major cases in both Australia and the United Kingdom. In *Zhu* the High Court of Australia approved Kitto J's 'quasi-proprietary analysis' from *Attorney-General (NSW) v Perpetual Trustee Co Ltd*.[123] It did so on four bases. First, the Court referred to Erle J's broad rights based analysis in *Lumley v Gye*.[124] Second, the Court referred to American case law.[125] Third, the Court referred to the availability of specific performance and the right to performance in a contract.[126] Fourth, the Court refers to the availability of injunctive relief to restrain certain breaches of contract as establishing that contract gives rise to a chose in action and is thus quasi-proprietary.[127] However, as the High Court notes in *Zhu*, there is a certain circularity in saying a contractual interest is 'quasi-proprietary' because it has protection against third party interference.[128]

In *OBG v Allan*, the Court also sees inducing breach of contract as being based in the proprietary nature of contractual rights. Thus, Lord Hoffmann says:

> It [the tort of inducing breach of contract] treats contractual rights as a species of property which deserve special protection, not only by giving a right of action against the party who breaks his contract but by imposing secondary liability on a person who procures him to do so.[129]

The quasi-proprietary analysis has also found favour in academic circles,[130] and recent statements by Lord Reed in *One Step (Support) Ltd v Morris-Garner* suggest that breach of contract may result in the loss of a 'valuable asset created or protected by the right which was infringed'.[131] However, as Carty has noted, 'any policy that simply focuses on the protection of contract rights runs the risk of being too wide'.[132] I will suggest a potentially more workable proprietary theory below.

[123] *Attorney-General (NSW) v Perpetual Trustee Co Ltd* (1952) 85 CLR 237 (HCA), 294–95, discussed in *Zhu* (n 58) [123]–[125].

[124] *Zhu* (n 58) [126].

[125] *Ibid* [127].

[126] *Ibid* [128].

[127] *Ibid* [129]–[134].

[128] *Ibid* [125].

[129] *OBG* (n 64) [32]. This bears some similarity to Lord Reed's analysis of contractual rights as property: see *One Step (Support) Ltd v Morris-Garner* [2018] UKSC 20, [2018] 2 WLR 1353 [30], [79], [81] (Lord Reed, with whom Lady Hale and Lord Wilson agreed, and Lord Carnwath in a separate judgment rejecting Lord Sumption's analysis).

[130] See, eg, R Epstein, 'Inducement of Breach of Contract as a Problem of Ostensible Ownership' (1987) 16 *Journal of Legal Studies* 1; R Bagshaw, 'Inducing Breach of Contract' in J Horder (ed), *Oxford Essays in Jurisprudence 4th Series* (Oxford University Press, 2000) 135 (using an analogy with property); Waddams (n 19) 449–50; Lee (n 98); Simester and Chan (n 114) 143; JW Neyers, 'The Economic Torts as Corrective Justice' (2009) 17 *Torts Law Journal* 162; P Benson, 'The Basis for Excluding Liability for Economic Loss in Tort Law' in DG Owen (ed), *Philosophical Foundations of Tort Law* (Clarendon Press, 1993) 427; Deakin and Randall (n 98) 535.

[131] *One Step (Support) Ltd v Morris-Garner* [2018] UKSC 20, [2018] 2 WLR 1353 [92] (Lord Reed).

[132] Carty (n 51) 59.

C. A Different Approach to the Justifications for Inducing Breach of Contract?

The typical approach to justifying inducing breach of contract according to either the social theory or the quasi-proprietary theory is to say that *all* breaches of contract are important, or *all* (or most contracts) give rise to quasi-proprietary rights, and that this means that all contracts are subject to the doctrine of inducing breach of contract.[133] Certainly, this is what seems to have been intended by at least some of the majority in *Lumley v Gye*, and by the High Court in *Zhu*.

In this context, Harder's concept of the unauthorised use of an 'exclusive entitlement' can be useful, as he seeks to explain why and when contractual rights can appear to be 'quasi-proprietary'.[134] Harder argues that exclusive entitlements are of two kinds: (1) exclusive entitlements *erga omnes* (against the whole world – including property rights, reputational rights, rights to bodily integrity); and (2) exclusive entitlements *inter partes* (against the defendant only – for example, specifically enforceable contracts of sale of land or chattels).

Harder's analysis helps us understand that, if one looks at the kinds of contract which give rise to a proprietary right which is enforceable *inter partes*, the contracts which do give rise to a proprietary interest of this kind are those where a constructive trust is imposed upon entry into a specifically enforceable contract of sale.[135] There are admitted issues with the constructive trust analysis, as I have noted elsewhere,[136] but the essence of the reason why such a constructive trust is held to arise (and why specific performance is granted) is because of a lack of substitutability of the subject matter of the contract. Damages are inadequate because the plaintiff cannot easily purchase a substitute performance from elsewhere.

It is also notable that, in *Zhu*, the cases the Court concentrates on are those where specific performance or an injunction would be awarded (either to restrain breach or to enforce the contract). As discussed at the outset, if we look at the historical situations in which inducing breach of contract has been instituted, often the cases in which it has been awarded are those where the subject matter of the contract is not substitutable. Moreover, it is suggested that concerns about substitutability and unavailability of substitute performance have been at the heart of the tort from its very inception. During the Black Death, there was a temporary scarcity of labour which gave rise to the development of the tort from a

[133] *Ibid* 31.

[134] S Harder, *Measuring Damages in the Law of Obligations: The Search for Harmonised Principles* (Hart Publishing, 2010) 216.

[135] See *Lysaght v Edwards* (1876) 2 Ch D 499, 510 (Jessel MR); *Holroyd v Marshall* (1862) 10 HL Cas 191, [1862] 11 ER 999. *cf Wall v Bright* [1820] 37 ER 456, 459 (Plumer MR): the vendor is 'in progress towards' bare trusteeship. An analysis which adopts substitutability as a criterion for the award of proprietary rights is E Bant and M Bryan, 'A Model of Proprietary Remedies' in E Bant and M Bryan (eds), *Principles of Proprietary Remedies* (Thomson Reuters, 2013) [12.170].

[136] Barnett (n 108) 89–94.

statutory basis.[137] Similarly, the precursor to *Lumley v Gye*, *Lumley v Wagner*, is another case where the performance in question is sufficiently unique to render damages inadequate. This has continued to be reflected in the case law dealing with injunctions to restrain a breach of negative covenant in services contracts.[138] The true reason why contracts where a court will award an injunction to restrain a breach of negative covenant are 'quasi-proprietary' is because the court gives the plaintiff a right which is enforceable against the breaching party: it is again enforceable *inter partes*.

It is suggested that one of the reasons why the 'union breaking' cases are discomforting to at least some of us[139] is that the services rendered in the primary contracts in those cases were *not* sufficiently unique as to ordinarily give rise to specific relief of any kind, and because the law has a policy of not forcing ordinary workers to continue in employment when relations have broken down.[140] There seems to be a kind of sophistry in saying, 'we are not forcing workers to work, or even restraining them via a negative covenant; we are just telling their unions not to encourage them to do so'.[141] Employers might argue in response that, in the particular context of a strike, labour becomes temporarily scarce that the nature of the employer's interest in performance becomes sufficiently strong so as to give rise to accessorial liability.[142] However, if the problem is disruption of industrial activity, inducing breach of contract seems to be a tool ill-suited to fixing this issue given the considerable uncertainty around its operation and the available defences described in section III. It has been suggested to me that the constant legislative 'to and fro' on industrial relations is why the economic torts still have considerable currency.[143]

On the other hand, it might be questioned why the tort should always be used in a way which favours employers, and whether some kind of *quid pro quo* use of the doctrine could be applied by employees who are wrongfully sacked by employers at the behest of third parties.[144] Suppose, for example, that an employee makes

[137] Partlett notes that a similar situation gave *Lumley v Gye* an impetus in the United States, as the American South suffered from a labour shortage after the American Civil War and the emancipation of slaves: Partlett (n 53) 785.

[138] See Barnett and Harder (n 6) and the discussion of cases therein.

[139] Other than myself, there is Howarth (n 46); Dietrich and Ridge (n 3) 170, fn 9; Keeton et al (n 36) 979; P Cane, *The Anatomy of Tort Law* (Hart Publishing, 1997) 151.

[140] P Saprai, 'The Principle against Self-Enslavement in Contract Law' (2009) 26 *Journal of Contract Law* 25.

[141] *cf* Heydon (n 1) 9.

[142] One of the temporary scarcity of goods cases in which a court was prepared to order specific relief for ordinary goods involved a union strike: *Howard Perry & Co v British Railways* (n 11).

[143] In other words, one party tightens up industrial relations and limits the conditions upon which workers can strike, and the next party loosens them again, such that the only consistent doctrines are the common law doctrines.

[144] It is worth noting that courts have said that an employee may sometimes specifically enforce a contract against an employer in the Australian context: see *Quinn v Overland* [2010] FCA 799, (2010) 199 IR 40 [97]–[101]; *Automotive, Food, Metals, Engineering, Printing and Kindred Industries Union v McCain Foods (Aust) Pty Ltd* [2012] FCA 1126 [48].

a comment on social media which causes third parties to call for the employee to be sacked.[145] In breach of contract, and bowing to pressure from individuals such as politicians or radio shock jocks, the employer wrongfully terminates the employee's employment. It could be asked whether the employee should have an additional action (above and beyond any action under employment legislation) against those who have called for her sacking.

The difficulties with regard to the normative justification of the tort also flow through to the operation of the defence of justification and when it is appropriate to allow a party to induce a breach of contract. *If* the subject matter of the contract is substitutable, it is suggested that this goes to justifiability: the 'victim' of the breach can get a substitute performance from elsewhere and the inducement, no matter how knowing, is not one for which liability should attach. On the other hand, if the subject matter of the contract is not substitutable, then there is greater scope for arguing that there was no justification for inducing breach. At present, in my opinion, the Australian defence as proposed in *Zhu* is unduly narrow, and needs to include policy discussion as to the importance of relative contractual interests, precisely because the common law does *not* treat all contracts in the same way remedially (regardless of whether one adopts my view on rights to performance or not).

Finally, with regard to remedies, it is suggested that the primary remedy for inducing breach of contract should be an injunction (in line with the requirement that the subject of the performance of the contract should be non-substitutable) but that if specific relief is no longer available, then compensatory damages or disgorgement should be considered, depending upon the circumstances. It is also suggested that the dissenting judgment of Emmett J in *Hospitality Group Pty Ltd v Australian Rugby Union Ltd* is correct: an account of profits can be an exceptional remedy for inducing breach of contract,[146] particularly in light of the substitutability argument above (which, in my view, is key to why disgorgement can sometimes be allowed for breach of contract). If the primary contract is one where performance is not substitutable, it also follows that if the defendant makes a profit by deliberately encouraging the other party to the contract to breach, then the

[145] An instance of this happened in relation to a news reporter who criticised ANZAC Day and Australian soldiers on Twitter. See M Whitbourn, 'SBS Presenter Scott McIntyre Sacked Over "Inappropriate" ANZAC Day Tweets' (*Sydney Morning Herald*, 26 April 2015), available at www.smh.com.au/national/sbs-presenter-scott-mcintyre-sacked-over-inappropriate-anzac-day-tweets-20150426-1mtbx8.html. SBS and McIntyre later settled a claim for unfair dismissal under the *Fair Work Act 2009* (Cth): see L Visentin, 'Sacked Reporter Scott McIntyre and SBS Resolve Dispute Over Anzac Day Tweets' (*Sydney Morning Herald*, 11 April 2016), available at www.smh.com.au/business/companies/sacked-reporter-scott-mcintyre-and-sbs-resolve-dispute-over--anzac-day-tweets-20160411-go37vt.html. One of those who stridently criticised McIntyre at the time of the comments on ANZAC Day was the then Communications Minister Malcolm Turnbull (later erstwhile Prime Minister). Could the fact that a Communications Minister who spoke out against the comments be regarded as pressure to sack the employee? I do not offer a concluded view here, but merely ask the question.

[146] *Hospitality Group Pty Ltd* (n 54) [166]–[173].

defendant should disgorge that profit, subject to discretionary defences (justification may be a consideration in this specific context, particularly in light of the role of deterrence outlined by Emmett J).

V. Conclusion

The common law does *not* treat all contracts in the same way when awarding remedies, and it is suggested that a similar approach should be taken in regard to the tort of inducing breach of contract. If one conceives of inducing breach of contract as accessorial, it is only where the 'performance interest' is of sufficient importance to warrant specific relief (or disgorgement) for the primary breach that accessorial liability should be considered. Given the accessorial nature of inducing breach of contract, it is *not* appropriate that all breaches of contract should be covered by the tort, and it is the non-substitutable subject matter of the contract which renders the inducement wrongful. It might be argued in rebuttal to this that the tort of inducing breach of contract is already limited by the requirement that the tort be committed intentionally,[147] but the difficulties in proving knowledge and the uncertainty around the exact test suggest that by itself, it is not enough to provide a coherent limitation.

Consequently, the concept of 'substitutability' is essential to provide a limitation upon liability: it is only where the breaching party could not obtain a substitute for performance from elsewhere that liability for inducement should be established, and perhaps, even, to those situations where an adequate remedy cannot be obtained from the primary wrongdoer.[148]

[147] I think Carty would make this argument: Carty (n 51) 60–62.

[148] Note that this was given as a justification for the modern incarnation of the tort in *Lumley* (n 1) 754–55 (Crompton J), 756 (Erle J).

6

Cross-Border Civil Conspiracy

DR BOBBY WM LINDSAY

I. Introduction

Private international law provides a range of remedial responses which a litigant may invoke in the face of oppressive or wrongful conduct by a counterparty. An anti-suit injunction may be sought which orders the counterparty to desist from 'vexatious and oppressive' conduct before a foreign court.[1] Such an injunction frequently is granted where proceedings are brought in breach of an exclusive jurisdiction clause.[2] To supplement this, the law of contract has been drawn upon, and now it is commonly accepted that the breach of a forum selection clause gives rise to a claim in damages.[3]

However, these remedies are often limited by the bounds of privity.[4] As a result, the economic torts have been pressed into action to counter the obfuscation and evasion which may easily be injected into international commercial litigation. Most prominently, the tort of inducing breach of contract has been used to fortify jurisdiction clauses, permitting a party to such a clause to pursue third parties who have advised or assisted the counterparty in raising proceedings before a non-designated court. For example, a professional adviser who advises their client to issue proceedings outside the contractually-designated forum can be pursued under the inducement tort.[5] There may also be a role for the 'infliction' or 'causing loss by unlawful means' tort, particularly where speculative or

[1] See M Douglas, 'Anti-Suit Injunctions in Australia' (2017) 41(1) *Melbourne University Law Review* 66; T Raphael, *The Anti-Suit Injunction*, 2nd edn (Oxford University Press, 2019).

[2] *Donohue v Armco* [2001] UKHL 64, [2002] 1 All ER 749.

[3] See, eg, *Starlight Shipping v Allianz ('The Alexandros T')* [2013] UKSC 70, [2014] 1 All ER 590; *cf Airbus v Generali Italia SAS* [2019] EWCA Civ 805 (no breach on the facts). Similar protection has not, however, been extended to choice of law clauses: *Ace Insurance v Moose Enterprise* [2009] NSWSC 724; *Navig8 Pte Ltd v Al-Riyadh Co for Vegetable Oil Industry* [2013] EWHC 328 (Comm).

[4] Although an injunction sometimes may bind parties beyond the jurisdiction agreement: *Kallang Shipping v AXA Assurances Senegal* [2006] EWHC 2825 (Comm).

[5] As in *AMT Futures Ltd v Marzillier, Dr Meier & Dr Guntner Rechtsanwaltsgesellschaft GmbH* [2017] UKSC 13, [2018] AC 439.

vexatious proceedings are commenced against a third party with the object of causing loss to the claimant.[6] If unlawful means – such as the tort of malicious prosecution[7] or interference with a dispute resolution agreement – are employed against the third party, and those means restrict that third party's ability to deal with the claimant,[8] then this tort may provide the claimant an avenue for redress on the basis of the defendant's civil wrong against the third party. This may prove useful as – unlike the inducement tort – there likely is no defence of justification for the infliction tort.[9]

This chapter, however, focusses on the tort of conspiracy. Conspiracy may have at least three functions in this context of cross-border litigation. First, pleading conspiracy may ensnare a party who otherwise would not be amendable to the jurisdiction of the claimant's preferred court. The establishment of jurisdiction over one conspirator provides a good reason for the assertion of jurisdiction against co-conspirators, and therefore the ability to formulate a claim in conspiracy may yield practical advantage where otherwise it would be difficult to 'tag' the third party. This tactical benefit is increased if the directors of a company and the company itself are capable of conspiring with one another.[10]

Second, conspiracy may provide a residual remedy beyond the limitations of a specialised remedial regime. For instance, a statutory recovery mechanism may be limited to defendants who are domiciled within the jurisdiction or may only apply to conduct within the jurisdiction. This 'gap-filling' function may be seen in *Customs and Excise Commissioners v Total Network SL*.[11] There, the statutory mechanism for collecting unpaid VAT could not be used against the defendant

[6] For cross-border claims using this tort, see *Future Investments SA v Federation Internationale De Football Association* [2010] EWHC 1019 (Ch), [2010] ILPr 34; *Marex Financial v Sevilleja* [2017] EWHC 918 (Comm), [2017] 4 WLR 105.

[7] Expanded to include the institution of civil proceedings in *Willers v Joyce* [2016] UKSC 43, [2018] AC 779. As the tort applied to foreign *criminal* proceedings (see A Jones, AM Dugdale, and M Simpson (eds), *Clerk and Lindsell on Torts*, 23rd edn (London, Sweet & Maxwell, 2020), with second supplement (2019) [15-65]), it is suggested that it also may apply to the institution of foreign *civil* proceedings. There is a germ of this principle in admiralty law: see *Castrique v Behrens* (1861) 3 E & E 709; *Congentra v Sixteen Thirteen Marine* [2008] EWHC 1615 (Comm) [38]–[45].

[8] This remains a requirement in English law: *Secretary of State for Health v Servier* [2021] UKSC 24; *cf*, for Canada, *AI Enterprise v Bram Enterprise* [2014] 1 SCR 177 [87].

[9] *Palmer Birch (a partnership) v Lloyd* [2018] EWHC 2316 (TCC), [2018] 4 WLR 164 [183]–[186], [201].

[10] A recent decision favouring this possibility is *Palmer Birch*, *ibid*. See also *Thames Valley Housing Association v Elegant (Guernsey) Ltd* [2011] EWHC 1288 (Ch) and *Domestic & General Group v Global Appliance Care* [2019] EWHC 1550 (QB). See, for other corporate contexts, *McLeod v Rooney* [2009] CSOH 158, 2010 SLT 499 [22]; and more generally C Witting, 'Intra-Corporate Conspiracy: An Intriguing Prospect' [2013] *CLJ* 178. While the rule prohibiting reflective loss may prevent recovery of certain losses in this context (see, eg, *Magdeev v Tsvetkov* [2019] EWCA Civ 1802), it now is important to reconsider these decisions in light of the restriction of this rule only to claims for loss brought by shareholders. It does not apply to claims brought by creditors who do not hold shares: *Sevilleja v Marex Financial* [2020] UKSC 31, [2021] AC 39.

[11] *Customs and Excise Commissioners v Total Network SL* ('*Total Network*') [2008] UKHL 19, [2008] 1 AC 1174.

Spanish company, as it was not VAT registered in the United Kingdom. By a bare majority, it was held that it was legitimate to use the tort of unlawful means conspiracy to overcome the limitations of the statutory remedy.

Third, it may be used to reinforce orders issued by the English court in the face of debtor intransigence. Assume, for instance, that a creditor obtains judgment against a debtor in England, and also obtains a worldwide freezing order to aid the enforcement of that judgment. What is the creditor to do if the debtor and a third party combine to defeat that freezing order by dissipating assets in a manner which puts them outside of its reach? And what if the debtor has disappeared from the reach of the English courts at the time that the scheme is discovered? In *JSC BTA Bank v Khrapunov*,[12] the UK Supreme Court unanimously held that, in such circumstances, the creditor may, in principle, have a claim in unlawful means conspiracy against the debtor and the third party.

This chapter first considers the tort of conspiracy post-*Khrapunov* and suggests that the emphasis on the conspiratorial agreement and the 'absence of a just cause or excuse' placed therein obscures the operation of tortious conspiracy. The chapter then will offer the first detailed consideration of cross-border civil conspiracy. This issue sits at the intersection of tort law and private international law, but has received no sustained attention in the literature. This is despite the immense practical significance of such claims, which are growing in incidence. The chapter systematises the treatment of these claims across three issues. First, the chapter analyses how jurisdiction may be asserted against parties to a conspiracy claim. Second, it will argue that the scant analysis of choice of law for conspiracy which has been undertaken so far erroneously conflates two issues. The question of which law governs the framework of conspiratorial liability must be detached from the question of which law may supply the 'unlawful means'. Third, the chapter will consider this latter, novel, question. It argues that, in principle, foreign crimes or civil wrongs should be capable of supplying 'unlawful means' for the purposes of conspiracy, and the limited authority bearing on this question will be surveyed. While the chapter is written from the standpoint of English law, its observations hopefully illustrate the cross-border potency of the tort of conspiracy across the common law world.

II. The Present State of the Conspiracy Tort(s)

A. Background: *Khrapunov*

The UK Supreme Court handed down judgment in *Khrapunov* ten years after the speeches of the Appellate Committee of the House of Lords in *Total Network*,[13]

[12] *JSC BTA Bank v Khrapunov* ('*Khrapunov*') [2018] UKSC 19, [2020] AC 727. See also the somewhat similar case, reached without reference to *Khrapunov*, of *Talacko v Talacko* [2021] HCA 15 (conspiratorial design to place foreign properties out of hands of prospective judgment creditors).

[13] *Total Network* (n 11).

the last decision on civil conspiracy from the apex British court. The intervening decade demonstrated that the tort remains controversial. One key debate is the definition of 'unlawful means', and the relationship between the expansive definition given in *Total Network* and the narrower definition of the same term, in the context of the tort of causing loss by unlawful means, given ten months prior in *OBG v Allan*.[14] Another, more existential, debate concerns whether the tort of conspiracy is at all necessary, or whether it merely duplicates what can be achieved through the rules of joint tortfeasorship.[15]

Khrapunov concerned litigation on a behemothic scale. It involves Mukhtar Ablyazov and the fallout from the nationalisation of the Kazakh state bank (BTA) of which he once was chairman. Against a background of much political intrigue,[16] allegations of asset stripping were made against Ablyazov and he fled, initially to London, pursued all the while by BTA. All in all, Westlaw lists over 75 decisions involving BTA and Ablyazov. BTA obtained a default judgment for $4.6 billion, as well as a worldwide freezing order to assist in retrieving this sum.[17] Ilyas Khrapunov, Ablyazov's son-in-law, allegedly had directed connected Swiss, Russian, and Belizean companies to dissipate their assets beyond the effective scope of the bank's freezing order. The bank alleged that this amounted to unlawful means conspiracy. At that point, Ablayzov could not be traced, but Khrapunov was domiciled in Switzerland. As such, an action could be brought against Khrapunov in England if it were established that there was a good arguable case that a tort had been committed and that England was the place where the 'harmful event' occurred.

Teare J held that (i) a breach of a court order could not constitute wrongful means and (ii) that the English courts did not have jurisdiction over the conspiracy claim.[18] The Court of Appeal reversed both of these conclusions,[19]

[14] *OBG v Allan* [2007] UKHL 21, [2008] 1 AC 1. See, eg, R Stevens, *Torts and Rights* (Oxford, Oxford University Press, 2007) 190; H Carty, 'The Economic Torts in the 21st Century' (2008) 124 *LQR* 641; H Carty, *An Analysis of the Economic Torts*, 2nd edn (Oxford, Oxford University Press, 2010) 23–29, 164–81, 318–28; R Bagshaw, 'Lord Hoffmann and the Economic Torts' in PS Davies and J Pila (eds), *The Jurisprudence of Lord Hoffmann* (Oxford, Hart Publishing, 2015) 59 72–79; R Stevens, 'Salvaging the Law of Torts' in Davies and Pila (eds), *ibid* 85, 96; H Carty, 'The Tort of Conspiracy as a Can of Worms' in SG Pitel, E Chamberlain, and JW Neyers (eds), *Tort Law: Challenging Orthodoxy* (Oxford, Hart Publishing, 2013) 391, 401–404; H Carty, 'The Modern Functions of the Economic Torts: Reviewing the English, Canadian, Australian and New Zealand Position' [2015] *CLJ* 261; *cf* P-W Lee, 'Unravelling Civil Conspiracy' [2018] *Lloyd's Maritime and Commercial Law Quarterly* 508.

[15] See, eg, P Sales, 'The Tort of Conspiracy and Secondary Civil Liability' [1990] *CLJ* 491; H Carty, *An Analysis of the Economic Torts*, 1st edn (Oxford, Oxford University Press, 2001) 26 (not pursued in the second edition (2010)); Stevens, *Torts and Rights* (n 14) 249–51; PS Davies and Sir P Sales, 'Intentional Harm, Accessories and Conspiracies' (2018) 134 *LQR* 69 86–94.

[16] For more on the efforts of BTA Bank, see T Burgis, 'Spies, Lies, and the Oligarch: Inside London's Booming Secrets Industry' *Financial Times* (London, 28 September 2017), available at www.ft.com/content/1411b1a0-a310-11e7-9e4f-7f5e6a7c98a2.

[17] The scope of the freezing order was disputed before the Supreme Court: *JSC BTA Bank v Ablyazov (No 10)* [2015] UKSC 64, [2015] 1 WLR 4754.

[18] *JSC BTA Bank v Khrapunov* ('*Khrapunov*') [2016] EWHC 230 (Comm), [2017] QB 853, 859–82.

[19] *JSC BTA Bank v Khrapunov* ('*Khrapunov*') [2017] EWCA Civ 40, [2017] QB 853 882–914. Sales LJ gave the only substantive judgment, with which Gloster and Beatson LJJ concurred.

but Khrapunov was granted permission to appeal both grounds by the Supreme Court.[20] That Court's conclusions as to the domestic tort question will now be discussed; this chapter will consider the jurisdiction outcome below.

B. Conspiracy: All in the Agreement?

Previously, the wrongdoing in civil conspiracy was thought to arise when actions were taken pursuant to the agreement.[21] This differs from the position in criminal conspiracy, where 'the essence of the crime is the agreement or understanding that the parties will act unlawfully, whether or not it is implemented'.[22] The judgment in *Khrapunov* aligned civil and criminal conspiracy, observing that the requirement for actions pursuant to the agreement was not the 'essence' of the tort of conspiracy, but rather a manifestation of the general notion that a tort must cause loss before 'the cause of action will be complete'.[23]

This reorientation was undertaken seemingly for two reasons. First, the reconfiguration of conspiracy may serve to counter the objections levelled at the very existence of the tort, which view it as a redundant duplication of the doctrine of joint tortfeasorship. In joint tortfeasorship, the wrongdoing occurs when the joint tortfeasors take concerted acts pursuant to a common design; whereas, in the reconfigured guise of conspiracy, the wrongdoing is all bottled up in the conspiratorial agreement.[24] The degree of difference here is slight, and it may respectfully be suggested that the three reasons advanced for the survival of the conspiracy tort do not remove force from the redundancy objection. First, the fact that conspiracy is 'actionable as a distinct tort'[25] simply describes, and does not justify, the present position. If that distinct tort was lost, joint tortfeasorship would – depending on the scope accorded to 'unlawful means' – cover the same ground.[26] Second, the fact that liability for civil conspiracy is primary, and not secondary or accessory, again simply restates the present position. Of course, it is too much to expect the Supreme Court to engage with this question which was, at best, tangentially related to an issue to be determined on a summary basis; but the only justification given

[20] *Khrapunov* (UKSC) (n 12). Judgment jointly was given by Lords Sumption and Lloyd-Jones JJSC, with the concurrence of Lord Mance DPSC and Lords Hodge and Briggs JJSC.

[21] *Lonhro v Shell Petroleum* [1982] AC 173 188 (Lord Diplock). See also eg *Marrinan v Vibart* [1963] 1 QB 234 238–29; *Midland Bank v Green (No 3)* [1979] 1 Ch 483 524; *Grupo Torras SA v Al-Sabah (No 5)* [1999] CLC 1469 1635–37; *Kuwait Oil Tanker Co v Al-Bader (No 3)* [2000] 2 All ER (Comm) 271 [110].

[22] *Khrapunov* (UKSC) (n 12) [9].

[23] *Ibid.*

[24] *Ibid.*

[25] *Ibid.*

[26] *cf* the position in criminal law, where a separate crime of conspiracy is necessary because a decision by *one* party to commit a crime is not in itself punishable, and therefore accessorial liability cannot attach to such a decision. In tort, however, the availability of injunctive relief does not depend on whether an independent or accessorial approach to conspiracy is taken.

for the primary nature of liability is the citation of previous apex authority. Third, it is said that 'the fact of combination may alter the legal character and consequences of the overt acts'.[27] But, remedially, it is difficult to envisage a situation in which the damages awarded for an unlawful means conspiracy would differ from those awarded in respect of the joint commission of the wrongful acts.[28]

The second, less explicit, reason is that focussing on the agreement – as opposed to the concerted acts – simplifies the jurisdictional analysis. This question – and choice of law considerations – will be returned to below, but for now it may be worth considering whether there are any other procedural consequences of this reconceptualisation. It makes no difference for limitation purposes, as the clock runs from when the cause of action accrues,[29] which, as can be inferred from what is said by the UK Supreme Court, is the date on which loss is caused. Nor does it seem that the re-orientation of conspiracy to focus on the agreement has altered the circumstances in which a *qua timet* injunction will be granted.[30] Therefore, aside from private international law implications, the reformulation may be of little practical import.

C. Just Cause or Excuse?

Having altered traditional understandings of conspiratorial liability, the Supreme Court then sought to explain when such an agreement would be actionable. As is well known, there are two forms of tortious conspiracy. With lawful means conspiracy, an agreement to carry out acts which the parties otherwise would be at liberty to perform may be actionable if the *predominant* motive behind those acts is to injure the claimant.[31] By contrast, if unlawful means are used, the intentionality requirement is relaxed: all that must be shown is that the conspirators employing those means had *an* intention to injure the claimant.[32]

In *Khrapunov*, the Supreme Court described both forms of conspiracy as being actionable in the 'absence of a just cause or excuse'.[33] The starting point

[27] *Khrapunov* (UKSC) (n 12) [9].

[28] For prescient criticisms of this justification, see Davies and Sales (n 15) 91–93. See also *easyGroup v Easyfly* [2020] EWHC 40 (Ch) [85] (theoretical difference between conspiracy and joint tortfeasorship recognised, but practical difference 'not immediately evident').

[29] *Limitation Act 1980* s 2(1).

[30] In *Ineos Upstream v Persons Unknown* [2019] EWCA Civ 515, [2019] 4 WLR 100, it still was stated, post-*Khrapunov*, that 'it is of the essence of the tort that it must cause damage': [40]. See latterly *Cuadrilla Bowland v Persons Unknown* [2020] EWCA Civ 9, [2020] 4 WLR 29 [69], where it was held that a *qua timet* injunction must be limited to conduct which is intended to cause damage to the claimant.

[31] *Quinn v Leathen* [1901] AC 495; *Crofter Hand Woven Harris Tweed Co Ltd v Veitch* ('*Veitch*') [1942] AC 435.

[32] *Lonhro v Al Fayed (No 1)* [1992] 1 AC 448.

[33] *Khrapunov* (UKSC) (n 12) [10]. The formulation is resurrected from *Veitch* (n 31).

for *lawful* means conspiracy is that '[a] person has a right to advance his own interests by lawful means even if the foreseeable consequence is to damage the interests of others'.[34] That 'right affords a just cause or excuse'.[35] But there is no such excuse where, rather than being a foreseeable consequence, damage to the interest of others is the predominantly-intended object of the conspirator's actions. With *unlawful* means conspiracy, the Supreme Court observed that there is no right to 'seek to advance [one's own] interests by unlawful means',[36] and therefore the use of unlawful means necessarily connotes the absence of a 'just cause or excuse'.

With respect, there is little to commend a test based on the lack of 'just cause or excuse'. In the lawful means context, why must – in the absence of a predominant intention to injure – a party rely on the 'right'[37] to advance their interest by legitimate means to 'excuse' actions which they were at liberty to conduct in the first place? The pursuit of legitimate ends need not be excused. As for unlawful means, there is little explanatory force in the statement that a defendant has 'no right' to advance their interests by unlawful means. For one, this suggests that it is the employment of unlawful means by themselves which is actionable. But there is no general tort of infliction of loss by unlawful means,[38] and, in the conspiracy context, those unlawful means still must be accompanied by an intention to injure the claimant.

Moreover, the test does not assist much in determining what constitutes unlawful means. The judgment simply states that the determination of when such means will negate a 'just cause or excuse' pivots on, first, 'the nature of the unlawfulness' and, second, 'its relationship with the resultant damage to the claimant'.[39] Leaving aside the somewhat jarring notion that targeted unlawful conduct may in some circumstances be excusable, the second limb effectively is a 'targeting' test: the unlawful means must actually be the instrumentality through which the claimant is harmed. As for the first limb, there is little exploration of this in the Supreme Court's judgment. In fact, the reasoning driving the conclusion that the contemptuous violation of a freezing order sufficed as unlawful means is, with respect, opaque. The judgment focusses on the intent to harm the bank through defeating its ability fully to enforce its claim, and the correlation between the bank's loss and Abylazov's gain, before stating that 'we conclude that the cause of action in conspiracy to injure the bank by unlawful means is made out'.[40]

[34] *Ibid.*
[35] *Ibid.*
[36] *Ibid.*
[37] The juridical classification of this as a 'right' can be doubted; what, for instance, is the correlative duty, and by who is it owed? The formulation calls to mind Hohfeld's criticisms of the usage of 'right' in *Allen v Flood* [1898] AC 1 and *Quinn* (n 31): WH Hohfeld, 'Some Fundamental Legal Conceptions as Applied in Judicial Reasoning' (1913) 23(1) *Yale Law Journal* 16, 33.
[38] At least, if Lord Hoffmann's approach in *OBG* (n 14) is followed. *cf* P Sales and D Stilitz, 'Intentional Infliction of Harm by Unlawful Means' (2001) 115 *LQR* 411.
[39] *Khrapunov* (UKSC) (n 12) [11].
[40] *Ibid* [16].

Little is said about the nature of instrumentality through which this intention was targeted at the claimant. A substantial part of the judgment concerns the rejection of the argument that the public policy behind denying the independent actionability of contempt of court also compelled a refusal of the actionability of a conspiracy founded on contempt.[41] However, this presupposed that, all other things being equal, contempt would furnish unlawful means to which conspiratorial liability might attach. There is no discussion of why this might be so: is it because contempt is penal in nature; or because the acts deliberately were directed at frustrating the process of the English court; or because the means were directed at impeding the effect of an order which had been obtained by the claimant? Would any of these singularly deny a 'just cause or excuse' for the combination, or does the conclusion depend on the cumulation of some of these factors? Which sources generally may furnish a just cause or excuse? And what is the distinction – if any – between a cause (or 'just cause'?) and an excuse?

The test was elaborated upon in *Palmer Birch v Lloyd*,[42] but no real answers to these questions were forthcoming. There, HHJ Judge Russen QC observed that, while the test was not immediately illuminating, its essence was that:

> there may be categories of unlawfulness which a combiner may be excused from agreeing to perpetrate either because of the classification of the unlawful act (identified by reference to the purpose or duty which it subverts) or because it is too incidental to the claimant's position to be actionable.[43]

The parenthetical gloss on *Khrapunov* is not explicit in the judgment of the UK Supreme Court. One of the questions in *Palmer Birch* was whether a breach of contract constituted 'unlawful means'. Unfortunately, the positive conclusion on this point is not reached through the application of the 'just cause or excuse' test or the gloss. It instead is based on the view that the inducement tort may not always provide a remedy against additional parties behind a concerted effort to induce a breach of the contract.[44] The 'purpose or duty' subverted by a breach of contract clearly is a very specific one where that duty has been voluntarily assumed towards the claimant by (at least one of) the conspirators, and so it is justifiable to treat such a breach as a form of 'unlawful means'.

The formulation of the test also gives rise to the impression that unlawful means conspiracy may have a defence of justification. In *Palmer Birch*, the judge rejected this: as conspiracy was a tort of primary liability, liability would only arise where 'the defendant has himself been guilty of conduct … which is to be categorised as independently actionable …'[45] Instead, justification within conspiracy

[41] *Ibid* [17]–[24].

[42] *Palmer Birch* (n 9).

[43] *Ibid* [189]. *Cf Global Display Solutions Ltd v NCR Financial Solutions Group Ltd* [2021] EWHC 1119 (Comm) [125] (rejecting, without deciding the general availability of, potential defence of justification in relation to the particular facts of that case, which involved a conspiracy to commit deceit).

[44] *Ibid* [229]–[235], especially [232].

[45] *Ibid* [185].

would be accommodated within both the intentionality requirement and the need for unlawful means: the intentional targeting of a claimant through unlawful means never could be justified, as there always would be an absence of 'just cause or excuse' in such a circumstance.[46] Again, however, this gives little indication of how the new test is to be applied in determining the threshold for *unlawful* means.

D. Knowledge?

Another question arising is whether a lack of knowledge of the fact of unlawfulness on the part of a conspirator constitutes a 'just cause or excuse'. Prior to *Khrapunov*, there was Court of Appeal authority favouring[47] and opposing[48] such a conclusion. The issue since has been considered in two decisions of interest.[49] The first decision – another judgment of HHJ Judge Russen QC – *Stobart Group v Tinkler*[50] concerned alleged unlawful means in the form of breaches of contract and fiduciary duties. The judge held that it was irrelevant that the conspirators were unaware of the fact that their conduct amounted to these breaches.[51] The question was approached not as one of intention, but one concerning the scope of unlawful means.[52] To establish liability for conspiracy, 'it is enough to show that [the conspirator] had sufficient knowledge of the essential facts, that acts which were unlawful were to be carried out so as to implicate him in liability for them'.[53] The judge clearly believed that a stricter test dependent on the defendant's knowledge of legality would be inappropriate where clear intention to harm the claimant was present on the facts.[54]

However, a more granular conclusion was reached in *The Racing Partnership v Done Brothers (Cash Betting)*.[55] In this case, the alleged unlawful means were breaches of confidence. Zacaroli J concluded that the claimant required to prove that the conspirators knowingly perpetrated a breach of confidence before liability would attach.[56] However, His Lordship did not see this as a necessary requirement in all forms of unlawful conspiracy claims, stating that:

> … It might well be said that it is consistent with enforcing basic standards of behaviour to find a person who conspires to perform criminal acts liable even if … he or she did

[46] *Ibid* [190]–[192].
[47] *British Industrial Plastics v Ferguson* [1938] 4 All ER 504; *Meretz Investments NV v ACP Ltd* [2007] EWCA Civ 1303, [2008] Ch 244.
[48] *Belmont Finance v Williams Furniture* [1980] 1 All ER 393.
[49] The point was left open in *Alesco Risk Management Services v Bishopsgate Insurance Brokers* [2019] EWHC 2839 (QB).
[50] *Stobart Group v Tinkler* [2019] EWHC 258 (Comm).
[51] *Ibid* [554]–[573]
[52] *Ibid* [553]–[555].
[53] *Ibid* [573].
[54] *Ibid* [568], [573].
[55] *The Racing Partnership v Done Brothers (Cash Betting)* [2019] EWHC 2678 (Ch), [2020] Ch 289.
[56] *Ibid* [258]–[287].

> not know that the acts were unlawful. But where … the unlawful conduct consists of infringing the claimant's private law rights, then I consider it is consistent with enforcing basic standards of civilised behaviour that a person is liable for conspiring to injure through such unlawful means only if he or she knows (to the requisite standard) that the claimant's rights are being infringed.[57]

His Lordship thought it reasonable to allow an honest belief in the civil lawfulness of one's actions to negate liability, not least because otherwise the tort of conspiracy potentially would 'risk trespassing on legitimate competitive business practices'.[58] His Lordship also inclined towards the view that the knowledge of wrongdoing must be shared by at least two parties to the conspiracy.[59]

However, Zacaroli J's judgment was reversed on this point by a majority in the Court of Appeal.[60] Arnold LJ concluded that the passages in prior Court of Appeal authorities which suggest that knowledge of unlawfulness on the part of at least one of the conspirators was a requirement of the tort of conspiracy were *obiter* on that point and need not be followed.[61] Knowledge of unlawfulness is not a requirement in the realms of criminal conspiracy,[62] and Arnold LJ did not see any reason why the approach to tortious conspiracy should be different.[63] His Lordship also observed, following the affirmation in *Khrapunov*, that conspiratorial liability is not a form of accessory liability, that the test for liability should not depend on whether the underlying unlawful means required the particular form of mental element to be independently actionable or prosecutable.[64]

Turning to broader concerns, Arnold LJ recalled the axiom that 'ignorance of the law is generally no defence in either crime or in the civil law' and opined there was no cause to create an exception for the tort of conspiracy.[65] Counsel had also argued that a lack of a knowledge requirement in the unlawful means conspiracy court would allow parties and pleaders to get around the stricter requirements of the inducing breach of contract tort which did require knowledge to be established. Arnold LJ thought that the differences between the two torts were sufficient to guard against any evasive pleading.[66] Phillips LJ, while noting that the 'interplay

[57] *Ibid* [277].

[58] *Ibid* [284]. See also *Pepe's Piri Piri v Junaid* [2019] EWHC 2097 (QB), where, at [76], the judge proceeded (without argument or discussion) on the basis that knowledge that the defendants would be bringing about a breach of contract was necessary to establish an unlawful means conspiracy.

[59] *Ibid* [293].

[60] *The Racing Partnership v Done Brothers (Cash Betting)* [2020] EWCA Civ 1300, [2021] FSR 2.

[61] *Ibid* [122]; [133]–[134] (preferring the decision in *Belmont Finance* (n 48) to *British Industrial Plastics* (n 47), as the point was not in issue in the latter case); [135]–[139] (characterising the observations on this point in *Meretz* (n 47) as *obiter*, relating to intention, and without reference to prior authority on the question in the context of tortious conspiracy). Phillips LJ concurred with these observations at [171].

[62] *Churchill v Walton* [1982] 2 AC 224, discussed in *ibid* [123]–[126].

[63] *The Racing Partnership* (n 60) [134]. Lewison LJ opined to the opposite effect at [231].

[64] *Ibid.*

[65] *Ibid* [141].

[66] *Ibid* [142].

between unlawful means conspiracy and inducing breach of contract … may merit further examination in a future case', nevertheless observed that the ability of a defendant to take advantage of the lower standard in the conspiracy context might not be one which could be exercised – or abused – in many cases.[67] Finally, Arnold LJ cast doubt on the value of Zacaroli J's distinction between crimes and infringement of private law rights, noting that both the criminal and the civil law admitted strict liability wrongdoing.[68] However, in dissent on this point,[69] Lewison LJ developed the reasoning of Zacaroli J and strongly was of the opinion that a knowledge requirement should be imposed where the unlawful means constituted only a breach of a private right as these did not have 'the same societal effect' as a violation of the criminal law.[70]

It seems settled that knowledge need not be a requirement where the means are unlawful in criminal terms, but there is less unanimity as to whether knowledge is required where the means are civilly wrongful. One may doubt whether the drawing of such distinctions within the tort is helpful. Requiring 'enlightened' intention, ie the intention to harm the claimant through means which are knowingly breaches of private law duties – for civilly unlawful means may be consistent with the tort of inducing breach of contract, but the accessory nature of that tort should caution against making too ready a comparison with the tort of conspiracy. In any event, this dispute demonstrates how hollow the 'just cause or excuse' test is: as Lewison LJ states in his dissenting judgment, the test 'does not answer … the question whether it is a "just excuse" that the actor did not intend to use unlawful means; and did not appreciate that the means that were used were in fact unlawful'.[71]

E. What Remains of Lawful Means Conspiracy?

One situation which clearly involves an absence of a just cause or excuse is where the conspirators act with the predominant motive of injuring the claimant. But the Ablyazov saga also demonstrates just how narrow the tort of lawful means conspiracy is.[72] An experienced Lord Justice in one branch of the litigation remarked that it was 'difficult to imagine a party to commercial litigation who has acted with more cynicism, opportunism and deviousness towards court orders than Mr Ablyazov'.[73] The same sentiment might – if the alleged facts were proven – be expressed about Mr Khrapunov: after all, with the knowledge of (i) the bank's

[67] *Ibid* [171]. Lewison LJ was far more concerned by this point in his dissent: [240]–[245].
[68] *Ibid* [143].
[69] *Ibid* [231]–[265].
[70] *Ibid* [264].
[71] *Ibid* [224].
[72] For a general exploration of this tort, and its relationship with other malice-orientated torts, see J Murphy, 'Malice as an Ingredient of Tort Liability' [2019] *CLJ* 355.
[73] *JSC BTA Bank v Ablyazov (No 8)* [2012] EWCA Civ 1411, [2013] 1 WLR 1331 [202] (Maurice Kay LJ).

claims and (ii) the orders of the English court, he allegedly assisted his father-in-law by dissipating corporate assets to put these beyond the scope of the orders of the Court in an attempt to defeat, devalue, or at least impede the enforcement of the bank's claim. Nevertheless, the strictness of the 'predominant motive' test is such that it was thought so obvious that the defendants were acting with the predominant motive of self-preservation that the claimants did not raise lawful means conspiracy at first instance. Moreover, the observations of Sales LJ[74] and the UK Supreme Court[75] suggest that the illegitimacy of the actions are neither here nor there.[76] So long as their actions would bring some benefit to themselves, then that self-benefit, and not injury to the claimant, constituted the predominant motive. Immoral rationality cannot ground a claim in lawful means conspiracy: what is required is conduct which has no rational benefit to the defendant. Given that a human being rarely cuts off her own nose to spite her face, the lawful means variety of conspiracy seems liable – at long last – to fall into desuetude.

F. Conclusion

Although the judgment on the substantive law of tort in *Khrapunov* perhaps raises more questions than it answers, it clearly does evidence the practical utility of the tort of conspiracy in cross-border cases. First, it demonstrates that conspiracy may be used to fortify freezing orders, to provide a civil violation for their transgression over and above the normal sanction of contempt of court. It cannot be the case that the reasoning within is limited to breaches of a freezing order: the same result may follow in respect of the breach of any form of court order: say, for instance, an anti-suit injunction. The case also demonstrates the 'gap-filling' function of conspiracy. Typically, a worldwide freezing order contains a provision precluding its having effects on third parties outside of the jurisdiction.[77] Mr Khrapunov was protected by the benefit of such a provision,[78] but, nevertheless, the tort of conspiracy subjected him to (non-penal) consequences for facilitating a breach of the order.[79] That conclusion makes the tort of conspiracy a valuable weapon in the creditor's armoury in cross-border litigation.

It therefore is unfortunate that the rules of jurisdiction and choice of law which apply to conspiracy claims have – until now – not been the subject of sustained discussion. The focus of this chapter now moves away from the domestic

[74] *Khrapunov* (EWCA) (n 19) [10]–[11].

[75] *Khrapunov* (UKSC) (n 12) [16].

[76] If one were minded to argue for the retention of lawful means conspiracy, it might be enquired whether this reasoning overlooks the emphasis in the constitutive authorities on the need for the conspirator's predominant interest to be a *legitimate* one before liability will attach: see, eg *Veitch* (n 31) 445, 447 ('the lawful protection … of any lawful interest …' or the '*bona fides* of the avowed purpose': Viscount Simon LC); 469 ('legitimate benefit': Lord Wright).

[77] The so-called *Babanaft* proviso: *Babanaft International v Bassante* [1990] Ch 41.

[78] Confirmed by *Khrapunov* (EWCA) (n 19) [14].

[79] *Ibid* [51].

formulation of the conspiracy torts, and instead considers the application of private international law rules to a conspiracy claim. The next section considers the jurisdictional rules which determine where such claims should be brought; the next section how choice of law rules operate in the conspiracy context. This chapter then will return to the 'just cause or excuse' test in the context of asking whether norms from a foreign legal system may undermine a conspirator's claim to justification.

III. Jurisdiction

A. Introduction

Three types of jurisdictional rule demand specific consideration when dealing with conspiracy: rules which clothe the court with jurisdiction over all of the conspirators on the basis that at least one of the defendants is amenable to the jurisdiction of the court; rules which focus on the tortious nature of conspiracy; and, finally, those which apply where the conspiracy claim may be said to relate to a contract or be caught by a contractual choice of court provision. This section will consider not only the rules under the English national rules of jurisdiction, but also will still consider the position under the Brussels I Recast Regulation[80] despite the cessation of its direct effect following Brexit. This is for three reasons: first, there is the possibility that those rules will again become relevant if the UK again accedes to the Lugano Convention;[81] second, the Scottish national rules of jurisdiction in Schedule 8 of the *Civil Jurisdiction and Judgments Act 1982* are closely mirrored on the Brussels rules; and, third, the Brussels case law has been influential in the context of the English national rules of jurisdiction for tort, and remain important in determining the application of the retained choice of law rules for non-contractual obligations.[82]

B. Procedural Consolidation: Brussels I Recast, Art 8 and CPR PD 6B para 3.1(3) ('Necessary or Proper Party')

As a conspiracy claim often will involve a multiplicity of defendants, grounds of jurisdiction which permit the procedural consolidation of actions against multiple parties are of particular importance. Under the Brussels I Recast, if one of the

[80] *Regulation (EU) No 1215/2012 of the European Parliament and of the Council of 12 December 2012 on Jurisdiction and the Recognition and Enforcement of Judgments in Civil and Commercial Matters* (recast) [2012] OJ 351/1.

[81] Although the prospects of this appear dim in light of the EU Commission's refusal to give consent to the UK's accession: Commission, *Communication – Assessment on the application of the United Kingdom of Great Britain and Northern Ireland to accede to the 2007 Lugano Convention* COM(2021) 222 final.

[82] See section IV.B.ii.

conspirators was shown to be domiciled[83] in a Member State,[84] then it was possible for the claimant[85] to use Article 8(1) of the Brussels I Recast Regulation to establish jurisdiction over co-conspirators who were domiciled in other Member States; in fact, much recent jurisprudence on Article 8(1) has concerned conspiracy claims. The provision requires that the claims against the defendants be 'so closely connected that it is expedient to hear and determine them together to avoid the risk of irreconcilable judgments resulting from separate proceedings'.

It has been observed that '[t]he prospect of irreconcilable findings in different courts on relevant issues of fact in an alleged conspiracy is an unpalatable one',[86] and the risk is increased in the conspiracy context by the 'multiple overlapping questions of fact and law' which are presented by the claims against each defendant.[87] All that this requires is that there is a serious issue to be tried against the anchor conspirator.[88] There is no need to establish that there is a serious issue to be tried as against the non-domiciled co-conspirators[89] and the test may be 'plainly satisfied' where the anchor claim is one of conspiracy.[90] This may even be established if the applicable law views the liability of the co-conspirators on an individual, as opposed to accessory or combinational, basis.[91] It is difficult to locate a case in which the English courts have held that an action against one conspirator is not 'so closely connected' with the action against the anchor conspirator:[92] the sole case refusing that it was 'expedient' to hear the case against the conspirator and the anchor defendant together was because in truth no claim in conspiracy was levelled against the latter.[93] A similarly permissive approach to Article 8(1) has been taken

[83] For an application of the English test for civil and commercial domicile in the conspiracy context, see *Khrapunov* (EWCA) (n 19) [57]–[65]; *Tugushev v Orlov* [2019] EWHC 645 (Comm) [112]–[185].

[84] The relevant time is when the proceedings originally are issued against the anchor defendant: *Petrotrade Inc v Smith* [1999] 1 WLR 457. Service on the anchor defendant need not, however, come before service on the co-conspirators: *Canada Trust v Stolzenberg (No 2)* [2002] 1 AC 1.

[85] The claimant, of course, must be the same in respect of each of the advanced claims: *Madoff Securities International v Raven* [2011] EWHC 3102 (Comm), [2012] 2 All ER (Comm) 634.

[86] *Sabbagh v Khoury* [2017] EWCA Civ 1120 [222].

[87] *Ibid* [221].

[88] *Ibid* [68] (Gloster LJ on this point dissented on the basis that it should not be necessary to demonstrate a serious issue to be tried against the anchor defendant). For further application in the conspiracy context, [2019] EWHC 2414 (Comm).

[89] *Joint Stock Company 'Aeroflot-Russian Airlines' v Berezovsky* [2013] EWCA Civ 785 [105]–[110] (Aikens LJ).

[90] *Ibid* [111]–[113].

[91] See the first instance judgment of Carr J in *Sabbagh v Khoury* [2014] EWHC 3233 (Comm) [219]–[224], a point which was not challenged before the Court of Appeal (see (n 86) [20]).

[92] See the following cases on Art 8(1) or its antecedents: *Bank of Tokyo-Mitsubishi v Baskan Gida Saayi Ve Pazarlama* [2004] EWHC 945 (Ch) (expediency found as defendants involved in 'single conspiracy': [216]–[217], [221]); *Montani v First Directors* [2006] IEHC 92, [2008] ILPr 2 (expediency found: [25]–[26]); *Apax Global Payment & Technologies v Morina* [2011] EWHC 2983 (expediency found: [13]–[14]); *Sibir v Haener* [2012] EWHC 1844 (QB) (expediency conceded: [12]) *Linuzs and Others v Latmar* [2013] EWCA Civ 4 (expediency found: [35]–[46]); *Tchenguiz v Grant Thornton UK LLP* [2015] EWHC 1864 (Comm) (expediency conceded: [13]); *Media-Saturn Holding GmbH v Toshiba* [2019] EWHC 1095 (Ch) ([269]–[283]).

[93] *Shahar v Tsitsekkos and Others* [2004] EWHC 2659 (Ch) [54].

in the competition law context in relation to cartels.[94] Moreover, it has been held that it is irrelevant if the proceedings against the anchor conspirator have been instituted solely to remove the other conspirators from their domiciliary fora.[95]

Post-Brexit, the English national rules retain a provision similar to Article 8(1) in the form of the 'necessary or proper party' gateway under the service out of the jurisdiction regime.[96] This requires:[97]

i. a real issue to be tried between the claimant and the anchor defendant which it is reasonable for the court to try;[98]
ii. that there is a 'good arguable case' that the third party who is domiciled outside of England is a 'necessary or proper party' to that claim;[99] and
iii. that England is clearly or distinctly the appropriate forum in which for the action to proceed.[100]

It is readily accepted that one co-conspirator is a necessary or proper party to a conspiracy claim against an anchor defendant.[101] This provision is broader than Article 8 of Brussels I Recast as jurisdiction over the anchor defendant need not be based on its domicile; such jurisdiction might, for instance, also be based on the tortious jurisdiction ground discussed in the next section.

C. Tort: Brussels I Recast Art 7(2) and CPR PD 6B para 3.1(9)

It may be, however, that there is no anchor defendant domiciled in England, and therefore the conspiracy claim must be brought on some other basis.

[94] *Cooper Tire & Rubber Company Europe v DOW Deutschland* [2010] EWCA Civ 864 (expediency 'self-evident': [44]); *Nokia v AU Optronics* [2012] EWHC 731 (Ch) (expediency not challenged); *Cartel Damage Claims (CDC) Hydrogen Peroxide SA v Akzo Nobel NV* (Case C-352/13) [2015] QB 906.

[95] *JSC Commercial Bank Privatbank v Kolomoisky* [2019] EWCA Civ 1708 (David Richards and Flaux LJJ; Newey LJ dissenting).

[96] Civil Procedure Rules (CPR) Practice Direction (PD) 6B, para 3.1(3).

[97] See, eg, *AK Investment CJSC v Kyrgz Mobil Tel* [2011] UKPC 7, [2012] 1 WLR 1804 [71].

[98] This presupposes that jurisdiction may be established against the anchor defendant on some other basis. Note that it will not be reasonable for the court to try such an action if it deems the claimants to already have submitted to foreign proceedings on essentially the same point: see, for the conspiracy context, *Erste Group Bank AG London v JSC VMZ Red October* [2015] EWCA Civ 379 [59]–[60], [77]–[82].

[99] Which will be the case if the claims against all parties involve 'one investigation', are 'closely bound up', and/or share a 'common thread': *AK Investment* (n 97) [87].

[100] See section III.E.

[101] *Alliance Bank JSC v Aquanta* [2012] EWCA Civ 1588, [2013] 1 All ER (Comm) 819 [76] (*obiter* as no anchor defendant amenable to jurisdiction of court); *Republic of Angola v Perfectbit Ltd* [2018] EWHC 965 (Comm) (concession recorded at [112]); *Gulf Air v One Inflight Ltd* [2018] EWHC 1019 (Comm) [32] ('little doubt' that actions against co-conspirators shared common thread); *Eurasia Sports Ltd v Tsai* [2018] EWCA Civ 1742, [2018] 1 WLR 6089 [49] (co-conspirator 'obviously' a proper party); *Tugushev* (n 83) [253] (conspiracy claims all 'inextricably bound up, [arose] from the same facts and [required] a common inquiry'); *ED&F Man Capital Markets v Come Harvest Holdings* [2019] EWHC 1661 (Comm) (concession recorded at [37]); *Domestic and General Group v Premier Protect Holdings* [2021] EWHC 135 (QB) [27]. See also, for a cartel under EU competition law, *Iiyama (UK) v Samsung Electronics* [2018] EWCA Civ 220.

The most logical basis would be the tortious jurisdiction grounds. Brussels I Recast, Article 7(2)[102] permitted a claim to be brought in England if this was the place where 'the harmful event occurred or may occur', which, as is well known, has been interpreted as encompassing both the place (a) where the event giving rise to the harm occurred and (b) where the ensuing damage directly was felt. In *Khrapunov*, location (a) was interpreted for conspiracy as coinciding with the 'place where the conspiratorial agreement was made …'[103] As for location (b), the relevant direct damage was identified as the reduced ability of the creditor to execute against the assets, which occurred in the jurisdictions where the assets were located prior to their dissipation.[104]

Outside the purview of the EU rules, the service out of the tortious gateway[105] is bifurcated similarly to Article 7(2): it must either be shown that damage was sustained in England,[106] or that the damage sustained resulted from an act committed or to be committed within England.[107] The application of the second limb to a conspiracy claim is relatively settled. It has been held that this limb requires a 'substantial and efficacious act' within England.[108] Recently, *Khrapunov* has been applied by analogy to the effect that the conspiratorial agreement is such an act, so therefore the hatching of a conspiracy in England will be enough to trigger this part of the gateway.[109]

What is more unclear is the application of the first limb, which requires damage to be sustained in England. Is this satisfied – as with Article 7(2) – only by the occurrence of *direct* damage in England, or does indirect or consequential damage suffice? While, in the personal injury context, earlier decisions countenanced a more permissive approach to 'indirect damage', the Court of Appeal in *Erste* cautioned against this expansiveness in the conspiracy context.[110] However, it did not go so far as to overrule these earlier decisions.[111] Nevertheless, in *Eurasia Sports Ltd v Aguad*, it was held that it was necessary to show that *direct* damage

[102] See also, for Scotland, *Civil Jurisdiction and Judgments Act 1982*, Sch 8, Rule 2(c).

[103] *Khrapunov* (UKSC) (n 12) [41]; *cf Shahar* (n 93) [56], which appears to focus on the acts taken pursuant to the conspiracy. On the evidence required to prove the location of the place where the agreement is entered, see *LIC Communications v VTB Capital* [2019] EWHC 1747 (Comm) [294]–[296].

[104] *Khrapunov* (EWCA) (n 19) [69]. The UK Supreme Court refused to permit a cross-appeal on this basis: *Khrapunov* (UKSC) (n 12) [29]. See also *Bank of Tokyo-Mitsubishi v Baskan Gida Saayi Ve Pazarlama* [2004] EWHC 945 (Ch) [219]; *Sunderland Marine Mutual Insurance Company v Wiseman* [2007] EWHC 1460 (Comm) [36]; *Actial Farmaceutica LDA v De Simone* [2016] EWCA Civ 1311 [34]–[37]; *LIC Communications, ibid* [297]–[299]; *easyGroup* (n 28) [142]–[151].

[105] CPR PD 6B para 3.1(9)(a) and (b).

[106] Broadly equating to location (b) under Art 7(2).

[107] Broadly equating to location (a) under Art 7(2).

[108] *Metall und Rohstoff v Donaldson Lufkin & Jenette* [1990] 1 QB 391 437.

[109] *Tugushev* (n 83) [211]–[215]. See also the similar conclusion in *Claimants Listed in Schedule 1 v Spence* [2021] EWHC 276 (Comm) [75].

[110] *Erste* (EWCA) (n 98) [104]. See also *ABCI v Banque Franco-Tunisienne* [2003] EWCA Civ 205 [44]–[45], focussing on *direct* damage in its application of the tort gateway to a conspiracy claim (payment made from Geneva bank account).

[111] *Ibid* [105].

had occurred in England before the tort gateway would be satisfied on this basis in respect of a conspiracy claim.[112] The Court of Appeal did not refer to *Erste*, but proceeded on the basis that it would not follow the earlier, more claimant-friendly line of authority. There is no mention of the sentiments of the majority of the UK Supreme Court in *Brownlie v Four Seasons Holdings Inc*[113] which adopted – in *obiter* comments[114] – reasoning resuscitating the wide scope for indirect damage to satisfy the tort gateway, even, it seems, in respect of financial loss.[115] Following *Brownlie*, there are signs that, despite its adoption in *Eurasia Sports*, first instance decisions in the conspiracy context are inclining away from the conflation of the tort gateway and Article 7(2).[116]

The point therefore requires clarification. The present situation appears to treat economic loss differently from physical or psychiatric injury, which is unprincipled at the jurisdiction stage. This is especially so where there exists the further requirement to show that England is the *forum conveneiens*,[117] which curtails the excesses of founding jurisdiction on indirect loss. When the general approach to damage under the tort gateway eventually is confirmed, this distinction at the very least should be rejected: direct damage either should be unnecessary for founding jurisdiction in England for all torts or should be necessary when applying the tort gateway to all torts. We will return to the problem of identification of damage in section IV.B.ii. below in considering choice of law for conspiracy claims.

D. Contract?

Can a claim in conspiracy be brought under a jurisdiction or arbitration agreement between the parties? It has been held that a clause through which parties agreed to 'submit any potential disputes regarding the performance or the interpretation of this Contract' to arbitration in Paris covered a tortious claim formulated in conspiracy based on the defendant's attempts to undermine the main contract.[118] A similar conclusion was reached in respect of cartel conspiracy claims where the clause between the parties read that '[any] disputes related to this Agreement or its enforcement shall be resolved and settled by arbitration'.[119] Therefore, if the

[112] *Eurasia Sports Ltd v Aguad* [2018] EWCA Civ 1742, [2018] 1 WLR 6089 [21].

[113] *Brownlie v Four Seasons Holdings Inc* [2017] UKSC 80, [2018] 1 WLR 192.

[114] However, a majority of the Court of Appeal since followed these *obiter* remarks, thereby adopting a wider approach to the tort gateway: *FS Cairo (Nile Plaza) v Brownlie* [2020] EWCA Civ 996 (Arnold LJ dissenting) (appeal outstanding).

[115] *Brownlie* (n 113) [55] (Lady Hale DPSC), endorsed in more general terms by Lords Wilson ([64]) and Clarke ([68]–[69]).

[116] *Tugushev* (n 83) [214]. See also *Shahar* (n 93) [40] (counterfactual concession that indirect damage in the form of loss of value of shareholding in an English company would trigger the tort gateway).

[117] Discussed below at section III.E.

[118] *ET Plus SA and others v Welter and Others* [2005] EWHC 2115 (Comm) [40]–[45]. See also *Fundando Soberano de Angola v Dos Santos* [2018] EWHC 2199 (Comm) [37].

[119] *Microsoft Mobile Oy (Ltd) v Sony Europe Ltd* [2017] EWHC 374 (Ch), [2018] 1 All ER (Comm) 491.

conspiratorial conduct has a sufficiently close connection to a contract between the parties (eg also plausibly constitutes a breach of that contract),[120] the common sense approach of English law[121] to arbitration and jurisdiction agreements[122] may mean that an ensuing conspiracy claim has to be litigated in accordance with those agreements.[123] However, the question of the closeness of the connection clearly is one of degree: it has been held that, if only one of the various unlawful means which have been pleaded relates to a contract containing an arbitration clause, then that alone is insufficient to subject the conspiracy claim as a whole to that clause.[124]

There also has been considerable discussion of whether or not a conspiracy claim brought by an employer against an (ex)-employee falls within the protective employment contract grounds of the Brussels I Recast Regulation.[125] The UK Supreme Court referred this question – which the Court of Appeal had answered in the negative[126] – to the Court of Justice of the EU (CJEU) in *Arcadia Petroleum Ltd v Bosworth*.[127] However, the CJEU held that it was possible that the director's contracts could not be characterised as one of employment,[128] and thus did not discuss the question of the substantive scope of the protective provisions.[129] We are therefore left with the Advocate General's preliminary observations, which first indicated a preference for claims under the general, non-protective provisions to be classified according to the substantive legal basis on which those claims are advanced.[130] However, the employment provisions necessitated a different approach: to fulfil their protective purpose, an employer could not be allowed to escape their operation by formulating a claim in tort where the claim arose out of 'alleged wrongdoings on the part of the employee in the performance of

[120] For an application of the 'close connection' test, see *ibid* [70]–[73]. The approach under the Brussels I Recast Regulation, Art 25 is narrower: Case 352/13 *Cartel Damage Claims (CDC) Hydrogen Peroxide v Akzo Nobel* [2015] QB 906 [67]–[72].

[121] See *Fiona Trust v Privalov* [2007] UKHL 40, [2007] 4 All ER 951.

[122] See also *Erste Group Bank AG London v JSC VMZ Red October* [2013] EWHC 2926 (Comm) [118] (conspiracy claim brought under jurisdiction clause; not challenged on appeal: *Erste* (EWCA) (n 98) [20]); *VTB Commodities Trading v JSC Atipinsky Refinery* [2019] EWHC 3292 (Comm) [57] (conspiracy claim "very clearly caught" by arbitration clause).

[123] This may even be so if the conspiracy claim does not fall within the four corners of the clause but is closely related to a claim between the same parties which is covered by the clause: *AstraZeneca UK Ltd v Albemarle* [2010] EWHC 1028 (Comm) [84]–[87].

[124] *Republic of Mozambique v Credit Suisse International* [2020] EWHC 2012 (Comm) [108]–[109].

[125] See, in addition to the next-discussed case, *CEF Holdings v Mundey* [2012] EWHC 1524 (QB) [164]–[173], disagreeing with the negative conclusion in *Swithenbank Foods Ltd v Bowers* [2002] EWHC 2257 (QB), [2002] 2 All ER (Comm) 974.

[126] *Arcadia Petroleum Ltd v Bosworth* [2016] EWCA Civ 818.

[127] *Arcadia Petroleum Ltd v Bosworth* Case ID: UKSC 2016/0181.

[128] In fact, on the case's return to the English courts, it was held that there was no relationship of subordination on the facts, and therefore the employment provisions did not apply: *Alta Trading v Bosworth* [2020] EWHC 2757 (Comm), affirmed [2021] EWCA Civ 687.

[129] Case C-603/17 *Bosworth v Arcadia Petroleum Ltd* ECLI:EU:C:2019:310, [2019] ILPr 22 [29]–[35].

[130] *Ibid* [AG83]–[AG90].

his duties'.[131] This would encompass a conspiracy claim on the facts of that case. However, the Advocate General's opinion is not binding, and may be departed from by the English courts. The point remains relevant post-Brexit as the civil jurisdiction rules contain employment contract grounds based on the Brussels provisions.[132] The Court of Appeal's more rigid approach recently has been applied in the non-protective context to exclude a conspiracy claim from Article 7(1), the contractual ground of special jurisdiction under the Brussels I Recast.[133] A similarly restrictive approach to the contractual service out gateway[134] has been taken in respect of conspiracy claims.[135]

E. The Proper Forum and Conspiracy

If the conspiracy claim is held to fall within one of the CPR gateways[136] on the basis of a good arguable case, then the claimant must also convince the court that England is the proper forum in which that action should proceed. Space precludes an exhaustive analysis of the factors taken into account when applying this test.[137] However, in the conspiracy context, it would seem that the possibility of having a 'composite' conspiracy action against all co-conspirators before a single forum will be a powerful factor in demonstrating the appropriateness of that forum.[138] It would also seem that, following *Khrapunov*, the place where the conspiratorial agreement was entered into will be relevant.[139] Moreover, the identity of the applicable law may well be a factor of some importance, and it is to considerations of choice of law that this chapter now turns.

[131] *Ibid* [AG95]. The Advocate General suggested ([AG98]) excluding from the scope of this rule claims which were 'not connected by any objective circumstance pertaining to time, place, means or purpose with the duties performed by the employee'.

[132] The *Civil Jurisdiction and Judgments (Amendment) (EU Exit) Regulations* (SI 2019/479), para 26, inserting s 15C into the *Civil Jurisdiction and Judgments Act 1982*.

[133] *LIC Communications* (n 103) [276]–[286]. Argument in this case proceeded after both the Advocate General's opinion and the judgment of the Court in *Arcadia* (n 129). It is, however, consistent with the Advocate General's approach to the Art 7(1)/7(2) division.

[134] CPR PD 6B para 3.1(6)–(8).

[135] *Alliance Bank* (n 101) [60] (conspirator a stranger to the background contract and therefore claim not made in respect of a contract); applied in *Erste* (EWHC) (n 122) [136]–[140]. Compare *Cecil v Bayat* [2010] EWHC 641 (Comm) [135].

[136] Or, for Scotland, Sch 8 of the *Civil Jurisdiction and Judgments Act 1982*; alternatively, for disputes between Scotland and England, Sch 4 of that Act.

[137] See for a general exploration within the conspiracy context, *KMG International v Chen* [2018] EWHC 1078 (Comm); *Fundando Soberano de Angola* (n 118) [38]–[44]; *Traxys Europe v Sodexmines Nigeria* [2020] EWHC 2195; *Dili Advisors v Production Investment Management* [2020] EWHC 2669 (Comm) [205]–[215]; *Domestic & General* (n 101) [28].

[138] *ED&F Man* (n 101) [42]–[54], upheld by [2019] EWCA Civ 2073.

[139] See also the consideration in *VTB Capital v Nutritek* [2013] UKSC 5, [2013] 2 AC 337, which proceeded on the assumption that English law governed the conspiracy claim.

IV. Choice of Law

A. Introduction

Two issues require separation here. In this section, we will examine the question of which law supplies the 'framework' for a conspiracy claim. This law will supply the answer to 'framework' questions such as:

i. what degree of combination is required before parties will become ensnared in the conspiracy?;
ii. what is the requisite degree of intention?;
iii. is there a distinction between unlawful and lawful means?;
iv. if so, what are the consequence of that distinction?; and
v. how is that distinction – if present – to be demarcated?

This should be kept distinct from the question of whether or not means which are unlawful under a foreign law can anchor a claim in conspiracy brought before the forum, which may or may not be applying its own law to the 'framework' of conspiracy. That issue – relating to the use of foreign law as *datum*[140] – will be considered in detail in the next section.

It first is necessary to justify the above bifurcation. In *Irish Response v Direct Beauty*,[141] Richard Seymour QC HHJ was faced with a conspiracy claim anchored on the defendant's alleged acts of perjury before a Danish court. No attempt was made to prove the content of Danish law as to the 'framework' question, so English law applied to this by default.[142] However, the Deputy Judge did not take kindly to the claimant's attempts to nevertheless make Danish law relevant as providing the unlawful means for the conspiracy. This was denigrated as 'wholly artificial'[143] and as an attempt to create 'a hybrid Anglo-Danish cause of action, in which English law supplied the conspiracy and Danish law supplied the crime'.[144] With respect, there is a preferable way to construe this submission: English law supplies the framework of the conspiracy. It is up to English law to decide whether or not the unlawful means may be supplied by a foreign legal system: that question is not answered, or excluded from arising, by the fact that English law governs the conspiracy framework.

To generalise: despite the application of one legal system to a particular matter, it is possible for account to be taken of another legal system if the applicable law permits this. For example, in assessing the standard of care to be owed under the applicable law, account might be taken of standards prevailing at the *locus* of the

[140] ie treating a situation obtaining under foreign law as an observable fact: see HH Kay, 'Conflict of Laws: Foreign Law as Datum' (1965) 53 *Californian Law Review* 47 59–63.
[141] *Irish Response v Direct Beauty* [2011] EWHC 37 (QB).
[142] *Ibid* [141]–[142], [151].
[143] *Ibid* [135].
[144] *Ibid* [153].

accident if that system does not also constitute the applicable law.[145] In fact, *Dicey, Morris and Collins* approve the general principle that, where the 'governing law demands reference to the law of another country as a matter of fact in the application of its rule … the Rome II Regulation should not be taken to preclude such reference'.[146]

Having justified the separation of the unlawful means question from the framework choice of law question, this section now will first consider the conspiracy framework in the context of two choice of law regimes: first, the *Rome II Regulation*[147] with its general rule focusing on the place of *loss*, before considering the *lex loci delicti* rule which is common in other Commonwealth jurisdictions and which focuses on the place of the *tort*.

B. Rome II: *lex loci damni*?

i. General or Specific Rule?

Before turning to the general rule of Rome II, it first is important to dispose of the specific rule provided for torts affecting unfair competition in Article 6. While conspiracy may in some circumstances police the boundaries of what is fair competition, it will not fall under the specific rule as it is disapplied by Article 6(2) where 'an act of unfair competition affects exclusively the interests of a specific competitor'. Although this exclusion is somewhat opaque, it sensibly has been suggested that this includes an economic tort such as conspiracy which is targeted at a particular individual, as opposed to wrongdoing which is aimed to affect an entire market.[148]

ii. Article 4(1)

The effect, therefore, is that the general rules in Article 4 apply.[149] Article 4(1) has as its connecting factor the place where the damage directly occurs. This is the

[145] See, for a specific provision permitting this, *Regulation (EC) No 864/2007 of the European Parliament and of the Council of 11 July 2007 on the law applicable to non-contractual obligations* [2007] OJ L199/40 *('Rome II')* Art 17.

[146] Sir L Collins et al (eds), *Dicey Morris and Collins on the Conflict of Laws* (5th Supplement to the 15th edn (London, Sweet & Maxwell, 2018) [34-069]. In addition to cases involving conspiracy and illegality further discussed in the next section, this paragraph also cites *Weller v Associated Newspapers* [2015] EWCA 1176, [2016] 1 WLR 1541, where, at [19] and [67]–[71], the Court of Appeal discussed the possibility of taking into account the content of foreign law when determining a claimant's reasonable expectation of privacy when in that foreign jurisdiction.

[147] Post-Brexit, Rome II takes effect as 'retained EU law' in terms of the *European Union (Withdrawal) Act 2018*. See, for related modifications, *The Law Applicable to Contractual Obligations and Non-Contractual Obligations (Amendment etc.) (EU Exit) Regulations 2019* (SI 2019/834).

[148] A Dickinson, *The Rome II Regulation* (Oxford University Press, 2008) [6-29]–[6-30].

[149] A conspiracy to cause injury which occurs in a pre-contractual context probably does not fall within the special rule in the Regulation (Art 12) for *culpa in contrahendo*: *Perfectbit* (n 101) [198]–[200].

same[150] as the 'damage' limb of Article 7(2) of the Brussels I Recast Regulation.[151] So, in *Khrapunov*, the English court could have been invited to apply Swiss, Russian and Belizean law in determining liability for assisting the company registered in each jurisdiction to obscure its assets. Those where the places which the court identified as the relevant place of damage for Article 7(2) and, so, *mutatis mutandis*, also would be designated under Article 4(1).

The first post-*Khrapunov* applicable law decision confirms the real risk of fragmentation. In *MX1 Ltd v Farahzad*,[152] it was alleged that the defendant conspired with ex-employees of the claimants (a Luxembourgish satellite company and its Israeli media subsidiary) to tweet out a series of defamatory allegations and references to confidential documentation. One aspect of the damage alleged by the claimants was the cost of unmasking who was behind the Twitter account,[153] but clearly other damage occurred elsewhere. Marcus Smith J rejected the notion that Article 4(1) looked for the locus of the 'predominant' damage. Instead, 'where damage occurs across several jurisdictions, there will be several applicable laws'.[154]

Fragmentation raises particular issues in the context of English law's approach to foreign law. As is well known, foreign law is a question of fact, which must be proved to the satisfaction of the judge before it is to be applied; absent such proof, English law is applied by default.[155] It has been held that this approach allows a claimant simply to allege that conspiratorial conduct under various potentially applicable laws is unlawful in terms of English law, placing the burden on the defendant to prove contrary position under the laws of the various places where damage was suffered to defeat the claim.[156] Clearly, the more wide-ranging the conspiracy is in its geographical effect, the more difficult it will be for the defendant to discharge that burden. The obvious practical implications of this fragmentary approach may, however, be obviated by use of the exceptions to Article 4(1) discussed below.[157]

MX1 also contains a suggestion as to how we identify the place of damage. On this, Marcus Smith J adopted Dickinson's criterion of reversibility: with economic loss, the damage occurs where the 'act or omission becomes irreversible by [the claimant's] own actions'.[158] As for the costs of investigating the Twitter account, this occurred when and where the claimants engaged English lawyers to

[150] Although see the note of caution in *Erste* (EWCA) (n 98) [91].

[151] Which was referred to as 'location (b)' above: see section III.C.

[152] *MX1 Ltd v Farahzad* [2018] EWHC 1041 (Ch), [2018] 1 WLR 5553. The applicable law discussion concerns a lawful means conspiracy allegation, but nothing turns on this.

[153] *Ibid* [36].

[154] *Ibid* [44].

[155] See generally *Dicey Morris and Collins* (n 146) Ch 9; R Fentiman, *Foreign Law in English Courts* (Oxford University Press, 1998).

[156] *Iranian Offshore Engineering and Construction v Dean Investment Holdings* [2018] EWHC 2759 (Comm), [2019] 1 WLR 82; *Qatar Airways v Middle East News FZ* [2020] EWHC 2975 (QB) [171]–[190]; *Suppipat v Narongdej* [2020] EWHC 3191 (Comm).

[157] See section IV.B.iii.

[158] *MX1* (n 152) [39], citing Dickinson (n 148) [4.67].

make investigations. It was at that point that it could no longer disengage advisors without incurring cost. However, the reversibility test was not referred to by Cockerill J in *FM Capital Partners v Marino*.[159] Instead, her Ladyship adopted as a general principle the *Dolphin Maritime*[160] test. This poses a counterfactual: what would have occurred if the tort did not take place? If the claimant would have received money, or avoided loss,[161] in a particular place, then that may be the place of direct harm for the purposes of the Regulation. In that case, absent the conspiracy, the claimant would have received the payment of commissions in England, and so England was the place of direct harm. It is true that Cockerill J did not ascribe a monopoly to the counterfactual test: 'it is simply one of the permissible methods of trying to discern the country where the damage occurs'.[162] Moreover, the distinction between the two tests may be artificial: for instance, there would be no difference on the facts of *MX1* if the counterfactual test was applied. But the difficulty of identifying the exact place of economic loss – when combined with the raw potential for fragmentation – are perhaps just specific instantiations of the limitations of a loss-focussed choice of law rule in the context of economic torts.

iii. Articles 4(2) and 4(3)

A different form of fragmentation may arise as a result of Article 4(2): this displaces the general rule where claimant and defendant have the same habitual residence. This could especially be problematic in a conspiracy claim: if some of the conspirators happen to share a habitual residence with the claimant, then their liability will be determined by the law of the common habitual residence. The liability of the other conspirators will, however, still be determined by the general rule, meaning that there may a fragmentation of applicable laws within the one conspiracy claim even if all of the damage directly is felt within a single jurisdiction.

As observed in the previous section, fragmentation – either as a result of multiple places of damage, or as a result of a common habitual residence between the claimant and some, but not all, of the defendants – does not make much practical or conceptual sense. It can, however, be avoided within the Regulation using Article 4(3)'s escape clause. This can be used to designate a legal system which is manifestly more closely connected to that designated by Articles 4(1) or 4(2) and can also be used to displace Article 4(2) in favour of the legal system designated

[159] *FM Capital Partners v Marino* [2018] EWHC 1768 (Comm). The choice of law point was not discussed on appeal: [2020] EWCA Civ 245.

[160] *Dolphin Maritime & Aviation Services v Sveriges Angfartygs Assurans Forening* [2009] EWHC 716 (Comm), [2010] 1 All ER (Comm) 473.

[161] A generalisation extracted from *Dolphin Maritime, ibid* by Cockerill J in *FM Capital* (n 159) [493]–[497].

[162] *FM Capital* (n 159) [497]. It was, however, the method approved in relation to the conspiracy claim in *Qatar Airways v Middle East FZ* (n 156) ([169]).

by Article 4(1).[163] It requires a 'clear preponderance of factors' connecting the case with the 'other' legal system when compared to that designated by either Article 4(1) or Article 4(2).[164]

In *FM Capital*, Cockerill J was not persuaded that the escape clause applied: while some of the documentation in that case was governed by Swiss law and some of the conspirators were domiciled in Switzerland, the target of the conspiracy was based in England and that is where its effects were felt.[165] As England – the law of which had been designated by Article 4(1) – was the 'centre of gravity of the wrongdoing', there was no case for displacement.[166] However, in *Erste*,[167] the Court of Appeal accepted that Article 4(1), which designated New York law (being the place where the conspiracy led to the non-payment of contractually-due sums) should be displaced under Article 4(3), as it was 'as Russian a conspiracy as it is possible to imagine'.[168] This was because all conspirators were Russian; the scheme was hatched there; the unlawful means involved inappropriate application of Russian insolvency law, all the acts took place in Russia, and resulted in the extraction of Russian assets and their vesting in a Russian company.[169] While it is rare that there will be such a culmination of factors favouring a particular jurisdiction, this does give an indication of the factors which may be taken into account under Article 4(3) in a conspiracy claim.[170]

C. *Lex loci delicti*?

Choice of law rules elsewhere in the Commonwealth[171] – and the pre-Rome II position in the UK[172] – focus not on the place of loss, but on the place where the tort occurred. Following *Khrapunov*, there is a good argument that at least the starting point of this analysis should be the place where the conspiracy was hatched or where the conspiratorial agreement was entered.[173] In Singapore,

[163] *Pickard v Marshall* [2017] EWCA Civ 17 [20].
[164] *Winrow v Hemphill* [2014] EWHC 3164 (QB).
[165] *FM Capital* (n 159) [512]–[518].
[166] *Ibid* [519].
[167] *Erste* (EWCA) (n 98) [97]–[100].
[168] *Ibid* [99].
[169] *Ibid* [100].
[170] See also *Dili Advisors* (n 137) [98], highlighting (under reference to *Avonwick Holdings v Azitio Holdings* [2020] EWHC 1844 (Comm) [156]) the importance of where those 'pulling the strings' and where the 'heart' of the wrongdoing were located.
[171] For Australia, see *Regine Nationale des Usines Renault v Zhang* (2002) 210 CLR 491 (and, for its application to the inducement tort, see *Daebo Shipping Co v The Ship Go Star* (2012) 207 FCR 220). For Canada, see *Tolofson v Jensen* [1994] 3 SCR 1022.
[172] *Private International Law (Miscellaneous Provisions) Act 1995*, ss 11–12. See, for its application to conspiracy, *Fiona Trust v Privalov* [2010] EWHC 3199 (Comm) [163]–[175].
[173] *cf Fiona Trust*, *ibid* [166].

the following factors have been identified as having particular relevance in the conspiracy context:

> the identity, importance and location of the conspirators; the locations where any agreements or combinations took place; the nature and places of the concerted acts or means; the location of the plaintiff; and the places where the plaintiff suffered losses.[174]

There is no reason why such factors also cannot be considered when determining the proper forum for a conspiracy claim, or under Article 4(3) of the Rome II Regulation.

V. Unlawful Means under Foreign Law?

A. Introduction

A final question which requires consideration is whether the 'unlawful means' at the core of an unlawful means conspiracy may include means which are unlawful according to foreign law. In other words, may the violation of a foreign norm exclude a 'just cause or excuse' for acting in concert? Of course, in many situations, tortious or criminal conduct under a foreign law may be also be considered as such in domestic law, negating the need for the claimant to assert the relevance of the foreign position. However, domestic law will not contain a close analogue for every situation of foreign 'unlawfulness', and there may be technical reasons why the defendant's conduct cannot be held to fall within the scope of the domestic law of tort or crime.

The position in criminal conspiracy is clear. The common law rule, reflected in statute, was that a charge of conspiracy required an envisaged offence which was 'triable in England and Wales'.[175] However, subsequent amendment has created a new ground of conspiratorial liability in respect of offences contrary to the criminal law of a foreign jurisdiction;[176] such a conspiracy may be prosecuted in England and Wales provided that, *inter alia*, steps in pursuance of the conspiracy were taken within the jurisdiction.[177]

However, the position in civil conspiracy is far from settled: may foreign torts, crimes, or breaches of foreign regulatory statutes underpin a claim in conspiracy? This is a question of English domestic law, but it cannot be resolved without at least a brief detour into principles of private international law; namely, the axiom that

[174] *EFT Holdings v Marinteknik Shipbuilders* [2014] 1 SLR 860 [53]; applied in *Kioumji & Eslim Law Firm v Rotary Engineering* [2016] SGHC 218 [38]–[41].

[175] *Criminal Law Act 1977* s 1(4).

[176] *Ibid* s 1A (inserted by the *Criminal Justice (Terrorism and Conspiracy) Act 1998*). Identical provision was made for Scots law: *Criminal Procedure (Scotland) Act 1995* s 11A (as amended).

[177] In particular, the accused must have joined the conspiratorial scheme in England or done something in anticipation of, or pursuant to, the scheme there.

one nation will not enforce the penal laws of another and the doctrine of comity. A supposed analogy with breach of statutory duty will then be refuted, before the limited case law bearing on this question is discussed.

B. The Penal Law Rule?

Rule 3(1) of *Dicey, Morris and Collins* states, in so far as is relevant, that 'English courts have no jurisdiction to entertain an action …. For the enforcement, either directly or indirectly, of a penal … law of a foreign state'.[178]

This prohibition – the 'penal law rule' – was held to be firmly established by 1892 decisions of the Privy Council[179] and US Supreme Court.[180] It seemingly is an extraction from the territorial nature of criminal jurisdiction: '[c]rimes are in their nature local, and the jurisdiction of crimes is local'.[181] Therefore, the reasoning proceeds, it would be a flagrant excess of jurisdiction to seek to assert the application of one nation's criminal law within the territory of another sovereign state.

Reasoning along these lines has been employed to doubt the inclusion of foreign law within 'unlawful means': 'to allow an action to be founded in tort under English law on such a basis would effectively amount to a back-door exercise of extra-territorial jurisdiction'.[182] However, it is submitted that – leaving aside the inadequacies of the justifications for the penal law rule[183] – the rule is not triggered by using unlawful means conspiracy in this manner, and treating breaches of foreign law as 'unlawful means' involves no unjustified excess of jurisdiction.

It is submitted the penal law rule is not engaged because determining a tortious claim in conspiracy formulated by reference to a foreign penal law can in no circumstances be said to amount to the 'enforcement' of that law. 'Enforcement', in these circumstances, has a technical meaning: it requires the existence of an outstanding claim under the foreign penal law, which allowing the claim to proceed to a judgment in favour of the claimant would satisfy or otherwise extinguish.[184]

This reasoning can be supported by drawing an analogy with cases concerning the sister to the penal law rule: the rule which precludes the enforcement of foreign revenue laws. As mentioned above, the House of Lords in *Total Network*[185]

[178] Sir L Collins et al (eds), *Dicey, Morris and Collins on the Conflict of Laws*, 15th edn (London, Sweet & Maxwell, 2012) [5-019].

[179] *Huntington v Attrill* [1893] AC 150.

[180] *Huntington v Attrill* 146 US 657 (1892).

[181] *Rafael v Verelst* (1776) 2 Bl W 1055, 95 ER 621.

[182] G Stirling, 'It's a Conspiracy! Or Is It? The Difficulty with the Economic Torts as 'Alternative' Causes of Action for Competition Law Damages Actions in UK Courts' (2017) 8(4) *Journal of European Competition Law & Practice* 233 240.

[183] These are explored in more detail in B Lindsay, *Cross-Border Public Law Claims: Private International Law's Exclusionary Rules* (Oxford University Press, forthcoming).

[184] *Williams and Humbert Ltd v W&H Trademarks (Jersey) Ltd* [1986] AC 368 440F-441C.

[185] *Total Network* (n 11).

confirmed that, as a matter of domestic English law, the common law crime of cheating the revenue would suffice as 'unlawful means' for the conspiracy tort, and therefore the UK tax authorities could rely on that tort to recover unpaid output VAT from parties beyond the reach of the statutory recovery mechanisms. This authority was relied upon by HM Revenue and Customs (HMRC) in respect of an almost identical carousel fraud involving the Sunico group of companies.[186] In support of English proceedings, HMRC sought assistance from the courts in Hong Kong in the form of a supporting freezing injunction against two of the defendants in the English action. The striking out of the application was sought on the basis that, as the value of the conspiracy claim was identical to the value of the unpaid VAT, the English action obviously was an attempt to enforce the revenue laws of the United Kingdom. Therefore, the granting of the freezing injunction in Hong Kong would be tantamount to the 'enforcement' of a foreign revenue law, and thereby would be precluded by the revenue law rule. This argument was rejected at first instance[187] and on appeal:[188] the fact that the 'unlawful means' pled as part of the English action related to a revenue offence did not alter the fact that it was an action in private law, despite the equivalence between the compensation craved and the unpaid VAT.[189]

This conclusion was echoed in the reasoning of the CJEU in dealing with a Danish court's preliminary reference as to whether or not it would be bound to recognise a judgment from the English *Sunico* proceedings.[190] In concluding that the conspiracy claim was a 'civil and commercial one' despite the nature of the unlawful means alleged, the CJEU focussed on the following factors: (i) the power to pursue the conspiracy claim did not 'accrue to the state in its capacity as an organ of sovereign power'; (ii) HMRC was victim of a tortious act 'whose victim can in principle be anyone'; (iii) satisfaction of the conspiracy claim would have no bearing on the amount of outstanding VAT left unpaid; and (iv) therefore it was irrelevant that there was an equivalence between the value of the claim and the value of the tax.

This reasoning is unaffected if we shift the form of the unlawful means involved from the crime of cheating the revenue to any other possible crime under a foreign system. In fact, as submitted above, it may even apply with heightened force where: (i) the action is brought by a private party; and (ii) where there is no

[186] Proudman J found the conspirators liable: *Commissioners for Her Majesty's Revenue v Sunico and others* [2013] EWHC 931 (Ch). The Court of Appeal gave permission to appeal ([2014] EWCA Civ 1008); but permission was revoked when the defendants did not comply with an order to pay a sum into court: [2014] EWCA Civ 1563.

[187] *Commissioners for Her Majesty's Revenue v Sunico* [2010] HKCFI 962.

[188] *Commissioners for Her Majesty's Revenue v Sunico* [2011] HKCA 369.

[189] Compare this, however, with the negative conclusion reached by Andrew Baker J in *Skatteforvaltningen v Solo Capital Partners LLP (In Special Administration)* [2021] EWHC 974 (Comm) in respect of claims in deceit and conspiracy brought by the Danish tax authority in respect of allegedly-fraudulent tax rebate applications. The judge ruled the claims to be precluded by Dicey's Rule 3 as an attempt to enforce Danish tax law. Whatever the merits of that decision, it is submitted that it does not impact the argument in the text in relation to foreign unlawful means for the purposes of conspiracy.

[190] Case C-49/12 *Revenue and Customs Commissioners v Sunico* [2014] QB 391.

close correlation between the compensation claimed for and the punitive monetary sanction which would attach under the foreign law for use of those unlawful means. In this instance, the transgression of a foreign criminal law simply is an observable fact – a piece of *datum* – which can be recognised and processed through the conspiracy framework in order to reach a conclusion as to liability.

C. Comity?

The law of illegality may provide an instructive inversion of the issue under consideration here. There, instead of unlawful means under foreign law providing a part of a successful cause of action, the presence of foreign illegality may provide a reason to preclude an otherwise good claim. This has been long-established in contract law: the English courts will not enforce an English contract where the effect would be to 'assist or sanction the breach of the laws of other independent States'.[191] In tort law, it has been said that 'the principle of international comity suggests' that illegality under foreign law should have the potential to preclude a claim in tort,[192] and there is authority rejecting an unjust enrichment claim because of the presence of foreign illegality.[193]

If foreign unlawful means may negate a cause of action *per* the doctrine of illegality, then it may be logical – so long as the conspiracy framework supplied by the *lex causae* permits it and provided that the public policy of the forum is not infringed – for such means being able to *support* a cause of action in conspiracy. However, there is a distinction between the two situations which alters the effect of comity. It is far more invidious for an English court to refuse to take foreign unlawful means into account in the illegality context, as the effect may be to fail to deter, or positively sanction, the violation of foreign law. That degree of offence would not be present in the conspiracy context, where the court's unwillingness to consider foreign unlawful means does not involve any approbation of the conduct which violated the foreign law. However, the awkward refusal to take account of an intentional conspiratorial transgression of a foreign law hardly is in keeping with the spirit of comity.

[191] *Ralli Bros v Compania Naviera Sota y Aznar* [1920] 2 KB 287 304 (Scrutton LJ). The other two seminal cases are *Foster v Driscoll* [1929] 1 KB 470 and *Regazzoni v Sethia* [1958] AC 301.

[192] *Lilly Icos LLC v 8PM Chemists Ltd* [2009] EWHC 1905 (Ch), [2010] FSR 4 [271] (Arnold J); the position in contract is set out at [261]–[266], and see the statement at [287] that '[a]s a matter of international comity, it does not matter for this purpose [i.e. the refusal to enforce a cross-undertaking] whether the acts in question are unlawful under English law or under foreign law'. These observations were not departed from by the Court of Appeal in *Les Laboratoires Servier v Apotex* [2012] EWCA Civ 593 [69] (Etherton LJ). The UK Supreme Court ([2014] UKSC 55, [2015] AC 430) reversed the Court of Appeal, but did not refer at all to the *foreign* nature of the illegality involved: the illegal act in question (a patent infringement) was said not to be sufficiently 'quasi-criminal' to engage the public interest protected by the illegality defence.

[193] *Barros Mattos Junior v MacDaniels* [2004] EWHC 1188 (Ch), [2005] 1 WLR 247.

D. Analogy with Breach of Statutory Duty?

The non-actionability of foreign unlawful means also has been justified on the basis of an analogy with the tort of breach of statutory duty. It is said that, as there is no evidence of an English court finding liability for the breach of a duty imposed by a foreign statute, it follows that there should be no liability for loss incurred via a conspiratorial breach of a foreign statute.[194] Although both breach of statutory duty and conspiracy are 'framework' torts, it is not self-evident that what goes for the one must go for the other. Moreover, there have been instances where claims for breach of a duty imposed by a foreign statute have been raised without adverse comment from the bench.[195] It is also unclear why so much should turn on the *statutory* nature of the foreign norm: first, the foreign unlawful means conceivably might be founded in a common law tort or crime; second, it creates an unjustified distinction which hinges on the juristic source of the foreign means: the actionability of foreign unlawful means should not turn on whether or not they have been legislatively enacted.[196] This objection, therefore, should be rejected.

E. Judicial Consideration

i. Emerald Supplies

So much for principle. The only direct consideration of this question – and albeit only at the level of a strike out application – is found in *Emerald Supplies v British Airways*.[197] This involved claims made against 31 airlines which allegedly were involved in a price-fixing cartel. The EU Commission made an infringement decision against the airlines in 2010, and the claimants thereafter brought an action alleging unlawful means conspiracy based upon alleged breaches of EU competition law and various foreign laws. British Airways sought for these actions to be struck out on the basis that foreign unlawful means could not ground an English conspiracy claim, or, in the alternative, that they could only be used as such if an independent action could be brought for any violations in the foreign system.

[194] Stirling (n 182) 240.

[195] See, in passing, *Middle Eastern Oil LLC v National Bank of Abu Dhabi* [2008] EWHC 2895 (Comm), [2009] 1 Lloyd's Rep 251 [17]; *Shannon v Global Tunnelling Experts UK* [2015] EWHC 1267 (QB) [9]; *O'Keefe v Caner* [2017] EWHC 1105 (Ch); *Fundando Soberano de Angola* (n 118) [32]; *Vedanta Resources v Lungowe* [2019] UKSC 20, [2019] 2 WLR 1051 [63]–[65]. This is in addition to the cases discussed in section V.E.ii. below, particularly *Digicel (St Lucia) v Cable and Wireless* [2010] EWHC 744 (Ch), where statutes from seven jurisdictions were examined to determine whether a breach of their provisions would afford an action for breach of statutory duty either under English or foreign law: see [22]–[23].

[196] Such an approach may unduly restrict the actionability of unlawful means from civilian or federal systems, where codification is more common than in the English system.

[197] *Emerald Supplies v British Airways* [2014] EWHC 3513 (Ch).

Peter Smith J observed that in a previous judgment[198] he was content to proceed on the basis that violations of Zambian law could found an English conspiracy,[199] but acknowledged that there was 'no clear decision' made with the benefit of argument on the actionability of foreign unlawful means.[200] He therefore refused to decide the point on a summary judgment basis, a decision which was not challenged before the Court of Appeal.[201]

However, the Court of Appeal held that – whatever the status of foreign unlawful means – the requisite degree of intention would not be made out on the facts, so it struck out the claim on this basis.[202] But one can sense that the Court of Appeal would be wary of allowing the foreign competition laws to constitute unlawful means, for this would extend the scope of those competition laws beyond their intended scope and provide a remedy where the foreign law was silent.[203] Of course, that would only be so if: (i) there was no public policy objection to such a course; and (ii) if the law applicable to the conspiracy framework would supply a remedy in the circumstances.[204] However, conspiracy is not a direct replacement for a specialised regime: it provides a remedy for intentional concerted harm which has been directed at the claimant and which has caused it loss. In any event, in *Total Network*,[205] the majority of the Appellate Committee was content to allow the conspiracy tort to fill the gap left by a statutory recovery regime, so the objection based on undermining the drafter's intention rings a little hollow in the wider context of English tort law. And, as we shall see, the Court of Appeal's wariness is out of step with the (albeit limited) indications which can be gleaned from cases where the issue was not subject to active debate and consideration.

ii. Early Consideration of Foreign Conduct

The first case in which foreign conduct appears to have been rendered actionable as part of the economic torts is *Tarleton v McGawley*,[206] which considered what we now would consider the tort of causing loss by unlawful means. The claimants attempted to trade with Cameroon and anchored their ship off the coast. The defendants were rival traders who opened fire on Cameroonians as they attempted to board the claimant's ship, striking their canoe with a cannon and killing one of the occupants. As a result, the claimant lost the benefit of the prospective trade,

[198] *Attorney General of Zambia v Meer Care & Desai* [2007] EWHC 952 (Ch), reversed on other grounds on appeal ([2008] EWCA Civ 1007).
[199] *Emerald Supplies* (EWHC) (n 197) [98].
[200] *Ibid* [101].
[201] *Emerald Supplies v British Airways* [2015] EWCA Civ 1024, [2016] Bus LR 145 [127].
[202] *Ibid* [159]–[173].
[203] *Ibid* [132], [174]
[204] If a foreign statute excluded a residual common law action, this exclusion could be applied: *Allen v Depuy International* [2015] EWHC 926 (QB).
[205] *Total Network* (n 11).
[206] *Tarleton v McGawley* (1794) Peake 270, 170 ER 153.

and it was held that the defendant could be held liable for this. Admittedly, it is not clear from the judgment of Lord Kenyon CJ as to whether this conclusion was because: (i) the attack was 'illegal' under English law; (ii) the attack was a battery under English law; (iii) the attack was against the criminal laws of Cameroon; (iv) the attack was civilly actionable under Cameroonian law; (v) the attack was contrary the law of nations; or (vi) a combination thereof.[207] The primitive state of private international law in 1794 perhaps should caution against trying to infer too much from this decision;[208] but it does suggest that there should be no instinctive reason why a foreign crime or tort should not supply 'unlawful means' for the conspiracy tort.

Relatedly, in *Machado v Fontes*,[209] it was held that criminality under Brazilian law provided the second limb of the double actionability requirement in respect of a statement which was libellous under English law. The tenor of this reasoning supports the instinct that account should be taken of foreign unlawfulness, albeit this decision since has been overruled.[210]

iii. Modern Inferences

In the last three decades, several decisions have touched on conspiracy claims with foreign elements. What inferences, if any, regarding the actionability of foreign unlawful means can be gleaned from these? In *Grupo Torras v Al-Sabah (No 5)*,[211] Mance J considered a conspiracy claim partly alleging the violation of the *Spanish Companies Act 1989* as unlawful means. While noting that the point was not subject to specific argument, His Lordship concluded that the scheme involved 'the doing of an act or the use of means illegal under Spanish law, and that, if necessary, may be relied upon [by the claimant] as an unlawful act or means in relation to the conspiracy claim'.[212] Violations of the *US Securities Exchange Act 1934* arising out of the Enron scandal were at the heart of the conspiracy counterclaim in *Mahonia v JP Morgan Chase Bank*.[213] Cooke J was content to proceed on the basis that if 'foreign law unlawfulness is sufficient', then 'the acts in question must be actionable under foreign law by the alleged victim'.[214] However, the judgment begs that initial, fundamental question as the claimants did not press argument on the non-actionability of foreign unlawful means.[215] In other cases, the actionability

[207] As would be required by the double actionability rule for choice of law in tort which was developed in the 19th century: *Philips v Eyre* (1870) LR 6 QB 1.

[208] Especially as there appears to have been no attempt to argue the applicability of, or prove the content of, Cameroonian law.

[209] *Machado v Fontes* [1897] 2 QB 231.

[210] *Boys v Chaplin* [1971] AC 356.

[211] *Grupo Torras v Al-Sabah (No 5)* [1999] 1 CLC 1469.

[212] *Ibid* 1651.

[213] *Mahonia v JP Morgan Chase Bank* [2004] EWHC 1938 (Comm).

[214] *Ibid* [253].

[215] *Ibid* [364].

of foreign unlawful means has been assumed[216] or asserted in argument.[217] The following cases are, however, discussed in more detail for the light which they may shade on the instinctive response of English law to conspiracy claims grounded in allegations of foreign unlawfulness.

In *Digicel (St Lucia) Ltd v Cable and Wireless Plc*,[218] the claimants alleged that the defendants conspired to cause them loss through conduct which violated the telecommunications licensing regimes in seven Caribbean jurisdictions. This claim ultimately failed on the basis that Morgan J held that 'unlawful means' required that these regulatory violations either gave rise to civil actionability or criminal liability,[219] which, in his interpretation, was not the case. At no point was the foreign source of these regulations considered to be a knock-out blow: it was the *nature* of those foreign regulations that the case hinged upon.

The case nevertheless is interesting for its approach to the international dimension to this elaborate conspiracy claim. First, it is notable that there was no challenge to the jurisdiction of the English court. Second, Morgan J felt that he did not have to definitively resolve the identity of the law applicable to each claim in conspiracy because the parties had agreed that all seven potentially applicable foreign laws were (for the most part) to be treated as being identical in content to English law. However, in relation to a potential conflict for limitation purposes, Morgan J – while not deciding the point – commented that the claimants would face an 'uphill struggle' in persuading him that the law of anywhere other than the place where the regulatory breaches occurred should apply.[220] This contentedness to discuss the case as if English law applied, suggests quite clearly that foreign unlawful means may ground a conspiracy claim under English law. If the position were otherwise, His Lordship would either: (i) have definitively to settle the identity of the applicable law (foreign means relevant if foreign law applicable, but irrelevant if English law applied); or (ii) have been relieved of the task of considering, in detail, the nature of the alleged unlawful means across the seven legal systems. If the case could have been disposed of simply on the basis of the non-actionability of foreign unlawful means, then one suspects Morgan J may have taken this course.[221]

[216] *Lebara Mobile v Lycamobile* [2015] EWHC 3318 (Ch) (for the purposes of the granting of an interim injunction, it was held that 'serious issue to be tried' in relation to conspiracy alleging unlawful means under four foreign jurisdictions and generally under EU law: [86]–[89]); *Apollo Ventures v Machanda* [2016] EWHC 1416 (Comm); [2020] EWHC 2006 (Comm) (unlawful means under Thai law held to be 'serious issue to be tried' which grounded the granting of a worldwide freezing order).

[217] *Loches Capital v Goldman Sachs International* [2020] EWHC 2327 (Comm) [50] (application for pre-action disclosure).

[218] *Digicel (St Lucia) Ltd v Cable and Wireless Plc* [2010] EWHC 744 (Ch).

[219] *Ibid* [186]–[187], expanded upon in [4]–[69] of Annexe I (ie the ninth(!) annexe) to the judgment.

[220] *Ibid* [221].

[221] Lest this be taken to be glib, it is worth noting that outline consideration of the actionability (or otherwise) of the foreign means occupies [98]–[565] of the judgment, and detailed consideration occupied seven annexes to the judgment (from pages 142 to 520 of the Westlaw PDF version). See also *Emerald Supplies* (EWHC) (n 197) [95] (commenting on the fact that the shortcut of excluding foreign unlawful means *holus bolus* was not taken in *Irish Response* (below)).

Of course, the forum still will retain the power to disregard foreign unlawful means where the creation of a cause of action in respect to the foreign transgression would be contrary to forum public policy. A good example of such a situation – albeit not reasoned in such a manner – is *Irish Response v Direct Beauty*.[222] Danish litigation ensued between the claimant and a party with which it had entered into an exclusive distribution agreement, and the claimant made allegations that the defendants conspired with the counterparty to have it lead false evidence in the Danish proceedings. The 'critical question', as framed by the judge, was 'whether a conspiracy to commit perjury in a court in Denmark is actionable in this court'.[223] Given that there was no proof as to whether Danish law recognised conspiratorial liability,[224] English law fell to be applied to the framework of the conspiracy claim.[225] The scant evidence of Danish law disclosed no immunity from suit for a witness in civil proceedings corresponding to the rule found in English law.[226] The judge held that the claim failed, not because the unlawful means on which the conspiracy pivoted were foreign, but because of the English rule that perjury before a competent court was not actionable as a tort. Although not expressed as such[227] – the judge's framework approach to conspiracy has been criticised above – this has the same effect as concluding that a long-held and clearly formulated strand of English public policy – such as that relating to witness immunity[228] – may step in to defeat such a claim regardless of the inconsistent approach of foreign law.

Constantin Media v Ecclestone[229] concerned allegations that Bernie Ecclestone had paid a bribe to a German bank employee in order to bring about a sale of shares in the Formula One Group. The claimants were a German media company which stood to benefit if the shares were sold over a certain price, and it was alleged that they suffered a loss because of the low sale price of the shares as facilitated by the bribe. Newey J held that the conspiracy claim was governed by German law but failed on account of: (i) the failure to show that the claimant had suffered any loss; (ii) the fact that any such losses would fall foul of the German equivalent of the reflective loss principle, and (iii) the lack of sufficient proof of intention to harm the claimant.[230] Newey J also added that the claim would fail as a matter of English law for much the same reasons.[231] His Lordship, however, did

[222] *Irish Response* (n 141).
[223] *Ibid* [140].
[224] *Ibid* [141].
[225] *Ibid* [151].
[226] *Ibid* [136]–[139].
[227] This is how Peter Smith J interpreted this decision in *Emerald Supplies* (EWHC) (n 197) [94]–[96].
[228] Another example might be what is left of advocate's immunity. In *King v Stiefel* [2021] EWHC 1045 (Comm) an English law conspiracy claim which would have impinged on a barrister's immunity from suit would fall to be struck out by the court as an abuse of process if it had not already been struck out on other grounds: [319]–[335].
[229] *Constantin Media v Ecclestone* [2014] EWHC 387 (Ch).
[230] *Ibid* [362]–[367].
[231] *Ibid* [337]–[338].

not identify the precise nature of the unlawful means which were being fed into the English conspiracy framework, and so we do not know whether these were to be supplied by English or German law. In fact, his judgment says very little about the 'unlawful means' component of the English tort: the sole point elaborated upon is the test for intention. However, the case at least may be taken as authority for the proposition that the law governing the conspiracy framework sets the standard for what is and what is not unlawful.[232] If an English court is willing to recognise unlawful means under German law when German law applies to the conspiracy claim, then this further undermines the 'extraterritoriality' objection attacked above.

These decisions demonstrate, at the very least, that there is no instinctive abhorrence in English law of the notion that foreign law may provide the requisite unlawful means for a conspiracy claim. Given what was said above about the policy factors justifying such a conclusion, this demonstrates that the case law should not constitute a barrier. However, the final decision considered here demonstrates that, even if such a prohibition on foreign unlawful means does exist, there may be a route in many cases to circumvent this. In *Mbasogo v Logo*, the President of Equatorial Guinea issued a conspiracy claim against those who had attempted to foment an armed coup against him. The claim ultimately was struck out on grounds of non-justiciability (again exemplifying that the forum ultimately has the power to refuse to deal with conspiracy claims which it does not wish to entertain). At first instance, the claim was based on crimes and civil wrongs under the laws of England and Equatorial Guinea, and no adverse comment was raised in respect of the inclusion of foreign unlawful means at first instance,[233] or in the Court of Appeal.[234] However, it is notable that one of the English offences alleged was under the *Criminal Law Act 1977*. As mentioned above, this creates a criminal offence of conspiring to commit an offence prohibited by foreign law. Not only does this again underline the lack of an extraterritoriality objection to taking account of foreign unlawful means,[235] but it provides a potential means for converting foreign unlawful means into domestic unlawful means. As this provision, in certain circumstances, creates a *domestic* offence of conspiring to commit a foreign offence, then a claim in conspiracy framed with that domestic offence as unlawful means would, in principle, fall outside any objection based purely on the foreign nature of the offence involved.

[232] In German law, the question being whether the means employed were *contra bones mores*: *Ibid*, [339]–[356].

[233] *Mbasogo v Logo* [2005] EWHC 2034 (QB) [12], [52].

[234] *Mbasogo v Logo* [2006] EWCA Civ 1370, [2007] QB 846.

[235] Albeit that statute does so with the imprimatur of statutory authority, which would not necessarily be the case with a common law conspiracy claim.

F. Conclusion

Therefore, there is no sound reason why a foreign tort or crime should not be capable of excluding a 'just cause or excuse' for a conspiratorial agreement. Such a conclusion is not an imperialistic intrusion into the territory of other sovereign states; it is consistent with prevalent concepts of comity; and it further increases the value of the conspiracy tort. If a careful consideration of the foreign norm leads to the conclusion that it applies to the conduct in question, and the application of that foreign norm does not offend the forum's public policy, then a claim in unlawful means conspiracy should lie even if the framework of the conspiracy claim is governed by English law.

This conclusion is much more easily reached on the basis of an independent tort of conspiracy – as confirmed in *Khrapunov*[236] – than would be the case with an accessorial conception of conspiracy liability. One question which remains, however, is whether the claimant must prove that the conspirators were aware that their actions violated foreign law before conspiratorial liability will attach. It might be argued that the absence of such a requirement would put parties at the potentially severe cost of having to satisfy themselves as to the content of the legal position in each jurisdiction in which their combined acts may have consequences. This raises similar issues to our discussion of the knowledge requirement which,[237] it will be recalled, was repudiated in relation to both criminal and civil wrongs by a majority of the Court of Appeal in *The Racing Partnership*.[238] To require knowledge in the context of foreign unlawful means may be thought to be a useful control mechanism. However, it would again create distinctions in the framework tort of conspiracy which may not be justified. For one, it is difficult to see how ignorance of domestic law should not be an excuse, but ignorance of foreign law may be excused; such a conclusion would offend against the notion of comity. It may also be difficult to prove the requisite knowledge, presumably being most obviously evidenced where the alleged conspirators had sought legal advice on the foreign law position. But it seems unlikely that such a smoking gun will be unearthed in many cases, and it may be that a knowledge requirement in the context of foreign means would denude the conspiracy tort of the very real utility it may have in this context.

VI. Conclusion

The versatility of the tort of conspiracy makes it no surprise that it has proved a popular tool in cross-border litigation. The above, however, has demonstrated the

[236] Discussed at section II.B.
[237] See section II.D.
[238] *The Racing Partnership* (n 60).

difficulties in applying domestic tort law and private international law rules to such claims. Academic consideration of cross-border conspiracy virtually is non-existent, and the judicial consideration is fragmented, unfocussed, and tucked away within voluminous judgments where the assessment of facts far outweighs legal analysis. *Khrapunov* has, in theory, made significant alterations to the English tort of conspiracy, and this chapter has highlighted some problematic areas within that judgment. It also can be observed that the independent nature of the tort of conspiracy is reflected in its private international law sphere: the triggering event still is conceived to be the entering into the agreement, and not the acts taken pursuant to that agreement which would be the focus of an accessorial conception. This emphasises the importance of looking to the international dimension when considering the internal, domestic, formulation of private law concepts and doctrines.

The growing number of conspiracy claims present a challenge to the classically-bipartite conception of private international law rules. The reality in litigation often strays far from the simple claimant versus defendant archetype, and a significant challenge facing the future operation of jurisdiction and choice of law rules is how they fairly can corral a multitude of defendants in such cases. This chapter has sought to distil guidance from the judgments as to how successfully they presently do so. Moreover, it has provided the first sustained argument favouring the 'actionability' of foreign unlawful means. In other words, the tort of conspiracy should provide a remedy where the conspirators seek to inflict harm on the claimant through a violation of foreign criminal law or a civil wrong governed by foreign law. This further would increase the utility of the economic torts in the international arena.

7

Economic Wrongs and Private Nuisance: A Common Law Perspective

PAULA GILIKER*

I. Introduction

The tort of private nuisance[1] seeks to protect the plaintiff from unlawful interference with his or her use or enjoyment of land, or of some right over, or in connection with it. As a tort protecting land rights, it is often termed a 'property' tort[2] and this trait influences who can sue and the remedies provided. Only plaintiffs with a legal right to, or exclusive possession of, the land, will be able to sue.[3] Remedies equally respond to an 'undue' interference with the plaintiff's land rights. Compensation will be awarded for diminution in value of the plaintiff's land and for loss of its 'amenity value'.[4] In the leading nineteenth century case of *St Helen's Smelting Co v Tipping*,[5] Lord Westbury made it clear that private nuisance would not only remedy physical (material) damage to property (for example damaged crops and buildings), but would extend to sensible personal discomfort (caused, for example, by fumes and noxious gases). In this latter category, however,

* Professor of Comparative Law, University of Bristol.

[1] This chapter will not cover the law relating to the rule in *Rylands v Fletcher* which is part of private nuisance in the law of England and Wales, but is treated as part of the tort of negligence in Australia: see *Burnie Port Authority v General Jones Pty Ltd* (1994) 179 CLR 520 (HCA). To avoid clumsy duplication, the chapter will also use the term 'plaintiff' in relation to English and Australian law, although English law now prefers the term 'claimant'.

[2] D Nolan, '"A Tort Against Land": Private Nuisance as a Property Tort' in D Nolan and A Robertson (eds), *Rights and Private Law* (Oxford, Hart Publishing, 2011) 459.

[3] *Hunter v Canary Wharf Ltd* [1997] AC 655 (HL). For complications this may cause to business plaintiffs, see *Colour Quest Ltd v Total Downstream UK Plc* [2010] EWCA Civ 180, [2011] QB 86.

[4] The latter has been defined broadly as 'the personal inconvenience and interference with one's enjoyment, one's quiet, one's personal freedom, anything that discomposes or injuriously affects the senses or the nerves': *St Helen's Smelting Co v Tipping* (1865) 11 HLC 642, 650, (1865) 11 ER 1483, 1486 (Lord Westbury).

[5] *Ibid*. For critique, see AWB Simpson, *Leading Cases in the Common Law* (Oxford, Clarendon Press, 1995) Ch 7; JPS Maclaren, 'Nuisance Law and the Industrial Revolution – Some Lessons from Social History' (1983) 3 *OJLS* 155; JF Brenner, 'Nuisance Law and the Industrial Revolution' (1974) 3 *Journal of Legal Studies* 403 on the tensions underlying judicial decisions in nineteenth century nuisance cases.

liability would only arise if the harm was over and above what would be expected of the locality in question. Equity also permits injunctive relief to protect the plaintiff's rights over the land when appropriate. Authors such as John Wightman have observed, however, that while the origins of private nuisance lie in the protection of rights over land, it has been used since the nineteenth century by plaintiffs to preserve their estates, laying down the basis for protection of a broader range of interests, giving it, what he terms, a double life.[6]

Where does the protection of economic interests fit into this legal framework? This topic is under-researched in that most claims focus on material harm to property and personal discomfort. The typical plaintiff, in student textbooks at least, is the harassed householder unable to sleep due to noise or whose life is blighted by toxic fumes from a neighbouring property. However, as in all areas of tort, the question of protection of economic interests needs to be addressed. As will be seen, businesses and developers will not only be the defendant pursued by the harassed householder, but also, at times, the plaintiff bringing an action due to interference with their use and enjoyment of land leading to loss of profit. This chapter therefore will address the extent to which private nuisance provides for the vindication and protection of economic interests in the laws of England and Wales and Australia.

The choice of these two jurisdictions for comparison is based on a number of factors. They are closely related. Sharing the same common law legal tradition, they are bound historically. It is therefore unsurprising that, as a long-standing tort traceable back to the thirteenth century,[7] the early cases on private nuisance are still influential in both legal systems. On this basis, the starting point for analysis in both jurisdictions is the same. Further, the fact that this is an area of law where reported cases in the upper courts are infrequent means that it makes sense for both jurisdictions to seek authority where they can. Despite the termination of formal ties between the jurisdictions, English case law is still regarded as persuasive authority by the Australian courts.[8] In examining comparatively the core principles arising in private nuisance in both jurisdictions, this chapter will provide a clearer picture of the extent to which economic interests are protected in the common law. It will inevitably also consider the extent to which we see common approaches or divergence. As we shall see, private nuisance is a tort where the facts of the case are particularly important. Attention should be paid, therefore, to the extent cases arising in a rural, agrarian context and those arising in urban, built-up areas where the need for 'give and take' becomes a fact of daily life reflect different approaches to the role of private nuisance in our society.

[6] J Wightman, 'Nuisance – the Environment Tort? *Hunter v Canary Wharf* in the House of Lords' (1998) 61 *MLR* 870.

[7] See PH Winfield, 'Nuisance as a Tort' (1931) 4 *CLJ* 189.

[8] See, generally, M Kirby, 'The Old Commonwealth' in L Blom-Cooper, B Dickson and G Drewry (eds), *The Judicial House of Lords 1876–2009* (Oxford, Oxford University Press, 2009) Ch 19; M Vranken, 'Australia' in JM Smits (ed), *Elgar Encyclopaedia of Comparative Law*, 2nd edn (Cheltenham, Edward Elgar Publishing, 2012).

One further potential obstacle to comparison needs, however, to be addressed straightaway. Between 2002 and 2003, Civil Liability Statutes were introduced across Australia.[9] There is no equivalent in UK law. Nevertheless, in relation to private nuisance, leading authors have indicated that because nuisance is directed at the harm caused, rather than the conduct causing it, and does not as a matter of form require a failure to exercise reasonable care, the civil liability statutes in Australia do not apply.[10] A comparison based on case law is still, therefore, valid.

In examining the tort of private nuisance in England and Wales and Australia, this chapter will assess the extent to which the 'double life' of nuisance might enable developers, businesses and other parties to argue that undue interference with their rights should entitle them to protection of their economic interests either by means of compensation or injunctive relief. It will also highlight private nuisance's uneasy relationship with the tort of negligence which has yet to be satisfactorily resolved.

II. Interference with Economic Interests in Private Nuisance

A. Private Nuisance as a Threat to Economic Interests

We can consider the question of interference with economic interests in private nuisance in two alternative ways. First, the tort itself may impact negatively on the economic interests of the developer or business. Private nuisance protects against undue interference with the plaintiff's use or enjoyment of land and, in so doing, businesses and developers are likely defendants who may find themselves liable to pay damages or ordered to refrain from further development. The question, then, is the extent to which the pursuit of economic gain is deemed wrongful by the courts. Second, and perhaps more conventionally, the tort may be relied upon by businesses in their capacity as plaintiffs. Here, the question is the extent to which private nuisance protects economic interests, notably loss of profits resulting from the interference with the plaintiff's rights over land.

The first is, in fact, the most common scenario. Any tort which protects the land rights of plaintiffs has the potential to interfere with the desire of business

[9] See B McDonald, 'Legislative Intervention in the Law of Negligence: The Common Law, Statutory Interpretation and Tort Reform in Australia' (2005) 27 *Sydney Law Review* 443.

[10] See H Luntz et al, *Torts: Cases and Commentary*, 8th edn (Sydney, LexisNexis Butterworths Australia, 2017) [14.1.1], citing *Southern Properties (WA) Pty Ltd v Executive Director of the Department of Conservation and Land Management* [2012] WASCA 79 [329] (Pullin JA). See also *Dimitrios Michos v Council of the City of Botany Bay* [2012] NSWSC 625, (2012) 189 LGERA 25 [68] in relation to the *Civil Liability Act 2002* (NSW). See, however, section IV below on the relationship between negligence and private nuisance.

defendants to use their land for profit. Going back to the industrial revolution, the classic case of *St Helen's Smelting* involved Tipping, the landowner of Bold Hall, bringing a claim against a copper smelting operation. The Court faced a number of questions relating to the extent to which an individual could restrict the operation of a commercial enterprise. Lord Westbury LC drew a distinction between a nuisance causing material injury to property and one which is productive of sensible personal discomfort. Case law has long accepted that where the defendant's interference causes the plaintiff material damage, this will generally be regarded as an unreasonable use of land, permitting the plaintiff to claim damages regardless of the nature of the locality.[11] Immaterial loss, however, is less clear-cut. As stated by Lord Westbury, the question:

> … must undoubtedly depend greatly on the circumstances of the place where the thing complained of actually occurs. If a man lives in a town, it is necessary that he should subject himself to the consequences of those operations of trade which may be carried on in his immediate locality, which are actually necessary for trade and commerce, and also for the enjoyment of property, and for the benefit of the inhabitants of the town and of the public at large.[12]

This qualified protection of amenity rights is potentially beneficial to enterprises operating in an industrial location. It is also possible that defendants may be able to avail themselves of the defence of statutory authority, provided, of course, that the nuisance can be shown to be an inevitable consequence of the authorised undertaking.[13] Major industrial enterprises may have statutory protection for their actions even if material harm is caused to another. In, for example, *Southern Properties (WA) Pty Ltd v Executive Director of the Department of Conservation and Land Management*,[14] smoke from a prescribed fire which damaged grapes cultivated for wine production was not actionable due to a defence of statutory authority.

However, the nature of private nuisance as a tort can lead to problems for business defendants. First, as seen in *St Helen's Smelting*, the courts take no notice of the fact that the business had been in operation when the plaintiff acquired his estate. Coming to a nuisance, even where the plaintiff arrives with full knowledge of the potential interference, is no defence. This well-established rule[15] has been

[11] 'As a general proposition, the infliction of physical damage is more likely to be adjudged unreasonable than any other types of interference': *Marsh v Baxter* [2015] WASCA 169, (2015) 49 WAR 1 [260] (McLure P).

[12] *St Helen's Smelting* (n 4) 650 (HLC), 1486 (ER). Steel argues that to the extent the locality principle requires individuals to bear substantial burdens that they would not have to bear were collective interests set aside, without compensation, it is difficult to justify: S Steel, 'The Locality Principle in Private Nuisance' (2017) 76 *CLJ* 145.

[13] *Allen v Gulf Oil* [1981] AC 1001 (HL); *Bankstown City Council v Alamdo Holdings Pty Ltd* [2005] HCA 46, (2005) 223 CLR 660 [16].

[14] *Southern Properties* (n 10) [120].

[15] *Elliotson v Feetham* (1835) 2 Bing NC 134, (1835) 132 ER 53; *Bliss v Hall* (1838) 4 Bing NC 183, (1838) 132 ER 758.

confirmed recently by the UK Supreme Court[16] and in Australia,[17] despite its seeming injustice to established businesses.[18] The nature of private nuisance as a property tort means, therefore, that the right to allege a nuisance runs with the land.

Second, under the test for loss of amenity, the courts will have regard to what an ordinary average resident of the district ought reasonably to have expected under the circumstances.[19] This does render businesses vulnerable to the balancing of interests by the court. Planning permission to engage in the activity in question will rarely assist defendants in that it is regarded as an administrative matter, rather than a defence.[20] The case of *Barr v Biffa Waste Services Ltd*[21] provides a good illustration of the tensions involved. Here, the English Court of Appeal faced a classic battle of interests between a business whose waste disposal business led to unsavoury odours in the neighbourhood. The Court rejected the argument that complying with the terms of a statutory permit[22] meant that the use of the site had been reasonable. The test for private nuisance is that of a 'reasonable user'. In applying that test, the courts are trying to strike a balance between the right of the defendant to use his or her property for his or her own lawful enjoyment and the right of the plaintiff to the undisturbed enjoyment of his or her property.[23] This is a question of degree based on the ordinary usages of mankind on the facts of each individual case. What the courts do not factor into this equation, in terms of strict law at least,[24] is the broader community benefits which the defendant enterprise might provide in terms of employment, prosperity, etc to the neighbourhood. It is not a defence to show that the business or activity of the defendant is a useful one, even if the activity is highly desirable

[16] *Coventry v Lawrence* [2014] UKSC 13, [2014] AC 822.

[17] *Campbelltown Golf Club v Winton* [1998] NSWSC 257.

[18] See, eg, *Sturges v Bridgman* (1879) 11 Ch D 852 (CA) where an injunction was granted against a confectioner who had for more than 20 years used a pestle and mortar in his back premises, whose noise and vibration only became a problem when his neighbour chose to erect a consulting room at the end of his garden. It was, suggested in *Coventry v Lawrence* (n 16), however, that the rule should no longer continue to apply where the plaintiff had altered his or her use of property after the activity in question has started if the activity would not have been a nuisance had the alteration not occurred: [53] (Lord Neuberger).

[19] *Marsh v Baxter* (n 11). See also *Munro v Southern Dairies Ltd* [1955] VLR 332 (VSC); *Walter v Selfe* (1851) 4 De G & Sm 315, 322, (1851) 64 ER 849, 852: whether it is 'an inconvenience materially interfering with the ordinary comfort … of human existence'.

[20] *Coventry v Lawrence* (n 16).

[21] *Barr v Biffa Waste Services Ltd* [2012] EWCA Civ 312, [2013] QB 455. This was a group action where Biffa, whose major commercial interests lay in waste-tipping, were keen to resolve its responsibilities to the local community in this and similar cases. See also *Bamford v Turnley* (1860) 3 B & S 62, (1860) 175 ER 1037; *Adams v Ursell* [1913] 1 Ch 269 (Ch).

[22] The UK Environment Agency, exercising its statutory powers, had granted a waste management permit for the tipping of pre-treated waste on the site.

[23] *Sedleigh-Denfield v O'Callaghan* [1940] AC 880 (HL) 903 (Lord Wright); *Cambridge Water Co v Eastern Counties Leather Plc* [1994] 2 AC 264 (HL) 299 (Lord Goff).

[24] See M Lee, 'The Public Interest in Private Nuisance: Collectives and Communities in Tort' (2015) 74 *CLJ* 329.

in the public interest.[25] However, much lies at the discretion of the court and it is possible to find dicta that indicate that, in reality, benefit to the community may play some role in determining whether the use of land is 'reasonable'.[26] In *Biffa* itself, a group action had been brought by 152 households living near a waste tip. The Court emphasised that there is no absolute standard in private nuisance; it is a question of degree. This was to be decided by reference to all the circumstances of the case. Despite the grant of a specific waste permit, the Court of Appeal held that the introduction of 'pre-treated' tipping which led to a series of episodes of unpleasant smells over a five-year period, affecting the ordinary enjoyment of residents' houses and gardens, amounted to a reasonably clear-cut private nuisance.

This is not the end of the story, however. In determining the appropriate remedy, the courts seem to be more receptive to the argument that the benefits provided by the enterprise to the local community should be taken into account in determining whether the court will award an injunction against the defendant.[27] Allegations, therefore, that the grant of an injunction may lead to the closure of the defendant's business (with loss of jobs) or that the wider community interests had influenced the grant of planning permission,[28] may encourage the court to refrain from injunctive relief and award damages instead.[29] Lord Sumption was more forthright in *Coventry v Lawrence*:

> There is much to be said for the view that damages are ordinarily an adequate remedy for nuisance and that an injunction should not usually be granted in a case where it is likely that conflicting interests are engaged other than the parties' interests. In particular, it may well be that an injunction should as a matter of principle not be granted in a case where a use of land to which objection is taken requires and has received planning permission.[30]

Private nuisance then provides plaintiffs with a potential means of halting (if injunctive relief if given) or making more expensive (if damages are awarded) the activities of the defendants, thereby harming their economic interests. As seen above, while the main focus initially was on material harm to property, as *Biffa* testifies, claims for loss of amenity, particularly if brought as a class action, can prove problematic. The Court of Appeal noted in that case that the successful claims were unlikely to add up to more than a few tens of thousands of pounds. Nevertheless, by the time the case reached the Court of Appeal, the costs were of the order of £3 million on each side.[31] Even if

[25] See, generally, M Jones (ed), *Clerk and Lindsell on Torts*, 23rd edn (London, Sweet and Maxwell, 2020) [19-107].
[26] *Southern Properties* (n 10) [118]–[120]; *Coventry v Lawrence* (n 16) [96].
[27] See now in UK law, *Coventry v Lawrence* (n 16).
[28] *Ibid* [124]–[125] (Lord Neuberger).
[29] See also *Miller v Jackson* [1977] QB 966 (CA).
[30] *Coventry v Lawrence* (n 16) [161].
[31] *Barr v Biffa* (n 21) [48].

injunctive relief is not granted, therefore, the finding of a nuisance can have significant financial implications for a business.

B. Private Nuisance Protecting Economic Interests

The second, and perhaps most obvious, way of addressing economic wrongs and private nuisance is to examine the extent to which private nuisance *protects* the economic interests of the plaintiff. Here we are examining a conventional claim for private nuisance, but the injury is not that of property damage but rather financial loss. Classically the law regards private nuisance as falling into three categories:

1) nuisance by encroachment on a neighbour's land;
2) nuisance by direct physical injury to a neighbour's land; and
3) nuisance by interference with a neighbour's quiet enjoyment of his land.[32]

Should any of these three heads be established, a claim may be made for encroachment, physical injury or loss of amenity and consequential economic loss.[33]

However, we can identify three particular obstacles which will reduce the plaintiff's ability to protect his or her economic interests. First, the interference complained of must negatively affect the plaintiff's use or enjoyment of land. This is fundamental. Second, the plaintiff's use of land must not be regarded as 'extra-sensitive'. This is the way in which the tort of private nuisance balances the interests of ordinary citizens against those who seek to impose their own personal idiosyncrasies on others and therefore fail to 'give and take'. Third, the economic loss suffered by the plaintiff must be reasonably foreseeable. As will be seen, this final condition is significant in that it applies across both nuisance and the tort of negligence.

All three obstacles will be examined below.

i. Has There Been an Interference Causing Harm to the Plaintiff's Use or Enjoyment of Land?

The 'nuisance' must be shown to interfere with the plaintiff's use or enjoyment of the land, causing damage to the plaintiff's interests. There is clear authority that simple interference with the profitable conduct of a business on the land will not amount to a private nuisance.[34] Where, for example, the defendant used his land to construct a platform to enable a broadcasting station to report the results of horse-racing taking place on the plaintiffs' neighbouring land, leading to a loss of income to the plaintiffs due to a fall in spectator numbers, this was not regarded

[32] *Hunter v Canary Wharf Ltd* (n 3) 695 (Lord Lloyd).

[33] See Lord Hoffmann in *Hunter v Canary Wharf, ibid* 704–706, giving examples of loss of profits resulting from inability to use the land for the purposes of his business.

[34] *Victoria Park Racing and Recreation Grounds Co Ltd v Taylor* (1937) 58 CLR 479 (HCA) 508. See also *Bradford Corp v Pickles* [1895] AC 587 (HL).

as a nuisance in law. There had been no interference with an identifiable right over land. The onus in such cases is on the plaintiff to find an alternative cause of action in such circumstances such as harassment.[35] More recently, the English Court of Appeal in *Fearn v The Board of Trustees of the Tate Gallery*[36] held that installing a viewing platform from which visitors to the Tate Gallery would, in addition to the sights of London, be able to look into nearby flats did not amount to an actionable nuisance, even where, as here, it was likely to affect the resale value of the properties. It was an issue for planning or privacy law, not the tort of private nuisance.

Further, to bring a claim for private nuisance the plaintiff must show damage. While this can be material or immaterial damage, until damage is caused, as a matter of strict law, no nuisance exists, only the potentiality of a nuisance.[37] The recent English case of *Network Rail Infrastructure Ltd v Williams*[38] highlighted the potential difficulties of identifying actionable 'damage' when the primary concern is the plaintiff's financial loss. In this case, an infestation of Japanese knotweed had spread from the defendants' land to that of the plaintiffs, although it had yet to cause any physical damage. A notoriously invasive weed, the plaintiffs alleged that its presence had affected their ability to sell their properties at a proper market value.[39] The question was therefore to what extent the inability of the householder to dispose of his or her property at a proper value was actionable when the 'blight' had been caused by the defendant. The Court of Appeal found the concept of 'damage' in private nuisance to be 'a highly elastic one',[40] but that the tort did not extend to protecting the value of property as an investment or financial asset. This would, says the Court, extend the tort to *pure* economic loss: 'that would not be an incremental development of the common law by way of analogy but a radical reformulation of the purpose and scope of the tort'.[41] As Sandy Steel graphically illustrates in his example, well-known gangsters moving next door to you may negatively affect the market value of your property, but it is not an actionable nuisance as it has no effect on your ability to use the land.[42] However, by interpreting the loss as that arising due to the immediate burden the presence of knotweed would place on the landowner in terms of an increased difficulty in the ability to develop, and in the cost of developing, the land, should the owner wish to do so, the Court was able to grant recovery.

[35] See *Bernstein of Leigh (Baron) v Skyviews & General Ltd* [1978] 1 QB 479 (QB), although that question did not arise in this case.

[36] *Fearn v The Board of Trustees of the Tate Gallery* [2020] EWCA Civ 104, [2020] Ch 621, overturning [2019] EWHC 246 (Ch), [2019] Ch 369.

[37] *Sedleigh-Denfield v O'Callaghan* (n 23).

[38] *Network Rail Infrastructure Ltd v Williams* [2018] EWCA Civ 1514, [2019] QB 601.

[39] The plaintiffs indicated that mortgage lenders, since around 2012, had been reluctant or had refused to provide mortgages where Japanese knotweed was found to be within seven metres of the property's boundary.

[40] *Williams* (n 38) [42] (Sir Terence Etherton MR).

[41] *Ibid* [48] (Sir Terence Etherton MR).

[42] S Steel, 'The Gist of Private Nuisance' (2019) 135 *LQR* 192, 194.

Such a 'natural hazard' should be regarded, said the Court, as a classic example of an interference with the amenity value of the land.[43]

It remains the case, however, that an interference that cannot be proven substantially to interfere with a property right, but merely affects the profitability of the plaintiff's enterprise will not give rise to an action in nuisance.

ii. Extra-Sensitive Plaintiffs

Businesses suffering economic loss as a result of a nuisance render themselves vulnerable also to the accusation that their losses are due to the specific trade or enterprise in which they are engaged. In *Robinson v Kilvert*,[44] for example, by engaging in an 'exceptionally delicate trade'[45] – here taking the premises as a warehouse for paper and twine – the tenant was unable to establish that his landlord, by heating the cellar underneath and drying out his brown paper and making it less valuable, had committed a nuisance. Such heat would not injure paper generally and so the plaintiff could not sue for the diminution of profits in consequence of rendering the paper brittle. Equally, in the Australian case of *Marsh v Baxter*,[46] the plaintiffs claimed for economic loss of AUD $85,000 resulting from their organic farm being contaminated by the harvesting of genetically modified (GM) canola in a neighbouring farm. The canola was not dangerous to people, livestock or property (including the Marshes' own livestock), so the only loss was the organic certification. The majority refused to regard the growth of GM crops as an unreasonable method of farming[47] (and argued, in contrast, that the plaintiffs' use of land was abnormally sensitive ('an isolated practice in the area')). Commentators regard the failure of the Marshes' case as a significant defeat for opponents of GM crops and their farming.[48]

The English case of *Network Rail Infrastructure Ltd v Morris*[49] does suggest a more flexible approach could be taken. In this case, Network Rail's signalling system was found to affect the sound of the electric guitars in Morris' recording

[43] *Williams* (n 38) [55].

[44] *Robinson v Kilvert* (1889) 41 Ch D 88 (CA). See also *Bridlington Relay Ltd v Yorkshire Electricity Board* [1965] Ch 436 (Ch) (interference with special radio and television relay system); *E & S African Telegraph v Cape Town Tramways* [1902] AC 381 (PC) (electrical interference with the transmission of messages in a submarine cable).

[45] *Robinson* (n 44) 97 (Lopes LJ): 'A man who carries on an exceptionally delicate trade cannot complain because it is injured by his neighbour doing something lawful on his property, if it is something which would not injure anything but an exceptionally delicate trade.'

[46] *Marsh v Baxter* (n 11). The High Court dismissed the Marshes' application for leave to appeal.

[47] It had been licensed under statute. A claim for negligence also failed.

[48] A Bunn, and M Douglas, 'Breaking New Ground? Nuisance, Negligence and Pure Economic Loss in *Marsh v Baxter*' (2014) 22 *Torts Law Journal* 160. See also K Ludlow, 'The Economic Impact of Genetically Modified Organisms as Actionable Damage in Torts' (2005) 13 *Torts Law Journal* 159; CP Rodgers, 'Liability for the Release of GMOs into the Environment: Exploring the Boundaries of Nuisance' (2003) 62 *CLJ* 371, 378–80.

[49] *Network Rail Infrastructure Ltd v Morris* [2004] EWCA Civ 172.

studio (80 metres from the main track).[50] The Court of Appeal was critical of using the concept of extra-sensitivity to exclude activities which were part of modern life, describing it as 'outmoded'. In its view it was difficult to say, in the modern era, that the type of recording studio involved was so unusual as *necessarily* to disqualify Morris from the protection of the law of nuisance. Nevertheless, the Court of Appeal stressed that businesses would have to show an undue interference leading to foreseeable harm. On the facts of the case, expert evidence had indicated that it was not reasonable to foresee interference as far away as 80 metres and so the claim failed.

Where, however, a private nuisance has been established and damage to the plaintiff's economic interests is reasonably foreseeable, there is authority that remedies by way of damages or an injunction can extend to delicate and sensitive operations such as the commercial growing of orchids.[51] Equally, there is dicta indicating that a sensitive use might be converted into a nuisance where the interference is motivated by malice. In *Hollywood Silver Fox Farm Ltd v Emmett*,[52] for example, the plaintiff company carried on the business of breeding silver foxes on their land. During the breeding season the vixens are very nervous, and liable if disturbed either to refuse to breed, to miscarry, or to kill their young. The defendant, an adjoining landowner, intentionally caused his son to discharge guns on his own land as near as possible to the breeding pens for the purpose of injuring the plaintiffs by interfering with the breeding of the foxes. Here, the Court rejected the extra-sensitive user argument: the defendant acted for the purpose of annoyance, and it was not a legitimate use of the defendant's land to use it for the purpose of vexing and annoying his neighbours.

iii. Damage Must be Reasonably Foreseeable

In *Wagon Mound (No 2)*,[53] the Privy Council (dealing with an appeal from Australia) found that the remoteness test in negligence was equally applicable to claims in private and public nuisance. Only loss of a kind that was reasonably foreseeable could be claimed. This test has been followed in England and Wales and Australia, despite being a Privy Council decision, and, as Harold Luntz et al point out, strictly obiter in relation to private nuisance.[54] Commentators have noted

[50] As a result of the noise interference with amplifiers in the studio, Morris lost customers at the studio and claimed to have lost £60,000 in income.

[51] *McKinnon Industries Ltd v Walker* [1951] 3 DLR 577, 581.

[52] *Hollywood Silver Fox Farm Ltd v Emmett* [1936] 2 KB 468; *Marsh v Baxter* (n 11) [787]: 'it was clearly relevant that the appellants did not deliberately cause the swathes to be released on to the appellants' land'.

[53] *Overseas Tankship (UK) Ltd v Miller SS Co Pty* [1967] 1 AC 617 (PC) ('*Wagon Mound (No 2)*'). On its implications for the law of tort, see RWM Dias, 'Trouble on Oiled Waters: Problems of The Wagon Mound (No.2)' [1967] *CLJ* 62.

[54] Luntz et al (n 10) [14.4.4].

the breadth of this principle.[55] In *Cambridge Water*,[56] therefore, liability did not arise under the rule in *Rylands v Fletcher* (which is still part of private nuisance in English law)[57] where a chemical from the defendants' factory escaped and contaminated the local water supply, rendering it unfit for human consumption. The defendants' tanning works were about 1.3 miles away from the borehole, the chemical having seeped into the ground beneath the works and thence conveyed in percolating water in the direction of the borehole. The House of Lords held that the firm could not have possibly foreseen at the relevant time this turn of events and that the defendants should not be under any greater liability than that imposed for negligence.[58]

The problems this may cause to plaintiffs are ably demonstrated in the case of *Gales Holdings Pty Ltd v Tweed Shire Council*.[59] *Gales* highlights that even where a nuisance is proved, the full extent of the plaintiffs' economic losses may not be recoverable. In this case, stormwater runoff had flowed onto the plaintiffs' land which had caused a substantial wetting up, which in turn resulted in the development of a habitat for the Wallum Froglet, which is a protected species. This led to conditions being imposed on development approval, diminishing the value of the land. While the Council was found guilty of nuisance for changes in drainage systems that they had approved or made,[60] the Court was of the view that the increase in the froglet population was not foreseeable. While only the kind of damage in question need be foreseeable and it was not necessary to establish the reasonable foreseeability of the creation of a habitat for a *particular* vulnerable species, it was necessary nevertheless to establish the reasonably foreseeable possibility that *some* vulnerable species might establish itself.[61] In this case, therefore, the plaintiffs did obtain injunctive relief to minimise the stormwater flow and some damages, but this specific head of loss was not recoverable. The New South Wales Court of Appeal added that the reasonable foreseeability test would apply regardless of whether the nuisance was intentionally or negligently caused.[62]

iv. Concluding Remarks

Essentially the dilemma facing businesses seeking to protect their economic interests in private nuisance is whether the interference harming the rights over land will be regarded as 'extra-sensitive' or give rise to particular forms of harm which

[55] For example the precise accident or harm need not be foreseeable: Jones (n 25) [2-156]ff.

[56] *Cambridge Water* (n 23).

[57] See *Transco Plc v Stockport MBC* [2003] UKHL 61, [2004] 2 AC 1.

[58] *Cambridge Water* (n 23) 307 (Lord Goff).

[59] *Gales Holdings Pty Ltd v Tweed Shire Council* [2013] NSWCA 382. Leave to appeal to High Court refused.

[60] This led to directing the flow of stormwater runoff onto the land in greater quantities and in greater volumes than would flow naturally.

[61] *Gales* (n 59) [281] (Leeming JA; Sackville AJA concurring).

[62] *Ibid* [144].

are not reasonably foreseeable to the defendant. Otherwise, the ordinary principles of private nuisance will apply. The above cases demonstrate that despite businesses being more obviously the defendant rather than the plaintiff in nuisance cases, they can and do resort to private nuisance claims. The question then arises as to what extent they are able to obtain remedies for their financial losses.

III. Interference with Economic Interests: Remedies

The remedial response of the courts to private nuisance will be determined by the type of harm suffered. Damage to property is normally assessed according to diminution in value of the land. Equally, damage to personal property may be recovered as consequential loss and assessed similarly.[63] Interference with the utility and amenity value is more problematic.[64] If the interference reduces the value of the plaintiff's property, substantial damages for reduction in value may be awarded. Where it does not, the rights holder will be able to sue for an award determined by the court which represents the diminished utility value of the land.[65] In a number of cases, the courts have recognised that financial loss *consequential* on property loss or loss of amenity is recoverable, for example, where the interference prevents the plaintiff from using the land for the purposes of his or her business.[66] In *Andreae v Selfridge & Co Ltd*,[67] therefore, the owner of a hotel was allowed to recover damages for the loss of custom suffered by her business due to noise and dust caused by the defendants' construction work. Equally, in *Jan de Nul (UK) Ltd v AXA Royale Belge SA (formerly NV Royale Belge)*,[68] the Court of Appeal permitted the Hampshire Wildlife Trust to recover over £100,000 for an investigation into silting of feeding grounds at the head of an estuary. Although the report had indicated no long-term damage would occur, the Court found that it had acted reasonably in commissioning such a report and the cost of the survey was consequential on physical interference with its property rights. A decision of the Supreme Court of Canada, *Antrim Truck Centre Ltd v Ontario (Transportation)*,[69] provides a further example. Here damages covering business losses and diminution of property value were recoverable when a new road construction project substantially interfered with the use and enjoyment of the appellant's restaurant and gas bar at a truck stop complex.

[63] *Hunter v Canary Wharf Ltd* (n 3) 706 (Lord Hoffmann).

[64] Jones (n 25) [19-29].

[65] *Bone v Seale* [1975] 1 All ER 787 (damages awarded to compensate for loss of amenity caused by smells from an adjacent pig farm).

[66] See, eg, Lord Hoffmann (obiter) in *Hunter v Canary Wharf* (n 3) 706.

[67] *Andreae v Selfridge & Co Ltd* [1938] Ch 1 (CA). See also Lawton J in *British Celanese v Hunt* [1969] 1 WLR 959 (QB).

[68] *Jan de Nul (UK) Ltd v AXA Royale Belge SA (formerly NV Royale Belge)* [2002] EWCA Civ 209, [2002] 1 Lloyd's Rep 583.

[69] *Antrim Truck Centre Ltd v Ontario (Transportation)* 2013 SCC 13, [2013] 1 SCR 594.

It is clear then that once a nuisance is proven, the courts are able to compensate for economic loss, subject of course to the rule of remoteness. It must, however, be seen as a result of the interference with the use of land. This means for example that, in England and Wales, and it is generally assumed in Australia,[70] damages for personal injury are not recoverable in the tort of private nuisance. This is justified on the basis that it is a tort dedicated to the protection of property interests. Personal injury does, however, remain recoverable in the non-property tort of public nuisance (and, of course, negligence).[71] Private nuisance provides a rare example in the law of tort where economic interests receive greater protection than injury to the person.

The above framework reflects the particular characteristics of the tort of private nuisance. Despite the fact that, private nuisance shares a common remoteness test with negligence and is often pleaded alongside negligence claims, the courts have not sought to draw analogies between the treatment of economic loss in both these torts. It seems to be regarded as a non-issue given that they are distinct torts. However, as will be seen in the next section, this becomes problematic when it becomes clear that negligence (or, perhaps more accurately, fault-based reasoning) plays a not insignificant role in the tort of private nuisance in both jurisdictions. As the division between the two torts becomes blurred, how do we justify, for example, the fact that financial losses suffered when a hotel is forced to close due to noise and vibrations from nearby building work are recoverable in nuisance (*Andreae*[72]), but not where the closure is due to the negligent acts of the defendant requiring vital structural repairs (*Murphy v Brentwood DC*[73])? As John Fleming posits:

> This can result in odd distinctions: a road repairer who paralyses an adjoining hotel by negligently cutting a connecting electric cable will not be liable, but one who does so through vibrations, noise and dust will be.[74]

The next section will address tensions between the treatment of economic loss in private nuisance and the tort of negligence.

[70] The position is less clear in Australia where certain cases do not seem to have viewed the award of damages for the personal impact of the nuisance as a problem: *Cohen v Perth* [2000] WASC 306, (2000) 112 LGERA 234 (damages for sleep deprivation caused by noise nuisance); *Broken Hill City Council v Tiziani* [1997] NSWSC 20 (flooding of home causing mental distress). It is possible, however, to regard these cases as compensating broadly for loss of amenity: see *Dobson v Thames Water Utilities Ltd* [2009] EWCA Civ 28 which held that the actual impact of the nuisance upon the occupiers of the land would in practice be relevant to the assessment of common law damages for loss of amenity in many cases.

[71] *Corby Group Litigation v Corby BC* [2008] EWCA Civ 463, [2009] QB 335.

[72] *Andreae* (n 67). See also Lawton J in *British Celanese* (n 67).

[73] *Murphy v Brentwood DC* [1991] 1 AC 398 (HL). Woolcock Street Investments Pty Ltd v CDG Pty Ltd (2004) 216 CLR 515.

[74] C Sappideen and P Vines (eds), *Fleming's The Law of Torts*, 10th edn (Sydney, Thomson Reuters Australia, 2011) [21-260].

IV. Interference with Economic Interests: Tensions with Negligence?

In this section, we will examine two questions. First, to what extent is there an overlap between the torts of negligence and private nuisance, and second, given this overlap, can the different approaches to economic loss be reconciled? We will also consider why, despite some attention by academic writers, the tensions between negligence and private nuisance have yet to be fully addressed by the courts.

A. Negligence and Private Nuisance: An Overlap?

Traditionally private nuisance has been regarded as a strict liability tort. Classically in *Rapier v London Tramways Co*,[75] the Court held that even where a defendant acts with all due care and skill, if a nuisance occurs, this is no defence.[76] In modern law, however, the situation is less clear-cut.[77] A body of law renders occupiers of land liable for the nuisances created by others, whether by trespassers or natural events, if they fail to take reasonable steps to abate the nuisance.[78] Lest this be regarded as exceptional, in the second half of the twentieth century, courts came to realise that 'although negligence may not be necessary, fault of some kind is almost always necessary and fault generally involves foreseeability'.[79]

Generally, then, while fault, which may extend from carelessness to the deliberate or reckless use of land in a way the defendant knows is likely to cause harm, is not a condition of liability, its presence renders a finding of an actionable nuisance more likely. President McLure expresses well in the *Southern Properties* case the tension between the strict liability character of private nuisance and the reality of court decisions:

> Although the 'fault' of the defendant may be a relevant consideration in an assessment of whether the interference with the claimant's enjoyment of land is unreasonable, the

[75] *Rapier v London Tramways Co* [1893] 2 Ch 588 (CA).

[76] See Luxmoore J in *Vanderpant v Mayfair Hotel Co* [1930] 1 Ch 138 (Ch) 166: 'the making or causing of such a noise as materially interferes with the comfort of a neighbour when judged by the standard to which I have just referred, constitutes an actionable nuisance, and it is no answer to say that the best-known means have been taken to reduce or prevent the noise complained of, or that the cause of the nuisance is the exercise of a business or trade in a reasonable and proper manner'.

[77] See M Lee, 'What is Private Nuisance?' (2003) 119 *LQR* 298; C Gearty, 'The Place of Private Nuisance in a Modern Law of Torts' (1989) 48 *CLJ* 214. Winfield also highlights that an overlap between nuisance and negligence had existed historically, see PH Winfield, 'The History of Negligence in the Law of Torts' (1926) 42 *LQR* 184, 197–98.

[78] Jones (n 25) [19-42]; K Barker et al, *The Law of Torts in Australia*, 5th edn (Sydney, Oxford University Press, 2012) 213–17.

[79] *Wagon Mound (No 2)* (n 53) 639 (Lord Reid). Approved in *Elston v Dore* (1982) 149 CLR 480 (HCA) 488.

> duty not to expose one's neighbours to nuisance is not necessarily discharged by the exercise of reasonable care. Liability in nuisance is strict.[80]

For occupiers, however, special rules apply. In *Sedleigh-Denfield v O'Callaghan*, the defendants were held liable for the overflow of water onto the plaintiffs' land causing damage when trespassers had interfered with the draining system on their land. By knowing (through their employees) of the problem and failing to take reasonable steps to abate it, the defendants were liable.[81] Equally, in *City of Richmond v Scantelbury*,[82] the roots of elm trees had encroached on neighbouring land, extracting water and moisture from the subsoil and undermining the structuring of a neighbouring property. The Supreme Court of Victoria found liability to arise where the occupier (here the Council) had known or should have been aware of the nuisance and the real possibility of damage occurring. In all cases, fault is a condition for liability.[83]

In both jurisdictions, *Goldman v Hargrave*[84] offers guidance when an occupier will find him or herself liable for failing to take reasonable steps to safeguard the interests of their neighbours, here in abating a fire which had been started by lightning striking a tree on his land. In so doing, the Court made no attempt to resolve whether the liability of the occupier should be classified as arising under nuisance or placed in a separate category:

> [T]he tort of nuisance, uncertain in its boundary, may comprise a wide variety of situations, in some of which negligence plays no part, in others of which it is decisive. The present case is one where liability, if it exists, rests upon negligence and nothing else; whether it falls within or overlaps the boundaries of nuisance is a question of classification which need not here be resolved.[85]

We can identify, however, two distinctions between *Goldman* liability and that of ordinary negligence principles. First, in negligence there is no general liability for a failure to act (often stated as the rule of 'no liability for pure omissions'). Lord Goff in *Smith v Littlewoods*[86] distinguished *Goldman* as one of the exceptions to this rule in that it places a person under an *affirmative* duty to prevent harm being caused by a source of danger which has arisen without his fault.[87] In the context of the case, where vandals had set fire to a derelict cinema on

[80] *Southern Properties* (n 10) [119] (McLure P).

[81] *Sedleigh-Denfield v O'Callaghan* (n 23). See also *Montana Hotels Pty Ltd v Fasson* [1987] VR 147 (VSC) (aff'd (1986) 69 ALR 258 (PC)).

[82] *City of Richmond v Scantelbury* [1991] 2 VR 38 (VSC).

[83] Such claims failed in *Montana Hotels v Fasson* (1986) 69 ALR 258 (PC) (occupier could not reasonably be expected to know of seepage traced to a broken drainpipe next door) and *British Road Services v Slater* [1964] 1 WLR 498 (occupier had no reason to realise that a high branch protruding into the road from one of his trees constituted a hazard to passing trucks piled 16 feet high).

[84] *Goldman v Hargrave* [1967] 1 AC 645 (PC appeal from Australia).

[85] *Ibid* 657. See also Megaw LJ in *Leakey v National Trust for Places of Historic Interest or Natural Beauty* [1980] QB 485 (CA) 514–15.

[86] *Smith v Littlewoods* [1987] AC 241 (HL) 271.

[87] See BS Markesinis, 'Negligence, Nuisance and Affirmative Duties of Action' (1989) 105 *LQR* 104.

the defendants' land, such liability would only arise where the defendants had the knowledge (or means of knowledge) that the vandals had created the risk of fire and then had failed to take reasonable steps to prevent it damaging the plaintiffs' land. This was not the case on the facts.[88]

Second, the duty on the occupier is a 'measured' one: it is not identical to that found in the tort of negligence. As explained by Lord Wilberforce:

> The law must take account of the fact that the occupier on whom the duty is cast has, ex hypothesi, had this hazard thrust upon him through no seeking or fault of his own. His interest, and his resources, whether physical or material, may be of a very modest character either in relation to the magnitude of the hazard, or as compared with those of his threatened neighbour. A rule which required of him in such unsought circumstances in his neighbour's interest a physical effort of which he is not capable, or an excessive expenditure of money, would be unenforceable or unjust ... In such situations the standard ought to be to require of the occupier what it is reasonable to expect of him in his individual circumstances.[89]

Where, therefore, the defendant is poor, and abatement will require vast expense, the defendant will not be considered liable. Equally, less will be expected of the infirm than of the able-bodied. In *Holbeck Hall Hotel Ltd v Scarborough BC* (No 2),[90] the Court of Appeal applied the test to a local authority that had been sued for loss of support. Here, a massive landslip in 1993 had led to the collapse of part of the four-star Holbeck Hall Hotel, which was situated at the top of a cliff overlooking the North Sea. As a result, the hotel had to be demolished. The hoteliers sued the local council, which owned the land forming the undercliff between the hotel and the sea, for loss of support, claiming that they should have taken measures to prevent the damage caused. The council had been aware of the danger of landslips due to marine erosion, and had undertaken works in the past, but had not foreseen a landslip of this magnitude. The Court of Appeal rejected the claim. Applying Lord Wilberforce's test, the Council would not be found liable for failing to undertake measures which only a geological expert could have identified as necessary. A defendant would thus not be liable where he or she was unable to foresee the extent of the loss suffered. Even if the loss had been foreseeable, in view of the extensive and expensive nature of the works necessary, the Court suggested that the scope of the duty might be limited to warning neighbours of the risks the Council were aware of or ought to have foreseen and sharing such information.[91]

[88] It was no more than a merely foreseeable possibility that trespassers would gain access to land and cause damage to the property of neighbouring owners.

[89] *Goldman* (n 84) 663. Also explained in *Smith v Littlewoods* (n 86) 275 (Lord Goff).

[90] *Holbeck Hall Hotel Ltd v Scarborough BC (No 2)* [2000] QB 836 (CA). Comment: MP Thompson, 'Coastal Erosion and Collapsing Hotels' [2001] *Conveyancer and Property Lawyer* 177.

[91] See *Holbeck Hall Hotel, ibid* 863 (Stuart-Smith LJ). See also *Lambert v Barratt Homes Ltd* [2010] EWCA Civ 681, [2010] 33 EG 72 where the Court expressly recognised that most local authorities operate under a degree of financial pressure and held that the measured duty of care involved, here, only a duty to cooperate in a solution which involved the construction of suitable drainage.

B. Negligence and Private Nuisance: Protecting Economic Interests

We have highlighted above two ways in which fault-based reasoning manifests itself in the tort of private nuisance. First, while fault is not required to establish an unreasonable use of land, it helps and is often present on the facts. As Bryson JA stated in *Sutherland Shire Council v Becker*, '[a]lthough there may be some exceptions, fault of some kind is now usually necessary for liability in nuisance'.[92] Second, we have seen that, for occupiers, a 'measured' duty arises to abate a nuisance where the occupier has adopted or continued a nuisance created by another or a natural event. This is a distinctive duty in that the resources of the defendant are taken into account. As stated recently in the English Court of Appeal, the issue here is what is fair, just and reasonable between the two neighbouring landowners; the Court regarding all the relevant circumstances which here include the extent of the foreseeable risk, the availability of preventative measures, the costs of such measures and the resources of both parties.[93] Finally, it should be recalled that negligence and nuisance share the same test for remoteness, based on the view that it would be unjust to place too great a burden on the defendant to remedy unforeseeable loss.

Given the close relationship between nuisance and negligence, one might question why financial losses do not seem to have raised the same concerns as found in the tort of negligence. All tort lawyers will be familiar with the general reluctance of the tort of negligence to allow recovery for economic loss premised on the fear of indeterminate liability.[94] That this discussion does not take place in private nuisance might seem surprising. Case law, as seen above, tends to be more concerned with matters of remoteness rather than wider concerns of indeterminate liability.

Two reasons can be found to explain why the common law courts have not sought to resolve the tensions between private nuisance and negligence in this field. First, under the common law system of nominate torts, there is no duty to reconcile the approaches of different torts. This may be contrasted with the position taken in civil law systems where there is a greater tendency to seek general principles of tort law and thus remove inconsistencies. In such systems, the State's civil (or private law) code will generally include a specific section on tort law which will set out the rules of tort law collectively.[95] This is taken a step further in systems based on the French legal system which conceptualise tort law

[92] *Sutherland Shire Council v Becker* [2006] NSWCA 344 [119]. See also *Robson v Leischke* [2008] NSWLEC 152, (2008) 72 NSWLR 98 [44].

[93] See *Vernon Knight Associates v Cornwall Council* [2013] EWCA Civ 950 [49] (Jackson LJ).

[94] The so-called 'floodgates' argument: see *Ultramares Corp v Touche*, 174 NE 441 (NY, 1931) (Cardozo CJ).

[95] U Magnus, 'Tort Law in General' in JM Smits (ed), *Elgar Encyclopaedia of Comparative Law*, 2nd edn (Cheltenham, Edward Elgar Publishing, 2012).

through the use of general clauses setting out principles of fault-based and strict liability.[96] The civilian approach prioritises the need to identify rules applicable across the law of tort when possible.[97] The very different historical development of the common law through the writ system means that rather than seeking general principles of tort law, the common law courts' focus is on the rationalisation of individual torts. This difference in approach may be seen in the treatment of the nineteenth century rule in *Rylands v Fletcher* over the last 30 years. Both the English and Australian courts have sought to review its validity as a distinct tort (reaching, interestingly, different results),[98] but have avoided the creation of any general principle of extra-hazardous liability.[99] In this light, it is unsurprising that the courts have not seen it as their role to resolve the conceptual tension between negligence and private nuisance.[100] Lord Justice Megaw, for example, in *Leakey v National Trust* stated that:

> [T]here is an allegation of a breach of duty, and the duty asserted is, in effect, a duty to take reasonable care to prevent part of the defendants' land from falling on to the plaintiffs' property. I should, for myself, regard that as being properly described as a claim in nuisance. But even if that were, technically, wrong, I do not think that the point could or should avail the defendants in this case. If it were to do so, it would be a regrettable modern instance of the forms of action successfully clanking their spectral chains.[101]

His Lordship's point, it will be noted, is one of civil procedure, not legal coherence. It is not therefore a problem that the *Wagon Mound* test applies to negligence and public and private nuisance. Under the nominate system of tort law in England and Wales and Australia, it is simply a matter of setting out the rules for each tort. Rules are not regarded as a general framing device for tortious liability and so it is not a problem that other torts, such as deceit, have different rules of remoteness.[102]

Second, it is possible conceptually to explain the cautious approach of negligence compared to the *sangfroid* of nuisance towards claims for economic loss. The concern of negligence is with pure economic loss and the threat of indeterminate

[96] See *Code Civil* [Civil Code] (France) Arts 1240–1242 (renumbered in 2016 from earlier Arts 1382–1384). For an overview, see E Steiner, *French Law: A Comparative Approach*, 2nd edn (Oxford, Oxford University Press, 2018) Ch 14.

[97] In relation to the treatment of economic loss in civil law, see S Banakas, 'Liability for Incorrect Financial Information: Theory and Practice in a General Clause System and in a Protected Interests System' (1999) 7 *European Review of Private Law* 261 comparing English, French and German law.

[98] See *Transco* (n 57); *Burnie Port Authority* (n 1).

[99] *Cf* US Restatement (Second) of Torts, §§ 519–520 (1977) and now Restatement (Third) of Torts: Liability for Physical and Emotional Harm § 20 (2010). See, generally, E Reid, 'Liability for Dangerous Activities: A Comparative Analysis' (1999) 48 *ICLQ* 731.

[100] A similar example may be found in *Fowler v Lanning* [1959] 1 QB 426 (relationship between torts of trespass and negligence).

[101] *Leakey v National Trust* (n 85) 514 (occupier's liability for a naturally caused nuisance).

[102] See *Doyle v Olby (Ironmongers) Ltd* [1969] 2 QB 158.

liability. In *Spartan Steel v Martin*,[103] the Court of Appeal drew a line between consequential and pure economic loss; only the latter raising floodgates concerns. In both England and Wales and Australia, losses consequential on negligently caused physical injury have long been compensated. In the case of nuisance, what is important is that the financial losses recoverable are triggered by either material loss to the property or loss of amenity. They are therefore 'consequential'. What is distinct from negligence is that financial losses consequential on loss of amenity do not require injury to material property or the person, but are nevertheless regarded as acceptable consequential loss.[104] The torts therefore are consistent; the only difference being that consequential loss in negligence follows from material harm to the person or property, while in nuisance it derives from material loss or loss of amenity. We can explain this more generous approach by looking at the nature of the tort of private nuisance. It protects injury to the plaintiff's *rights* over land. Hence where the economic loss can be seen to result from an actionable nuisance – for example, in *Andreae*[105] noise, dust or vibrations from nearby building work causing substantial interference with the operation of a hotel – financial loss is recoverable. The rule of remoteness ensures that no risk of indeterminate liability arises as a result. Arguments against recovery of pure economic loss in negligence are thus irrelevant.

Given the above analysis, why have the courts not addressed this question in the manner indicated above? For a civil lawyer, accustomed to taking a more holistic view of the law of tort, the current position, in which imprecision is allowed to persist, is hard to justify. Civilian lawyer and legal theorist, Pierre Legrand, for example, is on record for criticising the common law for deciding not to fashion itself systematically, with a preference for making its courts 'masters of fact'.[106] Whilst an obvious generalisation, it is notable that the resolution of contradictions and potential inconsistencies in the law of torts have been side-stepped by the courts, as Fleming's example at the end of section III above demonstrates. The tension between nuisance and negligence is thus seen as a matter for academic treatises, rather than the day-to-day task of the courts. Nevertheless, as this section has shown, tensions between negligence and private nuisance in relation to the treatment of economic interests can quite easily be resolved.

V. Conclusions

Private nuisance protects plaintiffs in their use or enjoyment of land. While priority is naturally given to material loss, this chapter has shown that immaterial loss is

103 *Spartan Steel v Martin* [1973] QB 27. For an interesting Australian example, see *Rail Corp of New South Wales v Fluor Australia Pty Ltd* [2009] NSWCA 344, (2009) Aust Torts Reports 82-038.

104 See *Williams* (n 38) above as to the divide between consequential and unacceptable pure economic loss in nuisance.

105 *Andreae* (n 67).

106 P Legrand, 'Against a European Civil Code' (1997) 60 *MLR* 44, 48–49.

taken broadly and can extend to consequential damage to personal property and financial loss, although not harm to the person. It is a tort, therefore, where money matters more than physical harm to the person! Whilst classified as 'consequential' economic loss, rendering it formally reconcilable with the tort of negligence, we have seen that the very nature of private nuisance means that matters such as noise, smoke or vibrations not causing physical damage to the property may nevertheless provide a basis for recoverable economic loss flowing from a finding of loss of amenity to the property rights of the plaintiff. As noted above, this conceptual difference is logical, but perhaps puzzling to the lay person faced with similar fact scenarios in private nuisance and negligence. While the torts of private nuisance and negligence overlap, there are still distinctions between these two torts which prevents merger occurring.

Whilst possible, then, in private nuisance, recovery of economic loss is subject to barriers as outlined above. Plaintiffs labelled extra-sensitive or subject to unforeseeable losses or losses not resulting from harmful interference with their land rights cannot recover. In *Gales*, this meant that a significant head of recovery was excluded from the claim. While cases such as *Williams* show some ingenuity in enabling householders to protect their main financial asset by characterising the source of the losses as 'damage' to their proprietary rights, the willingness of the courts to engage in such creative thinking cannot be guaranteed.

Private nuisance can therefore be regarded as a tort which protects against both material and immaterial harm which will extend to some financial loss. It would be misleading to claim however that it is an 'economic' tort. Such losses are incidental to a focus on protecting property rights and not seen as an issue per se. What this chapter has noted is a lack of conceptual clarity. While academics may seek to find connections across tort law and bemoan the conceptual incoherence of the 'measured duty of care', the courts are just doing what they regard as 'their job' in deciding cases on the facts. Indeed, one of the challenges of writing this chapter has been to bring together the cases protecting economic interests in nuisance which are rarely identified as such by the courts (or indeed in most textbooks). Nevertheless, by examining private nuisance from this novel angle, we gain an insight into the operation of this fascinating tort, its underlying justifications as well as judicial blind spots. By gathering together the limited case law on this topic in England and Wales and Australia, it is hoped to provide a practical insight into how this tort can be used to protect economic interests, in addition to flagging its limitations. The tort of private nuisance, as recent cases such as *Gales* and *Williams* highlight, has been used to protect the economic interests of businesses, developers and ordinary householders and the dynamic reasoning of the Court of Appeal in *Williams* suggests that it will continue to evolve. Finally, in view of the limited authoritative case law on this topic, it is suggested that comparative common law perspectives are useful, even if we do need to factor in the significance of context and individual circumstances. As illustrated again by *Williams* and *Gales*, urban development contrasts with the construction of a shopping development in a village with a potential risk to the rainforest population. Private nuisance remains a tort where the factual circumstances are important and this needs to be taken into consideration when reviewing the applicability of judgments across different jurisdictions. Nevertheless, it cannot be doubted that in reviewing private nuisance in English and Australian law we gain a greater insight into the operation of this long-standing tort in today's commercial environment which will help us to understand its potential in protecting a plaintiff's economic interests.

8

Revisiting Injurious Falsehood

HILARY YOUNG*

I. Introduction

When a person suffers economic harm due to a false statement of fact, a number of causes of action may apply. In Canada, those causes of action include defamation, injurious falsehood, negligent misrepresentation, deceit, passing off, and statutory causes of action in the *Competition Act*[1] and *Trademarks Act*.[2] This does not include causes of action that might apply in relation to false statements of fact but are not predominantly aimed at such statements, such as conspiracy, unlawful interference with economic interests and breach of contract.

The current landscape differs significantly from that when torts such as defamation and injurious falsehood (then known as slander of title) first emerged. Over the centuries, new causes of action have been added and the scope of existing causes of action has expanded. For example, since 1963 negligence has permitted recovery for false statements of fact causing pure economic loss,[3] and since 1915 defamation has been available to corporate plaintiffs in Canada.[4]

This chapter examines the tort of injurious falsehood. While the focus is on Canadian law, much of the analysis will reflect the law in other common law jurisdictions. There is uncertainty with regard to several elements of injurious falsehood. The chapter considers how to resolve confusion over the meaning of some of those elements, and what the scope of the tort should be in light of modern realities, including the importance of freedom of expression, the role of corporations in twenty-first century society and the existence of other torts addressing false statements of fact. The chapter also describes the results of a small empirical study of injurious falsehood, which shows that while the tort is not pleaded as often as defamation, defamation has not effectively eclipsed the tort of injurious falsehood.

* Professor, University of New Brunswick Faculty of Law. I wish to thank Chantalle Briggs for her research assistance.

[1] *Competition Act* (Revised Statutes of Canada (RSC) 1985, c C-34) ss 36(1), 52.

[2] *Trademarks Act* (RSC 1985, c T-13) s 22.

[3] *Hedley Byrne & Co Ltd v Heller & Partners Ltd* [1964] AC 465 (HL).

[4] *Price v Chicoutimi Pulp Co* 1915 51 SCR 179.

Ultimately, this chapter argues that there remains a role for injurious falsehood, but that it is rightly a narrow one. So long as defamation remains as plaintiff-friendly as it currently is, many cases best conceived of as involving injurious falsehood will be pleaded as defamation. That is the result of a problem with the scope of defamation law, which in my view should not apply to protect corporate reputation, rather than a problem with the law of injurious falsehood. Further discussion of the scope of Canadian defamation law is beyond the scope of this chapter. Rather, it focuses on clarification and minor changes that ought to be made to the law of injurious falsehood to ensure it achieves its intended goals.

II. The Tort of Injurious Falsehood

Injurious falsehood is an under-examined tort, 'curious in its origin, its history and its present features'.[5] It goes by several names: injurious falsehood, malicious falsehood, slander of goods (and quality), trade libel, and slander of title.[6] It is an 'action on the case for words'.[7] Of these descriptions, Fleming says that 'injurious falsehood', coined by Sir William Salmond, is the 'best and most inclusive'.[8] Certainly, as we shall see, the scope of the tort has expanded well beyond false claims about the plaintiff's title to land or goods and is not limited to spoken words.[9]

It is widely accepted that injurious falsehood, malicious falsehood, slander of goods (and quality), trade libel, and slander of title are different names for the same tort:

> Actions for injurious falsehood originally arose under such names as slander of title, slander of goods, trade libel, interference with prospective advantage, disparagement of goods, title or property and commercial disparagement. The term "injurious falsehood" was coined by Sir William Salmond and has gradually been accepted as a more accurate characterization of the interests being protected.[10]

[5] A Dowling, 'Early Reported Cases on Slander of Title' (2006) *57 Northern Ireland Legal Quarterly* 246, 246.

[6] 'Actions for injurious falsehood originally arose under such names as slander of title, slander of goods, trade libel, interference with prospective advantage, disparagement of goods, title or property and commercial disparagement. The term "injurious falsehood" was coined by Sir William Salmond and has gradually been accepted as a more accurate characterization of the interests being protected.': R Brown, *Brown on Defamation*, 2nd edn (Thomson Reuters, 1994) Vol 10, 28.1(1) cited in *311165 B.C. Ltd v Canada (Attorney General)*, 2016 BCSC 2068 [35].

[7] *Ratcliffe v Evans* [1892] 2 QB 524 (CA).

[8] J Fleming, *The Law of Torts*, 7th edn (The Law Book Company, 1987) 671 cited in *Elliott v Canadian Broadcasting Corp*, 1993 CanLII 5508 (ONSC), 46.

[9] Slander is not technically limited to spoken words. The distinction between libel and slander relates to the permanence of the communication. See A Mullis and R Parkes, *Gatley on Libel and Slander*, 12th edn (Sweet & Maxwell, 2013) [1.5].

[10] Brown (n 6) 28.1(1). See also *Bentley Aviation Ltd v Homelife Benchmark Realty Corp*, 2017 BCSC 1332 [37]: '[i]njurious falsehood and slander of title are different names for the same tort'.

Slander of title emerged in the late fifteenth century 'in cases involving a challenge of the plaintiff's title to land and thereby prejudicing his efforts to dispose of it'.[11] Its origins coincided with those of libel and slander, as the name 'slander of title' suggests. However, by no later than 1623, slander of title was a distinct cause of action from slander.[12]

The modern elements of the broader tort of injurious falsehood were set out by the Ontario Court of Appeal, citing Raymond Brown: 'There must be a showing that the published statements are untrue, that they were made maliciously, that is without just cause or excuse, and that the plaintiff suffered special damages.'[13]

A. Untrue

The element of untruth is relatively straightforward and requires little explanation, but two points concerning that element are worth making. First, not all untrue statements fall within the scope of injurious falsehood: statements falsely comparing products do not give rise to liability for injurious falsehood.[14] Second, that a statement must be false perhaps implies that the impugned statement must be a statement of fact. This would distinguish injurious falsehood from defamation, which also applies to statements of opinion and comment.[15] While Prosser refers to injurious falsehood as relating to 'untrue statement[s] of fact *or opinion*',[16] I could find little other support for that proposition other than generic statements referring to 'comment' where factual assertions were at issue.[17]

Injurious falsehood should only apply to statements of fact. Setting aside the question of what it even means for a comment or opinion to be false (as opposed to unfair), the tort should be limited to facts for the same reason that false comparisons do not constitute injurious falsehood. Permitting injurious falsehood actions in relation to comment would unjustifiably expand its scope. It would

[11] Fleming (n 8) 671; Dowling (n 5) 247.

[12] Dowling (n 5) 256.

[13] *Lysko v Braley*, 2006 ONCA 9038 [133].

[14] *Rust Check Canada Inc v Young et al* (1988) 47 CCLT 279 (OHC) [63]:

> If, for example, the only false statement of which complaint is made is that the defendant's goods are *better* than those of the plaintiff, such a statement may not give rise to a cause of action, at all events, in the absence of any false representation as to the quality or character of the plaintiff's goods. See, for example, *Gatley*, supra, para. 319, p. 140; and *Hubbuck & Sons v. Wilkinson, Heywood & Clark*, [1899] 1 Q.B. 86 at 93, [1895-9] All E.R. Rep. 244 (C.A.) per Lindley M.R.

[15] That said, defamation's application to comment has shrunk over the years. Fair comment now provides a broad defence to statements that amount to comment on a matter of public interest. See *WIC Radio Ltd v Simpson*, 2008 SCC 40. Fleming (n 8): malice is a 'weasel word' that is the source of uncertainty and confusion, 697.

[16] W Prosser, 'Injurious Falsehood: The Basis of Liability' (1959) 59 *Columbia Law Review* 425, 439 (emphasis added).

[17] But see *Hahn v Duveen* 133 Misc 871, 234 NY Supp 185 (Sup Ct 1929), in which the defendant told a reporter that the plaintiff's painting was not painted by Leonardo DaVinci. The Court treated this as opinion but did not view that as negating a claim in injurious falsehood. See Prosser, *ibid* 434.

encourage suits over negative online reviews, for example, which would likely have a chilling effect on legitimate non-malicious reviews. The expression of opinions is less blameworthy than spreading lies, even where the opinions are communicated maliciously, and should therefore have less of an economic impact. In any event, defamation remains available for unfair comment;[18] it is unnecessary for injurious falsehood to be expanded where another action already covers that field.

B. Malice

While it is clear that malice is required for injurious falsehood, what that means 'is a matter not entirely free from controversy'.[19] There are at least two areas of potential uncertainty: the first is the meaning and relevance of an absence of just excuse and the second is whether malice means knowledge of falsity, an intent to injure, both, or something else.

i. Absence of Just Excuse

On the first issue, there is uncertainty as to whether positive proof of malice is required or whether an absence of just excuse satisfies the malice element. One of the leading Canadian cases on injurious falsehood states, citing Raymond Brown, that '[t]here must be a showing that the published statements … were made maliciously, *that is without just cause or excuse*'.[20] This, in my view, means that a lack of just cause or excuse satisfies the malice element. However, this may simply be a misstatement of other versions of the test which posit that malice is required *in addition to* a lack of just cause or excuse. Brown himself states elsewhere that malice and a lack of just cause are required, and cases such as *Bentley Aviation* say that the tort may be committed 'maliciously *and* without just cause or excuse'.[21] These different phrasings may be the cause of confusion.

To say that an absence of just excuse counts as malice is inconsistent with most of the case law and with the ordinary meaning of 'malice'. In ordinary usage,

[18] By 'unfair comment' the law really means comment without a basis in fact or that no one could honestly believe on the underlying facts. See *WIC Radio* (n 15). I do note that if my recommendation below that defamation not be available for corporate reputation were adopted, defamation would no longer be available to corporate plaintiffs in relation to unfair comment.

[19] *Rust Check* (n 14) [64]. See also *Petten et al v EYE Marine Consultants et al*, 1994 NL SC 10293 [168] where a court refused to grant summary judgment dismissing a case where only carelessness was pleaded: '[b]ecause there is uncertainty in the scope of the role of malice in the tort of injurious falsehood, the court ought to be reluctant to refuse an amendment based on it, where applying the principles in *Hunt v. Carey Canada Inc.*, supra, there is any possibility of success'.

[20] *Lysko* (n 13) [133], citing Brown (n 6) 28.1(1) (emphasis added). See also *Activators Methods Inc v Chiropractors Association of Saskatchewan*, 1992 SK QB 7906 [27], which states the relevant element in the following terms: 'that it was published maliciously in the sense of without lawful justification or excuse or with a dishonest or improper motive'.

[21] Brown (n 6) 28.5; *Bentley Aviation* (n 10) [37] (emphasis added).

malice can mean a range of things, such as knowledge of falsity, intent to injure or an improper motive. It cannot, however, properly be understood as the absence of an excuse. This would import a significantly lower threshold for liability. The absence of a good reason for making a statement is not the same thing as having a bad reason for doing so. In *British Railway Traffic & Electric Co v CRC Co*, McCardie J stated that 'the mere absence of just cause or excuse is not of itself malice. Malice in its proper and accurate sense is a question of motive, intention, or state of mind'.[22] A standard of 'no just cause', rather than positive evidence of malice, may allow malice to be inferred from proof of falsity combined with the defendant's failure to raise a justification. This would be inconsistent with the case law, which makes it clear that malice is an element for the plaintiff to prove and cannot be inferred from proof of falsity alone.[23] Thus, the plaintiff must adduce positive evidence of the defendant's malice. The courts or legislatures should clarify that a lack of just cause or excuse alone does not constitute malice.

That said, the difficulty of the plaintiff proving what motivated the defendant is such that inferences should be drawn where appropriate. I do not mean to suggest that affirmative proof of a specific improper motive must be proven if the plaintiff adduces evidence from which a malicious motive can be inferred.

ii. Malice as Knowledge of Falsity versus Intent to Harm

On the second issue, whether malice means knowledge of falsity, an intent to injure, both, or something else, there is some uncertainty as to whether malice is really about knowledge of falsity or a desire to cause economic harm to the plaintiff. It seems that either will suffice. In the United States, Langvardt noted uncertainty as to whether the fault standard in injurious falsehood is intent or malice. He therefore says that '[i]n its present state, the common law of injurious falsehood is badly in need of coherence and direction with regard to the fault issue'.[24]

For the purposes of injurious falsehood, knowledge of falsity means knowledge or willful blindness,[25] but also includes recklessness.[26] However, it does not include carelessness. The New Brunswick Court of Appeal has recently stated that the malice element of injurious falsehood requires 'evidence of a dishonest or improper motive *which goes beyond mere carelessness*'.[27] The position would seem to be the same in England; Gatley stated that 'it is thought that [liability for negligence]

[22] *British Railway Traffic & Electric Co v CRC Co* [1922] 2 KB 260, 269 (McCardie J).

[23] See *Petten* (n 19) [166]. As for whether evidence of knowledge of falsity can satisfy the malice element, see the discussion of what counts as malice in section II of this chapter.

[24] A Langvardt, 'Free Speech versus Economic Harm: Accommodating Defamation, Commercial Speech, and Unfair Competition Considerations in the Law of Injurious Falsehood' (1989) 62 *Temp Law Review* 903, 917–18.

[25] *Procor Ltd v USWA*, 1989 71 OR (2d) 410 (ONSC) [65], OJ No 2156.

[26] *Manitoba Free Press Co v Nagy* (1907) 39 SCR 340, 349; Mullis and Parkes (n 9) 21.; *Boehringer Ingelheim (Canada) Ltd v Bristol-Myers Squibb Canada Inc*, 1998 ONSC 14787ONSC [12].

[27] *O'Neill et al v Edmanson*, 2017 NBCA 33 [46] (emphasis added).

should not be the case in malicious falsehood … [m]ere negligence is not malice'.[28] This makes sense, because liability on a fault standard of negligence for false statements causing economic harm raises many of the same proximity and policy issues that have led to limited liability for negligent misrepresentations.[29] Allowing injurious falsehood on the basis of negligence would greatly expand liability for false statements, particularly given that other aspects of the tort have been interpreted broadly.

I now turn to the question of malice as knowledge of falsity (including recklessness) versus an intent to injure. Several courts refer to the need for 'actual malice' in injurious falsehood,[30] but they seem to have understood 'actual malice' in different ways. Since *Sullivan v New York Times*, acting with 'actual malice' – at least in defamation law – has been understood to mean acting with knowledge of falsity or recklessness as to falsity.[31] The Supreme Court of Canada has referred to actual malice in the injurious falsehood context as meaning 'a predetermined intention to injure the plaintiff'.[32] However, in context, it is clear that the Court was distinguishing malice from situations of careless or accidental publication, not distinguishing knowledge of falsity from intent to harm. In *Petten*, the Newfoundland Supreme Court stated that older cases tended to require 'actual malice', which it interpreted to mean an intention to harm the plaintiff.[33] The Ontario Court of Appeal in *Siopiolosz v Taylor* stated that '[t]o make the act malicious it must be done with the direct object of injuring that other person's business'.[34] To be sure, publishing with knowledge of falsity will often coincide with an intent to injure, but not always, and the cases discussed in this paragraph are not particularly helpful in resolving the issue.

Is it necessary to have both knowledge of falsity and an improper purpose or just one of these? The Supreme Court of Canada has held that knowledge of, or recklessness as to, falsity is sufficient to satisfy the malice element:

> Actual malice in the sense of a predetermined intention to injure plaintiff or his property cannot be necessary to be proved … The reckless publication by a defendant of an untruth respecting the complainant's property the natural result of which is to produce and where it does produce actual damage is sufficient evidence of the absence of bona fides and of the malice required by law.[35]

Fleming stated that '[i]t is sufficient evidence of malice that the defendant knew the disparaging statement to be false'.[36] However, the example provided for this

[28] Mullis and Parkes (n 9) 21.7. However, the American position may be different. See Mullis and Parkes (n 9) 21.7 at fn 47, pointing to the Restatement 2d, Torts [630].

[29] See, eg, *Deloitte & Touche v Livent Inc (Receiver of)*, 2017 SCC 63, [2017] 2 SCR 855, which narrowed liability by requiring an invitation to rely in order for there to be a duty of care.

[30] See, eg, *Almas et al v Spenceley*, 1972 ON CA 609.

[31] *Sullivan v New York Times* (1964) 376 US 254 (1964).

[32] *Manitoba Free Press* (n 26) [349].

[33] *Petten* (n 19) [167].

[34] *Siopiolosz v Taylor*, 1944 ON CA 99 [20].

[35] *Manitoba Free Press* (n 26) 349, cited in *Petten* (n 19) [167].

[36] Fleming (n 8) 698. See also *Wilts United Dairies v Thomas Robinson Sons & Co* [1957] RPC 220.

proposition involves a landlord's intent to drive his tenant out of business so that the tenant would no longer resist a notice to quit. This is hardly mere knowledge of falsity. That knowledge of falsity is sufficient is further buttressed by s 17 of the Ontario *Libel and Slander Act*[37] (and the equivalent provisions in other provinces' legislation and in other common law countries). That section provides that special damages need not be proven where written words were 'calculated to cause pecuniary damage to the plaintiff' or where words were 'calculated to cause pecuniary damage to the plaintiff' in respect of one's profession. While the scope of the provision is not quite as broad as a desire to cause economic loss to the plaintiff generally, the overlap is such that the legislature arguably understood the malice element not to *require* evidence of a desire to cause economic harm. Otherwise, almost all injurious falsehood cases would satisfy the requirements of section 17.

This makes a certain amount of sense, in that one should be responsible for the economic consequences of one's deliberate lies. While the scope of recovery for negligent misstatements has wisely been contained, there is less, or arguably even no need to do so in relation to deliberate lies. There is perhaps a parallel to intentional versus negligent torts causing physical injury. Recovery is only permitted for negligently caused injury where such injury was foreseeable, whereas there is no such limitation on recovery in intentional torts such as battery.[38]

Yet if knowledge of falsity were sufficient to establish malice, the following might constitute injurious falsehood: a deliberate lie spread without any intention of hurting anyone but that ends up hurting the plaintiff; or where an author makes up an unpleasant character or product in a novel and some people understand it to refer to an actual person or product. There is knowledge of falsity, in a sense, since the author knew she was creating a fiction. This kind of publication has been held to constitute defamation[39] because defamation is strict liability, but is not consistent with the general understanding of malice. Thus, were malice established solely on the basis of knowledge of falsity, this would expand the scope of injurious falsehood beyond what it is normally understood to encompass. More to the point, it would erode injurious falsehood's fault requirement, thereby imposing greater restrictions on speech for no apparent reason.

Therefore, in my view, at least some improper purpose must be required. Other limiting factors, such as foreseeability of harm to the plaintiff or that the expression be *about* the plaintiff or her goods are insufficient. These might still capture the author who knows her novel to be 'false', and on an objective standard, the falsity could be said to be about the plaintiff or her goods. It may also be foreseeable that a person or product with the same name would suffer economic loss.

As for whether intent to harm in the absence of knowledge of falsity is sufficient to constitute malice, in my view, it cannot be. However, the case law is not always clear. On one hand, '[m]alice cannot be inferred merely upon proof that

[37] *Libel and Slander Act* (RSO 1990, c L.12) s 17. See also *United Kingdom Defamation Act 1952*, s 3.
[38] *Bettel et al v Yim*, 1978 ONSC 1580.
[39] *Hulton v Jones* [1910] AC 20. See also Mullis and Parkes (n 9) [7.5].

the words were calculated to injure the plaintiff'.[40] On the other hand, 'even where the defendant believes the incorrect statement there may still be malice if he was prompted by some indirect, dishonest or improper motive to make the statement'.[41] If the defendant believes the statement to be true, it should not constitute injurious falsehood to publish that statement (though it might constitute a different tort, such as negligent misrepresentation), even if she does so to cause harm. Injurious falsehood requires subjective fault, not merely negligence. That subjective fault must, in my view, relate to *deliberately* spreading lies, not to trying to cause harm with the truth. Given this, malice should be interpreted as requiring knowledge of falsity or recklessness, as well as some improper purpose. Improper purpose should have the same meaning as it does in defamation law, where malice is not an element but may defeat certain defences.[42]

C. Special Damage

That injurious falsehood requires special damage is not controversial, but there is an issue as to how strictly special damage must be proven. (I address the question of whether general damages are recoverable below in section E.) Note that in many jurisdictions, such as Ontario, special damage need not be proven where the words are calculated to cause financial loss regarding an 'office, profession, calling, trade of business', or where written words are calculated to cause financial loss.[43]

According to the Ontario Superior Court of Justice, 'although it is not necessary to establish the precise amount of damage, the actual fact of damage, or of loss of business, it must be proven and not speculated'.[44] *Bentley Aviation* provides examples:

> while it is not sufficient to allege, in general terms, that the value of the plaintiff's property depreciated or that the plaintiff lost the opportunity to sell the property, it is sufficient to expressly allege some specific pecuniary loss such as the loss of a particular sale.[45]

[40] *Captain Developments Ltd v Nu-West Group Ltd*, 1982 ONSC 1747 ONSC [36].

[41] *Balden v Shorter* [1933] 1 Ch 427.

[42] *Ibid* 430 (Maugham J): 'it is now apparently settled that malice in the law of slander of title and other forms of injurious falsehood means some dishonest or otherwise improper motive'. See also *Spring v Guardian Assurance Plc* [1993] 2 All ER 273 (CA), 288; *International Sausage House v Hammer* (2015) BCSC 1155 [209]: '[t]his improper purpose satisfies the requirement for actual malice: see *Western Surety* at paras. 52, 54, 64'. As for what an improper purpose is, Fleming, albeit speaking in the context of malicious prosecution, says that it has a 'wider meaning than spite, ill-will or a spirit of vengeance, and includes any other improper purpose, such as to gain a private collateral advantage': Fleming (n 8) 609, cited in *Oniel v Marks* [2001] OJ No 90 (ON CA) [43].

[43] *Libel and Slander Act* (n 37) s 17. See also *United Kingdom Defamation Act 1952* (n 37) s 3. According to *Joyce v Sengupta* [1992] EWCA Civ 9, 347, '[t]he whole purpose of section 3 [of the Defamation Act 1952] was to give the plaintiff a remedy in malicious falsehood despite the difficulty of proving actual loss'.

[44] *Boehringer* (n 26) [14].

[45] *Bentley Aviation* (n 10) [41]. *Bentley* concerned a motion to dismiss for disclosing no cause of action, so for those purposes an allegation was as good as proof. Proof and not mere allegations are required for liability.

Citing Brown, the Court goes on to say that

> [i]f the plaintiff is claiming special damages as a result of the loss to an intending purchaser of his or her property, particulars must be provided as to the name of the intended purchaser, the date on which he or she received notice of the publication, and the amount of damages claimed to be lost as a result of the slander of title.[46]

Langvardt refers to this as the 'rigid "loss of particular sales" approach'.[47] The existence of special damage must be strictly proven.[48]

Other cases, however, take a less strict approach and Langvardt refers to a movement in the United States away from having to strictly prove special damage in injurious falsehood 'when it would be unreasonable to insist upon the rigid "loss of particular sales" approach'.[49] This is reflected in Canadian law in *Frank Flaman Wholesale Ltd v Firman, Patton, Stephens and SF Kennedy New Products Inc*, for example, which held that 'Under present circumstances, a general loss of custom or business, as distinct from loss of specific customers, is admissible in evidence, and is sufficient special damage to maintain an action of this kind'.[50]

The 'present circumstances' included that 'the plaintiff swears that that result has followed and no evidence to the contrary has been adduced'.[51] It should be noted, however, that while the evidence of a general loss of custom seems to have been one or more affidavits by the plaintiffs attesting to a general loss of custom, there was, in that case, at least some evidence to the contrary: the defendant filed an affidavit saying that there was no loss of business, but if there was, it was because he and his co-defendants were no longer selling the product for the plaintiff.[52] Thus, to find that the evidence satisfies the special harm element here suggests a fairly low threshold.

Similarly, in *Petten*, the Newfoundland Supreme Court cited *Frank Flaman* with approval for the proposition that evidence of general loss of custom can satisfy the special damage element (though perhaps only if there is no evidence to the contrary). The Court further noted that: '[t]he nature of the dissemination of the falsehood may dictate the degree of particularity of the loss of business that must be pleaded and proved'.[53] Langvardt also notes that how widespread the publication is influences how strictly special damage need be proven.[54] If the suggestion

[46] *Ibid* [40] citing Brown (n 6) 28.1.
[47] Langvardt (n 24) 918.
[48] *Galand Estate v Stewart*, 1992 ABCA 334 [48] citing Fleming (n 8): '"special" refers to the fact that the damage is capable of more or less exact calculation and that the claimant may therefore not unfairly be put to pleading and proving it strictly'.
[49] Langvardt (n 24) 918.
[50] *Frank Flaman Wholesale Ltd v Firman, Patton, Stephens and SF Kennedy New Products Inc*, 1982 SK QB 2487 [10].
[51] *Ibid.*
[52] *Ibid* [5].
[53] *Petten* (n 19) [174]. In *Petten* the Court relied on the annotation to *Frank Flaman* (n 50) 20 CCLT 247–49 by J Irvine.
[54] Langvardt (n 24) 959.

is that an inference of special damage may be drawn from the fact of publication alone where publication was widespread, this would be contrary to logic. Even widespread lies do not always cause injury, such as where they are disbelieved or where they are already widely known. However, the Court in *Petten* may simply have meant that the degree of precision required in the pleadings and evidence is less where there was widespread publication, because, for example, one does not need to point to each of thousands of lost sales. However, this would seem to be more relevant to quantifying damages than to establishing the element of special damage. It is not clear why one should be able to plead and prove *some* economic loss with less specificity simply because the publication was widespread. It may be that the issue of sufficient evidence to satisfy the threshold of some special damage is being confused with what counts as sufficient evidence of damages under the head of special damages.

If the rules around proof of special damage are being relaxed by courts, this may be as a result of the influence of defamation. In defamation, injury (albeit not economic injury) is presumed from the publication of a libel. In addition, a successful plaintiff is entitled to greater than nominal damages without any proof of actual loss. This is because it is thought difficult to prove a causal connection between a libel and specific reputational or other harm.[55] This is no less true with respect to injurious falsehoods.[56] For example, even if the plaintiff can prove a loss of income, there may have been a general economic downturn such that the plaintiff would have earned less this year than in previous years regardless of any injurious falsehood. Indeed, the difficulty of proving a causal connection to a pecuniary loss is said to be one reason why plaintiffs prefer to sue in defamation than in injurious falsehood where they have that option.[57] To the extent that defamation and injurious falsehood are often pleaded together and share several features, and to the extent that there is a 'blurring of the line between claims of defamation and injurious falsehood',[58] courts may be inclined to relax the requirements for proving special damage in injurious falsehood.

It must be recalled, however, that special damage is 'the gist of the action' in injurious falsehood.[59] To allow special damage to be inferred from the widespread publication of a false statement, for example, would significantly alter the tort, making it more about the wrongfulness of publishing the false statement than about recovery for economic loss. It would also further blur the line between

[55] '[I]t is generally impractical for a claimant to seek out witnesses to say that they read the words complained of and thought the worse of the claimant': *Ames v Spamhaus Project* [2015] EWHC 127 (QB) [55].

[56] Langvardt suggests that the difficulty of proving special damage is one reason why plaintiffs prefer to sue in defamation where they have the option: Langvardt (n 24) 919. See also *Fortress Real Developments v Franklin*, 2018 ONSC 296 [61].

[57] Langvart (n 24) 919.

[58] *Ibid* 906.

[59] *Frank Flaman* (n 50) [10], citing Mullis and Parkes (n 9) [327].

injurious falsehood and defamation. Therefore, any attempts to lower the threshold of proof of special damage in injurious falsehood should be resisted.

In any event, it should rarely be hard to point to *some* economic loss as a result of the widespread publication of a falsehood. As always, the standard is the balance of probabilities and a trier of fact may infer the existence of a loss, or its causal connection to the publication, by taking a robust and pragmatic approach to the evidence.[60] There must be some affirmative evidence: (a) of a loss; and (b) that the loss was caused by the publication of a falsehood. However, the evidence need not be conclusive. This is Langvardt's view as well; he suggests special damage could be proven 'by means of circumstantial evidence demonstrating a decline in sales since the publication of the disparaging statement, so long as the plaintiff eliminates other causes for the decline in sales'.[61]

D. Identification

Although this section began with a quote from the Ontario Court of Appeal saying that the elements of injurious falsehood are an untruth, published with malice causing special damage, there is also an element of identification.[62] However, this element is different in injurious falsehood than in defamation, where the test is simply whether an ordinary person would think the plaintiff was being referred to. In injurious falsehood, identification can be satisfied by showing the plaintiff's wares, property or business (as opposed to the plaintiff herself) are identifiable.[63] Thus, an action lies for a falsehood naming a business even if an ordinary person would not connect the plaintiff to the business.[64]

This makes sense, given that injurious falsehood is about economic losses due to false statements of fact rather than the plaintiff's reputation. If the plaintiff is not identified, her reputation cannot be harmed, whereas false statements of fact that do not refer to the plaintiff *can* lead to economic losses. However, there must be some connection between the falsehood and the plaintiff. A false statement about a product that incidentally causes harm because the plaintiff *relies* on the statement to her detriment potentially gives rise to a claim in negligent or fraudulent misrepresentation, but not in injurious falsehood. It is unclear precisely what the limits of the necessary connection are, but the case law involves statements about plaintiffs themselves, their goods or their property. The scope of identification is probably not much broader than that.

[60] See *Snell v Farrell*, 1990 SCC 70, [1990] 2 SCR 311 for a commonsense approach to proving causation where the evidence is not definitive.

[61] Langvardt (n 24) 919.

[62] Mullis and Parkes (n 9) [21.1], [21.4].

[63] 'In a tort claim for injurious falsehood, it is essential that the plaintiff, and/or its wares, be identifiable from the offending statements': *Beatrice Foods Inc v Ault Foods Ltd*, 1995 ONSC 7308 [35].

[64] Mullis and Parkes (n 9) [21.4].

Note that to the extent that courts sometimes state that the falsehood must relate to title to the plaintiff's property,[65] they are distinguishing the narrower slander of title tort from the broader injurious falsehood tort. For example, in 1966 the Supreme Court of Canada cited a nineteenth century English case for the proposition that the subject of a slander of title is 'real or personal property'.[66] In 2007 a British Columbia court, citing *Gatley*, stated:

> For slander of title to be actionable the statement … must operate as a cloud upon the plaintiff's rights to the property at issue which makes third parties 'shun and avoid' the plaintiff's property from a commercial point of view.[67]

However, it is clear that injurious falsehood is simply a broader category of wrong for publishing false statements of fact and includes slander of title and slander of goods. Injurious falsehoods need not specifically impugn title to land or goods.

Osborne frames the scope as requiring proof of damage to the plaintiff's 'trade, business or property interests'.[68] Even this may be too narrow. The elements as set out by the Ontario Court of Appeal in *Lysko v Braley* above suggest that the scope is limited only by the requirement of a false statement of fact causing special damage. Liability has been found in injurious falsehood where the statement was a false allegation of customs fraud[69] and where posters were put up saying that an accompanist was playing on a certain date, causing him to lose another engagement.[70] While these examples can be understood as affecting business interests, Fleming cites the example of a loss of marriage due to the defendant's false claim that he was already married to the prospective bride.[71] This would not satisfy the requirements of 'damage to trade, business or property interests' (unless 'property interests' is understood very broadly – arguably as broadly as pecuniary interests, which must already be affected per the special damage element). It would seem that the tort's scope is now 'broad enough to encompass any damaging falsehood which interferes with prospective advantage, even of a non-commercial nature'.[72] Similarly, '[a] broad scope of economic interests may serve as the basis of an injurious falsehood claim, if adversely affected by a defendant's false statement'.[73]

[65] *Western Surety Company v Hancon Holdings Ltd et al*, 2007 BCSC 180 [49]:

> Slander of title involves slanderous remarks cast upon a person's property. It is akin to the tort of defamation in that it involves a false statement about the plaintiff; however, it differs from defamation in that the false words do not reflect upon the character of the plaintiff, but on the plaintiff's property.

[66] *S & S Industries Inc v Rowell*, 1966 SCC 53, [1966] SCR 419, 427 citing *Skinner v Perry* (1893) 10 RPC 1, 6.

[67] *Western Surety* (n 65) [50] citing P Milmo et al, *Gatley on Libel and Slander*, 10th edn (Sweet & Maxwell, 2004) 591–92.

[68] P Osborne, *The Law of Torts*, 3rd edn (Irwin Law, 2007) 302.

[69] *Procor* (n 25).

[70] *Shapiro v La Morta* (1923) 40 TLR 201 CA.

[71] Fleming (n 8) 671 cited in *Elliott v Canadian Broadcasting Corp*, 1993 ONSC 5508 ONSC [46].

[72] *Ibid*.

[73] Langvardt (n 24) 914.

That said, we must assume that typical cases of fraudulent misrepresentation are excluded from the scope of injurious falsehood. That is, to constitute injurious falsehood, the false statement must relate in some way to the plaintiff's economic interests – it is not enough that the statement has caused harm to those interests. Therefore, a malicious and false credit statement about X relied on by Y to her detriment should not constitute injurious falsehood. We already have distinct torts (fraudulent misrepresentation, deceit, negligent misrepresentation) to address false statements causing harm through detrimental reliance.

One consequence of this greater scope of recovery in injurious falsehood is the further blurring of distinctions between it and defamation. Though the distinction between reputation – the proper subject of a defamation action – and economic interests is clear enough in theory, with the former implicating dignity and sociality[74] while the latter only implicates financial interests, in practice they bleed into each other. Langvardt has stated that '[r]ecent years have witnessed a blurring of the distinction between reputation and economic interests that separates defamation from injurious falsehood'.[75] There is a fine line between

> the statement that tends to harm a plaintiff's reputation and a statement that harms interests of pecuniary value to a plaintiff but stops short of inflicting a reputational injury … [j]udicial mixing of the torts of defamation and injurious falsehood may occur as a result.[76]

Further, given the lesser onus on defamation plaintiffs and the availability of damages without proof of loss, where a plaintiff can plead either defamation or injurious falsehood, she will usually prefer to plead defamation.

One way to address the conceptual overlap between the two doctrines would be to remove from the scope of injurious falsehood those economic effects that flow from reputational harm, as opposed to those that do not flow from reputational harm. This seems impractical, however, given the difficulty in distinguishing between a falsehood that affects reputation and one that merely affects the bottom line directly. Instead, I suggest below denying corporations the ability to sue in defamation, since their reputational interests are of a different kind than those of human beings.

E. Availability of Damages other than Special Damages

Having addressed the elements, I turn to two remedies issues relating to injurious falsehood. First is the availability of damages other than special damages. This can also be thought of as the availability of damages for consequential losses, as

[74] The term 'sociality' comes from D Howarth, 'Libel: Its Purpose and Reform' (2011) 74 *MLR* 845. On defamation and dignity, see Langvardt (n 24) 907.

[75] Langvardt (n 24) 904. See sources cited for this proposition.

[76] *Ibid* 904–905.

opposed to the pecuniary loss that is the gist of the injurious falsehood action. The second is the availability of injunctive relief, particularly compared to the availability of such relief in defamation. I addressed above the need for proof of special damage in order to establish injurious falsehood. That is a liability issue. However, there is also a remedies issue with regard to special damage: whether recovery should extend beyond special damage. In particular, should damages be available for non-pecuniary losses such as emotional distress?

There is case law to the effect that non-pecuniary damages are not recoverable in injurious falsehood. The Ontario Court of Appeal has stated that 'the plaintiffs on this head of claim can recover only damages for their probable money loss, and not for their injured feelings'.[77] The same Court affirmed this in 2006 with reference to an Australian case:

> The importance of actual damage as an element of the tort of injurious falsehood is that, because the tort is not concerned with injury to either reputation or feelings, *damages for injurious falsehood would appear to be restricted to the recovery of that actual damage*.[78]

The England and Wales Court of Appeal cites the same rule.[79] In the US context, Langvardt has stated that 'consequential damages … fall outside the scope of recoverable special damages, as do damages for emotional distress'.[80]

Yet all of these sources other than Langvardt (who cites the American Restatement (Second) of Torts) rely on Lord Denning's statement in *Fielding* that: '[t]he plaintiffs on this head of claim [ie injurious falsehood] can only recover damages for their probably money loss, and not for their injured feelings'.[81] However, in that case the injurious falsehood claim was brought by the corporate plaintiff, not the individual one. It is therefore possible that Lord Denning rejected damages for injured feelings simply because the corporate plaintiff had no feelings to be injured. This is not a firm foundation for a rule about the availability of damages for emotional distress.

Regardless of what the rule was historically, there is now at least some judicial interest in allowing damages for emotional distress in injurious falsehood. The English Court of Appeal in *Joyce v Sengupta* stated that if such damages were not available, 'it could lead to a manifestly unsatisfactory and unjust result in some cases'.[82] The Court indicated that where there is special damage, general damages should also be recoverable where proven. To do otherwise would be

[77] *Almas* (n 30) [21] citing *Fielding et al v Variety, Inc* [1967] 2 All ER 497, 499 (Lord Denning).

[78] *Haines v Australian Broadcasting Corp* (1995) 43 NSWLR 404, 408, cited in *Lysko* (n 13) [135] (emphasis added). See also *Procor* (n 25) [51]: '[t]he damage must be monetary. There can be no compensation for injured feelings'; J Kee, 'Injurious Falsehood' in LD Rainaldi (ed), *Remedies in Tort* (Carswell, 1987) Vol 1, 1–20.

[79] *Joyce* (n 43) 347–48.

[80] Langvardt (n 24) 919.

[81] *Fielding* (n 77) 850.

[82] *Joyce* (n 43) 347.

to 'fail[] to do justice'.[83] Although it is not sufficient in injurious falsehood to prove only non-pecuniary losses (ie, pecuniary loss is an element of the action), Nichols VC asked: 'ought not the law to take [injury in the form of anxiety and distress] into account when it is connected with financial damage inflicted by the falsehood?'[84] While this is all obiter, it opened the door for the same Court to award general damages for emotional distress in injurious falsehood in a subsequent case, *Khodaparast v Shad*.[85]

Both *Joyce* and *Khodaparast* invoked section 3 of the *Defamation Act 1952* which provides that special damage need not be proven where certain motives are present. It would be odd to provide for liability without proof of economic loss but then restrict recoverable damages to proven economic loss. Thus, it might be tempting to read these cases as limiting damages for emotional distress to section 3 cases (or section 3's equivalents, such as section 17 of the *Ontario Libel and Slander Act*). However, in my view that would be a mistake. The logic of these cases is premised on the unfairness of denying damages for emotional distress where such loss flows from the relevant unlawful conduct. There is no reason, on this logic, to limit the rule to cases invoking section 3 of the *Defamation Act 1952* or its equivalents.

Should, then, courts allow recovery for emotional distress in injurious falsehood? The answer ultimately depends on one's theory of remedies. While theorising on the availability of damages for emotional distress is beyond the scope of this chapter, it is interesting to note the lack of any principled approach in the context of injurious falsehood. On one side is the argument that torts focused on economic harms should preclude recovery for emotional distress. In the deceit context, the Iowa Supreme Court said: 'though strong men may cry at the loss of money, separate recovery for mental anguish is usually denied in deceit cases'.[86] On the other side is the principle that one should be able to recover for losses that flow directly from a legal wrong.[87] Without more, it is hard to know which approach to prefer. Looking to other causes of action is not especially helpful; recovery for emotional distress is at least sometimes available in breach of contract and intentional interference with economic relations[88] but not for violations of section 36(1) of the *Competition Act*[89] or in lawful act conspiracy.[90]

[83] *Ibid* 348.
[84] *Ibid.*
[85] *Khodaparast v Shad* [2000] 1 WLR 618 [34]–[46].
[86] *Cornell v Wunschel* 408 NW 2d 382, cited in AL Merrit, 'Damages for Emotional Distress in Fraud Litigation: Dignitary Torts in a Commercial Society' (1989) 42 *Vanderbilt Law Review* 1, 6.
[87] Eg, a successful plaintiff 'is entitled to recover in a tort action those damages which result directly, naturally and proximately from fraud': *Kneip v Unitedbank-Victoria*, 734 SW 2d 130, 136. This is the approach taken in *Joyce* (n 43) 347–48.
[88] *Grand Financial Management Inc v Solemio Transportation Inc*, 2016 ONCA 175. See also *Khodaparast* (n 85) 629.
[89] *Competition Act* (n 1). This has been interpreted as limiting damages to special damages. See, eg, *Polar Ice Express Inc v Arctic Glacier Inc*, 2007 ABQB 717 [115].
[90] *Lonrho Plc v Fayed (No 5)* [1993] 1 WLR 1489 CA 1509.

Wrongful death claims traditionally excluded general damages, at least for emotional distress, although many provinces now do allow such damages.[91]

The trend in tort is toward awarding damages for consequential emotional distress, but that trend is less robust in the business torts, where special damage is the gist of the action. To further complicate things, whether a tort is intentional or requires malice would also seem to be relevant.[92] So too is whether the tort was committed in a commercial or personal context.[93]

In the injurious falsehood context specifically, the fact that the Libel and Slander Acts and Defamation Acts provide for liability where special damage is not proven suggests that at least in those cases where a written falsehood is intended to cause pecuniary harm, or where the words are intended to cause pecuniary loss regarding one's profession, damages other than those for pecuniary losses must be available. Further, the Court of Appeal stated in *Joyce* that the purpose of the English equivalent, section 3 of the *Defamation Act 1952*, would be defeated if only nominal general damages were available under that provision.[94]

In my view, given the lack of coherent doctrinal approach, courts should resist expanding the scope of injurious falsehood to provide for damages for emotional distress. The gist of injurious falsehood is special damage. This helps maintain the distinction between defamation and injurious falsehood. That said, a compelling doctrinal approach to recovery for consequential emotional distress may justify a change to the status quo.

If damages for emotional distress are to be available in injurious falsehood, such damages should be limited to cases in which false statements causing special damages cause *significant* emotional distress.[95] The threshold must remain more than annoyance or upset, rising to the threshold of compensable injury. Second, such damages should obviously not be available to corporate plaintiffs, because they are unable to suffer emotional distress. The same is true in defamation.[96]

Whether aggravated damages are available in injurious falsehood is somewhat unclear and likely depends on whether general damages for emotional distress are available. If general damages for emotional distress are not available, neither should aggravated damages be, because they are effectively compensatory damages for emotional distress.[97] If emotional distress *is* compensable, however, one might assume aggravated damages should then be available. This was the conclusion in *Khodaparast*.[98] However, I strongly disagree. Aggravated damages are a troubling

[91] See, eg, *Fatal Accidents Act* (RSA 2000, c F-8) s 4.1(1); *Family Law Act* (RSO 1990, c F.3) s 61(2).

[92] *Joyce* (n 43) 348; Merrit (n 86) 6 citing eg *Rosener v Sears, Roebuck & Co*, 110 Cal App 3d 755.

[93] In the deceit context, see Merrit (n 86) 10–12.

[94] *Joyce* (n 43) 347.

[95] On this point, in the deceit context, see Merrit (n 86) 7–9.

[96] See *Walker v CFTO*, 1987 ONCA 126, 59 OR (2d) 104, 113; *Pinewood Recording Studios Ltd v City Tower Development Corporation* (1998) 40 CLR (2d) 84 (BCCA) 72; *Lewis et al v Daily Telegraph Ltd* [1963] 2 All ER 151 (HL) 156.

[97] On this point, see *Joyce* (n 43) 348–49.

[98] *Khodaparast* (n 85) [42].

category of damages that result in overcompensation by duplicating awards for general damages for emotional distress and by importing a punitive aspect without meeting the high threshold required to be entitled to punitive damages. They are 'absurd in theory and mischievous in practice'.[99] In my view, they should be done away with in all areas of law.[100] Even if readers disagree with this view of aggravated damages generally, such damages are especially dangerous in the context of a tort with an actual malice element. The conditions for an award of aggravated damages will effectively always be met where the plaintiff is human and there is liability in injurious falsehood. To go from never compensating for non-pecuniary injuries to awarding aggravated damages as a matter of course would be inappropriate.

At least in Canada, where the availability of punitive damages follows general principles rather than particular causes of action,[101] punitive damages should be available simply because there is no reason to deny the plaintiff access to them where the facts warrant such an award. However, they should not, of course, simply follow from a finding of malice.

The next issue is the availability of general damages for reputational harm. Notwithstanding the general rule that '[d]amages at large may be awarded in cases of intentional torts, and to corporations in such circumstances where there has been injury to the corporation's reputation and associated economic loss',[102] I am of the view that general damages for reputational loss should, in accordance with the status quo, not be available in injurious falsehood. Injurious falsehood is distinguishable from defamation in large part by not being about reputational loss. Historically, the tort has not permitted recovery for such loss. *Gatley* has stated that 'the claimant may not recover general damages for injury to reputation as such in malicious falsehood'.[103] This reflects the fact that injurious falsehood is not about reputation but rather about economic injury and is an important distinction between defamation and injurious falsehood.[104] Even the English Court of Appeal in *Joyce*, which otherwise wanted to extend the availability of general damages, said '[i]t would be going too far to hold that all non-pecuniary loss suffered by a plaintiff is recoverable in a malicious falsehood action, because that would include injury to reputation at large'.[105] While reputational injury can certainly flow from an injurious falsehood, this will virtually always constitute defamation. To allow recovery for reputational harm in injurious falsehood would further blur the lines between the two torts.

[99] R Brown, *Defamation Law: A Primer*, 2nd edn (Carswell, 2013) 330.

[100] *Ibid*. Brown notes that this is especially the case where there is no cap on punitive damages, though I do not think there is any justification for them in any event.

[101] *Whiten v Pilot Insurance Co*, 2002 SCC 18 [67].

[102] *Grand Financial Management* (n 88) [82].

[103] Mullis and Parkes (n 9) [21.3].

[104] The history of malicious falsehood as a cause of action shows it was not designed to provide a remedy for such injury: the remedy for such loss is an action for defamation in which, incidentally, damages for injury to feelings may be included in a general award of damages: see *Fielding* (n 77) 851, 855 (Salmon LJ and Lord Denning MR).

[105] *Joyce* (n 43) 348.

Although general damages for reputational injury are not, and should not be, allowed in injurious falsehood, the law treats corporate goodwill differently than reputation. Goodwill can be compensated by an award of general damages,[106] though it flows from injury to corporate reputation. However, what counts as goodwill for this purpose may be understood narrowly. For example, in *Lonrho*, Dillon LJ stated that compensable goodwill is limited to goodwill as defined in *Trego v Hunt*. That case essentially defines goodwill as the value of the ability to attract customers.[107] Dillon LJ continued: 'It cannot mean some airy-fairy general reputation in the business or commercial community which is unrelated to the buying and selling or dealing with customers which is the essence of the business of any trading company'.[108]

Specifically, a decline in share price was found not to be compensable as damage to goodwill.[109]

In other words, compensable goodwill is quite different from reputation in the defamation sense. Damages for injury to goodwill represents 'the court's best assessment of financial loss in fact suffered and proved'.[110]

F. Availability of Injunctions

The discussion to date has revealed injurious falsehood to have relatively strict requirements that make a defamation action preferable for plaintiffs where that is feasible. However, there is one respect in which a plaintiff may prefer injurious falsehood and where the boundary between the torts is not blurred: the availability of interlocutory injunctions.[111] I address in this section whether the different approach to interlocutory injunctions in injurious falsehood versus defamation remains appropriate.

[106] Mullis and Parkes (n 9) [21.3], fn 23 referring to *Lonrho* (n 90): '[one cannot recover general damages for damage to reputation …] [a]s opposed to loss of business goodwill with customers which leads, or is likely to lead, to loss of trade'. See also *Dentec Safety Specialists Inc v Degil Safety Products (1989) Inc*, 2014 ONSC 2449 [34]: '"General damages", then, is a term used in passing off cases to refer to approximations of the quantum of damages in circumstances where there has been some damage to the plaintiff's reputation or goodwill, but where it is very difficult to attach a quantum to that damage'. Neither of these cases is an injurious falsehood case (*Lonrho* was a lawful means conspiracy case and *Dentec* a passing off case), but there is no reason to think that injurious falsehood is different than these torts in this respect.

[107] *Trego v Hunt* [1896] AC especially 17–18.

[108] *Lonrho* (n 90) 1496.

[109] *Ibid* 1496–97.

[110] *Ibid* 1509 (Evans LJ).

[111] 'In certain circumstances an injunction to restrain a publication may have a greater chance of success if framed in injurious falsehood rather than defamation. A plaintiff may, for instance, be able to readily prove that the published matter was undeniably false, but not that it was unarguably defamatory': A Gemmell, 'Injurious Falsehood Emerges from the Wings: Will the Poor Cousin to Defamation Please Step Up?' (2008) 46(9) *Law Society Journal* 69, 70, citing *Kaye v Robertson & Anor* [1991] FSR 62.

For a number of reasons, interlocutory injunctions are rarely available in defamation cases. These reasons include the important free speech implications of such orders, interference with the role of the jury and the fact that the usual balance of convenience test would too often lead to injunctions in cases involving speech.[112] It is one thing to award damages as a result of a libel but another thing to tell someone they may not speak on pain of contempt of court. The test for an interlocutory injunction in defamation is as follows:

> For at least one hundred years and certainly since ... the leading case of Bonnard v. Perryman, [1891] 2 Ch. 269, it has been universally and consistently held by British and Canadian Courts that such an interim injunction will never be granted where the defendant expresses his intention to justify unless the words in question are so clearly defamatory and so obviously impossible to justify that the verdict of a jury accepting a plea of justification as a defence would of necessity have to be set aside as a perverse finding on appeal.[113]

The test for an interlocutory injunction in injurious falsehood is less rigorous; the usual *American Cyanamid Co v Ethicon Ltd* approach is taken, which simply requires a serious case to be tried, irreparable harm and that the balance of convenience favour an injunction.[114] The rules differ because of the commercial as opposed to 'pure speech' nature of the words targeted by the two torts: '[t]he kind of commercial free speech at issue here, is qualitatively different' than in the cases in which the special defamation rule evolved.[115]

Although the distinction is phrased as turning on commercial versus pure speech, it could also be said to rest on the different consequences of an injurious falsehood and defamation. The former implicates economic interests while the latter implicates reputation, which itself often implicates human dignity and sociality.[116] Society may tolerate a greater infringement of freedom of expression

[112] *Canada (Human Rights Commission) v Canadian Liberty Net* [1998] 1 SCR 626, 1998 818 (SCC) [47]–[49] citing *Herbage v Pressdram Ltd* [1984] 1 WLR 1160. In the context of enjoining references to people's criminal records, Griffiths LJ stated that if the court were to apply the *American Cyanamid* test for injunctions:

> the practical effect would I believe be that in very many cases the plaintiff would obtain an injunction, for on the *American Cyanamid* principles he would often show a serious issue to be tried, that damages would not be realistic compensation, and that the balance of convenience favoured restraining repetition of the alleged libel until trial of the action. It would thus be a very considerable incursion into the present rule which is based on freedom of speech.

[113] *Canada Metal Co Ltd et al v Canadian Broadcasting Corp et al*, 1975 ONSC 661 ONSC.

[114] *American Cyanamid Co v Ethicon Ltd* [1975] AC 396. For the application of the rule in that case in Canada, see *Demone Monuments and Granite Products Ltd, v Heritage Memorials Ltd*, 2015 NSSC 314 [35]–[41].

[115] *Demone Monuments, ibid* [32].

[116] See Howarth (n 74) and R Post, 'The Social Foundations of Defamation Law: Reputation and the Constitution' (1986) 74 *California Law Review* 691, 707–19. See also *Rosenblatt v Baer*, 383 US 75, 92 (1966): '[t]he right of a man to the protection of his own reputation from unjustified invasion and wrongful hurt reflects no more than our basic concept of the essential dignity and worth of every human being – a concept at the root of any decent system of ordered liberty'.

to prevent the latter than the former. (The situation is more complicated than this, in that corporate plaintiffs, which have no dignity or sociality, are generally subject to the restrictive *Bonnard v Perryman*[117] rule, despite the interests at stake being purely economic. Denying corporations standing to sue in defamation would solve that problem.)

While some courts have applied the wrong test (both the *American Cyanamid* test to defamation injunctions[118] and the restrictive defamation approach to injurious falsehood),[119] the rules are fairly clear and settled. Courts should continue to apply the usual *American Cyanamid* test to injurious falsehood cases. It is the default test for interlocutory injunctions and the reasons to depart from it, whether those in *Bonnard v Perryman* or the 'pure speech' rationale in *Canadian Liberty Net*, do not apply to injurious falsehood. In the latter case, the Supreme Court stated that in the commercial context, 'the criteria of "balance of convenience" and "irreparable harm" [have] some measurable meaning'[120] and do not inevitably lead to the injunction being granted. The Court therefore distinguished those situations from ones involving 'pure speech', where the balance of convenience will generally favour an injunction despite its speech-infringing effect.

Whether the much more restrictive *Bonnard v Perryman* approach is still warranted in defamation cases is a more difficult issue that I will leave for another day. Suffice it to say that there are increasing calls to broaden the availability of interlocutory injunctions in defamation,[121] particularly in light of the persistence and geographical reach of internet publications.

III. Empirical Study of Injurious Falsehood

As noted above, there is significant overlap between injurious falsehood and other torts, especially defamation. Defamation in particular imposes a far lesser onus on the plaintiff. I therefore hypothesised that injurious falsehood claims would be relatively rare and would generally be pleaded alongside defamation. I suspected that there was little scope left to be covered by injurious falsehood alone. This might then have implications for changes to the tort landscape regarding false statements of fact. This section describes a small empirical study conducted to test those hypotheses.

[117] *Bonnard v Perryman* [1891] 2 Ch 269. This is the same as the *Canada Metal Co* approach noted above.

[118] There are several examples of this kind of error. See, eg, *Manson v John Doe*, 2011 ONSC 4663 [11]; *SR v LR* 2010 ONSC 5229 [14]–[20]; *Yaghi v WMS Gaming Inc*, 2003 ABQB 680 [33]–[48].

[119] *Raimondi v Ontario Heritage Trust*, 2017 ONSC 3389 [163].

[120] *Canadian Liberty Net* (n 112) [47].

[121] See 'Bonnard v Perryman (1891)' in D Rolph (ed), *Landmark Cases in Defamation Law* (Hart Publishing, 2019) 56–57. And courts have sometimes refused to apply the restrictive test for interlocutory injunctions in defamation cases. See, eg, *Friesen v Chiu*, 2006 BCSC 2104, especially at [24]; *Rosemond Estates Inc v Levy*, 2003 ONSC 44868 ONSC; 65 O.R. (3d) 79.

I searched CanLII (a freely accessible database of Canadian cases)[122] for 'injurious falsehood' or 'malicious falsehood' or 'slander of title' or 'slander of goods' or 'trade libel'. This returned 718 results. I categorised the first 154 of these, representing the 100 most recent injurious falsehood cases[123] (once false positives and multiple proceedings from the same case were deleted). These 100 cases were decided between April 2013 to July 2019.

Of the 100 cases, 60 were finally decided on the injurious falsehood issue, as opposed to being interlocutory. Of those 60, only four resulted in liability. Damages were assessed in only one case and were awarded in the amount of approximately \$276,000.[124] In the other three cases, injurious falsehood damages would duplicate defamation damages and so were not ordered[125] or were to be determined at a later date.[126]

There was less overlap between injurious falsehood and defamation than I would have predicted. Although it is sometimes hard to tell from reasons for judgment what causes of action were pleaded, it appears that of the 100 most recent cases involving injurious falsehood claims, 44 also included claims for defamation. While this is a significant number, it is clear that these two torts do not always go hand in hand. Causes of action other than injurious falsehood were pleaded in the vast majority of the injurious falsehood cases (91/100), but it is not uncommon for plaintiffs to plead multiple causes of action. Other than defamation, causes of action frequently pleaded alongside injurious falsehood in the cases sampled included breach of contract (at least 21 cases),[127] intentional interference with economic interests (at least 25 cases) and conspiracy (at least 12 cases).

Not surprisingly, injurious falsehood is less litigated than defamation. Although it is hard to prove such statements empirically given the dearth of data on civil actions in Canada, the following should be enough to make the point. Whereas a search of terms related to injurious falsehood returned 718 hits in CanLII, a similar search of terms related to defamation ('defamation' or 'libel' or 'slander') returned 13,660 hits on CanLII. Defamation is clearly the more litigated tort.

One final result of the empirical study relates to the identity of injurious falsehood plaintiffs. Although both human beings and corporations can have their economic interests injured by false statements, one might expect injurious falsehood plaintiffs to more often be corporations than people. After all, injurious falsehood is often considered a business tort or a matter of unfair competition.[128]

[122] CanLII, 'What's CanLII', available at www.canlii.org/en/info/about.html.

[123] CanLII is not a complete database, and so these 100 cases do not reflect all of the most recent case law. However, CanLII is quite comprehensive, especially with regard to more recent cases.

[124] Damages were assessed as interest on \$2.3 million at a rate of 5% from March 2013 to the date of judgment, being July 2015. Calling this 2.4 years, I arrived at a figure of \$276,000. *International Sausage House* (n 42) [215].

[125] *British Columbia Recreation and Parks Association v Zakharia*, 2015 BCSC 1650.

[126] *Cana International Distributing Inc., c.o.b. as Sexy Living v Standard Innovation Corporation*, 2016 ONSC 7197.

[127] I say 'at least' because some decisions refer to causes of action 'including' or 'inter alia'.

[128] Langvardt (n 24) 947.

Thirty of the 100 injurious falsehood plaintiffs were solely corporate; 37 were solely human and 33 involved both human and corporate plaintiffs. So, while corporate injurious falsehood claims are quite common, it is certainly not rare for human plaintiffs to bring claims in injurious falsehood.

IV. Final Thoughts

This chapter has been largely descriptive, while also indicating how uncertainties in the law should best be resolved. This final section notes some related subjects for further consideration.

A. Denying Corporations Access to Defamation Law

The first such subject is whether the distinction between injurious falsehood and defamation should be made clearer by denying corporate plaintiffs the ability to sue in defamation, and leaving them to sue in injurious falsehood. This is what Australia has done for larger corporations.[129] This would prevent corporations from obtaining the benefit of more plaintiff-friendly aspects of defamation law, which exist to protect reputation, despite their claim really being about economic harm.

In my view, defamation should not be available for claims primarily involving economic harm and there should be changes to both defamation and injurious falsehood to better reflect the substantive requirements appropriate to causes of action involving different kinds of injuries. To be clear, my objection does not rest on the fact that the torts overlap. It is not problematic for the same facts to lead to liability in multiple torts:

> English law has marked out causes of action on which plaintiffs may rely. Many causes of action overlap. On one set of facts a plaintiff may have more than one cause of action against a defendant. He may have a cause of action in tort and also for breach of contract. This is an everyday occurrence with some claims for negligence, or with claims for breach of confidence …. Or a plaintiff may have more than one cause of action in tort: a factory accident may give rise to a claim in negligence and for breach of statutory duty. These instances could be multiplied. When more than one cause of action is available to him, a plaintiff may choose which he will pursue … He may pursue one to the exclusion of another, even though a defence available in one cause of action is not available in another. Indeed, the availability of a defence in one cause of action

[129] *Civil Law (Wrongs) Act 2002* (ACT) s 121; *Defamation Act* (NT) s 8; *Defamation Act* (NSW) s 9; *Defamation Act* (Qlt) s 9; *Defamation Act* (SA) s 9; *Defamation Act* (Tas) s 9; *Defamation Act* (Vic) s 9; *Defamation Act* (WA) s 9.

> but not another may be the very reason why a plaintiff eschews the one and prefers the other .... I have never heard it suggested before that a plaintiff is not entitled to proceed in this way, and take full advantage of the various remedies English law provides for the wrong of which he complains. I have never heard it suggested that he must pursue the most appropriate remedy, and if he does not do so he is at risk of having his proceedings struck out as a misuse of the court's procedures. In my view those suggestions are as unfounded as they are novel.[130]

Rather, my objection is that the plaintiff-friendly nature of defamation, which limits freedom of expression, is not appropriate where economic harm is the gist of the tort. It strikes the wrong balance between expression and reputational interests and is inconsistent with the requirements of other torts involving false statements causing economic harm, such as negligent misrepresentation, deceit and the tort created by section 52(1) of the *Competition Act*.[131] The status quo does not reflect a principled approach, but rather results from independent and incremental developments to both torts over the past century or so. There has been remarkably little justification of the law of defamation applying to corporations. Courts did not thoughtfully analyse the similarities between corporate and human reputation or the benefits and detriments of extending libel law to non-human entities. Rather, in Canada, the rationales were that corporations are legal persons with the same rights as humans[132] and that it would be unacceptable for corporations not to have any recourse when a libel was spread.[133] While I agree that corporations should have legal recourse when their reputations are unfairly harmed, this hardly means that defamation (or a tort that strikes the same balance as defamation) need apply to corporate reputation, nor that the law that applies must be substantively the same for corporate plaintiffs as for human ones.

It does not seem likely, if one were to create a tort to protect corporate reputation in 2020, that it would look anything like defamation. Courts in the twenty-first century are showing greater concern for freedom of expression than they did 100 years ago. Rather, I expect it would look more like injurious falsehood.

B. Eliminating Injurious Falsehood Altogether

Common law jurisdictions have generally resisted denying corporations access to defamation law on the basis that such a change would go too far and leave

[130] *Joyce* (n 43) 342–43.

[131] *Competition Act* (n 1).

[132] *Price* (n 4) 214.

[133] *Ibid* 197. This case, which first recognised a corporation's right to sue in defamation, was about an allegation that Chicoutimi Pulp had wrongfully tried to acquire title to property. This is squarely within the scope of injurious falsehood, so the company would not necessarily have been left without a remedy had it not sued in defamation.

corporations largely unprotected from lies spread about them.[134] If Canada continues to allow corporations to sue in defamation, one might wonder whether injurious falsehood performs any important function that would justify its continued existence. Thus, one possibility would be simply to eliminate the tort of injurious falsehood. It is seldom litigated (at least successfully for the plaintiff) and overlaps to a great degree with other torts (eg, defamation, s 52(1) of the *Competition Act*, and passing off). It is likely that few would miss it if it were abolished.

This argument is perhaps even stronger in light of a potential new false light privacy tort. In December of 2019, an Ontario court recognised Prosser's false light privacy tort, defined as follows:

> One who gives publicity to a matter concerning another that places the other before the public in a false light is subject to liability to the other for invasion of his privacy, if
>
> (a) the false light in which the other was placed would be highly offensive to a reasonable person, and
>
> (b) the actor had knowledge of or acted in reckless disregard as to the falsity of the publicized matter and the false light in which the other would be placed.[135]

I do not think it likely that the false light privacy tort will come to be widely recognised in Canada. It does not fill a gap in the law. Indeed, the *Yanovkian* case could easily have been resolved on the basis of defamation. However, if it does take hold, it will overlap with injurious falsehood almost completely. False light requires malicious publication of words that convey a false impression. The advantage of the false light tort, from a plaintiff's perspective, is that there is no need to prove special damage and general damages are clearly available. The only injurious falsehoods that would not amount to false light are those that would not be highly offensive to a reasonable person. While that may sound like a high threshold, it has not necessarily been interpreted that way in other privacy cases. For example, in *Vanderveen v Waterbridge Media Inc*,[136] the Court found that element to be made out where a two second video clip, showing the plaintiff jogging on a public trail, was used in a commercial video. Although the emphasis of the false light tort is on privacy rather than economic loss, historical experience with defamation shows that those lines are blurry.

Yet I believe there is still a role for injurious falsehood. The appropriate response to the tort's decline is not to abolish it but to give it new life – to push back against

[134] The Law Commission of Ontario, a law reform body in that province, undertook a major defamation reform project and recommended against denying corporations standing to sue in defamation. See Law Commission of Ontario, 'Defamation Law in the Internet Age' (2020) 66–68, available www.lco-cdo.org/wp-content/uploads/2020/03/Defamation-Final-Report-Eng-FINAL-1.pdf. The UK also resisted calls to take Australia's approach and, in its *Defamation Act 2013*, c. 26 s 1(2) eliminated the presumption of damage for corporate defamation plaintiffs, otherwise leaving their right of action intact.

[135] *Yanovkian v Gulian* 2019 ONSC 7279 [170].

[136] *Vanderveen v Waterbridge Media Inc*, 2017 ONSCSM 77435ONSC.

defamation and other torts' encroachment and its own expansion. Langvardt, who has written about the same issue in the American context, agrees that there is a role for injurious falsehood.[137] Note, however, that much of his reasoning is grounded in First Amendment jurisprudence that has little relevance outside the United States.

If we start from first principles, namely that injurious falsehood is about economic harm caused by false statements while defamation is about reputational harm caused by false statements, some of the elements of each tort should be modified better to reflect those principles. Further, the fact that there is only a very narrow range of conduct that constitutes injurious falsehood and not some other tort is not a reason in and of itself to eliminate the cause of action. Nor is the fact that its requirements are stringent and plaintiffs who plead it rarely succeed. It carves out its own range of unlawful conduct, albeit narrow, and we might as well keep it. That said, continued confusion about its elements does a real disservice to litigants who expend resources perhaps because of confusing and contradictory statements in the law. This confusion should be eliminated. One simple way of limiting confusion is to abandon reference to 'slander of title', 'slander of goods' or malicious falsehood, and to always refer to the tort as injurious falsehood.[138]

V. Conclusion

This chapter has described the current state of the law of injurious falsehood, particularly in Canada, emphasising areas in which the law is unclear or unsatisfactory. In such areas, I have suggested how that confusion should be resolved. For example, the existence of special damage should still have to be strictly proven. As for quantum, by definition special damages need to be proven specifically. Nevertheless, the approach should be contextual and a 'robust and pragmatic approach'[139] should be taken to proving special damages where the nature of the loss, or its causal connection to the falsity, make it especially difficult to prove.

The second goal of the chapter was to examine empirically how injurious falsehood is being litigated. It has not been totally eclipsed by defamation, though there is no doubt that the latter is the more popular tort and is generally preferred where facts permit either tort to be pleaded. Rates of success for the plaintiff appear to be quite low in injurious falsehood and even where liability is established, no additional damages will be ordered where they would duplicate defamation damages.

[137] Langvardt (n 24) 906.

[138] 'The problem of nomenclature is a substantial one in researching the law in this area': *Frank Flaman* (n 50) 257.

[139] In *Snell* (n 60), the Supreme Court of Canada adopted a robust and pragmatic approach – essentially a common sense approach to proving causation where the evidence is not definitive.

Finally, I showed that both human and corporate plaintiffs regularly avail themselves of the tort.

Finally, I considered ways in which changes to current law might improve the status quo. My preference would be to deny corporations access to defamation law, since that tort's elements, in my view, are only justifiable given the significant dignitary and social interests at stake. These do not arise (or not to the same extent) where corporate reputation is involved. If this change were made, the effect would likely be to breathe new life into the tort of injurious falsehood.

That said, this seems unlikely in the present context, so I also considered whether, in that case, injurious falsehood it worth retaining at all. I ultimately conclude that its slice of the tort pie is very small, and that it rarely results in liability. However, that is not a sufficient to eliminate injurious falsehood. The expansion of tort liability over the past 100 years or so has left injurious falsehood with relatively little to do, but there are occasions when it is just the right thing. For example, where an interlocutory injunction is sought, defamation's free speech focus may make an injunction unobtainable, but injurious falsehood, with its focus on economic loss, permits such injunctions where the balance of convenience favours them. Given that, I see no reason to interfere with the tort of injurious falsehood beyond clarifying uncertainties about its elements and remedies.

9

Regulation of GM Farming via Private Nuisance

ANNA BUNN* AND MICHAEL DOUGLAS**

I. Introduction

Economic torts perform an important function in protecting against the infliction of economic harm in the context of certain competitive practices.[1] This chapter focuses on a particular species of competitive practice that has emerged in recent years: the use of genetically modified organisms ('GMOs') in agriculture, particularly with respect to crop farming. It considers how a particular economic tort may regulate the farming of GMOs ('GM farming').[2]

The chapter focuses on the tort of private nuisance.[3] In her chapter, Professor Giliker considers that nuisance is not an economic tort.[4] However, while the primary concern of the tort of nuisance is regulation of 'the reciprocal rights and duties of private individuals, where there is conflict over competing uses of land',[5] nuisance can provide protection for economic interests and even protect against excessive competition.[6] Through a functionalist lens, it is an economic tort,[7] and one that farming businesses negatively impacted by GM-farming neighbours have turned to in an attempt to vindicate their economic interests.[8]

The significance of nuisance for GM farming turns on a backdrop of statutory regulation. Regulation of GMOs varies around the world; we focus on our native Australia, and Western Australia in particular. Regulators must grapple

* BA (Oxf), MA (Oxf), PhD (UNDA), Senior Lecturer, Curtin Law School, Curtin University, Western Australia.

** BA (Hons) LLB LLM (Dist) MBA (Dist) (W.Aust), Senior Lecturer, UWA Law School, University of Western Australia.

[1] H Carty, *An Analysis of the Economic Torts*, 2nd edn (Oxford, Oxford University Press, 2010) 4.

[2] The use of genetically modified livestock in agriculture is not considered in this chapter.

[3] Referred to below as simply 'nuisance'.

[4] See chapter 7 of this volume.

[5] *Marsh v Baxter* [2015] WASCA 169, (2015) 49 WAR 1 [242] (McLure P). *Marsh* was a case concerning the impact of GM farming on a neighbouring organic farmer. The case is discussed throughout this chapter.

[6] Carty (n 1) 2.

[7] *Contra* Giliker, chapter 7 of this volume.

[8] For a brief discussion of such cases, see section IV.A. of this chapter.

with the unique risks to the environment and to other forms of agriculture posed by GM farming.[9] In Australia, some of those risks are managed by a national regulatory framework underpinned by the *Gene Technology Act 2000* (Cth) and corresponding State and Territory legislation.[10] Although the framework considers risks to the environment and to human health and safety, it does not address other socio-economic impacts of GM farming.[11] This is a purposeful omission. It has been argued that the common law, and torts in particular, can protect affected farmers and other persons who incur damage from GMOs.[12] This chapter tests that argument. With reference to *Marsh v Baxter* – a Western Australian case in which organic farmers did not succeed in their nuisance claim against their GM-farming neighbour – we argue that while nuisance has some role in regulating the socio-economic impacts of GMOs, its role is limited. In practice, if not in theory, it is unlikely that those dealing in GMOs will be held liable in nuisance for any of the economic consequences of their activities.

The chapter is structured as follows. Section II briefly considers the potential socio-economic impacts of GM farming and provides an overview the statutory framework regulating GMOs in Australia. Section III briefly considers how nuisance may serve as a vehicle for regulation.[13] Section IV considers whether nuisance is capable of filling gaps in the regulatory scheme, and section V offers some conclusions.

II. GM Farming and its Regulation

The use of GMOs in farming is a modern step in a long tradition of human beings tinkering with plants.[14] Some crops, like the corn we know today, could not exist without our intervention.[15] Science has taken our ability to manipulate

[9] K Ludlow, 'Gene Technology Regulation and the Environment Protection and Biodiversity Conservation Act 1999 (Cth)' (2004) 30(2) *Monash University Law Review* 165, 167–73.

[10] See section II.

[11] Ludlow (n 9) 166, 172; K Ludlow, 'The Economic Impact of Genetically Modified Crops as Actionable Damage in Torts' (2005) 13 *Torts Law Journal* 159, 162. Impacts on health and the environment can themselves be considered socio-economic considerations relevant to GM technology: see, eg, K Ludlow, SJ Smyth and J Falck-Zepeda, 'Introduction to Socio-Economic Considerations in the Regulation of Genetically Modified Organisms' in K Ludlow, SJ Smyth and J Falck-Zepeda (eds), *Socio-Economic Considerations in Biotechnology Regulation* (New York, Springer, 2014).

[12] See Senate Committee on Community Affairs, Parliament of Australia, *A Cautionary Tale: Fish Don't Lay Tomatoes – A Report on the Gene Technology Bill 2000* (2000) 151–52; Department of Health and Ageing, Australian Government, *Statutory Review of the Gene Technology Act 2000 and The Gene Technology Agreement* (2006) 38; Ludlow Economic Impact (n 11) 162; D Dalton, 'Transgenic Crops and Genetic Contamination: Assessing the Need for a Regulatory Response to Protect Organic Farmers' (2003) 8(2) *Australian Journal of Natural Resources Law and Policy* 129, 142.

[13] The principles of nuisance are also considered by Giliker, in chapter 7 of this volume.

[14] B Glass-O'Shea, 'The History and Future of Genetically Modified Crops: Frankenfoods, Superweeds, and the Developing World' (2011) 7(1) *Journal of Food Law & Policy* 1, 3.

[15] *Ibid*; JA Thomson, *GM Crops – The Impact and Potential* (CSIRO Publishing, 2006) 1.

crops to another level. Through use of biotechnology, humans can now change the characteristics of living organisms to create GMOs for various ends, including enhanced productivity, improved weed and pest control, and more flexible crop management.[16] GM farming has great potential; it provides the opportunity to improve food security[17] against a backdrop of climate risk.[18] Importantly for present purposes, it may also massively increase the productivity, and so profitability, of many agricultural businesses. Over the 17 years from 1996–2013, GM crop farming generated $117.6 billion income for farm businesses, increasing global yield by 22 per cent.[19] Increased productivity provides a strong incentive for farming businesses to incorporate GMOs into their farming practices.

Despite those benefits, GM farming remains controversial. There is conflicting scientific evidence concerning the impact of GMOs on health and the environment.[20] One clear risk of GM farming practices concerns herbicide resistance.[21] For example, herbicide-resistant GM canola may improve crop yields but may lead to the emergence of herbicide-resistant weed species in the long term.[22] Another risk concerns the economic impact of GM farming on other farming practices. Organic farming business models may be particularly vulnerable; organic produce may attract a substantial price premium that is unavailable to traditional (ie, non-organic) and GM produce.[23] The premium may turn on 'certification' of the produce by an appropriate body. GM farming in proximity to organic farming puts that certification at risk.[24] Whenever there is an unwanted spread of GMOs to those involved in non-GM or GM-free production,[25]

[16] United Nations Conference on Trade and Development, 'International Trade in GMOs and GM Products: National and Multilateral Legal Frameworks' (Policy Issues in International Trade and Commodities, Study Series No 29, United Nations, 2005) 1, available at https://unctad.org/system/files/official-document/itcdtab30_en.pdf.

[17] K Jamil, 'Biotechnology – A Solution to Hunger?' (*UN Chronicle*, United Nations, 2020), available at www.un.org/en/chronicle/article/biotechnology-solution-hunger.

[18] R Raman, 'The Impact of Genetically Modified (GM) Crops in Modern Agriculture: A Review' (2017) 8(4) *GM Crops & Food* 195, 205.

[19] *Ibid* 198.

[20] See A Tsatsakis et al, 'Impact on Environment, Ecosystem, Diversity and Health from Culturing and using GMOs as Feed and Food' (2017) 107(A) *Food and Chemical Toxicology* 108.

[21] See G Schütte et al, 'Herbicide Resistance and Biodiversity: Agronomic and Environmental Aspects of Genetically Modified Herbicide-Resistant Plants' (2017) 29(5) *Environmental Sciences Europe* 1.

[22] *Ibid.*

[23] European Commission, 'Financial Competitiveness of Organic Agriculture on a Global Scale' (Knowledge for policy, 8 November 2018), available at https://ec.europa.eu/knowledge4policy/publication/financial-competitiveness-organic-agriculture-global-scale_en.

[24] Legislative Council Western Australia, Standing Committee on Environment and Public Affairs, *Mechanisms for Compensation for Economic Loss to Farmers in Western Australia caused by Contamination by Genetically Modified Material*, Report 49 (February 2019) 18.

[25] An explanation of the difference between the terms 'GM-free food' and 'non-GM food' is provided by the Standing Committee on Environment and Public Affairs, *ibid* 14 [3.14]. Essentially, GM-free food contains no GM materials, whereas non-GM food contains no GM material above a particular tolerance level. The tolerance level for non-GM canola in Western Australia is 0.9 and this level is 'widely accepted as the international standard for exported canola': Standing Committee on Environment and Public Affairs, *ibid* 9 [2.46].

the potential costs to those affected include costs of testing and re-certification, loss of markets, brand damage, clean-up costs, audit costs and loss of profits.[26]

A. Statutory Regulation of GM Farming in Australia

The risks of GM farming have justified regulation of GMOs by Australian legislators. The *Gene Technology Act* was established to 'protect the public health and safety of people and to protect the environment from risks associated with gene technology'.[27] The Act is the centrepiece of a regulatory scheme established with the cooperation of the States and Territories.[28] The Act also establishes the Gene Technology Regulator ('Regulator'), an independent statutory office holder, whose role is overseen by the Gene Technology Ministerial Council established by the Gene Technology Agreement of 2001.[29]

The *Gene Technology Act* achieves its risk-averse object by establishing the default position that dealing with GMOs is prohibited in Australia.[30] The concept of 'dealing' is very broad, and includes breeding, propagating, using, growing, transporting and disposing of GMOs.[31] If a farmer were to grow and harvest a GM crop, it would be a 'dealing' (or multiple 'dealings') within the meaning of the Act.[32]

[26] *Ibid* 18.

[27] Explanatory Memorandum, *Gene Technology Bill 2000* (Cth) 2; *Gene Technology Act 2000* (Cth) s 3. Section 47(3) reaffirms that the Act is primarily concerned with risks to the health and safety of people, and to the environment.

[28] See *Gene Technology Act 2000* (Cth) s 5, pt 2 div 4; *Gene Technology Regulations 2001* (Cth); *Gene Technology Act 2003* (ACT); *Gene Technology (Northern Territory) Act 2004* (NT); *Gene Technology (New South Wales) Act 2003* (NSW); *Gene Technology Act 2001* (Qld); *Gene Technology Regulation 2002* (Qld); *Gene Technology Act 2001* (SA); *Gene Technology Regulations 2002* (SA); *Gene Technology Act 2001* (Tas); *Gene Technology Regulations 2003* (Tas); *Gene Technology Act 2001* (Vic); *Gene Technology Regulations 2001* (Vic); *Gene Technology Act 2006* (WA); *Gene Technology Regulations 2007* (WA). The scheme is also comprised of the Gene Technology Regulator (*Gene Technology Act 2000* (Cth) pt 3; see Department of Health, Office of the Gene Technology Regulator, Australian Government, Office of the Gene Technology Regulator (13 November 2014), available at www.ogtr.gov.au/>); the Gene Technology Agreement (Department of Health, Australian Government, 13 November 2014), available at www.health.gov.au/internet/main/publishing.nsf/Content/gene-tech-agreement); the Gene Technology Ministerial Council, (Australian Government, Gene Technology Ministerial Council (GTMC) (13 November 2014), available at www.directory.gov.au/directory?ea0_lf99_120.&organizationalUnit&8cce654a-b00b-4c4d-8183-b8de6687730d); the Gene Technology Technical Advisory Committee; and the Gene Technology Ethics and Community Consultative Committee (*Gene Technology Act 2000* (Cth) pt 8; see Department of Health, Office of the Gene Technology Regulator, Australian Government, The Gene Technology Technical Advisory Committee (GTTAC) (13 November 2014), available at www.ogtr.gov.au/internet/ogtr/publishing.nsf/Content/gttac-2; Department of Health, Office of the Gene Technology Regulator, Australian Government, The Gene Technology Ethics and Community Consultative Committee (GTECCC) (13 November 2014), available at www.ogtr.gov.au/internet/ogtr/publishing.nsf/Content/gteccc-2; LexisNexis, *Halsbury's Laws of Australia*, 330 Primary Industry (at Service Number 386, March 2014) [330-3300].

[29] *Marsh* (n 5) [45]–[46] (McLure P).

[30] *Gene Technology Act 2000* (Cth) s 32; *cf Gene Technology Regulations 2001* (Cth) reg 6. There are equivalent provisions in the State and Territory legislation, eg *Gene Technology Act 2006* (WA) s 32.

[31] *Gene Technology Act 2000* (Cth) s 10 (definition of 'deal with').

[32] See *Marsh v Baxter* [2014] WASC 187, (2014) 46 WAR 377 [154]–[162].

Despite the default prohibition on dealing with GMOs, the Act permits some dealings under licence from the Regulator.[33] The Regulator has issued several licences since the introduction of the Act.[34] This chapter only considers the impact of dealings with GM crops pursuant to these licences.[35] A critical feature of such cases is that a legislature has approved the kind of agricultural activity in question. However, the fact that GM dealings are conducted pursuant to a licence will not necessarily preclude the possibility of liability in tort.[36]

B. Gaps in the Regulatory Scheme

The *Gene Technology Act* does not make provision for compensation of farmers or other third parties affected by GMOs. As noted by a committee of the Western Australian Legislative Council, the protection of the Act is 'confined to certain persons or classes of persons who are affected by the Regulator's decision to not issue a licence or to issue one subject to conditions, rather than third parties who may be affected by such a decision'.[37]

A person who suffers damage as the result of 'contamination' by GM material may be able to sue the person responsible to recover compensation.[38] That responsible person could be the farmer responsible for the contamination event; a company through which the responsible farmer conducts his or her business; or, arguably, the licensor of GM crops.[39]

As there is unlikely to be any contract between the parties or their respective business entities, in the absence of statutory relief, the causes of action most likely applicable are those arising in tort. Given that loss is most likely to be an indirect result of a person's act or omission, the most relevant causes of action are

[33] The Act also permits a dealing with a GMO that is exempt; that is a notifiable low risk dealing; or that is on the Register of GMOs: *Gene Technology Act 2000* (Cth) pt 4, s 31; Explanatory Memorandum, *Gene Technology Bill 2000* (Cth), 2.

[34] See Department of Health, Office of the Gene Technology Regulator, *Table of Applications and Authorisations for Dealings Involving Intentional Release (DIR) into the Environment* (6 June 2014), available at www.ogtr.gov.au/internet/ogtr/publishing.nsf/Content/ir-1.

[35] The economic impact of the *unauthorised* release of GMOs into the environment may be amenable to claims framed in terms of other economic torts, including the so-called unlawful means tort.

[36] A person may drive negligently but with a drivers' licence. In the context of an action in private nuisance, the defence of statutory authorisation may preclude liability provided that the interference complained of was the inevitable result of the activity authorised by statute, *cf* the defence of statutory authority which is discussed further below. See generally J Murphy, *The Law of Nuisance* (Oxford, Oxford University Press, 2010) 100–104 [5.02]–[5.10].

[37] Standing Committee on Environment and Public Affairs (n 24) 4.

[38] As noted by Ludlow: 'Neither the national regulatory scheme created by the Gene Technology Act 2000 (Cth) … nor the State moratorium legislation gives immunity to those who comply with the legislation but nevertheless cause harm to others': K Ludlow, 'Genetically Modified Organisms and Private Nuisance Liability' (2005) 113 *Tort Law Review* 92, 94.

[39] For example, Bayer Australia Ltd.

negligence and nuisance, although depending on the particular factual matrix at hand, other causes of action are also possible. For example, a farmer who purchases seed on the understanding that it is GM-free when it is not may have an action for misleading or deceptive conduct or false or misleading representations under the Australian Consumer Law.[40] Where the person whose act or omission is responsible for the GM contamination intended harm, other causes of action might also lie.[41] The remainder of this chapter focuses on the tort of nuisance.

III. Private Nuisance as a Vehicle for Regulation

A. Nuisance

The tort of nuisance is an activity or a state of affairs that causes a substantial and unreasonable[42] interference with a person's land or with the use and enjoyment of that land.[43] It balances the rights of occupiers to use their land freely with the rights of their neighbours not to be interfered with.[44] In doing so it provides a vehicle for the regulation of land use and the environment: it has been described as the 'environmental tort' *par excellence*.[45]

The cause of action may be distilled into three elements.[46] First, the plaintiff must have a proprietary interest in land. This is necessary so that the plaintiff has standing to sue in respect of interference with the use and enjoyment of *that* land.[47] Second, there must be interference with the plaintiff's land or the plaintiff's use and enjoyment of that land.[48] Third, the interference must be substantial and unreasonable.[49]

It is sometimes said that nuisance is not actionable per se, and that damage must be proved before the cause of action is established.[50] However, in

[40] Australian Consumer Law s 18(1) and ss 29 and 33; *Competition and Consumer Act 2010* (Cth) sch 2.

[41] For example, trespass.

[42] *Grand Central Car Park Pty Ltd v Tivoli Freeholders* [1969] VR 62, 72 (McInerney J).

[43] *Sedleigh-Denfield v O'Callaghan* [1940] AC 880, 896–97 (Lord Atkin). See Murphy (n 36) 5 [1.05].

[44] *Sedleigh-Denfield*, *ibid* 903 (Lord Wright), cited in *Elston v Dore* (1982) 149 CLR 480, 487–88 (Gibbs CJ, Wilson and Brennan JJ).

[45] J Wightman, 'Nuisance – The Environmental Tort? *Hunter v Canary Wharf* in the House of Lords' (1998) 61(6) *MLR* 870, 870; see also NJ Benson, 'What to Do about Useful Nuisances? *Antrim Truck Centre* and its Implications for Toxic Torts' (2012) 20 *Tort Law Review* 107, 107, fn 1.

[46] See LexisNexis, *Halsbury's Laws of Australia*, 415 Tort (at Service Number 389, May 2014) [415–635].

[47] *Hunter v Canary Wharf* [1977] AC 655; *Benning v Wong* (1969) 122 CLR 249, 320 (Windeyer J).

[48] *Southern Properties (WA) Pty Ltd v Executive Director of the Department of Conservation and Land Management* [2012] WASCA 79, (2012) 42 WAR 287 [118] (McLure P).

[49] *Kine v Jolly* [1905] 1 Ch 480, 489 (Vaughan Williams LJ); *cf Southern Properties* (n 48) [118]–[119] (McLure P), 346 [315] (Pullin JA).

[50] C Sappideen and P Vines (eds), *Fleming's The Law of Torts*, 10th edn (Pyrmont, Lawbook Co, 2011) 497.

Williams v Network Rail Infrastructure Ltd,[51] Sir Etherton MR commented that the 'frequently stated proposition that damage is always an essential requirement of the cause of action for nuisance … must be treated with considerable caution'.[52] The Master of the Rolls went on to comment that the objective impact on the amenity value of the land occasioned by the interference constituting the nuisance 'satisfies any requirement to show damage'.[53] On this view, it is interference with the property right – the right to the use and enjoyment of land free from substantial and unreasonable interference – that constitutes damage.[54] There is thus no requirement that the plaintiff prove damage above and beyond the harm to their property right, albeit that where the plaintiff suffers consequential losses these may be recoverable. The diminution in the quality of the plaintiff's use and enjoyment of their property as a result of nuisance has real economic value even in the absence of physical damage, justifying the characterisation of that diminution in terms of economic loss.[55]

B. Nuisance's Regulatory Role

The law of nuisance seeks to regulate environmental and other harms by striking a balance between competing interests: the plaintiff's interest in the use and enjoyment of land, on the one hand, and the defendant's freedom to pursue activities (often, but not always, on their own land), on the other. It does this by attributing value to externalities – that is, to the effects that a transaction has on people that were not party to the negotiations that led to it.[56]

Nuisance can shift the economic costs of a particular activity. For example, all other things being equal, unless a factory is liable in tort for damaging a neighbouring property, the market will assess any damage as zero.[57] Nuisance can transpose what would otherwise be a mere externality to be borne by the neighbour into a cost for the individual responsible for the damage.[58] According to a liberal framework, individuals will be motivated to minimise costs in pursuit of material self-interest, and in doing so, will avoid producing harmful, and costly,

[51] *Williams v Network Rail Infrastructure Ltd* [2018] EWCA Civ 1514, [2018] 3 WLR 1105.
[52] *Ibid* [42].
[53] *Ibid* [43].
[54] A view expressed by D Nolan, '"A Tort against Land": Private Nuisance as a Property Tort' in D Nolan and A Robertson (eds), *Rights and Private Law* (Oxford, Hart Publishing, 2011) 481.
[55] *Cf* the characterisation of defects in other kinds of property, including defective products or buildings, as economic loss: R Bernstein, *Economic Loss*, 3rd edn (London, Sweet & Maxwell, 2013) Vol 1 [1-007].
[56] P Dagupta, 'Facts and Values in Modern Economics' in H Kincaid and D Ross (eds), *The Oxford Handbook of Philosophy of Economics* (Oxford, Oxford University Press, 2009) 580, 588.
[57] D Campbell, 'Of Coase and Corn: A (Sort Of) Defence of Private Nuisance' (2000) 60 *MLR* 197, 199.
[58] *Ibid* 199; see, also, KN Hylton, 'The Economics of Nuisance Law' (Boston University School of Law Working Paper No 09-05, Boston University, May 2010) 2, available at https://scholarship.law.bu.edu/cgi/viewcontent.cgi?article=1442&context=faculty_scholarship.

externalities.[59] Riskier activities will mean higher chances of nuisance liability, and so if actors are well informed, nuisance law will make them more careful.[60]

While the regulatory function of private nuisance serves economic ends, however, it also has a broader function. For example, in relation to GMOs, private nuisance has a role in ensuring that coexistence between GM systems and GM-free systems is sustained. Co-existence, in turn, affords consumers with a choice between GM and GM-free products: a choice which may be motivated by concerns for health or the environment.[61]

IV. Application to GM Farming

A. Case Examples

The only Australian case to have considered the availability of a nuisance action to a non-GM farmer in respect of the impact of GMOs on farming operations is *Marsh v Baxter*.[62] The Marshes grew cereal crops, but not canola, and raised sheep on their farm in Kojonup, Western Australia. In 2006, the majority of their farm was certified as organic by an organisation accredited by the Commonwealth of Australia to certify produce as organic for the purpose of sale, provided that produce meets certain standards.[63] Some years after they had achieved organic certification, and after it had become legal to grow GM canola in Western Australia, the Marshes' immediate neighbour, Baxter, decided to grow GM canola on his farm for the first time.[64] Baxter elected to harvest this GM crop by a method known as swathing.[65] Swathing involves cutting the canola stalks and stacking the cut swathes in 'windrows' to ripen, before harvesting the seed. After Baxter had left the GM canola in windrows to ripen, several of the swathes were picked up by wind and blew across onto the Marshes' farm.[66] The Marshes informed the organic certifying body of the presence of GM canola swathes and seeds on their property.[67] After inspecting the Marshes' property, the organic certifying body decertified a large proportion of the Marshes' farm,[68] as a result of which the organic crops grown in those areas were unable to be

[59] DM Hausman, 'Philosophy of Economics' in EN Zalta (ed), *The Stanford Encyclopedia of Philosophy* (Winter 2013 Edition) (16 November 2014), available at http://plato.stanford.edu/entries/economics/.

[60] See generally Hylton (n 58) 2.

[61] K Kariyawasam, 'Legal Liability, Intellectual Property and Genetically Modified Crops: Their Impact on World Agriculture' (2010) 19(3) *Pacific Rim Law & Policy Journal* 459, 461–63.

[62] *Marsh* (n 32) and *Marsh* (n 5).

[63] *Marsh* (n 5) [389]–[390] (Newnes and Murphy JJA).

[64] *Ibid* [402]–[403] (Newnes and Murphy JJA).

[65] *Ibid* [415] (Newnes and Murphy JJA).

[66] *Ibid* [446] (Newnes and Murphy JJA).

[67] *Ibid* [416] (Newnes and Murphy JJA).

[68] *Ibid* [418], [419], [420], [424].

sold as certified organic and attracted a lower market price than they would otherwise have done. The Marshes sought to recover this pure economic loss by way of an action brought in negligence and nuisance against Baxter. They also sought a perpetual injunction in nuisance to restrain Baxter from harvesting his GM canola by swathing within a certain distance from their farm.[69]

In a lengthy first instance judgment, Kenneth Martin J dismissed claims in nuisance and negligence.[70] On appeal, the appellant organic farmers were unsuccessful as regards both claims.[71] The Western Australian Supreme Court of Appeal was divided in their judgment. McLure P dissented in the appellants' favour on both causes of action. The remaining justices, Newnes and Murphy JJA, dismissed the appeal on both actions. The appellants subsequently sought special leave to appeal this decision to the High Court, which was refused.[72] Aspects of the Court of Appeal's judgment pertaining to the nuisance action are discussed further below.

Actions brought in nuisance by non-GM farmers affected by the unwanted spread of GMOs in other jurisdictions have enjoyed mixed success. In *Hoffman v Monsanto Canada Inc*,[73] a group of Canadian organic farmers pursued a class action against Monsanto Canada Inc and Bayer Crop-Science Inc, the companies behind the commercial release of GMOs to farmers. The farmers claimed damages as a result of that commercial release.[74] Their claim in nuisance was dismissed,[75] although this was a weak test-case, given that the defendant–respondent companies did not actually grow any GM crops.[76] The Court of Appeal of Saskatchewan affirmed the words of Smith J in the judgment below: '[t]he implications of holding a manufacturer, or even inventor, liable in nuisance for damage caused by the use of its product or invention by another would be very sweeping indeed'.[77] Smith J further held that 'where the activity complained of is not an activity of one who is not in occupation or control of adjoining land, and no malfeasance is alleged, then, direct causation of the damage alleged must be alleged [sic]'.[78] That was not the case in the action before the Court.

[69] *Marsh* (n 32) [726].

[70] *Ibid.*

[71] *Marsh* (n 5).

[72] *Marsh v Baxter* [2016] HCATrans 22 (12 February 2016).

[73] *Hoffman v Monsanto Canada Inc* [2005] SKQB 225, [2005] 264 Sask R 1.

[74] *Ibid* [1] (Smith J).

[75] *Ibid* [99]–[124]. Leave to appeal to the Supreme Court of Canada was refused in *Hoffman v Monsanto Canada Inc* [2007] SKCA 47, (2007) 293 Sask R 89. The claimants also pursued (inter alia) claims in negligence, trespass and the rule in *Rylands v Fletcher* [1868] UKHL 1, (1868) LR 3 HL 330, all of which failed: *Hoffman* (n 73) [88] (as to negligence), [97] (as to *Rylands v Fletcher*) and [133] (as to trespass) (Smith J).

[76] *Hoffman* (n 73) [1].

[77] *Hoffman v Monsanto Canada Inc* [2007] SKCA 47, (2007) 293 Sask R 89 [63] (Cameron JA), quoting *Hoffman* (n 73) (Smith J).

[78] *Ibid*, quoting *Hoffman* (n 73) [122] (Smith J).

In contrast to the decision in *Hoffman*, the plaintiffs in the US *StarLink* litigation[79] claimed that companies behind 'StarLink' GM corn should be liable in private nuisance for marketing GM seeds for a type of corn ('StarLink') not approved for human consumption, knowing those seeds would cross-pollinate with neighbouring corn crops.[80] The central issue for the plaintiffs' nuisance claim was whether the defendants 'were responsible for contamination caused by their product after sale'.[81] On a motion to dismiss the nuisance action and other claims, the defendants argued that they could not be liable for any damage caused to farmers after the sale of GM seeds to farmers.[82] The Court disagreed and held that there was a valid claim in nuisance.[83] Important to that decision was the fact that the defendants were in a position to control the nuisance; their failure to do so could amount to a 'substantial contribution' to the nuisance, sufficient to ground liability.[84] The fact that one of the defendants (Aventis) had been granted limited registration by the United States Environmental Protection Agency created an affirmative duty to ensure that farmers to whom the GM corn was supplied complied with grower agreements which outlined field management requirements.[85] According to the Court, this 'arguably gave the plaintiffs some measure of control over StarLink's use, as well as a means to abate any nuisance caused by its misuse'.[86] Ultimately, however, the StarLink litigation was settled before a determination on liability was made by the courts.[87]

The plaintiffs in *Marsh* could have named Monsanto as a defendant but did not. This would have been ambitious on two fronts. First, unlike the litigation pursued against distributors in *Hoffman* and *StarLink*, the Marshes would not have the benefit of participating in a class action.[88] Second, although it is not a requirement of liability in nuisance that the 'nuisance' emanated from land belonging to the defendant,[89] where the nuisance emanates from property in the possession of

[79] *In re StarLink Corn Products Liability Litigation, Marvin Kramer v Aventis Crop Science USA Holding Inc*, 212 F Supp 2d 828 (ND Ill, 2002).

[80] L Beebe, 'In re StarLink Corn: The Link between Genetically Damaged Crops and an Inadequate Regulatory Framework for Biotechnology' (2004) 28(2) *William & Mary Environmental Law and Policy Review* 511, 524; *StarLink* (n 79) [844].

[81] *StarLink* (n 79) [845].

[82] *Ibid* [845] (Moran SDJ).

[83] *Ibid* [847] (Moran SDJ).

[84] *Ibid*. Note, however, that the Court did not rule on whether there *had* been a substantial contribution: 'On a motion to dismiss we may not speculate whether the as yet undeveloped facts will constitute substantial contribution': *StarLink* (n 79) [847] (Moran SDJ).

[85] *StarLink* (n 79) [874] (Moran J).

[86] *Ibid*.

[87] M Baram, 'Governance of GM Crop and Food Safety in the United States' in M Baram and M Bourrier (eds), *Governing Risk in GM Agriculture* (Cambridge, Cambridge University Press, 2010) 51.

[88] As to the benefits of class actions in GMO cases, see generally H McLeod-Kilmurray, '*Hoffman v Monsanto*: Courts, Class Actions, and Perceptions of the Problem of GM Drift' (2007) 27(3) *Bulletin of Science, Technology & Society* 188.

[89] *Goldman v Hargrave* (1963) 110 CLR 40, 60 (Windeyer J). *Cf Gales Holdings Pty Ltd v Tweed Shire Council* [2013] NSWCA 382 [132], where Emmett JA described nuisance as the 'wrongful interference with another's enjoyment of land by the use of other land owned or occupied by the alleged wrongdoer'.

another liability will not be imposed upon the alleged tortfeasor unless it was in a position to control what occurred on the land.[90] Where the alleged tortfeasor *was* in a position to control what occurred on the land but failed to do so, the relevant question becomes 'whether the person ought to have exercised control over the other'.[91] In those parts of Australia in which GM canola is licenced, Bayer Australia Ltd, which purchased the Monsanto brand in 2018,[92] has the ability to control to some extent the on-farm practices of growers of GM canola, through its crop management plan.[93] For example, Bayer recommends separation distances of at least five meters between GM canola and all other canola.[94] While, arguably, Bayer is in a position to control growing practices, at least to some extent, its liability in tort remains to be tested.[95]

Marsh shows that GM-affected persons pursuing nuisance claims face several challenges, which are explored in the remainder of this section.

B. Interference of the Relevant Kind

The essence of an action in private nuisance is that it involves interference with a property right. In the recent English case of *Williams*, Sir Etherton MR observed that the 'purpose of the tort of nuisance is not to protect the value of property as an investment or a financial asset' but 'to protect the owner of land (or a person entitled to exclusive possession) in their use and enjoyment of the land as such as a facet of the right of ownership or right to exclusive possession'.[96] Thus, a distinction must be made between interferences which merely diminish the market value of a property or the ability to profit from a business carried on from the land, which are not actionable,[97] and interferences which affect the legal rights of or

[90] *Eastern Asia Navigation Co Ltd v Fremantle Harbour Trust Commissioners* (1950) 83 CLR 353, see especially 394 (Fullagar J) and 397 (Kitto J).

[91] F Trindade, P Cane and M Lunney, *The Law of Torts in Australia*, 4th edn (South Melbourne, Oxford University Press, 2007) citing *Club Italia (Geelong) Inc v Ritchie* (2001) 3 VR 447.

[92] R Neate, 'Monsanto to Ditch its Infamous Name after Sale to Bayer' *The Guardian* (4 June 2018), available at www.theguardian.com/business/2018/jun/04/monsanto-to-ditch-its-infamous-name-after-sale-to-bayer.

[93] Bayer Australia Ltd, 'Roundup Ready® Canola Technologies: Crop Management Plan', available at www.roundupreadycanola.com.au/prod/media/4094/m0450-roundup-ready-canola-cmp_02.pdf ('Bayer Crop Management Plan'). It is likely that licensees of Roundup Ready® canola have agreed to comply with the Crop Management Plan as part of the licence agreement. It was a term of Baxter's licence of GM canola that he agreed with the (then Monsanto) crop management plan: see *Marsh* (n 5) [399] (Newnes & Murphy JJA).

[94] *Marsh* (n 5) [89] (McLure J) and see Bayer Crop Management Plan, *ibid* 3.

[95] That prospect may turn on principles of accessorial liability beyond the scope of this chapter.

[96] *Williams* (n 51) [48]. See also *Victoria Park Racing v Taylor* [1937] 58 CLR 479, 513: Evatt J citing Street to emphasise that the tort of nuisance involves an 'interference with some right incident to the ownership or possession of realty'. For a detailed discussion of the property law basis of nuisance; see Nolan (n 54).

[97] *Williams* (n 51) [46], [48]; *Victoria Park*, *ibid* 493 (Latham CJ), 508 (Dixon J), 523 (McTiernan J).

interests in land or the use and enjoyment of land – its 'amenity value' – which may be actionable.[98]

The question as to the underlying rights protected by a nuisance action received little attention both in the trial judgment of *Marsh*[99] and on appeal.[100] At trial, the plaintiffs contended that, due to the presence of GM canola seeds on their land, and the resulting decertification of a portion of their land, they were unable to sell a certain amount of their produce as 'certified organic' for a period of time.[101] The defendants did not dispute that. The focus of the inquiry, both during trial and on appeal, was upon whether the interference should be considered unreasonable, and upon issues of causation, rather than on the anterior question as to whether there was an interference with a property right.[102]

Despite the absence of analysis as to the underlying legally protected rights in *Marsh*, it is possible that other actions for nuisance may be argued in such a way that more attention will need to be directed to this fundamental issue. If so, an argument that there has been no interference with land, but only with a business conducted on the land, could present a hurdle for famers seeking to bring an action for nuisance in respect of non-physical damage to their land caused by the incursion of GM material. Such arguments, of course, do not lie if the plaintiff can satisfy the court that the interference affects the *objective* amenity value of the land,[103] which may more readily be established in respect of, but which is not limited to, interferences that cause material (or physical) damage to the land.

C. Interferences not Entailing Physical Damage to Land

An incursion of GM material that impacts upon the profitability of a farming business, but which does not cause material damage or otherwise affect the use and enjoyment of the land, will not be considered sufficient to ground a nuisance action. That proposition is illustrated in the classic case of *Victoria Park*.[104] The plaintiff racecourse complained that the defendants' act of watching the races from a platform overlooking the park and broadcasting those races to others interfered

[98] *Williams* (n 51) [40]; *Victoria Park* (n 96) 493 (Latham CJ), 508 (Dixon J), 523 (McTiernan J).

[99] *Marsh* (n 32)(Martin J).

[100] *Marsh* (n 5).

[101] *Marsh* (n 32) [290] (Martin J).

[102] Although the Plaintiff's Outline of Opening Submissions ahead of the first trial asserted that 'while the GM material remained on the land it could not be used for the cultivation of crops consistently with the organic standard': *Marsh v Baxter* (n 32) [48].

[103] In some cases, the distinction between material damage and harm to amenity value of land is not always clear cut. See, eg, *Williams* (n 51) [55].

[104] *Victoria Park* (n 96).

with the suitability of the racecourse for its purposes and, being an unnatural user of land, constituted a nuisance and gave rise to a claim for damages.[105] The High Court majority held that there had been no interference with the use and enjoyment of the plaintiff's land.[106] According to Latham CJ, the racecourse was:

> as suitable as ever it was for use as a racecourse. What the defendants do does not interfere with the races, nor does it interfere with the comfort or convenience of any person who is on the racecourse. The alleged nuisance cannot be detected by any person upon the land as operating or producing any effect upon the plaintiff's land.[107]

Similarly, in *Shogunn Investments v Public Transport Authority of Western Australia*,[108] the alleged interference with the plaintiff's use of their car-park, occasioned by the redevelopment of a section of road that made it more difficult for customers to access the car-park, was held not to constitute a nuisance. Martin J, adapting the words of Latham CJ in *Victoria Park*, held that the car park was 'as suitable as ever it was' for use as a car-park[109] and that the plaintiff's complaint was ultimately one that 'goes to interference not with the enjoyment of the land but with the profitable conduct of its business'.[110]

It may be analogously argued that an incursion of GMOs onto organic or GM-free farmland, at least where there is no risk of genetic trait-transfer by the GMOs, does not interfere with the use or enjoyment of the land but merely with business interests associated with the particular use. Nolan, for example, suggests that the finding of no nuisance in *Marsh* 'seems intuitively to be correct'[111] and argues that

> given that in fact there was no risk of any transfer of genetic material, this would seem to blur the important distinction drawn in the earlier cases between interfering with the *land* and 'interfering with' (or making less profitable) a *business* conducted on it.[112]

There is insufficient opportunity here to explore arguments as to whether plaintiffs who have suffered loss due to the incursion of GMOs, without being exposed to the risk of genetic transfer between GMOs and produce grown or raised on the land, could overcome an argument that there has been no relevant interference with land but only with a business conducted upon it. For present purposes, it is sufficient to note that both *Victoria Park* and *Shogunn* can be distinguished from *Marsh* on the basis that there was no physical incursion upon the plaintiff's land.

[105] *Ibid* 492 (Latham CJ).
[106] *Ibid* 493 (Latham CJ), 508 (Dixon J), 523 (McTiernan J).
[107] *Ibid* 493 (Latham CJ).
[108] *Shogunn Investments v Public Transport Authority of Western Australia* [2016] WASC 42 (12 February 2016).
[109] *Ibid* [247].
[110] *Ibid* [281].
[111] D Nolan, 'The Essence of Private Nuisance' in B McFarlane and S Agnew (eds), *Modern Studies of Property Law* (Oxford, Hart Publishing, 2019) Vol 10, 76.
[112] *Ibid*.

Where there has been a physical incursion it may more readily be argued that there has been an interference with the amenity value of the plaintiff's land, not least because the removal of the GMOs entails inconvenience, and potentially expense.[113]

Even assuming that a plaintiff is able to overcome the initial hurdle of establishing an interference with *land*, those affected by GM farming still face several obstacles to successfully establishing a nuisance. Considerations of locality and hypersensitivity present particular challenges for organic or GM-free plaintiffs.

D. Locality and Hypersensitivity

While the absence of physical damage is not fatal to a plaintiff's case in private nuisance, in its absence, and unless the spread of GMOs occurs in an area designated GM-free, or where the growing of GM crops is restricted,[114] considerations of locality are more likely to favour those dealing in GMOs. Indeed, the court may take the view that, if anything, the organic or GM-free farmers are 'hypersensitive', a factor which will count against a finding that the interference is unreasonable.[115]

In *Marsh* the majority took the view that the locality in which the plaintiffs and defendant were located (the district of Kojonup in Western Australia) was one in which crop farming, including the farming of canola, was 'a common and ordinary use of the land'.[116] They found that the method of harvesting chosen by the defendant, and at the heart of the plaintiff's complaint, was 'the generally preferred method of harvesting canola crops, and formed part of the common and ordinary use of the land'.[117] This was despite the fact the farming of genetically modified canola, even at the time of writing, counts for the minority of Australian grown canola[118]

[113] See, eg, *Williams* (n 51).

[114] Such as in ACT, Tasmania and South Australia: Office of the Gene Technology Regulator, *Genetically Modified (GM) Crops in Australia* (undated) 1, available at www.ogtr.gov.au/internet/ogtr/publishing.nsf/Content/9AA09BB4515EBAA2CA257D6B00155C53/$File/11%20-%20Genetically%20modified%20(GM)%20crops%20in%20Australia.pdf.

[115] As per *Marsh* (n 5) [788] (Newnes and Murphy JJA).

[116] *Ibid* [779] (Newnes and Murphy JJA).

[117] *Ibid*. *Cf* the judgment of McLure P who observed (at [272]) that the trial judge's finding that swathing was not 'unique or aberrant in the context of "ordinary usages of broadacre farming in the Kojonup locale"' did not account for the fact that 'in 2010 GM canola was being grown in [the] State for the first time and was accompanied by public warnings from the Ag Department as to the care required to ensure the co-existence of organic, non-GM and GM farming'.

[118] According to the Department of Primary Industries and Regional Development, since 2010 GM canola plantings account for 34% of grower plantings: Department of Primary Industries and Regional Development, 'Genetically Modified Crops in Western Australia' (13 July, 2020), available at www.agric.wa.gov.au/genetic-modification/genetically-modified-crops-western-australia>.

and would have been even less prevalent at the time of the incursion giving rise to the claim in *Marsh*.[119]

The co-majority in *Marsh* clearly regarded organic farming as hypersensitive, a factor that by itself was considered sufficient to defeat an action in nuisance.[120] Certainly, the hypersensitivity of the plaintiff must be factored in when weighing where the balance between competing interests should be struck. In the words of Lord Robertson, 'a man cannot increase the liabilities of his neighbour by applying his own property to special uses, whether for business or pleasure'.[121] However, where a particular practice (such as swathing of GM canola) has the capacity to affect conventional crop growing operations as well as organic or GM-free ones, an argument that organic farms are hypersensitive is less persuasive.[122] There is, for instance, acknowledgement on the part of Bayer that GM canola poses a risk, albeit a low one, of cross-contamination with conventional canola and certain other species.[123] Any cross-contamination that did occur would be capable of significantly affecting farming operations, at least where the unintentional presence of GM material is in excess of tolerance thresholds.[124] Accordingly, if the potential consequences of a particular practice in relation to GMOs have the capacity to prejudicially affect any ordinary trade carried on within the locality (even if they

[119] *Marsh* (n 5) [279]: 'in 2010 the cultivation of GM canola was wholly novel' (McLure P).

[120] *Ibid* [783] (Newnes and Murphy JJA). A different view would hold hypersensitivity as being just one consideration to be factored into the equation: a view that, in fact, appears to be held by McLure P [291] but which has not been firmly settled.

[121] *Eastern & South African Telegraph Co Ltd v Cape Town Tramways Companies Ltd* [1902] AC 381, 393.

[122] A point also made by M Lee and R Burrell, 'Liability for the Escape of GM Seeds: Pursuing the "Victim"?' 65 (2002) *MLR* 532.

[123] Bayer Crop Management Plan (n 93) 2. Indeed, certain crop management practices, such as separation distances, are recommended in order to control that risk: see, eg, Bayer Crop Management Plan (n 93) 3. See, also, Standing Committee on Environment and Public Affairs (n 24) 43 [6.3].

[124] Both McLure P and the co-majority make reference to the tolerance levels of GM canola in non-GM Canola seed at a level of 0.9%: *Marsh* (n 5) [240], [277] and [641]. It appears that the tolerance level may, in fact, refer not to the presence of GM canola in seed but to the presence of GM canola in non-GM canola product (grains): see, eg, Australian Oilseeds Federation, *Grain Industry Common GM Declarations* (November, 2008) 2, available at www.australianoilseeds.com/__data/assets/pdf_file/0020/5537/GM_Declaration_Update_Nov_08.pdf. The tolerance level of GM canola in non-GM canola seed for planting is currently 0.5%: Government of Western Australia, Department of Agriculture and Food, 'On Farm Segregation of Canola Varieties' (20 September, 2019), available at www.agric.wa.gov.au/canola/farm-segregation-canola-varieties. There is some evidence that non-GM canola attracts a premium price in certain export markets: K Anderson, *Independent Review of the South Australian GM Food Crop Moratorium*, Report to the SA Minister for Primary Industries and Regional Development (March 2019) xi. In *Marsh* (n 5) [205], McLure P noted that the evidence at trial established 'economically significant domestic and export markets for non-GM agricultural produce, both conventional and organic'. In Australia, labelling of food as GM is not required where 'there is no more than 1% (per ingredient) of an approved GM food unintentionally present as an ingredient or processing aid in a non-GM food' unless the GM food has altered characteristics: Food Standards Australia and New Zealand, *GM Food Labelling* (August 2019), available at www.foodstandards.gov.au/consumer/gmfood/labelling/Pages/default.aspx. As to the potential effect on non-GM farmers generally, see also Lee and Burrell (n 122) 518–19.

do not in fact do so),[125] then arguably, a plaintiff impacted by that practice is not actually hypersensitive.[126]

Even so, there is the possibility that as more GM crop varieties are licensed for dealing in Australia, and as the uptake of GM crops continues to increase,[127] the farming of GMOs will be considered simply 'conventional' – making it more likely that organic and GM-free farmers could be considered hypersensitive.

E. Nuisance Nonetheless has Potential

One of the advantages of a private nuisance action is that a plaintiff who is able to successfully establish an interference with amenity should be entitled to damages, even in the absence of a finding that particular consequential losses (such as those occasioned by decertification of organic status) were a foreseeable consequence of the incursion. That is because tort damages are, in the words of Stevens, 'awarded as a substitute for the right infringed'[128] and, as Nolan has further observed, unlike consequential losses (such as loss of profits) that have to be proven, that 'core "substitutive" award is generally assessed objectively, so whether or not there is a loss to the claimant is irrelevant'.[129] Nevertheless, there is some uncertainty as to how the objective measure of damages for loss of amenity is to be assessed in the absence of physical harm to the property.[130] A private nuisance action may also be particularly useful for plaintiffs who wish to prevent an ongoing interference (or the threat of one) occasioned by GM farming or activities associated with it. For these plaintiffs, provided they can establish that the interference was unreasonable and substantial, injunctive relief should be available regardless of whether or not the harm was, up to that point in time, foreseeable.[131]

Nuisance also has a role in ensuring that coexistence between GM systems and non-GM or GM-free systems is sustained. As noted by a committee of the Legislative Council of WA, finding ways to ensure the coexistence of GM and non-GM crops 'enables industry to meet the different requirements of their domestic and export

[125] See *Robinson v Kilvert* (1889) 41 Ch D 88, 94 in which Cotton LJ noted that 'it would … be wrong to say that doing something not in itself noxious is a nuisance because it does harm to some particular trade in the adjoining property, although it would not prejudicially affect any ordinary trade carried on there, and does not interfere with the ordinary enjoyment of life …'.

[126] This argument was not apparently pursued in *Marsh*.

[127] Agricultural Biotechnology Council of Australia, *Statistics: GM Canola Uptake* (2021), available at www.abca.com.au/materials/statistics/.

[128] R Stevens, *Torts and Rights* (Oxford, Oxford University Press, 2007) 60.

[129] Nolan (n 54) 476, citing Stevens, *ibid*.

[130] As Nolan has also alluded to: Nolan (n 54) 476–77, citing Stevens (n 128).

[131] As noted by Lord Goff in *Cambridge Water*, 'where an injunction is claimed, its purpose is to restrain further action by the defendant which may interfere with the plaintiff's enjoyment of his land, and ex hypothesi the defendant must be aware, if and when an injunction is granted, that such interference may be caused by the act which he is restrained from committing': *Cambridge Water Co v Eastern Counties Leather plc* [1994] 2 AC 264, 300.

markets, some of whom demand an absence of GMOs'.[132] Bayer, which now licenses Roundup Ready® Canola in Australia, regards coexistence as achievable and notes that successful coexistence 'depends on communication, cooperation, flexibility and mutual respect for each system among growers'.[133] There is evidence that, even though the Marshes were unsuccessful in establishing nuisance, the very fact that the matter was litigated may have effected some change. For one thing, the Bayer Crop Management Plan notes that:

> it may be appropriate for neighbouring farmers to consider and discuss how they might each use additional management measures to help ensure reasonable coexistence, such as a seed production minimum distance or direct heading, where a neighbour is growing an organic or other specialty crop.[134]

While the Monsanto Crop Management Plan to which the Baxter – the GM farmer in the *Marsh v Baxter* litigation – was subject, also urged GM growers to talk with their neighbours about their cropping intentions,[135] there was no mention in that document of the use of direct heading as a management strategy. Direct heading is a specific means of harvesting GM canola which, in contrast to the swathing method adopted by Baxter, does not present a risk of cut swathes blowing onto neighbouring properties. The specific reference to direct heading in the Bayer Crop Management Plan was likely included as a direct response to the issues raised in the *Marsh v Baxter* litigation and has the potential to effect practical change by alerting GM farmers of the need to consider this as an alternative means of harvest of GM canola. This illustrates that the very fact of litigating an action in nuisance, regardless of the outcome, has the potential to effect practical change and demonstrates that, in this way, the tort can be regarded as indirectly regulating one of the socio-economic impacts of GM farming.

V. Conclusion

This chapter has sought to test the proposition that private law will protect those who suffer damage from GMOs. Despite its limitations, the tort of nuisance is theoretically capable of filling in some of the gaps left by the regulatory scheme for

[132] Standing Committee on Environment and Public Affairs (n 24) 14. See also McLure P in *Marsh* (n 5) [283]: 'In lifting the prohibition on the cultivation of GM canola, the State Government's intention, as evident in the Second Reading Speech to the GM Free Act, the Ag Department information sheets and the terms of the Monsanto Agreement and Monsanto Management Plan, was that GM canola farming, conventional (non-GM) canola farming and organic farming coexist within the agricultural regions of this State. The sole reason for this policy was economic, namely to ensure the State could continue to maintain and service all demand particularly in its large export market'.

[133] Bayer Crop Management Plan (n 93) 1.

[134] *Ibid.*

[135] Monsanto Australia Ltd, 'Roundup Ready® Canola: Crop Management Plan' 3, available at www.croplife.org.au/wp-content/uploads/2013/05/Roundup-Ready-canola-Crop-Management-Plan.pdf.

GMOs in Australia. However, the reality for individuals and entities affected by the unwanted spread of GMOs is that only those with deep pockets, or who enjoy the financial backing of others,[136] should consider proceeding to a trial. While the same might be said in respect of anyone considering pursuing a civil action through the courts, the very flexibility of private nuisance,[137] as well as its still uncertain boundaries, renders the outcome particularly unpredictable.

The split decision in *Marsh* illustrates that different judges have different views as to how the balance between the competing interests of plaintiffs and defendants should be struck. These differing views owe perhaps as much to different interpretations of the principles of private nuisance as they do to the application of the principles to a given set of facts. As noted above, there is evidence, in *Marsh*, of the co-majority deciding that hypersensitivity of the plaintiff should preclude a finding that there has been an unreasonable interference,[138] rather that hypersensitivity being but one relevant factor. Likewise, there are different views about the extent to which 'fault', in the sense of foreseeability of harm, should be considered an element of the cause of action rather than a matter going only to the liability of the defendant in damages.[139] Further, while McLure P was critical of the trial judge for failing to consider whether harm to the plaintiffs 'could have been avoided without appreciable prejudice to the respondent's interests',[140] the co-majority did not allude to this consideration at all in determining the nuisance action. Still, even when judges do agree on the applicable principles, the inherent need to balance interests by taking into account a variety of considerations means it is often likely to be difficult to predict with any certainty what outcome will be reached on application of those principles to the facts. While the judgment in *Marsh* is of limited precedential value given the specific factual matrix, it may well act as a further deterrent for otherwise would-be plaintiffs affected by the unwanted spread of GMOs.

The assumption that private law will protect those who suffer damage from GMOs is, to a large degree, misplaced: not necessarily because the cause of action is inherently incapable of affording protection, but because structural barriers,

[136] See, eg, *Marsh v Baxter [No 2]* [2016] WASCA 51, 22 noting Baxter had the benefit of an indemnity from Monsanto Australia Ltd in relation to the costs incurred in relation to the trial (but not the appeal).

[137] M Lee, 'What is Private Nuisance?' (2003) 119(2) *Law Quarterly Review* 298.

[138] *Marsh* (n 5) [788] (Newnes & Murphy JJA).

[139] The co-majority in *Marsh* found that the respondent did not have actual knowledge or foresight of the fact that the appellant was at risk of decertification and economic loss due to the swathing of the crop: *Marsh* (n 5) [666], [671], and that this fact would be sufficient to dispose of both the negligence and the nuisance claim [673]. The co-majority also observed that '[w]hile negligence is not essential to a claim in nuisance, fault of some kind is almost always necessary. Fault generally involves foreseeability' ([768] references omitted). By contrast, McLure P held that the risk of economic loss to the appellants was reasonably foreseeable [350]. However, this finding was made in the context of determining the negligence action only, and made only after she had disposed of the nuisance action, without any reference to foreseeability. See also *Southern Properties* (n 48) in which McLure P was clearly of the view that fault is not part of the nuisance action [126].

[140] *Marsh* (n 5) [271].

such as the cost and uncertainty of pursuing legal action through the courts, mean it is unlikely to do so. While that may be true of any private law remedy,[141] structural barriers are particularly acute when it comes to actions brought by those affected by GM farming. Farmers may not just be pitted against their neighbours, but against the 'might' of big business involved in the GM farming industry.[142] In the *Marsh v Baxter* litigation, for example, the respondents were funded, at least to the initial trial, by Monsanto, the company which was then behind RR canola, the subject of the action.[143]

Given the limitations of a nuisance action there is a question as to whether the socio-economic impacts associated with the unwanted spread of GMOs need to be better or differently regulated. The answer to that question will depend on various considerations, including but not limited to economic analysis of the broader impacts of imposing liability for the unwanted spread of GMOs on those responsible for it, as well as on what particular perspective is adopted. It is a question the answer to which this chapter has not sought to address. Rather, our purpose has been to demonstrate that the shortcomings of the action in private nuisance, whether inherent or structural, be acknowledged. Only once the gaps in the statutory scheme are clearly identified can sensible consideration be given to the question of whether and, if so, how they should be filled.

[141] Standing Committee on Environment and Public Affairs (n 24) 20 [4.6].

[142] C Gearty, 'The Place of Private Nuisance in a Modern Law of Torts' (1989) 48(2) *Cambridge Law Journal* 214, 216, observing that obstacles such as costs, causation, the burden of proof and rules on standing may be 'especially relevant' in a private nuisance action 'where often a big business concern is the defendant'.

[143] *Marsh [No 2]* (n 136) 22. Bayer Australia Ltd has since acquired the Monsanto Brand: see Neate (n 92).

10

Misfeasance by Directors: Past, Present and Future

THE HON GEOFFREY NETTLE AC QC AND DANIEL FARINHA

I. Introduction

The basic problem underpinning directors' duties of care and skill was articulated by Adam Smith, some two centuries ago and with characteristic perspicuity, as follows:

> The directors of [joint-stock] companies ... being the managers rather of other people's money than of their own, it cannot well be expected, that they should watch over it with the same anxious vigilance with which the partners in a private copartnery frequently watch over their own. Like the stewards of a rich man, they are apt to consider attention to small matters as not for their master's honour, and very easily give themselves a dispensation from having it. Negligence and profusion, therefore, must always prevail, more or less, in the management of the affairs of such a company.[1]

The problem – known in the economic literature as the problem of 'agency costs'[2] – arises wherever beneficial ownership of an asset is divorced from practical control over it, irrespective of whether that position follows, in legal terms, from bailment, trust, incorporation or any similar institution. The answer to the problem traditionally adopted by the law is to impose enforceable obligations on the bailee, trustee, director or other 'agent' (in a non-technical sense) to take care in dealing with the asset. In formulating the standard of care required, however, further difficulties arise.[3] If the standard is too lax, the prospect of liability will not outweigh the natural incentive to be neglectful. If the standard is too onerous, the same prospect will discourage profitable risk-taking; and, once liability is imposed

[1] A Smith, *An Inquiry into the Nature and Causes of the Wealth of Nations*, 5th edn (London, Strahan & Cadell, 1789) Vol 3, Bk 5, 124.

[2] MC Jensen and WH Meckling, 'Theory of the Firm: Managerial Behaviour, Agency Costs and Ownership Structure' (1976) 3 *Journal of Financial Economics* 305.

[3] See CA Riley, 'The Company Director's Duty of Care and Skill: The Case for an Onerous but Subjective Standard' (1999) 62 *MLR* 697.

for risks beyond the agent's control, he or she will be deterred from undertaking the position, at least without further remuneration.[4]

In times past, courts of common law and equity sought to navigate these difficulties by applying a subjective standard of care derived, by successive analogies, from Roman jurisprudence. Although, eventually, the liability of trustees and bailees came to depend on an objective test, that of company directors was conspicuously resistant to change, even after legislative intervention. Ultimately, after an extreme period of corporate excess and its financial consequences, an objective standard of care was firmly imposed by statute – albeit that, when the full effects of that came to be appreciated, an attempt was made to alleviate the burden by the enactment of a 'business judgment rule'. In the way in which that rule has since been interpreted, however, it is of little (if any) effect, and, despite proposals for further statutory reform based on American precedent, it does not seem likely that there will be any such reform within the foreseeable future. In the result, even if the objective standard of care required of directors is too onerous, it appears set to stay.

II. Development of the Duty

A. 'Prehistory'[5]

The form of the modern director's duties of care and skill may be traced, ultimately, to a system of law which lacked any institution akin to the modern trading corporation.[6] Roman law, at least by the time of Justinian's compilations, distinguished the failure to take the same care in another's affairs as in one's own (*diligentia quam in suis*), which was gross negligence (*culpa lata*) tantamount to fraud (*dolus*), from the failure to take such care as a most conscientious householder (*diligentissimus paterfamilias*) would take in his own affairs.[7] Thus, the *Institutes* commissioned by Justinian for the instruction of law students explained that a borrower for use was 'under a duty to conform to the highest standard of care in keeping the thing safe, a requirement not satisfied by his own habitual standard if others could do better', but that the liability of a mere depositary extended 'only to deliberate wickedness, not to fault such as laziness or

[4] Such a standard – in effect requiring the agent to act as insurer – would, ordinarily, be inefficient wherever the 'principal' (eg the company) is better able to absorb or otherwise insure against losses: see *ibid* 705, 711, fn 77.

[5] D Kershaw, *The Foundations of Anglo-American Corporate Fiduciary Law* (Cambridge, Cambridge University Press, 2018) 1.

[6] See AM Fleckner, 'Roman Business Associations' in G Dari-Mattiacci (ed), *Roman Law and Economics* (Oxford University Press, 2020) Vol 1.

[7] T Mommsen, P (eds) and A Watson (tr), *The Digest of Justinian*, revised edn (Philadelphia, University of Pennsylvania Press, 1998) Vol 2, 20 [16.3.32], *cf* Vol 1, 405 [13.6.18.pr]. See R Zimmermann, *The Law of Obligations: Roman Foundations of the Civilian Tradition* (Oxford, Oxford University Press, 1990) 209–12, *cf* 192–93.

negligence': for one 'who gives something to a negligent friend to look after should blame his loss on his own complacency'.[8]

Much influenced by continental learning on the rediscovered Roman law,[9] the thirteenth century treatise known as *Bracton* asserted that this distinction formed part of the common law of England: that, whereas the borrower was 'to show the standard of care that a most conscientious householder shows in his own affairs', the depositary was liable only for 'some wrongful act', not for 'carelessness', again on the basis that one who trusted a 'negligent friend' could 'only blame himself'.[10] Some four-and-a-half centuries later, the same distinction was adopted in Lord Holt CJ's canonical judgment in *Coggs v Bernard*, which required 'gross neglect' – 'looked upon as an evidence of fraud' – for an unrewarded bailee to be liable for carelessness in an action upon the case.[11] For over a century thereafter, that standard of care was regularly applied and endorsed.[12]

Seeing, moreover, an analogy between gratuitous bailments and early trusts, Chancery employed the same standard to define the scope of the trustee's liability to account. Lord Nottingham LC, the 'father of Modern Equity',[13] concluded that a trustee was 'not to be charged with any Loss in putting out Money at Interest, or for Money raised out of the Estate without his wilful Negligence or Default',[14] and thus that he was 'to keep' trust property 'but as his own'.[15] That doctrine was substantially maintained for almost two centuries,[16] except in one decision of Lord Northington LK, who thought even it was too exacting.[17] By the mid-eighteenth century, the assumption underlying this doctrine that trusteeship was invariably uncompensated was made explicit by Lord Hardwicke LC – 'the greatest of the English chancery judges', in Pomeroy's view, and 'far more than Lord Eldon penetrated by the genius of equity':[18]

[8] P Birks and G McLeod (trs), *The Institutes of Justinian* (Duckworth, 1987) 107 [3.15], *cf* 115 [3.24].

[9] See P Vinogradoff, 'The Roman Elements in Bracton's Treatise' (1923) 32 *Yale Law Journal* 751.

[10] SE Thorne (tr), *Bracton on the Laws and Customs of England* (Cambridge, Belknap, 1968) Vol 2, 284, *cf* 184. See SD Elliott, 'Degrees of Negligence' (1933) 6 *Southern California Law Review* 91, 103–107.

[11] *Coggs v Bernard* (1704) 2 Ld Raym 909, 915, (1704) 92 ER 107, 111; *cf Southcote's Case* (1576) 4 Co Rep 83b, 83b, (1576) 76 ER 1061, 1062. See CA Wright, 'Gross Negligence' (1983) 33 *University of Toronto Law Journal* 184, 194–95, 202–10, 239–41.

[12] eg *Moore v Mourgue* (1776) 2 Cowp 479, 480, (1776) 98 ER 1197, 1198 (Lord Mansfield CJ); *Shiells v Blackburne* (1789) 1 Bl H 158, 162, (1789) 126 ER 94, 96 (Lord Loughborough); W Jones and W Theobald (eds), *An Essay on the Law of Bailments*, 4th edn (New York, Sweet & Maxwell, 1833) 9, 21–22, 118. But see D Ibbetson, '"The Law of Business Rome": Foundations of the Anglo-American Tort of Negligence' (1999) 52 *Current Legal Problems* 74, 93, 104.

[13] DEC Yale (ed), *Lord Nottingham's Chancery Cases* (Selden Society, 1957) Vol 1, vii.

[14] *Hussey v Markham* (1676) Rep t Finch 258, (1676) 23 ER 142.

[15] *Morley v Morley* (1678) 2 Chan Cas 2, (1678) 22 ER 817; *cf Palmer v Jones* (1678) 79 SS 649.

[16] eg *Palmer v Jones* (1682) 1 Vern 144, (1682) 23 ER 376 (North LK); *Brown v Litton* (1711) 1 P Wms 140, 141, (1711) 24 ER 329, 329 (Harcourt LK); *Crookshanks v Turner* (1723) 7 Bro PC 255, 258, (1723) 3 ER 166, 168 (Darnell and Talbot) (*arguendo*); *Jones v Lewis* (1750–1751) 2 Ves Sen 240, 241, (1750) 28 ER 155, 155 (Lord Hardwicke LC); *Massey v Banner* (1820) 1 Jac & W 241, 247, (1820) 37 ER 367, 369 (Lord Eldon LC).

[17] *Harden v Parsons* (1758) 1 Eden 145, 148, (1758) 28 ER 639, 641.

[18] J Norton Pomeroy, *A Treatise on Equity Jurisprudence, as Administered in the United States of America* (San Francisco, Bancroft-Whitney, 1881) Vol 1, 50 § 50.

> If there is no *mala fides*, – nothing wilful in the conduct of the trustee, the Court will always favour him. For as a trust is an office necessary in the concerns between man and man, and which, if faithfully discharged, is attended with no small degree of trouble, and anxiety, *it is an act of great kindness* in any one to accept it: to add hazard or risque to that trouble, and to subject a trustee to losses which *he* could not foresee, and consequently not prevent, would be a manifest hardship, and would be deterring every one from accepting so necessary an office.[19]

B. Recognition

Only five years earlier, in 1742, Lord Hardwicke had decided *Charitable Corporation v Sutton*,[20] later described by Williston as 'the basis, mediate or immediate, of all subsequent decisions' on the requirement that 'directors of a corporation shall manage its affairs honestly and carefully'.[21] The plaintiff in that case – a corporation established by charter to provide credit to the 'industrious poor' – was defrauded by a 'Partnership of Five' officers obtaining loans on fictitious pledges.[22] Of the defendants, the five conspirators were held 'liable to make good the losses which the corporation have sustained', and the other 45 'committee-men' and other officers were held at most liable 'in the second degree', for 'not making use of the proper power invested in them by the charter, in order to prevent the ill consequences arising from such a confederacy'.[23]

Applying 'the limited legal vocabulary of the day', in which the generic term 'fiduciary' was not yet current,[24] the Lord Chancellor identified these directors as 'trustees' and held that '*gross* negligence' by them would constitute 'breaches of trust'.[25] Characteristically, his Lordship essayed to justify this doctrine in terms of policy, by identifying the two competing 'mischiefs … to be avoided':

> first, not to make it unsafe or too perilous for honest men to accept offices of trust, by making them liable to losses in the execution of them; and secondly, to prevent the frauds of dishonest men in such employments.[26]

[19] *Knight v Earl of Plymouth* (1747) Dick 120, 126–27, (1747) 21 ER 214, 216 (emphasis added). See also *Ex parte Belchier* (1754) Amb 218, 219, (1754) 27 ER 144, 145 (Lord Hardwicke LC); *A-G v Corporation of Exeter* (1826) 2 Russ 45, 54, (1826) 38 ER 252, 256 (Lord Eldon LC).

[20] *Charitable Corporation v Sutton* (1742) 2 Atk 400, (1742) 26 ER 642, (1742) 9 Mod 349, (1742) 88 ER 500.

[21] S Williston, 'The History of the Law of Business Corporations Before 1800' in Committee of the Association of American Law Schools (ed), *Select Essays in Anglo-American Legal History* (Boston, Little Brown, 1909) Vol 3, 226.

[22] See P Brealey, 'The Charitable Corporation for the Relief of Industrious Poor: Philanthropy, Profit and Sleaze in London, 1707–1733' (2013) 98 *History* 708.

[23] *Charitable Corporation v Sutton* (n 20) Atk 406, ER 645.

[24] LS Sealy, 'The Director as Trustee' [1967] *CLJ* 83, 85–86.

[25] *Charitable Corporation v Sutton* (n 20) Mod 356, ER 504 (emphasis added).

[26] *Ibid.*

He also recognised the danger of judicial hindsight in determining the proper balance thus:

> it is by no means just in a judge, after bad consequences have arisen from such executions of their power, to say that [the committee-men] foresaw at the time what must necessarily happen; and therefore were guilty of a breach of trust.[27]

The doctrine thus established had a wide and enduring influence. In the former half of the nineteenth century, it was applied not only to public corporations,[28] but also to joint stock companies,[29] in which the property of the venture was often held by trustees in the strict sense.[30] After the enactment of laws providing for general incorporation by registration[31] and limited liability,[32] which were later consolidated,[33] the doctrine was further applied to modern trading corporations.[34] The result was embodied in Lord Hatherley LC's aculeated apophthegm in *The Overend & Gurney Co v Gibb* that the liability of directors for an unsuccessful transaction 'simply reduced to' whether they had 'exceeded the powers entrusted to them' or displayed '*crassa negligentia*', being

> cognisant of circumstances of such a character, so plain, so manifest, and so simple of appreciation, that no men with any ordinary degree of prudence, acting on their own behalf, would have entered into such a transaction as they entered into.[35]

C. Divergence

In hindsight, the analogies underpinning this development, from bailee to trustee to director, may, no doubt, be considered an instance of equity regarding substance over form: each is held accountable for misfeasance because of his practical control over the property of another, whether in the form of possession, ownership or mere custody; but each is judged by his own capacities, not those of

[27] *Ibid* Atk 405, ER 644. See also *Carlen v Drury* (1812) 1 V&B 154, 158, (1812) 35 ER 61, 62 (Lord Eldon LC).

[28] See also *Harman v Tappenden* (1801) 1 East 555, 562, (1801) 102 ER 214, 217 (Lawrence J).

[29] *Benson v Heathorn* (1842) Y & CCC 326, 341–42, (1842) 62 ER 909, 916 (Knight Bruce LJ); *cf Re German Mining Co; Ex parte Chippendale* (1854) 4 De G M & G 19, 34–35, (1854) 43 ER 415, 421 (Knight Bruce LJ).

[30] See M Schmitthoff, 'The Origin of the Joint-Stock Company' (1939) 3 *University of Toronto Law Journal* 74.

[31] *Joint Stock Companies Act 1844* (7 & 8 Vict c 110).

[32] *Limited Liability Act 1855* (18 & 19 Vict c 133).

[33] *Companies Act 1862* (25 & 26 Vict c 89).

[34] *Turquand v Marshall* (1869) LR 4 Ch App 376 (CA) 386 (Lord Hatherley LC); *Re County Marine Insurance Co (Rance's Case)* (1870) LR 6 Ch App 104 (CA) 110 (Lord Romilly MR), 119 (James LJ), 122–23 (Mellish LJ); *The Overend & Gurney Co v Gibb* (1872) LR 5 HL 480 (HL) 493 (Lord Hatherley LC); *Lagunas Nitrate Co v Lagunas Syndicate* [1899] 2 Ch 392 (CA) 435 (Lindley MR). See Kershaw (n 5) 40–44, 237–43.

[35] *The Overend & Gurney Co v Gibb*, *ibid* 486–87.

an ideal person, in order to avoid deterring beneficial undertakings.[36] The legal system, appearing instinctively to understand the common economic problem, posited a common solution which plausibly balanced the competing incentives at stake. As SFC Milsom reminded, however, '[t]he "necessities of the time" make demands which cannot always be met; and when they are met, the effectiveness of the response depends upon the logic of the time'.[37]

Since the nineteenth century, the logics of the common law and of equity have competed over the scope of the liability of bailees, trustees and directors for negligence. Under the modern law, a bailee's failure to take care causing damage has been conceived of as an actionable tort or breach of contract;[38] and, accordingly, the bailee's liability has come to be limited by elementary notions of causation and remoteness at common law,[39] derived from Bacon's maxim *in jure non remota causa sed proxima spectatur*.[40] By contrast, the trustee was and is liable in equity to account for his or her stewardship; and, traditionally, upon receiving the account, beneficiaries could require the trustee to make good any loss to the trust fund from misconduct, even from a mere failure to take care, 'however unexpected the result, however little likely to arise from the course adopted, and however free such conduct may have been from any improper motive'.[41] Only in the last 30 years have common law notions of causation and remoteness been applied – not without controversy[42] – to claims for so-called 'equitable compensation' for breach of the non-fiduciary equitable duties of care and skill owed by directors,[43] and trustees.[44]

Of more immediate relevance, however, is the progressive application of objective standards of care to bailees and trustees, but not directors. In the law

[36] But see W Gummow, 'The Equitable Duties of Company Directors' (2013) 87 *Australian Law Journal* 753, 754–755.

[37] SFC Milsom, 'Reason in the Development of the Common Law' (1965) 81 *LQR* 496, 498, quoting OW Holmes, *The Common Law* (Boston, Little, Brown & Co, 1881) 1.

[38] On the longstanding controversy as to which, see, eg, NE Palmer, 'Gratuitous Bailment: Contract or Tort?' (1975) 24 *ICLQ* 565. On the medieval conception of bailees as accountable parties, see S Stoljar, 'The Early History of Bailment' (1957) 1 *American Journal of Legal History* 5.

[39] *Davis v Garrett* (1830) 6 Bing 716, 722–724, (1830) 130 ER 1456, 1459 (Tindal CJ); *Lilley v Doubleday* (1881) 7 QBD 510 (DC) 511 (Grove J), 512 (Lindley J); *James Morrison & Co Ltd v Shaw Savill & Albion Co Ltd* [1916] 2 KB 783 (CA) 795–796 (Swinfen Eady LJ), 800 (Phillimore LJ); J Story, *Commentaries on the Law of Bailment, with Illustrations from the Civil and the Foreign Law* (London, John Richards & Co, 1839) 332.

[40] F Bacon, *The Elements of the Common Lawes of England* (London, 1630) 1. See *National Insurance Co of New Zealand Ltd v Espagne* (1961) 161 CLR 569 (HCA) 592 (Windeyer J).

[41] *Clough v Bond* (1838) 3 My & Cr 490, 496, (1838) 40 ER 1016, 1018 (Lord Cottenham LC). See also *Caffrey v Darby* (1801) 6 Ves Jun 489, 495–496, (1801) 31 ER 1159, 1162 (Lord Eldon LC).

[42] See, eg, *Youyang Pty Ltd v Minter Ellison Morris Fletcher* [2003] HCA 15, (2003) 212 CLR 484 [38]–[40] (Gleeson CJ, McHugh, Gummow, Kirby and Hayne JJ); JD Heydon, 'Are the Duties of Company Directors to Exercise Care and Skill Fiduciary' in S Degeling and J Edelman (eds), *Equity in Commercial Law* (Sydney, Lawbook, 2005).

[43] eg *Permanent Building Society v Wheeler* (1994) 11 WAR 187 (WASC) 237–238 (Ipp J); *Bell Group Ltd (in liq) v Westpac Banking Corporation (No 9)* [2008] WASC 239, (2008) 39 WAR 1 [4375] (Owen J).

[44] *Bristol and West Building Society v Mothew* [1998] Ch 1 (CA) 16–18 (Millett LJ); *Bank of New Zealand v New Zealand Guardian Trust Co Ltd* [1999] 1 NZLR 664 (CA) 681–682 (Gault J for the Court of Appeal).

of bailment, Tindal CJ advocated adherence to a rule requiring 'in all cases' such caution 'as a man of ordinary prudence would observe',[45] and Rolfe B criticised the term 'gross negligence' as being 'the same thing' as negligence 'with the addition of a vituperative epithet'.[46] This 'assault'[47] on the traditional standard was later reinforced by the 'imperial march of modern negligence law'[48] following *Donoghue v Stevenson*,[49] until (to mix metaphors) 'the current of judicial opinion' had begun 'to run in favour of affixing the depositary with an obligation of reasonable care'.[50] The English law of trusts – influenced, it seems, by the reference to 'reasonable and proper' investment in Lord St Leonards' Act[51] – also belatedly[52] took this step, requiring trustees 'to conduct the business of the trust' as 'an ordinary prudent man of business would conduct his own'.[53]

By contrast, the standard for directors remained avowedly subjective, as emphasised in Romer J's three well-known propositions in *Re City Equitable Fire Insurance Co Ltd*.[54] First, although a director was bound to act honestly, he was not required to exercise any greater degree of skill than that which might reasonably be expected from a man of the director's knowledge and skill. So, it was said, he might 'undertake the management of a rubber company in complete ignorance of everything connected with rubber, without incurring responsibility for the mistakes which may result from such ignorance'.[55] Second, a director was not bound to give continuous attention to the affairs of the company, though, if he chose to be present at a board meeting, he was there required 'to be awake'.[56] His perverse incentive, therefore, was to act as did the Marquis of Bute, who attended only one meeting in the 38 years after he inherited the *de facto* presidency of the Cardiff

[45] *Vaughan v Menlove* (1837) 3 Bing NC 468, 475, (1837) 132 ER 490, 493.

[46] *Wilson v Brett* (1843) 11 M&W 113, 115–116, (1843) 152 ER 737, 739. See also *Beal v South Devon Railway Co* (1864) 3 H&C 337, 341–342, (1864) 159 ER 560, 562 (Crompton J for the Exchequer Chamber); *Grill v General Iron Screw Collier Co* (1866) LR 1 CP 600 (CP) 612 (Willes J); *Giblin v McMullen* (1868) LR 2 PC 317 (PC) 336–338 (Lord Chelmsford for the Board).

[47] N Palmer, *Palmer on Bailment*, 3rd edn (London, Sweet & Maxwell, 2009) 578.

[48] *Astley v Austrust Ltd* [1999] HCA 6, (1999) 197 CLR 1 [48] (Gleeson CJ, McHugh, Gummow and Hayne JJ).

[49] *Donoghue v Stevenson* [1932] AC 562 (HL).

[50] Palmer (n 47) 583.

[51] *Law of Property Amendment Act 1859* (22 & 21 Vict c 35) s 32. See C Stebbings, *The Private Trustee in Victorian England* (Cambridge, Cambridge University Press, 2002) 151–52.

[52] *cf Harvard College v Amory*, 9 Pick 446, 461 (Putnam J for the Supreme Judicial Court of Massachusetts) (Mass Sup Ct, 1830); *Lamar, v Micou* 112 US 452, 467–469 (Gray J for the Supreme Court) (1884). See Ibbetson (n 12) 103–105.

[53] *Re Speight; Speight v Gaunt* (1883) 22 Ch D 727 (CA) 739–740 (Jessel MR). See also *Speight v Gaunt* (1883) 9 App Cas 1 (HL) 4 (Earl of Selborne LC), 19 (Lord Blackburn); *Re Whiteley* (1986) 33 Ch D 347 (CA) 350 (Cotton LJ), 355 (Lindley LJ), 358 (Lopes LJ); *Learoyd v Whiteley* (1887) 12 App Cas 727 (HL) 731–732 (Lord Halsbury LC), 737 (Lord Watson).

[54] *Re City Equitable Fire Insurance Co Ltd* [1925] Ch 407 (Ch) 428–429. See MJ Trebilcock, 'The Liability of Company Directors for Negligence' (1969) 32 *MLR* 499, 502–508.

[55] *Re Brazilian Rubber Plantations & Estates Ltd* [1911] 1 Ch 425 (Ch) 437 (Neville J). See also *Re Denham & Co* (1883) 25 Ch D 752 (Ch) 766–767 (Chitty J).

[56] *Land Credit Co of Ireland v Lord Fermoy* (1870) LR 5 Ch App 763 (CA) 770 (Lord Hatherley).

Savings Bank at six months old.[57] Third, in the absence of grounds for suspicion, a director was allowed to trust other company officials to perform their duties. Thus, it could be remarked that attempts 'to render directors personally liable, on the ground … that they have failed to detect and been misled by misrepresentation or concealment' by company officers had 'not been successful'.[58]

Notwithstanding the developments in bailment and trusts, the standard of care for directors continued to be justified in terms reminiscent of Justinian. Loss arising from the mere negligence of directors was attributed to 'the misfortune of the company that they chose such unwise directors',[59] even though the ownership of capital and voting rights, and thus shareholders' responsibility for the selection of the directors, was already diffuse in Victorian times.[60] Reliance was placed on the fact that impugned directors had 'receive[d] no remuneration',[61] even though paid directors appear not to have been subjected to any more onerous standard. Where, occasionally, the company director's position was distinguished from that of a trustee, it was by reference to the 'speculative character' of, or 'hazard' attending, decision-making by trading corporations,[62] without explanation of how that fact afforded a reason for allowing directors to be ill-informed, absent and credulous.

III. Statutory Intervention

A. The Victorian Attempts

Generally speaking, company law in the Australian colonies followed that in England, albeit with some local innovations.[63] Local legislatures enacted general incorporation statutes, modelled on successive English Acts.[64] Entrepreneurs took up the corporate form, at first mostly in the banking and mining sectors.[65] In Victoria, lax disclosure requirements contributed to a major boom in the 1880s

[57] *Re Cardiff Savings Bank (Marquis of Bute's Case)* [1892] 2 Ch 100 (Ch) 102, 108 (Stirling J). See also *Re Montrotier Asphalte Co (Perry's Case)* (1876) 34 LT 716 (Ch) 717 (Bacon V-C).

[58] *Prefontaine v Grenier* [1907] AC 101 (PC) 109 (Sir Arthur Wilson for the Board). See also *Dovey v Cory* [1901] AC 477 (HL) 486 (Earl of Halsbury LC).

[59] *Turquand v Marshall* (n 34) 386; *Grimwade v Mutual Society* (1885) 52 LT 409 (Ch) 416 (Chitty J); *Lagunas Nitrate* (n 34) 426.

[60] GG Acheson et al, 'Corporate Ownership and Control in Victorian Britain' (2015) 68 *Economics History Review* 911.

[61] *Re Forest of Dean Coal Mining Co* (1878) 10 Ch D 450 (Ch) 455 (Jessel MR).

[62] *Sheffield & South Yorkshire Building Society v Aizlewood* (1890) 44 Ch D 412 (Ch) 454 (Stirling J). See also *Forest of Dean*, *ibid* 451–52.

[63] See P Lipton, 'A History of Company Law in Colonial Australia: Economic Development and Legal Evolution' (2007) 31 *Melbourne University Law Review* 805.

[64] eg *Companies Statute 1864* (Vic), based on the *Companies Act 1862* (25 & 26 Vict c 89).

[65] Lipton (n 63) 814–16.

and crash in the 1890s.[66] Significantly for what follows, in 1892, the Mercantile Bank of Australia collapsed, and summonses charging conspiracy were issued against the chairman of its board of directors, Sir Matthew Davies, the Speaker of the Legislative Assembly, as well as its manager and auditors.[67] When, in the following year, the recently commissioned Patterson government refused to proceed with indictments, the Solicitor-General for Victoria – a young Isaac Isaacs – announced his intention to consider exercising his independent authority to prosecute,[68] but was forced to resign.[69] After successfully recontesting his seat, Isaacs was appointed Attorney-General in the new Turner government, with a mandate to reform Victorian company law.[70]

Beginning in 1894, Isaacs introduced a series of controversial Bills to the Victorian Parliament. While the debate progressed, the Davey Committee in England handed down its report, recommending the following provision as 'right in principle', although perhaps going 'beyond any actual decision of the courts':

> Every director shall be under an obligation to the company to use reasonable care and prudence in the exercise of his powers, and shall be liable to compensate the company for any damage incurred by reason of neglect to use such care and prudence.[71]

A later Bill introduced by Isaacs included a provision in those terms,[72] but the clause was rejected by the Legislative Council as overbroad.[73] In support of an amended version limiting compensation to cases of '*gross* neglect', Isaacs asserted, with reference to Lord Hatherley LC's judgment in *Overend & Gurney*, that the provision required only 'the same amount of prudence which, in the circumstances, [the director] would exercise on his own behalf'.[74] A provision to that effect was enacted with the word 'culpable' substituted for 'gross' and, even still, with opponents asserting that judges would be influenced by hindsight[75] and that directors would be deterred from taking up office.[76] The whole episode illustrated, rather neatly, Karr's epigram – '*plus ça change, plus c'est la même chose*'[77] – and, more particularly, what Professor Krygier has called the

[66] J Waugh, 'Company Law and the Crash of the 1890s in Victoria' (1992) 15 *University of New South Wales Law Journal* 356.

[67] Z Cowen, *Isaac Isaacs* (Brisbane, University of Queensland Press, 1967) 30.

[68] *Crimes Act 1890* (Vic) s 388. See and compare *Taylor v A-G (Cth)* [2019] HCA 30, (2019) 93 ALJR 1044 [63]–[73] (Nettle and Gordon JJ).

[69] Cowen (n 67) 31–34.

[70] *Ibid* 38, 41.

[71] Board of Trade (UK), *Report of the Departmental Committee Appointed by the Board of Trade to Inquire What Amendments Are Necessary in the Acts Relating to Joint Stock Companies Incorporated with Limited Liability under the Companies Acts, 1862 to 1890* (C (2nd series) 7779, 1895) para 32.

[72] *Companies Act Further Amendment Bill (No 3)* 1986 (Vic) cl 51(2).

[73] Vic LC Deb 28 February 1896, eg 6159 (Sargood), 6160.

[74] Vic LA Deb 4 March 1896, 6232.

[75] eg Vic LA Deb 3 March 1896, 6218 (Murray Smith).

[76] eg Vic LA Deb 4 March 1896, 6230 (McIntyre).

[77] A Karr, 'Juillet 1848' in *Les Guêpes* (Paris, Lecou, 1853) 403.

'traditionality of statutes',[78] even those backed by considerable public support for change. As it happened, Isaacs' provision was repealed in 1910:[79] a neo-colonial enthusiasm for the idea that Victoria's company law should remain as one with that of England carried the day.[80]

The next attempt at reform occurred some 40 years later, when the Parliament of Victoria enacted section 107 of the *Companies Act 1958* (Vic), which has generally been considered the *fons et origo* of statutory directors' duties in Australia,[81] and which pioneered the conception of breach of directorial duty as a public wrong, rather than solely within the law of private obligations.[82] Most significantly, perhaps, the Act empowered the Attorney-General to bring proceedings for breach of a duty under section 107, engendering a public appetite for the enforcement of economic duties by state authorities which was, and to an extent remains, unique to Australia and has arguably been the most substantial factor in shaping the subsequent development of company law in this country.[83] Further, whereas breach of a director's duty had never before been conceived of as a criminal offence, section 107 made it punishable by a penalty of up to £500, in addition to any civil liability. In addition, a contravention of section 107 rendered a director liable to the company for any profits made as a result of the contravention, whereas, to that point, it had been arguable that a director was only liable for losses suffered by the company.[84]

In terms of standard of care, however, section 107(1) did little more than reiterate the law as stated in *Re City Equitable Fire Insurance*.[85] Indeed, the Explanatory Memorandum that accompanied the 1958 Bill purposefully declared that section 107 was declaratory of the existing law; and the courts proceeded accordingly.[86] In 1964, in *Byrne v Baker*, the Full Court of the Supreme Court of Victoria concluded that, because of Romer J's second proposition, that a director was not ordinarily bound to give continuous attention to the affairs of the

[78] M Krygier, 'The Traditionality of Statutes' (1988) 1 *Ratio Juris* 20.

[79] *Companies Act 1910* (Vic) s 2.

[80] eg Vic LA Deb 4 August 1910, 479–480 (Mackey).

[81] *Angas Law Services Pty Ltd (in liq) v Carabelas* [2005] HCA 23, (2005) 226 CLR 507 [55], [57] (Gummow and Hayne JJ); KM Hayne, 'Directors' Duties and a Company's Creditors' (2014) 38 *Melbourne University Law Review* 795, 804; *Ford, Austin and Ramsay's Principles of Corporations Law* [8.305.3] (service 134, May 2018).

[82] See R Teele Langford, I Ramsay and M Welsh, 'The Origins of Company Directors' Statutory Duty of Care' (2015) 37 *Sydney Law Review* 489, 499, 505–18.

[83] eg *Treasury Laws Amendment (Strengthening Corporate and Financial Sector Penalties) Act 2019* (Cth); S Hughes, 'ASIC's Approach to Enforcement After the Royal Commission' (36th Annual Conference of the Banking and Financial Services Law Association, Gold Coast, 30 August 2019). See MJ Whincop and ME Keyes, 'Corporation, Contract, Community: An Analysis of Governance in the Privatisation of Public Enterprise and the Publicisation of Private Corporate Law' (1997) 25 *Federal Law Review* 51, 88; M Welsh, 'Realising the Public Potential of Corporate Law: Twenty Years of Civil Penalty Enforcement in Australia' (2014) 42 *Federal Law Review* 217.

[84] See HAJ Ford, *Principles of Company Law* (Sydney, Butterworths, 1974) 321–23 [1512].

[85] *Re City Equitable Fire Insurance* (n 54).

[86] See *Carabelas* (n 81) [62]; Langford, Ramsay and Welsh (n 82) 504.

company, section 107 was to be construed as concerned with negligence referable 'to identifiable acts or omissions, not to any general characterisation of the conduct of a director over a selected period'.[87] And that was said to be so notwithstanding that the words 'at all times' were included in section 107 in relation to the duty to 'use reasonable diligence'.

Because section 107 was re-enacted in the same form as section 124 of the Uniform Companies Acts 1961–62, the influence of *Re City Equitable Fire Insurance* thus continued up to and beyond the publication of the first edition of Ford's *Principles of Company Law* in 1974.[88] Yet, though the change to an objective standard of care was slow in coming, it was, of course, inevitable. Throughout the 1970s, there were a number of proposals for reform, and finally section 229 of the *Companies Act 1981* (Cth) emerged.[89]

B. The Australian Advance

Section 229(2) subjected a director to a statutory duty to 'exercise a reasonable degree of care and diligence in the exercise of his powers and the discharge of his duties'. It also imposed a criminal penalty of up to $5,000 or, where the director acted with intent to deceive or defraud, $20,000 or five years' imprisonment or both.[90] And, significantly, it provided that, if the court was satisfied that the corporation had suffered loss or damage as a result of the act or omission constituting the offence, the director could be ordered to pay compensation to the corporation in addition to a penalty, and such order was enforceable as if it were a judgment of the court.[91] Section 229(2) was later re-enacted, without substantial amendment, as section 232(4) of the *Corporations Act 1989* (Cth), which continued to operate until the enactment of the *Corporate Law Reform Act 1992* (Cth).

When section 229(2) was enacted, few in practice had much doubt that it was intended to impose an objective standard of skill and care. That also appeared to be the view of the courts. Consistently with the idea that the age of the objective standard of care had arrived, courts in New South Wales and Victoria held that a director could not rely on ignorance of facts which ought to have been known in his or her defence to liability for insolvent trading,[92] notwithstanding contrary High Court authority on predecessor legislation.[93] In that context, Tadgell J remarked

[87] *Byrne v Baker* [1964] VR 443 (VSC) 453.

[88] See *Australian Securities and Investments Commission v Vines* [2003] NSWSC 1116, (2003) 48 ACSR 322 [10]–[14] (Austin J); *Carabelas* (n 81) [63].

[89] See *Vines, ibid* [15]–[18].

[90] *Companies Act 1981* (Cth) s 229(1)(b).

[91] *Ibid* s 229(6).

[92] eg *Metal Manufacturers Ltd v Lewis* (1986) 11 ACLR 122 (NSWSC) 129 (Hodgson J), affd (1988) 13 NSWLR 315 (NSWCA) and *Morley v Statewide Tobacco Services Ltd* [1993] 1 VR 451 (VSC) 465 (Crockett, Southwell and Hedigan JJ), applying *Companies (Victoria) Code* s 556.

[93] *Shapowloff v Dunn* (1981) 148 CLR 72 (HCA) 85 (Wilson J), applying *Companies Act 1961* (NSW) s 303.

in *Commonwealth Bank of Australia v Friedrich*, by reference to the comments of Sir Douglas Menzies a generation earlier,[94] that surely the law had progressed to the point that a director was bound to exercise an objectively reasonable standard of skill in discharging the duty to understand the financial statements and affairs of the company and to take reasonable steps to place himself in a position to guide and monitor the management of the company by reference to information appropriate for that purpose.[95]

It was, therefore, a little against the tide that Professor Ford wrote in the fifth edition of *Principles of Company Law*, published in 1990, that the statutory provisions of the 1980s had merely added the word 'care' to the pre-existing requirement to exercise 'reasonable diligence' and extended the duty to corporate officers other than directors, but that neither required a particular level of skill nor envisaged a model reasonably competent non-executive director.[96] His conclusion, that previous case law as to the demands of skill would continue to apply,[97] directed one back to *Re City Equitable Fire Insurance*. But, despite such comfort as Professor Ford's view of the matter might have brought to company directors of the day, Parliament was not to be denied its goal of establishing an objective duty of skill and care.

In a Discussion Paper published in April 1989, the Companies and Securities Law Review Committee stated:

> There has been no clear indication that [s 229 of the 1981 Act] changes the standard of care to be achieved by officers. Just as the common law standard has had to operate without there being a recognised calling of company directors so this provision is subject to the same impediment. Hence it seems that in assessing a director's performance attention would have to be given to his own training and experience rather than some objective standard.[98]

In November 1989, the Senate Standing Committee on Legal and Constitutional Affairs recommended, in the *Cooney Report*, that legislation be enacted to make plain that company directors were subject to an objective standard of care.[99] Those developments led to the insertion by the *Corporate Law Reform Act 1992* (Cth) of a new section 232(4), which provided:

> In the exercise of his or her powers and the discharge of his or her duties, an officer of a corporation must exercise the degree of care and diligence that a reasonable person in a like position in a corporation would exercise in the corporation's circumstances.

[94] See D Menzies, 'Company Directors' (1959) 33 *Australian Law Journal* 156.

[95] *Commonwealth Bank of Australia v Friedrich* (1991) 5 ACSR 115, 125–26.

[96] HAJ Ford, *Principles of Company Law*, 5th edn (Sydney, Butterworths, 1990) [1527].

[97] *Ibid.*

[98] Companies and Securities Law Review Committee (Cth), *Company Directors and Officers: Indemnification, Relief and Insurance* (CSLRC DP No 9, 1989) [28].

[99] Senate Standing Committee on Legal and Constitutional Affairs, Parliament of Australia, *Company Directors' Duties: Report on the Social and Fiduciary Duties and Obligations of Company Directors* ('*Cooney Report*') (PPS 1989, 395) [3.28].

As was stated in the Explanatory Memorandum to the 1992 Bill, that amendment was intended 'to reinforce that the duty of care is an objective one'.[100]

And, as was to be expected, subsequent case law construed it accordingly. Fortified by this legislative advance, in *Daniels v Anderson* in 1995,[101] the New South Wales Court of Appeal held that a director owed not only a statutory duty of care but also a common-law duty of care, primarily by reference to the notion of proximity then in vogue. Whether that conclusion accorded with 'what the Parliament had determined to be "the appropriate balance between competing claims and policies"',[102] and whether it requires re-examination now that 'proximity is no longer seen as the "conceptual determinant" in this area',[103] need not be considered. What matters, for present purposes, is that both duties were not limited by the director's subjective knowledge and experience or ignorance and inaction, but rather required directors to discharge their duties in good faith and with the degree of diligence, care and skill which an ordinary prudent person would exercise under similar circumstances in a like position. Hence, it was said that a director should acquire at least a rudimentary understanding of the business of the corporation or refuse to act; that a director was not permitted to shut his or her eyes to corporate misconduct and then claim that, because he or she did not see it, there was no duty to look; and that a director was only to delegate powers where he or she had reasonable grounds to believe, after making any necessary inquiries, that the delegate was reliable and competent.

C. The American Transplant

Subject to one qualification, that remains, in effect, the position today. What was said in *Daniels v Anderson* forms the basis of the duty to exercise 'the degree of care and diligence' of a reasonable person in similar circumstances that is now to be found in section 180(1) of the *Corporations Act 2001* (Cth). The one qualification is the statutory business judgment rule that now finds expression in section 180(2).

The origin of that rule, as of such much else in this area, was Lord Hardwicke's judgment in *Charitable Corporation v Sutton*. As has been seen, in England (and Australia), that judgment was responsible for the persistent doctrine that a 'director is obliged only to do as much as could be expected from someone as incompetent and foolish as he happens to be'.[104] Across the Atlantic, however, it

[100] Explanatory Memorandum to the Corporate Law Reform Bill 1992 (Cth) [82].

[101] *Daniels v Anderson* (1995) 37 NSWLR 438 (NSWCA) 503 (Clarke and Sheller JJA).

[102] *Peters (WA) Ltd v Petersville Ltd* [2001] HCA 45, (2001) 205 CLR 126 [33] (Gleeson CJ, Gummow, Kirby and Hayne JJ), quoting *Moorgate Tobacco Co Ltd v Philip Morris Ltd (No 2)* (1984) 156 CLR 414 (HCA) 445 (Deane J).

[103] *Woolcock Street Investments Pty Ltd v CDG Pty Ltd* [2004] HCA 16, (2004) 216 CLR 515 [18] (Gleeson CJ, Gummow, Hayne and Heydon JJ), quoting *Bryan v Maloney* (1995) 182 CLR 609 (HCA) 619 (Mason CJ, Deane and Gaudron JJ).

[104] AL Mackenzie, 'A Company's Director's Obligations of Care and Skill' [1982] *Journal of Business Law* 460, 461.

also inspired a more nuanced rule, recognising that directors must take calculated risks, invariably subject to constraints of time, information and foresight. A conventional starting point is Chancellor Kent's dictum that a director is 'not supposed to have attained infallibility' and, therefore, not held 'responsible for mistake or error of judgment'.[105] The point was soon expressly identified with the 'leading case' of *Charitable Corporation v Sutton*,[106] and summarised as being that '[q]uestions of policy of management or expediency of contracts … are to be left solely to the honest decision of directors.'[107] By the mid-twentieth century, it was labelled the 'business judgment rule' and codified under that name in the American Law Institute's *Principles of Corporate Governance*.[108]

For reasons which, in retrospect, do not appear very convincing, in the early 1990s, the Commonwealth Parliament made a conscious decision not to legislate for the introduction of such a rule.[109] As was explained in the Explanatory Memorandum accompanying the *Corporate Law Reform Bill 1992* (Cth), the view taken was that, just as the development of a business judgment rule in the United States had not been the subject of legislation, it was better to leave it to the courts in this country to develop similar principles.[110] But exactly how that was supposed to happen in the face of a newly introduced statutory provision strengthening the scrutiny of directorial decision-making in accordance with an objective standard of care is, to say the least, not clear. After all, section 232(4) was enacted in 1992 for the very purpose of overcoming the courts' thitherto established reticence about second-guessing business judgments. Then, as now, courts took the law to be as expressed in the terms of the statute, rather than as reflected in the high hopes of explanatory memoranda. Consequently, during the 1990s, courts became not at all hesitant in second-guessing business judgments and in holding directors liable for decisions with which those courts disagreed. The litigation associated with the Duke Group is one example which comes to mind.[111]

As a result, and as was recorded in the proposals for reform associated with the Corporate Law Economic Reform Program ('CLERP'),[112] by 1997 there had developed a good deal of concern and uncertainty among directors as to the scope of their liability, and not a little lobbying was undertaken to resolve that question.

[105] *Scott v Depeyster*, 1 Edw Ch 513, 535 (NY Ct of Ch, 1832), citing *Harman* (n 28), *Corporation of Exeter* (n 19) and *Crookshanks* (n 16). See also *Percy v Millaudon*, 8 Mart (NS) 82, 86–87 (Porter J for the Supreme Court of Louisiana) (La Sup Ct, 1829); *Godbold v Branch Bank at Mobile*, 11 Ala 191, 199 (Ormond J) (1847).

[106] *Spering's Appeal*, 71 Pa 11, 21 (Sharswood J for the Supreme Court of Pennsylvania) (1872).

[107] *Ellerman v Chicago Junction Railways*, 49 NJ Eq 217, 232 (Green V-C) (NJ Ct of Ch, 1891). See also *Elkins v Camden and Atlantic Railway Co*, 36 NJ Eq 241, 244 (Van Fleet V-C) (NJ Ct of Ch, 1882).

[108] American Law Institute, *Principles of Corporate Governance: Analysis and Recommendations* (1994) Vol 1, 166 § 4.01.

[109] *cf Cooney Report* (n 99) [3.35].

[110] Explanatory Memorandum to the Corporate Law Reform Bill 1992 (Cth) [89].

[111] eg *Pilmer v Duke Group Ltd (in liq)* [2001] HCA 31, (2001) 207 CLR 165.

[112] CLERP, *Directors' Duties and Corporate Governance: Facilitating Innovation and Protecting Investors* (Paper No 3, 1997) [5.2.1].

CLERP proposed that a statutory business judgment rule be enacted in order to overcome the problem. And, significantly in view of subsequent developments, the Reform Paper stated as follows:

> [a] statutory formulation of the business judgement rule would clarify and confirm the position reached at common law that *Courts will rarely review bona fide business decisions*. However, unlike the common law, it would provide a *clear presumption* in favour of a director's judgement thereby creating much more certainty for directors. Accordingly, while the substantive duties of directors would remain unchanged, directors would benefit from knowing that if they took decisions in good faith and in the company's interest, they would not be subject to challenge.[113]

CLERP added:

> the parameters of a statutory business judgement rule, or director *safe harbour* law, need to be very clearly expressed in legislation. A business judgement rule should not insulate directors from liability for negligent, ill-informed or fraudulent decisions.[114]

Hence, the statutory business judgment rule was justified as merely confirmatory on the assumption that courts, applying general law doctrines of liability, were already hesitant in reviewing directors' bona fide business decisions. Although that assumption was misplaced, it accorded with views which Professor Ford had expressed in the fifth edition of *Principles of Company Law*. There, he had set out what he described as the American 'so-called business judgment rule', as being that:

> a director or officer shall not be subject to liability under the duty of care standards with respect to the consequences of a business judgment if he (1) informed himself and made reasonable inquiry with respect to the business judgment; (2) acted in good faith and without a disabling conflict of interest; and (3) had a rational basis for the business judgment.[115]

Professor Ford proceeded to observe that, although the business judgment rule had *not* been adopted in Australia at that time, Australian courts had in effect applied an aspect of the rule by acknowledging that the business decisions of directors would not be reviewed on their merits and by generally not impugning a board decision that could have been made by reasonable directors.[116] He cited the 1968 decision of the High Court in *Harlowe's Nominees Pty Ltd v Woodside (Lakes Entrance) Oil Co*[117] and the 1974 decision of the Privy Council in *Howard Smith Ltd v Ampol Petroleum Ltd*[118] in support of his conclusion.

[113] *Ibid* [5.2.2] (citations omitted; emphasis added).
[114] *Ibid.*
[115] Ford (n 96) [1527].
[116] *Ibid* [1437].
[117] *Harlowe's Nominees Pty Ltd v Woodside (Lakes Entrance) Oil Co* (1968) 121 CLR 483 (HCA) 493.
[118] *Howard Smith Ltd v Ampol Petroleum Ltd* [1974] AC 821 (PC) 832.

But the difficulty with CLERP proceeding on that basis was that what Professor Ford had written in the fifth edition concerned the position in 1990: that is, before the changes to section 232(4) imposed an express statutory objective standard of skill and care, and before *Daniels v Anderson* recognised that the same standard applied in relation to a director's common-law duty of care. *Harlowe's Nominees* and *Howard Smith v Ampol Petroleum* were decided before those later developments and, therefore, had nothing to say about them. Each had involved an essentially different issue of whether a decision to raise capital by an issue of shares which diluted the percentage holding of existing members was a decision made bona fide in the best interests of the company as a whole. Duties of good faith differed from duties of care, especially after the latter came to be judged against an objective standard. Thus, paradoxically, the CLERP proposal for a business judgment rule, although ostensibly calculated to pull back from common-law developments like *Daniels v Anderson*, which were said to be productive of uncertainty, at the same time asserted that the statutory formulation of the business judgment rule would do little more than clarify and confirm the position that had been reached at common law.

The CLERP proposal led to the enactment of a statutory business judgment rule[119] in the form of section 180(2) of the *Corporations Act 2001* (Cth). That section relevantly provides that a director 'is taken to meet' his or her statutory, common-law and equitable duties to act with reasonable care and diligence where the director has made a business judgment in good faith for a proper purpose, without material interest in the subject matter, after informing himself or herself to the extent reasonably believed appropriate, and with a rational belief that the judgment was in the best interests of the corporation. As will be apparent, the terms of the provision are closely modelled on the American business judgment rule as codified in the American Law Institute's *Principles of Corporate Governance* in 1992.[120] Correspondingly, the Explanatory Memorandum to the Bill which enacted it predicted:

> the statutory formulation will provide a clear presumption in favour of a director's judgment. In particular, while the substantive duties of directors will remain unchanged, absent fraud or bad faith, the business judgment rule will allow directors the benefit of a presumption that, in making business decisions, if they have acted on an informed basis, in good faith, and in the honest belief that the decision was taken in the best interests of the company, they will not be challenged regarding the fulfilment of their duty of care and diligence.[121]

In the events which have since occurred, however, none of that has come to pass. On the present state of authority, section 180(2) does not provide a clear

[119] *Corporations Law* s 180(2).

[120] *cf Principles of Corporate Governance* (n 108). See DA DeMott, 'Legislating Business Judgment: Comment from the United States' (1998) 16 *Company and Securities Law Journal* 575.

[121] Explanatory Memorandum to the Corporate Law Economic Reform Program Bill 1998 (Cth) [6.4].

presumption or, indeed, any presumption in favour of directors. Following the decision of Austin J in *Australian Securities and Investments Commission (ASIC) v Rich*,[122] it has been generally accepted that section 180(2) operates only as a defence, casting the onus on the director to justify his or her decision-making.[123]

Justice Austin considered that there were two reasons which favoured that construction over one requiring the plaintiff to rebut a presumption in favour of the defendant director by proving additional facts.[124] First, his Honour considered that such a requirement would run counter to what he considered to be the clear intention expressed in the Explanatory Memorandum, and Second Reading Speech, that there should be no reduction in the duties demanded of directors. Second, his Honour took the view that it would be unusual if, as part of the burden of establishing breach of the statutory duty of care and diligence in section 180, a plaintiff might be required to establish that the defendant's business judgment was made otherwise than in good faith for a proper purpose, because that would amount to proving the more serious contravention of the duty in section 181.

The decision in *ASIC v Rich* was also bad news for directors hoping that the concept of business judgments would be construed generously. Justice Austin noted that it was not clear how far 'the concept of business judgment [was] extended into the realm of management, organisation and planning'.[125] Though accepting that, on account of the broad statutory language and the position adopted in the United States, a wide interpretation of the definition in section 180(3) of business judgments appeared attractive, his Honour determined that the concept was limited by the reference to a decision 'to take or not to take action'.[126] That directed attention to 'whether the director or officer has turned his or her mind to the matter'.[127] And thus, his Honour concluded:

> the discharge by directors of their 'oversight' duties, including their duties to monitor the company's affairs and policies and to maintain familiarity of the company's financial position, is not protected by the business judgment rule, because the discharge or failure to discharge those duties does not involve any business judgment as defined.[128]

[122] *Australian Securities and Investments Commission (ASIC) v Rich* (2009) 236 FLR 1, [2009] NSWSC 1229.
[123] See, eg, *Australian Securities and Investments Commission v Fortescue Metals Group Ltd* (2011) 190 FCR 364, 427, [2011] FCAFC 19 [197]–[198] (Keane CJ, Emmett J and Finkelstein J agreeing); *Australian Securities and Investments Commission v Mariner Corporation Ltd* (2015) 241 FCR 502, 589, [2015] FCA 589 [485].
[124] *ASIC v Rich* (n 122) [7266]–[7269].
[125] *Ibid* [7272].
[126] *Ibid* [7271].
[127] *Ibid* [7277].
[128] *Ibid* [7278].

Although the conclusions in *ASIC v Rich* have been followed consistently in subsequent cases,[129] some commentators have observed that, apart from the passages of the extrinsic material which expressed an intention not to lessen the duties of directors, there were other stronger passages, to which Austin J did not refer, that left little doubt that the legislature intended the provision to operate as a presumption in favour of providing directors with the benefit of the doubt unless the identified additional elements could be proved.[130] Equally, as some commentators have observed, if the provision only created a defence, it would be, at best, a defence of marginal utility in view of the relief-from-liability provisions in sections 1317S and 1318.[131] Nonetheless, as matters now stand, although the enactment of section 180(2) of the *Corporations Act 2001* (Cth) was unquestionably motivated by an intention to create a presumption in favour of directors, and the drafting of the provision was modelled on the more generous American business judgment rule, the effect of section 180(2) according to *ASIC v Rich* is entirely different and of little (if any) practical utility.

These points are amply illustrated in a study conducted by Jenifer Varzaly. Writing in October 2012, she recorded that, following the introduction of section 180(2) in March 2000, the provision was not considered in any reported decision of an Australia court until 2003.[132] The greatest number of decisions in which it was considered took place between 2006 and 2010 – the end of that period corresponding to the effects of the global financial crisis. In the 10 years following the enactment of the statutory business judgment rule, there was only one case in which the defence was successfully invoked, and that was by a receiver, not a director.[133] She concluded that section 180(2) has provided neither business confidence nor legal certainty.

IV. Prospects for the Future

Of course, that is not to overlook that there are powerful arguments against the business judgment rule. In each jurisdiction which has adopted it, whether by statute or by judicial decision, the rule has presented a number of problems in

[129] eg *Australian Securities and Investments Commission v Adler* (2002) 168 FLR 253, [2002] NSWSC 171, [387], [406], [511]; *Gold Ribbon (Accountants) Pty Ltd (in liq) v Sheers* [2006] QCA 335 [247]–[248]; *Fortescue Metals* (n 123) [197].

[130] See W Bainbridge and T Connor, 'Another Way Forward? The Scope for an Appellate Court to Reinterpret the Statutory Business Judgment Rule' (2016) 34 *Company and Securities Law Journal* 415, 425–26.

[131] See N Young, 'Has Directors' Liability Gone Too Far or Not Far Enough? A Review of the Standards of Conduct Required of Directors under Sections 180–184 of the Corporations Act' (2008) 26 *Company and Securities Law Journal* 216, 222–23.

[132] J Varzaly, 'Protecting the Authority of Directors: An Empirical Analysis of the Statutory Business Judgment Rule' (2012) 12 *Journal of Corporate Law Studies* 429, 439.

[133] *Ibid* 456.

interpretation and application, which have given rise to considerable differences in practice between jurisdictions.[134] More fundamentally, Professor Gevurtz has argued that the rule is 'meaningless' in so far as the duty of reasonable care allows for the exercise of reasonable business judgment and 'misguided' in so far as directors are not required to exercise the same objective standard of care as any other professional.[135] The argument has logical appeal, and it might well be accepted in von Jhering's *Begriffshimmel*, or Heaven of Juristic Conceptions.[136] For mere mortal judges and advisers, however, the business judgment rule may at least serve as a heuristic, cautioning against the danger of hindsight bias so percipiently identified by Lord Hardwicke.

Alive to the practical aspect of the rule, Julie Margaret posited of *ASIC v Rich* that the process and its outcome were such as to suggest that something might be seriously wrong with the system.[137] The case took eight years, generated in excess of 16,000 pages of transcript, occupied three years in hearings and two further years to produce the 3,000-page judgment, cost $40 million, and concluded with the dismissal of the claim. As Margaret also observed, and as indeed Austin J ultimately found, such cases are not always the result of directors deceiving others for their own gain, or, it might be added, doing less than is required of them. Often, much of the financial suffering that results from corporate failure is due to the economic system, national and international conditions, and the limitations of generally accepted accounting standards. Business can be inherently risky. Therefore, should not the statutory business judgment rule be more attuned to those considerations?

Sir Owen Dixon famously wrote of what a court might do, consistently with traditional methods of judicial reasoning, when it has the feeling that there is something wrong with the conclusion dictated by a hitherto accepted understanding of the law.[138] Speaking in the context of the rule in *Foakes v Beer*,[139] Sir Owen posited that it would be in complete accordance with orthodox judicial method for the court to re-examine the essentials of the formation of a simple contract at common law and the elements inherent in the theory of estoppel with a view to ascertaining whether in truth, upon a correct analysis of the situation, the objectionable conclusion that a creditor cannot bind himself to take less than the whole

[134] See, eg, A Gurrea-Martínez, 'Re-Examining the Law and Economics of the Business Judgment Rule: Notes for Its Implementation in Non-US Jurisdictions' (2018) 18 *Journal of Corporate Law Studies* 417, 419.

[135] FA Gevurtz, 'The Business Judgment Rule: Meaningless Verbiage or Misguided Notion?' (1994) 67 *Southern California Law Review* 287.

[136] R von Jhering and CL Levy (tr), 'In the Heaven for Legal Concepts: A Fantasy' (1985) 58 *Temple Law Quarterly* 799. See J Stone, *Legal System and Lawyers' Reasonings* (Sydney, Maitland Publications, 1964) 226–27.

[137] JE Margaret, *Solvency in Financial Accounting* (New York, Routledge, 2012) 100–101.

[138] O Dixon, 'Concerning Judicial Method' in S Crennan and W Gummow (eds), *Jesting Pilate, And Other Papers and Addresses*, 3rd edn (Sydney, Federation Press, 2019) 119.

[139] *Foakes v Beer* (1884) 9 App Cas 605 (HL).

of the debt inevitably flowed from the logical application of principle properly understood.[140] Granted that is a long way from directors' duties. But might it be that an analogous approach could be invoked if the correct construction of section 180(2) were ever to be put in issue in a court of appeal? Of course, the latter is a question of statutory construction, which is not entirely the same as the correct approach to the ascertainment of what Sir Owen described as true legal principle. But to go back some 70 years to another area of law, is it possible that then-Justice Dixon's approach to statutory construction in *Brennan v The King* offers an insight into how something similar could be done in this context?[141]

Either way it is doubtful that it will be decided within the near future. A decade has passed since *ASIC v Rich* was decided, and no one has yet challenged the construction of section 180(2) endorsed in that decision in an appellate court. Further, apart from the enactment of a safe harbour provision allowing for reasonable risk taking in insolvent trading,[142] there has been no indication from a government of either persuasion of an inclination to amend section 180(2) to bring it into line with what was originally said to be intended. So far as appears, no one suggests that the considerations which led CLERP to favour the introduction of the statutory business judgment rule in 1997 are no longer valid. But the realpolitik of the situation appears to be that the will to grapple with them has gone.

[140] Dixon (n 138) 120–22.

[141] *Brennan v The King* (1936) 55 CLR 253 (HCA) 263.

[142] *Corporations Act 2001* s 588GA, inserted by *Treasury Laws Amendment (2017 Enterprise Incentives No 2) Act 2017* Sch 1, item 2.

11

Fiduciaries, Equitable Compensation and Lost Commercial Opportunity: Reconciling the Need for Financial Loss

SIMONE DEGELING*

The equitable rules circumscribing the conduct of fiduciaries in Anglo Australian law are well documented. A fiduciary has an obligation of loyalty to their principal. A fiduciary must 'not obtain … any unauthorised benefit from the relationship and not … be in a position of conflict'.[1] A fiduciary must therefore avoid placing themselves in a position of conflict[2] or a real or substantial possibility of conflict[3] between [their] personal interests and 'those whom the fiduciary is bound to protect'[4] or between their duties to multiple principals.[5] Additionally, a fiduciary must not profit by reason or use of their fiduciary position.[6] The fiduciary who

* Orcid id, https://orcid.org/0000-0001-7498-8590. I am indebted to Jessica Hudson for her comments on a draft version of this chapter. All errors are mine.

[1] *Breen v Williams* [1996] HCA 57, (1996) 186 CLR 71, 113 (Gaudron and McHugh JJ), approved in *Pilmer v Duke Group Ltd (in liq)* [2001] HCA 31, (2001) 207 CLR 165 [74] (McHugh, Gummow, Hayne and Callinan JJ) and *Youyang Pty Limited v Minter Ellison Morris Fletcher* [2003] HCA 15, (2003) 212 CLR 484 [41] (Gleeson CJ, McHugh, Gummow, Kirby and Hayne JJ). See also *Bristol & West Building Society v Mothew* [1998] Ch 1, 18 (Millett LJ); *Bray v Ford* [1896] AC 44, 51 (Lord Herschell).

[2] *Commonwealth Bank of Australia v Smith* (1991) 42 FCR 390, 392 (the Court); *Breen* (n 1)135; *Pilmer* (n 1) [78] (McHugh, Gummow, Hayne and Callinan JJ). See also *Maguire v Makaronis* [1997] HCA 23, (1997) 188 CLR 449, 461 (Brennan CJ, Gaudron, McHugh and Gummow JJ); *Beach Petroleum NL v Abbott Tout Russell Kennedy* [1999] NSWCA 408, (1999) 48 NSWLR 1, 47 (Spigelman CJ, Sheller JA, Stein JA); *Howard v Commissioner of Taxation* [2014] HCA 21, (2014) 253 CLR 83 [59] (Hayne and Crennan JJ).

[3] *Commonwealth Bank of Australia v Smith* (n 2) 392 (the Court); *Breen* (n 1) 135 (Gummow J); *Birtchnell v Equity Trustees and Agency Co Ltd* (1929) 42 CLR 384, 408 (Dixon J); *Boardman v Phipps* [1967] 2 AC 46, 124 (Lord Upjohn); *Hospital Products Ltd v United States Surgical Corporation* [1984] HCA 64, (1984) 156 CLR 41, 103 (Mason J); *Pilmer* (n 1) [79] (McHugh, Gummow, Hayne and Callinan JJ); *Australian Careers Institute Pty Ltd v Australian Institute of Fitness Pty Ltd* [2016] NSWCA 347, (2016) 340 ALR 580 [3]–[5] (Bathurst CJ), [132] (Sackville AJA, with whom Meagher JA agreed).

[4] *Breen* (n 1) 135 (Gummow J).

[5] *Commonwealth Bank of Australia v Smith* (n 2) 392 (the Court); *Breen* (n 1) 135 (Gummow J).

[6] *Howard* (n 2) 107 [62] (Hayne and Crennan JJ); *Regal (Hastings) Ltd v Gulliver* [1967] 2 AC 134, 143 (Lord Russell). As discussed in section II below, Smith argues that the no profit rule is not a secondary obligation to disgorge the fiduciary's unauthorised profit, but is rather a rule of primary attribution. See L Smith, 'Fiduciary Relationships: Ensuring the Loyal Exercise of Judgment on Behalf of Another' (2014) 130 *LQR* 608.

is unwilling or unable to meet their fiduciary obligations may seek to rely on the equitable defence of informed consent.[7] Transactions entered into in breach of these prohibitions are vulnerable to rescission.[8] Further, subject to the doctrine of election,[9] a fiduciary may be required to account for any profits made by reason or use of their position[10] and to hold any bribe or secret commission for the principal on constructive trust.[11] As with all equitable remedies, the nature and extent of relief is given in the discretion of the court. Of relevance to this chapter is the remedy of equitable compensation, which is potentially available to the principal for loss caused by breach of a fiduciary's obligation of loyalty.[12]

The heads of loss recognised by an award of equitable compensation include the loss of a commercial opportunity, where the lost chance is itself a *valuable* commercial opportunity.[13] Thus, it is necessary for the principal to demonstrate that a lost opportunity to contract 'had real value because the prospect of a successful outcome was substantial rather than speculative'.[14] Similarly, in a claim for equitable compensation for the lost opportunity to obtain funding, the court's starting point is that the raising of funds would only have been of benefit to the principal if it could have done something useful with the funds.[15] Therefore, it is necessary to consider 'not only [the claimant's] prospects of obtaining funding, but also whether, if obtained, that funding would have been put to profitable use'.[16]

This chapter explores the requirement of a *real loss* or *productive of financial loss* in relation to an award of equitable compensation against a defaulting fiduciary for the principal's lost commercial opportunity. It is argued that these requirements arise at the point of calculation of the remedy of equitable compensation and are part of equity's method of making certain the principal's losses. The chapter also attempts to understand these requirements of a *real loss* or *productive of financial loss* in the light of various normative accounts of fiduciary obligation. For example, it might erroneously be thought that the need for the principal to suffer a financial loss may pose challenges for accounts of fiduciary relationships which rest on controlling those who hold power in relation to the autonomy of

[7] *Maguire* (n 2) 466 (Brennan CJ, Gaudron, McHugh, and Gummow JJ).

[8] *Ibid* 467, 475 (Brennan CJ, Gaudron, McHugh, and Gummow JJ).

[9] Election is not required when remedies are cumulative rather than alternative. However, where remedies are alternative and inconsistent, the principal must elect between them. See generally *Tang Man Sit v Capacious Investments Ltd* [1996] AC 514, 520–21 (the Board).

[10] *Warman International Ltd v Dwyer* [1995] HCA 18, (1995) 182 CLR 544, 560 (Mason CJ, Brennan, Deane, Dawson and Gaudron JJ).

[11] *Grimaldi v Chameleon Mining NL [No 2]* [2012] FCAFC 6, (2012) 200 FCR 296, 346–47 [183]–[185] (Finn, Stone and Perram JJ); *FHR European Ventures LLP v Cedar Capital Partners LLC* [2015] AC 250 [7], [50] (the Court).

[12] *Youyang* (n 1).

[13] *Ramsay v BigTinCan Pty Ltd* [2014] NSWCA 324, (2014) 101 ACSR 415 [72] (Macfarlan JA with whom McColl JA agreed at [2]); *Hart Security Australia Pty Ltd v Boucousis* [2016] NSWCA 307, (2016) 339 ALR 659 [165]–[167] (Meagher JA, with whom Bathurst CJ and Beazley P agreed).

[14] *Hart Security, ibid* [166] (Meagher JA, with whom Bathurst CJ and Beazley P agreed).

[15] *BigTinCan* (n 13) [69] (Macfarlan JA).

[16] *Ibid* [72] (Macfarlan JA with whom McColl JA agreed at [2]).

the principal. Smith argues that, '[i]n every fiduciary relationship, the fiduciary acquires control over a part (or in some cases, all) of another person's autonomy'[17] and the requirement of loyalty 'is imposed to control decision-making power held for, or on behalf of, another person'.[18] If it is the autonomy of the principal which is being protected via, for example, the no-conflict rule, why is it that only lost opportunities which are themselves productive of financial losses may be recovered? The answer is that analysis must take care not to elide breach and loss. Contrary to the statement of Macfarlan JA in *Ramsay v BigTinCan Pty Ltd*, that in assessing equitable compensation:

> the same question as arises when assessing equitable compensation: namely, whether loss has flowed from identified breaches of duty (*Nicholls v Michael Wilson & Partners Ltd* [2012] NSWCA 383). In this respect it does not matter whether the breaches were of common law, statutory or equitable duties ...[19]

This chapter argues that equity's response to breach of the fiduciary obligation of loyalty is particular. In assessing equitable compensation, it is necessary to keep firmly in mind the distinction between breach and loss. This is because a plaintiff asserting an equity for relief for breach of fiduciary duty does not need to establish loss. Rather, breach of fiduciary obligation exists when the defendant has placed herself in a position of actual or serious possibility of conflict of duty and self-interest or conflicting duties.[20] The existence and quantum of loss may be relevant in determining the appropriate remedy to meet the principal's equity for relief, but is not part of the inquiry in establishing breach. Thus, the requirement that any lost opportunity is a *real loss* or *productive of financial loss* is consistent, or at least neutral, with an account of fiduciary relationships that rests on the need to supervise the decision maker's (ie the fiduciary's) 'legal controls of part or all of the other person's [the principal's] autonomy'.[21] As will be explained in section III below, this conclusion also follows in relation to the undertakings account and the legitimate expectations account of fiduciary obligations.

This chapter proceeds in three parts. Section I sets out an explanation of the requirement that any lost opportunity be a real loss or productive of financial loss. In section II, the discussion demonstrates how this requirement may be understood to be part of equity's approach to making certain the principal's loss. Finally, section III considers the significance of the requirement that the principal's lost opportunity itself be productive of real or financial loss for various normative accounts of fiduciary relationships.

[17] Smith (n 6) 614.
[18] *Ibid.*
[19] *BigTinCan* (n 13) [71] (Macfarlan JA).
[20] *Commonwealth Bank of Australia v Smith* (n 2) 392 (the Court); *Breen* (n 1) 135 (Gummow J); *Pilmer* (n 1) [78]–[79] (McHugh, Gummow, Hayne and Callinan JJ); *Birtchnell* (n 3) 408 (Dixon J); *Boardman* (n 3) 124 (Lord Upjohn); *Hospital Products* (n 3) 103 (Mason J). See also *Maguire* (n 2) 461 (Brennan CJ and Gaudron, McHugh and Gummow JJ); *Beach Petroleum* (n 2) 47 (the Court); *Howard* (n 2) [59] (Hayne and Crennan JJ).
[21] Smith (n 6).

I. Is the Lost Commercial Opportunity Productive of Financial Loss?

The requirement that in order to be met by an award of reparative equitable compensation, the lost commercial opportunity flowing from a breach of fiduciary obligation must be a real loss, or productive of financial loss, is shown by two decisions of the New South Wales Court of Appeal. As discussed below, in each case the fiduciary was in breach of fiduciary obligation.

In *Hart Security Australia Pty Ltd v Boucousis*[22] the appellant, Hart Security Australia ('HSA'), sought to enter into a contract with Norther Territory Airports Pty Ltd ('NTA') for the provision of security services to airports in the Northern Territory. NTA would only enter into a contract if a $1 million bank guarantee were provided by HSA securing HSA's performance. HSA was unable to agree to that requirement, as the major shareholder of HSA (Hart Cyprus, who was providing funding) refused. As a result, the negotiations reached an impasse.

Boucousis was a director of HSA and the ultimate minority shareholder in HSA. An alternative arrangement, involving another entity, was eventually entered into by Boucousis. Pursuant to this alternative arrangement, without the knowledge or consent of Hart Cyprus, HSA, Boucousis and ATMAAC agreed to make a rival bid for the contract, with the necessary guarantee being given by Investec Bank. Pursuant to the proposal, a new entity, ATMAAC Aviation, would be incorporated, which would by a share issue become the holding company of HSA. ATMAAC Aviation would enter the security contract with NTA, thus displacing HSA. Boucousis would receive a shareholding and directorship in ATMAAC Aviation and employment in the ATMAAC group. However, Boucousis' scheme failed and neither ATMAAC Aviation nor HSA entered into a contract with NTA. HSA brought proceedings against Boucousis for breaches of equitable fiduciary duties and statutory duties under sections 181(1), 182(1) and 183(1) of the *Corporations Act 2001* (Cth).

Of interest is HSA's equity for relief against Boucousis for breach of fiduciary obligations. The Court found that Boucousis had breached his fiduciary obligation to HSA as, through his conduct, there was an actual or substantial possibility of conflict between his fiduciary duty to HSA and his self-interest.[23] Further, Boucousis had not obtained informed consent to any breach of fiduciary obligation.[24] HSA alleged that it had lost an opportunity to enter into a contract with NTA, as 'the opportunity for further negotiation included a real prospect that NTA might not insist on [the requirement for a $1million bank guarantee]'.[25]

[22] *Hart Security* (n 13).
[23] *Ibid* [123] (Meagher JA). Pursuant to the proposed transaction, Boucousis was to receive 'significant personal benefits' (see [122]), including a directorship, shareholding and employment with ATMAAC.
[24] *Ibid* [12], [109], [123] (Meagher JA).
[25] *Ibid* [169] (Meagher JA).

HSA therefore sought, inter alia, equitable compensation for the lost opportunity to negotiate a successful contract with NTA. The claim failed.

Meagher JA (with whom Bathurst CJ and Beazley P agreed) held that:

> HSA had to establish to the required standard that the opportunity to continue to negotiate with NTA, in the absence of the pursuit by HSA of the ATMAAC proposal, had *real value* because the prospect of a successful outcome was substantial rather than speculative; and that it was lost by Mr Boucousis' conduct.[26]

The evidence did not support HSA's argument. The Court relied on the trial judge's findings that, on the balance of probabilities, the trial judge was not satisfied either that Hart Cyprus may have been prepared to support the $1 million bank guarantee required by NTA, nor that NTA would have been prepared to relax the requirement for a guarantee.[27] It therefore followed that HSA had not established, on the balance of probabilities, that the opportunity for further negotiation included any real or substantial prospect of agreement between HSA and NTA. Thus, HSA had not proved that it had lost a valuable opportunity to negotiate a contract with NTA by reason of Mr Boucousis's conduct.[28] Equitable compensation was not awarded.

The same, or a similar, requirement was articulated in the earlier case of *Ramsay v BigTinCan*.[29] BigTinCan ('BTC') was a company established to develop smart phone applications. Although BTC had enjoyed some success and its products were approved by Blackberry, Apple and Google, BTC required capital. Ramsay was a director of BTC who with his wife held 20 per cent of the shares in BTC. Ramsay's primary task was to assist BTC in obtaining funding, in particular by developing and marketing the app called BigTinCanConnect. During 2009 Ramsay regularly reported to BTC that he was confident he could secure funding of up to $1.2 million. In March 2009, Pollers was engaged by BTC as an app developer.

It turned out that Ramsay and Pollers were not to be trusted. In late 2009 and early 2010 Pollers and Ramsay formulated and implemented a plan to acquire BTC's assets at a discounted value, to develop BTC's business through a new entity ('Newco') and to divert funding and business opportunities from BTC to Newco.[30] The trial judge, Ball J, found that Ramsay had breached his fiduciary obligations as director of BTC, thereby causing BTC to lose an opportunity to raise finance. Ball J awarded equitable compensation of $300,000 reflecting the value of that loss.[31] By majority, the New South Wales Court of Appeal confirmed the quantum awarded, but held that Ball J was in error in treating BTC's lost opportunity to

[26] *Ibid* [166] (Meagher JA) (emphasis added).
[27] *Ibid* [168]–[169] (Meagher JA).
[28] *Ibid* [170] (Meagher JA).
[29] *BigTinCan* (n 13). Special leave to appeal to the High Court of Australia was refused: s268/2014, [2015] HCATrans 059.
[30] *Ibid* [12] (Macfarlan JA).
[31] *Ibid* [13] (Macfarlan JA).

obtain funding itself as the real or substantial financial loss. Rather, BTC was also required to demonstrate that the funding, if obtained, would have been put to a profitable use. It was only in such circumstances that the lost opportunity to obtain funds could be regarded as a 'real' loss.[32] Macfarlan JA stated:

> … the raising of funds would only have been of benefit to BTC if it could have done something useful with them. Otherwise, whilst [BTC] would have received money, it would have incurred a liability to the investor to repay an equivalent amount, either as a debt due to a creditor or as share capital ultimately to be returned to a shareholder. If the evidence established that funding would, or might, have enabled BTC to earn profits, the absence of that funding might fairly be regarded as causally related to a financial loss. Otherwise, it could not be so regarded.[33]

In result, a majority of the Court confirmed the amount awarded by Ball J, albeit via applying the above principle.[34] Taking into account 'the very significant business contingencies to which the prospect of deriving the anticipated profits was subject'[35] and the fact that the parties would not have committed their time and energy had they not assessed the prospects of business success at greater than 10 per cent or estimated returns in excess of $650,000, the award of $300,000 in equitable compensation awarded at trial was confirmed.

II. Certainty of Loss and Equitable Compensation

This chapter argues that the requirement that any lost opportunity be a real loss, or productive of financial loss, are inquiries driven by the need to make certain the principal's loss. Legal analysis is familiar with a requirement of certainty of loss in relation to some claims for compensatory damages at law. For example, in an action for compensatory damages for breach of contract, or for the tort of negligence, the plaintiff bears the legal burden of establishing her claim for damages on the balance of probabilities, which may be taken to imply an obligation on the plaintiff to establish the nature and extent of her losses.[36] Thus, '[t]o justify an award of substantial damages where loss is asserted the claimant must satisfy the court both as to (i) the fact of damage, that is an adverse consequence; and (ii) as to its amount'.[37] The principal's lost commercial opportunity is an inherently

[32] *Ibid* [69] and [72] (Macfarlan JA) with whom McColl JA agreed (at [2]).
[33] *Ibid* [69] (Macfarlan JA) (emphasis added).
[34] *Ibid*. Gleeson JA agreed that BTC's lost opportunity was not itself a substantial financial loss, and that BTC needed to demonstrate that the funding would, or might, have enabled BTC, for example, to earn profits. However, on the facts (at [123]–[141]), Gleeson JA valued the lost opportunity significantly lower than Macfarlan JA at 0.1 x $650,000 = $65,000, taking into account various contingencies affecting the possible trajectories of Ramsay's capital raising strategies. Therefore, per Gleeson JA's calculation, $300,000 awarded by Ball J at trial was not a fair assessment of BTC's loss.
[35] *Ibid* [84] (Macfarlan JA).
[36] M Tilbury, *Civil Remedies: Principles of Civil Remedies* (Butterworths, 1990) Vol 1, 149.
[37] J Edelman, *McGregor on Damages*, 20th edn (Sweet & Maxwell, 2018) [10-001].

uncertain loss. Uncertainty may arise as the nature and extent of this loss may depend, for example, on the hypothetical conduct of a third party,[38] the hypothetical conduct of the plaintiff in deciding whether or not to pursue the lost opportunity[39] and the actions of the defendant.[40] Depending on the contingency involved, the court will discount the value of the lost commercial opportunity to reach a certain value of loss in order to award compensatory damages. Following *Hart Security* and *BigTinCan*, this chapter takes the view that a similar inquiry occurs in equity following breach of a fiduciary obligation. Assuming the court is satisfied that the principal has lost a commercial opportunity in a manner attributable to the breach of fiduciary obligation, such that causation is satisfied,[41] it remains necessary to place a certain value on the principal's lost commercial opportunity. Equitable compensation may only be awarded once the principal's loss has been rendered certain.

Previous work[42] identifies that equity has two methods of making certain the principal's loss when awarding equitable compensation following breach of fiduciary obligation. The first, as shown by *Hart Security* and *BigTinCan*, employs a method of probabilistic reasoning. The second embeds certainty within equity's discretion and according to equity's assumed standards of conduct about the fiduciary.

A. Probabilistic Inquiry

The reasoning and result in both *Hart Security* and *BigTinCan* rest on the view that in order to obtain equitable compensation for a lost commercial opportunity, the

[38] *Sellars v Adelaide Petroleum NL* [1994] HCA 4, (1994) 179 CLR 332; *Heenan v Di Sisto* [2008] NSWCA 25, (2008) 13 BPR 25,213 [28] (Giles JA with whom Mason P and Mathews AJA agreed); *Hendriks v McGeoch* [2008] NSWCA 53, (2008) Aust Torts Reports 81-942 [87]–[99] (Basten JA with whom Spigelman CJ and Giles JA agreed); *Falkingham v Hoffmans* [2014] WASCA 140, (2014) 46 WAR 510 [44] (Pullin and Murphy JJA) [219] (Buss JA), special leave to the HCA refused: [2015] HCATrans 066 (multiply by the degree of probability).

[39] *Heenan*, *ibid* [28], [32] (Giles JA with whom Mason P and Mathews AJA agreed) (assess on a balance of probabilities).

[40] See the following contract cases which indicate support for both a balance of probabilities and a degree of probabilities approach in taking account of the conduct of the defendant: *Commonwealth v Amann Aviation Pty Ltd* [1991] HCA 54, (1991) 174 CLR 64; *Chaplin v Hicks* [1911] 2 KB 786.

[41] There is not one approach to causation in equity: see, eg, *Ancient Order of Foresters in Victoria Friendly Society Limited v Lifeplan Australia Friendly Society Limited* [2018] HCA 43, (2018) 265 CLR 1 [9] (Kiefel CJ, Kean and Edelman JJ). Rather, as stated in *O'Halloran v RT Thomas & Family Pty Ltd* (1998) 45 NSWLR 262, 275 (Spigelman CJ), '[i]t is necessary to identify the purpose of the particular rule to determine the appropriate approach to issues of causation'. See also *Agricultural Land Management v Jackson [No 2]* [2014] WASC 102, (2014) 48 WAR 1 [392]–[396] (Edelman J). Accordingly, common sense causation reasoning is applied in order to connect the breach of fiduciary duty with the principal's loss, with the 'but for' test being applied to ensure that loss which would have occurred in any event is not compensated.

[42] S Degeling, 'Loss of a Chance and Breach of Fiduciary Duty' (2016) 28 *Singapore Academy of Law Journal* 825.

principal must demonstrate that a 'real' loss has been suffered, such that the award reflects both the likelihood and value of the lost opportunity. In *Hart Security* and *BigTinCan*, the New South Wales Court of Appeal relied on the decision of the High Court of Australia in *Sellars v Adelaide Petroleum NL*[43] in which Adelaide Petroleum NL ('ADP') successfully recovered damages under section 82 of the *Trade Practices Act 1974* (Cth) for a lost commercial opportunity. As outlined below, a percentage-based probabilities approach was employed to make certain ADP's loss.

ADP was a mining exploration company which by early 1988 was beginning to run into financial difficulty. ADP had had little success in locating oil and mineral deposits and had insufficient working capital or income. ADP's directors sought another company willing to buy out the directors' shareholding as part of a restructuring arrangement. With this in mind, ADP entered parallel negotiations with two companies for the sale of the directors' shareholding: Poseidon Ltd ('Poseidon') and Pagini Resources NL ('Pagini'). Sellars was an executive of Poseidon. In the course of negotiations between ADP and Poseidon, Sellars made several misrepresentations, the effect of which was to induce ADP to discontinue negotiating with Pagini. These misrepresentations constituted misleading conduct in breach of section 52 of the *Trade Practices Act 1974* (Cth). However, after a hiatus, negotiations resumed and led to an agreement between ADP and Pagini of the 'type originally contemplated but [ADP argued] … on terms less favourable that those which would have resulted if the original Pagini negotiations had been pursued to a conclusion'.[44] ADP therefore sued Poseidon and Sellars under section 82 of the *Trade Practices Act 1974* (Cth) for the 'loss of the benefit represented by the Paganini Resources Agreement [the originally proposed agreement], less the benefit able to be obtained with alternative arrangements …',[45] or 'the loss of chance'.[46] At trial, French J held that there was a 40 per cent chance that Pagini would have contracted on terms more favourable to ADP had their negotiations not been disrupted by the misleading conduct of Sellars and Poseidon.[47] The High Court of Australia held that the Full Federal Court was not in error in dismissing an appeal against this finding.[48]

The High Court confirmed that, irrespective of whether the deprivation of a commercial opportunity occurs by reason of breach of contract, tort or contravention of section 52 of the *Trade Practices Act 1974* (Cth), damages should be assessed by reference to 'the prospects of success of that opportunity had it been pursued'.[49] Therefore, the plaintiff must prove:

[43] *Sellars* (n 38).
[44] *Ibid* 341 (Mason CJ, Dawson, Toohey and Gaudron JJ).
[45] *Adelaide Petroleum NL v Poseidon Ltd* (1990) 98 ALR 431, 529 (French J).
[46] *Ibid* 531 (French J).
[47] *Ibid* 532 (French J).
[48] *Sellars* (n 38) 356 (Mason CJ, Dawson, Toohey and Gaudron JJ). Brennan J at 369 similarly held that the plaintiff's case was established and dismissed the appeals.
[49] *Ibid* 355 (Mason CJ, Dawson, Toohey and Gaudron JJ).

> … on the balance of probabilities that he or she has sustained *some* loss or damage. However, in a case such as the present, the applicant shows *some* loss or damage was sustained by demonstrating that the contravening conduct caused the loss of a commercial opportunity which had *some* value (not being a negligible value), the value being ascertained by reference to the degree of probabilities or possibilities. It is no answer to that way of viewing an applicant's case to say that the commercial opportunity was valueless on the balance of probabilities because to say that is to value the commercial opportunity by reference to a standard of proof which is inapplicable.[50]

On the facts, 'by reference to the degree of probabilities or possibilities',[51] French J's award was not overturned. The Pagini contract would have been entered into but for the defendants' contraventions of section 52: 'Although, on the probabilities, it would not have been completed, there was a significant chance that it would be completed.'[52] French J discounted to allow for the probability that the agreement would not have proceeded, reaching a certain value of loss at a 40 per cent chance of contracting and a monetary value was according assigned.

The reasoning in *Sellars* refers to damages for the deprivation of a commercial opportunity by reason of a breach of contract, tort or contravention of section 52 of the *Trade Practices Act 1974* (Cth). As discussed below, the reasoning in both *BigTinCan* and *Hart Security* adopt the percentage-based probabilities approach identified in *Sellars* in quantifying equitable compensation for breach of fiduciary duty.[53]

In *BigTinCan*, in confirming the quantum of Ball J's award of equitable compensation (albeit via a reassessment),[54] Macfarlan JA for the majority held that the Court is required to consider 'not only BTC's [the principal's] prospects of obtaining funding, but also whether, if obtained, that funding would have been put to profitable use'.[55] Applying this principle, Macfarlan JA took into 'account the very significant business contingencies to which the prospect of deriving the anticipated profits was subject'.[56] His Honour did not specify what these contingencies were, but we may interpolate that they included the conduct of third parties who would be involved in 'exploitation of [BTC's] new technology',[57] including parties in the industry or considering entering the industry. Macfarlan JA, with whom McColl JA agreed, reassessed BTC's equitable compensation at $1,200,000 ((underlying value of lost chance) x 0.25 per cent (per cent chance of raising the funds + prospect of putting funds to profitable use, including discounting for business contingencies) = $300,000 equitable compensation).

[50] *Ibid.*
[51] *Ibid.*
[52] *Ibid.*
[53] *BigTinCan* (n 13) [70]–[72] (Macfarlan JA) (citing and applying *Sellars* (n 38)); *Hart Security* (n 13) [139]–[141] (Meagher JA) (citing and applying *Sellars* (n 38) with whom Bathurst CJ and Beazley P agreed).
[54] *BigTinCan* (n 13) [77] (Macfarlan JA).
[55] *Ibid* [72] (Macfarlan JA).
[56] *Ibid* [84] (Macfarlan JA).
[57] *Ibid* [80] (Macfarlan JA).

Gleeson JA in dissent also purported to follow *Sellars*,[58] but came to a different conclusion, reassessing equitable compensation at the lesser amount of $65,000. Unlike Macfarlan JA, Gleeson JA granulated the different contingencies to which BTC's ability to obtain projected future profits (which was said to be the 'profitable use' associated with the lost chance), all of which concerned the conduct of third parties.[59] In addition, Gleeson JA aligned the valuation of the lost opportunity with the value of the *profitable use itself*.[60] Taking the view that the evidence supported the conclusion that BTC's nominal *loss of profits* was $650,000,[61] Gleeson JA discounted 'this nominal loss to take into account the multiple, and to some degree, independent, contingencies affecting the possible outcome'.[62] Therefore, Gleeson JA reassessed equitable compensation at $650,000 ((underlying value of lost chance) x 10 per cent (prospects of success or of earning the profit, adopting a discount of 90 per cent) = $65,000). Gleeson JA therefore uniquely identified a different conceptual basis for the valuation of BTC's underlying lost commercial opportunity.

The Court in *Hart Security* similarly applied *Sellars* and required the principal HSA to establish the existence of the lost opportunity on a balance of probabilities and then establish that the lost opportunity 'had *some* value (not being a negligible value) … or which involved a "substantial, and not merely speculative" prospect of producing a benefit'.[63] However, although breach of fiduciary of duty was found,[64] in result HSA did not obtain equitable compensation.[65] It is not clear on the reasoning if this was because HSA failed to establish causation or whether the lost opportunity was too uncertain. The evidence indicated that the parties had reached an impasse: NTA insisted on a guarantee and there was no indication that Hart Cyprus would agree. HSA had not established on the balance of probabilities that it had '"lost" a valuable opportunity to negotiate a contract with NTA by reason of Mr Boucousis' conduct'.[66] Was the difficulty of proof that HSA could not demonstrate the link between the breach of fiduciary duty and the lost opportunity, or that the opportunity had some real value? Irrespective of whether the obstacle in *Hart Security* was causation or certainty of loss, the point is to observe that HSA was required to make certain its loss through the probabilistic mode of reasoning.

In applying the probabilistic approach outlined, I have previously argued that there is an important limit when using this method of making certain the principal's (or claimant's) lost opportunities which may be claimed following a breach of

[58] *Ibid* [125] (Gleeson JA).
[59] *Ibid* [126]–[138] (Gleeson JA).
[60] *Ibid* [134] (Gleeson JA).
[61] *Ibid* [138] (Gleeson JA).
[62] *Ibid* [139] (Gleeson JA).
[63] *Hart Security* (n 13) [141] (Meagher JA with whom Bathurst CJ and Beazley P agreed).
[64] *Ibid* [123] (Meagher JA).
[65] *Ibid* [171]–[172] (Meagher JA).
[66] *Ibid* [170] (Meagher JA).

fiduciary obligation. This limit is that in determining the nature and extent of the principal's lost opportunity, and therefore in making certain the lost opportunity, judicial reasoning should not discount the value of the lost opportunity for the risk that the *principal* would not have pursued it.[67] Consistently with the fiduciary's obligation not to put themselves in a position of conflict or possibility of conflict between duty and self-interest or conflicting duties owed to more than one principal and not to make a profit, the fiduciary has no escape route from liability by arguing that the opportunity was one which the principal was 'unwilling, unlikely or unable'[68] to pursue. Thus, for example, in *Boardman v Phipps*,[69] the solicitor to the trustees, Boardman, had to account for the profit he made on shares he acquired in Lester & Harris. The reasoning of the House of Lords rest on the observations that

> (1) the trustees could not have made any offer [for the shares] without the sanction of the court, as such shares were not an authorised investment [under the testamentary trust]; [and] (2) that Mr Fox [the 'active' trustee] said in evidence that he would not consider the trustees buying these shares under any circumstances.[70]

However, the inability of the trustee to purchase the shares made 'no difference to the liability of [Boardman], if liability otherwise exists'.[71] Unlike the position at law, in which a defendant would be permitted to raise an argument about whether the claimant would have taken up the lost opportunity in any case,[72] such arguments should not be available in making certain the lost opportunity caused by a breach of fiduciary obligation. This is because to do so permits an argument running contrary to the fiduciary obligation itself.

Therefore, in discounting the value of an opportunity lost as a result of a breach of fiduciary obligation, the hypothetical conduct of third parties may be included in the calculation. Thus, in *BigTinCan*, Macfarlan JA discounted for the 'significant business contingencies to which the prospect of deriving the anticipated profits was subject'[73] which must have included the third-party risk. This reasoning is most explicit in the judgment of Gleeson JA, who granulates the particular third-party factors, albeit that this discount is then applied to a different underlying value of the lost chance.[74]

[67] Degeling (n 42) 839 ff. See also S Degeling, 'Certainty in Calculating Monetary Remedies for Breach of Fiduciary Duty' in K Barker and R Grantham (eds), *Apportionment in Private Law* (Hart Publishing, 2019) 221, 230–39 which suggests a parallel inquiry into certainty, with the same limit to reasoning, in relation to hypothetical gains made by the fiduciary and the calculation of an account of profits.

[68] *Warman* (n 10) 558 (the Court).

[69] *Boardman* (n 3).

[70] *Ibid* 96 (Lord Cohen).

[71] *Ibid* 109 (Lord Hodson).

[72] *Heenan* (n 38) [29] (Giles JA).

[73] *BigTinCan* (n 13) [84] (Macfarlan JA).

[74] ie, for Gleeson JA, the base value of the lost chance was the financial return associated with the lost chance. Discussed above (n 59). *Ibid* [126]–[138] (Gleeson JA).

B. Equitable Discretion

Consistently with the position that equitable compensation is a discretionary equitable remedy, given to meet the plaintiff's equity for relief and fashioned to meet the circumstances and facts of the case, authority also establishes an approach to certainty in which the Court may 'be robust and do rough and ready justice without having to justify the amount of its award with any degree of precision'.[75] Therefore, rather than applying probabilistic reasoning, as explained by Ribeiro PJ in *Libertarian Investments Ltd v Hall* (quoting and adopting *Houghton v Immer (No 155) Pty Ltd* (1997) 44 NSWLR 46, 59 (Handley JA)) the Court may embed certainty within equitable discretion:

> [i]n my judgment the Court should assess the compensation in a robust manner, relying on the presumption against wrongdoers, the onus of proof, and resolving doubtful questions against the party 'whose actions have made an accurate determination so problematic'. See *LPJ Investments Pty Ltd v Howard Chia Investments Pty Ltd* (1990) 24 NSWLR 499 at 508.[76]

In *Libertarian*, the defaulting fiduciary (Hall) was required to pay equitable compensation to the principal (Woods/Libertarian). At the end of 2002, Hall and Woods embarked on a project of acquiring a substantial interest in an English Company called The Sporting Exchange (TSE) which was at the time not publicly listed but later listed on the London Stock Exchange. In order to fund this acquisition, €50 million and GBP5,949,994 was transferred from Woods and his companies, including Libertarian Investments Ltd (a company wholly owned by Woods), to a trust account established by Hall at his solicitors, Berwin Leighton Paisner (BLP) to be held for the benefit of Hall's company Axdale as client. Woods was unaware of this arrangement, believing the funds were being held by BLP for a client entity which was one of Wood's companies.

Hall transferred funds in and out of the BLP trust account without the authority of Woods. In October 2003, Hall withdrew GBP5,463,508.46, suggesting that these funds would be used to purchase 1,777,700 shares in TSE (the so-called 'third tranche') at GBP3.11 per share. This was a lie. Although Hall had falsely confirmed to Woods that he had used the funds to purchase the third tranche for Wood's benefit, Hall had in fact not purchased the shares and no explanation was given as to how the money was used.[77] Woods/Libertarian had an equity for relief against Hall for breach of fiduciary obligation. Libertarian's loss was said to be the lost opportunity to on-sell the third tranche of TSE shares, assuming that they had all along been purchased for Woods. This loss was hypothetical as it necessarily assumed a notional purchase date by Woods/Libertarian of the shares. Further, there was inherent uncertainty of valuation in the 'guesswork' and 'evidential'

[75] *Libertarian Investments Ltd v Hall* [2013] HKCFA 93, (2013) 16 HKCFAR 681 [174] (Millett NPJ).
[76] *Ibid* [138] (Ribeiro PJ). See also [123] (Ribeiro PJ), [174] (Millett NPJ).
[77] *Ibid* [30] (Ribeiro PJ).

gaps in ascribing a price a potential buyer would have been willing to pay for a hypothetical shareholding in TSE, especially considering, at the time of the hypothetical transactions more than 10 years prior, when the breaches occurred, there were many transactions affecting TSE's share register.

Taking the 'robust' approach described by Ribeiro PJ, Millett NPJ stated:

> Where the absence of evidence is the consequence of the fiduciary's own breach of duty the court is not without resource, for it can have resort to three principles. First, it may be able to take the fiduciary at his own word and use his falsehoods to establish the facts as if they were true even though they are known to be untrue. Secondly the court is entitled to make every assumption against the party whose conduct has deprived it of necessary evidence. And thirdly the court is entitled to be robust and do rough and ready justice without having to justify the amount of its award with any degree of precision.[78]

Accordingly, the Court was entitled to treat the fiduciary, Hall, as if he had purchased the third tranche, with a correlative assumption that Woods/Libertarian would have put the whole parcel of 1,777,700 shares up for sale, ultimately realising GBP18,970,565.54. Equitable compensation was ordered on this basis.[79] The Court made certain the value of Woods/Libertarian's lost opportunity to sell the shares by reference to the standards of conduct and conscience expected of Hall according to his fiduciary obligation.

III. Normative Accounts of Fiduciary Obligations

The discussion above sets out an understanding of the requirement that the principal's lost opportunity be a real loss, or productive of financial loss, according to the need to make certain the principal's hypothetical lost commercial opportunity. This section explores the implications of the requirement for various normative accounts of fiduciary obligations. In particular, those accounts which rest, at least in part, on the autonomy of the principal and equity's response in supervising those with the ability to make legally effective decisions affecting the principal. We may ask why, if it is the autonomy of the principal which is being protected via, for example, the no-conflict rule, it is that only lost opportunities

[78] *Ibid* [174] (Millett NPJ).

[79] In *Zhang Hong Li v DBS Bank (Hong Kong) Limited* [2019] HKCFA 45 the Hong Kong Court of Final Appeal considered *Libertarian* (n 75) in the context of the general principles relevant to the determination of equitable compensation for breach of trust and breach of fiduciary duty. At [115] the plurality (Riberio PJ, Fok PJ and Lord Neuberger NPJ) analysed the approach to equitable compensation by reference to the nature of the breach: (a) breaches leading directly to damage to or loss of the trust property; (b) breaches involving infidelity or disloyalty which engage the conscience of the fiduciary and (c) breaches involving a lack of skill and care. However, the Court did not consider the particular difficulties for a plaintiff wishing to obtain equitable compensation for a lost opportunity. At [136] (Cheung PJ) and [137] (Tang NPJ), Cheung and Tang agreed with the plurality.

which are themselves productive of financial losses may be recovered via equitable compensation? Does the requirement therefore challenge various normative and interpretive accounts of fiduciary obligations?

The short answer is that it does not. The requirement of financial loss must be understood in the particular fiduciary context. Loss is not an integer in demonstrating a breach of fiduciary obligation. Unlike, for example, the tort of negligence, where the claimant's action is not complete without proof of actual damage or injury,[80] the principal is not required to show loss in order to raise an equity for relief founded on the fiduciary's breach of fiduciary obligation. Rather, breach of fiduciary obligation arises on actual or potential conflict, such that the fiduciary must avoid a position of a conflict, or real or substantial possibility of conflict, between duties or between their self-interest and duty to the principal.[81] In addition, as stated in *Howard v Commissioner of Taxation*,[82] 'a fiduciary cannot profit from the relationship', which encompasses profits or other benefits obtained or received by reason or use of position.[83] Thus, in *BigTinCan*, the Court that found Ramsay had breached his fiduciary obligations in the conflict between his duty to BTC and his self interest in 'seeing BTC's attempts at raising capital fail and … in diverting whatever capital he could raise from BTC to [Newco]'.[84] Similarly, in Hart Security, the Court found that Boucousis had breached his fiduciary obligations to HSA, as there was an actual or substantial possibility of conflict between Boucousis' duty to HSA and his self-interest.[85] The proposed conflicted transaction would have given Boucousis a directorship, shareholding and employment in the ATMAAC group. In neither case was the principal required to demonstrate the real loss associated with the lost commercial opportunity in order to establish the fiduciary's breach of fiduciary obligation.

Therefore, the principal's equity for relief for breach of fiduciary obligation does not depend on finding that the lost opportunity is itself productive of financial loss.

[80] *Williams v Milotin* (1957) 97 CLR 465, 474 (the Court). A difficult question thereby arises, which is to determine what constitutes actionable damage for the purposes of the tort(s) of negligence. Clear examples (as in *Williams*) include personal injury. Psychiatric injury also qualifies as recoverable loss (*Tame v New South Wales* [2002] HCA 35, (2002) 211 CLR 317). However, the loss of an opportunity to obtain a better medical outcome (rather than the underlying physical injury) is *not* recognised as a relevant head of loss: see *Tabet v Gett* [2010] HCA 10, (2010) 240 CLR 537 [124] (Kiefel J) with whom Crennan J agreed at [100]. See also [68] where Hayne and Bell JJ agreed the lost chance of a better medical outcome should not be recognised as a form of actionable damage. Within confined limits, pure economic loss may also be recoverable. See generally S Sugarman, 'Damage' in P Vines and C Sappideen (eds), *Fleming's The Law of Torts*, 10th edn (Lawbook Co, 2011).

[81] *Commonwealth Bank of Australia v Smith* (n 2) 392 (the Court); *Breen* (n 1) 135 (Gummow J); *Birtchnell* (n 3) 408 (Dixon J); *Boardman* (n 3) 124 (Lord Upjohn); *Hospital Products* (n 3) 103 (Mason J); *Pilmer* (n 1) 199 (McHugh, Gummow, Hayne and Callinan JJ); *Australian Careers Institute* (n 3) [3]–[5] (Bathurst CJ), [132] (Sackville AJA with whom Meagher JA agreed).

[82] *Howard* (n 2) [62] (Hayne and Crennan JJ).

[83] *Ibid* [62]–[64] (Hayne and Crennan JJ). See also *Regal (Hastings)* (n 6) 143 (Lord Russell).

[84] *BigTinCan v Ramsay* [2013] NSWSC 1248 [80] (Ball J). On appeal, the fiduciary (Ramsay) did not challenge Ball J's finding of breach of fiduciary duty: *BigTinCan* (n 13) [52] (Macfarlan JA).

[85] *Hart Security* (n 13) [123] (Meagher JA).

The latter element is only required where the remedy sought, equitable compensation, is designed to meet *loss*. Thus, for example, other remedies such as rescission may be available to meet the principal's equity without requiring proof that the lost opportunity was itself productive of financial loss. Arguably, therefore, as discussed below, the requirement of financial loss does not undermine the autonomy accounts of fiduciary obligations. It is only when we elide breach with loss, and in error take the view that 'it does not matter whether the breaches were of common law, statutory or equitable duties',[86] that analysis may lead us in the opposite direction. The discussion below explores the requirement that the principal's lost commercial opportunity be productive of financial loss, or be a real loss, in the context of various accounts of fiduciary obligation.

A. Relational Account

Smith proposes what he describes as a 'relational theory' of fiduciary relationships as best explaining or interpreting the cases.[87] Smith's account starts by identifying the distinctive quality of the fiduciary relationship, which he identifies is that the fiduciary holds powers for and on behalf of another, and which therefore demands and explains the particular incidents equity attaches to that relationship.[88] Importantly, Smith emphasises that fiduciary relationships are bilateral. Consistently with this observation, he argues that the incidents of the relationship are 'not a means of enforcing some wider social policy or goal',[89] but are rather the law's means of giving effect to the bilateral relationship which exists between the parties.[90]

Thus, Smith argues that '[i]n every fiduciary relationship, the fiduciary acquires control over a part (or in some cases, all) *of* another person's autonomy'[91] and the requirement of loyalty 'is imposed to control decision-making power held for, or on behalf of, another person'.[92] The fiduciary obligation is one of loyalty and the prohibitions against profit and conflict are rules which support and complete the obligation of loyalty, rather than themselves being the fiduciary duty.[93] Pursuant to

[86] *BigTinCan* (n 13) [71] (Macfarlan JA).
[87] L Smith, 'Parenthood is a Fiduciary Relationship' (2020) 70 *University of Toronto Law Journal* 395.
[88] *Ibid.*
[89] *Ibid.*
[90] *Ibid.*
[91] Smith (n 6) 614 (emphasis added), noting also Smith states that 'autonomy itself cannot be transferred'.
[92] *Ibid.*
[93] *Ibid* 625. Smith argues that the no-conflict rules 'tell a fiduciary when judgment cannot be safely exercised in relation to a fiduciary power'. Breach of the no-conflict rules render a transaction, inter alia, voidable by the principal. The no-profit rule is explained at 628 as a rule of primary attribution pursuant to which profit obtained by the principal is attributed to the principal from the moment of acquisition. The no-conflict rule is thus about the vitiation of the principal's consent and the no-profit rule about the carrying out or enforcement of the principal's primary right to the profit. On this view, the no-profit rule (at 608) 'does not provide a remedy for wrongful conduct'.

this view, loyalty is an overarching concept which is required and determined by law,[94] whenever a person holds power over another and exercises judgment over their interests such that judgment must be exercised in what the fiduciary believes to be the best interests of the other.[95]

Smith's thesis therefore rests on the 'levers'[96] by which the autonomy of the principal is realised. Fiduciary loyalty is engaged where some power or discretion has been entrusted to the fiduciary such that 'the decision-maker [the fiduciary] holds the legal controls of part or all of the other person's autonomy'.[97] Smith describes autonomy as 'a person's ability to control what happens in his or her life',[98] it is the principal's 'choice making ability'.[99] Even in the more contentious category of adviser, in which we might conclude that the principal retains control of their levers of autonomy, since it is up to the principal whether to accept or reject the advice, Smith argues that a fiduciary relationship exists where the relationship is 'truly advisory'.[100] These instances are said to be where it is 'as if'[101] the adviser holds a factual power to transform the position of the principal, such that the law assimilates the factual power to a legal power.[102]

The requirement that the principal's lost commercial opportunity must be productive of financial loss in order to be met by equitable compensation is consistent with Smith's thesis. Returning to the facts of *Hart Security*, in virtue of his position as director of HSA, Boucousis held the power and authority to transform the legal and factual position of HSA. Boucousis held the 'levers' to realising HAS's autonomy. Therefore, Boucousis was bound by the requirement of fiduciary loyalty. The no-conflict rule constrained Boucousis in the exercise of his powers, and Boucousis' breach of fiduciary duty lay in the actual or substantial possibility of conflict between his duty to HSA and his self-interest.[103] Despite the fact that 'HSA had not proved that it had "lost" a valuable opportunity to negotiate a contract with NTA by reason of Boucousis' conduct',[104] the supervisory impact of the no-conflict rule arguably remained in the finding that Boucousis was in breach. Moreover, depending on the facts, other remedies may have been available. For example, had HSA discovered Boucousis' conduct early enough,

[94] *Ibid.* Although determined by law, the obligation of loyalty, on Smith's thesis, arises from the requirements of the relationship. It is not a function of the consent of the parties.
[95] *Ibid* 613, 616.
[96] *Ibid* 614.
[97] *Ibid* 614.
[98] *Ibid* 614.
[99] *Ibid* 628.
[100] *Ibid* 619.
[101] Smith (n 87), section IV C.
[102] *Ibid*, main text near fn reference 130. Therefore, it may be argued that doctrinal tests which determine whether or not an adviser client relationship is fiduciary are directed to determining the existence of this factual power, or 'as if' power is held by the adviser for the client. See, eg, *Daly v Sydney Stock Exchange* [1986] HCA 25, (1986) 160 CLR 371, 377 (Gibbs CJ), 385 (Brennan J).
[103] *Hart Security* (n 13) [123] (Meagher JA).
[104] *Ibid* [170] (Meagher JA).

Boucousis might possibly have been injuncted against breaching his fiduciary obligations. As stated by Mason J in *Hospital Products Ltd v United States Surgical Corporation*,[105] '[e]ach breach, had it been discovered in time, might have been restrained by injunction'. Further, a mere finding or declaration of breach of fiduciary itself arguably serves a vindicatory remedial function. As stated by the plurality of the High Court of Australia in *Maguire v Makaronis*:

> Equity intervenes, particularly where the fiduciary is a solicitor, not so much to recoup a loss suffered by the [principal] as to hold the fiduciary to, and vindicate, the high duty owed to the [principal].[106]

Finally, there remains the obvious point that if Boucousis had made a profit by reason or use of his fiduciary position, he would have been accountable for this profit.

B. Other Accounts of Fiduciary Obligations

The discussion below deals briefly with the undertakings theory of fiduciary obligations and the legitimate expectations account of Finn. As above, the requirement of a real loss on the part of the principal is consistent with these approaches.

The undertakings account holds that fiduciary obligations arise because of an undertaking by the putative fiduciary. The leading exponent of this approach is Edelman, who argues that the necessary but not sufficient condition for the existence of fiduciary obligations is that the conduct of the fiduciary 'has manifested an undertaking such that the principal is entitled, "in an objective sense, to expect that the other will act in his or their interests in and for the purposes of the relationship"'.[107] Fiduciary duties are terms which are expressed or implied into these 'manifested undertakings'.[108] Edelman argues that the same is true of status based fiduciaries, in which it is argued that the status or office held by a person is an important circumstance in determining the scope of obligations which the office-holder may reasonably be held to have undertaken.[109] Therefore, according to this theory, fiduciary obligations arise from, and give effect to, the fiduciary's undertaking, objectively construed.

Finn's scholarly work tells us that fiduciary obligations are recognised where the actual circumstances of a relationship demonstrate that 'one party is entitled

[105] *Hospital Products* (n 3)106 (Mason J) citing *In re Thomson* [1930] 1 Ch 203. See also *Pacifica Shipping Co Ltd v Andersen* [1986] 2 NZLR 328, 352 (Davison CJ).

[106] *Maguire* (n 2) 465 (Brennan CJ, Gaudron, McHugh and Gummow JJ).

[107] J Edelman, 'The Importance of the Fiduciary Undertaking' (2013) 7 *Journal of Equity* 128, 133 quoting *Red Hill Iron Ltd v API Management Pty Ltd* [2012] WASC 323 [361] itself quoting *News Ltd v Australian Rugby Football League Ltd* (1996) 64 FCR 410, 541.

[108] J Edelman, 'When Do Fiduciary Duties Arise?' (2010) 126 *LQR* 302, 316 and 326.

[109] J Edelman, 'The Role of Status in the Law of Obligations Common Callings, Implied Terms, and Lessons for Fiduciary Duties' in A Gold and P Miller (eds), *Philosophical Foundations of Fiduciary Law* (Oxford University Press, 2014) 21.

to expect that the other will act in his or her interests in and for the purposes of the relationship'.[110] These circumstances are said to be informed by considerations of public policy 'aimed at preserving the integrity and utility of such relationships given the expectation that the community is considered to have of behaviour in them, and given the purposes they serve in society'.[111]

Does the requirement that, to be met by an award of equitable compensation, the principal's lost commercial opportunity must have been productive of financial loss have any significance for these approaches? The answer is no. Consistent with the key observation that fiduciary analysis keeps separate questions of breach and loss, such that loss is not an integer in demonstrating breach of fiduciary obligation, the requirement of financial loss has no relevance for a theory that derives the source and content of the fiduciary relationship from the fiduciary's undertaking or the principal's legitimate expectation.

[110] P Finn, 'Fiduciary Reflections' (2014) 88(2) *Australian Law Journal* 127, 139. See also P Finn, 'The Fiduciary Principle' in TG Youdan (ed), *Equity, Fiduciaries and Trusts* (Carswell, 1989) 46.
[111] *Ibid.*

12

Lawful Act Duress: Part of the Solution to Problematic Banking Practices?

CLAUDIA CARR

I. Introduction

In 2019, the Royal Commission into Misconduct in the Banking, Superannuation and Financial Services Industry confirmed something long suspected: Australia's financial sector is rife with misconduct and problematic, predatory behaviour. The Commissioner's final report, submitted 1 February 2019 ('Report'),[1] lamented 'the pursuit of short-term profit at the expense of basic standards of honesty' and made 76 wide-ranging recommendations. Ultimately, the Commissioner considered that existing legislation was sufficient, but was not being adequately enforced.

The Royal Commission shows that banks and other financial services providers are too often exploiting, coercing and preying on consumers. The Commissioner's final Report made several recommendations as to how to remedy that state of affairs. Those recommendations have been criticised for their light touch and are predicted by some to be ineffective. Yet the need to address problematic conduct in this sphere is more important than ever in light of the challenges facing consumers of financial products in the twenty-first century, which has already seen a global financial crisis and recession in Australia and the United Kingdom.

While the legislature and relevant regulatory bodies certainly have key roles to play in fixing the problematic practices of financial institutions, the courts too must have a hand in addressing the issue. This is particularly so considering that the Australian Securities and Investments Commission ('ASIC'), in light of the Royal Commission, has adopted a 'why not litigate' approach to enforcement – meaning that once ASIC is satisfied that there is more likely than not to have been a breach of the law and the facts of the case show that litigation would be

[1] Royal Commission into Misconduct in the Banking, Superannuation and Financial Services Industry, 'Final Report' (Submitted to Governor-General of the Commonwealth of Australia on 1 February 2019 and tabled in Parliament on 4 February 2019), available at https://financialservices.royalcommission.gov.au/Pages/reports.html#final.

in the public interest, then ASIC will actively ask itself why it should not litigate the matter.[2] In order for this new enforcement approach to be effective, ASIC and other litigants must be armed with appropriate causes of action that address the conduct of banks.

In that context, this chapter considers the role that lawful act duress might play in addressing problematic banking practices. The doctrine, which has not yet been embraced by Australian courts, concerns lawful acts that nevertheless constitute duress. This chapter suggests that lawful act duress is well-suited to address problematic banking practices and should be accepted by courts and litigants as such. Aspects of the doctrine that have previously been criticised, such as its uncertainty, are precisely what make it flexible enough to address circumstances in which banks or other financial services providers are applying unacceptable pressure on customers or potential customers. In particular, the flexibility of the doctrine would assist in closing 'loopholes' which banks are so determined to find and exploit – problematic conduct has so often gone unpunished as it is technically within the bounds, but not the spirit, of the law, despite being clearly unfair. It is such scenarios that are likely to fall within the scope of lawful act duress, making the doctrine a useful tool for ASIC and others litigating against financial institutions.

Section II provides a brief overview of some of the problematic banking practices uncovered by the Royal Commission. Section III considers how those practices could be addressed through the application of the doctrine of lawful act duress. Section IV concludes that lawful act duress should form part of the courts' armoury when it comes to the misconduct of financial entities.

II. Problematic Banking Practices

Inequality of economic and bargaining power and differing levels of commercial sophistication are hallmark features of relationships between financial institutions and the majority of their consumers. Such circumstances make for ripe ground for lawful act duress. This chapter is primarily concerned with conduct and issues in respect of what the Report described as 'traditional banking services' – lending, deposit taking and the provision of transaction services.[3] Banks and bank-owned entities featured heavily in the Royal Commission in connection with, among other things, financial advice, lending, superannuation and insurance.

[2] Sean Hughes, 'ASIC's Approach to Enforcement After the Royal Commission' (Banking in the Spotlight: the 36th Annual Conference of the Banking and Financial Services Law Association, Gold Coast, Queensland, 30 August 2019), available at https://asic.gov.au/about-asic/news-centre/speeches/asic-s-approach-to-enforcement-after-the-royal-commission/.

[3] Final Report (n 1) 51.

Ultimately, the Royal Commission revealed systemic misconduct and the failure of the current regulatory regime.[4] The Commissioner made the following observations with respect to the financial services industry in Australia:[5]

1. In almost every case, the impugned conduct was driven by the entity's pursuit of profit and an individual's pursuit of gain. Financial services companies reward misconduct through incentives, bonuses and commission schemes.
2. 'Entities and individuals acted in the ways they did because they could … There was a marked imbalance of power and knowledge between those providing the product or service and those acquiring it'.[6]
3. Consumers often deal with financial services entities through an intermediary who is often paid by and may act in the interests of the financial services entity. The interests of the client and the intermediary are opposed.
4. Financial services entities that broke the law are often not held to account. It seems that entities do not believe that misconduct will be detected, denounced and justly punished.

With respect to lending, various issues were uncovered with respect to, for example, the use of mortgage brokers or other intermediaries. The Report noted that '[t]he intermediary may pass on information to the lender that is wrong; the intermediary may join forces with either the would-be borrower or with one or more employees of the lender to deceive the lender'.[7] The fact that a broker is paid only if a loan application succeeds motivates brokers to engage in misconduct in order to get would-be lenders to take out loans – as stated in the Report, 'payments by banks to intermediaries have induced some to engage in other forms of dishonest conduct'.[8]

Similar problems arise with 'vendor introducers' – retail dealers, such as car dealers, who are entitled to act as agents for lenders.[9] Many will be familiar with the pressure applied by car dealers at the point of potential sale. Misconduct is encouraged by the use of 'flex commissions', where the lender fixes a base rate of interest charged under the loan agreement. If the dealer can persuade the borrower to agree to pay a higher rate of interest, the dealer will receive a large part of the interest payable over and above the base rate. Before 1 November 2018, that conduct was not unlawful.[10] Most borrowers know little or nothing of these arrangements.[11]

[4] See D Russell, '2018 WA Lee Equity Lecture: Equity in an Age of Uncertainty' (2018) 18(2) *QUT Law Review* 137, 152.
[5] Final Report (n 1) 2.
[6] *Ibid.*
[7] *Ibid* 64.
[8] *Ibid* 65.
[9] *Ibid* 84.
[10] *ASIC Credit (Flexible Credit Cost Arrangements) Instrument 2017/780* (Cth).
[11] Final Report (n 1) 85.

The Report also identified issues that arise as a result of differing degrees of access to banking services:

> It is unsurprising that large entities, carrying on their businesses in all parts of Australia, apply the same policies and procedures whenever they can. But, as the Commission's inquiries showed, not all Australians can always resort to those standard policies and procedures. Not all Australians have the same access to telephone or internet banking. Not all Australians can 'step into the nearest branch' to sort out some issue that has emerged. Not all Australians have English as a first language or are as adept in using the English language as others. Not all Australians can easily produce standard identification records. Not all Australians need, or benefit from, 'standard offerings' like informal overdrafts.[12]

Many Australians who fall within one or more of these categories will live in regional or remote locations.[13] Often, those Australians will be most at risk of being harmed by problematic banking practices.

The Report pointed out that a financial adviser in Australia is something between a salesperson and a professional adviser,[14] going on to say that '[t]he industry has moved from scandal to scandal, causing financial harm to clients, and damaging public confidence in the value of financial advice'.[15] In particular, the Report notes the vertical integration of major backs and fund managers – during the late 1990s and early 2000s, each of the major banks acquired or merged with a fund manager.[16]

The Royal Commission uncovered an inordinate amount of problematic behaviour in the financial services industry. There are, indeed, too many to describe in detail in this chapter. The following, however, are examples that might be considered particularly relevant for present purposes:

- In a report concerning life insurance, ASIC found that 20 per cent of all policies taken out between 2012 and 2017 were cancelled during the cooling-off period. ASIC's view is that this may mean that 'customers had immediately realized they had made a bad decision *or had been pressured into buying a policy they did not need*'.[17]
- Several issues were identified in respect of inappropriate sales practices used when dealing with Aboriginal and Torres Strait Islander customers, particularly misrepresentations and pressure selling tactics.[18]

[12] *Ibid* 88–89.
[13] *Ibid* 89.
[14] *Ibid* 120.
[15] *Ibid*.
[16] *Ibid* 124–25.
[17] *Ibid* 281 (emphasis added).
[18] Royal Commission into Misconduct in the Banking, Superannuation and Financial Services Industry, 'Interim Report' (Submitted to the Governor-General of the Commonwealth of Australia on 28 September 2018 and tabled in Parliament on 28 September 2018) 262.

- In one case study, it was found that an insurance company trained sales agents to engage in unfair sales practices, including through aggressive objection handling approaches.[19]
- Several issues were identified in respect of parental guarantors. Even where parents received legal advice, they often did not understand the details of the financial arrangement to which they agreed and had a limited recollection of the circumstances surrounding the signing of the guarantee.[20]
- Several instances of financial services entities applying unfair pressure to borrowers were uncovered.[21]

The findings of the Royal Commission made it clear that the laws and regulations in place in Australia have not been robust enough to protect consumers from the predatory behaviour of financial services industries. It remains to be seen whether the recommendations of the Royal Commission will be enough to deter, prevent and punish future misconduct.

The Report has been criticised for making relatively conservative recommendations. While it was recommended that there be certain changes or additions to the law,[22] none of the suggested changes are particularly dramatic or significant. In many areas, the Report did not recommend any changes to rules. Immediately after the handing down of the Report, news articles appeared, accusing it of 'holding back'.[23] In one article in particular, Long describes Commissioner Hayne as having 'squibbed' the Report, calling the 'mild recommendations for change' as 'striking'.[24] There were obvious remedies that the Report side-stepped. Vertical integration was a contributing cause to much of the misconduct considered in the Report, but with respect to remedies, enforced structural separation of financial services entities was not even contemplated.

The approach taken in the Report was evidently a cause for relief on the part of the banks – if more evidence were needed to show that the Report let banks off easily in terms of remedies for consumers, share prices surged the day after the Report was handed down. Financial stocks had their best day in nearly a decade after a leading analyst described the Report as 'a clear win for the banks'.[25] Bankers themselves criticised the Report – a UBS analyst described the final recommendations as falling well short of market expectations, saying that

[19] Final Report (n 1) Vol 2, Case Studies, 296.
[20] Interim Report (n 18) Vol 2, Case Studies, 264.
[21] See, eg, *ibid* Vol 2, Case Studies, 313.
[22] Final Report (n 1) 49–50.
[23] See, eg, S Long, 'Kenneth Hayne's Final Royal Commission Report Held Back "Heavy Hits" from the Banks' (*ABC*, 26 February 2019), available at www.abc.net.au/news/2019-02-26/hayne-banking-royal-commission-squib/10832620.
[24] *Ibid.*
[25] M Janda, 'Banks Win from "Disappointing" Royal Commission Report, Shares Surge' (5 February 2019), available at www.abc.net.au/news/2019-02-05/banks-win-from-disappointing-royal-commission-report/10781288.

'we do not believe that any of the 76 recommendations by themselves will have a material financial impact on the banks'.[26] Of course, the purpose of the Royal Commission was never to impose pecuniary punishment directly or indirectly on banks; ultimately, the goal should be consumer protection. Yet one might wonder why the Report would have no material financial impact on banks when it is now known that banks' profits have, in many instances, been inflated by the fruits of misconduct.

A notable feature of the Report is its failure to recommend changes to lending processes. The cases considered later in this chapter in which banks have applied unfair pressure to consumers primarily concern lending. However, the Report made no recommendations of change to the responsible lending laws. Addressing the misconduct of the financial services industry with respect to lending is particularly important during times of crisis, such as the global financial crisis and the COVID-19 pandemic. Society is especially reliant on banks acting properly in times of crisis. Inequality of economic power makes lawful act duress possible;[27] such inequality has been, and will continue to be, increasingly prevalent in the context of the rise of the multinational enterprise.[28]

The Report found that regulators are lacking in effectiveness. The recommendations made 'seek to improve the effectiveness of the regulators in deterring misconduct and ensuring that there are just and appropriate consequences for misconduct'.[29] One of the main remedies relied on by the Report in that respect is self-regulation. This is peculiar, to say the least, given that the Report contains ample evidence that Australia's financial services industry is largely incapable of, or unwilling to, self-regulate. The Interim Report stated that:

> When misconduct was revealed, it either went unpunished or the consequences did not meet the seriousness of what had been done. The conduct regulator, ASIC, rarely went to court to seek public denunciation of and punishment for misconduct. The prudential regulator, APRA, never went to court. Much more often than not, when misconduct was revealed, little happened beyond apology from the entity, a drawn out remediation program and protracted negotiation with ASIC of a media release, an infringement notice, or an enforceable undertaking that acknowledged no more than that ASIC had reasonable 'concerns' about the entity's conduct. Infringement notices imposed penalties that were immaterial for the large banks. Enforceable undertakings might require a 'community benefit payment', but the amount was far less than the penalty that ASIC could properly have asked a court to impose.[30]

[26] *Ibid*.
[27] C Carr, 'Lawful Act Duress in Australia' (2020) 13 *Journal of Equity* 292, 294.
[28] See, eg, R Blanco, 'Reconsidering the Self-Regulatory Approach to Corporate Social Responsibility' (2017) 35 *Companies and Securities Law Journal* 7, 8–9; G Nettle, 'The Changing Position and Duties of Company Directors' (2018) 41 *Melbourne University Law Review* 140; Interim Report (n 18).
[29] Final Report (n 1) 46.
[30] Interim Report (n 18).

Given those damning findings, it is naïve to think that the problematic behaviour uncovered by the Royal Commission will be improved or solved by self-regulation. Ultimately, it will be ASIC and hard law that forces the industry to change.

III. Addressing the Issue through Lawful Act Duress

A. The Nature and Development of Lawful Act Duress and Duress as a Tort

Duress has two elements: (1) pressure amounting to compulsion of the will; and (2) illegitimacy of the pressure exerted.[31] Contracts procured by duress are rendered voidable. It is well-established that unlawful threats and actions are illegitimate for the purposes of duress.[32] However, whether lawful threats and actions can be illegitimate is not yet settled in Australia.[33] The term 'lawful act duress' was coined by Steyn LJ in *CTN Cash and Carry Ltd v Gallaher Ltd* and refers to lawful acts constituting duress.[34]

In *Thorne v Kennedy*, the plurality of the High Court described the question of whether lawful threats or conduct might constitute duress as one 'which has chiefly arrested the modern development of the law of duress'.[35] A detailed examination of the historical treatment of lawful act duress has been carried out elsewhere and is beyond the scope of this chapter. Suffice it to say that in *Thorne v Kennedy* the plurality declined to clarify the Australian position on lawful act duress.[36] However, in a separate judgment, Nettle J said he would have found lawful act duress to be present but for the decision in *Karam*.[37] His Honour said he could not depart from *Karam* without detailed submissions, which he did not have in *Thorne*.[38] I have made a detailed argument in favour of the acceptance

[31] *Universe Tankships Inc of Monrovia v International Transport Workers Federation* [1983] 1 AC 366 (HL) 400 (Lord Scarman) ('*The Universe Sentinel*'); *McIntyre v Nemesis DBK Ltd* [2009] NZCA 329, [2010] 1 NZLR 463; *Crescendo Management Pty Ltd v Westpac Banking Corp* (1988) 19 NSWLR 40, 45 (McHugh JA, Samuels and Mahoney JJA agreeing); *Electricity Generation Corp v Woodside Energy Ltd* [2013] WASCA 36 [24] (McLure P, Newnes JA agreeing); *Doggett v Commonwealth Bank of Australia* [2015] VSCA 351, (2015) 47 VR 302 [73] (Whelan JA, Garde AJA agreeing) (Doggett).

[32] *Beerens v Bluescope Distribution Pty Ltd* [2012] VSCA 209, (2012) 39 VR 1 [145] (Tate JA, Redlich JA agreeing); *Crescendo Management* (n 31) 46 (McHugh JA); *Ford Motor Co of Australia Ltd v Arrowcrest Group Pty Ltd* [2003] FCAFC 313, (2003) 134 FCR 522; J Edelman and E Bant, *Unjust Enrichment*, 2nd edn (Hart Publishing 2016) 212.

[33] See *Australia and New Zealand Banking Group Ltd v Karam* [2005] NSWCA 344, (2005) 64 NSWLR 149 ('*Karam*'); *Tsarouhi v Tsarouhi* [2009] FMCAfam 126; *Thorne v Kennedy* [2017] HCA 49, (2017) 350 ALR 1, [70]–[73] (Nettle J).

[34] *CTN Cash and Carry Ltd v Gallaher Ltd* [1994] 4 All ER 714 (CA) 718 (Steyn LJ).

[35] *Thorne v Kennedy* (n 33) [27].

[36] *Ibid* [29].

[37] *Ibid* [70].

[38] *Ibid* [73].

of lawful act duress elsewhere.[39] This chapter argues that lawful act duress is well-suited to addressing the problematic banking practices uncovered by the Royal Commission.

There is some controversy as to whether duress is a tort.[40] There is dicta to the effect that while in some circumstances duress may be actionable as a tort, but it is not a tort per se, nor does conduct need to be tortious to constitute duress.[41] Arguably, the nature of duress is that an ultimatum threatening wrongful harm wrongfully deprives the victim of his or her ability to choose. Beever posits that, with respect to economic torts, '[t]he *wrong* is not the causing of the loss, it is *coercion*'.[42] The wrongdoing with which lawful act duress is concerned is the coercion of the plaintiff by the defendant.

It is worth considering whether those deeply concerned with legal taxonomy might be more comfortable with the concept of lawful act duress if it went by a different name. Bowley notes the very expression 'lawful act duress' poses conceptual difficulties and, expounding an understanding of economic duress, identifies what he refers to as the 'tort of malicious bargaining, a form of interpersonal wrongdoing which … arises from the harmful application of illegitimate pressure'.[43] Since the concept of lawful act duress began to emerge, the doctrine has been conceptualised as a broadening of duress.[44] Bowley argues that 'an explanation for the doctrine of duress that focusses on illegitimate pressure unjustifiably attaches a contract law remedy, voidability, to tortious conduct'.[45] He posits that there are two types of economic duress cases: (1) 'Brigand Cases', which involve 'your money or your life' ultimatums and have been recognised as constituting duress for centuries; and (2) 'Monopolist Cases', which is what Bowley calls cases that are usually recognised as lawful act duress cases. Bowley describes lawful act duress as 'the illegitimate imposition of a choice between two losses, neither of which would itself be a tortious loss'.[46]

Bowley describes lawful act duress cases as involving a legal phenomenon distinct from duress in the sense of Brigand Cases, being a 'wrongfully imposed

[39] Carr (n 27) 294.

[40] See, eg, *Berezovsky v Abramovich* [2010] EWHC 647 (Comm) [191] (Sir Anthony Colman); *The Universe Sentinel* (n 31) 385 (Lord Diplock), 400 (Lord Scarman); *Dimskal Shipping Co SA v International Transport Workers Federation (No 2)* [1992] 2AC 152 (HL) 169 (Lord Goff) ('*The Evia Luck (No 2)*'); *Nehayan v Kent* [2018] EWHC 333 (Comm) [224] (Leggatt LJ); *Investec Bank (Channel Islands) Ltd v The Retail Group Plc* [2009] EWHC 476 (Ch) [122] (Sales J); J Dietrich, 'Lawful Coercive Threats and the Infliction of Harm' (2000) 8 TLJ 187; J Murphy, 'Duress as a Tort Law Defence?' (2018) 38 *Legal Studies* 571.

[41] *Berezovsky* (n 40) [191] (Sir Anthony Colman J); *The Universe Sentinel* (n 31) 385, 400 (Lord Scarman); *The Evia Luck (No 2)* (n 40) 169 (Lord Goff); *Nehayan* (n 40) [224] (Leggatt LJ); *Investec Bank (Channel Islands) Ltd v The Retail Group plc* [2009] EWHC 476 (Ch) [122] (Sales J); Dietrich (n 40).

[42] A Beever, *A Theory of Tort Liability* (Hart Publishing, 2016) 124 (emphasis added).

[43] G Bowley, '"You Leave Me (Almost) No Choice": Duress in Contract and the Tort of Malicious Bargaining' (2019) 36 *Journal of Contract Law* 22, 22.

[44] *Ibid.*

[45] *Ibid.*

[46] *Ibid* 23.

choice'.[47] As a result, he says that lawful act duress is fundamentally a tortious legal concept, as it identifies deficient interpersonal conduct.[48] One of the key consequences of conceptualising lawful act duress in such a way is that lawful act duress would not identify circumstances in which contractual obligations have been created or should be discharged. Thus, the well-accepted result of voidability for duress would fall away in lawful act duress cases – to produce that result 'would be well beyond the ordinary scope of any tort doctrine'.[49]

The view that duress is actionable as a tort is not a new one. In *The Universe Sentinel*, Lord Scarman stated:

> It is, I think, already established law that economic pressure can in law amount to duress; and that duress, if proved, not only renders voidable a transaction into which a person has entered under its compulsion but is actionable as a tort, if it causes damage or loss: Barton v Armstrong [1976] AC 104 and Pao On v Lau Yiu Long [1980] AC 614. The authorities upon which these two cases were based reveal two elements in the wrong of duress: (1) pressure amounting to compulsion of the will of the victim; and (2) the illegitimacy of the pressure exerted.[50]

It might be said that lawful act duress currently conflates contract, tort and equity. Whether conduct is wrongful is determined, in some ways, through the employment of equitable concepts; the identification of wrongful or tortious conduct is then seen to affect the existence of contractual rights and remedies. Bowley's view is that lawful act duress cases can only be properly analysed from the perspective of tort – he states that lawful act duress 'can only be coherently thought of as a tort doctrine that has been, for the last four decades, masquerading as a doctrine of contract law'.[51]

Bowley therefore refers to lawful act duress as the tort of malicious bargaining. Bowley characterises it as arising where there is a causal link between illegitimate pressure applied and harm alleged to have been suffered as a result.[52] The rationale given for distinguishing between traditional duress and a 'new' tort of malicious bargaining (which would really be lawful act duress rebranded) is that it would allow 'both categories of conduct to retain some measure of internal coherence and justifiability, neither of which has been a notable feature of economic duress jurisprudence'.[53]

It should be accepted that lawful act duress, at least in the contexts contemplated by this chapter, involves the wrongful application of economic pressure. For the purposes of this chapter, it is not necessary to determine whether lawful

[47] *Ibid.*
[48] *Ibid* 24.
[49] *Ibid.*
[50] *The Universe Sentinel* (n 31).
[51] *Ibid* 24–25.
[52] *Ibid.*
[53] *Ibid.*

act duress ought to be characterised as a tort that can only result in tortious liability, a contract law doctrine that can affect contractual rights and liabilities, an equitable doctrine that can affect contractual rights and liabilities, or a hybrid that fits within two or all three of those categories. While Bowley rightly notes that economic duress jurisprudence lacks coherence, this is arguably a result of conflicting decisions concerning the existence of a doctrine of lawful act duress and inconsistent use of language,[54] rather than a lack of justifiability. Perhaps it is most useful to accept that, as espoused by Lord Diplock and Lord Scarman, the form that duress takes may, or may not, be tortious.[55] Whether lawful act duress results in tortious liability or the voidability of a contract, it is capable of providing redress in circumstances where financial institutions have exerted illegitimate pressure on a customer.

B. The Adoption of Lawful Act Duress is Comparatively Simple

Addressing the issues identified above through the adoption of the doctrine of lawful act duress would be consistent with the Report's view that change should be made carefully and simply and that adding a new layer of regulation will not assist.[56] It is unlikely that any comparable legislative reform will be introduced in the foreseeable future, making it all the more necessary for courts to be well-equipped to deal with misconduct in this sphere – particularly in circumstances where ASIC has been encouraged to litigate more often. Further, as stated in the Report, legislative simplification can be a long and difficult task.[57] Embracing a known general law doctrine is a much simpler, quicker method of addressing misconduct. The Report sets out several reasons for not recommending dramatic legislative change.[58]

The Report states that '[t]he more complicated the law, the harder it is to see unifying and informing principles and purposes … boundary-marking and categorisation may promote uncertainty'.[59] I have made the point elsewhere that, given the current uncertainty as to the status of lawful act duress, it is not possible to ascertain with certainty whether one has applied illegitimate pressure to a person.[60]

[54] Eg, the term 'economic duress' is sometimes used to describe lawful act duress, but lawful act duress and economic duress are not the same. While a lawful threat may be applied against a person's economic wellbeing, it is not limited to that scenario. A lawful threat might also be applied, for example, against a person's emotional wellbeing. While economic duress might involve a lawful threat against a person's economic wellbeing, it might also involve an unlawful threat. For that reason, arguably, the term economic duress merely serves to identify the type of harm a threat is posed to cause and is of little use.

[55] *The Universe Sentinel* (n 31) 385 (Lord Diplock), 400 (Lord Scarman).

[56] Final Report (n 1) 16, 43–44.

[57] *Ibid* 16.

[58] *Ibid* 16–19.

[59] *Ibid* 44.

[60] See Carr (n 27).

The unequivocal adoption of lawful act duress would introduce further certainty for both financial entities and consumers – in particular, it would set out clearer guidelines for financial entities as to acceptable levels of pressure.

The field covered by lawful act duress is not wholly covered by any other doctrine or statutory provision. In particular, lawful act duress may be necessary to address circumstances that do not fall within the scope of undue influence or unconscionable conduct. This is particularly relevant to problematic banking practices – banks' misconduct may not be captured by undue influence as there may not clearly be a relationship between the parties where the bank has assumed a position of dominance.[61] Whereas undue influence is concerned with whether advantage was taken of a position of dominance in a relationship, duress focuses on the nature of pressure applied.[62] As a result, duress may be better suited to actions against banks, where the bank may not be in a position of 'dominance' per se (particularly where the plaintiff is a sophisticated corporate entity or individual), but nevertheless has exerted pressure on the plaintiff that should properly be considered unjust or unconscionable.

Misconduct will fall outside the scope of unconscionable conduct if the plaintiff is not subject to a 'special disadvantage'. Duress does not require impaired judgmental capacity; a person might be well aware that entering into a transaction is not in his or her best interests but nevertheless accede to a demand due to pressure. While a person subjected to lawful act duress may also be subject to a special disadvantage, that will not always be the case.[63] The term 'special disadvantage', as it is used in the context of the doctrine of unconscionable conduct, is unlikely to encompass most scenarios in which lawful act duress may be engaged. Unconscionable conduct will generally not be made out in circumstances of 'market exploitation in relation to volitional disabilities such as "pressing need", financial or otherwise'.[64] Those 'volitional disabilities' are precisely the kind of factors which give rise to a vulnerability to predatory banking practices. Duress is thus well-suited to this context.[65]

Lawful act duress is also not currently covered by statutory provisions. The *Contracts Review Act 1980* (NSW) ('CRA') permits courts to grant relief in respect of 'unjust' contracts. Where a court finds a contract or contractual provision to be 'unjust', it can grant various forms of relief to avoid 'as far as practicable an unjust consequence or result'.[66] Section 9(2) lists non-exhaustive matters to which a court

[61] *Johnson v Buttress* [1936] HCA 41, (1936) 56 CLR 113 (HC), 134 (Dixon J); JD Heydon, MJ Leeming and PG Turner, *Meagher, Gummow & Lehane's Equity: Doctrines & Remedies*, 5th edn (LexisNexis Butterworths, 2015) 492–93 [15-105].

[62] NC Seddon and RA Bigwood, *Cheshire & Fifoot: Law of Contract*, 11th Australian edn (LexisNexis Butterworths, 2017) 794, [14.1].

[63] See further R Bigwood, 'Throwing the Baby out with the Bathwater? Four Questions on the Demise of Lawful-Act Duress in New South Wales' (2008) 27(2) *University of Queensland Law Journal* 41, 75.

[64] *Ibid* 83.

[65] GE Dal Pont, *Equity and Trusts in Australia*, 6th edn (Lawbook, 2015) 313 [9.45].

[66] *Contracts Review Act 1980* (NSW) s 7.

may have regard in determining whether such relief should be granted, including whether the contractual provisions impose conditions that are not reasonably necessary for the protection of the legitimate interests of any party to the contract. However, the legislation only applies to contracts if the proper law of the contract is that of New South Wales.[67] Other Australian states and territories do not have parallel legislation. Relief under the CRA is also subject to statutory limitation periods different to those that would apply to a lawful act duress claim.[68] There are no statutory provisions that cover the field in the same way as lawful act duress.

At the federal level (and adopted by all states and territories), parts 2–3 of the Australian Consumer Law[69] provides protection from unfair contract terms by rendering such terms void.[70] A term will be 'unfair' where it:

(1) would cause a significant imbalance in the parties' rights and obligations under the contract;
(2) is not reasonably necessary to protect the legitimate interests of the party advantaged by it; and
(3) would cause detriment to a party if it was to be applied or relied upon.[71]

However, this protection only applies to consumer contracts and small business contracts.[72] 'Consumer contracts' are defined as contracts for the supply of goods or services or a sale or grant of an interest in land to an individual whose acquisition of the goods, services or interest is wholly or predominantly for personal, domestic or household use or consumption.[73] The fair trading legislation at state level that supplements the Australian Consumer Law is subject to the same limitations.[74] As a result, those legislative provisions are not capable of covering the field in the same way as lawful act duress.

Section 12DJ of the *Australian Securities and Investments Commission Act 2001* (Cth) ('ASIC Act') provides that a person may not use physical force or undue harassment or coercion in connection with the supply or possible supply of financial services to a consumer or the payment for financial services by a consumer. While that provision may overlap with lawful act duress, it nonetheless differs in a number of respects. First, the elements and formulation are different; section 12DJ does not utilise the test of disproportionality. Most potential lawful act duress cases, in the context of the behaviour contemplated by the Royal Commission, will not involve physical force, nor will they necessarily involve undue harassment or coercion (though they might). Second, the few cases that deal with section 12DJ

[67] *Ibid* s 17(3).
[68] *Ibid* s 16.
[69] *Competition and Consumer Act 2010* (Cth) sch 2 ('Australian Consumer Law').
[70] *Ibid* s 23.
[71] *Ibid* s 24.
[72] *Ibid* s 23.
[73] *Ibid* s 23(3).
[74] See, eg, *Fair Trading Act 2010* (WA) pt 2–3.

generally concern the misconduct of debt collectors.[75] In the context of the section, 'undue harassment' has been interpreted in a way that diverges from lawful act duress, being 'persistent disturbance or torment' or conduct where 'the frequency, nature or content of such communications is such that they are calculated to intimidate or demoralise, tire out or exhaust a debtor'.[76] Similarly, the word 'coercion' has been understood particularly narrowly in the context of section 12DJ; for example, in *ACCC v Excite Mobile Pty Ltd* coercion was found where a company created a fictitious complaints handling body and a fictitious debt collection agency in order to obtain payment from a debtor.[77] While these elements may be present in cases of lawful act duress, they are not necessary. There is a clear pattern of section 12DJ only being relied upon and engaged in cases involving conduct that is relatively extreme in nature.[78] As a result, section 12DJ is considerably narrower in scope than lawful act duress.

Section 12CB of the ASIC Act provides that a person must not, in trade or commerce, in connection with the supply or possible supply of financial services to a person or the acquisition or possible acquisition of financial services from a person, engage in conduct that is, in all the circumstances, unconscionable. This section, too, is arguably incapable of fulfilling the role that lawful act duress would play. The concept of statutory unconscionability has proven unwieldy; the inquiry is broad and value-laden.[79] In particular, section 12CB has been narrowly interpreted by the High Court.[80] In *ASIC v Kobelt*, Gageler J described 'unconscionable conduct' as 'conduct proscribed by the section as unconscionable is conduct that is so far outside societal norms of acceptable commercial behaviour as to warrant condemnation as conduct that is offensive to conscience'.[81] The reference to societal norms of 'commercial behaviour' is critical – currently, as shown by the Royal Commission, misconduct and conduct that is offensive to conscience too often *is* the norm of commercial behaviour. The meaning that has been given to section 12CB unconscionability is unduly restrictive in a way that lawful act duress is not. Indeed, the minority decisions in *ASIC v Kobelt* characterised the majority interpretation of unconscionability under section 12CB as narrow and restrictive.[82]

[75] See, eg, *ASIC v Accounts Control Management Services Pty Ltd* [2012] FCA 1164 (where the conduct of debt collectors that Perram J found to be in breach of s 12DJ involved, among other things, threats to humiliate debtors by sharing the fact of the debtor's indebtedness with friends, family, employers and colleagues); *ACCC v Davis* [2003] FCA 1227; *ACCC v Capalaba Pty Ltd* [2003] FCA 1226 (where the conduct in breach of s 12DJ involved the violent physical holding of the debtor to the ground).

[76] *ACCC v Maritime Union of Australia* [2001] FCA 1549 [60].

[77] *ACCC v Excite Mobile Pty Ltd* [2013] FCA 350.

[78] Perhaps as a result of this, only 17 cases to date contemplate s 12DJ and the section has received little attention from appellate courts.

[79] See, eg, *Commonwealth Bank of Australia v Kojic* (2016) 249 FCR 421, 434–37 [55]–[60] (Allsop CJ).

[80] In particular, see *Australian Securities and Investments Commission v Kobelt* [2019] HCA 18, (2019) 93 ALR 743. *Cf* the minority decision in that case, which took a view of the provision more closely aligned with lawful act duress.

[81] *Ibid* [92].

[82] *Ibid* [247] (Nettle and Gordon JJ) [311] (Edelman J).

Further, unconscionability is not the key or only consideration in relation to lawful act duress; the relevant inquiry is broader in scope and more flexible.

Given that Australia's current legal and regulatory regime is clearly ill-equipped to deal with problematic banking practices, more needs to be done to protect the community from financial services entities that may exert improper pressure for profit. This chapter suggests that lawful act duress, while not a complete answer to the problems in this sphere, should comprise part of the courts' armoury when it comes to dealing with problematic banking practices.

C. Lawful Act Duress in the Context of the Conduct of Financial Services Entities

i. Example Cases

The fact that a threat is lawful does not necessarily make the pressure legitimate.[83] The following section considers conduct on the part of financial services entities that may amount to lawful act duress. Doing so illustrates the types of cases in which lawful act duress might be made out.

The case in which the New South Wales Court of Appeal rejected the doctrine of lawful act duress, *Karam*, concerned a problematic banking practice of the precise type that lawful act duress is apt to address. The case concerned the provision by the Australia and New Zealand Banking Group ('ANZ') of financial accommodation to a family business over several years. ANZ took various securities from the company and its directors, including what was described as 'unlimited guarantees' from four members of the family operating the business: two brothers and their spouses. The company subsequently failed. ANZ sought to recover the company's debt from the personal assets of the brothers and their spouses. The Karams commenced proceedings against ANZ, seeking that the securities given to the bank be set aside for, among other things, duress.

At first instance, Santow J held that the security documents were vitiated 'by unconscionability or illegitimate pressure amounting to duress'.[84] Particularly salient was the fact that ANZ, while putting 'maximum pressure' on the Karams to sign acknowledgments pertaining to securities given many years ago, failed to provide the original security documents to the Karams' solicitor and thus rendered the independent advice received inadequate.[85] Further, the enormous pressure placed on the Karams by the bank was calculated to prevent the Karams from disclosing to their solicitor the original circumstances in which the securities documents were

[83] That same position was taken by the Privy Council in *R v A-G (England and Wales)* [2003] UKPC 22, [2004] 1 LRC 132 [16]. *Cf Karam* (n 33).

[84] *Karam v Australia & New Zealand Banking Group Ltd* [2001] NSWSC 709 [218], [389], [399].

[85] *Ibid* [373]–[374].

signed.[86] Santow J said that the 'illegitimacy' of the lawful pressure exerted derived from the bank's unconscionable exploitation of the known financial vulnerability of the company and the Karams.[87]

The Court of Appeal reversed Santow J's decision, holding that ANZ was entitled to recover the company's debt from the Karams. The Court said the way in which lawful act duress fits in with unconscionable conduct and undue influence is unclear, and that concepts of illegitimate pressure and unconscionability, where not referring to equitable principles, lack clarity.[88] Ultimately, the Court considered that lawful act duress and the terms 'economic duress' and 'illegitimate pressure' should be abandoned altogether in favour of relying on unconscionable conduct and undue influence.[89] The Court stated that the only three categories of lawful threats that might constitute duress are:

1) threats made maliciously, without any interest in the outcome;
2) threats made in the context of a protected relationship (ie, a fiduciary relationship); and
3) threats made in a public law context where principles of fairness and rationality apply.[90]

The Court considered that, rather than accepting any doctrine of lawful act duress, 'the principled approach is to adopt equitable principles relating to unconscionability' by pursuing a claim for undue influence or unconscionable conduct.[91] It was said that the vagueness of the terms 'economic duress' and 'illegitimate pressure' could be avoided by treating the concept of duress as limited to threatened or actual unlawful conduct.[92]

A more flexible approach, and one that would have been able to relieve the Karams of their obligations to ANZ, was set out in *Crescendo Management Pty Ltd v Westpac Banking Corp*:

> The proper approach in my opinion is to ask whether any applied pressure induced the victim to enter into the contract and then ask whether that pressure went beyond what the law is prepared to countenance as legitimate?[93]

More recently, in *Morgan Stanley Wealth Management Australia Pty Ltd v Detata (No 3)*, Banks-Smith J applied the 'test of disproportionality' to determine whether lawful pressure was illegitimate.[94] Noting that the impugned conduct

[86] *Ibid* [374].
[87] *Ibid* [93].
[88] *Ibid* [166].
[89] *Ibid* [166].
[90] *Ibid*, citing Keith Mason and JW Carter, *Restitution Law in Australia* (LexisNexis Butterworths, 1995) 184, para 540.
[91] *Ibid* [167].
[92] *Ibid* [66].
[93] *Crescendo Management* (n 31) 46 (McHugh JA).
[94] *Morgan Stanley Wealth Management Australia Pty Ltd v Detata (No 3)* [2018] WASC 32.

was not unlawful, her Honour reasoned that it was 'not a case of there being no reasonable or justifiable connection between the pressure allegedly being applied and the demand which that pressure supports'.[95] The test of disproportionality, which asks whether the impugned lawful threat is proportionate to the defendant's legitimate interest in the subject of the threat, is arguably an appropriate mechanism for determining whether the threat is one that the law is prepared to countenance as legitimate. McLure P succinctly stated the test in *Verve*: '[i]f the pressure is lawful, it may be illegitimate if there is no reasonable or justifiable connection between the pressure being applied and the demand which that pressure supports'.[96] In this way, lawful act duress is capable of restraining financial services entities from applying illegitimate pressure to consumers.

Perhaps one of the most important reasons for using lawful act duress to address problematic banking practices is to reduce the number of loopholes available to financial services entities. Problematic banking practices are not always unlawful. For example, the Consumer Action Law Centre submitted, and the Commissioner agreed, that:

> the watered-down antihawking requirement has seen unsolicited selling take place within structures and systems which do not ensure compliance with the law. This type of non-compliance is an inevitable risk of any laws which are relatively complex and contain loopholes which may enable businesses to go further with their practices than the 'spirit' of the law dictates.[97]

Restricting illegitimate pressure to unlawful acts is likely to restrict courts' ability to do justice in accordance with contemporary expectations of fairness. Birks said that if duress was restricted to unlawful conduct, then 'those who devise outrageous but technically lawful means of compulsion must always escape restitution until the legislature declares the abuse unlawful'.[98] Although Birks was not referring specifically to problematic banking practices, it is a particularly apt description of much of the misconduct uncovered by banks. Often, banks were not doing things that were *technically* unlawful, but they were doing things that were outrageous, and at which a reasonable honest person would baulk.

Two of the case studies considered in the Interim Report concerned the ways in which lenders exercised their powers during the currency of a loan or when seeking to have the loan repaid.[99] In both cases, the bank told the borrower that the borrower could not have access to the proceeds of the sale of a property unless the borrower agreed to restructure existing loan arrangements.[100] In the first case, the bank's witness said the bank had acted inappropriately and unfairly.[101]

[95] *Ibid* [409].
[96] *Electricity Generation Corp* (n 31) [25] (McLure P, Newnes JA agreeing).
[97] Final Report (n 1) 282–83.
[98] P Birks, *An Introduction to the Law of Restitution*, revised edn (Clarendon Press, 1989) 177, cited in *CTN Cash* (n 34) 718 (Steyn LJ).
[99] Interim Report (n 18) Vol 2, Case Studies, 308.
[100] *Ibid.*
[101] *Ibid.*

That case concerned two loans made by the Bank of Melbourne (a brand name of Westpac) to Thir Pty Ltd ('Thir'), a family company controlled by Mr and Mrs Wallis.[102] In April 2016, Thir applied for a loan to assist in the purchase of a 20-acre property containing a bed-and-breakfast business. The loan was to be secured by a mortgage over the property. In June 2016, Thir agreed to refinance an existing mortgage over a residential investment property. The bed-and-breakfast business began to struggle and the Wallis family decided to relocate and rent out the business and property. Mr Wallis asked the bank to revalue the property, hoping to borrow against any equity that might have accrued to purchase a new family home.

Upon receiving the request, the Bank of Melbourne credit team told Mr Wallis that the property had been improperly classified as a residential loan, rather than a commercial loan secured by commercial property, and that as a consequence the bank considered that it had a security shortfall under the loan of around $100,000. Mr Wallis decided to sell Thir's residential investment property to free up some capital and requested that the bank discharge the mortgage over that property. The bank refused to agree to discharge the mortgage unless $100,000 from the proceeds of the sale was deposited and held in a Bank of Melbourne term deposit account as collateral for the potential security shortfall. Mr Wallis gave evidence that he felt 'held for ransom' by the Bank of Melbourne.[103] The Interim Report concluded that 'to apply commercial pressure to the borrower in those circumstances was at least unfair'.[104]

There are various other findings of arguably illegitimate pressure throughout the Interim Report, in which victims of that pressure felt that they had no choice but to agree to terms put to them by financial institutions. Another example in the Interim Report is the case of the Brauers.[105] The Brauers owned a property called Kia Ora in Queensland, where they kept cattle and grew hay. They became customers of Rabobank in 2005, using a $700,000 facility with a 15-year term to refinance their prior facilities and rebuild their cattle years. That facility was increased several times. Subsequently, the Brauers sold their cattle and leased out Kia Ora. In December 2010 and January 2011, Kia Ora experienced significant flooding and the lessee elected not to renew the lease of Kia Ora. As a result, the Brauers experienced significant financial pressure and returned to Kia Ora. They enquired about borrowing a further $300,000 from Rabobank to restock Kia Ora. The bank agreed on the condition that $3 million be repaid within two years. At the time, the Brauers' income was insufficient to meet their loan repayments; they had to outlay capital to restock the property so as to earn an income. Mrs Brauer gave evidence to the Commission that 'she felt they had no choice but to accept the offer given their dire need for additional finance at that time'.[106] In its written

[102] *Ibid.*
[103] *Ibid* 312.
[104] *Ibid* 313.
[105] *Ibid* 388.
[106] *Ibid* 395.

submissions, Rabobank accepted that by failing to consider the Brauers' hardship in circumstances where the Brauers' business had been affected by both flood and a live export ban, the bank 'engaged in conduct that fell below community standards and expectations'.[107]

A third case concerned Mr and Mrs Ruddy, who owned two farms, Sunrise and Arranfield. Mr and Mrs Ruddy were aggressively pursued by a bank manager of Bankwest.[108] The Ruddys agreed to move their financial business to Bankwest in 2011 after the bank manager offered free property valuations for Sunrise and Arranfield. It later came to light that the bank manager was engaging in serious misconduct. There was no record of the manager's customers ever being informed of that misconduct. With respect to the Ruddys, it became clear to the bank that the bank manager had valued the property on the basis that it was 869 hectares, when in fact it was 72 hectares.

Subsequently, the Ruddys' farming businesses experienced hardship. Mr Ruddy experienced a period of ill health, a ban was placed on live cattle exports, cattle prices dropped and the region experienced a drought. Despite these hardships resulting in financial challenges, Bankwest continued to extend credit to the Ruddys. In 2013, Bankwest notified the Ruddys that the bank wanted to revalue Sunrise and Arranfield and that the Ruddys would be required to pay for the revaluations. Prior to receiving the revaluations, Bankwest issued two offers to the Ruddys to extend their facilities.

The revaluations valued Arranfield at $900,000, down from $1.1 million, and Sunrise at $750,000, down from $1.2 million. Bankwest informed the Ruddys that, as a result of the revaluations, the Ruddys were in breach of their loan-to-value ratio and that they would have to sell Sunrise. The parties proceeded to debt mediation and, ultimately, the Ruddys agreed to sell Sunrise within six months and pay Bankwest 75 per cent of the net sale proceeds. They also agreed to pay Bankwest an additional $410,000 to discharge their mortgage over Arranfield. Tellingly, as in the cases above, Mr Ruddy said that he felt that doing so was his only choice.[109] The bank accepted that it was not fair to rely on the loan-to-value ratio breach occasioned by the 2013 revaluations to require the Ruddys to sell Sunrise.

Each of the cases above could conceivably be considered cases of lawful act duress. None of the cases fit clearly within existing doctrines. There is no clear relationship of influence between the parties – and in any event, the issue in both cases is with the nature of the pressure applied by the banks, rather than advantage being taken of a particular relationship between the parties. Nor are the parties likely to be considered subject to any kind of special disadvantage for the purposes of the doctrine of unconscionable conduct.

[107] *Ibid* 400.
[108] *Ibid* 405.
[109] *Ibid* 408.

The argument could be made that in cases such as those set out above, the aggrieved parties ultimately *had* a choice – their will was not 'overborne' in the sense of the overborne will theory of duress. Historically, the prevailing view was that duress should be understood as compulsion to the extent that the will of the plaintiff was completely overborne by the will of the defendant. The overborne will theory has been the subject of significant criticism in recent decades. Those criticisms are valid – duress generally should not be understood through the lens of the overborne will theory. The fact that the law treats contracts procured by duress as valid and binding from conception, but voidable on a finding of duress, rather than void *ab initio*, undermines the overborne will theory. As stated by Bowley:

> At the core of that argument is the contention that, in order for a valid contract to be created in the context of an ultimatum, the common law must have recognised that position as a moment of autonomous agency for the target, an understanding which, if accepted, eviscerates any understanding of duress as placing the target under any substantive form of other-directed compulsion.[110]

The overborne will theory is inconsistent with the proper conceptualisation of duress more generally – it does not produce a condition of true involuntariness. A person subjected to duress may be reluctant or deeply unhappy about performing the act he or she is being pressured to do, but the act is undoubtedly voluntary and the person is aware of what he or she is doing.[111] In *The Universe Sentinel*, Lord Scarman stated, in the context of describing duress:

> There must be pressure, the practical effect of which is compulsion or the absence of choice. Compulsion is variously described in the authorities as coercion or the vitiation of consent. The classic case of duress is, however, not the lack of will to submit *but the victim's intentional submission arising from the realisation that there is no other* ***practical*** *choice open to him*.[112]

Atiyah posited that, as a matter of fact, generally there are other options available to a person who submits to duress – the overborne will theory is unpersuasive.[113] Atiyah proposed a better view that duress is 'only partly a question of fact. Once it is appreciated that the victim of duress has chosen between evils, it becomes necessary to examine the nature and acceptability of the choice he was presented with'.[114] Such an examination would allow courts to review the nature and acceptability of options available to customers on the receiving end of unfair pressure from banks and other financial institutions.

[110] Bowley (n 43) 27.

[111] *Lynch v Director of Public Prosecutions of Northern Ireland* [1975] AC 653, 678 (Lord Morris), 679–80 (Lord Wilberforce), 695 (Lord Simon), 703 (Lord Kilbrandon), 709–10 (Lord Edmund-Davies).

[112] *The Universe Sentinel* (n 31) 400 (emphasis added).

[113] PS Atiyah, 'Economic Duress and the "Overborne Will"' (1982) 98 *LQR* 197, 200.

[114] *Ibid* 202.

ii. Addressing Inequity

These cases clearly demonstrate violations of societal norms and expectations – so much was stated in the Report. In each case, the bank applied pressure on the customer that was at least inappropriate and, at worst, illegitimate. The general law can and should provide redress in those circumstances, even where the pressure applied was prima facie lawful. Lawful act duress is capable of doing so. The wrongdoing with which lawful act duress is concerned is the coercion of the plaintiff by the defendant. It is not a violation of the plaintiff's property or contractual rights; it is a violation of the plaintiff's innate right to *choose*.

If we accept that lawful act duress concerns the violation of a plaintiff's innate right to choose, it follows that lawful act duress is aligned with, and supports, contract law's foundational concern with freedom of contract.[115] While some might worry that lawful act duress is oppressive with respect to negotiation behaviour and therefore offensive to the notion of freedom of contract, arguably the exact opposite is true. Lawful act duress supports the position that transactions should be voluntary even when entered into out of economic necessity. Where the perpetrator of a threat seeks to take away a plaintiff's right to choose, lawful act duress would step in to offer relief. Tamblyn aptly describes lawful act duress as concerning the abuse of rights.[116] It involves the 'exploitation of the freedoms delineated by rights, in bad faith and contrary to the reasons for their recognition'.[117] The recognition of lawful rights should never be abused to enable predation.[118]

Lawful act duress is suited to address situations of inequity. Equity has had a pervasive influence on the law of duress – the line between common law duress and 'equitable pressure' is unclear (and arguably unimportant). There is even a school of thought that duress originated in the Court of Chancery and is a solely equitable doctrine. Lawful act duress is therefore an appropriate mechanism to deal with unconscionable behaviour of banks – not in the sense of the equitable doctrine of unconscionable conduct, but the broader notion of conduct that is 'against conscience'. In *Progress Bulk Carriers*, Cooke J said lawful act duress allows judges to give effect 'to the reasonable expectations of honest people'.[119] Leggatt LJ said that 'no apology is needed for intervening in [lawful act duress] cases, as the enforcement of basic norms of commerce and of fair and honest dealing is an essential function of a system of commercial law'.[120]

[115] Bigwood (n 63) 49–50.

[116] N Tamblyn, 'The Tort of Intimidation and Breach of Contract' (2015) 23 *Tort Law Review* 164, 166. See further M Krauze, 'English Law and the Doctrine of Abuse of Rights' [2012] 1 *Oxford University Undergraduate Law Journal* 1.

[117] Tamblyn, *ibid* 166.

[118] *Ibid.*

[119] *Progress Bulk Carriers Ltd v Tube City IMS LLC* [2012] EWHC 273 (Comm), [2012] 2 All ER (Comm) 855 [32] (Cooke J).

[120] *Nehayan* (n 40) [187] (Leggatt LJ).

Lawful act duress is flexible enough to be used to ensure that financial services entities are acting in accordance with societal expectations of justice and fairness. This is a controversial aspect of lawful act duress, as set out by Steyn LJ, citing Birks, in *CTN Cash*:

> Can lawful pressures also count? This is a difficult question, because, if the answer is that they can, the only viable basis for discriminating between acceptable and unacceptable pressure is not positive law but social morality. In other words, the judges must say what pressures (though lawful outside the restitutionary context) are improper as contrary to prevailing standards. That makes judges, not the law or legislature, the arbiters of social evaluation.[121]

It is true that, when assessing the legitimacy of lawful pressure, courts must apply a 'standard of impropriety'.[122] Yet it is this very standard that would make lawful act duress such a useful tool in the context of problematic banking practices, given that the Royal Commission investigated conduct which 'does not meet community standards and expectations'.[123] It would allow courts to decide, with appropriate flexibility, whether the conduct of financial services entities is 'illegitimate' in novel circumstances. Sourdin and Atherton noted that 'in terms of the Royal Commission's work, it seems clear that a specific focus on vulnerability is required'.[124] However, this focus 'should not be conceived as a fixed category but rather as a state that is highly dependent on the circumstances of consumers at the time of the transaction and the market in which they find themselves dealing'.[125] For that reason, causes of action such as undue influence and unconscionable conduct may not be appropriate when dealing with banks' misconduct – the circumstances may not be able to be shoehorned into a relationship of undue influence or special disadvantage.

This flexibility need not be cause for anxiety on the part of banks – in cases concerning two commercial parties dealing with one another at arms' length, courts should encourage 'fair dealing' but not 'set its sights too highly when the critical inquiry is not whether the conduct is lawful but whether it is morally or socially unacceptable'.[126] Indeed, the threshold for a threat to constitute lawful act duress should not be easy to cross. Perhaps a bank's conduct should not be

[121] *CTN Cash* (n 34) 718, citing Birks (n 98). See also Seddon and Bigwood (n 62) 777 [13.1]; P Atiyah, 'Duress and the Overborne Will Again' (1983) 99 *LQR* 353, 356; D Tiplady, 'Concept of Duress' (1983) 99 *LQR* 188.

[122] *CTN Cash* (n 34) 718 citing Birks (n 98) 177.

[123] Letters Patent from Queen Elizabeth the Second to The Honourable Kenneth Madison Hayne AC QC, 14 December 2017, (c).

[124] T Sourdin and M Atherton, 'Treating Vulnerable Consumers 'Fairly' When They Make a Complaint About Banking or Finance in Australia' (2020) 32 *Bond Law Review* 1, 17.

[125] *Ibid* 17–18.

[126] *Aponso v Sea Corp Pty Ltd* [2018] FCCA 339 [48] (Wilson J); *Barton v Armstrong* [1976] AC 104 (PC) 121 (Lord Wilberforce and Lord Simon); *Bloomingdale Holdings Pty Ltd v 63 Buckley Street Pty Ltd* [2008] VSC 168 [427]–[428] (Hargrave J); *Commonwealth Bank of Australia v Doggett* [2014] VSC 423 [200] (Hargrave J); *Commercial Base Pty Ltd v Watson* [2013] VSC 334 [38] (Almond J).

considered illegitimate unless it amounts to 'unconscionability', which has the added benefit of being a concept that is already familiar to courts and included in statutory provisions.[127] Determining whether a threat is unconscionable ultimately requires a judge to undertake a normative characterisation of the threat.[128]

Further, to suggest that pressure is only illegitimate if it is unlawful could be described as a fallacy. Whether pressure is 'lawful' turns on whether a party has the 'right' to do as he or she threatens. However, rights are rarely so simple as to be had or not had. Rights are often contingent, conditional or defeasible. Until one has examined the pressure and the relevant demand in detail, one cannot be sure whether a party truly has a right to do a particular thing in the particular circumstances.[129] 'Legitimacy' is not coterminous with 'lawfulness' and lawfulness is not black and white.[130]

Several inferences may be drawn from the cases set out above, and from duress jurisprudence more generally, as to when a financial institution will be deemed to have applied illegitimate pressure to a customer. In *CTN Cash & Carry*, the seminal case in which Steyn LJ coined the phrase 'lawful act duress', the Court of Appeal considered that the defendant's conduct was not illegitimate because it was performed in good faith in furtherance of what the defendant believed to be its legal rights.[131] This suggests that where a bank is negotiating or applying pressure in bad faith, this might properly lead to a finding of lawful act duress. This is supported by the case examples above – consider, for example, the bank's conduct in the case of the Ruddys, where the bank's demand for repayment could ultimately be traced back to the bank manager's own misconduct which was effectively hidden from customers. Further, the Court's focus on the nature of the defendant's demand, rather than the position of the plaintiff, indicates that it is the conduct of the bank and not the will of the plaintiff that is in issue. As a result, cases like those of the Ruddys, where realistically there were other, albeit undesirable, options open to the Ruddys, may still give rise to a finding of lawful act duress.

iii. Considerations of Morality

No doubt some will claim that to adopt lawful act duress would hinder the legitimate commercial activities and pursuits of financial services entities. This is a slippery slope argument. Courts will not use lawful act duress as a wildcard to

[127] See, eg, *Competition and Consumer Act 2010* (Cth), sch 3, pt 2-2; *Australian Securities and Investments Commission Act 2001* (Cth), ss 12CA–12CB; *Retail Leases Act 1994* (NSW), s 62B; *Business Tenancies (Fair Dealings) Act 2003* (NT), ss 78–79; *Retail Leases Act 2003* (Vic), s 77; *Commercial Tenancy (Retail Shops) Agreements Act 1985* (WA), s 15C; *Fair Trading Act 2010* (WA), ss 20–22.

[128] *Australian Competition and Consumer Commission v CG Berbatis Holdings Pty Ltd (No 2)* [2000] FCA 2, (2000) 96 FCR 491 [26] (French J).

[129] G Lamond, 'The Coerciveness of Law' (2000) 20 *OJLS* 39, 50–51.

[130] The disagreement over whether a breach of contract will always be unlawful, as discussed above, is one example of this.

[131] *CTN Cash* (n 34) 719.

punish any and all conduct deemed morally reprehensible. Rather, courts will be restrained by the test of disproportionality and must ask whether the threat was reasonably necessary for the protection of legitimate interests. That test is not unfamiliar to courts; it is already applied in other contexts.[132] Precedents maintain that 'mere commercial pressure' is not illegitimate.[133] There is a difference between a threat and a statement of a realistic position; for example, it may not be illegitimate for a bank to state that it will withdraw its support for a debtor who has proved unable to make repayments.[134] There is no general doctrine of inequality of bargaining power in Australia, nor does lawful act duress purport to be such a doctrine; that a party happens to be in a strong position relative to another cannot alone amount to duress, even where pressure is present.[135]

These precedents, and the application of the test of disproportionality, are capable of ensuring that the acceptance and application of lawful act duress is consistent with the dominant philosophical underpinnings of contract law: freedom of contract and the idea that transactions are voluntary, even when entered into out of economic necessity.[136] Australia's capitalist market 'generally expects and condones the use of economic strength to extract favourable [contractual] terms'[137] – this chapter does not suggest that lawful act duress should alter that position.

Further, the test of disproportionality need not refer to morals and is already familiar to courts.[138] It is disproportionality between a threat and the perpetrator's legitimate interest in the corresponding demand that results in lawful act duress, not disproportionality in bargaining power. Further, it is not necessarily duress for one party, faced with the prospect of the exercise of legal rights by another, to act in accordance with the other's wishes because they consider themselves to have little or no choice.[139] In *Thorne*, Nettle J suggested that *Karam* was incorrect, saying 'it would better accord with equitable principle, and better align with English and American authority, if the test of illegitimate pressure were whether the pressure goes beyond what is reasonably necessary for the protection of legitimate interests'.[140]

[132] *Australian Building and Construction Commissioner v Construction, Forestry, Mining and Energy Union* [2017] FCA 157, (2017) 267 IR 130.

[133] *Aponso* (n 126) [48] (Wilson J); *Barton* (n 126) 121 (Lord Wilberforce and Lord Simon); *Bloomingdale* (n 126) [427]–[428] (Hargrave J); *Commonwealth Bank of Australia v Doggett* (n 126) [200] (Hargrave J); *Commercial Base Pty Ltd* (n 126) [38] (Almond J).

[134] *Bank of New Zealand v Equiticorp Finance Ltd* (1992) 29 NSWLR 260 (SC) 298–99 (Giles J); *Equiticorp Finance Ltd (in liq) v Bank of New Zealand* (1993) 32 NSWLR 50 (CA) 150–51 (Clarke and Cripps JJA).

[135] *CTN Cash* (n 34) 717 (Steyn LJ).

[136] Bigwood (n 63) 49–50.

[137] *Ibid* 50.

[138] See, eg, the use of the test in *Australian Building and Construction Commissioner v Construction, Forestry, Mining and Energy Union* (n 132); *Morgan Stanley* (n 94).

[139] *Frederick v South Australia* [2006] SASC 165, (2006) 94 SASR 545 [181] (White J), referring to *Smith v William Charlick Ltd* (1924) 34 CLR 38 (HC) and *Westpac Banking Corporation v Cockerill* (1998) 152 ALR 267 (FC); *Magnacrete Ltd v Douglas-Hill* (1988) 48 SASR 565 (SC).

[140] *Thorne* (n 33) [71] (Nettle J).

That unconscionable behaviour is unacceptable is also a proposition that is already more than familiar to Australian law.[141] The very notion of unconscionability, which pervades our law and is now included in statutory provisions, is a moral concept: 'the description embodied in the word "unconscionable" ultimately refers to the normative characterisation of conduct by a judge having jurisdiction in the relevant class of case'.[142] There is little strength to the argument that lawful act duress involves excessive considerations of social morality; all substantive law ultimately reflects or aspires to moral standards. For example, concepts such as 'disadvantage', as they are used in the context of unconscionable conduct, also involve questions of social morality, at least in the context of more difficult cases identifying novel types of disadvantage.[143]

Lawful act duress is simply a tool to ensure fairness – 'the foundation of any practical and just legal system' – of the conduct of financial services entities.[144] It is consistent with contemporary societal expectations of fairness with respect to banks.[145] In the English case *of Huyton SA v Peter Cremer GmbH & Co*, Mance J said that the degree of flexibility involved in determining lawful act duress was not open to the reproach that it introduces a judicial discretion because courts must often form judgments regarding inequitability or unconscionability.[146] In doing so, judges give effect 'to the reasonable expectations of honest people'.[147]

In the Report, it is evident that the behaviour of financial services entities is not consistent with societal norms – the reasonable expectations of honest people are not being met. Indeed, in the example cases above, the Report uses the term 'unfair' repeatedly to describe banks' conduct. Perhaps, in lawful act duress cases, it is appropriate to consider whether banks' conduct is morally or socially unacceptable. Lawful act duress can be applied to cases which involve a high level of moral obloquy. Restricting illegitimate pressure to unlawful acts is likely to restrict courts' ability to do justice in accordance with contemporary expectations of fairness.

iv. Self-Regulation

Once it is established that lawful pressures may be illegitimate, the mere acceptance of lawful act duress may encourage self-regulation of negotiation behaviour.

[141] This is evident in the equitable doctrines and statutes discussed above.

[142] *Australian Competition and Consumer Commission v CG Berbatis Holdings Pty Ltd (No 2)* [2000] FCA 2, (2000) 96 FCR 491 [26] (French J).

[143] See, eg, *Louth v Diprose* (1992) 175 CLR 621 (HC).

[144] A Phang, 'Doctrine and Fairness in the Law of Contract' (2009) 29 *Legal Studies* 534, 535.

[145] See, eg, similar comments to that effect concerning economic duress generally in *South Caribbean Trading Ltd v Trafigura Beheer BV* [2004] EWHC 2676 (Comm), [2005] Lloyd's Rep 128 [112] (Colman J); see further T Ciro and V Goldwasser, 'From Private Law to Public Regulation: A New Role for Courts?' (2003) 15(2) *Bond Law Review* 154, 160; *Renard Constructions (ME) Pty Ltd v Minister for Public Works* (1992) 26 NSWLR 234 (CA) 268 (Priestley JA).

[146] *Huyton SA v Peter Cremer GmbH & Co* [1998] EWHC 1208 (Comm), [1999] 1 Lloyd's Rep 620, 637–38.

[147] *Progress Bulk Carriers* (n 119) [32] (Cooke J).

Bentham imagined a panopticon prison, which allowed the warden, obscured from view in a watchtower, to observe the activities of prisoners day and night. While the prisoners might not know when the warden is watching, the possibility of being watched at all times is enough to encourage good behaviour.[148] In the same way, the possibility of lawful pressure being deemed illegitimate for the purposes of duress might be enough to encourage self-regulation of behaviour – particularly negotiation behaviours of banks.[149]

IV. Conclusion

The Royal Commission uncovered serious misconduct and problematic practices on the part of financial services institutions. Even if each of the recommendations of the Report were to be adopted, the underlying challenges would remain. More is needed to protect consumers of financial services and products. The unequivocal adoption of lawful act duress would provide recourse to victims of unfair pressure applied by banks. The doctrine's focus on the *wrongful* nature of a demand is distinct from the focus of other doctrines that are thought to be 'similar' to duress, such as undue influence and unconscionable conduct.

Much of the Report focused on the fact that the financial sector is failing to meet community expectations – the behaviour of the sector falls short of what a reasonable person in Australia would consider socially and morally acceptable. The very nature of the inquiry required in a case in which lawful act duress is alleged directs courts to consider whether the demand and the pressure applied is socially and morally acceptable. That aspect of the doctrine, which is sometimes considered to be a flaw, is in fact what makes it so well-suited to addressing scenarios in which a bank has applied pressure which should properly be considered illegitimate.

[148] See M Bozovic (ed), *Jeremy Bentham: The Panopticon Writings* (Verso, 2010); M White, 'Bentham and the Panopticon: Totalitarian or Utilitarian?' [1995] *University College London Journal of Law and Jurisprudence* 67; S Halborg, 'Panopticon: A Critique' [1995] *University College London Journal of Law and Jurisprudence* 28; J Pratt, 'This Is Not a Prison: Foucalt, the Panopticon, and Pentonville' (1993) 2(4) *Social & Legal Studies* 373; JT Gentry, 'The Panopticon Revisited: The Problem of Monitoring Private Prisons' (1986) 96 *Yale Law Journal* 353.

[149] See further Ciro and Goldwasser (n 145).

13

Developing a Rational Law of Misleading Conduct

ELISE BANT AND JEANNIE MARIE PATERSON*

I. Introduction

A broad-based concern to prohibit misleading conduct underpins a vast swathe of common law, equitable and statutory rules that seek to forbid, prevent and remedy the consequences of this misconduct. The reasons for the law's consistent focus on this issue are not difficult to identify: it is unfair and inefficient for a person to be misled, and to suffer loss because of such conduct. At its worst, misleading conduct may be deliberate, amounting to deceit. Deceit is wholly without social utility, prompting the law's maxim that 'fraud unravels all'.[1] However, even in its most innocuous forms, such as where misleading conduct is innocently committed or based on reasonable grounds, misleading conduct must be remedied and deterred. A plaintiff who enters into a transaction or otherwise changes her position in reliance on misleading information has been denied the opportunity to make a genuinely welfare-enhancing decision and may be financially worse off.[2] A defendant who benefits from misleading conduct undermines the efficient operation of the market by distorting the price and quality signals that drive competition.[3] In this light, the law's prohibition on misleading conduct is not only a fundamental legal norm shared at common law, in equity and under statute, but is necessary to promote a successful market economy.

* This chapter forms part of an Australian Research Discovery Grant project DP180100932 on 'Developing a Rational Law of Misleading Conduct' and seeks to synthesise and disseminate the project findings to date. To that end, it references more extended discussions and analysis developed pursuant to that project and its predecessor, DP140100767 on 'Remedies under the Australian Consumer Law and the Common Law: Evolution and Revolution'. Our sincere thanks to Priyanka Banerjee for her research assistance. All remaining errors are our own.

[1] *United City Merchants v Royal Bank of Canada* [1983] AC 168 (HL) 184 (Lord Diplock). The interaction between specific and the more general expression of the law's prohibition of fraud is explored in E Bant, 'Unravelling Fraud in the Wake of *Hayward v Zurich Insurance*' [2019] *Lloyd's Maritime and Commercial Law Quarterly* 91.

[2] MJ Trebilcock, *The Limits of Freedom of Contract* (Cambridge, Harvard University Press, 1993).

[3] AJ Duggan, *The Economics of Consumer Protection: A Critique of the Chicago School Case against Intervention* (Adelaide, Adelaide Law Review Association, 1982) 22.

Throughout common law jurisdictions, this concern to address conduct that misleads is expressed in a range of general law rules, including the common law torts of deceit, negligent misrepresentation, injurious falsehood, passing off, defamation and rescission for fraudulent misrepresentation, while in equity, the doctrines of estoppel, rescission for misrepresentation, unilateral mistake and breach of fiduciary duty may also respond to circumstances of misleading conduct.[4] Many long-standing statutory regimes concerned with protecting intellectual property rights, such as copyright and trademarks, routinely operate in circumstances involving misleading conduct. In Australia, the law's prohibition on this form of misconduct is also given central prominence through the explicit and wide-ranging statutory prohibition on conduct in 'trade or commerce' that is 'misleading or deceptive or likely to mislead or deceive'. The central expression of this core prohibition is found in section 18 of the Australian Consumer Law (ACL) (found in schedule 2 of the *Competition and Consumer Act 2010* (Cth)), previously section 52 of the *Trade Practices Act 1974* (Cth) (TPA). The prohibition is then repeated in slightly different forms and with varying coverage in dozens of other legislative instruments at state, territory and commonwealth levels. In most cases,[5] the prohibition is accompanied by a remedial smorgasbord designed to provide powerful private rights of redress. The wide variety of orders operate to compensate for, reduce or avoid loss or damage caused by contravening conduct.[6] Beyond these extensive remedies, regulators are given powers to seek a range of orders in response to contraventions of the prohibition, including (in relation to more specific instances of contravening behaviour) the option to seek civil pecuniary penalties.[7]

Although the law's continued focus on regulating this form of misconduct might appear laudable, unfortunately the resultant interaction of statute and general law has become almost unmanageably complex – a labyrinth that defies navigation, let alone rational analysis.[8] Responsibility for the growing tangle of statutory and common law principles concerning misleading conduct arguably

[4] While some doctrines such as estoppel will often operate to remedy misleading conduct, that is not to say that the prevention of this misconduct is the purpose of the doctrine.

[5] In some iterations, such as pursuant to the food acts, the regulator is the only proper plaintiff: see, eg, *Food Act 2006* (Qld).

[6] Found in *Competition and Consumer Act 2010* (Cth) (CCA) sch 2 ch V ('Australian Consumer Law' or ACL); see especially at ss 236, 237–38, 243.

[7] JM Paterson and E Bant, 'Intuitive Synthesis and Fidelity to Purpose?: Judicial Interpretation of the Discretionary Power to Award Civil Penalties under the Australian Consumer Law' in P Vines and S Donald (eds), *Statutory Interpretation in Private Law* (Leichhardt, Federation Press, 2019).

[8] *Wingecarribee Shire Council v Lehman Brothers Australia Ltd (in liq)* [2012] FCA 1028, (2012) 301 ALR 1, 247 [947]–[948] (Rares J). An analysis of the statutory prohibitions on misleading conduct is currently underway: J Sabbagh, JM Paterson and E Bant, 'Navigating the Labyrinth of Misleading Conduct: A Roadmap for Reform' (forthcoming). The raw data will be posted to www.uwa.edu.au/projects/developing-a-rational-law-of-misleading-conduct. For an initial taxonomy of the general law and statutory norms and principles that regulate misleading conduct within private law, see E Bant and JM Paterson, 'Silence and the Regulation of Misleading Conduct: A Taxonomy' in E Bant and JM Paterson (eds), *Misleading Silence* (Oxford, Hart Publishing, 2020) 3.

rests with the ongoing failure of parliaments and, to a lesser but still significant degree, courts and commentators to treat those principles as contributing parts of a holistic system of regulation of a social wrong (misleading conduct). This in turn undermines the opportunities for the development of a *coherent* law of misleading conduct, precluding a comprehensive jurisprudence that applies across discrete doctrines and which provides a blueprint for rational and effective law reform. The High Court of Australia has, in recent years, emphasised the principle of coherence[9] as an overriding aim and requirement both of general law (here, comprising common law and equitable rules and doctrines) and statutory development. In the context considered here, coherence requires consideration of the 'fit' between a wide range of overlapping statutory and general law principles all concerned to, or operating so as to forbid, deter and remedy misleading conduct. It also requires consideration of how to promote coherence between our overlapping statutory frameworks.[10] Only from this perspective can we hope to arrive at any clarity in our understanding of the existing law and identify the gaps and overlaps worthy of law reform.

The chapter begins by giving a brief outline of the core statutory prohibition on misleading conduct, section 18 of the ACL, which provides the template for all subsequent legislative interventions. It identifies the key features of the prohibition and contrasts the clear and categorical standard it imposes – prohibiting conduct in trade or commerce that is misleading or deceptive or is likely to mislead or deceive – with another well-known legislative intervention in the field: the *Misrepresentation Act 1967* (UK). This statutory starting point is appropriate as it is the power of the core Australian prohibition which arguably highlights

[9] *Miller v Miller* [2011] HCA 9, (2011) 242 CLR 446, 454 [15] (French CJ, Gummow, Hayne, Crennan, Keifel and Bell JJ); *Equuscorp Pty Ltd v Haxton* [2012] HCA 7, (2012) 246 CLR 498, 518 [34], 520 [38], 523 [35] (French CJ, Crennan and Kiefel JJ).

[10] The growing interest in the role of statute in an integrated legal system has produced a swell of literature, but some influential examples include (in chronological order): P Finn, 'Statutes and the Common Law' (1992) 22 *University of Western Australia Law Review* 7; J Beatson, 'Has the Common Law a Future?' (1997) 56 *CLJ* 300; W Gummow, *Change and Continuity: Statute, Equity and Federalism* (Oxford, Oxford University Press, 1999); J Beatson, 'The Role of Statute in the Development of Common Law Doctrine' (2001) 117 *LQR* 247; P Finn, 'Statutes and the Common Law: The Continuing Story' in S Corcoran and S Bottomley (eds), *Interpreting Statutes* (Annandale, Federation Press, 2005) 52; J Dietrich, 'What is "Lawyering"? The Challenge of Taxonomy' (2006) 65(3) *CLJ* 549; S Gageler, 'Common Law Statutes and Judicial Legislation: Statutory Interpretation as a Common Law Process' (2011) 37(2) *Monash University Law Review* 1; A Burrows, 'The Relationship of Common Law and Statute in the Law of Obligations' (2012) 128 *LQR* 231; M Leeming, 'Theories and Principles Underlying the Development of the Common Law: The Statutory Elephant in the Room' (2013) 36 *University of New South Wales Law Journal* 1002; D Wright, *Common Law in the Age of Statutes: The Equity of the Statute* (Chatswood, LexisNexis Butterworths, 2015); E Bant, 'Statute and Common Law: Interaction and Influence in Light of the Principle of Coherence' (2015) 38(1) *University of New South Wales Law Review* 367; A Mason, 'A Judicial Perspective on the Development of Common Law Doctrine in the Light of Statute Law' in A Robertson and M Tilbury (eds), *The Common Law of Obligations: Divergence and Unity* (Oxford, Hart Publishing, 2016) 119; R Grantham and D Jensen, 'Coherence in the Age of Statutes' (2016) 42 *Monash University Law Review* 360. The critical nature of the enquiry in the 'age of statutes' was examined and the term coined in G Calabresi, *A Common Law for the Age of Statutes* (Cambridge, Harvard University Press, 1982).

the need for integration of statutory and general law principles. It is also the proliferation and fragmentation of the original statutory norm that has done so much to exacerbate the complex existing system of regulation to the point of incoherence, which is the subject of the following section. The chapter concludes by making some recommendations with a view to clearing a pathway through the thicket, through statutory reform and through closer consideration of the evolving interaction between general law and legislative regimes that respond to misleading conduct.

II. The Core Statutory Norm Prohibiting Misleading Conduct

A. The Regime Outlined

The ACL, like its predecessor, the TPA, was introduced with the express aim of changing commercial behaviour in Australia, with a stated purpose of enhancing 'the welfare of Australians through the promotion of competition and fair trading and provision for consumer protection'.[11] The central provision in the regime is section 18(1) of the ACL. It states simply: 'A person must not, in trade or commerce, engage in conduct that is misleading or deceptive or is likely to mislead or deceive'.

The alternate 'likely to mislead' makes it clear that no person need actually have been misled for the prohibition to have been contravened. Emphasising this point, the legislation empowers the regulator to bring actions for statutory relief (such as injunctions, education orders and penalties) against a contravening defendant, simply where the defendant's actions were likely to lead the public or some portion of it into error.[12] The divergence from general law claims also concerned with misleading conduct, which are dependent on finding a plaintiff affected by the defendant's misconduct, is clear.

The statutory prohibition revolutionised Australian private law in other ways. The prohibition is strict: it may be contravened by conduct that was unintentionally misleading. Further, the statute provides extensive private rights of redress for victims of misconduct who suffer loss or damage because of contravening behaviour, supported by a veritable remedial 'smorgasbord'. Thus, plaintiffs are entitled as of right to damages for 'loss or damage' caused by misleading conduct pursuant to section 236 of the ACL (TPA section 82), but also may ask the court to make wide-ranging and discretionary compensatory orders under sections 237 and 243 of the ACL (TPA section 87) where required to 'compensate', 'prevent or reduce' loss or damage (including loss or damage that is 'likely' to occur) because of the

[11] CCA s 2.
[12] See ACL ch 5.

misleading conduct. Section 243 of the ACL, which replicates the earlier provision under section 87 of the TPA, provides a non-exhaustive list of the kinds of orders that may be made:

> 243 Kinds of orders that may be made
>
> Without limiting section 237(1), 238(1) or 239(1), the orders that a court may make under any of those sections against a person (the *respondent*) include all or any of the following:
>
> (a) an order declaring the whole or any part of a contract made between the respondent and a person (the *injured person*) who suffered, or is likely to suffer, the loss or damage referred to in that section, or of a collateral arrangement relating to such a contract:
>
> (i) to be void; and
>
> (ii) if the court thinks fit – to have been void ab initio or void at all times on and after such date as is specified in the order (which may be a date that is before the date on which the order is made);
>
> (b) an order:
>
> (i) varying such a contract or arrangement in such manner as is specified in the order; and
>
> (ii) if the court thinks fit – declaring the contract or arrangement to have had effect as so varied on and after such date as is specified in the order (which may be a date that is before the date on which the order is made);
>
> (c) an order refusing to enforce any or all of the provisions of such a contract or arrangement;
>
> (d) an order directing the respondent to refund money or return property to the injured person;
>
> (e) except if the order is to be made under section 239(1) – an order directing the respondent to pay the injured person the amount of the loss or damage;
>
> (f) an order directing the respondent, at his or her own expense, to repair, or provide parts for, goods that had been supplied by the respondent to the injured person;
>
> (g) an order directing the respondent, at his or her own expense, to supply specified services to the injured person;
>
> (h) an order, in relation to an instrument creating or transferring an interest in land, directing the respondent to execute an instrument that:
>
> (i) varies, or has the effect of varying, the first mentioned instrument; or
>
> (ii) terminates or otherwise affects, or has the effect of terminating or otherwise affecting, the operation or effect of the first mentioned instrument.

The discretionary remedies include proprietary and personal orders that find counterparts under the general law. For example, courts have long made use of orders that declare a contract void from a certain date and require restitution of money and property transferred pursuant to the impugned transaction (sections 243(a), (c) and (d)), to effect a statutory equivalent to rescission.[13] However, other statutory

[13] *Demagogue Pty Ltd v Ramensky* [1992] FCA 851, (1992) 39 FCR 31.

remedies contained within the smorgasbord are traditionally foreign to the general law, such as an order to vary a contract pursuant to section 243(b).[14]

B. Legislative Design

There are striking features of this statutory regime which, as we will see, have been copied to its general and more particular legislative counterparts: namely the use of principles-based legislative design; the adoption of a clear, 'dualist' position on the relationship between the prohibition and its remedial scheme; and the consequential embrace by Australian courts of substantive over formal modes of reasoning to promote the protective aims of the regime.

i. Principles-Based Prohibitions

The first distinctive feature is the legislative style of drafting, which is based around a set of standard-based prohibitions directed at a range of misconduct including misleading conduct,[15] unconscionable conduct[16] and unfair contract terms.[17] As Justice Rares has noted, '[p]rinciples-based drafting of legislation, in general, identifies the broad nature of the target that Parliament wants to hit and leaves it to the Courts to work out answers, in the pragmatic cauldron of litigious situations dealing with specific facts'.[18] Early iterations of the prohibition on misleading conduct and their supporting remedial provisions were extremely effective on this count. They established a broad-based normative standard that arguably liberated judges to engage directly with the substantive and shared principles and policies that underpin the various doctrines responding to misleading conduct under statute, at common law and in equity.[19]

The central prohibition on misleading conduct is supported by a remedial scheme, again expressed in open-ended terms, that provides for a wide range of orders designed to 'compensate', 'prevent or reduce' 'loss or damage' suffered 'because of' 'conduct that is misleading or deceptive'.[20] None of these terms is defined in the Act. However, they all echo well-known concepts from the surrounding general law context. This has led courts to draw upon common law

[14] The potential for the statutory scheme to influence the evolution of related general law remedies is briefly explored below at section II.B.i.

[15] ACL s 18.

[16] *Ibid* ss 21–22.

[17] *Ibid* s 23.

[18] Justice Rares, 'Striking the Modern Balance between Freedom of Contract and Consumer Rights' (2014) 28 *Commercial Law Quarterly* 7, 13.

[19] E Bant and JM Paterson, 'Misleading Conduct before the Federal Court: Achievements and Challenges' in P Ridge and J Stellios (eds), *The Federal Court's Contribution to Australian Law: Past, Present and Future* (Annandale, Federation Press, 2018) 165.

[20] See ACL ss 23–29, 236.

and equitable doctrines to the extent that they are consistent with and promote the language and protective purpose of the statute.[21] This has been a very good thing for promoting discerning and coherent treatment of related statutory and general law doctrines.[22] Thus the common law torts of deceit[23] and negligent misstatement[24] have provided guidance on the measure of 'loss or damage' that must be compensated under s 236 of the ACL. But the requirements of plaintiff reliance found under those common law doctrines have rightly been recognised as foreign to the statute and likely to undermine its protective purposes.[25] Here, insights from the torts of passing off and injurious falsehood have, instead, confirmed that the statutory requirement of causation is satisfied where the plaintiff suffers damage because, for example, third parties (rather than the plaintiff) have relied on the defendant's misleading conduct.[26] Similarly, courts have actively drawn on equitable principles to help guide the award of orders akin to equitable rescission, available under section 87 of the TPA (section 243 of the ACL).[27] However, their approach has not been slavish. As Gummow J observed in *Marks v GIO Australia Holdings Ltd*,[28] '[t]he principles regulating the administration of equitable remedies afford guidance for, but do not dictate, the exercise of the statutory discretion conferred by s 87'.[29] Thus, courts making orders akin to rescission have been astute to temper the requirements of *restitutio in integrum* applicable to equitable rescission where necessary to protect victims of misleading conduct, in accordance with the statute.

[21] See, eg, *Elna Australia Pty Ltd v International Computers (Australia) Pty Ltd* [1987] FCA 376, (1987) 75 ALR 271, 279 (Gummow J); *Marks v GIO Australia Holdings Ltd* [1998] HCA 69, (1998) 196 CLR 494, 529 [103] (Gummow J); *Henville v Walker* [2001] HCA 52, (2001) 206 CLR 459, 470 [18] (Gleeson CJ). The nuanced interpretive process is examined in E Bant and J Paterson, 'Limitations on Defendant Liability for Misleading or Deceptive Conduct under Statute: Some Insights from Negligent Misstatement' in K Barker, R Grantham and W Swan (eds), *Law of Misstatements: 50 Years on from Hedley Byrne v Heller* (Oxford, Hart Publishing, 2015) 159.

[22] *Demagogue* (n 13) 37–38 (Gummow J):

> As Professor Finn has pointed out, s 52 of the [Trade Practices] Act epitomises both the encroachment by statute upon areas previously left to the general law and the challenge which now exists to bring into relative harmony with the body of case-law construing s 52, general law doctrines whose deficiencies (for example, as to the legal consequences of pre-contractual statements) this case law has exposed: Finn, "Statutes And The Common Law" (1992) 22 UWA L Rev 7 at 11, 25 …

[23] See *Kizbeau Pty Ltd v W G & B Pty Ltd* [1995] HCA 4, (1995) 184 CLR 281, 291 (Brennan, Deane, Dawson, Gaudron and McHugh JJ); *Kenny & Good Pty Ltd v MGICA (1992) Ltd* [1995] HCA 25, (1999) 199 CLR 413, 460–1 [129] (Kirby and Callinan JJ).

[24] *Gates v The City Mutual Life Assurance Society Ltd* [1986] HCA 3, (1986) 160 CLR 1, 11 (Mason, Wilson and Dawson JJ). The law of negligent misstatement has perhaps been under-utilised by courts to date: see the discussion in Bant and Paterson (n 21) 159.

[25] *Campbell v Backoffice Investments Pty Ltd* [2009] HCA 25, (2009) 238 CLR 304, 351 [143] (Gummow, Hayne, Heydon and Kiefel JJ). See also *Caason Investments Pty Ltd v Cao* [2015] FCAFC 94, (2015) 236 FCR 322, 333–34 [68] (Gilmour and Foster JJ), 352 [153] (Edelman J) in the context of the *Corporations Act 2001* (Cth) s 729.

[26] *Caason Investments, ibid* 352 [155] (Edelman J); *Chowder Bay Pty Ltd v Paganin* [2017] FCA 332 [380] (Barker J); *Janssen-Cilag Pty Ltd v Pfizer Pty Ltd* [1991] FCA 649, (1992) 37 FCR 526.

[27] *Munchies Management Pty Ltd v Belperio* [1988] FCA 779, (1988) 58 FCR 274, 288.

[28] *Marks v GIO Australia Holdings Ltd* (n 21).

[29] *Ibid* 535 (Gummow J) (citations omitted).

Australian courts have, therefore, actively but also discriminatingly drawn on related general law concepts to give content to the broadly-framed prohibition and its remedial counterpart. This statutory jurisprudence provides, in turn, a rich source of insights for courts seeking to explore the boundaries of analogous general law remedies. A good example of the creative potential of this form of 'gravitational' influence of the statutory regime is *Vadasz v Pioneer Concrete (SA) Pty Ltd*,[30] where the High Court of Australia, in a unanimous judgment, drew upon a number of authorities on cognate statutory fields to support its view that equity permitted partial rescission of a contract. This form of remedial flexibility is clearly permitted under the ACL.[31]

Indeed, this integration of related general law and statutory principle, enabled by the form of and curial approaches to the core statute, stands in stark contrast to another well-known statutory incursion into the regulation of misleading conduct: the *English Misrepresentation Act 1967*. By contrast with the TPA or the ACL, the Misrepresentation Act does not disturb the general law that identifies when conduct is misleading, but rather regulates the *consequences* of misrepresentations that induce entry into a contract. It does so through technical, rules-based drafting that leverages off the existing common law rules in a manner quite at odds with the dominant Australian approach. Thus, section 2(1) of the Misrepresentation Act provides:

> Where a person has entered into a contract after a misrepresentation has been made to him by another party thereto and as a result thereof he has suffered loss, then, if the person making the misrepresentation would be liable to damages in respect thereof had the misrepresentation been made fraudulently, that person shall be so liable notwithstanding that the misrepresentation was not made fraudulently, unless he proves that he had reasonable ground to believe and did believe up to the time the contract was made the facts represented were true.

Like the Australian scheme, section 2(1) provides a right to damages without a representee needing to establish fault or a duty of care. Also, similarly to the Australian scheme, it was enacted to give greater protection to victims of misleading conduct who were not, prior to the statute, entitled to compensation for non-fraudulent misrepresentations.[32] However, the highly restrictive, formal and rules-based drafting of the provision has tended to import all of the categorical restrictions of the common law doctrines of misrepresentation and to isolate the operation of the statute from its evolving common law context. The consequence has been to undermine the protective operation of the statute.[33]

[30] *Vadasz v Pioneer Concrete (SA) Pty Ltd* [1995] HCA 14, (1995) 184 CLR 102. On the intersections between statutory rescission and restitutionary relief, see E Bant, 'Rescission, Restitution and Compensation' in S Degeling and J Varuhas (eds), *Equitable Compensation and Disgorgement of Profit* (Oxford, Hart Publishing, 2017) 277, 305–307.

[31] Indeed, the statutory scheme permits the court to make orders 'varying' a contract: *Trade Practices Act 1974* (Cth) s 87 (TPA); ACL s 243.

[32] Law Reform Committee, *Innocent Misrepresentation* (Tenth Report, Cmnd 1782, 1962) para 17.

[33] J Cartwright, *Misrepresentation, Mistake and Non-Disclosure*, 3rd edn (London, Sweet & Maxwell, 2012) [7-33]. JM Paterson and E Bant, 'Misrepresentation, Misleading Conduct and Statute through the

The 'quite extraordinarily tortuous and obscure'[34] language of the provision relies on a 'fiction of the fraud' device to extend the remedy of compensatory damages to innocent plaintiffs.[35] Adopting a strongly literal approach to the interpretation of the provision, English courts have consistently held[36] the relevant measure of damages to be that for the tort of deceit.[37] It follows that the remoteness rules in deceit will also apply, so that the defendant will be liable for all loss that is an intended or direct and natural consequence of the misrepresentation, regardless of whether such loss was reasonably foreseeable.[38] The result is that a tortious remoteness rule tailored to highly culpable defendants has been transferred holus-bolus to a provision designed to capture and remedy innocent misrepresentations.[39] In stark contrast with the Australian position, the statutory form of damages under the Misrepresentation Act is disconnected from and unresponsive to the normative foundations of and ongoing developments in related general law remedies.

The distinctive, open-ended style of legislative drafting underpinning the Australian regime has given courts the room required to interpret the regime purposefully, to give effect to its protective aims. This has further enabled courts to overcome traditional, common law limitations to relief for misleading conduct, such as the distinction between representations of fact and law, and between active representations and omissions or silence, which find no express place in the statute and arguably would operate to undermine its protective operation.[40] Again, the contrast with the restrictive design and consequential protective operation of the Misrepresentation Act is striking.[41] Guided by the

Lens of Form and Substance' in A Robertson and J Goudkamp (eds), *Form and Substance in the Law of Obligations* (Oxford, Hart Publishing, 2019) Ch 17.

[34] PS Atiyah and GH Treitel, '*Misrepresentation Act 1967*' (1967) *MLR* 369, 369, 378.

[35] Cartwright (n 33) [7-33].

[36] *Royscot Trust Ltd v Rogerson* [1991] 2 QB 297 (CA) 304–305 (Balcombe LJ). See also *South Australia Asset Management Corp v York Montague Ltd* [1997] AC 191 (HL) 216; *Smith New Court Securities Ltd v Citibank NA* [1997] AC 254 (HL) 267, 283.

[37] *Royscot Trust*, *ibid* 304–305 (Balcombe LJ). See also *William Sindall Plc v Cambridgeshire County Council* [1994] 1 WLR 1016 (CA) 1037; *Bridgegrove Ltd v Smith* [1997] 2 EGLR 40 (CA) 42; *Spice Girls Ltd v Aprilia World Service BV* [2002] EWCA Civ 15, [2002] EMLR 27 [12]; *Ng Buay Hock v Tan Keng Huat* [1997] 1 SLR(R) 507; *South Australia Asset Management*, *ibid* 216. The question was, however, left open in *Smith New Court Securities*, *ibid* 267 (Lord Browne Wilkinson), 283 (Lord Steyn).

[38] *Doyle v Olby (Ironmongers) Ltd* [1969] 2 QB 158 (CA) 167 (Lord Denning MR); *Smith New Court Securities* (n 37) 264–67 (Lord Browne Wilkinson), 283 (Lord Steyn).

[39] The nuanced responses of the common law to the spectrum of misleading conduct are discussed below at section IV.A.

[40] *Demagogue* (n 13) 32 (Black CJ), 40–41 (Gummow J, Cooper J concurring on this point).

[41] On the distinction between active misrepresentations and silence, see generally E Bant and JM Paterson (eds), *Misleading Silence* (Oxford, Hart Publishing, 2020) and for specific discussions, *André & Cie v Ets Michel Blanc & Fils* [1979] 2 Lloyd's Rep 427 (CA) 434 (Geoffrey Lane LJ); Atiyah and Treitel (n 34) 369; Cartwright (n 33) [7-07]; Bant and Paterson (n 8) 3. On the fact/law distinction, see Cartwright (n 33) [3-33], [5-08], [7-10]; *André & Cie*, *ibid* 435 (Geoffrey Lane LJ) and the recent shift in *Pankhania v Hackney LBC* [2002] EWHC 2441 (Ch), [2002] All ER (D) 22 [57] (Rex Tedd QC), approved in *Brennan v Bolt Burden* [2004] EWCA Civ 1017, [2005] QB 303 [10] (Maurice Kay LJ).

form of the provision, English courts and commentators have tended to assume that the technical word 'misrepresentation' reflects its traditional common law meanings, which generally embrace words or conduct but not silence.[42]

A restrictive approach similarly marked English courts' original responses to the question of whether section 2(1) captured misrepresentations of law. Notwithstanding that the law of deceit arguably does so extend,[43] a point which could be used to expand the protective operation of the provision, courts initially held that the provision followed the general law and was restricted to misrepresentations of fact.[44] This view was fortified by the provision's explicit reference to the measure of recovery, in the concluding words of the provision, in terms of the 'facts represented'. Notwithstanding this initially restrictive interpretation, there is now significant support for the view that the provision captures misrepresentations of law as well as misrepresentations of fact.[45] Significantly, this change was largely dictated by the need for coherence between the statute and its evolving general law context,[46] a requirement at the heart of the parallel Australian jurisprudence.

ii. The Relationship between Prohibition and Remedy

The second distinguishing feature of the core prohibition on misleading conduct in Australia is that it is separated both structurally and normatively from the remedial consequences of its contravention. Thus, taking the modern incarnation of the scheme under the ACL as our exemplar,[47] we have seen that fault is irrelevant to the primary issue of contravention for the purposes of section 18 of the ACL, found in Chapter 2 'Unfair practices'. By contrast, questions of culpability and responsibility strongly inform the remedial enquiry following a finding of contravention, both in relation to regulator actions and to private claims for redress, made under Chapter 5 'Enforcement and Remedies'.[48] The statute also expressly endorses the role of judicial discretion in awarding remedies in response to contraventions of the primary prohibitions.

In these respects, the statute clearly adopts a 'dualist' approach to right and remedy, in which a range of considerations may legitimately guide judicial discretion in the award and measure of appropriate remedies for wrongdoing.[49]

[42] *André & Cie*, *ibid* 434 (Geoffrey Lane LJ), adverting to the significance of the title to the Act in making that assumption. See also Atiyah and Treitel (n 34); Cartwright (n 33) [7-07].

[43] Cartwright (n 33) [3-33], [5-08], [7-10].

[44] *André & Cie* (n 41) 435 (Geoffrey Lane LJ).

[45] See *Pankhania* (n 41) [57] (Rex Tedd QC), approved in *Brennan* (n 41) [10] (Maurice Kay LJ): 'a lucid and trenchant judgment'.

[46] *Pankhania* (n 41) [57] (Rex Tedd QC).

[47] Under the TPA, the prohibition was found in s 52 and private rights to compensation under ss 82 and 87.

[48] Bant and Paterson (n 21); Paterson and Bant (n 7).

[49] G Hammond, 'Rethinking Remedies: The Changing Nature of the Conception of the Relationship between Legal and Equitable Remedies' in J Berryman (ed), *Remedies: Issues and Perspectives*

This may be contrasted with a 'monist' vision of right and remedy, in which a remedy is considered to be a right 'contemplated from the other end'.[50] The monist approach recognises very little room for judicial discretion in the award of relief, or for importing considerations at the point of remedy that do not appear in the primary claim. Rather, the nature of the right dictates the form and measure of relief. An example is the view that a plaintiff's contractual right can be defined in terms of the defendant's obligation to perform or pay compensation for the loss of the right to performance.

When taken with the broad range of remedial options offered by the statute, and the inevitable overlap with the areas of operation of cognate general law claims, Australia's statutory scheme provides a powerful paradigm of remedial reasoning that may be expected to exert its influence across the spectrum of private law doctrines that regulate misleading conduct. Paul Finn has identified the imprint of the statutory scheme on areas as varied as the remedial constructive trust and equitable compensation.[51] Others include recognition of partial rescission in equity, discussed below, and early attempts by the Mason High Court to develop a unified doctrine of estoppel.[52] This reflexive relationship between the statute and general law is encouraged by the open-ended legislative design of the scheme, discussed earlier, and the styles of judicial reasoning it promotes. This is the final distinctive feature of the regime, to which we now turn.

iii. Substance, Form and Predictability in the Law

A notable feature of the regime is its influence on forms of judicial reasoning, with consequences for certainty and predictability in the law. It might well be feared that such a novel regime, which adopts broadly-framed and undefined terms of reference, will have an inevitable tendency to undermine commercial confidence and even the rule of law. However, perhaps counter-intuitively, the very breadth of the statutory regime has demanded courts engage transparently from the outset with the substantive policies and issues informing the statutory schemes and engaged by the particular disputes before the courts.

(Toronto, Carswell, 1991) Ch 4. The broader implications of the statute's design for broader debates concerning the law of remedies are explored in E Bant and JM Paterson, 'Evolution and Revolution: The Remedial Smorgasbord for Misleading Conduct in Australia' (2020) 14 *Florida International University Law Review* 25.

[50] P Birks, 'The Law of Restitution at the End of an Epoch' (1999) 28 *University of Western Australia Law Review* 13, 55. See also P Birks, 'Definition and Division: A Meditation on Institutes 3.13' in P Birks (ed), *The Classification of Obligations* (Oxford, Clarendon Press, 1997) 24: 'The secondary obligation to pay compensatory damages is … the same thing as the right looked at from the other end.'

[51] P Finn, 'Unity, then Divergence: The Privy Council, the Common Law of England and the Common Laws of Canada, Australia and New Zealand' in Robertson and Tilbury (eds) (n 10) 37, 56–57. See also P Finn, 'Common Law Divergences' (2013) 37 *Melbourne University Law Review* 509.

[52] *Demagogue* (n 13) 37–38 (Gummow J). Changing judicial attitudes have arguably halted this advance: see below at section III.D. and E Bant and J Paterson, 'Estoppel, Misleading Conduct and Equitable Fraud' (2019) 13 *Journal of Equity* 183.

A good example is parties' efforts to 'contract out of', or otherwise engage in defensive drafting techniques to avoid or restrict the protective operation of, the statute. Australian courts have consistently held that parties cannot directly exclude liability for misleading conduct under the Australian prohibitions, as it is considered that this would be contrary to public policy.[53] Courts have accepted, in principle, that parties may use contractual devices to define the scope of their relationship, specifying the kinds of information that can be relied upon and those that cannot,[54] typically through the use of 'basis', 'non-reliance' and 'no-representation' clauses.[55] However, importantly, these kinds of terms are not treated as absolute in achieving their stated goal. Rather, any clause is considered at the outset, as an evidential factor only, as part of a matrix of considerations relevant to determining whether the plaintiff has been misled.[56] Here, the form of the regime has produced a principled approach to the attempts of parties to define the scope of their relationship. The approach is entirely consistent with the consumer protection purposes of the provisions, while also respecting the autonomy of parties of equal bargaining power to define their own relationship.

Again, the contrast with the more rules-based approach of the Misrepresentation Act is striking. As part of its protective scheme, section 3 of the Act provides that:

> If a contract contains a term which would exclude or restrict—
>
> a) any liability to which a party to a contract may be subject by reason of any misrepresentation made by him before the contract was made; or
>
> b) any remedy available to another party to the contract by reason of such a misrepresentation,
>
> that term shall be of no effect except in so far as it satisfies the requirement of reasonableness as stated in section 11(1) of the Unfair Contract Terms Act 1977; and it is for those claiming that the term satisfies that requirement to show that it does.

The English experience with this provision has been tortuous. It has taken decades of an almost impenetrable forest of authorities to get to the point that English judges no longer will take 'no reliance' statements at face value, but rather will

[53] *Henjo Investments Pty Ltd v Collins Marrickville Pty Ltd* [1988] FCA 42, (1988) 39 FCR 546, 561.

[54] Paterson and Bant (n 33).

[55] Non-reliance clauses are contractual statements where one or both parties have not relied on any or specified statements of the other party in making the decision to enter into the contract. No representation clauses similarly deny any representation has been made beyond those contained in the contract.

[56] See *Campbell* (n 25) 348 [130]; *Butcher v Lachlan Elder Realty Pty Ltd* [2004] HCA 60, (2004) 218 CLR 592, 638–39 [152] (McHugh J); *Havyn Pty Ltd v Webster* [2005] NSWCA 182, (2005) 12 BPR 22,837, 22, 852–22, 854 [86]–[96] (Santow, Tobias JJA and Brownie AJA). See also *Westpac Banking Corporation v Lee* [2013] NSWCA 375, [175], [177] (Barrett, Emmett and Gleeson JJA); *Jewelsnloo Pty Ltd v Sengos* [2016] NSWCA 309 (Beazley ACJ, Macfarlan and Payne JJA); *Re Colorado Products Pty Ltd (in prov liq)* [2014] NSWSC 789, (2014) 101 ACSR 233, 272 [124]; *Guirguis Pty Ltd v Michel's Patisserie System Pty Ltd* [2017] QCA 83, [28]–[29], [63]–[64] (Fraser JA, McMurdo JA and Boddice J agreeing); *Shah v Hagemrad* [2018] FCA 91 [106]–[107].

engage with the substantive question of whether such clauses constitute an attempt to limit liability so as to enliven the *Unfair Contract Terms Act 1977* (UK). In the meantime, in seeking to uphold contractual autonomy in the face of what appears to be a fairly clear direction, English courts have relied on novel doctrines of contractual estoppel and applied muddied distinctions between exclusion provisions and those that define the scope of the contract,[57] before more recently recognising that the integrity of the legislative regime demands a more holistic response to the clear legislative intent. Thus, in *First Tower Trustees Ltd v CDS (Superstores International) Ltd*, the English Court of Appeal clarified that any clause, regardless of form, that has the effect of avoiding or reducing liability under the Misrepresentation Act must satisfy the test of reasonableness in the Unfair Contract Terms Act.[58]

In summary, Australia's original statutory prohibition of misleading conduct has been remarkably successful in promoting an effective and principled regulation of that misconduct, across common law, equity and statute. The statutory prohibition has promoted integration of related general law and statutory concepts. In contrast to the English position, Australia's statutory prohibition on misleading conduct has also encouraged a style of judicial reasoning which favours substance over form and recognises a valued role for principled judicial discretion in crafting relief.

III. Wrong Turns Taken

Unfortunately, from this relatively positive starting position, affairs have degenerated. There are two main causes for this deterioration, both attributable to the enthusiastic burst of legislative activity in the field: namely the risk of incoherence through too many iterations of and variations on the core prohibition and, largely for the purpose of containing enforcement powers, a shift in legislative design towards more rule-based and specific prohibitions of misleading conduct.

A. Statutory Overkill and Incoherence

First, and rather ironically, it is arguable that the very success of ACL section 18 has led to its undoing. The original regime has been taken up with enthusiasm by successive

[57] G McMeel, *McMeel on the Construction of Contracts: Interpretation, Implication and Rectification*, 3rd edn (Oxford, Oxford University Press, 2017). See, eg, *Raiffeisen Zentralbank Osterreich AG (RZB) v Royal Bank of Scotland plc* [2010] EWHC 1392 (Comm), [2011] 1 Lloyd's Rep 123 [314] (Christopher Clarke J). See also *IFE Fund SA v Goldman Sachs International* [2006] EWHC 2887 (Comm), [2007] 1 Lloyd's Rep 264, [68]–[69] (Toulson J), affirmed by the Court of Appeal: *IFE Fund SA v Goldman Sachs International* [2007] EWCA Civ 811, [2007] 2 Lloyd's Rep 449 [28].

[58] *First Tower Trustees Ltd v CDS (Superstores International) Ltd* [2018] EWCA 1396.

governments at federal, state and territory levels, which have enacted equivalent schemes in slightly different forms, with varying coverage, in dozens of other legislative instruments. These include major statutory regimes such as the *Corporations Act 2001* (Cth), *Australian Securities and Investments Commission Act 2001* (Cth) ('ASIC Act'), the National Credit Code (schedule 1 to the *National Consumer Credit Protection Act 2009* (Cth)), as well as a raft of more specific counterparts ranging across subjects as varied as retail tenancies, food, protection of sporting images and the regulation of the legal profession.[59] Rather than cementing the central role of the original regime, as we will see, a nasty legislative environment of overlapping and conflicting provisions has developed. This outcome risks encouraging unhelpful 'regulatory arbitrage' as parties seek to take advantage of the resultant uncertainty.

This increasingly irrational landscape has only been rendered more problematic through the introduction of numerous exceptions and carve-outs to the core prohibition. Thus, as discussed further below, penalties for misleading conduct are generally limited to contraventions of more specific prohibitions on misleading conduct in the provision of named goods and services,[60] and sometimes expressly exclude particular contexts in which the general norm would be naturally applicable, such as misleading conduct in the context of company disclosure documents.[61] As Commissioner Hayne in the Final Report of the Royal Commission into Misconduct in the Banking, Superannuation and Financial Services Industry observed, 'much of the complication comes from piling exception upon exception, from carving out special rules for special interests'.[62] However, some carve-outs and exceptions may also reflect a genuine failure by parliament to understand that courts are quite capable of, and accustomed to, drawing appropriate distinctions between minor and major forms of contravening conduct and adjusting the outcomes for defendants accordingly. Whatever the motivation, however, the end result is the same: a morass of overlapping rules of stupendous complexity. This outcome undermines the role of principle-based drafting in a regulatory regime as the balance between specific rules applicable to particular contexts and overarching principle-based standards expressing the aspirational values of the market are lost in a 'porridge'[63] of general and specific prohibitions.

Moreover, this burgeoning regulation has led to exponential growth in the length of the statutory scheme, with no obvious signs of success in its educative aims.[64] As Justice Rares has observed, when the TPA was first enacted, it was

[59] See, eg, *Corporations Act* s 1041H; *Australian Securities and Investment Commission Act 2001* (Cth) s 12DA; *Retail Leases Act 1994* (NSW) s 62D; *Commercial Tenancy (Retail Shops) Agreements Act 1985* (WA) s 16C; *Food Act 2006* (Qld) s37.

[60] ACL ss 29–34, 37.

[61] See, eg, ASIC Act ss 12DA(1A), 12DB(2).

[62] Royal Commission into Misconduct in the Banking, Insurance and Financial Services Industry, 'Final Report' (Commonwealth of Australia, 1 February 2019) 16 ('Royal Commission Final Report').

[63] Rares (n 18) 10, extracted immediately below.

[64] See also E Bant and J Paterson, 'Statutory Interpretation and the Critical Role of Soft Law Guidelines in Developing a Coherent Law of Remedies in Australia' in R Levy et al (eds), *New Directions for Law in Australia: Essays in Contemporary Law Reform* (Acton, ANU Press, 2017) 301.

88 pages long.[65] The ACL has since quadrupled in size (not including endnotes). In *Wingecarribee Shire Council v Lehman Brothers Australia Ltd (in liq)*, his Honour summarised the problem neatly:

> For many years all one had to know was that the elegantly simple s 52(1) of the *Trade Practices Act 1974* (Cth) prohibited a corporation from engaging in conduct, in trade or commerce, that was … likely to mislead or deceive. For some purpose that is not evident the parliament decided to remove elegant simplicity in its statutory drafting some years ago. Now the community and the courts must grapple with a labyrinth of statutes, all prohibiting such conduct, in relatively general fields … and also in particular fields … Since the end result of this legislative morass seems to be the same, it is difficult to discern why the public, their lawyers (if they can afford them) and the courts must waste their time turning up and construing which of these statutes applies to the particular circumstance. … Why does a court have to waste its time wading through this legislative porridge …?[66]

B. Inconsistent Legislative Design

The second cause of deterioration in the state of our laws of misleading conduct lies in inconsistencies in the design of the ACL itself. In particular, concerns about the detrimental effects of misleading conduct led the legislators from the time the TPA was first introduced to supplement the general prohibition in section 18 of the ACL (previously section 52 of the TPA) with prohibitions on specific and detailed types of misleading conduct.[67] Thus, section 18 of the ACL is accompanied by prohibitions on specific kinds of misleading conduct:

- false or misleading representations about goods or services;[68]
- false or misleading representations about the sale of land or grant of an interest in land;[69]
- misleading conduct in relation to persons seeking employment as to matters relating to employment;[70]
- misleading conduct in relation to the nature of goods;[71]
- misleading conduct in relation to the nature of services;[72] and
- misleading representations about certain business activities.[73]

[65] Rares (n 18) 10.
[66] *Wingecarribee Shire Council* (n 8) 247 [947]–[948].
[67] Originally in TPA ss 53, 53A and 53B.
[68] ACL s 29.
[69] *Ibid* s 30.
[70] *Ibid* s 31.
[71] *Ibid* s 33.
[72] *Ibid* s 34.
[73] *Ibid* s 37.

The initial reason for including these more specific iterations of the core prohibition was to make clear the scope of the protective legislation, in particular its application to land and employment.[74] More generally, it may be that a related aim was to make more explicit the kinds of acts captured by the general norm. These might be thought to encourage the regime to be more 'self-executing', by making explicit to traders and consumers alike the nature and consequences of serious misconduct.[75] When civil penalties were introduced in the ACL as an enforcement option available to regulators to deter contraventions of the law, these were limited to the specific prohibitions on misleading conduct. Presumably, this approach was based on the view that civil pecuniary penalties should only apply in defined cases, rather than under the more open-textured prohibition in section 18.[76]

These specific prohibitions expand upon the more general section 18 by applying misleading conduct in particular circumstances. Perplexingly, though, the language in which they are expressed varies subtly from that in the core prohibition.[77] The reference in several sections is to 'false or misleading representations' rather than the misleading conduct of section 18.[78] Usually we might expect different uses of language within a statute to prompt a different interpretation of the prohibition, on the assumption that drafters use language careful to convey shades of meaning which must then be given effect in the application of the provision. However, courts have taken the view that very little turns on the differences in language of the prohibitions on misleading conduct in the ACL.[79] Why, then, one might reasonably ask are those specific variations needed and, moreover, what would justify different enforcement responses applying to them?

C. Ramifications of an Increasingly Convoluted and Conflicting Landscape

These two factors have combined to produce statutory schemes of enormous complexity, which define and delimit their operation on instances of misleading conduct in ways that defy rational justification.

[74] Explanatory Memorandum to the Trade Practices Amendment (Australian Consumer Law) Bill (No 2) 2010 paras 6.14–6.18 ('TPA Explanatory Memorandum').

[75] R Grantham, 'To Whom Does Australian Corporate and Consumer Legislation Speak' (2018) 37 *University of Queensland Law Journal* 57.

[76] See ACL s 224. See similarly the criminal offences attaching to the equivalent of these provisions: ACL ss 151–56, 159.

[77] See also TPA Explanatory Memorandum (n 74) para 6.11 making the point that even greater variations in the language used were found in the TPA.

[78] A person must not make false or misleading representations in relation to goods and services, in relation to the sale of land or in relation to certain business activities: see ACL ss 29–30, 151–152, 159.

[79] *Australian Competition and Consumer Commission v Coles Supermarkets Australia Pty Ltd* [2014] FCA 634, (2014) 317 ALR 73 [40] (Allsop CJ); *Australian Competition and Consumer Commission v Dukemaster Pty Ltd* [2009] FCA 862 [14] (Gordon J).

One outcome of this excessive and ill-directed legislative activity is that parties are encouraged and sometimes forced to engage in protracted and cripplingly expensive litigation to determine who is covered by what prohibition. This is not an efficient or beneficial use of scarce legal resources. As noted by Keane CJ in the Full Federal Court of Australia decision of *Australian Securities and Investments Commission v Fortescue Metals Group Ltd*, '[t]he presentation of a range of alternative arguments is not apt to aid comprehension or coherence of analysis and exposition; indeed, this approach may distract attention from the central issues'.[80] Justice Edelman has similarly observed that the developing trend of pleading every possible permutation on the law relating to misleading conduct is likely in most cases to do little more than 'delay the proceeding and increase legal expenses'.[81]

Given the limited resources available to the regulators charged with investigating and prosecuting contraventions of the statutory prohibitions, the burden of holding those who mislead others for profit to account, increasingly falls on private victims. However, the prohibitive costs of litigating what has become an almost unnavigable statutory landscape is likely to prove a strong deterrent to most corporate claimants, let alone private consumers. The consequence is that, paradoxically, the sheer volume and complexity of regulation results in regulatory failure. It is notable that the recent Royal Commission into Misconduct in the Superannuation, Banking and Financial Services Industry revealed a culture of widespread and systemic failure to comply with the relevant statutory regimes. This trend may be symptomatic of the paradoxical consequences of the combination of legal uncertainty and incoherence in fundamental statutory prohibitions that aim to produce a fair and efficient market.[82]

It may be that the unhelpful 'demarcation disputes' between legislative schemes could nonetheless be tolerated if the various provisions were all likely to lead to the same result.[83] Indeed, given the statutory regimes (such as those introduced under the ACL, ASIC Act and Corporations Act) concerned with misleading conduct frequently apply in conjunction with claims in tort, contract and in equity,[84] some consistency in principle and in application seems at the least a bare minimum requirement if the rule of law is to be maintained. However, this seems an overly optimistic view. The idiosyncrasies and vagaries in legislative drafting at Commonwealth and state levels mean that different language is often used in a variety of overlapping scenarios to address what appear to be similar issues, to different effect. The general statutory prohibitions on

[80] *Australian Securities and Investments Commission v Fortescue Metals Group Ltd* [2011] FCAFC 19, (2011) 190 FCR 364 quoted with approval in *Forrest v Australian Securities and Investments Commission* [2012] HCA 39, (2012) 247 CLR 486, 503 [27] (French CJ, Gummow, Hayne and Kiefel JJ).

[81] *Kadam v MiiResorts Group 1 Pty Ltd (No 2)* [2016] FCA 1343 [35] (Edelman J).

[82] Royal Commission Final Report (n 62).

[83] See above accompanying text to n 67.

[84] See, eg, *ABN AMRO Bank NV v Bathurst Regional Council* [2014] FCAFC 65, (2014) 224 FCR 1.

misleading conduct are accompanied by their own, distinct rules on contributory negligence[85] and proportionate liability for concurrent wrongdoers in respect to economic loss or damage to property.[86] Moreover, each of these provisions has its own unique application criteria. For example, provisions for proportionate liability only apply to claims under the general prohibition on misleading conduct[87] and not to claims under the more specific prohibitions on false or misleading conduct.[88]

Similarly, foundational requirements for imposing liability for misleading conduct often differ between statutes without apparent rhyme or reason. In relation to each prohibition on misleading conduct, the chief statutes provide compensatory remedies for loss or damage suffered 'because' of or 'by' that conduct.[89] In this way, each statute requires that the loss has been caused by the defendant's misleading conduct. However, in each case, courts have exposed endemic uncertainty over how these causal requirements operate and have raised questions over the differences in language employed under parallel and overlapping legislative schemes.[90] Given the scope of these Acts, this degree of doubt is of considerable concern. However, the position is arguably far more complex and troubling than even this sketch suggests. Similar, but not always identical, wording is replicated in a myriad of more specialised legislation addressing specific commercial contexts.[91] Most recently, it has been realised that civil liability acts may combine with these elements to introduce a further degree of complication.[92]

These layers of rights and limitations have resulted in overarching and overlapping legislative leviathans of byzantine complexity. A further layer of incoherence is introduced through the ad hoc retentions of the state-based statutes such as those in the Australian Capital Territory and South Australia derived from the Misrepresentation Act, whose operation and relationship to the broader legislative schemes remains almost wholly unexplored.

[85] CCA s 137B; Corporations Act s 1041I(1B); ASIC Act s 12GF(1B). Moreover, the CCA provisions have not been replicated in their state and territory-based counterparts, providing a clear opening for regulatory arbitrage.

[86] See, eg, CCA s 87CC; Corporations Act s 1041M; ASIC Act s 12GQ, discussed in BMcDonald, 'Proportionate Liability in Australia: The Devil in the Detail' (2005) 26 *Australian Bar Review* 29.

[87] CCA s 87CC; Corporations Act s 1041M; ASIC Act s 12GQ.

[88] See, eg, Corporations Act s 729(1).

[89] See, eg, *ibid* ss 601MA, 601XAA, 670B, 1041I, 283F ('because'); ASIC Act s 12GF; TPA s 82 ('by'); ACL s 238 ('because of').

[90] *Caason Investments* (n 25).

[91] For example, pursuant to the *Retail Leases Act 1994* (NSW) s 62E using 'by reason of'; National Credit Code ss 154 and 179U using 'as a result of'; *Co-operatives (Adoption of National Law) Act 2012* (NSW) Appendix ('Co-operatives National Law') s 73, using both 'because of' and 'caused by'. *Superannuation Industry (Supervision) Act 1993* (Cth) ss 29VP, 29VPA, 55(3) using 'as a result of'.

[92] *Redmond Family Holdings v GC Access Pty Ltd* [2016] NSWSC 796 [167] (Black J).

D. Accompanying Common Law Chaos

Legislative incursions have also deeply complicated tracts of otherwise relatively stable, albeit evolving, common law doctrines.[93] For instance, in Australia, the common law tort of negligence, which is the foundation for claims of negligent misstatement, has been modified by the various state and territory Civil Liability and Wrongs Acts that prescribe criteria for establishing the standard of care, a framework for causation, defences, proportionate liability for economic loss and property damage, contributory negligence and limitations on damages.[94] These Acts are not all consistent and have undoubtedly contributed to the complexity of negligence actions.[95]

However, general law doctrines must also carry their fair share of blame for the current incoherent state of the law. For example, in the context of the doctrine of estoppel, the watershed High Court of Australia decision in *Waltons Stores (Interstate) Ltd v Maher*[96] arguably developed the law in a manner consistent with the core statutory prohibition on misleading conduct, in choosing to eschew formalist categories and seek to unite substantive principles shared amongst reliance-based estoppels.[97] However, nearly four decades later, Australian courts continue to divide (often seemingly along state lines)[98] over the foundational question of whether a misrepresentation that has been detrimentally relied upon by a plaintiff may found a positive source of rights against the representor. In some states, there has been a retreat to traditional categories and rejection of substantive commonalities of principle and policy in reliance-based estoppels.[99] Other courts and scholars have perceived a far greater unity of purpose in the conduct-based

[93] J Dietrich, 'Teaching Torts in the Age of Statutes and Globalisation' (2010) 18 *Torts Law Journal* 141, 144.

[94] *Civil Law (Wrongs) Act 2002* (ACT); *Civil Liability Act 2002* (NSW); *Civil Liability Act 2003* (Qld); *Civil Liability Act 1936* (SA); *Civil Liability Act 2002* (Tas); *Wrongs Act 1958* (Vic); *Civil Liability Act 2002* (WA). Compare more limited reforms in the *Personal Injuries (Liability and Damages) Act 2003* (NT).

[95] See B McDonald, 'Legislative Intervention in the Law of Negligence: The Common Law, Statutory Interpretation and Tort Reform in Australia' (2005) 27 *Sydney Law Review* 443.

[96] *Waltons Stores (Interstate) Ltd v Maher* [1988] HCA 7, (1988) 164 CLR 387.

[97] Bant and Paterson (n 52). For examination of the similarly complex interaction between the related fields of contract and consumer law, see JM Paterson and E Bant, 'Contract and the Challenge of Consumer Protection Legislation' in TT Arvind and J Steele, *Contract Law and the Legislature* (Oxford, Hart Publishing, 2020) 79.

[98] A Robertson, 'Three Models of Promissory Estoppel' (2013) 7 *Journal of Equity* 226.

[99] For a description of the shift and a powerful criticism, see *ibid.* See especially *Saleh v Romanous* [2010] NSWCA 373, (2010) 79 NSWLR 453; *DHJPM Pty Ltd v Blackthorn Resources Ltd* [2011] NSWCA 348, (2011) 83 NSWLR 728. A detailed case for *maintaining* continued separation between common law and equitable estoppels on the ground of coherence is made by J Hudson, 'The Price of Coherence in Estoppels' (2017) 39 *Sydney Law Review* 1.

estoppels.[100] Following *Waltons Stores*, the High Court has repeatedly refrained from clarifying the position.[101] The end result has been a proliferation of cases which may well have been decided differently had the case been brought before another court on another day. The early insights drawn from the overarching statutory schemes for the evolving general law seem to have been lost in a judge-led return to formalism.

IV. Getting Back on Track

A. Mapping the Current Law

Ideally, the route back to rationality requires a systematic analysis of the current maze of legislative and general law rules, with a view to producing a roadmap of misleading conduct operating across the field of regulated transactions. This foundational map would then be used to guide the development of a more coherent system, pursuant to which cases of misleading conduct would be subject to consistent and justified legal treatment following specific rules developed in light of relevant broader legal and statutory principles. This process of mapping and then rationalising the current law would not require the development of some uber-tort or overarching principle of misleading conduct. Rather, the analysis would support the consistent and nuanced regulation of misleading conduct in all its manifestations and varied contexts, retaining justified distinctions in treatment, while eradicating inconsistencies that undermine the law's effectiveness and validity. This conceptual and legal clarification would in turn reinvigorate the expressive power of the law, to give content and context to the powerful command 'do not mislead'. The ultimate beneficiaries of this process of rationalisation include victims, those engaging in corporate and commercial conduct, as well as protecting those in our broader legal, social and commercial communities. As we will see below, developing a detailed map of the existing complex landscape is also the critical first step to cutting through unnecessary litigation and statutory duplication, so as to achieve a more just, effective and coherent law of misleading conduct.

There is a myriad of ways in which this kind of systemic analysis could bring greater order to the mess of current law and to its future development. For example, simply identifying all the iterations of the statutory prohibition on misleading conduct would be a huge step forward; mapping the ways in which the prohibitions differ from one to the other. However, given the constraints of space, we paint only the broad outlines of one example of the sort of productive avenues

[100] E Bant and M Bryan, 'Fact, Future and Fiction: Risk and Reasonable Reliance in Estoppel' (2015) 35 *OJLS* 1.

[101] *Giumelli v Giumelli* [1999] HCA 10, (1999) 196 CLR 10; *Sidhu v Van Dyke* [2014] HCA 19, (2014) 251 CLR 505; *Crown Melbourne Ltd v Cosmopolitan Hotel (Vic) Pty Ltd* [2016] HCA 26, (2016) 260 CLR 1.

of enquiry possible and required for the future development of a rational law of misleading conduct. It concerns the identification and development of coordinated and coherent remedial rules that respond to misleading conduct, across common law, in equity and under statute.

In terms of mapping the current law, we have already noted that the general law articulates a spectrum of compensatory liability for misleading conduct. As we have explained elsewhere, the law recognises that for cases of 'decision causation' such as are generally engaged in cases of misleading conduct, the test of factual causation is one of 'a factor' contribution, rather than the 'but for' test.[102] However, the normative principles of responsibility (sometimes known as 'legal causation') rightly distinguish between forms and degrees of culpability and hence vary between categories of claim. Thus deceit, as a highly culpable form of wrongdoing, attracts generous remoteness rules that ensure that wrongdoers are held liable for intended, direct and 'natural and probable' losses arising from their misconduct, even though they are not reasonably foreseeable.[103] Consistently, the contributory negligence of the plaintiff is no defence to a claim of deceit.[104] After all, a fraudster's very business model is likely framed to target the gullible, weak, greedy or careless. Any other conclusion is likely to reward and encourage calculated and egregious misconduct. Indeed, the law's concern to deter this form of misleading conduct is revealed in the ready award of exemplary damages, designed not to compensate but to punish, deter and denounce the defendant's actions.[105] At the other end of the spectrum, innocent misrepresentation is not a form of wrong[106] and hence, at general law, attracts only restitutionary liability (included in this category is restitution following rescission), which seeks to return the parties to their former positions.[107] This limited form of liability is itself subject to defensive considerations such as the defendant's good faith changes of position, which prevents restitution operating to impose unmerited punishment on innocent defendants, by placing them in a worse position than they occupied prior to the impugned transaction.[108]

[102] E Bant and JM Paterson, 'Statutory Causation in Cases of Misleading Conduct: Lessons from and for the Common Law' (2017) *Torts Law Journal* 1. It follows that the different statutory forms of words signalling causation should not affect the factual enquiry: see eg *PT Patrol Pty Ltd as trustee for Amies Superannuation Fund v Myer Holdings Limited* [2019] FCA 1747 [1526] (Beach J) and above n 91. This is distinct from the scope of liability enquiry, as to which see below at n 116.

[103] *Doyle v Olby* (n 38) 167 (Lord Denning MR); *Palmer Bruyn & Parker Pty Ltd v Parsons* [2001] HCA 69, (2001) 208 CLR 388, 396 [13] (Gleeson CJ), 407–13 [63]–[80] (Gummow J).

[104] *Standard Chartered Bank v Pakistan Shipping Corporation* [2002] UKHL 43, [2003] 1 AC 959, approved in *Ancient Order of Foresters in Victoria Friendly Society Ltd v Lifeplan Australia Friendly Society Ltd* [2018] HCA 43 [9] (Kiefel CJ, Keane and Edelman JJ); *Jamieson v Westpac* [2014] QSC 32 [166] (Jackson CJ).

[105] *Musca v Astle Corporation Pty Ltd* [1988] FCA 4, (1988) 80 ALR 251, 268 (French J).

[106] *Tanwar Enterprises Pty Ltd v Cauchi* [2013] HCA 57, (2013) 217 CLR 315, 325 [25] (Gleeson CJ, McHugh, Gummow, Hayne and Heydon JJ).

[107] Bant (n 30) 277.

[108] *Ibid* 300–306; *Australian Financial Services and Leasing Pty Ltd v Hills Industries Ltd* [2014] HCA 14, (2014) 253 CLR 560.

Negligent misstatement and reliance-based estoppels, by contrast, occupy a middle ground, demanding more complex and subtle responses to the culpability of the defendant, harm to the plaintiff and corresponding scope of defendant liability.[109] Thus in negligent misstatement, a negligent but good faith defendant will be protected from excessive liability through a combination of limiting rules, including additional conditions required to attract a duty of care, as well as principles of contributory negligence, remoteness and mitigation.[110] This comprehensive combination is necessary to balance the inherent tendency of statements to be circulated well beyond their original audience and to produce purely economic losses,[111] with the need to maintain important norms of commercial responsibility.[112] By contrast, reliance-based estoppels are concerned to prevent the harm to the plaintiff that would be caused by allowing the defendant to act inconsistently with the assumption created by his conduct.[113] The loss is necessarily more specific and limited than the potentially unlimited liability that informs the law of negligent misstatement. However, similarly to such cases, a defendant to an estoppel may have induced the plaintiff's assumption in circumstances of relatively low culpability, which call for limitations on their scope of liability. While the limiting mechanisms employed by courts are yet to become fully settled, relief in equity is tailored to the circumstances of the case and may be subject to such conditions as the giving of reasonable notice[114] and conceptions of proportionality. Beyond punishment, compensation and restitution, equity also recognises the value of deterrence of serious wrongdoing, including in cases of misleading conduct. This cognisance is exemplified in the sphere of breach of fiduciary duty, where orders requiring wrongdoers to account for and disgorge their profits operate to discourage secret and unauthorised profit-taking and to encourage the disclosure of fiduciary conflicts.[115]

Against this background of subtle general law remedial principles, the core prohibition of misleading conduct and its remedial scheme operates as an interactive overlay that both draws from and informs its evolving general law neighbours. To some extent, it is developing, and may yet develop further, to reflect sympathetic remedial principles of responsibility to those found in the general law. Thus, the new statutory provisions such as section 137B of the CCA, concerned

[109] Discussed in Bant and Bryan (n 100) 19–23.

[110] Bant and Paterson (n 21) 159, 161–70.

[111] See, eg, *Bryan v Maloney* [1995] HCA 17, (1995) 182 CLR 609, 618 (Mason CJ, Deane and Gaudron JJ), 632 (Brennan J).

[112] See, eg, *Perre v Apand Pty Ltd* [1999] HCA 36, (1999) 198 CLR 180, 200 [33] (Gaudron J), 219–20 [101]–[104], 223–25 [114]–[117] (McHugh J), 283 [279] (Kirby J).

[113] A Robertson, 'Protecting Reliance: The Emergent Doctrine of Equitable Estoppel' (2000) 24 *Melbourne University Law Review* 218, text following n 11.

[114] *Central London Property Trust Ltd v High Trees House Ltd* [1947] KB 130 (KB); *Ayayi (t/a Colony Carrier Co) v RT Briscoe (Nigeria) Ltd* [1964] 1 WLR 1326 (PC).

[115] *Ancient Order of Foresters in Victoria Friendly Society Ltd* (n 104) [9] (Kiefel CJ, Keane and Edelman JJ); *cf* at [78] (Gageler J) 'removing the incentive for the fiduciary to act other than in the sole interests of the principal'.

to apportion liability for careless conduct, do not apply in cases of fraud. Principles of mitigation that apply throughout the private law are also likely to be captured by those apportionment provisions but, in any event, have been held to inform and constrain the defendant's scope of liability under section 237.[116] Notwithstanding the unfettered language of the statutory scheme, private rights of redress that entitle plaintiffs to compensation for loss or damages suffered 'because of' misleading damage do not impose blanket obligations on the part of defendants to insure plaintiffs wholesale for all loss, however remote. Limitations apply, although they are yet to be fully articulated.[117] The civil penalties regime likewise reflects recognition of the need and value of orders sensitive to the range of misconduct, which denounce and deter misconduct by reference to a spectrum of culpability and which reflect conceptions of retribution, proportionality and deterrence.[118] Recent amendments build both on this jurisprudence and equity's use of disgorgement orders to recognise the critical role of profit-stripping orders by the regulator in effecting meaningful deterrence of serious misconduct.[119] At the other end of the spectrum of culpability, the role of restitutionary remedies in statutory orders, akin to rescission, highlights the need to go beyond compensatory remedies to reverse benefits received as a result of misleading conduct, no matter how innocent that conduct might have been.[120]

This obsfucated, but integrated, picture outlines the beginnings of a rational map of remedies for misleading conduct. However, it also immediately highlights further questions that need to be answered across the law, comprising common law, equity and statute: why are punitive and profit-stripping awards available only intermittently in response to the same or highly analogous, egregious misconduct;[121] why does compensation continue to monopolise remedial discourse across the spectrum of common law and statute;[122] how are the different purposes of the laws that prohibit misleading conduct (for example, those

[116] *Henjo Investments Pty Ltd* (n 53) 84–85 (Davies J), 89–97 (Lee J).

[117] Bant and Paterson (n 21) 159–90.

[118] Paterson and Bant (n 7) 154.

[119] *Treasury Laws Amendment (2018 Measures No 3) Act 2018* (Cth) and *Treasury Laws Amendment (Strengthening Corporate and Financial Sector Penalties) Act 2019* (Cth). For analysis of the relationship between, and lessons from, statutory and equitable regimes for proportionate punishment as a means of effecting deterrence, see E Bant and JM Paterson, 'Effecting Deterrence through Proportionate Punishment: An Assessment of General and Statutory Law Principles' in Bant et al (eds), *Punishment and Private Law* (Oxford, Hart Publishing, 2021) 255, in particular addressing the insights from *Ancient Order of Foresters in Victoria Friendly Society Ltd v Lifeplan Australia Friendly Society Ltd* [2018] HCA 43, (2018) 265 CLR 1.

[120] See, eg, ACL ss 237, 243(a), 243(c)–(d), discussed in E Bant and JM Paterson, 'Exploring the Boundaries of Compensation for Misleading Conduct: The Role of Restitution under the ACL' (2019) 1 *Sydney Law Review* 155.

[121] See further E Bant, and JM Paterson, 'Should Specifically Deterrent or Punitive Remedies Be Made Available to Victims of Misleading Conduct under the Australian Consumer Law?' (2019) *Torts Law Journal* 1.

[122] See, eg, *One Step (Support) Ltd v Morris-Garner* [2018] UKSC 20, [2018] 2 WLR 1353, 1365 [30], 1381 [92] (Lord Reed, Lady Hale, Lord Wilson and Lord Carnwath agreeing); see also at 1382–83 [94]–[95], particularly points (1) and (10). *Cf Turf Club Auto Emporium Pte Ltd v Yeo Boong Hua* [2018] SGCA 44, [210]–[215] (the Court), both discussed in Bant and Paterson (n 120) 175–78.

concerned to protect property-like or monopoly interests as opposed to those concerned to promote fair trading and consumer protection) to be accommodated within a rational and coherent legal system?[123]

To even begin to answer these questions is, of course, a massive undertaking which remains some way off from being realised. In the meantime, however, there are two other steps that merit far more concerted consideration than has been the case to date.

B. Back to First Principles of Legislative Design

The first relates to legislative design.[124] We have seen that principles-based drafting enables and promotes integrated regulation of misleading conduct across common law, equity and statute. Courts are able to draw from and 'connect' related general law and statutory principles as part of a broader and evolving legal context. Principles-based drafting also encourages overt judicial engagement with the key substantive principles and policies underpinning the law's intervention, in order to give content to broadly-framed legislative concepts. The shift to emphasise and promote more specific and prescriptive rules-based provisions, by contrast, has complicated the regulatory scheme massively and without any sign of achieving the desired educative aims. The result of this shift in legislative design has been that the statutory avenues to relief, once favoured over their more complex general law counterparts, are now assuming a back seat. Thus, in *ABN AMRO Bank NV v Bathurst Regional Council*[125] the conduct in question constituted both negligent misstatement[126] and contraventions of the prohibitions on misleading conduct found under sections 1041E and 1041H of the Corporations Act, as well as section 12DA of the ASIC Act.[127] However, in no large part because of the complexity and incoherence of the overlapping statutory treatments, the primary focus of the decision fell on the law of negligent misrepresentation.[128] Similarly, in the context of the Financial Services Royal Commission, Commissioner Hayne has powerfully argued that the current plethora of statutory rules reflect six core principles, of which a prohibition on misleading conduct is one.[129] The power of that

[123] An important question brought to our attention by Emeritus Professor Sam Ricketson.

[124] See also E Bant and JM Paterson (n 19) 165, 178–87.

[125] *ABN AMRO Bank NV* (n 84). See generally A Sahore, '*ABN Amro Bank NV v Bathurst Regional Council*: Credit Rating Agencies and Liability to Investors' (2015) 37 *Sydney Law Review* 437.

[126] *ABN AMRO Bank NV* (n 84) 147 [773].

[127] *Ibid* 195 [1006].

[128] The Full Federal Court spent 156 paragraphs analysing the claim in tort, and 50 paragraphs analysing misleading conduct contrary to statute, of which 42 paragraphs examined whether the legislation applied to the matters in dispute. See also JM Paterson and E Bant, 'In the Age of Statutes, Why Do We Still Turn to the Common Law Torts?: Lessons from the Statutory Prohibitions on Misleading Conduct in Australia' (2016) 23 *Torts Law Journal* 139.

[129] Royal Commission Final Report (n 62) 8–9. The six principles are: (1) obey the law; (2) do not mislead or deceive; (3) act fairly; (4) provide services that are fit for purpose; (5) deliver services with reasonable care and skill; and (6) when acting for another, act in the best interests of that other.

prohibition is, however, undermined and avoided by overly complex and convoluted regulatory regimes that invite wrongdoers to engage in regulatory arbitrage. The deleterious impact of the shift away from principle-based design has been further exacerbated by the introduction of carve-outs and exceptions discussed earlier.

Against that background, those charged with legislative design should be conscious of the consequence of adopting principles over rules-based statutory design, both for interpretation and operation of the specific provision and for the implications for the broader general law context. The temptation to introduce exceptions and carve-outs to the otherwise general application of key principles should be strenuously avoided.[130] Indeed, there is a strong case for the removal of these add-ons (or takeaways) from the statutes as a first step towards simplification and hence rationalisation of our regulatory landscape. As Commissioner Hayne observed, exceptions and carve-outs from the core norms rarely reflect principled distinctions.[131] Hence, they should, by and large, be removed. The professedly protective and educative aims that underpin carve-outs, exceptions and specific enactments of general norms are far more effectively realised through other routes, for example through the provision of soft-law guidelines, to which we now turn.

C. Decluttering the Legislation

A second and related step towards finding a pathway out of the current regulatory thicket arises from the evident value to all parties affected by the statutory regime of having clear and accessible guidance about its application. As we have noted, the recent Australian experiment of embedding detailed illustrations of the content and operation of the overarching norm against misleading conduct in a myriad of more particular provisions has not made their content more accessible or certain. Indeed, it may legitimately be concluded that the current consumer protection regime in Australia wholly fails to reach the consumer and business audiences at which it is aimed.[132] This is a considerable problem. The reality is that relatively few private litigants' claims for relief from proscribed conduct under the ACL reach courts and make it into the law reports. The dominant role of regulators in litigation, and the prevalence of alternative forms of dispute resolution, ensure that most cases are determined or compromised in the absence of curial oversight.[133]

[130] For a case study in poor statutory design in this sphere that makes active use of complex carve-outs, see JM Paterson and E Bant, 'Mortgage Broking, Regulatory Failure and Statutory Design' (2020) 31 *Journal of Banking and Finance Law and Practice* 7.

[131] Royal Commission Final Report (n 62) 16–19, 42–44. See recommendation 7.3 – Exceptions and qualifications and recommendation 8.3 – Simplification so that the law's intent is met: at 494–96.

[132] See also E Klotz, 'Misleading or Deceptive Conduct in the Provision of Financial Services: An Empirical and Theoretical Critique of the *Corporations Act 2001* (Cth) and the *Australian Securities and Investments Commission Act 2001* (Cth)' (2015) 33 *Company and Securities Law Journal* 451; Grantham (n 75).

[133] See further Paterson and Bant (n 97).

Those few cases that do currently reach the courts usually involve well-funded litigants and raise issues of considerable complexity and novelty.

Another approach is required if the statutory purposes of consumer protection and the promotion of fair-trading practices are not to be seriously undermined. Again, in the context of the Financial Services Royal Commission, Commissioner Hayne has suggested that the more specific iterations of the core prohibition on misleading conduct should be labelled within the legislative instrument, to reveal their relation to the key norm and provide guidance for those both subject to, and applying the statute.[134] However, while this would be an advance on the current situation, there is a danger that such a suite of amendments would only further burden an already engorged statutory framework.

Another route is to explore the role of soft law guidelines, expressed in plain English, located outside the body of the statute.[135] They may provide a ready source of guidance for stakeholders affected by the ACL, particularly individuals and small businesses who are unlikely to have the resources to pursue a case to court. In many of the disputes involving misleading conduct, such guidelines may provide real assistance to those parties in the resolution of their disputes, especially in the context of a statutory regime which has become notoriously difficult to navigate – for example, the placement of the apportionment provision introduced by section 137B in the CCA, not the ACL, or the division of responsibility discussed earlier between the ACL and the ASIC Act.

Soft law guidelines offer at least three benefits. First, they promote access to justice by enabling lay stakeholders to understand, in a broad sense, their potential rights and liabilities under the statutory scheme, without the need to resort to costly, uncertain and time-consuming litigation or dispute resolution. Second (and relatedly), soft law guidelines promote the 'self-execution' of the ACL, allowing parties more easily to assess where they stand, encouraging compliance and in turn promoting the protective purpose of the statute. Finally, the publication of soft law guidelines would allow courts to identify, review and correct shared conceptions of the ACL's operation, as these are enunciated in the guidelines, thereby promoting coherence in the application of the law both within and outside curial proceedings, and across jurisdictions.

Relocating the current detailed legislative directions and illustrations to new soft law guidelines would reduce the length and complexity of the statutory schemes, re-emphasising the generality and comprehensiveness of the overarching prohibition. This simple and powerful message – do not mislead whatever the commercial context – would then be supported by a range of representative illustrations for particular industries. This guidance would in turn promote low-cost access to justice under the regime for the large majority of relatively straightforward and small value disputes commonly affected by the legislation. A related benefit would be the freeing up of tribunal and court resources to focus on the

[134] Royal Commission Final Report (n 62) recommendation 7.4 – Fundamental norms.
[135] See Bant and Paterson (n 64) 30; Bant and Paterson (n 19).

more difficult cases that raise more subtle questions of statutory interpretation, and which require particular guidance on the scope of the open-ended prohibition and remedial regime for each statutory scheme.

V. Conclusion

This chapter offers insights into the necessary conditions for development of a rational law of misleading conduct, which integrates relevant common law, equitable and statutory principles into a coherent whole. It suggests that first steps towards addressing the current tangle of statutory and general law principles include 'mapping' the existing law and, importantly, returning to principles-based drafting in our legislative frameworks. This combination encourages an environment in which related statutory and general law principles can evolve in a mutually supportive manner and reinforce, rather than obscure, the expressive power of the law's foundational prohibition on misleading conduct. We further suggest that this reform agenda will be strongly supported by relocating the current detailed legislative directions and illustrations to soft law guidelines and by removing the excessive and unprincipled exceptions to the general prohibitions. If these steps are taken, it may be expected that the law will become more rational, transparent, accessible and efficient, to considerable public benefit.

14

Interference by Precedent

SAMUEL BESWICK*

I. Introduction

The law of economic wrongs protects people from improper interference with their economic interests by others. This chapter considers how common law might protect people from improper interference with their economic interests *by courts*. Two features of common law adjudication have long served to ensure that judges' rulings do not undermine private rights: stare decisis and the right of appeal. The former, the doctrine of precedent, ensures that judgments delivered today reflect the law that preceded them. Following precedent constrains judges from engaging in 'arbitrary, whimsical, capricious, unpredictable and autocratic decision making' that might otherwise interfere with established rights.[1] The right of appeal, meanwhile, provides an avenue for higher courts to correct errors of lower courts and thereby to oversee the consistent application of the law.

Stare decisis is not, however, a rigid shackle. Courts create law (the common law being 'judge-made') and effect changes in the law. But making law through court decision – by overturning precedent, recognising novel rights of action, or disapplying statute – can generate disruptive effects for past entitlements. That is because, unlike legislatures, which (largely) make laws that bear only upon future events, judicial law-making explicitly bears upon past disputes. Courts operate from the perspective of hindsight – declaring today what the principles of law were that governed the rights and duties of parties at the time a dispute before them arose. So-called 'judicial legislation' is invariably 'retrospective'.[2] The retrospective effect of judicial law-making imposes a cost on judicial innovation that weighs on judges' determinations of whether justice requires some change

* Assistant Professor, Peter A. Allard School of Law, The University of British Columbia. Thank you to Frederick Wilmot-Smith, Lael Weinberger, Heydon Wardell-Burrus and Gabriel Doble for their comments and critiques of an earlier draft.

[1] D Heydon, 'Judicial Activism and the Death of the Rule of Law' (2001) *Otago Law Review* 493, 515. See also Lord Devlin, 'Judges and Lawmakers' (1976) 39 *MLR* 1, 11.

[2] Heydon, *ibid* 509.

in the law. Thus, when delivering the historic *Practice Statement on Judicial Precedent*, which paved the way for the House of Lords to depart from its own decisions 'when it appears right to do so', the Lord Chancellor cautioned of 'the danger of disturbing retrospectively the basis on which contracts, settlement of property, and fiscal arrangements have been entered into …'.[3] Such costs rightly induce judicial restraint from departing from established law. Yet, when courts *do* depart from established law, who bears the cost?

Contemporary common law courts have on occasion characterised judicial decisions that change the law, or that contradict a previously established understanding of the law, as interfering with established private rights. And they have mooted doctrines that would shield parties from the effects of such judgments. These doctrines are dispersed across the law reports and often seem idiosyncratic. This chapter pulls together three landmark examples, arising in unjust enrichment, professional immunities, and property, each of which raises questions about judicial decisions seemingly interfering with economic interests. The doctrines proposed would provide litigants immunity from the effects of judicial changes in the law. Section II considers a 'settled view of the law' defence that has been proposed in response to actions for restitution of payments made under a mistake of law – the idea being that such payments should not be recoverable if the commonly understood view at the time of the transaction was that the law justified the payment. Section III discusses the landmark judgments that brought an end to the immunity of advocates from suit in the United Kingdom and New Zealand, and considers the argument that the immunity should have been overruled with prospective-only effect so as to protect from retrospective liability barristers and solicitors who had relied on the professional immunity in their practices. Section IV considers the doctrine of 'judicial takings', which purports to protect parties from the judicial elimination of vested property rights in complement to the law's protections from governmental expropriation of property rights. According to this proposed doctrine, when courts change an interpretation of a property rule, their ruling should not adversely bind those with property rights established prior to the judicial revision.

These doctrines can be understood as private immunities in the Hohfeldian sense: they would grant litigants a freedom from having an established legal relation altered by a subsequent judgment of a court.[4] A three-step analytical inquiry seemingly justifies such an outcome. That is to consider: (1) whether the legal

[3] *Practice Statement on Judicial Precedent* [1966] 1 WLR 1234 (HL). See L Blom-Cooper, '1966 and All That: The Story of the Practice Statement' in L Blom-Cooper, B Dickson and G Drewry (eds), *The Judicial House of Lords: 1876–2009* (Oxford, Oxford University Press, 2009). See also JP Salembier, 'Understanding Retroactivity: When the Past Just Ain't What It Used to Be' (2003) 33 *Hong Kong LJ* 99, 110 (describing property rights, contractual rights, rights to damages, legal defences, immunities from liability and rights of appeal as 'falling clearly within the category of vested rights').

[4] WN Hohfeld, 'Some Fundamental Legal Conceptions as Applied in Judicial Reasoning' (1913) 23 *Yale Law Journal* 16, 55, discussed in *Lai v Chamberlains* [2005] NZCA 37, [2005] 3 NZLR 291 [168] (Hammond J).

right in issue can be understood as established in the law; (2) whether a judicial change in the law can be understood to interfere with the established right; and, if so (3) whether the established right can be shielded from the (adverse) effects of the change in the law. Such inquiry is steeped in a realist conception of legal relations. The idea that judgments might *interfere* with *established* rights presumes that such judgments are doing more than interpreting and declaring the content of legal rights – they are changing those rights. Judicial scepticism of the declaratory theory of adjudication thus emanates from the cases. The explanatory force of the declaratory theory has long been,[5] and continues to be,[6] debated. It is understood by some scholars to reflect 'the law's conscience',[7] while it has been dismissed by others as a 'fairy tale'.[8] The discussion that follows shows – perhaps surprisingly – that, even when inquiries (1) and (2) can clearly be answered in the affirmative, common law courts have ultimately resisted recognising immunities from judicial interference with private rights. The declaratory theory seems to be an enduring feature of judicial law-making, even in 'hard' categories of cases where judges confront compelling reasons for limiting the retrospective effects of new precedent. The novel doctrines discussed in this chapter fall short of providing a bulwark against novel precedent determining the content of past rights. The discussion concludes with the observation that ultimately only robust time-bars can effectively ensure that rights once established in law remain settled.

II. Immunity from Retrospective Mistakes of Law?

The idea that defendants might be shielded from the effects of court decisions that change the law has been a prominent issue in contemporary unjust enrichment jurisprudence. For much of the nineteenth and twentieth centuries, common law courts held that a payment could not be recovered merely because it was made on the basis of a misunderstanding of the law. Mistake of law was not a ground for obtaining restitution, owing to the maxim *ignorantia juris non excusat* and the

[5] Compare W Blackstone, *Commentaries*, vol 1, 2nd edn (London, W Maxwell, 1856) 48 (when judges depart from prior precedent, they 'do not pretend to make a new law, but … vindicate the old one from misrepresentation') to J Bentham, *The Works of Jeremy Bentham*, vol 5 (edited by J Bowring) (New York, Russell & Russell, 1962) 235 (judges make laws '[j]ust as a man makes laws for his dog. When your dog does anything you want to break him of, you wait till he does it, and then beat him for it. … [T]his is the way the judges make law for you and me').

[6] Compare JS Masur and AK Mortara, 'Patents, Property, and Prospectivity' (2019) 71 *Stanford Law Review* 963, 1019 ('The notion that the courts only "find" what law the other branches have made is a legal fiction that fools few educated observers and is routinely contravened in public by other judges') to SE Sachs, 'Finding Law' (2019) 107 *California Law Review* 527, 527 ('Expecting judges to find unwritten law is no childish fiction of the benighted past, but a real and plausible option for a modern legal system').

[7] A Beever, 'The Declaratory Theory of Law' (2013) 33 *OJLS* 421, 443.

[8] Lord Reid, 'The Judge as Lawmaker' (1972–73) 12 *Journal of the Society of Public Teachers of Law* 22, 22. *cf* J Finnis, 'The Fairy Tale's Moral' (1999) 115 *LQR* 170, 172.

policy imperative of past transactions remaining settled.[9] Yet, many agreed with Judge Learned Hand that this mistake-of-law bar on restitutionary claims was a 'most unfortunate doctrine'.[10] It was criticised as contrary to coherent precedent, principle, and policy.[11] Steadily, common law jurisdictions abandoned the bar on recovery for mistakes of law. Some jurisdictions, like New York,[12] New Zealand,[13] and Western Australia,[14] enacted legislation that prohibited civil courts from denying relief for mistake to a party merely because the mistake was one of law rather than a mistake of fact. Other jurisdictions abrogated the mistake-of-law bar through the courts.[15] The presumptive position throughout the common law world today is that when an erroneous understanding of the law is an operative cause for enriching another, the mistake can provide ground for recovering the enrichment in restitution. (Or, in Canada, the lack of a valid legal basis justifying the enrichment amounts to an absence of juristic reason for retaining it.)[16] For example, if a taxpayer overlooks a statutory exemption when paying taxes to the Revenue, their mistake – which might have been apparent from simply reading the tax statute – may ground a right to restitution of the overpayment.[17]

Abolishing the bar on recovery for mistakes of law avoids what was once a fraught adjudicative problem of distinguishing legal from factual mistakes. But it has exposed a different conundrum. Some errors of law may become apparent only with hindsight – say, when a court rules upon a point of law under which parties previously transacted. If a court's ruling on the law contradicts the legal basis on which past transactions have been conducted, all such transactions would seem to become vulnerable to litigation on the grounds of mistake (save for those falling beyond the prescribed limitation period).[18] The doctrine of mistake of law

[9] *Bilbie v Lumley* (1802) 2 East 469, (1802) 102 ER 448. See J Halberda, 'Mistake of Law and Mistake of Fact in English Law of Restitution' (2014) *Legal History Review* 82.

[10] *St Paul & Marine Ins Co v Pure Oil Co*, 63 F.2d 771, 773 (2d Cir 1933).

[11] C Mitchell, P Mitchell and S Watterson (eds), *Goff and Jones: The Law of Unjust Enrichment*, 9th edn (London, Sweet & Maxwell, 2016) [9–101]; J Edelman and E Bant, *Unjust Enrichment*, 2nd edn (Oxford, Hart Publishing, 2016) 185.

[12] New York Civil Practice Law § 3005 (originally enacted 1942). See EW Patterson, 'Improvements in the Law of Restitution' (1955) 40 *Cornell Law Quarterly* 667, 676.

[13] *Judicature Act 1908* (NZ) (as amended by the *Judicature Amendment Act 1958* (NZ) s 2) s 94A(1) (since repealed and replaced by the *Property Law Act 2007* (NZ) s 74A(1)).

[14] *Law Reform (Property, Perpetuities, and Succession) Act 1962* (WA) s 23(1) (since repealed and replaced by *Property Law Act 1969* (WA) s 124(1).

[15] *Kleinwort Benson Ltd v Lincoln City Council* [1999] 2 AC 349 (HL); *Air Canada v British Columbia* [1989] 1 SCR 1161 (SCC); *David Securities Pty Ltd v Commonwealth Bank of Australia* (1992) 175 CLR 353 (HCA); *Willis Faber Enthoven (Pty) Ltd v Receiver of Revenue* 1992 (4) SA 202 (AD); *Morgan Guaranty Trust Co of New York v Lothian Regional Council* 1995 SC 151 (Court of Five Judges).

[16] M McInnes, 'The Reason to Reverse: Unjust Factors and Juristic Reasons' (2012) 92 *Boston University Law Review* 1049, 1056.

[17] *Pitt v Holt* [2013] UKSC 26, [2013] 2 AC 108; *Royal Canadian Legion Norwood (Alberta) Branch 178 v Edmonton* 1994 ABCA 37, 111 DLR (4th) 141; *Torrens Aloha Pty Ltd v Citibank NA* (1997) 72 FCR 581 (FCAFC).

[18] The proper solution to this problem divided the Supreme Court in *FII GLO Test Claimants v HM Revenue and Customs* [2020] UKSC 47 ('*FII* (SC II)'). See S Beswick, 'The Overpaid Tax Litigation: Roadblocked' (2021) 84 *MLR* _.

thus poses a threat to the stability of transactions and to parties' capacity to rely on settled law. How can parties protect themselves from the disruptive effects of court decisions that change the law?

A. Transacting under Established Settled Law

People invariably transact on the basis of, and against the background of, what are understood to be the established laws of the time. Taxes are paid because tax statutes enacted by Parliament are presumed validly to impose tax liability.[19] Contracts may be entered into in reliance on prior court precedent that establishes the interpretation of terms,[20] or in reliance on an established industry practice that has not previously been judicially questioned.[21]

There seem to be compelling rule-of-law reasons for holding parties to the law as it stood from their *ex ante* position. We might call this the 'transaction-time' law.[22] Holding parties to the transaction-time law presumptively promotes certainty and stability in transactions because it renders them subject only to existing law, not to principles of law articulated only by a future court. Applying transaction-time law also presumptively upholds parties' expectations and reliance interests in the settled or established laws of the time governing their transactions.[23] But to conclude that transactions should be determined according to the established law of the time is to beg the question. There may come to be disagreement as to what the 'transaction-time' law was. Only courts can authoritatively resolve the point. And courts can only do so from the ex post position.

B. Interference by Judicial Change in the Law?

How should we understand the effects of a court's ruling that departs from the premise of the law on which parties understood themselves to have transacted? The House of Lords confronted this problem in the seminal case of *Kleinwort Benson*.[24] Throughout the 1980s, local authorities had entered into interest rate swap agreements with banks as a form of financing. During this time, the prevailing legal view was that local authorities were legally competent to execute such

[19] *cf Deutsche Morgan Grenfell Group Plc v IRC* [2006] UKHL 49, [2007] 1 AC 558; *Air Canada v British Columbia* [1989] 1 SCR 1161 (SCC).

[20] *cf Re Spectrum Plus Ltd* [2005] UKHL 41, [2005] 2 AC 680; *Ipswich Town Football Club Co Ltd v Chief Constable of Suffolk Constabulary* [2017] EWCA Civ 1484, [2017] 4 WLR 195; *David Securities Pty Ltd v Commonwealth Bank of Australia* (1992) 175 CLR 353 (HCA).

[21] *Kleinwort Benson* (n 15); *Re Pallen Trust* 2014 BCSC 305.

[22] K Roosevelt III, 'A Little Theory is a Dangerous Thing: The Myth of Adjudicative Retroactivity' (1999) 31 *Connecticut Law Review* 1075, 1080–81.

[23] *Ibid* 1115.

[24] *Kleinwort Benson* (n 15), upheld by a majority in *FII* (SC II) (n 18).

agreements.[25] It was not until 1987 that their vires began to be questioned.[26] In 1989, the legality of the transactions was successfully challenged in the High Court,[27] whose decision the House of Lords affirmed in 1991.[28]

It is not necessarily intuitive that the House of Lords' decision in 1991 merely corrected a misapprehension of the law held by those transacting in the 1980s, ie that swaps agreements had *always* been unlawful. The issue was novel when it was argued before the courts. The Law Lords' judgment was certainly understood to be novel: even, a 'bombshell'.[29] Hundreds of swaps agreements had been executed and completed for the better part of a decade without protestation. The decision-time law articulated by the Law Lords seemed to have departed from the transaction-time law on which the swaps agreements had been premised. Against which understanding of the law should previously executed swaps contracts be interpreted?

The Law Lords split when they considered this issue in *Kleinwort Benson*. Lord Browne-Wilkinson and Lord Lloyd, in the minority, considered that the parties' actions had to be judged from their perspective at the time of transacting. Many scholars share this view.[30] On the transaction-time view, if a person makes a payment on the basis of settled law that is later overruled, they are not necessarily mistaken as to their present reason for making the payment. They have simply mispredicted the future change in the law.[31] The future development cannot undermine their present reason for transacting. So new precedent should not interfere with the parties' past bargain.

The Law Lords in the majority rejected this reasoning. Lords Goff, Hoffmann and Hope considered that the only coherent lens through which past actions can be judged in litigation is the court's decision-time perspective. When judges overturn precedent or impugn some established practice, they do so because that precedent or practice was both wrong today and wrong at the time the dispute before them occurred. If a court's ruling undermines the premise of the law on which parties believed themselves to have transacted, then, from this perspective of hindsight, the parties can be understood to have transacted under

[25] Purportedly on the basis of the *Local Government Act 1972* (UK) s 111, or, in Scotland, the *Local Government (Scotland) Act 1973* s 69. See *Westdeutsche Landesbank Girozentale v Islington London Borough Council* [1994] 4 All ER 890 (QB) 896–98 (Hobhouse J).

[26] *Kleinwort Benson* (n 15) 404 (Lord Hope).

[27] *Hazell v Hammersmith and Fulham LBC* [1990] 2 QB 697 (DC).

[28] *Hazell v Hammersmith and Fulham LBC* [1992] 2 AC 1 (HL).

[29] P Birks and F Rose (eds), *Lessons of the Swaps Litigation* (London, Mansfield Press, 2000) v.

[30] See references collected in F Wilmot-Smith, 'Retrospective Mistakes of Law' in PS Davies and J Pila (eds), *The Jurisprudence of Lord Hoffmann* (Oxford, Oxford University Press, 2015) 300, fn 75. See also C Sampford, *Retrospectivity and the Rule of Law* (Oxford, Oxford University Press, 2006) 212 (suggesting that the approach of the majority Law Lords in *Kleinwort Benson* had 'arguably unjust or anomalous consequences').

[31] G Virgo, *The Principles of the Law of Restitution*, 3rd edn (Oxford, Oxford University Press, 2015) 185. See W Seah, 'Mispredictions, Mistakes and the Law of Unjust Enrichment' [2007] *Restitution Law Review* 93. *cf* A Burrows, 'Restitution in Respect of Mistakenly Paid Tax' (2005) 121 *LQR* 540, 546.

a mistake of law. As a result, the blackletter rule is that '[a] person who acts on the basis of a settled understanding of the law, which is subsequently declared to be incorrect, makes a mistake of law'.[32] Where such mistakes have caused one party to enrich another, they may provide a basis for a claim in restitution of the enrichment.[33]

As a matter of policy, retrospective mistakes of law stand to undermine stability of transactions generally. As MacNeil has observed:[34]

> [F]ollowing the courts' recognition of the right to recover payments made under a mistake of law, there is a form of sleeping uncertainty inherent in every transaction in that the possibility of settled law being overturned is always present, even if it is not a regular occurrence.

Courts have grappled with whether they may provide certainty to parties by shielding from judicial changes in the law those who would otherwise be adversely affected.

C. Immunity from New Precedent?

A potential solution to the disruptive effects of retrospective mistakes of law is to recognise a 'defence' in respect of transactions that have been conducted on the basis of a 'settled' or 'common' understanding of the law.[35] This would immunise such transactions from the effects of future judge-made law. Such a defence is found in statutory form in several jurisdictions. New Zealand, for example, enacted legislation in 1958 that abolished the general common law bar on claims for recovery of payments made under a mistake of law. The legislation explicitly does not extend to enabling relief to be granted when *the law* as 'commonly understood' at the time of payment 'required or allowed' the payment and was only subsequently shown to have been wrong.[36] In other words, if people generally thought that the law justified the payment at the time, a subsequent clarification of or change in the law will not be a sufficient basis for reopening the transaction. This provision is a pragmatic barrier to revisiting old cases under new law.[37]

[32] Mitchell, Mitchell and Watterson (n 11) [9-112].

[33] A Burrows, *A Restatement of the English Law of Unjust Enrichment* (Oxford, Oxford University Press, 2012) [10(1)]; American Law Institute, *Restatement (Third) of Restitution and Unjust Enrichment* (2011) §19 cmt. d.

[34] I MacNeil, 'Uncertainty in Commercial Law' (2009) 13 *Edinburgh Law Review* 68, 82.

[35] See D Sheehan, 'What Is a Mistake?' (2000) 20 *Legal Studies* 538, 554–58; D Sheehan, 'Mistaken Overpayments of Tax' in S Elliott, B Häcker and C Mitchell (eds), *Restitution of Overpaid Tax* (Oregon, Hart Publishing, 2013) 62–68.

[36] *Property Law Act 2007* (NZ) s 74A(2) (replacing *Judicature Act 1908* (NZ) s 94A(2)).

[37] The provision has attracted surprisingly little judicial analysis. It would seem that the class of persons to be assessed as holding a 'common' understanding of the law will turn on the subject-matter of the enquiry: *Bell Bros Pty Ltd v Shire of Serpentine-Jarrahdale* (1969) WAR 104 and 155 (WASC); *McKenzie v Commissioner of Inland Revenue* (1979) 4 NZTC 61,614 (NZSC).

A provision with similar effect has, since 1927, existed in the United Kingdom's statutory regime for recovering mistakenly paid tax.[38] The *Taxes Management Act 1970* employs a 'prevailing practice defence', which provides that the Revenue can refuse a claim for recovery of tax if the tax was paid in accordance with the generally prevailing practice of the time.[39] It can do so even if the practice is subsequently held to have been wrong in law. (A New Zealand-style general 'settled view of the law' provision was also proposed in a report of the Law Commission of England and Wales,[40] although it was not taken up by Parliament and was later abandoned by the Law Commission.)[41]

It was against this legislative background that the House of Lords in *Kleinwort Benson* considered whether such a defence was reflected in the common law. The issue deeply divided the House – Lord Hoffmann admitting to having shifted his position following oral argument.[42] Some scholars attribute the split between the Law Lords to diverging positions in legal philosophy – ascribing to the majority position Dworkin's 'right answer' thesis,[43] and couching the minority's rejection of retrospective mistakes of law in a legal realist view that judicial changes in the law cannot 'falsify history'.[44] The split can more simply be explained by divergence in views regarding the explanatory force of the declaratory theory of adjudication. The minority Law Lords rejected the declaratory theory as an outmoded 'fairy tale'. Through their transaction-time lens, Lord Browne-Wilkinson and Lord Lloyd maintained that 'if there really was a settled understanding of the law, then that was the law at the time of payment', and a subsequent change in the law could not *ex hypothesi* create a mistake that did not exist at the relevant time.[45] Change in the law should simply have no bearing on transactions undertaken under prior law.

The three Law Lords in the majority, however, rejected the premise that payment under a settled view of the law was incompatible with a finding of retrospective

[38] M Bhandari, 'Recovering Mistakenly Paid Tax: Taxes Management Act 1970 Section 33 and the Prevailing Practice Defence' [2008] 4 *British Tax Review* 335, 336.

[39] *Taxes Management Act 1970* (UK) s 33(2), sch 1AB [2(8)].

[40] Law Commission of England and Wales, *Restitution: Mistakes of Law and Ultra Vires Public Authority Receipts and Payments* (Law Com No 227, 1994) 48. See L Flynn, '"No Taxation without Restitution" – The Law Commission's Proposals on Recovery of Overpaid Taxes' [1995] *British Tax Review* 15, 31.

[41] Law Commission of England and Wales, *Limitation of Actions* (Law Com No 270, 2001) 50.

[42] *Kleinwort Benson* (n 15) 398. See Wilmot-Smith (n 30) 289.

[43] Sheehan, 'What Is a Mistake?' (n 35) 559. *cf* A Nair, '"Mistakes of Law" and Legal Reasoning: Interpreting *Kleinwort Benson v Lincoln City Council*' in R Chambers, C Mitchell and J Penner (eds), *Philosophical Foundations of the Law of Unjust Enrichment* (Oxford, Oxford University Press, 2009) (outlining a positivist account).

[44] *Kleinwort Benson* (n 15) 358 (Lord Browne-Wilkinson) and 394 (Lord Lloyd), endorsed in C Mitchell, 'Retrospective Mistakes of Law' (1999) 10 *Kings College Law Journal* 121, 125–126.

[45] *Kleinwort Benson* (n 15) 397 (Lord Lloyd). See also Lord Browne-Wilkinson at 363 ('If, at the date of payment, it was settled law that payment was legally due, I can see nothing unjust in permitting the payee to retain moneys he received at a time when all lawyers skilled in the field would have advised that he was entitled to receive them and the payer was bound to pay them.').

mistake. To the contrary, they thought such a defence was incompatible with the declaratory theory of adjudication. Like the minority, the majority Law Lords rejected the parochial view that judges only ever 'find' law but do not 'make it'. Lord Goff acknowledged it was 'inevitable' that 'in reality ... the law is the subject of development by the judges'.[46] But because judges do so though adjudication of disputes, courts cannot separate their judgments of what the law holds from their determinations of what the law was. They cannot divorce the transaction-time law from the decision-time law, as the decision is what determines the law of the transaction. Thus, no matter how firmly people might have believed that a point of law justified a payment, if a court authoritatively rules otherwise, that must mean the payment was not due, and views to the contrary can only be understood as mistaken. Lord Goff summarised the logic of the majority's position as follows:

> The payer believed, when he paid the money, that he was bound in law to pay it. He is now told that, on the law as held to be applicable at the date of the payment, he was not bound to pay it. Plainly, therefore, he paid the money under a mistake of law, and accordingly, subject to any applicable defences, he is entitled to recover it.[47]

On this view, the idea that a 'settled understanding of the law' should operate as a defence to restitution contravenes the basic logic that holding an erroneous view of the law (as judicially determined) – even if commonly held – is a mistake.[48] It therefore provides no protection to defendants from the effects of judicial changes in the law.

In light of this contemporary common law position, the 'settled law' provisions that exist in statute seem to rest on 'insecure foundation[s]'.[49] Both in the United Kingdom and New Zealand, these provisions have come under criticism. The prevailing practice defence has also been found to contravene EU law.[50] It is ultimately a public policy defence that exists to ensure certainty of transactions and to protect public treasuries from restitutionary claims. But is it justified? Bhandari contends that the UK's statutory prevailing practice defence is indeterminate, excessively favourable to the Crown and burdensome on claimants who overpay tax, and unnecessary. The mischief of new precedent giving rise to floods of retrospective money claims can, she suggests, be avoided by simply having adequate limitation provisions.[51] Likewise, the New Zealand provision has been criticised as

[46] *Ibid* 377. See also *Robinson v Chief Constable of West Yorkshire Police (Rev 1)* [2018] UKSC 4, [2018] AC 736 [84] (Lord Mance): 'No-one now suggests that the common law has not changed since the Saxon era, merely to be revealed from time to time by an increasingly perceptive judiciary'.

[47] Kleinwort Benson (n 15). See A Burrows, 'Common Law Retrospectivity' in A Burrows, D Johnston and R Zimmermann (eds), *Judge and Jurist: Essays in Memory of Lord Rodger of Earlsferry* (Oxford, Oxford University Press, 2013) 548.

[48] See further *Deutsche Morgan Grenfell* (n 19) (overruled on the issue of limitation in *FII* (SC II) (n 18)).

[49] *Kleinwort Benson* (n 15) 383 (Lord Goff).

[50] *FII GLO Test Claimants v HM Revenue and Customs* [2012] UKSC 19, [2012] 2 AC 337 [204]–[205] (Lord Sumption). See Bhandari (n 38) 349.

[51] Bhandari (n 38) 340. This sentiment underpinned the decision in *FII* (SC II) (n 18).

overly broad and unjust, in that it precludes recovery to 'deserving' claimants who make payments on the basis of authority that an appellate court only later finds to be wrong.[52] In both jurisdictions, commentators have called for repeal of these statutes.[53] Grantham and Rickett have even questioned whether statutory 'settled law' provisions remain effective, or if they can simply be bypassed through claimants bringing purely common law claims in mistake.[54] The concept of a settled understanding of the law has proven an ineffective route to curbing the effects of retrospective mistakes of law.

III. Immunity from Abolition of Immunity?

The decisions of the House of Lords and of the New Zealand Supreme Court to bring an end to the common law immunity of advocates in their respective jurisdictions presented a stark occasion for tailoring a private immunity from the effects of judicial change in the law. The immunity of advocates from suit in respect of their conduct before the English courts was as old and established as the common law itself.[55] It travelled with the common law to the Antipodes, where it took root.[56] For the courts to abolish the immunity overnight, without limiting the retrospective effects of this change, would expose barristers and solicitors to potential liability in private law and to unexpected economic risk. Yet, when the issue was presented to the House of Lords in *Hall v Simons*, only Lord Hope favoured introducing a temporal limit. None of the six other Law Lords thought it necessary to shield the prior litigation conduct of barristers and solicitors from the abolition of advocates' immunity.[57] Nor did any judge on the New Zealand Supreme Court when they sealed the immunity's end in *Chamberlains v Lai*.[58]

A. Was Advocates' Immunity Established?

It is clear that by the turn of the millennium, advocates' immunity was recognised as an established doctrine in the United Kingdom, Australia and New Zealand. The immunity originated in ancient Roman law, which understood the relationship

[52] B Perham, 'Restitution for Mistaken Payments: Whither Mistakes of Law' (1995) 25 *Victoria University of Wellington Law Review* 373, 405.

[53] *Ibid*; Bhandari (n 38) 341.

[54] R Grantham and C Rickett, *Enrichment and Restitution in New Zealand* (Oxford, Hart Publishing, 2000) 132–33.

[55] A Emmett, 'Principles Relating to Advocate's Immunity following *Attwells v Jackson Lawyers* and *Kendirjian v Lepore*' (2016) 30 *Commercial Law Quarterly* 10, 10.

[56] Curiously, the same did not occur in North America's common law jurisdictions: *Demarco v Ungaro* (1979) 95 DLR (3d) 385 (OHC); *Ferri v Ackerman*, 444 US 193 (1979) (USSC).

[57] *Arthur JS Hall & Co v Simons* [2002] 1 AC 615 (HL). Although, partially dissenting, Lord Hope, Lord Hutton and Lord Hobhouse would have retained the immunity for criminal proceedings.

[58] *Chamberlains v Lai* [2006] NZSC 70, [2007] 2 NZLR 7.

between advocate and client as falling beyond the law of contract. As such, clients' obligations to pay barristers' fees, and barristers' obligations of diligence and competence, were not enforceable by private suit.[59] With the maturing of the law of obligations, and the recognition of special duties of care under the *Hedley Byrne v Heller* principle,[60] courts reconsidered the rationale for maintaining advocates' immunity as based, instead, in public policy. An advocates' immunity from suit by former clients reinforced the advocate's independence and duties to the court, the smooth functioning of the cab rank rule, and finality in litigation. It promoted the administration of justice. The House of Lords affirmed this rationale in *Rondel v Worsley*.[61] The Law Lords considered it 'long-established general policy' that the actions of judges, witnesses and counsel in litigation had immunity from suit.[62] In the words of Lord Pearson:

> The immunity of a barrister from legal liability for breach of his undertaking to appear for the client and from liability for negligence in the conduct of the case has been well established for more than a hundred years.[63]

Rondel v Worsley was endorsed by the New Zealand Court of Appeal in *Rees v Sinclair* and by the High Court of Australia in *Giannarelli v Wraith*.[64] The immunity extended, moreover, to pre-trial work provided such work was a necessary extension of the protected courtroom advocacy.[65] Bounded by that caveat, the firm precedent of these three jurisdictions established an immunity of advocates in respect of their courtroom conduct in both criminal and civil matters.

B. Interference with Advocates' Immunity by New Precedent?

The immunity of advocates was hardly a value-neutral doctrine. In submissions to the House of Lords in *Rondel v Worsley* in 1967, counsel for the appellant cited numerous opinions in public journals that were 'almost unanimously opposed to the conferment of the immunity'.[66] How was it good public policy to deprive individuals of a right to sue negligent counsel? It was far from obvious that advocates' immunity was necessary to guard against abuse of process and to safeguard the administration of justice. The issue inevitably returned to the courts. The High

[59] *Fell v Brown* [1820] Eng R 18, (1791) Peake 131.

[60] *Hedley Byrne & Co Ltd v Heller & Partners Ltd* [1964] AC 465 (HL) 502–503 (Lord Morris: 'if someone possessed of a special skill undertakes, quite irrespective of contract, to apply that skill for the assistance of another person who relies upon such skill, a duty of care will arise').

[61] *Rondel v Worsley* [1969] 1 AC 191 (HL).

[62] *Ibid* 284 (Lord Upjohn). See also 229 (Lord Reid).

[63] *Ibid* 288.

[64] *Rees v Sinclair* [1974] 1 NZLR 180 (NZCA); *Giannarelli v Wraith* (1988) 165 CLR 543 (HCA). See also, *Cabassi v Vila* (1940) 64 CLR 130, 140 (Starke J).

[65] *Rees, ibid* 187, endorsed in *Saif Ali v Sydney Mitchell & Co* [1980] AC 198 (HL) and *Giannarelli, ibid*.

[66] *Rondel* (n 61) 204 (Louis Blom-Cooper for the appellant).

Court of Australia in *D'Orta-Ekenaike v Victoria Legal Aid* reaffirmed the immunity,[67] and it has continued to do so in recent judgments,[68] to the chagrin of commentators.[69] The House of Lords in 2000, however, abandoned the doctrine.[70] The Court of Appeal of New Zealand followed in 2005, in a decision affirmed by the New Zealand Supreme Court the following year.[71] The Courts held that the public policy reasons that had grounded advocates' immunity simply no longer carried weight in their respective jurisdictions.

The judgments in *Hall* and *Chamberlains* clearly ushered a change in the law. None of the senior judges feigned to suggest otherwise. Lord Browne-Wilkinson, Lord Hutton and Lord Hobhouse considered that advocates' immunity could 'no longer' be 'justif[ied]'.[72] Lord Hoffmann, Lord Hope and Lord Millett considered the immunity to be 'abolish[ed]' by their judgment.[73] Lord Steyn held that 'the immunity no longer exists'.[74] Similarly, on the New Zealand Supreme Court, Elias CJ, on behalf of herself, Gault and Keith JJ, found 'the former justifications for the immunity [were] no longer convincing (if they ever were)' and the time had come to 'change' the law.[75] Justices Tipping and Thomas considered advocates' immunity to be 'abolish[ed]',[76] a development Thomas J hailed as 'long overdue'.[77]

This language is significant because it denotes a law-making function of courts that might seem at odds with the declaratory theory of adjudication. The judges did not, in the words of Lord Hope, 'go so far as to hold that *Rondel v Worsley* was wrongly decided'.[78] The new precedents of *Hall* and *Chamberlains* were not declaring that advocates' immunity had never been the law previously. Nor were they directly casting aspersions on the providence of the prior precedents that had recognised it. They did not purport to overrule *Rondel v Worsley*. Rather, *Hall* and *Chamberlains* were responding to a perceived change of circumstances in society and a shift in the balance of public interest. The circumstances had changed, and the present law needed to follow suit. By judicial decree, the old law was to give way to the new. That these judgments marked a clear break with the old law was explicitly put by Tipping J:

> We are changing the law in the present case. Hitherto barristers have had immunity from suit for protected work. Henceforth they will not have any such immunity.

[67] *D'Orta-Ekenaike v Victoria Legal Aid* [2005] HCA 12, (2005) 223 CLR 1.

[68] *Attwells v Jackson Lalic Lawyers Pty Ltd* [2016] HCA 16, (2016) 259 CLR 1; *Kendirjian v Lepore* [2017] HCA 13, (2017) 259 CLR 275.

[69] See n 104.

[70] *Hall* (n 57).

[71] *Lai v Chamberlains* (n 4); *Chamberlains* (n 58).

[72] *Hall* (n 57) 684 (Lord Browne-Wilkinson), 728 (Lord Hutton) and 735 (Lord Hobhouse).

[73] *Ibid* 707 (Lord Hoffmann), 713 (Lord Hope) and 752 (Lord Millett).

[74] *Ibid* 684. See B Juratowitch, *Retroactivity and the Common Law* (Oxford, Hart Publishing, 2008) 164; Sampford (n 30) 213.

[75] *Chamberlains* (n 58).

[76] *Ibid* [132] (Tipping J) and [224] (Thomas J).

[77] *Ibid* [224].

[78] *Hall* (n 57) 710.

> We are not declaring that in reality barristers have never had immunity; nor are we simply correcting a mistaken view of the law. Blackstone might have put it that way but we cannot. We are changing the law because of a change in perceptions over time of what public and legal policy require. If anyone had asked a properly qualified lawyer in 1995 whether barristers had immunity from suit in defined circumstances, the answer could only have been in the affirmative.[79]

The new precedents of *Hall* and *Chamberlains* replaced the old law of *Rondel v Worsley*. This threw up a puzzle regarding when the new precedent of no-immunity took effect. When did *Rondel v Worsley* cease to be good law? Ordinarily, courts 'make' law retrospectively by determining the law in the context of past disputes and applying their holdings to the parties before them. In the cases of *Hall* and *Chamberlains*, this would suggest treating advocates' immunity as expired at least by the time the disputes arose that precipitated the litigation before the respective apex courts. But this would then backdate the new law of no-immunity to a time when all well-informed barristers and clients would, as Tipping J averred, have understood advocates' immunity to apply. Can it be just and fair to apply a rule of no-immunity to parties who have relied and transacted on the basis of a rule of immunity? Conversely, if the new law took effect only from the date that the courts handed down their precedent-changing judgments – in 2000 and 2006, respectively – that would suggest that the parties appearing before the House of Lords and the New Zealand Supreme Court, whose disputes had both arisen by the mid-1990s, should be bound by advocates' immunity notwithstanding the plaintiffs' successful case against the immunity. In other words, barristers' past negligent courtroom actions would be shielded from the courts' new precedent.

C. Does Established Immunity Warrant Immunity from New Precedent?

At least from the perspective of courtroom lawyers, the stakes in *Hall* and *Chamberlains* were high. Abolishing the immunity would expose advocates to potential liability in respect of conduct (falling within the limitation period) that had previously been shielded from private suit. Appearing alongside the parties in *Hall* were counsel from the Solicitors Indemnity Fund and the Bar Council. Likewise, intervening in *Chamberlains* were the New Zealand Bar Association and the New Zealand Law Society. In both cases, counsel representing the interests of advocates argued that immunity remained good public policy. Two options were put forward, however, in the event the judges disagreed.

[79] *Chamberlains* (n 58) [136].

The first option was to leave abolition of the immunity to Parliament. The essence of the argument was that advocates' immunity was too well established in the common law for the courts simply to abandon it.[80] In both jurisdictions, legislation had been enacted on the assumption that advocates' immunity existed.[81] Parliaments of the United Kingdom and New Zealand had long had the opportunity to abolish it and neither had done so. The judges were thus urged to exercise restraint. Both apex courts rejected this invitation. They did not accept that parliamentary inaction presented any barrier to the judicial function. Advocates' immunity was 'a creature of the common law' and its interpretation and scope, as a matter of doctrine and statutory interpretation, fell within the province of the courts.[82] In the words of Lord Hoffmann, 'The judges created the immunity and the judges should say that the grounds for maintaining it no longer exist. *Cessante ratione legis, cessat lex ipsa*'.[83]

The second, alternative option presented to the judges was to abolish the immunity with prospective-only effect.[84] That is, to hold that the immunity should remain in effect over past actions of counsel (including the present conduct in dispute), but it should cease to govern future cases. Essentially, this would provide for past barristerial actions an immunity from the abolition of advocates' immunity. As signalled at the outset of this section, Lord Hope was alone in advocating such an approach in this context. Lord Hope premised his speech by stating:

> I consider it to be a legitimate exercise of your Lordships' judicial function to declare prospectively whether or not the immunity – which is a judge-made rule – is to be available in the future and, if so, in what circumstances.[85]

His Lordship proceeded to hold that the Law Lords 'should express our decision so that it applies only to the future – not to a period in the past as well'.[86] The date of handing down *Hall*, Lord Hope contended, should be taken to be the date

[80] See generally *Burnet v Coronado Oil & Gas Co*, 285 US 393 (1932) (USSC) (Brandeis J: '*Stare decisis* is usually the wise policy, because in most matters it is more important that the applicable rule of law be settled than that it be settled right'); *London Street Tramways Co Ltd v London County Council* [1898] AC 375 (HL) 380 (Lord Halsbury: 'there may be a current of opinion in the profession that such and such a judgment was erroneous; but what is that occasional interference with what is perhaps abstract justice as compared with the inconvenience – the disastrous inconvenience – of having each question subject to being reargued and the dealings of mankind rendered doubtful by reason of different decisions …').

[81] *Courts and Legal Services Act 1990* (UK) s 62; *Law Practitioners Act 1982* (NZ) s 61.

[82] *Chamberlains* (n 58) [128] (Tipping J). See also [94] (Elias CJ).

[83] *Hall* (n 57) 705.

[84] This is popularly known as 'prospective overruling', a term that is 'a misnomer since the law always operates prospectively; what is meant is that the overruling is not retrospective and so has prospective-only effect': *Chief Executive of the Department of Corrections v Gardiner* [2017] NZCA 608, [2018] 2 NZLR 712 [16] (Miller J). See Juratowitch, (n 74) 199. See generally E Steiner (ed), *Comparing the Prospective Effect of Judicial Rulings Across Jurisdictions* (Cham, Springer International Publishing, 2015).

[85] *Hall* (n 57) 710.

[86] *Ibid.*

on which advocates' immunity ended.[87] Lord Hope's explanation for so holding was brief, but it seemed to rest on two justifications. First, since in his view advocates' immunity was established doctrine in 1991 when the parties' dispute arose, it invariably must be taken to have expired at a later point in time.[88] Second, since it 'would be very difficult at this stage to identify' a cogent prior date on which the new rule of no-immunity could be said to have taken effect, the date of the House's judgment should operate as the law-changing moment.[89] It can be inferred that Lord Hope favoured a 'pure' prospective-only overruling approach and would not have lifted the immunity from the lawyer-defendants in the case before him.[90] This point was not necessary to decide, however, as all of the Law Lords agreed that, on the facts before them, the conduct in dispute – the allegedly negligent negotiation by solicitors of the terms of settlement of litigation – fell outside of the scope of the doctrine of advocates' immunity in any event.

In *Chamberlains*, the five Supreme Court judges were in agreement that the case for abolishing advocates' immunity in New Zealand only for the future had not been made out. Nevertheless, Tipping J opined that circumstances could arise where 'it would be wrong to extend the effect of a change' in the law to those who have acted on the basis of previously established law.[91] Justice Thomas concurred,[92] while Elias CJ for the majority thought the matter unnecessary to decide.[93] In extended obiter dicta, Tipping J outlined five signposts for guiding judges to determine when a novel judgment ought to apply only prospectively to future cases. His first point was that, prima facie, judgments should be understood to determine the law retrospectively 'unless they can clearly be said to change the law'.[94] Second, the point of law being changed must have been sufficiently established such that it could 'fairly be regarded as having settled the law'.[95] Third, 'citizens or society generally' must have sufficiently relied on the previously established point of law in ordering their affairs such that 'it would cause serious injustice to individuals, or would clearly not be in the best interests of society as a whole, for the law to be altered retrospectively'.[96] Fourth, the harm of retrospective changes in the law should be balanced against the harms 'to individuals or society' of not applying the new law to past cases.[97] Fifth, in order to preserve plaintiffs' incentives to litigate important points of law, the successful party to the law-changing decision ought

[87] *Ibid* 726.
[88] *Ibid.*
[89] *Ibid* 710.
[90] See *Re Spectrum Plus* (n 20) [72]–[73] (Lord Hope).
[91] *Chamberlains* (n 58) [140].
[92] *Ibid* [205].
[93] *Ibid* [95].
[94] *Ibid* [143].
[95] *Ibid.*
[96] *Ibid* [144].
[97] *Ibid.*

to receive 'the fruits of victory' through the judgment being selectively applied to their case, while the 'old' law is applied to other similarly situated non-parties.[98] (On this fifth point, Tipping J could be seen to differ from Lord Hope.)

I have elsewhere critiqued the coherence of the doctrine of prospective-only overruling.[99] Suffice it to say, all of these signposts are loaded with value-judgments. Thoughtful judges will inevitably disagree as to whether a point of law is sufficiently established, as well as whether a new judgment clearly *changes* or merely *refines* it. The *Chamberlains* judgment itself illustrates this: Tipping J thought that at the time the events in issue occurred, advocates' immunity 'was generally viewed as settled' law,[100] whereas Elias CJ considered that '[d]oubts about the justification for the immunity have always existed and have grown in recent years' such that it would not have been reasonable for 'legal practitioners [to] have ordered their practices' in reliance on it.[101] The same split in views occurred between Lord Hope and his fellow Law Lords in *Hall*.[102] (In any event, the formal rationale for the immunity was to benefit the public, not barristers, so practitioners' reliance interests rightly carried little weight.) Moreover, the reliance interests of citizens and society on principles of law are heterogeneous, change over time, and are irreducible to a simple balancing exercise. It is far from clear when, if ever, prospective-only overruling will be an appropriate course of action. The key takeaway, for the purposes of this chapter, is that prospective-only overruling presents as a (*tentative*) route for immunising parties from judicial changes in the law, while concomitantly withholding relief from those who might otherwise benefit from the court's holding.

One of the consequences of *Hall* and *Chamberlains* has been to compound reservations over the future of advocates' immunity in Australia. Advocates' immunity is clearly an established doctrine, it having been affirmed and refined by three judgments of the High Court of Australia in the past 15 years.[103] But this entrenchment is pushing against the tide of the rest of the common law world as well as fervent and frequent domestic calls for reform.[104] Justice Thomas in *Chamberlains* predicted that, 'in the fullness of time', the doctrine in Australia 'will be reversed by legislation or, possibly, a future Court'.[105] It might be thought

[98] *Ibid* [134].

[99] S Beswick, 'Retroactive Adjudication' (2020) 130 *Yale Law Journal* 276. See also, D Sheehan and TT Arvind, 'Prospective Overruling and the Fixed-Floating Charge Debate' (2006) 122 *LQR* 20. For a defence of *Chamberlains*, see J Wall, 'Prospective Overruling – It's about Time' (2009) 12 *Otago Law Review* 131.

[100] *Chamberlains* (n 58) [149].

[101] *Ibid* [95].

[102] See *Awoyomi v Radford* [2007] EWHC 1671, [2008] QB 793 [19].

[103] *D'Orta-Ekenaike* (n 67); *Attwells* (n 68); *Kendirjian* (n 68).

[104] S Charles, 'The Immunity of the Advocate' (2003) 23 *Australian Bar Review* 220, 225–26; P Gerber, 'Burning Down the House to Roast the Pig: The High Court Retains Advocate's Immunity' (2005) 28 *UNSW Law Journal* 646, 662; T Anthony, 'Australia's Anachronistic Advocates' Immunity' (2007) 15 *Tort Law Review* 11; M Kirby, 'Of Advocates, Drunks and Other Players: Plain Tales from Australia' (2011) 23 *Denning Law Journal* 47; C Green, 'A Case for Abolition' [2019] *Law Institute Journal* 44.

[105] *Chamberlains* (n 58) [203].

that the High Court has taken small steps in this direction by confining the scope of the immunity to exclude lawyers' advice on whether to settle litigation.[106] But the core of the doctrine remains. Even if the Court were inclined to revisit the continued suitability of the immunity in Australian law, judicial reform would face two obstacles. First, there is the argument that advocates' immunity is too firmly entrenched in Australian law for the Court now to abandon it. There is precedent of the High Court refusing to depart from prior (impugned) precedent that had 'stood without question for over fifty years', on the basis that 'commerce has, no doubt, been conducted on the footing of the correctness of what this Court has decided'.[107] Second, the economic consequences of an about-face could be particularly disruptive, as the High Court would hardly entertain shielding barristers from retrospective liability that might follow any decision to abolish advocates' immunity. The reasons given in *Hall* and *Chamberlains* for declining to do so are persuasive. Moreover, the High Court of Australia has rejected the doctrine of prospective-only overruling as 'inconsistent with judicial power'.[108] In *Ha v New South Wales*, the Court unanimously endorsed the declaratory theory – 'the making of binding declarations of rights and obligations arising from the operation of the law upon past events or conduct' – as a 'hallmark of the judicial process'.[109] Contrary to the positions expressed by Lord Hope and Tipping J, the High Court has maintained that: 'If an earlier case is erroneous and it is necessary to overrule it, it would be a perversion of judicial power to maintain in force that which is acknowledged not to be the law'.[110]

Barristers in Australia can count on no immunity defence if the High Court were to overrule *D'Orta-Ekenaike v Victoria Legal Aid*. But then, this being the case, in light of the pressures and speculation that advocates' immunity will eventually fall in Australia, perhaps professional indemnity insurance policies ought, as a matter of course, to cover the risk of suit over courtroom conduct. This would suit the interests of risk-averse barristers. A fair premium would be modest, since potential liability would be discounted by the expected risk of the High Court changing the law. This would then answer the economic disruption argument that drove the case for prospectively overruling advocates' immunity in other jurisdictions.

[106] Emmett (n 55) 18.

[107] *Geelong Harbour Trust v Gibbs, Bright & Co* (1970) 122 CLR 504 (HCA) 505. See Juratowitch (n 74) 167–71. See similarly, *Friedmann Equity Developments Inc v Final Note Ltd* [2000] 1 SCR 842 (SCC) [51].

[108] *Ha v New South Wales* [1997] HCA 34, (1997) 189 CLR 465, 503.

[109] *Ibid.*

[110] *Ibid* 504, *aff'd Bell Lawyers Pty Ltd v Pentelow* [2019] HCA 29, [55], [94]–[98]. See *FII* (SC II) (n 18) [99] and [293]. See generally J Edelman, 'Chief Justice French, Judicial Power and Chapter III of the Commonwealth Constitution' in H Jackson (ed), *Essays in Honour of Chief Justice French* (Alexandria, NSW, The Federation Press, 2019) 101–104 (describing Australia as 'one of the last holdouts against prospective overruling', and discussing *Re Spectrum Plus* (n 20) and the English mistake of law cases).

Alternatively, and perhaps more likely,[111] the demise of advocates' immunity in Australia may come from Parliament, not the Court. Since parliaments legislate with presumptively prospective-only effect, the problem of retrospective change in the law will simply not arise. There will be no question of Australian barristers needing immunity from the abolition of advocates' immunity. It would seem, then, that the novel doctrine that would immunise advocates from judicial interference with their immunity will remain consigned to legal theory, not to emanate in the common law.

IV. Immunity from 'Judicial Takings'? Two Paradigm Cases

When governments make laws that take private property, deprived owners are ordinarily due compensatory relief. This is the price of a democratic government's use of its expropriation power. When *courts* make laws that eliminate previously established rights to property, should affected persons be afforded similar protection? This section discusses two landmark judgments from the apex courts of the two most prominent common law jurisdictions – the United States and the United Kingdom – which appear to recognise a novel doctrine of 'judicial takings'. The premise of this doctrine is that those whose property rights are adversely affected by judicial decisions should receive similar protection as those adversely affected by governmental decisions. This doctrine, if accepted, would immunise private parties from detrimental judicial changes in the law governing their property. Despite garnering some judicial and scholarly support on both sides of the Atlantic, the content and scope of a judicial takings doctrine are far from established in common law reasoning.

A. *Stop the Beach Renourishment Inc v Florida Department of Environmental Protection*

Stop the Beach began as a fairly unremarkable property development dispute. It originated in a challenge by oceanfront property owners to a municipal plan to restore and expand around 11 kilometres of coastal beach in the State of Florida. Under Florida law, 'littoral' oceanfront property can be privately owned up to the mean high-tidewater line. The State owns in trust for the public the land extending past this line into the water. Coastlines, of course, change over time. Under the common law of Florida, oceanfront owners retain title over any gradual and

[111] Green (n 104) 46–47.

imperceptible 'accretions' to the dry sand area. But they do not benefit from 'sudden or perceptible' changes to the land from the water, which are called 'avulsions'.[112] The State retains title when formerly submerged land becomes dry land by avulsion.

The municipalities' proposal in *Stop the Beach* was to carry out massive sand dumps below the high-tidewater line so as to expand the beach area seaward by around 23 metres. This (now unsubmerged) beach area would be owned by the State. State legislation established the procedures for the project.[113] Once a restoration project was approved, a permanent erosion-control line would designate the boundary of oceanfront owners' property, replacing the common law boundary rules, including the right to accretions. The legislation preserved certain other 'common-law riparian rights', however, including 'rights of ingress, egress, view, boating, bathing, and fishing'.[114]

Oceanfront property owners who opposed the proposed development brought an administrative challenge, which they lost. But they succeeded before the Florida Court of Appeal, which held that the State, in approving the beach restoration project, had eliminated two littoral rights of oceanfront landowners: '(1) the right to receive accretions to their property; and (2) the right to have the contact of their property with the water remain intact'.[115] The Court held this was an unconstitutional 'taking' of property and it set aside the development approval. On appeal, the Florida Supreme Court reversed. It characterised the beach restoration project as a permissible act of avulsion, and rejected the contentions that any littoral rights to accretions or for property to touch the water had been unlawfully eliminated.[116]

Up until this point, this legal tussle was, as suggested, fairly unremarkable: the oceanfront landowners had exercised their rights to challenge a public works project and the highest state court had found that the landowners' property rights had not been violated. On further appeal to the Supreme Court of the United States, however, the owner-petitioners doubled down. Having failed to show that the Florida Government had unconstitutionally taken their property, the petitioners turned their sights on the Florida Supreme Court itself: they argued 'that the Florida Supreme Court's decision *itself* effected a taking' of their littoral rights contrary to the Federal Constitution's Takings Clause.[117] The Takings Clause, contained in the Fifth Amendment,[118] provides that 'private property' shall not

[112] *Stop the Beach Renourishment Inc v Florida Department of Environmental Protection*, 560 US 702, 708 (2010) (USSC).

[113] *Beach and Shore Preservation Act, 1961* Florida Laws ch 61–246, as amended, Florida Statute §§ 161.011–161.45 (2007).

[114] *Ibid* § 161.201.

[115] *Stop the Beach* (n 112) 711.

[116] *Ibid* 712.

[117] *Ibid* (emphasis added). See Note, 'Judicial Takings, Judicial Federalism, and Jurisprudence: An *Erie* Problem' (2020) 134 *Harvard Law Review* 808.

[118] And applied to the states through the Fourteenth Amendment: *Chicago, Burlington, & Quincy Railroad Co v Chicago*, 166 US 226, 236 (1897).

'be taken for public use, without just compensation'. The petitioners contended that the Florida Supreme Court's *judgment* had taken their property rights 'by declaring that those rights did not exist'.[119] Although the Supreme Court of the United States ultimately rejected this argument on the facts, one-half of the Court nevertheless endorsed the premise of the doctrine of judicial takings.

i. Were Property Rights Established?

None of the eight[120] justices on the United States Supreme Court who heard the appeal were satisfied that Florida law had ever recognised the property rights that the petitioners complained had been violated. The petitioners had relied on obiter dicta in a previous case of the Florida Supreme Court as grounding their rights to accretions and to a secure ocean boundary-line.[121] But the justices accepted that a legitimate consequence of avulsion could be to eliminate the conditions for accretion, and that there was 'no independent right of contact with the water' under Florida law.[122] Accordingly, no established property rights of the petitioners had been violated. The Florida Court of Appeal had simply gotten the law wrong.

Nevertheless, Scalia J, writing for a plurality of four justices,[123] considered in obiter what recourse the petitioners might have had had the Florida Court of Appeal's judgment correctly determined their rights under state law, yet still been overturned by the Florida Supreme Court. Justice Scalia framed the inquiry as turning on 'whether the property right allegedly taken was established'.[124] That is, whether the right in issue was 'private property under established law'.[125] The judgment sought to draw a line between established property rights, which may be protected by the Takings Clause, and non-established interests.[126] Problematically, Scalia J's analysis of how one ascertains when property rights are 'established' in law did not venture much further beyond stating, in a footnote, that '[a] property right is not established if there is doubt about its existence'.[127]

[119] *Stop the Beach* (n 112) 279.

[120] Justice Stevens, who owned property on a Florida beach, recused himself. In a speech given at Chicago-Kent College of Law after his retirement, Stevens J later criticised Scalia J's plurality opinion in *Stop the Beach*: JP Stevens, 'The Ninth Vote in the "Stop the Beach" Case' (Chicago, Illinois, 3 October 2012).

[121] *Board of Trustees of Internal Improvement Trust Fund v Sand Key Association Ltd*, 512 So 2d 934 (Fla 1987).

[122] *Stop the Beach* (n 112) 733.

[123] The other concurring judges did not reject the proposed judicial takings doctrine, but found it 'beyond the necessities of the case' to decide the issue, which was 'better left for another day': *Ibid* 737 and 742. See Masur and Mortara (n 6) 994 (noting that 'since *Stop the Beach Renourishment*, no court has held that a judicial decision effected a taking').

[124] *Stop the Beach* (n 112) 728.

[125] *Ibid.*

[126] LS Underkuffler, 'Judicial Takings: A Medley of Misconceptions' (2010) 61 *Syracuse Law Review* 203, 208; EM Penalver and LJ Strahilevitz, 'Judicial Takings or Due Process' (2011) 97 *Cornell Law Review* 305, 346.

[127] *Stop the Beach* (n 112) 726, fn 9.

The problem with this premise is that it is ordinarily courts – and in the United States, state courts – that interpret and determine the content of property rights. In order for a doctrine of judicial takings to take root, one must find a principled way to determine when a court is simply clarifying the law governing property rights and when it is changing that law. Property scholars[128] and practitioners[129] lament that the distinction is illusory. Perhaps a property right is only established once there is a 'baseline' of 'preexisting law' recognising it,[130] or 'prior case law' that has fully considered and ruled upon 'the competing public interests' implicated by the right.[131] But even these boundaries 'may be murky and contested', as evinced by the very fact of continued litigation over property rights.[132] If judges in good faith disagree over the nature of an asserted property right, does such divergence itself provoke sufficient doubt so as to undermine any finding that the right is 'established'?

ii. Interference with Established Property Rights by New Precedent?

Determining whether a novel precedent *interferes* with an established right would seem to present as fraught an inquiry as the determination of whether a right is established. According to the Court's plurality judgment, the Federal Constitution's Takings Clause, on its plain meaning, governs the actions of all branches of the State. Justice Scalia averred that 'the Takings Clause bars *the State* from taking private property without paying for it, no matter which branch is the instrument of the taking. … [T]he particular state *actor* is irrelevant'.[133] Accordingly:

> If a legislature *or a court* declares that what was once an established right of private property no longer exists, it has taken that property, no less than if the State had physically appropriated it or destroyed its value by regulation.[134]

The manner in which *a court* might 'take' property in such circumstances would be by declaring new law that changes or overrules authority under which property rights have been established. This idea of 'judicial legislation' sits in tension with the declaratory theory of adjudication. Justice Scalia grounded the judicial takings doctrine in a post-nineteenth century realist conceptualisation of courts as wielding 'the power to change the common law'.[135] While he acknowledged such a

[128] Penalver and Strahilevitz (n 126) 346.
[129] MJ Fasano, 'A Divided Ruling for a Divided Country in Dividing Times' (2010) 35 *Vermont Law Review* 495, 503.
[130] C Serkin, 'Transition Relief from Judge-Made Law: The Incentives of Judicial Takings' (2011) 21 *Widener Law Journal* 777, 783.
[131] DB Barros, 'The Complexities of Judicial Takings' (2010) 45 *University of Richmond Law Review* 903, 936.
[132] Penalver and Strahilevitz (n 126) 346.
[133] *Stop the Beach* (n 112) 715.
[134] *Ibid.* See F Bloom and C Serkin, 'Suing Courts' (2012) 79 *University of Chicago Law Review* 553.
[135] *Stop the Beach* (n 112) 722.

doctrine might not have been envisaged by the Blackstonian-influenced Framers of the Constitution – 'an era when courts had no power to "change" the common law' – it was now an appropriate response to modern adjudication in the United States.[136]

What is curious about this premise is that it appears to contradict Scalia J's own long-held jurisprudence on the declaratory theory as a fundamental feature of adjudication. In *James B Beam Distilling Co v Georgia*, Scalia J had intimated that neither he *nor* 'our forebears' were 'so naïve … as to be unaware that judges in a real sense "make" law'.[137] But, he maintained, they do not do so in the manner of legislatures. Legislatures make law for the future for all. Judges make law by adjudicating disputes that arose in the past. They are constitutionally constrained 'to say what the law is'.[138] Justice Scalia viewed the declaratory theory as a '[check] upon judicial law-making' that demanded adjudicatory discipline to make law only '*as judges make it*': [W]hich is to say *as though* they were 'finding' it – discerning what the law *is*, rather than decreeing what it is today *changed to*, or what it will *tomorrow* be.[139]

Viewed through this lens, judges' decisions cannot escape interpreting law and rights retrospectively because adjudication is fundamentally a backward-looking exercise.[140] This unbroken link between decisions of courts and their impact on past rights itself serves to ensure that judges do not lightly overrule prior precedent – because new law necessarily defines past rights.[141] The proposed doctrine of judicial takings, however, breaks this link. It purports to constrain judges from 'declar[ing] that what had been private property under established law no longer is'.[142] It requires judges to differentiate judgments that 'establish' property rights from those that 'eliminate' those same rights. But if, as the declaratory theory presumes, judges are fundamentally interpreters of the law (and of rights and duties under law), then such differentiation is paradoxical. The idea of judicial takings requires judges to separate their interpretive role from their 'law-changing' role. Yet, Scalia J denies that judge-made law can operate outside of the constraints of judicial interpretation. It is, then, perhaps not surprising that the judgment in *Stop the Beach* lacks guidance as to how the two judicial roles can be separated. Without such guidance, we are left in the dark as to when established rights should be understood to have been 'eliminated' rather than merely clarified by judge-made law. As Underkuffler laments:

[136] *Ibid* 721.

[137] *James B Beam Distilling Co v Georgia*, 501 US 529, 549 (1991) (USSC) (concurring opinion). See A Scalia, *A Matter of Interpretation: Federal Courts and the Law* (Princeton, Princeton University Press, 1997) 9–14.

[138] *Marbury v Madison*, 5 US 137, 177 (1803) (USSC).

[139] *James B Beam* (n 137) 549.

[140] Heydon (n 1) 509.

[141] Retroactivity acts as a check upon judicial law-making: *James B Beam* (n 137) 549. See P Cane, 'The Common Law, the High Court of Australia, and the United States Supreme Court' in P Daley (ed), *Apex Courts and the Common Law* (Toronto, University of Toronto Press, 2019) 77.

[142] *Stop the Beach* (n 112) 728. *cf* 737 (Justice Kennedy alluded to the declaratory nature of judicial law-making when noting that 'State courts generally operate under a common-law tradition that allows for incremental modifications to property law').

> Unless the court states that the prior decision established a right on which reliance was justified, and that its current decision eliminates that right, there is no way for an external 'takings' court to do anything more than impress its arbitrary characterization ('right' or 'no right', and 'elimination' or 'no elimination') on the events that have transpired.[143]

iii. Do Established Rights Warrant Immunity from New Precedent?

The plurality's proposed response to a judicial taking of property was, like the doctrine itself, unorthodox. The prescribed relief when *the state* takes private property is, as Kennedy J's concurring opinion noted, 'just compensation'.[144] One consequence of a judicial takings doctrine could thus be to saddle states with 'substantial' financial burden whenever their courts change the law.[145] Yet, awards of damages would not prevent novel judgments from applying to (and upending) past rights. To the contrary, Kennedy J surmised that a right to damages might even exacerbate 'sweeping' changes by courts to property rights since compensation would be seen to alleviate the burdens of change on those whose rights are impacted.[146]

The plurality, however, rejected the suggestion that compensation would be 'the exclusive remedy for a judicial taking'.[147] Instead, Scalia J averred that an appropriate response to a judicial taking would be to reverse the holding on appeal by disapplying the interfering precedent from 'the property in question'.[148] In other words, the plurality would not apply the new precedent to established property rights. This solution exposes a 'retroactivity problem' in the doctrine of judicial takings.[149] The plurality's solution was *not* to overturn the interfering precedent as wrong in law. It was merely to curb its scope. Presumably, the precedent would continue to govern non-established interests and future rights. Such a holding, then, looks suspiciously like overruling precedent with prospective-only effect – an adjudicative doctrine that Scalia J consistently admonished throughout his judicial career as 'incompatible with the judicial role'.[150] Prospective-only overruling

[143] Underkuffler (n 126) 210.
[144] *Stop the Beach* (n 112) 734.
[145] *Ibid* 739.
[146] *Ibid* 738.
[147] *Ibid* 723.
[148] *Ibid.*
[149] ME Brady, *Defining Navigability: Balancing State-Court Flexibility and Private Rights in Waterways* (2014) 36 *Cardozo Law Review* 1415, 1465.
[150] *American Trucking Associations Inc v Smith*, 496 US 167, 201 (1990) (USSC). See *James B Beam* (n 137) 548–49 (Scalia J: 'I would find both "selective prospectivity" and "pure prospectivity" beyond our power' and 'impermissible simply because it is not allowed by the Constitution'). Although prospective-only overruling came to prominence in jurisprudence of the United States Supreme Court, the Court has in recent decades considerably retracted the doctrine: *Harper v Virginia Department of Taxation*, 509 US 86, 97 (1993) (USSC); *Landgraf v USI Film Prods*, 511 US 244, 279, fn 32 (1994) (USSC); *Reynoldsville Casket Co v Hyde*, 514 US 749, 752 (1995) (USSC).

is inconsistent with the declaratory theory of adjudication in that it divorces the court's adjudicatory role from its law-making role. It purports to declare the law for the future without bearing upon rights and duties in the past. Justice Scalia considered the technique to be 'the handmaid of judicial activism, and the born enemy of stare decisis', because it allows courts to depart from precedent without consequences for past transactions.[151] It seems, then, remarkable that Scalia J would sanction a remedy to the perceived problem of judicial takings that would operate in the same way as overruling laws with prospective-only effect: allowing courts to determine new property rules for the future while shielding from such rules those with previously 'established' property rights.

Judicial takings is far from an established doctrine of US federal law. The key portions of Scalia J's opinion in *Stop the Beach* were ultimately delivered in obiter. But given the ideological shift of the Supreme Court since Scalia J's death, it is plausible that the doctrine could one day become federal precedent in America. If it is to take root, it seems beholden on the Court to articulate a more coherent jurisprudential framework on which to ground the judicial takings doctrine.

B. *Re Spectrum Plus Ltd*

There is similarity between the complaint that drove *Stop the Beach* and the issue that troubled the House of Lords in the landmark judgment of *Re Spectrum Plus*.[152] That case concerned the proper interpretation of a security created by a bank's standard form debenture. Specifically, whether a debenture executed by the company Spectrum Plus Ltd had granted to National Westminster Bank a fixed charge or a floating charge over the company's book debts. If the debenture created a fixed charge – which is what the parties had intended – then the liquidated company's book debts would be accounted to the bank. But if the bank held only a floating charge then claims by preferential creditors (namely, company employees and the Crown) would take precedence – meaning the value of the security would be significantly weaker than the parties had intended. *Re Spectrum Plus* was a test case, the outcome of which would determine the resolution of hundreds of pending company liquidations. The boilerplate language of the debenture in issue had, for some 25 years, been employed by banks to secure fixed charges over book debts. It was a matter of general importance if this understanding widely held in the market was to be disturbed by court decision.

The basis of this market understanding stemmed from a 1979 judgment of the Chancery Division of the High Court of England and Wales. In *Siebe Gorman & Co Ltd v Barclays Bank Ltd*,[153] Slade J addressed the nature of fixed and floating charges and held that a debenture that was materially similar to that in issue in

[151] *Harper v Virginia Department of Taxation* (n 150).
[152] *Re Spectrum Plus* (n 20).
[153] *Siebe Gorman & Co Ltd v Barclays Bank Ltd* [1979] 2 Lloyd's Rep 142 (Ch).

Re Spectrum Plus had created a fixed charge over a chargor's book debts. Twenty-five years later, Sir Andrew Morritt V-C, also sitting in the Chancery Division, reviewed the case law and concluded that *Siebe Gorman* had been wrongly decided.[154] At first instance in *Re Spectrum Plus*, the judge considered that the terms of the debenture were insufficiently restrictive to justify categorising the security as a fixed charge and that National Westminster Bank held in law only a floating charge over Spectrum Plus Ltd's book debts. The Court of Appeal overturned[155] on the basis that the Chancery Division had been bound to follow its precedent that was in line with *Siebe Gorman* (notwithstanding that that precedent had subsequently been criticised).[156] The issue presented to the House of Lords was whether the *Siebe Gorman* line of precedent ought to be affirmed so as to avoid interfering with banks' established property rights over secured book debts.

i. *Were Property Rights Established?*

The bank's argument was that *Siebe Gorman* had 'established the meaning and effect of' the debenture in issue.[157] It was 'an established decision which ha[d] caused neither serious inconvenience nor injustice'.[158] It was argued that for the House of Lords to '[alter] the law' by departing from this precedent would 'undermine title to property' as well as 'the effect of numerous commercial contracts'.[159] In order to preserve '[c]ommercial certainty', the Law Lords were urged to affirm the established precedent even if they themselves would not have decided *Siebe Gorman* the same way.[160] Lord Phillips of Worth Matravers MR in the Court of Appeal had been persuaded by this argument – his Lordship thought that years of 'customary usage' of the *Siebe Gorman* form of debenture had 'acquired the meaning and effect' of a fixed charge, and therefore courts ought to continue to treat it in this way.[161]

The House of Lords rejected the argument, at least for the context of the case before it. The Law Lords did not accept that *Siebe Gorman* could be taken to determine the property rights of banks which later relied upon that judgment in drafting debentures. *Siebe Gorman* was only a first instance decision.[162] As such, it was 'always open to correction' by an appellate court and so it 'cannot have

[154] *Re Spectrum Plus Ltd* [2004] EWHC 9, [2004] Ch 337.
[155] *Re Spectrum Plus Ltd* [2004] EWCA Civ 670, [2004] Ch 337 ('*Re Spectrum Plus Court of Appeal*').
[156] *Re New Bullas Trading Ltd* [1994] 1 BCLC 485 (CA), criticised in *Agnew v Commissioner of Inland Revenue* [2001] 2 AC 710 (PC) and by R Goode, 'Charges Over Book Debts: A Missed Opportunity' (1994) 10 *LQR* 592.
[157] *Re Spectrum Plus* (n 20) 687 (Gabriel Moss QC and Jeremy Goldring for the bank).
[158] *Ibid.*
[159] *Ibid* 688. See also *Geelong Harbour Trust* (n 107) [24] (Barwick CJ, dissenting, implying that if the impugned statutory interpretation in issue had 'affect[ed] the title to property or any matter of conveyancing' he would have been inclined not to overturn it).
[160] *Re Spectrum Plus* (n 20) 687.
[161] *Re Spectrum Plus Court of Appeal* (n 155) [97].
[162] *Re Spectrum Plus* (n 20) [122] (Lord Scott).

been regarded as definitively settling the law in this field'.[163] Lord Hope averred that while banks could not be faulted for taking guidance from *Siebe Gorman* in accepting securities over book debts, sophisticated parties should have understood that the principles of law that the judgment outlined could not be relied on as conclusive. The length of time for which the precedent remained undisturbed, and the eminence of the judge who wrote it, were not determinative factors.[164] On the facts of the case, the Law Lords determined that, properly understood, the only property right that the bank had in the disputed debenture was a floating charge over book debts. The prior precedent did not elevate the bank's rights any higher. *Siebe Gorman* was simply wrongly decided.[165]

ii. Interference with Established Property Rights by New Precedent?

Because the House of Lords rejected the contention that National Westminster Bank had established rights under *Siebe Gorman*, the Law Lords' ruminations on whether a judgment overruling prior precedent might interfere with established rights are obiter. Nevertheless, the Lords seemed surprisingly accommodating to the idea that the act of judicially overturning settled precedent might itself interfere with property rights. Much emphasis was placed on the point that *Siebe Gorman* was only a decision of a first instance court. Should it be inferred that if *Siebe Gorman* had previously been endorsed by a judgment of the House of Lords, that a subsequent judgment by the country's final court overruling it would – as National Westminster Bank had argued – 'undermine title to property'?[166] In other words, does *Re Spectrum Plus* lay the ground for a judicial takings doctrine in the United Kingdom?[167]

The germ of such a framework may be found in the judgments of Lord Nicholls of Birkenhead and Lord Hope of Craighead, with whom the other Law Lords expressly agreed. The Law Lords rested their concerns over disturbing past precedent on the pillars of stare decisis and commercial certainty. It was suggested that the fair administration of justice could warrant protecting from abrupt changes in the law those who have organised their affairs on the basis of previously settled precedent. Lord Nicholls envisaged that a case could arise where a court might have to overrule a longstanding principle or understanding of a statute, while also shielding those with rights established under the previous rule from the effects of its overruling decision so as to avoid imposing 'gravely unfair and disruptive consequences for past transactions or happenings'.[168]

[163] *Ibid* [64] (Lord Hope) and [43] (Lord Nicholls).
[164] *Ibid* [64] (Lord Hope).
[165] *Ibid.*
[166] *Ibid* 688.
[167] See Devlin (n 1) 11 (suggesting that 'for the method [of judicially changing the law] to work fairly, there should be some provision for the payment out of public funds for judicial lawmaking').
[168] *Ibid* [40].

Lord Hope seemed to suggest that, had *Siebe Gorman* itself been a decision of the House of Lords (rather than a judgment of first instance) which was then being overturned, the need for commercial certainty might justify treating previously executed debentures as securing fixed charges but future such arrangements as floating charges. His Lordship said:

> It is hard to think of an area of the law where the need for certainty is more important than that with which your Lordships are concerned in this case. The commercial life of this country depends to a large extent on the reliability of the security arrangements that are entered into between debtors and their creditors. The law provides the context in which these arrangements are entered into, and it lays down the rules that have to be applied when the arrangements break down. *Mistakes as to the law* can make all the difference between success and failure when the creditor seeks to realise his security. So a heavy responsibility lies *on judges* to provide the lending market with guidance that is accurate and reliable. This is so that mistakes can be avoided and transactions entered into with confidence that they will achieve what is expected of them.[169]

The implication seems to be that if judges through their decisions have caused parties to make mistakes about the law, *judges* are responsible for protecting parties from the unfair and disruptive consequences that might otherwise follow. So, if the law had been sufficiently settled such that it was reasonable for commercial parties to rely on the *Siebe Gorman* understanding of fixed charges in arranging their securities, their property rights ought to continue to be understood as having secured fixed charges notwithstanding the judicial overruling of *Siebe Gorman*. This premise rests on a heterodox assumption about the nature of private property rights: that the boundaries of such rights can be fixed in time by 'customary usage' *of a judicial interpretation*, such that if a future court on revisiting the issue takes a different position, the new judgment could be understood not merely to (re) interpret the property right but positively to *interfere* with established rights. It suggests that the content of a property right in some way subsists independent of the courts' interpretation of it, ie once *Siebe Gorman* established title to property in secured assets, for judges to depart from that precedent is not just to (re)interpret the law but to undermine title to property. As in *Stop the Beach*, this rubric strains the declaratory theory of adjudication to which English courts have otherwise remained wedded. Lord Scott recognised this when he expressed scepticism that there would ever be circumstances 'in which it would be proper for a court, having reached a conclusion as to the correct meaning of a statute, to decline to apply to the case in hand the statute thus construed'.[170] It is difficult to envisage how the idea of judicial takings might graduate from a tentative doctrine to a practical protection of private property rights.

[169] *Ibid* [63] (emphasis added). *cf* [122] (Lord Scott: 'If *Siebe Gorman* had been a decision of this House and therefore … a decision that settled the law with finality, I think your Lordships would have need to hesitate long before overruling').

[170] *Ibid* [126].

iii. Do Established Rights Warrant Immunity from New Precedent?

The legacy of *Re Spectrum Plus*, and the most jurisprudentially significant aspect of the judgment, has not been the House of Lords' pronouncements on securities law, but its discussion of its powers to protect parties from judicial changes in the law. Their Lordships were unanimous that in the case before them they would *not* restrain the effects of their decision to overrule *Siebe Gorman*. But they expressly declined to rule out a power to do so in an appropriate future case. If the Lords *had* understood *Siebe Gorman* as establishing the bank's right to a fixed charge over company book debts, there were two ways they might have responded to protect the bank.

The first possible response would have been to affirm the precedent of *Siebe Gorman*, on the basis that overruling the decision would have improperly interfered with established property rights. This approach was favoured by Lord Phillips in the Court of Appeal. His Lordship thought that since for 25 years banks and individuals had 'relied upon' an accepted understanding of the 'meaning and effect' of the standard form debenture, it was simply too late for the courts to change its meaning.[171] Not changing the law would have solidified *Siebe Gorman* as precedent at the highest level. It would mean that similarly-worded debentures over book debts, past and future, would continue to be treated as fixed charges, giving banks priority of security over preferential creditors, notwithstanding the House of Lords' unanimous view that the proper interpretation was that the debenture secured only a floating charge. This 'solution' would thus be overkill: it would deny to all future parties the courts' best determination on a point of law merely to protect the interests of a limited number of parties that can demonstrate prior-established rights. In essence, it would fix the common law in time for all parties once *a* party can establish reliance, or 'customary usage', on the point of law in issue – regardless of whether that established understanding reflected the courts' best interpretation of the law. It is not surprising that the Law Lords eschewed this approach in favour of a more tailored possible response.

The alternative possible response, considered by Lord Nicholls and Lord Hope, would have sought to change the law for future cases without affecting past established rights. This is what National Westminster Bank sought as an alternative to its primary argument that *Siebe Gorman* was good law. The bank argued that if *Siebe Gorman* was to be overruled, 'it should be done prospectively so that transactions entered into before the date of overruling are dealt with on the basis that it was correctly decided'.[172] This echoes the solution to 'judicial takings' that Scalia J favoured in *Stop the Beach*. The effect would be to immunise from the change in the law those with property rights 'established' prior to the judicial change. But it is easy to see why the Law Lords rejected this solution in the case before them. The problems of doctrinal coherence and inter-parties justice were patent, the

[171] *Re Spectrum Plus Court of Appeal* (n 155) [97]. *cf Geelong Harbour Trust* (n 107) 505.
[172] *Re Spectrum Plus* (n 20) 688.

issue before the Law Lords being the correct order of priority of creditors' rights in property. To overrule *Siebe Gorman* without giving retrospective effect to the House's considered interpretation of the debenture terms would simply protect banks at the expense of preferential creditors. It would deprive preferential creditors of a property right that, on the Law Lords' own reasoning, Parliament had intended they should have.[173] This encapsulates the fundamental tension within a doctrine of judicial taking of property: in striving to protect respondents' property rights from judicial 'interference', courts invariably risk interfering with the rights of claimants as established in the court's own judgment.

V. Limits on Uncertainty

The doctrines addressed in this chapter have a comparable function and form. Functionally, the doctrines are responses to the problem of uncertainty in the adjudication of rights. They try to promote certainty by fixing rights in time – shielding 'established' rights from retrospective interpretation by future courts. Formally, the doctrines depend on a conception of rights as being identifiable in positive law independent of subsequent judicial interpretation. The settled-view-of-the-law defence assumes that law at the time of a transaction can be distinguished from a court's decision-time law, and that in the case of conflict rights should be construed according to transaction-time law rather than by applying the adjudicating court's interpretation with hindsight. The doctrine of prospective-only overruling assumes that courts can change law for the future while concomitantly construing past rights according to such governing law as parties' might have expected and relied upon when they transacted. The idea of judicial takings assumes that, in the absence of temporal constraints, judgments that reinterpret property rights 'take' those rights. This realist conception of legal relations sits in tension with the idea that the judicial role is fundamentally interpretive. The outcome of each of the cases suggests that this interpretive role is not readily abandoned. To the contrary, the cases would seem to affirm Beever's contention that 'the modern law remains committed to' the declaratory theory of adjudication.[174]

It could be tempting to dismiss the idea of common law immunity from the retrospective effects of adjudication as a doctrinal misfire. Yet, the idea continues to enjoy judicial and scholarly support. That even a minority of judges at the highest level have endorsed these doctrines suggests that they will continue to be argued. So, it is important that these doctrines are understood. This chapter has cast the doctrines as seemingly pragmatic limits on uncertainty in adjudication: immunities from the effects of judicial changes in the law. I conclude with two thoughts on the problem of uncertainty in adjudication.

[173] *Ibid* [43] (Lord Nicholls) and [74] (Lord Hope).
[174] Beever (n 7) 423. See also L Shmilovits, 'The Declaratory Fiction' [2020] *King's Law Journal* 1, 23.

First, the problem of novel precedent creating uncertainty in the law may be overwrought. It cannot be assumed that some new judgment on a point of law invariably disrupts parties' prior reliance on the 'old' law.[175] Judicial change in the law is always foreshowed, either by prior cases or developments, or simply by the process of litigation that culminates in the law-change. As Lord Devlin recognised, it is rarely a judicial change in the law that causes uncertainty, but rather uncertainty that leads to the 'change' in the law:

> A judge-made change in the law rarely comes out of a blue sky. Rumblings from Olympus in the form of *obiter dicta* will give warning of unsettled weather. Unsettled weather is itself of course bound to cause uncertainty, but inevitably it precedes the solution of every difficult question of law.[176]

If the problem of uncertainty *precedes* a court's novel judgment, then it cannot adequately be resolved through doctrines that focus on limiting the effects of the court's judgment.

This leads to my second thought: that the extent of uncertainty should not be overstated. A degree of uncertainty over the content of one's rights and duties in law may be inevitable. But it is not perpetual. While most problems can be resolved by looking to precedent, statute and commentary, when intractable disagreement arises, ultimately it is only the courts that can conclusively resolve it. So long as the issue remains justiciable, residual uncertainty may persist. Uncertainty over a (trans)action is eliminated only once rights to litigate it have expired. Accordingly, within a statutory period of limitation, rights and duties may be in flux to the extent that they remain subject to the possibility of judicial (re)interpretation. Once a limitation period has expired, rights and duties in respect of a (trans)action become fixed (since adjudication of them cannot be compelled). When judges 'change' the law, then, the effects of such change drag into the past only until they hit the wall of limitation. Time-bars provide a bulwark against interference by precedent.

The law of limitation has long been underappreciated in the Commonwealth world; issues of limitation having been 'bedevilled by an unarticulated tendency to treat it as an unmeritorious procedural technicality'.[177] American jurists hold the better view. Chief Justice Marshall once proclaimed that a cause of action without a time limitation would be 'utterly repugnant to the genius of our laws'.[178]

[175] *Lymington Marina Ltd v MacNamara* [2007] 2 All ER (Comm) 825 [33] (Arden LJ).

[176] Devlin (n 1) 10. See also *Re Spectrum Plus* (n 20) [65] (Lord Hope: '[c]hanges in the law do not occur in a vacuum').

[177] *Abdulla v Birmingham City Council* [2012] UKSC 47, [2013] 1 All ER 649 [41] (Lord Sumption). See, eg, *Lovell v Lovell* [1970] 1 WLR 1451 (CA) 1454 (Salmon LJ: 'The courts are not particularly tender towards defendants who rely on the Statute of Limitations, but Parliament has given them this statutory defence.').

[178] *Adams v Woods*, 6 US 336, 342 (1805) (USSC), cited in *Gabelli v SEC*, 568 US 442, 452 (2013) (USSC).

Justice Story praised statutes of limitation as 'wise and beneficial law'.[179] Justice Rehnquist considered them 'fundamental to a well-ordered judicial system'.[180] Far from being a source of 'abuse',[181] limitation statutes implement a requirement of the rule of law 'that the past be settled'.[182] By providing closure over the past, limitation periods curb the backward reach of judicial developments in the law. This complements judicial law-making under the declaratory theory. When a court delivers what is perceived to be a novel precedent on an issue, it need not be understood as a statement on the (in)correctness of the legal rule for all past eras. The judgment does not bear upon all past rights and entitlements. The judgment impacts only those (trans)actions still justiciable before the courts. Its 'interference' with timely (trans)actions can be justified by the inference that the law must already have been trending toward a state of uncertainty on the issue warranting the court's intervention. In limiting the retrospective effects of adjudication to the 'timely' period, limitation statutes allow us to sidestep the puzzle of determining from when a change in the law takes effect. They allow us to accept, for instance, that advocates' immunity was well-established in the mid-twentieth century while also recognising, with hindsight, that the immunity 'could in 1991 no longer be justified on grounds of public policy'.[183]

A 'clean answer' as to whether the business of a court of law is '[t]o make law or to do justice according to law'[184] has been elusive because judgments have always done both: determining generally applicable principles of law through the resolution of individual disputes. The retrospective effects of judicial law-making give courts pause before departing from an established understanding of the law. But if a better understanding of a point of law is compelled by justice today, it is hard to see how it could not have also been compelled by justice yesterday, and the day before – regardless of whether such understanding can be found in the justice of a bygone era. From this perspective, rights and duties are established by courts applying their best understanding of the law to timely disputes. That courts do so with hindsight does not mean precedent interferes with private rights.

[179] *Bell v Morrison*, 26 US 351, 360 (1828) (USSC).

[180] *Board of Regents of University of State of New York v Tomanio*, 446 US 478, 487 (1980) (USSC).

[181] In *High Commissioner for Pakistan in the United Kingdom v Prince Mukkaram Jah* [2016] EWHC 1465 (Ch) [113], Henderson J suggested that in certain circumstances, 'in principle, it could be an abuse of the process of the court for a defendant to rely on a particular limitation defence'. On the other hand, in *FII* (SC II) (n 18) [72]–[82] a panel of seven Supreme Court judges held that it was not an abuse of process for the defendant to change its plea on limitation even at a very late stage in the proceedings.

[182] A Ripstein, 'The Rule of Law and Time's Arrow' in LM Austin and D Klimchuk (eds), *Private Law and the Rule of Law* (Oxford, Oxford University Press, 2014) 306.

[183] *Awoyomi v Radford* [2007] EWHC 1671, [2008] QB 793 [19].

[184] Devlin (n 1) 11.

INDEX

www.ingramcontent.com/pod-product-compliance
Lightning Source LLC
Chambersburg PA
CBHW071304180926
51613CB00001B/124
9781509934751